WE ALL FOLLOW THE PALACE

We All Follow the Palace

Edited and Designed by Tony Matthews.
Production team: John Ellis, Phil Huffer, Jonathan Scarlett, Laurie Dahl, Neil Witheroe, Steve Crisp, David Mearns, Jason Axell, Matthew Simmonds, Duncan Thompson.

Contributors: Steve Amos, Jim Austin, Peter Baars, Charles Bake, Paul Baker, Ed Barrett, Kevin Barthrop, Tony Baughen, B.K. Dighton, Chris Beale, Eric Bigg, Nick Booth, Keith Brody, Andy Brown, Dennis Brunskill, Andrew Bustard, Peter Butler, Jim Cannon, Darren Caplan, Steve Carleton, Peter Carpark, the other Carparks, Gary Chapman, Steven Chapman, Tom Chippington, Jim Chrystie, Jim Coombes, Louise Court, Diana Cowell, Steve Crisp, Nick Crivich, David Crosier, Mike Cunningham, John Curran, Alan Curtis, Sue Darnell, Roy Davies, Brian Davis, Matty Davis, Rod Deacon, Rob Deeks, Steve Dixon, Don the Landlord of the Railway Telegraph Thornton Heath (even though he's a Seaweed), Donny the Beastie Boy, Stuart Dunbar, Alan Dunlop, Bob Dunton, Eagle in Beds, Eagle in Beds' Mum, Trevor Edwards, Ian Evans, James Evans, Martin Evans, Neil Everitt, Paul Firmage, Andrew Fishleigh, John Fraser MP, Mark Gardiner, Peter Gee, Andy Gilbert, Billy Gilbert, Peter Gillman, Frank Glanz, John Golden, David and Olive Gowler, Michael Grace, Joe Grech, Barrie Greene, Alan Greenhow, Richard Gribble, Norman Grimes, "Guesty", Glenn Hallaway, Tony Halliday, Chris Hart, Faye Harvey, Geoff Haywood, John Henty, Vince Hilaire, Wayne Holton, Martin Huckle, Tony Humphreys, Peter Hurn, David Hynes, Andy Ingram, Cliff Jackson, Sheila Jackson, Paul James, Bjarne Johansen, Ray Kalinauskas, Simon Kane, David Kemp, Ian King, Jim Lee, Annette Legg, Cris Lehmann, Peter Lewis, David London, Kester Lovelace, Colin Machin, Pete Mahoney, Stanley Mann, Paul Mark, Keith Marriage, John McBride, Dave McClelland, Keith Miles, Hy Money, Phil Nicholson, Ron Noades, Gary O'Reilly, Stuart Panes, John Pateman, Jason Pipe, Anthony Powe, Glenn Pressnell, John Procter, Nick Rawling, Colin Readman, Red Ted, Tony Robertson, Declan Rogers, Ben Roxby, Ashley Royston, Dave Sargent, Jack Saunders, Chris Scargill, Martin Searle, Peter Sheeran, Gerry Simpson, Bob Sinclair, Keith Sinclair, Ken Sinclair, Paul Smith, Steve Smith, Ronald Spiers, Peter Spittles, Arron Trevor, Tor Øystein Vaaland, John C. Vallas, Dave and Hannah Van Spall, Gill Walsh, Ian Walsh, Andy Ward, Alex Warner, Stuart Watt, Neil Wensley, Tony West, Martin Whybrow, David Wilton, Peter Winfield, Chris Winter, George Wood, Guy Woodford, Paul Wright, Pete Wylie, Adam Young, Martin Young

Bibliography:
Soccer at War 1939-45 by Jack Rollin
Crystal Palace a Biased Commentary by Chris Winter
Crystal Palace: a Complete Record by Mike Purkiss
Eagle Eye, the Palace fanzine
Suffer Little Children/So Glad You're Mine fanzine
Light at the End of the Tunnel – Dartford FC fanzine.
The Crystal Palace Story by Roy Peskett

Photographs:
Hulton Deutsch, Colorsport, Allsport, Nuda, Neil Everitt, Hy Money, Gary Chapman, Norman Grimes, Eagle Eye.

ISBN No: 0 9522221 0 8

First published: November 1993 by Eagle Eye,

30 Manor Court, York Way, Whetstone, London N20 0DR

Printed by Juma, Trafalgar Works, 44 Wellington Street, Sheffield

The material in this book represents the views of the individual contributors and not necessarily those of Eagle Eye or any other body or individual.

The publishers have made every effort to contact all copyright holders of material in this book. As we have no wish to infringe copyright, could any unacknowledged copyright holder please contact us at Eagle Eye, 30 Manor Court, York Way, Whetstone, London N20 0DR

We would like to take this opportunity to thank Gill Pritchard and her team from Croydon Age Concern and the *Croydon Advertiser* newspaper for their support and assistance.

Addresses:
Palace Independent Supporters Association: Rosalind Poulson, 72 Beaumont Road, London W4 5AP

Eastern Eagles: 91 Lloyds Avenue, Kessingland, Lowestoft, Suffolk NR33 7TT

Northern Eagles: c/o Eagle Eye, 30 Manor Court, York Way, Whetstone, London N20 0DR

■ This book is dedicated to our families who mop our furrowed brows after Palace have lost (again).

Ian Wright: will you please hurry up and leave Arsenal, thanks

All profits from this book will be donated to Croydon Age Concern. Thank you.

Front cover picture by Hy Money: The Holmesdale on May 11, 1979. There were 21,193 people on that section out of a crowd of 51,801.

Back cover picture: F.A. Cup Final 1990. Andy Gray weeps as Palace lose in a replay. (photo: Colorsport)

Well, let's see what Palace can do about it now in the second half as they attack the Holte End here at Villa Park. John Pemberton, a lovely run early on. And a chance for Barber ... and Venison ... and it's a shot ... and it's a shot and ... it's there! By Bright. It's Mark Bright straight from the kick-off. After John Salako's shot didn't quite get there, Bright's certainly did and Palace are level. What a dramatic start to the second half and Liverpool are stunned.

JOHN MOTSON, BBC TELEVISION, APRIL 8, 1990

The supporters' guide to Crystal Palace

We could have taken the easy option and followed Arsenal, Spurs or Manchester United. As a matter of fact, many of us grew up surrounded by kids who did just that. But not for us glamour and glory – having to justify our support for Crystal Palace is a task we expect to take through life.

This book is not packed with tales of Cup Finals and internationals, although there are a couple later on. Instead it's about blokes like Len Choules, Percy Cherrett and Alan Pardew and supporters who are regularly forced to question their own sanity. Most of it is set in division three (south) rather than division one but that's not important either.

The history of Crystal Palace is as much about applying for re-election as it is about international footballers. It is as much about playing Accrington Stanley as it is about going to Wembley. It is about being part of shivering crowds of 4,000 but also about the comradeship of 50,000 voices. It is not only F.A. Cup glory against Liverpool that matters but League Cup defeat at Stockport. The history of Palace is a tale of genuine contrast. The only certainty is knowing that nothing is inevitable.

It is to be hoped that we will always retain our small club attitude, and all the romance that goes with it, but we also have the potential, some of it recently realised, to be a hugely successful club. We are privileged to have the best of both worlds. When something good happens to Palace it prompts celebrations that fans of big clubs will never experience. They think trophies fall off trees, but for us a piece of silverware is a fantasy. We can still live our dreams.

Crystal Palace is a real football club, supported by real people, not a corporate marketing exercise which is what many of English football's more 'glamourous' names have become. You can turn the pages of a hundred football history books and we will not be mentioned, but it is at Palace, and other clubs like us, that the real history of English football can be found. It has been ignored for too long.

The problem with football history books is that they rarely offer more than one person's view of events. But no matter how meticulously researched, we do not believe that one person can truly reflect the history of a football club simply by listing results, referring to old programmes or going throught the papers in a local library. For the real stories you need personal experience. Therefore this book is written by the people who were there – Crystal Palace supporters.

What is so special about Palace? The first thing that springs to mind is laughter. Black humour is the norm at Selhurst Park, we grew up with it. Even in our most successful spells and finest hours, the true Palace fan will always be immersed in the deepest pessimism. If things are going badly they'll get worse, if they're going well it can't last.

But though we laugh at them, there's nothing half hearted about supporting the Eagles. Scattered through this book you will find the word "love" and in many ways supporting the club is like a marriage. You share the joy, the hurt, the escapades and the excitement and, better than that, divorce never comes into it – only perhaps a trial separation.

It is rare for Palace to succumb to mid-table anonymity. We're either challenging at the top or struggling at the bottom. Some teams stay in the same division for years, but we are always on the move. Last season we were relegated and many of us cried because we thought we were good enough not only to survive but to improve. But the season before was tedious and in the end many of us would prefer to lose and be entertained than discover that our beloved Palace had become stale and boring. We are as happy now as we've ever been. No Palace fan wants to lose, but if you never taste defeat, how can you appreciate victory?

The editors would like to acknowledge the help and devotion of everybody who has contributed to this book. Crystal Palace for ever.

CONTENTS

its Jim Cannon's history of Crystal Palace

THEY SAY FOOTBALL WAS HARD IN THE EARLY DAYS...

..WHAT THEY SHOULD SAY IS THAT THE FOOTBALLS WERE HARD IN THE EARLY DAYS.
GRUNCH!!

OF COURSE CRYSTAL PALACE HAD A DIFFERENT NAME IN THOSE DAYS- GRANITE PALACE-AFTER OUR FIRST GROUND, STONEHENGE

OUR MANAGER AT THE TIME WAS TERRYDACTBLES...

HE MANAGED A VERY YOUNG PALACE TEAM, SO YOUNG INFACT THAT THEY HADN'T EVEN FORMED INTO A RECOGNIZABLE UNIFORM.

TRAVEL TO AWAY GAMES WAS DIFFICULT UNTIL THE INVENTION OF THE 'WAGON WHEEL'

THE ONLY PROBLEM WITH THE WAGON WHEEL WAS ON LONG TRIPS WHEN IT WOULD MELT...

AAAAY!!
LUCKILY THIS WAS ERAD-ICATED WHEN THE ICE AGE CAME ALONG. THIS PERIOD PALACE WERE KNOWN AS THE GLACIERS.

IT WAS HARDLY WORTH TRAVELLING TO AWAY GAMES WITH MANY POSPONEMENTS DUE TO THE WEATHER SUCH AS THE 4th ROUND OF THE CUP V NOTTS FROST WHICH BEGAN IN 47108 B.C. (BEFORE CLOUGH) AND TOOK 12 DECADES BEFORE THE DRAW WAS FINISHED.
AAAH CUM'N REF IT'S PLAYABLE!

THE NEXT NOTABLE PERIOD OF MY FOOTBALL CAREER WAS FAMOUS FOR IT'S GIANT KILLING!
THAT'S ONE IN THE EYE FOR DAVE
LOOKS LIKE GOLIATH'S DOWN AND OUT!

... EXCEPT AT FOREST WHERE FROG STOPS PLAY.
BUT REF ITS PLAGUBLE!

FIELD OF DREAMS

For Chris Hart, supporting Crystal Palace was a case of love at first sight.

I remember it like this. The sultry evening made light of the journey through Tooting; we were at Selhurst Park in no time at all. It was as if we had flown.

The brightest lights I had ever seen, four towering eyes burning down, casting a magical illumination on all below them. *Hey Jude* was playing over the loudspeaker system.

It was August 1968. The Russians had just rolled the tanks into Czechoslovakia, half the world was setting the streets alight with revolutionary fire and I was falling in love.

John Sewell, looking like a grammar school teacher, led the team out. They weren't the Eagles then, just a bunch of Glaziers. But unlike teams from different eras there was an almost eerie, timeless quality about them. They were wearing those magnificent claret shirts with thin blue stripes. I clutched the simple white programme like a ticket to wonderland.

Watching from the old stand, the grass was a glowing green, the light from the floodlights bouncing off it. It was as if there was a golden aura surrounding Palace's players that night.

It was the first football match I had ever been to and the fondness I had developed for West Ham United from watching them on TV immediately evaporated. The sound of a leather ball being hit, the dreamy smell of the grass, the shouts of the players, all were intoxicating. Palace beat Norwich 2-0. Mark Lazarus set up a goal and did a lap of honour.

The ground was more open then, with only one stand and grassy banks rising away behind each of the goals. It was a smallish crowd. But at times it was as if I was the only one there to witness this great drama; at others I felt the exhilaration of being totally lost in an army of supporters, united in their passion.

The following Saturday, Palace played Charlton, drew 3-3 and John Jackson saved a penalty. My love affair was confirmed.

Throughout that historic season the team never once let me down. We took to standing up on the bank of grass at the Whitehorse Lane End. Staring down from those dizzy heights I saw the unbelievable. Leeds, ready to crush all before them, crumpled before a team who were wearing the skins of lions, outplaying them throughout; that amazing run of 16 games without defeat to finish off the season, including the fairy tale of the last home match against Fulham; 0-2 down before winning 3-2.

One cold March night at home to Millwall, a gang of their fans decided to keep warm by wandering brazenly through the crowd, collecting up Palace fans' scarves and setting fire to them in a heap. To be 12 years-old and see those huge heaps of manhood walk away from the blokes who took me to matches was a god-like experience. Beating Millwall 4-2 became almost insignificant.

If John Jackson was solid, dependable and everything a young kid might want his father to be, Steve Kember was the star. There was a huge buzz around the ground whenever he got the ball. He made things happen that left you thinking that he had discovered the secret meaning of life in his right foot.

Kids from all over south London supported Chelsea then. They were a club that oozed glamour. Everyone had a story about how their older brothers drank with Chelsea players or their sisters knew them. Following Palace promised something different. It meant being different.

Because maybe the greatest thing about that team and that season was that they weren't glamourous and star studded. It was their very ordinariness that lifted them above other London teams.

They were artisans, as revealed in their nickname, who strode the stage of my imagination like giants.

John McCormick looked like he had been cast from Aberdeen's famous granite; Cliff Jackson, with his arm raised aloft after scoring; Bobby Woodruff, one of the great long throwers, who scored that night against Norwich; and Mel Blyth, who probably gave Clint Eastwood lessons in laconic cool. Heroes all.

The chase for promotion had looked too close to call at Easter. But that relentless undefeated run inexorably pulled Palace away from their rivals until they rose to glory, promoted to the top flight for the first time ever.

I remember it all, still, like a dream. The team was built around 13 players and I see them now, that glowing light surrounding them, floating over a surface as green as glittering emerald.

Everything that has followed – beating Ipswich to go top of division one, the play-off victory over Blackburn, the Wembley finals, even beating Liverpool at Villa Park – may have been more exciting or better football, but none of it compares, none of it retains that dreamlike quality. That's how I remember it.

Beginnings ... a club is born

The Victorian pioneers and their Edwardian successors

Any account of Crystal Palace Football Club should open with a brief introduction to the "original" club.

Most of us are aware that before the present club existed there was a much older one that played at the Crystal Palace exhibition ground. The *Rothmans Football Year Book,* among others, still includes the one appearance made by the original club in an F.A. Cup semi-final alongside the two made by its successors. This is clearly an anomaly and one should question why it is so important for us to mention the first club at all? After all, there is no evidence of any firm link between the present club and its predecessor other than a common name and the fact that, for the first ten years of its existence, the present club's home was the Crystal Palace.

Our knowledge of the first Crystal Palace FC is obviously sketchy, but it nevertheless offers an insight into the context in which football arrived in south London. The first Crystal Palace club is also important because it played a leading role in helping to establish the Football Association.

By the early 1860s, the British Empire was spreading across the globe. Europe was in the middle of a long period of peace and for the upper and middle classes of Victorian Britain it was a time of success and stability.

In 1851, to celebrate British commercial prosperity, a Great Exhibition was organised. Queen Victoria's beloved German Consort Prince Albert was an enthusiastic supporter of the scheme and the architect Joseph Paxton was commissioned to design a building not only to house the exhibition but to be its focal point. Paxton's structure, which used 400 tons of glass and 4,000 tons of iron, was tagged "the Crystal Palace" by the satirical magazine *Punch* when it was assembled in Hyde Park. It remained there for three years before it was moved to Sydenham Hill, a green open space in south London. The surrounding area immediately took its name from the new building – Crystal Palace.

Crystal Palace became a popular recreation spot and a major tourist attraction. Football at this time was still in its infancy and as befitted the ethics of the day the sport, which was once considered only suitable for a drunken rabble, became predominantly a game for amateur gentlemen. Matches were arranged on a friendly basis with frequent arguments over the interpretation of the rules. But from this shambles grew a desire on the part of some clubs – but by no means all – for greater organisation.

Did you know?

The Station End at Shrewsbury's Gay Meadow, where away fans stand, is equipped with a Victorian turnstile which is believed to have come from the old Crystal Palace ground where Palace played until 1915.

Many of the earliest teams originated in the public schools and universities but there were other clubs, one of which was Crystal Palace.

It is thought that employees of the Crystal Palace company first formed a football club in 1861. If this is correct, it would already have been established for some time before its secretary Mr F. Day attended a meeting of prominent clubs at the Freemason's Tavern, Great Queen Street, Lincoln's Inn Fields on October 26, 1863. Day joined delegates from Kilburn, No Names, Barnes, the War Office, Crusaders, Perceval House Blackheath, Forest Leytonstone, Blackheath, Kensington School, Surbiton, Blackheath Proprietary School and Charterhouse, and accepted on behalf of his club a broad agreement to form a Football Association.

The initial aim was simple – to devise a coherent set of rules. This proved to be a trying task, not least because the leading public schools, with the exception of Charterhouse, had refused to attend the meeting because of an earlier disagreement. Yet, even without the powerful voice of the public schools, the foundation of the association was a significant step. In those early years, Crystal Palace played their part to the full. The club remained prominent throughout its existence – their first committee member was Jas. Turner, who subsequently became treasurer during his second year of office. These are the men who represented Crystal Palace on those early F.A. committees:

1863	Jas. Turner
1864 - 1868	Jas Turner (treasurer) and W.J. Cutbill
1869-70	W.J Cutbill
1871 - 1873	D. Allport
1874	A. Morten
1875 - 1876	C.E. Smith and A. Morten (vice)

The F.A.'s rules remained widely ignored for some considerable time. A full three years after the first meeting, a representative of No Names F.C. complained that it was difficult to follow the fledgling rules because "only Crystal Palace and Barnes fully adhere to them". Nevertheless, football continued to advance. More and more clubs appeared, including many that are well known today.

In an attempt to stimulate greater interest in football and help introduce the F.A.'s coherent rules, such as they were, to a wider audience, a series of representative matches were organised at county level. The first of these took place between Middlesex and a combined team from Kent and Surrey at Battersea on Saturday, November 2, 1867.

Both sides called upon many of the leading players of the day and Crystal Palace's standing at that time can be gauged from the fact that they provided two players, W. Cutbill and W. Cockerell, for the Kent and Surrey team. The novel format of the match, which ended goalless, attracted great interest and drew a sizeable crowd, so a second game was arranged between Kent and Surrey on the West London Running Track on January 25 of the following year. How little developed the rules of football were at the time can be gathered from the following match report:

"At the end of an hour and a quarter's play, no goals had been scored and, after an additional quarter of an hour's play the game ended, as had the first, with no scoring."

The teams were:

Surrey: R.G. Graham (Barnes), J. Cockerell (Crystal Palace), C.C. Dacre (Clapham Grammar School), P. Rhodes (Wanderers), H. Richardson (Reigate Hill), F.B. Soden (C.C.C. Clapham), A. Thompson (Wanderers), R.W. Willis (Barnes), J, Turner (Crystal Palace), E.C. Morley (Barnes) and W. Collins (Barnes).

Kent: A.F. Kinnaird (Trinity College, Cambridge), E. Lubbock (West Kent), J.B. Martin (Wanderers), F.G. Paulson (Charterhouse) E.O Berens (Crusaders), W.J.C. Cutbill, D. Allport and A.C. Chamberlain (all Crystal Palace), P. Norman (Old Etonians), E.A. Hoare (St John's College, Cambridge) and J.T. Goldney (Old Harrovians).

The next step was to stage an international match. At the time of the first contests between England and Scotland, Crystal Palace were at the height of their powers and they provided several internationalists. The most famous of these was the first, Charles John Chenery, also of the Wanderers, who was included in the English team which travelled north for the inaugural international match against Scotland, who were represented by the entire Queen's Park team, at Partick in 1871.

In fact, Palace would have had a second player in the team had Alex Morten, along with three others originally chosen to play, been available. Morten had played in the unofficial international of 1870 when an English side met a loose Scottish team made up of London based players. Most of the England team stayed at the Carrick Royal Hotel, but four men, Chenery, C.J. Morice, R.C. Welch and J. Brockban, were unable to leave London until the Friday evening and had to endure an overnight journey to Partick. They were accompanied by C.W. Alcock, an important figure in the subsequent history of the Football Association, who acted as umpire on the English side.

Although it ended goalless the match was declared a success and a return fixture was arranged for the following year. The first full international to be played on English soil was staged at Kennington Oval, the home of Surrey County Cricket Club, and Chenery was selected once again, as was Morten. This time, the English were successful by four goals to two with Chenery scoring one of the English goals.

Crystal Palace provided two further players in those early matches: Charles Eastlake Smith was capped in the match of 1876 along with his club mate A.H. Savage. It was the only appearance for both men.

It is thought that selection for the England team was based as much on work done for committees as on any playing ability. But that should not detract from the achievements of these Crystal Palace pioneers.

Crystal Palace also enjoyed early success in the first years of the F.A. Cup, a competition the club played no small part in establishing. As football grew in popularity and the number of clubs increased, so the demand for greater organisation gathered momentum.

The idea for a knockout competition was first mooted at an F.A. meeting on July 20, 1871. *The History of the Football Association*, published in 1963, records: "There sat seven men, dressed in the height of fashion that befitted their place in society ... for each was a member of one or other of the best known teams of that period." The seven were: C.W. Stephenson of Westminster School, A. Stair of Upton Park, J.H. Giffard of Civil Service, M.P. Betts of Harrow, who would later become famous as "A.H. Chequer" the scorer of the first F.A. Cup Final goal, C.W. Alcock of Wanderers, captain Francis Marindin, who was later to become president of the Football Association, and D. Allport of Crystal Palace.

According to *The History of the Football Association*, the men spoke of the Prussian siege of Paris and other weighty matters and then of the exploits of their respective football clubs and of their desire for organised competition. It was agreed that a cup competition was a splendid idea and on October 16, a second meeting was held with more clubs in attendance. At a third meeting on February 1 of the following year, Alcock, Stair and Allport were given the task of purchasing the first ever F.A. Cup.

The silver trophy stood on an ebony plinth, had two handles, held little more than a quart, and had a figure of a player on the lid. It was designed by Martin Hall and Company and cost around £20.

In the first competition, Palace, who wore blue and white shirts and blue serge knickerbockers, were joined by Barnes, Civil Service, Clapham Rovers, Hampstead Heathens, Harrow Chequers, Hitchin, Maidenhead, Marlow, Queen's Park, Reigate Priory, Royal Engineers, Upton Park and Wanderers.

By modern standards, it was a strange competition. The early rounds were disrupted by byes and scratchings and Palace's progress relied as much on these factors as on ability to win matches. In the first round they were paired with Hitchin and the 0-0 draw immediately posed a problem as this report from the Committee explains:

"The progress of Crystal Palace and Hitchin into the second round and later of Crystal Palace and Wanderers into the semi-final round, in spite of drawn matches, is covered by rule 8 whereby in case of a drawn match the clubs shall be drawn again in the next ties or shall compete again at the discretion of the committee."

After Hitchin, Palace comfortably overcame Maidenhead in the second round by three goals to nil. Then, as the committee explained, they drew with the eventual winners, Wanderers, although there is no recorded score for this match. This took them into the semi-final, where unfortunately they were drawn against the foremost team of the day, the Royal Engineers. In their red and blue horizontal striped shirts, the Royal Engineers easily won 3-0 and went on to the final at Kennington Oval where they were rather surprisingly beaten by the Wanderers.

Crystal Palace were never able to follow up their initial success although they competed in the F.A. Cup for several more years. In the following year's competition, interest was shortlived – they were beaten by Oxford University in the first round. Palace also fell at the first hurdle in 1874 and 1875, when they lost first to Swifts by the only goal and then 2-1 to Cambridge University. As more and more clubs appeared, Palace's power waned. But before the record books closed on the original Crystal Palace FC for the last time, they enjoyed one last fling in the 1875-76 F.A. Cup. After a drawn game, they beat the 105th Regiment 3-0 to reach the second round. Perhaps fittingly, it was Wanderers, who had won the first three competitions and were about to win it again, who brought down the final curtain with a 3-0 victory.

Aside from the information here, we know nothing more of the club, although it has intrigued and puzzled fans of the current club for many years. In *Sports Gossip* in the *Croydon Advertiser* newspaper in May 1945, for instance, Alfred W. Apted (known by his pen-name "AWA") raised the topic:

"There has certainly been one other, many years before the present club was even thought of, and possibly there was another some time after that."

"The first Crystal Palace club took a hand in the formation of the Football Association and, in the 1872/3 season, supplied a player C.H. Chenery for the first recognised international between England and Scotland which was played on the West of Scotland Cricket Club ground at Partick and resulted in a draw.

"I have been trying to find out – and so far I am sorry to say without success – something about this first Crystal Palace club. I have been in communication with Sir Henry Buckland, general manager of the Crystal Palace, who has very kindly gone into the archives and made inquiries without finding any records or being able to gain any information about any other club.

"Like me, Sir Henry is forced to come to the conclusion that this first club was composed of players in the neighbourhood of the Crystal Palace, and took its name from the great glass house on the hill.

"In the course of my enquiries I was told, although my informant could not vouch for the authenticity of the statement, that there was a second Crystal Palace club which was in some way connected with the Anerley Congregational Church."

Crystal Palace's links with the F.A. Cup did not end with the demise of the original club, however. Until the 1891-92 season, the Final had been played at Kennington Oval. But, after Surrey County Cricket Club decided that the crowds were becoming too large and withdrew the Oval, there was no permanent home for the next two seasons. First it was played at the inadequate Fallowfield, Manchester, which was an unmitigated disaster, and then at Everton's Goodison Park.

But in 1895 it returned to a new permanent home in London – the Crystal Palace. That year, midland rivals Aston Villa and West Bromwich Albion competed for the cup and it went to Villa thanks to a fluke goal which went in off the knee of their captain John Devey after just 30 seconds. The goal came so swiftly that many of the 42,000 crowd, who stood on grassy slopes rather than terracing, were still outside and missed it. It remains the fastest ever Cup final goal.

Villa didn't hold the trophy for long. They displayed it in the window of boot and shoe manufacturer W. Shillcock, from where it was stolen and never recovered.

Despite the loss of the trophy – which was thought to have been melted down by the thieves – the final itself was voted a great success and remained at the Crystal Palace until the Admiralty intervened during the First World War and took it away from south London for ever.

The Crystal Palace was by this time one of the most famous and popular landmarks in London. The owners depended on tourist income and were always looking for fresh attractions.

It had already established cricket as an attractive diversion, first with the Crystal Palace Cricket Club and then with London County Cricket Club, who boasted the imposing figure of W.G. Grace, the famous Gloucestershire and England player, among their number.

Grace, such was his fame, was considered a major attraction in his own right, even though he was in the twilight of his cricketing career. He played many fine games for London. But the owners of the Crystal Palace wanted something with even greater pulling power and football seemed to be the very thing.

Despite the annual pilgrimage to the final and the great interest it generated in the game in south London, the Crystal Palace club, or clubs, were long gone. Nevertheless, it took fully ten years before anybody appeared to realise the potential of forming another football club in south London.

Perhaps the most obvious pointer to the potential was the attendance of 110,802 at the 1901 F.A. Cup final which saw a London club finally break the domination of the northern professionals in that competition. At that time, Tottenham Hotspur were a Southern League club, but they not only held first division Sheffield United but beat them in a replay to bring the cup south for the first time since the days of the early amateurs.

In 1904, the Crystal Palace Company proposed to establish a new club. It seemed a fine idea. The local population regularly supported the Cup Final so why not a team of their own? The Football Association, however, was not impressed with the prospect of the owners of the Cup Final ground possessing a club and refused permission. The idea was scrapped … but only for a year. Then a separate company was formed to establish the club and the ground was rented.

The first chairman was Sydney Bourne, who was offered the position in unusual circumstances as he recalled later in his life:

"Mr E.F. Goodman, our first secretary, was looking through the books of the Crystal Palace company dealing with the F.A. Cup Finals, and noticed that among those people who used to buy large numbers of tickets for the game was the name of Sydney Bourne. That seemed a good enough reason to ask me to become Chairman!"

In more cynical times, when Cup Final tickets are treated as a commodity by unscrupulous people, it might seem that a man who bought large numbers of tickets was someone to be treated with suspicion and contempt. But perhaps Mr Bourne was the product of a more innocent age and used proved such an attraction of the Colon... Indian Exhibition at the Crystal Palace, w... be given to-day (Saturday.)

CRYSTAL PALACE FOOTBALL CLUB.—To-day (Saturday) the first match will be played by this newly-formed club, the reserve team of the famous Southampton club being the visitors. Kick-off is timed for four o'clock. The Palace team will be as follows:—Heartson, Walker, Edwards, Innerd, Barnie (capt.), Astley, Thompson, Harker, Watkins, Needham, Roberts.

BROCK'S BENEFIT FIREWORK DISPLAY — ... display on Thursday next, will be a re- ...

them for genuine purposes.

Along with two other newly formed London clubs, Chelsea and Clapton Orient, Palace applied to join the second division of the Football League – which had been formed in 1888 and was now a flourishing and popular competition. Chelsea and Clapton were accepted, Palace were not.

This left the fledgling club with a problem. Having set out to join the league, they had to swiftly turn their attention to the Southern League, a powerful organisation in its own right, in order to secure a league in which to play. But they were too late and had to settle for a place in the second division of the competition. Not an auspicious start. To top up the fixtures, Palace also joined the United Counties League, and it was in this competition that they played their first competitive match.

To establish the club on a firm footing, Palace's officials turned to the leading club of the day, Aston Villa for help. Villa provided Palace with the services of their assistant secretary Edmund Goodman, who had played for them as a young man but had suffered an injury which necessitated the amputation of his right leg.

It was Goodman's hard work first as secretary and later as joint manager and secretary that did most to establish Crystal Palace F.C. as a healthy club. The first manager was John Robson, an experienced campaigner who had been Middlesbrough's manager in their first season in the football league in 1899/90 and who later led them into the first division. Robson brought 16 professionals to the club, mainly from Middlesbrough and other northern clubs with a couple of local lads thrown in for good measure.

Initial signs were far from encouraging. The club arranged a practice match to which, including the manager, trainer and secretary, only 12 people turned up. But when Palace kicked off in earnest they made a good start. On September 1, 1905 in the United Counties League, Palace visited New Brompton, who later became Gillingham, and were convincing 3-0 victors. Dick Roberts and Ted Birnie scored for Palace in the first half with "another point" added towards the close. The following day, Palace faced the more important task of challenging for the second division of the Southern League. The division was made up mainly of other clubs' reserve sides and a few exotic names such as Southern United, St Leonard's and Grays United.

Around 3,000 people paid 6d to stand and a shilling to sit for the opening fixture against Southampton Reserves. Robson opted to keep the same team that had been successful the day before. It seemed the right move as Palace roared into a three goal lead through Dick Roberts, after just four minutes, Archie Needham, and George Thompson. But towards the end of the game tiredness crept in and Southampton crept back. Palace lost inside right Dick Harker and the ten men were unable to keep the Saints at bay. Soy completed a hat-trick and close to the end Bert Hoskins netted the winner for the visitors. Happily, this set back was only temporary and two weeks later (we missed a week because the scheduled fixture with Southall was called off after they dropped out of the league) Palace secured their first victory at Swindon with goals by Harker and Ted Birnie. Then, after successive goalless draws with West Ham Reserves and Leyton Reserves, Palace set off on a winning streak. Seventeen straight victories took us to the top in a run which included outstanding performances against Fulham Reserves, who were on the receiving end of Palace's first five goal haul and Grays United who went down 9-1 at the Crystal Palace.

Of the attendances that were recorded, Palace regularly pulled in between two and three thousand spectators, although 4,000 attended the 4-0 roasting of Watford Reserves at the beginning of March. We also gained revenge over Southampton Reserves for their opening day defeat and although two points were dropped in the last three matches they became comfortable champions.

In the United Counties League, Palace enjoyed an equally good year, finishing runners-up to Watford. Incidentally, in April, the club also achieved its biggest ever victory when we beat West Beckenham 17-2 in a friendly.

If that wasn't enough, a good run in the F.A. Cup began with a seven goal pasting of Clapham, in which former Sunderland player Walter Watkins scored the first ever Crystal Palace hat-trick. The Palace team was: *Hewitson, Walker, Edwards, Innerd, Birnie, Astley, Wallace, Harker, Watkins, Needham and Roberts.*

In the second round, the same Palace line-up made short work of the Grenadier Guards, hammering three unanswered goals to set up a mouth watering tie with Chelsea. The Stamford Bridge club, remember, had been elected to the league while Palace were not considered good enough, so the match offered us an immediate chance to prove a point.

Chelsea were doing well in their first season of second division football and boasted several star attractions such as Willie "Fatty" Foulke, the legendary 21-stone goalkeeper, who was the biggest man ever to play in the Football League.

Sadly for Chelsea, and for Palace fans who relished the attraction, the west Londoners also had a league fixture to fulfil on the same day. With promotion to the first division a possibility, Chelsea elected to play their first team against Burnley at Stamford Bridge and sent a shadow team to face Palace in the Cup. Of the Chelsea side that faced the Glaziers, only left-back Miller and player-manager John Tait Robertson were regular first teamers.

It left Palace with an easy task and even though, Walter Watkins scored another hat-trick in a 7-1 canter, it could only be regarded as a hollow victory. The result produced an outcry and the F.A. subsequently introduced a rule that

Did you know?

In the early days of Palace's existence some papers tried to give them the nickname "Crystals" teams must always field their strongest line-ups in the F.A. Cup, although it is difficult to see what Chelsea were supposed to do in the circumstances.

Nevertheless, it meant Palace had reached the fourth qualifying round where they beat Luton. They now had every right to feel confident of further success against Blackpool – a fair to middling second division team. Having done the hard part by gaining a draw in Lancashire, Palace were unable to finish the Lancastrians off in the replay and in the third match at Villa Park it was Blackpool who went through. Despite the disappointment of the Cup exit, Palace had good reason to be satisfied with their first season and in the club handbook of 1906/7, Edmund Goodman noted:

"I consider that the Crystal Palace should, in time, get as big as any club in the South, or even in England, that is if our team is fairly successful from the playing point of view. To prove this I would point to the attendance at the various final ties which have been played on our ground, when from 60,000 to 110,000 persons have attended annually. Now with all due respects to the visiting teams which have from time to time appeared in the final, we know that they always bring a large following, but at the same time amongst the large crowd there are always thousands of south Londoners, which shows that if you provide them with first class football they will support it."

Our championship ensured a place in the first division of the Southern League, but after a brace of goals by George Woodger helped us to a flying start with a 3-0 victory over Northampton on the first day, things took a sudden turn for the worse.

Only two victories were gained in the next ten matches as Palace discovered they were not about to run off with the first division in the same way they had the second.

The highlight of the season was undoubtedly a 5-1 defeat of Queen's Park Rangers early in 1907, while the lowest ebb was a 6-0 thrashing at the hands of Portsmouth in April. But Palace's best form once again was saved for the F.A. Cup.

The Crystal Palace had already been earmarked for a rugby international by the time Palace got on the cup trail in a qualifying tie against Rotherham County. We were not unduly disturbed by having to move to Stamford Bridge to fulfil the fixture and still won 4-0. Hopes of further progress seemed to be dashed by the luck of the draw when Palace were paired with Newcastle United at St James' Park in the first round. The Magpies were the foremost team of the Edwardian era, having appeared in each of the previous two finals, and were on their way to a second league championship in three years. Furthermore, Frank Watt's team had not been beaten at home since November 25, 1905 and had the backing of 28,000 supporters packed in expecting to see a comfortable victory. Palace however had the advantage of an intimate knowledge of Newcastle. Wilf Innerd and Dick Harker had been at St James's Park before joining Palace and the Londoners also had several ex-Middlesbrough and Sunderland men on the staff. But initially, it seemed that Newcastle would make short work of Palace and the Geordies' Scottish international Jimmy Howie had a goal ruled out for offside.

Against the run of play, former 'Boro forward Horace Astley broke clear and set us on the way to one of the greatest Cup shocks ever. Newcastle huffed and puffed looking for a way back, but the Palace rearguard held firm and could even have extended their lead had it not been for three outstanding saves by Jimmy Lawrence, the goalkeeper who still holds Newcastle's appearance record.

It was a huge shock. *Athletic News*, the prominent sports journal of the day, carried the headline "Newcastle Mesmerised" and wrote: "It will be many a long day before the glorious victory will be forgotten." The *Croydon Advertiser and Surrey County Recorder* also joined in the praise for their local team: "The Crystal Palace players have just reason to be proud of their achievement," it said.

The Newcastle press were equally fulsome in their praise, as the *Advertiser* pointed out: "The *Morning Leader* man wrote: 'It would be invidious to single out anyone save Woodger on the Palace side for special mention. He was the undoubted star."

Newcastle must have hated Crystal Palace. They visited the ground five times in the opening decade of the century to play Cup Finals and never came came away winners – the best they could achieve was two draws, they won one replay and lost the other – and, to add insult to injury, a fledgling Crystal Palace barely one year old remember, had shattered their hopes of another final appearance. Palace didn't have so far to travel for the second round, where another 28,000 crowd saw Fulham held at Craven Cottage. Back in south London, Palace put their neighbours out with a goal from Woodger in front of a record attendance of 20,000. Fulham were not happy and claimed that a goal by Wheatcroft which had been disallowed for offside should have been allowed to stand. Palace couldn't give two hoots – they had already come up with their cup "gimmick". The *Croydon Advertiser* reported that … "the Palace players left for Brighton on Wednesday evening and are hoping that Mr Bourne, Mr Robson and Trainer Birch will 'dream dreams' about the Brentford tie. They had visions of the Newcastle and Fulham results even to the scores. Where's Old Moore after this?"

1905/6 Southern League Division Two

	P	W	D	L	F	A	Pts
C. Palace	24	19	4	1	66	14	42
Leyton	24	16	6	2	61	18	38
P'smouth Res	24	12	8	4	52	24	32
Fulham Res	24	11	6	7	52	39	28
S'thampton Res	24	7	9	8	39	41	23
Southern Utd	24	8	7	9	45	49	23
St Leonards U	24	9	4	11	54	50	22
Watford Res	24	8	5	11	43	47	21
West Ham Res	24	7	5	12	46	48	19
Grays United	24	8	3	13	24	77	19
Reading Res	24	6	5	13	36	49	17
Swindon Res	24	5	5	14	36	51	15
Wycombe Wdrs	24	5	3	16	36	83	13

Palace finished in second place in the United Counties League behind Watford

In the third round, another record crowd, this time 31,123, paid three shillings for Pavilion seats, 2s for reserved covered stand seats, 1s for unreserved seats and 6d in the uncovered stand to watch fellow Southern Leaguers Brentford hold us to a 1-1 draw. The *Croydon Advertiser* counted a continuous stream of heads and disputed the official gate stating it looked more like final day. Palace realised receipts of £820 17s. 6d.

On a slippery pitch, Harker gave Palace the lead with a cross shot but although there were opportunities to increase the advantage, Brentford were level before half-time, Hagan driving past Hewitson. The crowd cheered both sides on with "bell, bugle and rattle" but a tame second half ensured the visitors earned the draw that had always appeared to be the limit of their ambition. The replay at Griffin Park on the following Wednesday afternoon brought "little which could be termed classic football" and the game was marred by the sending off of Brentford's Taylor for a charge that almost rendered Wallace unconscious. The one man advantage turned the tide for Palace and, with time running out, Roberts completed a neat move with a left foot winner.

George Woodger. Not only a Palace hero, but a local boy. After several sparkling seasons for Palace he joined Football League club Oldham for around £800 and went on to represent England.
Illustration by Jason Axell

Cup holders Everton were next and Palace broke their attendance record. Thirty five thousand packed in hoping to see Palace topple the famous Liverpudlians. We played brilliantly and even took the lead but Everton pegged us back to gain a draw. The *Advertiser* could barely hide its disappointment. "Until the Cup holders got their rather lucky goal from a scramble in front of Hewitson, they were a demoralised team," it claimed. But the dream was over, Everton at Goodison were too strong and won 4-0.

Palace's plucky performances however drew praise from Everton's Jack Sharp. He told the *London Evening News*: "The Palace never once slacked, nor outwardly gave up hope. I have found this to be a characteristic of the Crystal Palace side which is handed down season after season and, if for no other reason, I shall always have a profound respect for the team." Kind words indeed, especially the bit about "season after season", Palace remember were only in their second year.

Equally impressed with Palace was Tityrus, columnist in the *Athletic News*. He called Palace a team of "one head, one purpose, one spirit, twenty two busy feet and a burning ambition – who play football with the sole purpose of victory. Everton were thoroughly held and extended and David very nearly slew Goliath."

Tityrus also liked the local hero George Woodger, who had joined the club at its inception from amateur team Thornton Heath Wednesday. The journalist thought him "the finest, trickiest most persevering forager at Sydenham". He added that "there is as much cunning in this fellow's toes as in many a man's head". Woodger, who had been given the nickname "Lady" by his school chums because of his dainty play, had played for Croydon Schools before playing for West Croydon and Croydon Wanderers with whom he toured Holland in 1902. He first represented Palace as an amateur and scored 21 goals. He turned professional the following season.

Jack of Clubs who wrote the *Croydon Advertiser's Sports Gossip* column noted that his transfer to Oldham had been the "talk of the town" because of the considerable sum of £800 which had been involved.

Jack of Clubs also said that Palace embarked on several continental tours in their early years including one to Austria "about which hangs a tale".

"In a match in Prague, the referee decided that Brearley, the old Spurs' player, had committed a foul and ordered him off the field. Brearley refused to obey the ruling and the end of the argument was the taking off of the entire team."

The 1907-08 season began with a new manager. Robson left Palace to take over at nearby Croydon Common and Edmund Goodman assumed the dual role of secretary and manager. Robson later managed both Brighton and Manchester United – no accounting for taste.

Goodman enjoyed a happy first season in charge of team affairs. Palace had further cause to celebrate when on March 7, 1908 Bill Davies became the first player from the club to win an international honour when he was selected for Wales against Scotland at Dundee. Scotland won 2-1.

There was also some recognition for Woodger's fine contribution. He was chosen as a reserve for England's match against Scotland but unfortunately did not play.

After finding the going tough in their first league season in the Southern League's top flight, Palace settled and although dogged by occasionally erratic results, they finished a

The Palace squad in 1909-10

creditable fourth in a division which strangely included Bradford Park Avenue. The Yorkshiremen had been drafted in to replace Fulham after the Cottagers had been elected to the Football League.

Palace again enjoyed a decent cup run. In the first round, they beat Coventry City away from home thanks to two Woodger goals and followed that by winning 3-2 at Plymouth Argyle in front of 17,830.

Hubert Swann opened his Palace account with a goal against his old club. In the third round, Palace were drawn away from home for the third successive time and they fell to the only goal at Grimsby Town. Had Palace won, they would have enjoyed a return visit to Newcastle. Grimsby didn't enjoy it, they got stuffed 5-1.

In 1908-09, Palace's form deserted them after a reasonable start which included a 4-0 win over Brighton in which new signing Charles McGibbon from Gillingham scored a hat-trick. There was also a 4-4 draw with old foes Southampton. Palace had trailed 3-0 and although McGibbon pulled one back before half time, the Saints restored their advantage from the penalty spot. Then McGibbon narrowed the gap again, Bill Lawrence reduced the arrears further and in the last minute, McGibbon stepped up to claim the equaliser with another penalty.

It was the only time during Palace's Southern League days that they would be involved in such a high scoring draw although there have been several 4-4 draws in the league. The team lost its rhythm and the two Woodger goals which earned a point against Reading marked the first of 13 games without a victory. Woodger brought that run to an end with a double to help beat Brentford 3-1 on the last day of March, but one win in the last five concluded a disappointing effort over all. Palace finished well down in 16th place.

Despite ragged form, we enjoyed another successful Cup run. On new year's day, Jimmy Bauchop, the former Celtic and Norwich player who holds the distinction of being the first Palace man to be sent off, surprised Wolves with two goals to bring the Black Country club back to London for a replay. Although, they were in the second division, Wolves had a fine tradition to uphold and had already visited the Crystal Palace earlier in the year to collect the F.A. Cup (and extend Newcastle's Crystal Palace cup jinx into the bargain). Palace's cup fighting reputation had already been upheld by the draw at Molineux, but again they were to surpass themselves.

But it was Wolves who drew first blood. With 60 seconds gone, Hedley put them ahead only for Palace to level within ten minutes, John Brearley setting up Bill Lawrence. Palace looked to have taken the lead when Bauchop, scored, but he was called offside.

Palace then faced the prospect of playing with ten men when Charlie Ryan limped off just before the interval. Fortunately he returned to the fray and Palace held on until half-time.

In the second half, with both side suffering from injuries, Wolves went on the offensive. Palace now had Ted Collins off the field although he returned to play a major part in Georgie Garratt's goal which seemed destined to give Palace another scalp but, with only eight minutes left, Hedley dashed Palace's hopes and took the game into extra time.

As both teams tired visibly it was the Glaziers who made the decisive breakthrough. Bauchop, the scourge of the Wolves' defence, was on target again. Then in the dying minutes, Palace finished it off with a remarkable goal. On a heavy pitch, right back Ted Collins who was still hurt was covered by Archie Needham, a great cup fighter who had appeared in three finals for Sheffield United. The story of this goal was recalled in the *Croydon Advertiser's* Sports Gossip column of March 22, 1946 by Mr Fred C. Fountain:

"I think that Archie Needham was the most versatile

and whole player that Palace ever had. For he played in nearly every position except goal and, if necessary, he would have done well there. He figured in what I consider to be the most exciting of many exciting Palace matches.

The Wolves had won the cup in the previous season. After playing through the qualifying rounds, the Palace were drawn against them in the first round proper away. They drew 2-2 at Wolverhampton and replayed on the following Thursday at the Crystal Palace.

At full time the score was again 2-2 and extra time had to be played.

In the first quarter of an hour Archie Needham playing at left back tackled and robbed a Wolves forward – a clever piece of play. Instead of passing the ball up field, he simply weaved his way through all the players and dribbled it right up to the Wolves' goal, putting in an unstoppable shot. The goalkeeper didn't have a chance."

The glory didn't end there for Palace. Second division Burnley were held to a draw in front of an attendance of 17,076 in the second round. Burnley's supporters came to London in force on an excursion train that set a record time of five and a quarter hours.

The visitors included Alec Leake, who had captained England in his Aston Villa days. Although he was coming to the end of his career he was still a fine player and gave a commanding performance.

Moffatt cleared off the Burnley line from Garrett and Bauchop hit the post, but with Woodger only hinting at his true abilities it was Burnley who did most of the attacking after half-time, forcing Josh Johnson to make a number of good saves to keep Palace on terms.

In the replay, Collins came in at right back and Needham moved to outside left. Lawrence, the amateur forward, moved to inside right which meant that Palace fielded exactly the same team that had beaten Wolves in the first round. Within three minutes Burnley were in front through Smith.

Johnson was already on a bonus for his heroics by the time the lead was doubled on the quarter hour – Smith again the scorer. In heavy conditions and with Palace already a beaten side, Burnley turned on the power and Harry Collyer deflected a shot from Moffat past Johnson for the third. Abbott added a fourth and just before half-time Cretney made it 5-0.

Palace weren't in it. Bauchop squandered our only opportunity of the half and the second period turned into a damage limitation exercise. For 20 minutes, with all hands to the pump, we kept things respectable but then Abbott, Smethams and Cretney scored in the space of five minutes and Smith nailed the coffin lid shut, completing his hat-trick with ten minutes left. The score was at least kept to single figures but it still represented our biggest defeat and Burnley's record victory.

George Payne, who joined Palace from Tottenham, scored the first goal of the 1909-10 campaign as Palace started with two wins and two draws. It was sufficient to beat Brentford although the Bees gained revenge twelve days later in what was to be our only defeat in the first 12 matches – a run that culminated in a 6-0 mauling of Southend, where another new forward, Jim Williams from Birmingham, scored five times. But our championship hopes were dashed in three separate spells of poor form – losing to Northampton, Portsmouth and QPR within a week in November and then going seven games without a win from New Year's day. We closed the season with only one victory in the last seven games which brought a final placing of seventh. Palace were equally disappointing in the Cup bowing out at Swindon by three goals to one.

During the season, Palace made news by appealing against compensation for injuries received in a match by former Wolves player George Walker, who had played in Palace's first ever match. He was awarded damages under the Workmans Compensation Act.

The club said he wasn't engaged in work but just playing a game while Walker's lawyers claimed their client had "surrendered to the club bodily labour of his arms and legs and that therefore he was a servant and had to obey the club's orders".

The Surrey County Court concluded that Walker was a workman within the confines of the 1906 Act and found for him but Palace appealed. *The Times* reported at the Court of Appeal that the Master of the Rolls Lord Justice Fletcher Moulton and Lord Justice Farwell concluded that Walker should be covered by the Act.

" ... his Lordship felt himself unable to entertain any doubt that this man had entered into a contract of service with the club, in his Lordship's opinion by way of manual labour, but whether that was so or not ...

The court would be narrowing the Act unduly if they were to say that this man was not within the Act.

It had been argued that it made a difference that this man contracted to exercise his skill, and that the company had no right to dictate to him how he should play.

Walker was, however, bound to obey the general instructions of the club. It was impossible that a man should be taken out of the Act because in doing the particular work which he was bound to do, and as to which he obeyed general instructions, and in particular he was bound in playing to obey the captain, who was the delegate of the club."

The appeal was dismissed. Appended to this case was a similar one brought by "Roberts v. The Crystal Palace Football Club (Limited). This time Palace claimed the player had not made an application within the time allowed by the compensation act. It was referred back to the County Court for judgement.

Palace also played in front of Norwich City's record crowd which was swelled by a visit by King Edward VII to the city on the day of the match. The King did not attend the match but most of the crowd had been to see him and were no doubt satisfied with Norwich's 1-0 victory.

Josh Johnson and Joe Bulcock played for the Southern League against the Football League in a representative match at Stamford Bridge on April 11. Johnson was a devout Christian and Sunday School teacher and regularly refused to play matches at Christmas and Easter because of his beliefs. We also faced serious local competition for the first time, attracting a record crowd (some 12,000) for the away game with Croydon Common, who'd been newly promoted to the Southern League first division. You can dispel any romantic visions of gentlemen sportingly competing in knickerbockers, this local derby was a "bad tempered" game according to the *Croydon*

Did you know?

On December 18, 1913 Lord Plymouth, who was the club's president, donated £35,000 to help purchase the Crystal Palace building for the nation for £230,000.

Advertiser, who had abandoned Palace in order to dedicate coverage to the Common. Palace were regarded as outsiders from a different area. "Football is a game in which one ought to be prepared to give and take hard knocks with good temper," it said. "But many of the modern footballers are very touchy individuals." So there you have it, they were moaning about the good old days back in 1910.

The *Advertiser* didn't seem to think the fans were much better. "When Balmer and Woodger came into collision, and the Palace captain was penalised for kicking his opponent, I thought it more accidental than intentional, although a good many of the spectators who were standing in the very immediate vicinity held very strong opinions to the contrary!" Players were accused of kicking, tripping, squaring up and striking opponents and "running amok".

The match went Palace's way when John Young scored to be "hailed with enthusiasm by the Palace supporters, who were present in full force".

Common were relegated after one season and Palace did the double over them.

We finished with a creditable draw at home to champions Brighton, who were managed by former Palace manager John Robson. Palace had beaten Robson's men away from home a week before Christmas.

At the start of 1910-11, Palace bade farewell to George Woodger who joined Oldham Athletic for a fee of around £800.

Oldham were strengthening the side that had just been promoted to Football League division one for the first time and Woodger proved a valuable acquisition for them, appearing for England before returning south with Spurs.

After an erratic opening, Palace's form was consistent enough to ensure that we equalled our best ever placing of fourth. But, again, occasional defeats punctuated the season and dashed any serious championship aspirations. The biggest win was a 6-1 stuffing of Plymouth, but despite a reasonable run of results, crowds were nothing special. The best attendance was just 12,000 for the Christmas fixture with Swindon.

Plymouth gained revenge in February when Palace had Harry Hanger and Ginger Williams sent off along with Plymouth's Butler in a brutal game that finished 5-1 to Argyle. All three were later suspended. In the Cup, Palace were drawn against old acquaintances Everton at home. It attracted a 35,000 crowd but there was to be no fairy tale and Palace went down 4-0.

There was only one defeat to mar the first 11 matches at the start of the 1911-12 season, but four draws limited our impact as once again we were found wanting in the race for the championship. In November, Charlie Woodhouse died after a short illness and his place was taken by a new signing from Hull, Ted Smith, who scored a record 111 goals in 155 matches for Palace and captained the side when we began our first league season 1920-21. But after 19 games, in which he scored nine goals, he lost his place and the captaincy. Smith and Peter Simpson are the only Palace players to score a hat-trick on their debuts.

Smith's came against West Ham in a 6-1 victory at Upton Park in which Dick Harker also scored three. Smith then went one better by scoring another three in his next match against Bristol Rovers. It was the most dramatic impact of any Palace player. Smith scored in each of the next five games but we didn't win any of them!

For the first time, Palace actually won the last match of the season, but it still only brought a final finish of seventh place. Brentford were also dispatched from the first round of the Cup, 4-0 after a replay which set up another glamour tie, this time with Sunderland, who included England internationals Charlie Buchan, F. Cuggy and J. Mordue. The north-easterners held us to a goalless draw and in front of 20,000 supporters at Roker Park, Palace went out to a single goal. In March, we gained another international honour when "Ginger" Williams was chosen to play for Wales against Scotland. This time the Welsh lost 1-0 although Williams played well enough to win a second cap against Ireland when Wales lost 3-2.

The long serving Harry Collyer and Josh Johnson were both given benefit games during 1912-13, a season which, again, was not one for trying to guess what Palace were going to do next.

There was great satisfaction in beating rivals Southampton 8-0, thanks to four goals from former West Bromwich man Charles Hewitt and a hat-trick from Williams, and, as usual, there was a cup run to add spice to another ultimately unfulfilling season.

Glossop and Bury, who ten years earlier had set a record score for a Cup Final but were now a mid-table second division side, were both beaten 2-0 in the early rounds before Palace drew Edmund Goodman's old team Aston Villa. But the Palace manager's return to Villa Park was not a happy one, the home side won comfortably and went on to lift the Cup.

Palace did have something to celebrate when they won the London Challenge Cup, which was a first team competition, for the first time, overcoming Croydon Common, Spurs and Fulham before beating West Ham 1-0 in the final.

The 1913-14 season was to be Palace's best ever, but it was one that would be played with the clouds of war gathering over Europe.

In the first 13 matches, only Swindon were able to beat us, which was to prove costly because the Wiltshire club were to pip us for the title. After a double setback against Coventry and QPR in November, Palace roared off on an 11 game unbeaten run. Unfortunately too many of those were draws and when the Glaziers had to settle for three draws in three days at Christmas the initiative was handed to Swindon.

Even four successive wins, which included a 2-0 victory over Swindon thanks to goals by John Bright and Ben Bateman, were insufficient. We finished unbeaten in the last eight matches including five more draws. Even on the last day, a victory would have been enough because Swindon could only draw with Cardiff, but Palace could do no better at Gillingham and we missed out on goal average.

One consolation was that Horace Colclough, who had signed from Crewe Alexandra in 1912, became the club's first England international when he played in the team that beat Wales 2-0 in Cardiff on March 16.

Colclough's form was such that it eventually led to the departure of crowd pleaser Joe Bulcock to Swansea. Another favourite on the move was Ginger Williams who in February made the short trip across town to play for Millwall Athletic (as they were then known).

Palace finished on a happy note to the season when they retained the London Challenge Cup, this time beating Spurs 2-1 at Highbury.

Palace repeated the dose in the Professional Footballers' Charity Fund Match at White Hart Lane, winning by the same margin.

The unease which surrounded European politics would grow during the summer and by the time the new football season kicked off in September, Britain would be at war.

The Palace in literature

The English language is a rich and beautiful vehicle for the expression of the greatest minds. Peter Carpark salutes those who have used their talents to recognise the role of Crystal Palace in book writing

Now that Nick Hornby has written *Fever Pitch* and says it's cool to like footie and be a member of the great literati (we always knew this, of course) how about a few tenuous links from Selhurst to Parnassus (look it up, learn something).

Just before we get going I'd like to say something about Arsenal. I hate them, they always beat us. Anyone who supports them must have a real problem. They have our best player at the moment and I'm not going to join in that chant – he has not got AIDS. He's just a bad tempered little sod. Well then, where do the lads stand on the shelves?

As far as I know, Palace do not feature significantly in the works of Chaucer, Malory or Spenser, although there is a rumour that the *Faerie Queene* was written with the late lamented Mick Hill in mind. When we come to the Bard though we're in for a bit of a treat.

It is obvious from the countless clues in the folio that Shakespeare was a Palace fan; and a lot of recent scholarship points the finger at Bert Head as the real 'author'. Now in these days of intentional fallacy and signifiers sliding under signifieds nothing, my friends, is certain. However, here are some give-aways.

i. The "lost" scene in *Macbeth* (Act III, Scene 9) featuring Gerry Queen, Willie Wallace and John Hughes as the three murderers. Here's an extract:

Queen: Oi, Willie did you bring the spanner?

Wallace: Christ no, that was Yogi's job.

ENTER BANQUO AND FLEANCE WITH A TORCH

Hughes: Oi, gotta light mate?

THEY RUN AWAY

Queen: That's blown it. The boss won't like this. You'll be on the bench next week.

All: Bert's a hard man. Let's away.

EXEUNT

Compelling evidence, I'm sure you'll agree.

ii. The scene where Richard the Second is 'nutmegged' by Bolingbroke with the triumphant cry of 'There's only one Jimbo Rimbo'.

The obvious references to Palace's lamentable spell during the 80s in the climactic Battle of Shrewsbury, which, fittingly enough, Hotspur loses one-nil at home.

iii. The argument in Ted Hughes' excellent critical study (*Shakespeare and the Goddess of Long Throws*) that if you read *Venus and Adonis* enough times you will start to find the initial letters of the Palace 1592 squad appearing in squiggly shapes in the white space in front of you.

Enough, I rest my case.

The next two centuries were barren years for Palace but with the emergence of the novel, things started looking up for us devotees: Dickens in his devastating critique of the Aylott days (*Donkey and Son*) and Virginia Woolf's searching metaphysical study of away supporters (*To the Whitehorse*) are typical of the genre.

The 20th century is awash with material for the Palace scholar: Graham Greene's *Brighton Ruck* and Samuel Beckett's *Waiting for Swindlehurst* are among many detailed nods in our direction.

William Trevor, the great Irish short story writer, seems to have a predelicition for the Eagles too, giving Charlie Cooke and the boys a mention in his story *Afternoon Dancing*. And Mike Leigh likes to mention Croydon in his work, even going so far as to make one of the characters in *Abigail's Party* an ex-Palace player. In fact, John Salthouse who played Tony, was actually on Palace's books as a youngster.

May I add we only have contempt for those who have shamed Palace through their public support. I am talking, of course, about Nookie the Bear, Ronnie Corbett and others too artistically bankrupt to mention.

I shall finish with the last words of Beckett's *Waiting for Swindlehurst*:

Flanagan: Well? Shall we go?

Allen: Yes, let's go.

THEY DO NOT MOVE (CURTAIN)

Initials

RSPCA – Ron Sold Palace Centurion to Arsenal
TSB – The Seaweed Bank
MSC – Manager Steve Coppell
AA – Alan's Anonymous
DTI – Don't Transfer Ian
CPFC – Couldn't Possibly Follow Chelsea
ITV – Integrity of Terry Venables
LBC – Liverpool Buried in Cup
RNLI – Ron Noades Loves Income
JCB – Jim Cannon's Brilliant

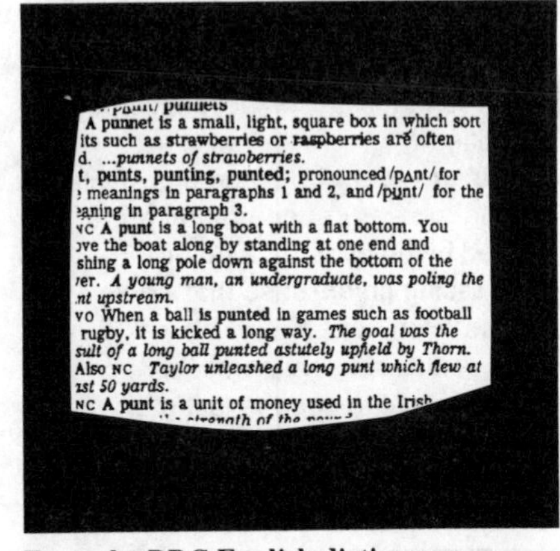

A punnet is a small, light, square box in which sort
its such as strawberries or raspberries are often
d. ...*punnets of strawberries.*
t, **punts, punting, punted;** pronounced /pʌnt/ for
meanings in paragraphs 1 and 2, and /pʊnt/ for the
aning in paragraph 3.
NC **A punt** is a long boat with a flat bottom. You
ove the boat along by standing at one end and
shing a long pole down against the bottom of the
ver. *A young man, an undergraduate, was poling the*
nt upstream.
VO When a ball is **punted** in games such as football
rugby, it is kicked a long way. *The goal was the*
sult of a long ball punted astutely upfield by Thorn.
Also NC *Taylor unleashed a long punt which flew at*
ast 50 yards.
NC **A punt** is a unit of money used in the Irish

From the BBC English dictionary

Crystal Palace

A RELIGIOUS GUIDE

Sic Transit Gloria Mundi: thus passes away the glory of this world. It came to Matthew Simmonds in a flash of blinding light. Supporting Crystal Palace is a holy experience

It came through my door unsolicited; about as welcome as the news that Mullery had got the Palace job. But, as I mooched towards the bin, I idly flicked through the pages. And it hit me; bang!

These loopy born-again bible bashers had all the answers. Their little book answered a lot of big questions. They didn't know it of course, but I did. Now it began to fall into place. There was some light at the end of the long dark tunnel. Eighteen years of supporting Palace, 18 years of faith largely unrewarded. A sign here and there, a minor miracle now and then; just enough to keep me going as I trudged wearily through the slough of despond.

Now, at last, I could see some pattern, some reason. My journey through purgatory, or Hartlepool, had meaning; the day I suffered in a car with a professional Scouser singing "one, two, one, two, three, one, two, three, four … five-nil", all the way back to South Wales; my four day away trip in 1989 to Nottingham (0-5) and Man City (0-3). The expense, the anguish, the despair. Not a goal, not a sniff, not a clue; bloody Clive Allen sliding in number three right in front of me. I could see the smile as he anticipated Perry's fumble.

What could it mean? So, a little book from some obscure evangelical cult proved to be the turning point, my conversion on the road to Holmesdale.

Palace serves a metaphysical purpose in our lives, above and beyond bodily suffering. Palace is a gateway to a spiritual dimension. We are not to bewail our fate, we must welcome it because we are closer to the meaning of life, the meaning of football than any permed, shell-suited, moptop berating Souness.

The natural condition of the football fan is to suffer. We have a lifetime's experience and they are uncomprehending. On the lush, green turf of human existence we are the veteran midfielders and they the YTS boys. How else do you explain my companion's gleeful comment, aimed to belittle and embarrass: "Every time Liverpool scored all Palace did was sing and wave their scarves around, ha ha."

See what I mean? They have not the slightest inkling, the merest grasp. Yet it was, perhaps, my proudest moment. It was above and beyond my friend. No spiritual dimension. Hard times nourish and strengthen us where they destroy the thousands of cling-ons to the Anfield bandwagon. I hope every time we play the 'Pool we continue to outsing, outdance, outballoon and outscarfwave them … and "give them a good kicking" as Mr Coleman of Swansea so touchingly put it, spiritually speaking of course.

Brother Simmonds presents the Crystal Palace guide to New Spiritualism

astral projection • existing beyond normal human perception: Steve Coppell's tactics in the Coca Cola Cup semi final first leg
clairvoyance • perception of things not seen: which explains those Liverpool penalties
conjurer • one who summons spirits:
crystal power • supernatural power gained by holding, rubbing or possessing crystals: so that's how "Uncle" Ron does it
ESP • extra sensory perception: enabling refs to see the last man playing Mark Hughes on side
incantation/mantra • prayers or words chanted to summon spirits: *Oh Palace We Love You* or *Red 'n' Blue Army* for example
meditation • mystical contemplation: such as why don't Palace bloody pass to each other?
medium • a go between for people wishing to communicate with the dead: such as the PA announcer at Wimbledon games
ouija board • board bearing symbols, used to spell out messages: "Lineker you're off, big nose get on!"
reincarnation • soul rebirth in another body: George Ndah is the new Vince Hilaire
tarot cards • set of 22 cards bearing pictures of people with symbolic meanings: I'll swap you Noades for Walker
telepathy • supernatural transfer of thought: Sinnott thinks "I'll knock it up the line", Row 17 of the Arthur Wait think: "Duck!"
visualisation • forming mental images of things not present: A pukka trophy in the Palace cabinet for instance
yoga • mystic Hindu discipline of exercising intense concentration: Unfortunately Jeff Hopkins failed to complete the whole course

Have you ever been taunted by a Tesco lorry?

Tony Matthews is not superstitious, until he goes to Palace. Then it's just as well not to offend the Gods

Many of us are superstitious about Palace – one woman wore the same shoes to every cup match in 1976 but changed them for the semi-final while Paul Bradbury, it was reported in *Rail Travellers' News* of September 18, 1976, wore "the same sweaty socks and the same overcoat to the majority of games in 1975-76 because they were "lucky", it was observed that if the tradition continued more people from coach four were expected to go by train.

It will always haunt me. The year I began attending Selhurst regularly we got relegated. After that my friends and I spent five seasons, hands thrust firmly in our pockets, shuffling from foot to foot trying to keep the tears of frustration at bay as our inept forwards ruined what little hope there was of a victory. During those years I often wondered if it was me. Was I a Jonah? After all, Palace had been doing fine until I took up my regular spot in the middle of the Holmesdale. I toyed with the idea that if I walked away from Palace forever perhaps the spell that hung over me would be lifted and Palace could continue as any other football club.

I am not naturally superstitious, I don't fear for my future if I walk under a ladder and I don't rush home for a pinch of salt if a black cat crosses my path, but where Palace are concerned it's as well not to tempt the Gods. Never do anything that might bring bad luck and this can range from not changing winning socks to drinking the same sort of drink (light and lager took us to Wembley, I swear it).

There was a time when lack of funds meant long journeys were out of the question, so I listened to the radio. To my alarm, I soon discovered that LBC "where news comes first" was a jinx on the Eagles. Whenever I tuned in we would lose. The usual pattern was for the commentator to spend most of the programme explaining that Palace were all over their opponents but just couldn't score, then, at about twenty to five, the breakthrough would come with those immortal words: "And it's bad news for Palace fans".

LBC's ability to lose us matches was uncanny. I tried to keep away, but by half-past-four I could hold out no longer. I'd just see how we were getting on. And as soon as I did, there would be news of another heartbreaking defeat. It was a major reason for my decision to travel everywhere to watch the team. I couldn't trust them to play properly unless I was there screaming, shouting and swearing at them. I couldn't stand the agony of having some faceless voice telling me ever-so-matter-of-factly that Palace were losing. But when I started going, I realised that luck wasn't confined to a tranny in my bedroom. Colours were unlucky too. If I wore a scarf or a shirt – defeat followed.

I took this belief to Wembley on Cup Final day. When all around were bedecked in glorious red and blue, faces and hair as well, I allowed myself a solitary badge (I have a collection of Palace badges, but there's only one which is safe to wear to a game - all the others are unlucky). I was like the ugly duckling, but how could I flirt with our chances just for the sake of my personal appearance? How I longed to put on a scarf or pick up a flag. But I knew to do so would mean inevitable defeat. After we lost the replay, I borrowed a friend's scarf as an act of defiance.

The worst example of the bad luck colours bring came in the 1988-89 promotion season when I plucked up sufficient courage to wear a scarf on a trip to Bristol City in the league cup. Not only did the coach break down but by the time we arrived, Palace were losing 3-0. I just want to apologise to all the other poor sods who were on the coach with me.

Since then, I have tried to break the spell and, on one occasion, I thought I'd succeeded. Anfield, November 1991, I wore my shirt. "What the hell? We're going to lose anyway, so I may as well make a futile gesture." Our 2-1 victory suggested the spell was broken. The same colours were worn to Forest shortly after and we were shafted 5-1, and it was my fault. The colours had to go back in the cupboard for casual wear only.

Equally sinister was the fear of Tesco lorries. While driving to away matches we began to notice that the number of Tesco trucks sighted coincided with the number of goals the opposition scored. By the same ruling, we discovered that a Sainsbury's lorry meant a goal for us. This we based on the proximity of Sainsbury's to Selhurst having a positive effect (although one would doubt whether they do in real life). As Brighton play in colours that resemble their carrier bags, Tesco's, are inextricably linked with all things evil.

Most superstitions don't tend to last long and are replaced by newer kinds. So it was that a feared 7-1 defeat at Notts County turned out to be a 3-2 win. We would never scream in terror at the sight of the huge Tesco's depot situated cruelly on the M1 again. Yet, as one superstition bites the dust so another comes along. Nigel Martyn cannot take the credit for his first ever penalty save for Palace because it would never have been achieved without the aid of my friend Louise Court's penalty saving hat. This furry item must now be worn each time he faces a spot kick.

Then there's the Shrewsbury-inspired fear of knowing the opposition's form. Never look in newspaper form columns to try to sus out how well opponents are playing. Any team that's gone, say, 56 matches since an away goal will definitely be coming to Palace next. Steve Coppell said "luck evens itself out over the course of a season". He's wrong. For Palace, luck never evens itself out. If it ever does, we will be champions. And the photo of the zebra crossing? It is the lucky crossing in Whitehorse Lane. *NEVER* use anything else!

The Great War and the Twenties

Palace join the Football League at last

Hulton Deutsch

Palace (in white) go out of the 1914 F.A. Cup at Upton Park

Against the background of increasing tension in central Europe, the 1913-14 season drew to a close with Palace celebrating their best season so far.

The peace that had reigned for so long was now fragile and when a Serbian nationalist shot dead Archduke Ferdinand of Austria in Sarajevo on June 28, Europe's armies mobilised.

On August 4, a month before the new football season was due to commence, Britain's Liberal Prime Minister Herbert Asquith declared war on Germany. The battles were soon raging. The British Expeditionary Force engaged the Germans at Mons and by the time the season began on September 5, the war was going badly – the Germans were within reach of Paris, the furthest extent of their advance of the whole war. Both sides began to dig their trenches.

Hopes that the season would see Palace go one better than the runners-up spot of the year before soon foundered. It didn't help that, at the onset of war, many players had joined the army. The first to go were the Reservists, former Army men, who were immediately called up. Nottingham Forest and Palace were hardest hit by this; both clubs losing three players. The speed with which British men were called to arms was remarkable. But this didn't satisfy some people and there were calls for football to cease altogether and for the 7,000 athletes from all clubs to be called to the colours.

In the light of what we know now, such a move would have been catastrophic. The number of footballers who would have been wiped out doesn't bear thinking about. Nevertheless, enthusiasm for the war was at its peak in the closing months of 1914 and football's apparently unpatriotic stance in refusing to halt for the duration won it little public sympathy. From Palace's point of view it might have been as well if football had stopped, because the team's winning touch deserted them and we finished in a lowly 15th place. A poor season hinged on a bad start in which only one victory was chalked up in the first ten games.

It would be wrong however to place the blame entirely on the war because it affected all clubs and many suffered as much as Palace. Nevertheless, attendances were swiftly affected and, as a result, the club began to experience serious financial problems. Such was their plight that in January 1915 Palace elected to play their third round F.A. Cup replay at Birmingham rather than come back to London. Birmingham were second in league division two at the time and were ripe for a giant killing but Palace, whose attendances had dipped as low as 1,000 for the visit of Norwich at Christmas, partly because of the war and partly because of bad weather, decided to "sell" the match and take the guarantee of healthy gate receipts.

In the first game, our problems were primarily on the playing side. The team was without captain Harry Hanger and Jimmy Hughes and at half time Ted Smith was unable to continue because of concussion. Facing ten men, Birmingham went ahead just after the hour with a penalty by Smith. Bill Davies equalised four minutes later from a Percy Keene centre and, within another three minutes, Palace were in front, Bill Middleton heading home. But a lapse of concentration brought the flurry of scoring to an end a minute later when Eyre equalised for Birmingham after a scramble. It was a gutsy performance nevertheless and Palace deserved more than a draw. Financially however, the result was a bonus. The takings for the first game were £429.2s, clearly the sort of money Palace needed. The club also had an uneasy relationship with the Admiralty, who had

A soldier who had been badly shell shocked while serving in the war, had not uttered a word since returning to Blighty. Then he went to watch Palace and got so involved in the game that he ended up cheering for the team and regained his powers of speech.

CRYSTAL PALACE CLOSED.

THE YEAR'S FIXTURES CANCELLED.

The following notice was issued at the Crystal Palace on Monday:—

"Owing to the steady increase in the numbers in the depot of the Royal Naval Division, the Lords Commissioners of the Admiralty have decided that in the interests of the Service the Palace and grounds will have to be entirely closed to the public from Wednesday, the 10th February.

"(Signed) R. WILLIAMS BULKELEY "(Commodore.)".

The General Manager of the Palace, Mr. H. J. Buckland, states that as the Admiralty were in occupation it was decided some weeks ago by the Commodore that it would not be possible for the proposed programme for 1915 to be carried out. The whole of the year's fixtures at the Palace were accordingly cancelled. The buildings have now been cleared of everything of interest to the public, and the Palace has been turned [illegible]

taken over the Crystal Palace ground while we remained as tenants, and so the board reluctantly agreed to stage the second game at St Andrew's.

On the following Saturday, January 16, 1915, with debutant John Bowler replacing Harry Collyer, who'd been injured in training, and John Whibley taking over from Davies, the Glaziers again held out for 90 minutes. But ten minutes into extra time Tinkler settled it for Birmingham, giving Johnson no chance. Further goals from Gibson and Smith gave the scoreline a harsh look.

The effect of the war on crowds can be gauged by comparing the Southern League encounter with West Ham in April 1915, which drew 6,000, with the corresponding fixture the following September, which attracted 3,500 less. The second match on September 25, coincided with the start of the Battle of Loos, where two British infantry divisions lost 8,000 men in a single attack – more than twice as many as had watched Palace that day. In March 1915, Palace were confronted with a more serious problem than poor form. The Admiralty, who had commandeered the Crystal Palace ground for military purposes ordered us out. The club was forced to find what it thought would be a temporary home (little realising we would never go back to our original ground). It also meant the end of Cup Finals in south London. The 1915 final between Chelsea and Sheffield United, known as the Khaki Cup Final because of the uniforms of the soldiers which coloured the crowd, was played at Old Trafford.

Palace were offered the chance to share with both Millwall and Croydon Common but instead moved to a small ground at Herne Hill, not far from Millwall's ground. Northampton were the first visitors and held the Glaziers to a 1-1 draw. Palace then suffered the ignominy of being destroyed 5-1 by their upstart neighbours Croydon Common in the next home match – it was a humiliating experience, although it was Croydon Common whose days were numbered.

On a Wednesday afternoon in March, the Common, battling against relegation, slaughtered us. The *Croydon Advertiser,* whose coverage was almost wholly restricted to the Croydon team's exploits rather than Palace's, crowed: "We have been accustomed to grumble at the failure of the Common's forwards, but compared with the five who represented Palace – well, comparisons are odious."

The response of the Palace fans to this latest misfortune was to chant *Are We Downhearted? No!* It would appear that this was a popular song among our support as it is mentioned on other occasions later in the 1920s. The result left Palace, marooned in 13th position, waiting for their first win at Herne Hill. Slowly we settled into the more homely surroundings and at last put together some decent results, winning four in a row against Plymouth, Gillingham, Southend and West Ham, before losing the last two matches of a disappointing season.

To see football through the rest of the hostilities, the Football and Southern Leagues ceased and a new regional competition was devised. All of London's major teams entered the London Combination, which began with a principal competition in September until the end of January. This was followed by a smaller, "supplementary" competition until the end of the season. In the principal competition, Palace didn't fare too well, finishing ninth, but in the supplementary competition they enjoyed better fortune. By now the F.A. had introduced a series of measures to cope with the rigours of wartime football as Jack Rollins explained in a chapter devoted to the first world war from his book *Soccer at War 1939-45*:

"The Registration Act came in during 1915 and this put more difficulties and pressure on football clubs. For 1915-16, it was decided that matches could only be played on Saturdays and public holidays. No mid-week games were permitted so as not to interfere with the making of munitions etc."

Rollin added: *"The League announced that there were to be no broken time payments, only genuine expenses, and that all footballers would be expected to take up bona fide work for the benefit of the country. It was decided during December 1915 that all games should be reduced to eighty minutes' duration. The referees could also dispense with the ten-minute interval. This applied in each of the following wartime seasons with the period being extended from about the middle of November to the middle of January."*

On through the hail of slaughter
Where gallant comrades fall
Where blood is poured like water
They drive the trickling ball
The fear of death before them
Is but an empty name
True to the land that bore them
The Surreys play the game

The above was written by Touchstone, the Daily Mail poet, about the charge of the 8th Battalion, East Surrey Regiment at Cental Maison. It was later reproduced in the Palace programme. One can only wonder at how many Palace fans there might have been in a Surrey regiment.

Football began to accept greater responsibility for helping the war effort and matches were occasionally used to raise money for such causes as the War Comforts Fund. Palace's first game in the London Combination against Croydon Common, which we lost 2-1 at the Nest, was played "without remuneration" for professionals. The *Advertiser* said: "There had been much speculation as to the drawing power of the game under the new conditions and the gate of 3,100 – exclusive of the wounded soldiers from the local military hospital who were accommodated with seats in one of the stands – must have set all doubt at rest."

Palace fared rather better in the supplementary league winning seven and losing only one of their first eight games including a 10-1 thrashing of Reading in which Sid Sanders scored six times. Crowds for most of the matches were not recorded, although 10,000 turned up to see Palace beat Spurs 4-0 on April 22. Such a crowd would have attracted the interest of the authorities, who regularly used football matches to look out for draft dodgers and the like. The season ended with the Allies bogged down at Gallipoli – a disaster which eventually prompted the resignation of the First Lord of the Admiralty Winston Churchill.

The first battle of the Somme began on July 1, 1916, when the new British Army, made up almost entirely of volunteers – three quarters of the regular army of 1914 had already been lost – attacked the Germans and suffered 60,000 casualties on the first day, including 20,000 dead. The battle was still raging as the new football season, 1916-17, began. Casualties ran at about 4,000 a day – comfortably exceeding average Palace crowds.

Reading, Southampton and Portsmouth were added to the London Combination which meant that, rather than a split between a principal and supplementary competition, there were now enough fixtures to play throughout the whole season. Palace played most (but not all) of the other teams four times opening with a 4-0 home win over Brentford, where the amateur player Lockton scored all our goals. We eventually finished a creditable eighth, even though the fixtures at home to Luton and away to Southampton were not played. Palace must have wished they hadn't bothered to play West Ham either, because they lost 8-1 at home.

The following week, on the day that the Somme finally drew to a sorry close, Palace lost 3-1 to Spurs. The Allies had won a strip of land 20 miles long and six deep at the cost of 420,000 British and 194,000 French casualties.

Palace were in the middle of a bad run – only one win out of 11. That came on December 9, when we beat Arsenal 2-1. Over Christmas and new year, we drew four times in succession with Portsmouth, Southampton, twice, and Millwall. It was a rare steady patch and form after Christmas was erratic although there were encouraging victories including four in a row finishing with a 2-1 victory at Portsmouth on the day the USA entered the war. The season ended early for Palace, because of the unplayed match at Southampton, so we finished with a disappointing 4-0 defeat at Arsenal, a team we'd actually beaten in the other three meetings. By the time the 1917-18 season began, the third battle of Ypres, Passchendaele, was under way. Loss of life was just as heavy as on the Somme.

If football was seen as a release valve from the rigours of war, the Palace supporters were given little to smile about. We lost our first four matches, including a 7-1 hiding by Fulham. But after 18 goals were conceded during those first four games Palace suddenly hit a rich vein with four straight wins. Despite the shaky opening, we recovered to finish a place higher than the season before. Nevertheless we still had to endure some heavy defeats including an 8-0 mauling by Tottenham. The worst, however, was saved until last. In a lamentable performance on the final day of the regular London Combination season, West Ham scored 11 times without reply in front of just 4,000.

Palace's contribution to the war effort continued after the end of the regular season when they had the chance to redeem themselves through a series of War Fund matches. The National Football War Fund had been established earlier that year to assist people associated with the game who had been bereaved or maimed. Two games against QPR ended with honours even, one win apiece, before Palace did the double over Clapton Orient, 2-0 both times.

With the weight of the American forces helping turn the tide, 1918-19 was the last season of war time soccer. The conflict was virtually at an end by the time the new football season started. Germany had the option to fight on but the Kaiser was advised to sue for peace.

Palace moved grounds again. This time to the Nest, near Selhurst station which had belonged to Croydon Common. The Robins' brief flirtation with Southern League first division football was over and they had gone into liquidation. It's strange to think that Palace were financially weaker and the loss of our ground might have forced us out of business. In which case, we might all be Croydon Common fans now.

Palace, who'd opened the season with a 2-1 win at Clapton Orient, christened the new ground with a 4-2 victory over QPR. The start to the season was as good as the previous one had been awful, but the last match of the first world war was a defeat – 3-2 in the return at QPR. Whitworth and Bates scored Palace's goals.

On the following Monday, November 11, 1918, the armistice was signed.

Palace had already put six past Orient and Spurs were similar victims, Whitworth helped himself to five goals in helping to erase the memory of the mauling of the previous year, but Palace conceded the same number against Brentford and finished the season without a win in the last nine matches – ten if you count the London Victory Cup defeat against Chelsea at Highbury. We finished seventh for the second year running. As Britain attempted to return to normality, football immediately resumed its pre-war format. For Palace and the other first division Southern League clubs, there was to be just one more season before they would all move on to greater things.

Harry Hanger had been killed in the fighting – as had former Palace men Ginger Williams and Joe Bulcock – but Edmund Goodman was still able to call on the experience of players such as Albert Feebury, Ernie Rhodes, Jimmy Hughes, the England amateur international Ben Bateman and Ted Smith, who would surely have become Palace's all-time record goalscorer had it not been for the intervention of the war. Despite this, Palace only managed two draws and a defeat from their opening three matches and by mid-October we'd still managed only one victory. Things picked up at Christmas with five straight wins, including a Christmas and Boxing Day double over Brighton. The second match at the Nest attracted more than 15,000, a figure that was exceeded by 2,000 the following day when Millwall were the visitors. Dick Cracknell's goal maintained Palace's impressive form. It was a platform on which to build and Palace did just that, only tasting defeat on four more occasions until the end of the season. As a result, we finished in a very creditable third position. In the Cup, Palace travelled to Newcastle but, in front of 15,000, were unable to repeat the victory of 1907. The Geordies eased through comfortably by two goals to nil.

For some time, the Football League had been ripe for expansion and there had been rumblings from many leading Southern League clubs who wished to join up. The League had already taken former Southern League clubs such as Stoke, West Ham and Fulham into the fold and Palace weren't the only ones with a strong case for being allowed to join them. The stumbling block was the argument over the composition of what would effectively be a new third division. The Southern League was stronger than its northern counterpart, but there was concern that a sudden influx of southern clubs would alter the balance of the league.

Eventually it was agreed that the Southern League would be taken into the third division *en bloc* and, if it proved a success, a northern third division would be established the following season. Palace, having been rejected at birth so to speak, were in the League at last.

The third division was hardly a novelty though. The only change to the composition of the division from that of the Southern League was that Cardiff City were elected straight into the second division to be replaced by Grimsby.

Having had such a successful final season in the Southern League, Palace had reason to be confident against the same opposition. During the summer, the squad was strengthened with players of international quality. A columnist in one of the leading papers of the day, *Football and Sports Favourite,* wrote: "J.T. Jones is Stoke's other loss. After a long stay with them, where he has gained international honours galore, he has gone to the Crystal Palace club. Methinks the 'Glaziers' are indeed lucky." Jones was an impressive signing and the paper added:

"Crystal Palace mean to fight their way into the second division this season or know the reason why. The 'Glaziers' have worked hard during the close season and they have caught some real big fish. Two of their captures are Jones and McCracken (not of Newcastle), Welsh and Irish Internationals respectively. Tommy Storey is wearing their colours too. It does one's heart good to see Tommy coming down the wing, and when he gets going things usually start to hum with a vengeance."

Storey, who joined Palace from Middlesbrough, made 33 appearances that season and scored four goals. More significant was the capture of centre-half Roy McCracken (sometimes spelt M'Cracken, depending on whose version of history you read). Although "not the famous McCracken", Roy was the cousin of the Newcastle star and, while at Palace, he shared international duties with his more illustrious relative. Born in Dromore County Down, McCracken signed for Palace from Distillery having served in Belgium and Italy during the war. His transfer was a controversial one. Distillery were annoyed that Palace had stepped in for their star man and the F.A. had to be called in to rule that everything was in order. Palace were instructed to pay the Irish club £800 for his services. McCracken gained three of his four Irish caps in the Home International championships of 1921-22, having made his debut in a 2-0 defeat by England at Sunderland in 1920 which brought him the honour of becoming the first ever third division international.

With Welsh international Jones also recognised as a quality player, Palace had reason for confidence. But there was a set back on the first day when Merthyr beat us 2-1. Captained by former Palace player Tommy Barber, Merthyr took the lead through Walker, although debutant A.G. Milligan secured a place for himself in the history books with Palace's first league goal to level the scores. The *Advertiser* said: "The equalising goal came quickly after the restart, and was mainly due to a clever effort by Conner, who worked through in clever fashion and centred almost from the goal-line. Milligan drove the ball past Lindon, who scooped it from the net, but the Palace inside left drove it back into the net to make sure." Merthyr struck back with an offside looking goal from Chesser to secure both points. Milligan's glory soon passed. He made one more appearance and then disappeared. In the first home match, Palace were equally disappointing being held to a goalless draw by Plymouth. But after that the season really took off. Six wins in a row, the first in the return with Merthyr, saw us surge to the top. Players didn't enjoy quite the luxury afforded stars of today. The visiting players "without waiting to change their 'footer' clothes, were out of the ground before the majority of the spectators and went full pelt in motors to Paddington, where they hoped to catch the six o'clock train to Merthyr".

Goalkeeper Jack Alderson, who'd signed in 1919 after making one pre-war appearance for Newcastle, added to his clean sheet against Argyle by remaining unbeaten in five of those victories and, although there were shock defeats against Bristol Rovers and Reading, both were swiftly avenged. Southampton gave chase but Palace finished comfortable champions.

Anyone who tells you that there was no crowd trouble in the "old days" is wrong. During the season, Palace's ground was closed because of trouble and we were forced to play the home game with Exeter at Southampton. The Palace programme noted after the 3-2 home midweek defeat by Southend that some fans had surrounded the visitors' right back who had played "a constantly over-vigorous match" and had been booked. That formed part of Palace's defence to the F.A. after they were called to account for the alleged assault of both Fairclough of Southend (who scored two

CRYSTAL PALACE FC THIRD DIVISION CHAMPIONS 1921

Hulton Deutsch

Athletic News **toasted Palace's promotion and its correspondent 'Nestor' offered some revealing pen-pictures of the players. These profiles are based upon his notes.**

JACK ALDERSON (goalkeeper): Stationed at Woolwich during the war, spotted by Edmund Goodman. Played for Palace in London Combination matches at Herne Hill. Turned pro after the armistice and played in every match in the last Southern League season and every match in the championship campaign. "Not showy, but sound, and extremely popular with all who know him. In his youthful days earned fame as a sprinter and one of the fastest men in the team."

JACK LITTLE (right back): Helped Croydon Common to promotion to the Southern League first division in 1913-14. Served in the Royal Artillery in the war and played for Arsenal and Palace. "A difficult man to beat especially at close quarters."

ERNIE RHODES (left back): "Dusty" came through the reserve ranks. "A cool defensive player, Rhodes is always 'all out'. Like most of the Palace players, a man of few words and takes the game seriously. Has a taste for music and at a festive gathering is able to keep the fun going by his pianoforte selections."

J.T. JONES (right half): Some time finding his form but one of the stalwarts. "Played for gallant little Wales against the three sister nations last season and also against England and Scotland this year. Also selected to play against Ireland but the club were unable to release him owing to important matches. A feeder of his forwards and a stumbling block to opponents."

PHIL BATES (centre-half): "Feeds his forwards like a waiter and can head a ball with the best. Is slightly handicapped by a wound in the shoulder – a memento of his war services – but is plucky and tackles like a terrier."

BERT FEEBURY (captain, left half): "A strong tackler and defender when danger threatens. Can shoot too. Feebury's 'specials' always cause anxiety to goalkeepers and rouse the Palace supporters to enthusiasm. 'Plays the game' on and off the field and a credit to his profession."

ROY M'CRACKEN (right half): "His departure from Belfast Distillery to the Palace caused quite a 'pother' but untroubled by these trifles, M'Cracken made a name at Selhurst and became a great favourite with the crowd. His opinions are always worth hearing. Young and level-headed should go far."

BEN BATEMAN (outside right): Gained amateur international honours in 1913-14. "Has fine speed and, given a partner, makes ground and middles a ball from the corner flag to perfection."

TOMMY STOREY (inside right): "Undoubtedly seen to more advantage on the wing but clever inside all the same. His footwork is neat and finished."

JOHN CONNER (centre-forward): Scottish junior international. "A capable centre, he holds the line together and has a 'swerve' which is disconcerting to opposing backs. Is fast, passes beautifully and never shirks the battle. Conner takes a serious view of life and commands respect from all who know him."

TED SMITH (centre-forward): "In his day one of the most consistent scorers in the country." Kept out of the team by ill-health and an operation.

JOHN WHIBLEY (outside-left): "He does not appear cut out for the hurly burly of strenuous football, but ability and pace enabled him to hold his own with most opponents. Quiet and unassuming he is the best type of professional."

A. WOOD (inside left): "Whole hearted and energetic, will be more of an asset when he learns discretion. A dangerous man to have on one's side."

BERT MENLOVE (centre-forward): Suffered ill-health during the season but "has great possibilities". A Reservist like Wood

BILL HAND (outside right): Hand came from Sutton in Ashfield where he was spotted by Edmund Goodman. "A box of tricks". A small player but "strongly built and full of pluck".

goals) and the referee. The upshot of this was that the Nest was closed for a fortnight and Palace banned from playing within a ten mile radius of their home ground. The reason we played at Southampton, our championship rivals who were in fact two points clear of us at the time, was that Palace hadn't been quick enough to take up the preferred options of playing at either Tottenham or Clapton Orient. There were some impressive attendances at the Nest though. At Christmas, 22,000 turned up to see Brighton beaten 3-2, completing the "double" over the seaside club. In the final 22 matches we suffered just one reverse, by one goal at Grimsby on February 5. We finished five points clear to complete a highly satisfactory first season in the League.

The foundation for this success was undoubtedly solid defence. Alderson and the full back pairing of "Dusty" Rhodes and Jack Little, who was described by the *Football and Sports Favourite* as "one of the star turns of Crystal Palace", were on their way to completing a century of consecutive matches together. Admittedly the total included friendlies and cup games, but it was still a remarkable record and gave Palace a great deal of stability. Not only was Little a "star turn", he remains one of Palace's greatest players. He was first choice right back for seven years after the war, having been a member of the Croydon Common defence which conceded just 14 goals in 30 matches when they won promotion to Southern League division one in 1913-14.

He also turned out for Arsenal during the war and also occasionally for Palace with whom he threw in his lot when normality returned. He made his Palace debut in the first match of the 1919-20 season, a 2-2 draw with Northampton, and remained ever present in our last season in the Southern League and first season in division three. His testimonial in April 1927 attracted 7,000 people when he fielded his own XI against Palace.

At the other end of the field , Scotsman John Conner led the scorers with 29 league goals.

Palace's championship was all the more remarkable because it was achieved for the most part without the services of our most important player, Roy McCracken, who broke his leg in a surprise home defeat by Swansea Town in mid-December and missed the rest of the season. The Irishman's value to Palace, it was said, could not be measured; yet the team still completed the season with only 34 goals against – a record which stood until it was bettered by the famous back four of 1978-79.

Palace were already well on their way to promotion when the *Football and Sports Favourite* sent their correspondent "Peeping Tom" *Behind the scenes with Crystal Palace.*

An article appeared in the issue of March 5, the day Palace chalked up their fifth win in a row, demolishing Gillingham 4-1. Yet, what Peeping Tom found was a homely club still coming to terms with league status: "Take a hop skip and jump and you are out of the Selhurst Railway station and into the Nest – the old ground of Croydon Common," he wrote. He was much taken with Edmund Goodman who "had a face as kindly and open as the sun shining above our heads". Goodman had lost his leg at 18 as an amateur while with Villa. He took a kick on the knee which he said himself "took bad ways". But there was plenty for Goodman to smile about, he had a super side, defensively outstanding and with Conner in predatory mood, Palace were on the up.

Conner scored in each of the last five matches as Palace surged towards division two and on four occasions he scored twice. Promotion was all but sealed with a 5-1 win over Northampton in torrential rain on April 23, the same day that King George V watched Spurs beat Wolves in the Cup Final at Stamford Bridge. Palace had saved their best performance of the season for the Cobblers and all that was required was a point from the return at Northampton County Cricket Ground the following Saturday.

The draw was not achieved without a scare. Northampton took an early lead before Palace came back to take the lead while "Bateman had a beanfeast with Hewison, who was beaten time after time". In the closing stages the Cobblers rallied and equalised but Palace were not to be denied and they held out for the precious point. The teams:
Northampton: Smith, Watson, Hewison, Bedford, Jobey, Tomkins, Pease, Burnand, Whitworth, Lockett, Chambers.
Palace: Alderson, Little, Rhodes, Jones, Bates, Feebury, Bateman, Storey, Conner, Hand, Whibley.

The celebrations were limited because the title was secured away from home. Away travel for supporters was rare although it was noted that "many supporters were going down by road" to the last game at Southend United. The officials and players dined together after the Northampton match and chairman Sydney Bourne congratulated the team on the "happy conclusion of a strenuous fight" while those who attended that day's friendly against Gillingham reserves at the Nest cheered when the score was announced. "There was hearty applause all round the ground," said the

Hulton Deutsch

1922: Palace get in some training at the Nest

Second division football at the Nest and Palace are on their way to defeat against South Shields. This was the last match in a dreadful spell which brought just one league win in 11 games. Yet Palace were still capable of travelling to Goodison Park and beating Everton 6-0.

Advertiser, "and the band, or as many of them as could be got together, played *For They Are Jolly Good Fellows*. But it wanted the players themselves to be there to stir up the enthusiasm." To ice the cake, Palace won the London Challenge Cup, defeating Clapton Orient, then a mid-table second division side, with a Conner goal at White Hart Lane.

In the F.A. Cup, 18,500 saw first division Manchester City humbled, even though they were heading for the runners-up spot in the league behind Burnley. Bert Menlove and Ben Bateman scored while the defence achieved another shut out.

It was a fabulous result, but in the end only served to heighten the disappointment of a surprise defeat by unfancied Hull in the next round.

Palace's success brought an incidence of law breaking. The *Advertiser* noted that it had become common practice for owners of motor vans to carry supporters to the ground. The law however did not provide for the picking up of "casual fares" and two brothers William and Albert Lawrence of Sydenham were each fined ten shillings for touting illegally for trade. The pair were unlucky enough to chance upon plain clothes sergeant Drayton of Penge police who spotted them plying their unlicensed van for hire.

"He stopped opposite to where witness was standing and called out 'Palace, Palace'. There were already about a dozen men in it. Witness and another police officer entered the vehicle with other men and were driven to Selhurst. The defendant Albert Lawrence stood at the back of the motor van and received the fares. They were each charged 1s."

William Lawrence claimed he'd brought the van load from the Dolphin pub in Sydenham and claimed he "hadn't worked for some time and was trying to earn a bit".

Palace began their second league season, their first as a second division club, in fine style. Nottingham Forest had been relegated from the first division the season before and, in an attempt to bounce straight back, had strengthened their team considerably with former Everton centre-half Fred Parker, Tinsley from Middlesbrough and Burton from Derby. They also had the ex-England keeper Sam Hardy, formerly of Liverpool and Villa, making his debut. But for all their supposed pedigree, Forest couldn't stop Palace chalking up a 4-1 victory. First on the scoresheet was J.T. Jones with a header after 25 minutes. Tinsley equalised, but before the interval Conner restored the advantage. Early in the second half, Ted Smith made things safe and John Whibley rounded it off with a magnificent solo run and shot past Hardy. Off to a flier, but defeats against Barnsley and in the return at Nottingham put paid to hopes of storming division two in the same way we had cruised through the third.

Crowds varied, but again touched 20,000 when Fulham were the visitors. Conner and Menlove scored to give Palace the points. At Craven Cottage in the return, 32,000 watched Palace share the spoils, Conner again scored in a 1-1 draw.

All-in-all the season turned into one of consolidation in which Palace learned a few hard lessons along the way but finished in a safe 14th place. Once again it was the F.A. Cup which provided the real excitement. When Palace, who had been out of sorts for some time, visited Everton in the first round, they pulled off one of the greatest shocks in F.A. Cup history. The Everton outside left did not touch the ball once as Palace delivered six unanswered blows to the mighty Toffees.

The Football and Sports Favourite of March 25, 1922 made Palace's captain Albert Feebury its cover star and included an appraisal. The reporting was made in the customary "jolly hockey sticks" fashion of the day (nothing was ever referred to in less than glowing terms) but it is still reasonable to assume that Feebury was a valuable member of the team.

"Whenever a penalty is to be taken by the 'Glaziers', the Selhurst crowd rise in a body and call for popular skipper Feebury, who is noted for his 'pile drivers'. If anybody can find the net Feebury can. Bert has a kick in his shooting boots that opposing goalies dread, and yet he is one of those very desirable half-backs who never over-shoot their forwards.

"He is a hefty fellow, is Bert, turning the scale somewhere around thirteen stone, and that's an unlucky figure for any opposing forward who tries to charge him. But, in spite of his weight, Feebury is never awkward or ungainly. It is one thing to have weight and stamina and quite another to know how to use them to best advantage."

Having stunned Everton in the Cup, Palace disappointed a 25,000 crowd by being held to a draw by neighbours Millwall, who were a division below us. We lost the replay 2-0.

Towards the end of the season, the team was strengthened by the acquisition of diminutive Albert Harry, who had been spotted playing for Kingstonian. Harry made his debut in the victory over Bury on March 25, 1922 and scored a couple of goals before the season finished.

It was hoped that Palace would improve considerably on their first showing in division two, but the dreams were soon dashed by our worst ever start to a season – 14 games without a win. This appaling record has only been matched on one subsequent occasion, in 1973-74. In both seasons, an identical record was achieved, if "achieved" is the word:

P8, W0, D2, L6, Pts 2.

The long awaited first victory did not arrive until November 11 when, in pouring rain on a muddy pitch, Bateman and Whitworth scored to beat The Wednesday. That was the first of three wins in a row. Palace were not satisfied though as the commentary in the programme explained: "We suffered on many occasions through the rather weak handling of the game by the referee and a stronger official would have seen to it that Gray, the old Norwich back, finished the match in the dressing room. A particularly bad and unnecessary foul on Whibley raised the ire of our supporters, but the referee did not consider the matter important enough to reprimand Gray.

"Gray is not too clean in his methods and when we played the Canaries at Norwich in a match in the old third division days, he once laid out both Bateman and Whibley." The programme added: "The Wednesday are about the roughest team seen at Selhurst this season." The Wednesday were more impressed, they later bought Whitworth, who had made 118 appearances for Palace scoring 50 goals.

In January, we won four matches on the trot, including a double over Southampton and, although we were still none too clever at times, made sufficient recovery to reach 16th place. The high spot was a stupendous performance at champions-to-be Notts County. We travelled to Meadow Lane in deep trouble but returned to London celebrating a splendid 4-0 victory. And there was another international honour when Jack Alderson was capped by England in a 4-1 end-of-season victory over France in Paris.

Could Palace maintain their improved form and mount a serious promotion push? The short answer for 1922-23 was no. In fact they finished only one place higher than the year before.

Frank Hoddinott had joined in the close season from Chelsea. The Pensioners had bought him to partner England centre-forward Jack Cock, but the pair didn't hit it off on the pitch so Palace moved in hoping the man everyone knew as "Tom" would find The Nest more to his liking.

Hoddinott opened his account with a consolation goal in a 2-1 home defeat by Port Vale on the first Saturday but reserved his best performance for Vale's neighbours Stoke who were overwhelmed by a first half hat-trick in 20 minutes at Selhurst at the end of November.

On the whole Hoddinott's form was rather disappointing and he finished with 13 goals from 32 games.

At Bradford in October, the club gave a debut to their new centre half Jimmy Hamilton, who was to become a mainstay of the side during the next six seasons.

Hamilton, from Hetton le Hole, County Durham, served with the Coldstream Guards during the war and signed for Palace after his demob from Caterham Barracks. Despite his undoubted abilities it was a disappointing season for Palace and we once again had to rely on the F.A. Cup to generate real interest. The victims this time were first division Tottenham, who were beaten by two goals from Bill Morgan in front of a "disappointing" crowd of 17,000. But it was half back Bobby Greener who did most to keep Spurs and England star "Fanny" Walden trussed up all afternoon. The reason for the relatively small crowd was not hard to find. The famous amateurs Corinthians defeated Blackburn Rovers 1-0 at the Crystal Palace on the same afternoon and drew 20,000.

"The Arsenal played a doubtful game towards the end and a stronger referee might have taken decisive steps. Turnbull in particular, manifested an unsportsmanlike disposition."

The Palace Programme Discussing a 1922 London Challenge Cup Match ... Same Old Arsenal

Greener, who had joined Palace from Birtley Colliery had only just established himself in the Palace side but would go on to make 290 league appearances for the Glaziers and would then serve the club faithfully as a member of the back room staff.

Palace now faced another first division club, Notts County, who we'd thrashed on our last visit to Meadow Lane. But this turned into a marathon – the longest cup tie in Palace's history. A goalless draw in front of 19,500 spectators at the Nest was followed by a similar result at Meadow Lane. The second replay at Villa Park also ended scoreless and so the teams took another crack at it on February 18 when County at last broke the deadlock. But straight from the kick off, Tom Hoddinott set off on a mazy dribble to score a magnificent solo equaliser. In the second half, Bill Hand grabbed the winner and an exhausted Palace returned to south London to face Swindon at the Nest on the following Saturday.

Had they been able to take a breather perhaps the result might have been different. Instead, Whitworth's goal wasn't enough and Swindon disappointed the watching 20,000 by snatching victory.

Selhurst Park

Roy Peskett was a *Daily Mail* sports journalist who wrote a regular column for the matchday programme in the 1960s and early 1970s.

A lifelong supporter, he also wrote the *Crystal Palace Story*, a history book published to celebrate Palace's promotion to the first division in 1969. In it he wrote of Selhurst Park: "Meanwhile, the Palace board was making every effort to give the club the ground it deserved. The first mention of the new ground came in the club's minute book when, dated 25th February, 1919.

The Secretary was instructed to get in touch with Mr Allen of the London, Brighton and South Coast Railway, in regards to getting the lease on the ground at Selhurst and to report." But, as Peskett explained, "To call it a 'ground' was perhaps a misnomer. It was a piece of waste land situated between Park Road, Whitehorse Lane and Holmesdale Road and valuable only to the railway company. At one time it

Chewing up the Toffees

What was the greatest cup shock in F.A. Cup history? Palace's 6-0 victory at Everton has been lost in the mists of time, but it remains the biggest victory by any team over higher division opponents

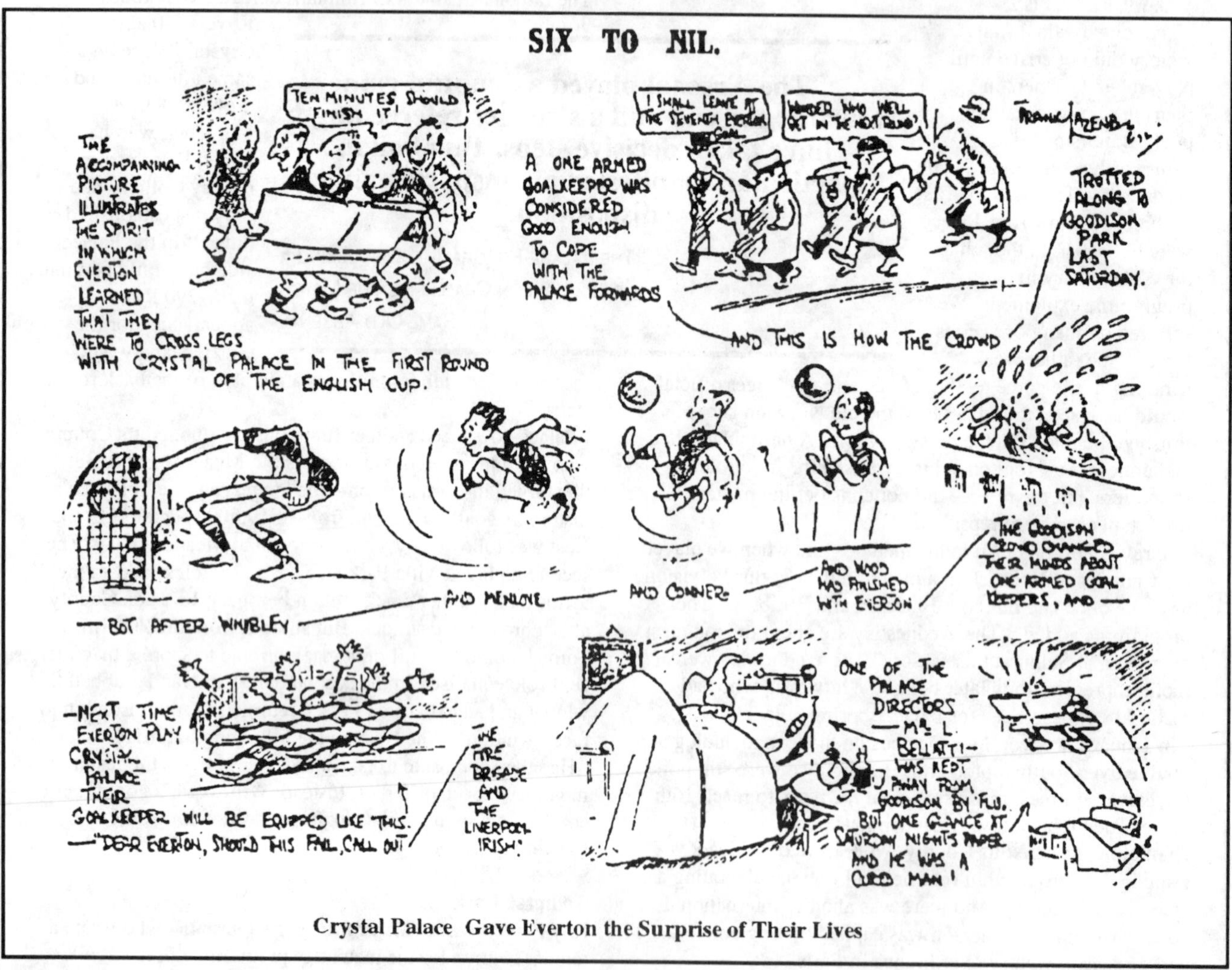

Crystal Palace Gave Everton the Surprise of Their Lives

Everton made no secret that they expected to win their first round tie against a Palace side finding life in the second division rather difficult. Certainly their programme editor, who seemed to be on a one man crusade to dispel the myth of the Scouse sense of humour, was in confident mood. He declared that the Toffees had "a fairly easy task on hand" adding: "Everton's chance is quite clear to us – clearer than Crystals in fact."

Labouring the feeble joke, he said: "Those who come from glass houses should be most circumspect." What a pity he didn't heed his own words, because Palace were to leave Everton's defence shattered.

After early rain, the sun came out and the "huge but orderly" Evertonian crowd were encouraged by the news that their goalkeeper Fern had passed a fitness test. He was cheered onto the pitch by the home followers as the teams arrived to the accompaniment of a band of "itinerant musicians".

Bert Feebery won the toss for Palace and Everton kicked off on the soft pitch. They were soon in trouble. From a corner won by Ben Bateman, John Whibley opened the scoring for the Glaziers.

Apparently the crowd cheered the goal because, in the words of a local pressman, they "expected to see Everton equalise". But nothing materialised from the home team's point of view and Palace were soon on the attack again only to be denied by some dubious refereeing.

An Everton defender handled near the penalty spot but the Glaziers were forced to settle for another corner from which Joe Jones headed on for Bert Menlove to net, but he was ruled offside. This double let off inspired Everton and Jack Alderson was called upon to make a save from Harrison.

The home side "passed prettily" but made little impression on the holding surface (it seems not much has changed at Goodison in 70 years). Palace were forced to defend in depth but Alderson was well protected by Jones and Jack Little and he was seldom called upon to deal with anything more than long range efforts.

In contrast, Palace were incisive and eager. Their fast running almost made the most of a poor back pass by Livingstone which Fern only just reached to clear before the "Palace pack" was upon him. The respite was temporary. Jones fed the ball to Menlove, who evaded a challenge by McDonald to drive the second goal beyond Fern.

Realising their predicament, Everton pressed forward with centre forward Irvine and his inside forwards Fazackerley and Wall causing some anxious moments.

Alderson beat out one close range shot from Fazackerley while Palace's riposte saw Bateman hit the crossbar. The ball rebounded to Whibley four yards out but, before he could react, McDonald took it off his toes.

Perhaps expecting to face a concerted onslaught, Palace started adventurously in the second half, but many of their moves foundered on the offside trap and they were forced back.

There were several hairy moments. Little hoofed clear from one home attack and Alderson saved a Harrison shot with his feet. He followed that with "a flying clearance" as Everton gave their followers hope of turning the tide.

The Croydon Advertiser correspondent wrote of the tension in the press box: "'They can't last,' said somebody close to me, but I assured him that the Palace could and would last, and would be playing at the last minute."

His words were more than prophetic and he continued: "Having got their second wind, they proceeded to smite Everton hip and thigh."

Whibley "dropped the ball on the net" as Palace returned to the offensive and Fern turned out a long range shot from Menlove. From the corner, Jones headed over.

John Conner then beat Fern with a shot that went narrowly wide, but he was soon on the scoresheet. From a Whibley run and cross, Fern could only parry and in the ensuing scramble the ball fell to Conner to hook in. Everton, in the words of one local reporter, were "a well beaten side" and with a quarter of an hour left, Bateman and Conner combined to set up Menlove. But his effort was again ruled out for offside. Then Jones, who had been getting on the end of corners all afternoon, put one just over the bar.

Menlove's disallowed goal looked to have been legitimate, so it was fitting that he should notch the fourth.

If the *Advertiser's* ecstatic report is to be believed, the Everton crowd had now changed sides and shouted "1-2-3-4, make it five," an unlikely scenario that was soon reality as Wood ran Whibley's pass into the net.

Everton's forwards strived for a consolation and, again, Alderson saved well to great cheers from the home supporters. Finally, in a scramble, Wood, protesting his innocence, was pulled up for an infringement. Justice was done when Fazackerley blasted the penalty yards wide to ironic cheers.

It was left to Conner to cap an unbelievable day for Palace by heading in number six just before the final whistle. The Everton crowd left the ground in "a sort of bewildered and bemused condition".

The *Advertiser* reported the following exchange: "'Here you are,' said one of the home crowd to a Palace supporter, taking off his blue favour, 'you've won it. Take it back to London.' And when the Palace officials and players drove away from Goodison Park, they were given a hearty send off by a large crowd.

"Bateman and Whibley have seldom played better. Menlove's dash and skill were great factors in the success while Conner, who played with nearly all his old confidence and spirit, and Wood were live members of a live line. Every name was praised to the high although Alderson had been tested more thoroughly."

Some reports dubbed Fern the "one handed goalkeeper", but *The Advertiser* said: "He was not in any way responsible for the defeat. He had no chance with any of the goals scored against him."

The Times reported the game on Monday January 9, 1922 in its usual sensationalist manner: "The most remarkable match of the day was that in which Crystal Palace beat Everton by six goals to none. There were over 45,000 people present to watch Everton win, and instead Crystal Palace simply ran over them.

"Crystal Palace has never threatened very strongly to achieve promotion this year, and yet they could play such a game in a Cup Tie, every man on the side playing above form!"

The local press wasn't quite so restrained. "Palace confound prophets and critics," the *Advertiser* crowed, and under the heading "Everton Eclipsed" the paper covered almost every second in the utmost detail.

Bearing in mind that Palace had had two goals disallowed for offside and, "even the Liverpool press men agreed" had legitimate claims for penalties when Menlove and Bateman were shoved off the ball, Everton could have been the victims of a double figure defeat.

"Here you are," said one of the home crowd to a Palace supporter, taking off his blue favour, "you've won it. Take it back to London."

A GREAT SPORTING MOMENT
RECOUNTED BY THE CROYDON ADVERTISER

Albert's joyful day out

The following appeared in the *Football and Sports Favourite* of December 24, 1923. Albert Menlove, the Palace centre forward, had joined Sheffield United. In a piece entitled *The Centre Forward in Cup Ties, Memories of a Marked Man he recalled the destruction of Everton.*

"What a joyful day we had in the first round. As perhaps you remember, we were drawn against Everton, rare old fighters in both cup and league, and with a host of traditions behind them.
"Poor old Palace" ... but the players didn't agree with that view at all. We went to Goodison Park and we whipped Everton by six goals to none. In Croydon they blinked when they read what had happened, and a story got about that one of the directors, who had been down with flu, was a cured man when the news came through on the Saturday evening."

How Mercer of the *Croydon Advertiser* saw Palace's giant-killing of Spurs

had been a brickfield, and two chimney stacks remained."

The site covered 15 acres and was within walking distance of three railway stations at Thornton Heath, Selhurst and Norwood Junction. Peskett recalled playing there as a child, as did the chairman when we were promoted to division one in 1969, Arthur Wait, who apparently "took part in pitched battles with brick ends, with shields of dustbin lids as protection". The deeds were secured just before the 1919-20 season. On June 25 chairman Sidney Bourne told a board meeting: "The club have been congratulated at all hands on having secured the ground. We will take with us the best traditions of the club and I feel sure that the crowd will be a good supporting one."

On January 3, 1922 an agent, Mr Richardson, was instructed to buy the ground at a cost of £2,750. Architect Archibald Leitch, who was the inspiration behind many football grounds of the time, was commissioned to design Selhurst Park. His previous work included the remodelling of Craven Cottage and the design of Tottenham's west stand. Leitch aimed big, stating that Palace would have the largest ground in London and the most modern in the country. The stand was designed along similar lines to the ones he'd built at Huddersfield, Craven Cottage and Stamford Bridge, but the Palace version had no roof gable (the triangular "attic" style part which adorns many grounds). The rest of the ground consisted of open banking and only the bottom parts were terraced, while the tops were covered in grass and became the "mud slides" so beloved of generations of Palace fans. When we eventually moved into Selhurst Park, the Nest was rented out to an amateur club Tramway FC on condition that they paid all expenses for the upkeep of the ground and also handed over ten per cent of their gate receipts to Palace.

Industrial disputes held up the construction work, by Humphrey's of Knightsbridge, who had built the Valley for Charlton, and when the ground was opened by the Lord

Mayor of London on the first day of the 1924/25 season the main stand was not finished although it didn't stop 25,000 turning up to see Palace take on the Wednesday. The visitors fielded their international stars Ernie Blenkinsop, George Wilson and Teddy Davidson. But, while Palace could still call upon McCracken, Jack Alderson was a notable absentee. He had departed under a cloud after a pay dispute to play a season for Pontypridd. He later he returned to League action with Sheffield United.

Palace's new keeper was Bill Harper, signed at the end of the previous season from Manchester City. He was beaten only once, by Wednesday's new signing from Sunderland Billy Marsden, but it was sufficient to give the visitors both points and spoil the party.

The boast of having a ground worthy of the team was about to slap Palace in the face. But initially there were no signs of the anguish to come. Indeed, in the run up to Christmas, Palace enjoyed their best spell as a second division side. Victories over Hull and Southampton attracted more than 15,000 and we gained a creditable draw with Chelsea at Stamford Bridge. Chelsea had just been relegated and were seeking a quick return to the top flight, yet Palace proved their equals and earned a point thanks to goals by Harry and Whitworth. We were in the middle of a six game unbeaten run and beginning to harbour promotion ambitions of our own.

Another visit from Peeping Tom of the *Football and Sports Favourite* was marked by the best victory of the season, a 4-1 drubbing of Bradford City on November 15, 1924. In that day's issue *Peeping Tom Peeps in on the Palace* gave a fascinating insight not only into the club but into the lives of the players.

"The Nest was just outside Selhurst railway station and now Selhurst Park has become the permanent home of the Glaziers, for presumably that name will always stick to the club."

Peeping Tom went on: *"It will be possible to extend so that 100,000 spectators will be able to obtain an uninterrupted view of the doings".*

He observed that the grandstand had room for 4,000 with another 6,000 in the covered enclosure. For the time Palace's new ground featured many "luxuries" including "offices, tea rooms, training quarters, plunge, slipper, shower and needle baths ..."

The correspondent then met some of the players, revealing that Roy M'Cracken was a cabinet maker by trade and enjoyed carpentry in his spare time, while Cecil Blakemore kept racing pigeons and Jack Little was regarded as "a fine billiards player". Presumably Bobby Greener's hobby was eating, because he was known to his team mates as "fat boy". Team spirit was clearly good and with a fine new stadium and a rich vein of form it seemed the only way was up.

The white space at the top of the map shows where Selhurst Park would be sited, the Nest is shown as "Athletic Ground" at the bottom.

But, in the end, Palace's second division status was simply thrown away, although a serious injury to centre-half Jimmy Hamilton, who was ruled out for the rest of the season after a haemorrhage to an eye injury in the home match with Blackpool, was a major reason for the loss of form. But there was no real excuse.

After gaining revenge on The Wednesday for that opening day defeat with a George Whitworth goal at Hillsborough, the Glaziers suddenly collapsed. A couple of weeks earlier, Palace had beaten Wolves 2-1 at Selhurst Park to go fifth.

After that we managed just three more wins and slipped rapidly down, so much so that even the tone of the *Football and Sports Favourite* changed: "Buck up Palace!" came the call although it qualified this abuse by saying "their record this season has not been one of the brightest, however better times lay ahead". The trouble was, better times didn't lay ahead. In January, the paper's correspondent Ken Bucknall

My Greatest Save

BY JACK ALDERSON
(taken from the *Football and Sports Favourite,* February 2, 1924)

"It was at Bradford, on the City's ground. We were leading 1-0 four minutes from time when the ball accidentally struck our inside right's arm in the penalty area. The referee pointed straight at the fated spot. I place myself three yards from the right hand side of the goal, expecting the ball to the left. Just as my opponents foot touched the ball I dived and turned it round the post."

Hysterical joke

...from the *Chelsea Chronicle* (match programme) September 27, 1924

"We are told that the Palace team are whole hearted players for the full ninety minutes. Natural enough that the Glaziers should be a panes-taking community."

put his finger on the problem: "The Crystal Palace have lost too many goals for them to be at all hopeful of continuing in the second league company," and he added "the Palace have had a lot of changes in their team and the forward play has been at fault on many occasions." Nevertheless, we still scored more goals than Stoke, Stockport and Oldham who finished immediately above us. Five of the last six matches were lost, with the other drawn, including a dramatic last day home defeat by fellow strugglers Oldham which sealed our fate.

The last two matches were at home and, against Fulham, Blakemore gave us the lead before we allowed them to come back. With hardly any time remaining, a Fulham defender handled Harry's centre and referee Mr Vickery pointed to the spot. Fulham's players surrounded the referee and persuaded him to consult the linesman, although he seemed to be in a less advantageous position. The linesman convinced the referee to change his mind and Palace's hopes of a vital point went out of the window.

The decision was compounded by more bad news. Both Oldham and Barnsley had won. Palace now faced Oldham in the last match needing a win to survive. The 1-0 defeat was one to regret for nearly 40 years.

The only consolation for Palace was international recognition for Selhurst Park, which staged the England versus Wales international on March 1, 1925. It remains the only full international ever held at the ground but the home supporters were disappointed, Wales won 3-1. Fowler scored twice, Walker replied for England while W. Davies got the other Welsh goal.

For 13 years, Albert Harry was a fixture on the right wing for Crystal Palace. He had been spotted playing in a Surrey Charity Shield final at the Nest, but had to wait through most of Palace's first season in division two before making his debut, after which his six appearances were enough to convince Edmund Goodman to make him a regular. In *The Crystal Palace Story*, Roy Peskett wrote that Harry was "a little man with a most unlikely shape for a footballer", but despite his diminutive build he steadily "won his way into the hearts of Crystal Palace supporters". Peskett described him as "5ft.6in., eight stone wringing wet, with a small hunched up body, bags of skill and the heart of a lion". He made a record 411 appearances for Palace, subsequently beaten by just two players, Terry Long and Jim Cannon.

Goodman moved him from centre-forward to outside right during the 1922-23 season and he stayed there for 12 years.

Any hopes of making a swift return to division two were dashed within five matches. We lost the lot and conceded 16 goals before recovering to bang in 11 in three straight wins. It was that kind of season. In November, after 18 years, Edmund Goodman decided to call it a day. He reverted to his administrative duties to make way for Alec Maley, who arrived from Hibernian.

Palace served up one of their more eccentric performances to welcome the new man, drawing 5-5 with Plymouth at Selhurst. Maley inspired a better spirit within the team, although it was one of Goodman's last signings Percy Cherrett who made the most difference to our fortunes. Cherrett's goals, 26 in 35 appearances, helped haul us up to 13th place.

While league form was disappointing, there was a return to the glory, glory days in the F.A. Cup. Palace had trailed Northampton by three goals in their third round tie, but fought back to take the tie to Selhurst Park where Cherrett earned us a home fourth round match with Chelsea. The Pensioners were again near the top of the second division and boasted famous names such as England's amateur goalkeeper B. Howard Baker, Albert Thain and Jack Harrow. It attracted a new Selhurst Park record of 41,000. And it proved to be Palace's day. Cherrett and Alf Hawkins gave us victory even though Thain hit the crossbar with a free kick from near the half way line. The reward was a difficult trip to Manchester City, who were struggling at the foot of division one with one of the creakiest defences in the league. City were in the process of conceding 100 league goals as they spiralled towards division two and there seemed no reason why our giant killers couldn't pull off another famous victory. But on February 20, 1926 in front of a crowd of 51,630 in Manchester, it was Palace who came unglued.

City were as capable of scoring goals as they were of letting them in and they wasted no opportunity to pay Palace back for their shock defeat of four years earlier. Within three minutes, we fell behind when Austin scored from the penalty spot. Before we could recover our composure we were five down. Browell grabbed two and Johnston and Roberts chipped in with one apiece. At half-time it was 7-0 and all over as a contest. Although plenty of Palace fans had made the trip, many more were watching the reserves at Selhurst. In those days the second string drew good crowds and it was customary for the half-time score from the first team game to be put on the scoreboard. This time, no score was forthcoming. It turned out that Palace didn't have a "7" in the box!

At least we could claim to have "drawn" the second half. Our rally was prompted by Cherrett, who opened our account, although Browell completed his hat-trick to make it 8-1. Palace fought back again. Cherrett scored his second and when Nobby Clarke reduced the arrears further and Roy McCracken scored the fourth there may have been some who could see a miracle looming. But City concluded with three more without reply. Roberts ended up with five and Hicks scored the 11th on the stroke of full time to ensure that every home forward had found the net. Peskett wrote: "My parents allowed me to make the momentous trip in an excursion train, which I think cost an all-in fare of 8/- from Thornton Heath Station. It was the saddest day of my life; Palace were overwhelmed and lost 11-4. Like the smallest pig, I think I cried all the way home!"

The setback didn't affect league form though, Palace recovered sufficiently to win their next five games. But the season ended with another thrashing, 6-1 at the hands of Bournemouth in a match which marked the end of Roy McCracken's Palace career.

It may have been a poor season but Palace still attracted some mighty crowds. The first day visit of Millwall pulled in 23,617, while more than 20,000 watched us entertain Norwich on Boxing Day and 20,578 saw the last home match against Reading. Percy Cherrett remained every bit as devastating in front of goal in 1926-27 as he had been during his first term at Palace. He set a club record of 32 goals in a season which helped us improve to a respectable sixth position. But with second division football still relatively fresh in the memory even that constituted something of a disappointment. Palace didn't have as much reason for anguish as Plymouth supporters who, for the sixth successive season, finished runners up. In those days only the champions were promoted. The number of goals scored reached ludicrous proportions as defenders still struggled to come to terms with the new offside laws. Cherrett's performances must be taken in this context and he was just one of many high scoring forwards of the period. The man who led the way was Middlesbrough's George Camsell who set a new league record of 59 goals out of his club's haul of 122 as they won the second division. Palace by comparison scored a mere 84, but they also conceded 81.

Our best form came at the start with only one defeat in the first eight. The best performance was a 4-2 win against Bristol City at Selhurst Park when Cecil Blakemore scored a hat-trick. There was only one goalless game all season – against Aberdare Athletic at Selhurst in October. Blakemore, a tall, fair haired inside left signed from Redditch in December 1922. He formed a powerful strike force with Cherrett and they shared over 100 goals between them. Goals may have been plentiful in the league but when we needed one in the Cup we couldn't get it. Norwich settled for a 0-0 draw at Selhurst and kept us out again in the replay to win by the only goal. Less than a month earlier, Cherrett had scored four times with his head in a 7-1 league annihilation of the Canaries. The Cup exit caused Palace to go to pieces suffering four straight defeats. High scoring became quite unexceptional. In November we came back from 1-3 down to beat Southend 5-3 with a Nobby Clarke hat-trick, followed by a 6-1 loss at Swindon. Against Bristol City at Ashton Gate, we went down 5-4, then lost 7-1 at Plymouth, beat Newport 6-2 at Selhurst, won 3-2 at Aberdare, lost to Brentford by three goals at Griffin Park, won 3-0 at home to Northampton and beat Bristol Rovers by 7-4 – all within the space of six weeks. In addition to Cherrett, Blakemore got 16 and red haired Clarke chipped in with 13. "Nobby" was a big, fast but "elegant" player, whose overall tally for the club remains second only to Peter Simpson, of whom there will be more later. We finished with a 6-1 defeat for the second year running but this one hurt more because it was against Millwall on home soil. It remains our heaviest ever home defeat.

In 1927-28, Palace improved further but were still unable to make any impact on the championship. More than anything, the season was ruined by a terrible start in which we showed the effects of losing Cherrett, who stepped up a division with newly promoted Bristol City. He'd scored 58 league goals in 75 appearances with seven more in six cup matches. Victories in the second and third games against Exeter and Northampton respectively were the only Palace triumphs in the first 11 games. We also suffered a couple of 6-1 defeats, first at Luton and then at Southend. The first of those hammerings signalled the end of the road for Alec Maley. He returned to Scotland to manage Clydebank and was replaced by Geordie Fred Mavin, who had been a Newcastle reserve before continuing his playing career with New Brompton, Fulham, Bradford and, after the war, Reading. After hanging up his boots he took over as manager of Exeter before moving to Palace. Mavin's reign began badly with three defeats against Millwall, QPR and Watford respectively, but then things began to pick up. We were unbeaten throughout November and started the month with a 5-0 pounding of Charlton in front of nearly 17,000. We lost just one of the next 11, a 5-1 defeat at Plymouth on Christmas Eve. That aberration aside, our form continued and six wins in a row in March and April underlined the improvement. This culminated in a 5-1 win at home to Walsall. Crowds however were not as good as Palace had come to expect. Visits by lowly Torquay and Gillingham both attracted little more than 4,000. In the F.A. Cup, we disposed of non-league Dartford but, having gained a draw at the County Ground, we lost the second round replay to Swindon in front of just 8,500 at Selhurst Park. Nevertheless the work Mavin had put in to turn the club's fortunes around had paid off and confidence was high for 1928-29 even though we got off to another indifferent start.

Twenty thousand turned up to see us dispose of Watford on the opening day but although we won five, drew two and lost two of the opening matches, a disastrous October and November did immeasurable damage to our championship hopes. Successive home defeats by bogey team Plymouth, in front of a crowd of almost 18,000, and Charlton were followed by a disastrous spell in which we conceded 16 goals in three games. Eight went past Billy Callender at Northampton, three at Coventry and five at Luton where Harry Havelock at least managed to reply on behalf of the forwards with a hat-trick in a 5-3 defeat.

It provided an odd prelude to a run of results that were as brilliant as the autumn had been appaling. Palace set a record 17 consecutive matches unbeaten (not improved upon until 1968-69) to take us within touching distance of the championship. But the crowds did not flock to Selhurst until we faced Northampton when 25,000 cheered Bert Butler's winner.

We also hit form in the Cup, defeating Kettering and Bristol Rovers in the early stages before chalking up our record F.A. Cup victory, seven without reply, against Luton in a third round replay. The architect of the Hatters' destruction was Havelock, who helped himself to another hat-trick. The other scorers were Jimmy Wilde, Bert Butler, Jimmy Hamilton and Lewis Griffiths.

As with Luton, we brought Millwall back to Selhurst Park following a goalless fourth round tie at the Den. This time it was Butler's turn to score a hat-trick as we ran out 5-3 winners. In the fifth round, we travelled to Huddersfield. The Terriers were just starting their decline after the glory years of the 20s. They were still a formidable proposition though, having been Wembley runners-up to Blackburn the season before, and they hadn't finished outside the top two in the first division for five seasons. Although Griffiths and Stan Charlton scored, we were beaten 5-2.

Our good form coincided with the arrival of centre-half Jimmy Wilde, who became a great servant to the club making 278 appearances in the half-back line.

Having done so well to re-establish themselves as candidates Palace suddenly blew up again and won just two of the next eight. Easter defeats at home to QPR and Exeter effectively finished us off. Before the holiday, we led Charlton. But in a topsy turvy battle, those Easter defeats meant we lost the initiative. Charlton beat Luton 4-1 at home while we were losing to QPR and this proved decisive because it gave them a superior goal average. Both teams won on March 30, Palace 4-2 at Brentford and Charlton 3-1 against Plymouth at the Valley.

On April 6, Palace lost to Bournemouth, something of a scourge in recent seasons, while Charlton were beating Fulham 5-2 at Craven Cottage. We gained a slender advantage again by beating Southend 3-2 at Selhurst while Bristol Rovers did the world a favour with a 3-0 win over Charlton.

But Palace's lead at the top only lasted until the Monday when Charlton played their game in hand against Brentford, scraping home 1-0 to go top on goal difference. The match turned on a bizarre incident in which a Brentford player, thinking he'd heard the whistle, picked the ball up and conceded a penalty.

Charlton stayed top, taking the championship and promotion by a fifth of a goal. It was agonising for Palace, the nearest we would come until we actually returned to division two in 1964.

IT'S JIM CANNON'S HISTORY OF THE PALACE PART II
THE MOST NOTED PLAYER OF THE TIME WAS ONE JESUS CHRIST....
...MOST PROBABLY THE BEST SAVIOUR PALACE EVER HAD, AN ALL ROUND BRILLIANT GOALIE...
THAT'S THE OLDEST FOOTBALL RELATED JESUS JOKE IN THE BOOK!
NO THAT'S THE OLDEST FOOTBALL RELATED JESUS JOKE IN THE BOOK!
I TELL YER THE F.A.'S GETTING TOUGH ON DISCIPLINE NOWADAYS!
AND I ONLY ASKED ABOUT THE REF'S PARENTS!
..EXCEPT, WHEN IT CAME TO CROSSES.
AROUND THIS TIME TEAMS ACROSS EUROPE WERE SPRINGING UP. IT WASN'T LONG BEFORE FRIENDLIES AGAINST FOREIGN TEAMS BEGAN.
THE FIRST INTER-CONTINENTAL TOURNAMENT PALACE PLAYED....
courtesy of dave's motors
...WAS IN NORTHERN FRANCE, WHERE I REMEMBER WE WERE TOLD TO BE CAREFUL OF THE HOSTILE NATIVES!
AND THUS THE NAME FOR SCORING IN FOOTBALL WAS BORN!
TURNIPS YUM YUM
OH NO IT'S A GAUL!

Palace fan Chris Beale from Banstead explains: "I hate Chelsea. I could never support them. When I lived in Epsom as a child, most of the other kids supported them and when my Mum and Dad got

Flashy, arrogant, aggressive and living in the past. Chelsea ... who else?

me my first Palace strip, the horrible white one with the claret and blue stripe down the middle, I was never chosen for any of the park teams because I wore a Palace kit and everybody else liked people like Osgood and Hudson.

"I hate them (I'm sobbing now), I've always hated Chelsea, they're horrible, they fornicate with the whore of Babylon. They ruined my childhood. My psychiatrist costs a lot."

Just one terrible tale of the team one Palace fan in *Eagle Eye* described as

Neil Everitt

Palace 3 Chelsea 1, League Cup 1993. A long awaited and richly enjoyed victory

CHELSEA BOOTS

"those flash bastards from the Bridge".

Another Palace man Dave Mearns puts his finger on the real problem. "Croydon is still crawling with Chelsea fans even though they haven't achieved anything for 20 years. Those people should support Palace."

Palace's links with Chelsea go back to the early days of this century. Both clubs were formed in 1905 and both immediately applied for election to the second division of the football league. Chelsea were accepted, Palace were refused.

Since then, Palace have always taken great delight in beating Chelsea, although it has to be said that the occasions when it happens seem to get rarer by the year.

The links have also be strengthened by the many players who have played for both clubs. The list is endless, Johnny McNicholl, Charlie Cooke, Bobby Tambling, Steve Kember, Alan Birchenall, Micky Droy, Gary Locke, Peter Nicholas, Tommy Langley and Trevor Aylott. In most cases this has been Palace taking Chelsea's veteran cast offs, although our rise has stemmed the flood.

Blimey, once I've met the husband it don't half put me off the wife. Like as not he'll turn out to be a really good bloke. As I'm having it off with her, I think about him hanging up his drip dry shirts or arguing in the pub about football or cricket. You get a lot of his sort ... Chelsea supporters.

– Michael Caine as Alfie (1966) discussing the problems of adultery

The object of Chelsea supporters hatred has always been Tottenham. It is a long standing passion fuelled by the Blues' defeat in the first Cockney Cup Final of 1967. For Palace, the last 20 years or so has been spent embroiled in a rivalry with Brighton initiated during a period when the Seaweeds were at their peak and we were at a low ebb. Only a calamity in Palace's fortunes it seems will restore parity with the "Seaweeds".

Chelsea seem to be greater potential rivals but neither set of fans wants it that way. Chelsea dispute it but these days Palace are of a similar stature, despite relegation, and perhaps it would only take a Mullery-esque incident on the part of a member of either club to ignite the potential. But then again the trouble with Chelsea fans is that they live in the past and think they are bigger than they really are. Perhaps the closest we ever came was during the Palace F.A. Cup run of 1976. A brilliant match in which Palace came out on top, just, was overshadowed by war on the terraces. The violence was certainly the worst ever experienced by a Palace crowd. If that's all Chelsea have to offer they can keep it.

Thirties ... depression all round

Palace in division three south

Crystal Palace and Fulham: Getting ready for the Cup Tie.

Another of the Advertiser's curious cartoons, this one looking at preparations for the Cup tie with Leeds

After the disappointment of missing out on promotion in the most unfortunate circumstances, Palace's hopes of making amends at the start of the 1929-30 season were understandably high. But results were not particularly good and, in the end, ninth place was the best we could manage.

Albert Harry was still going strong. He'd missed only seven games in five consecutive seasons for the club, while Jimmy Wilde remained as regular centre-half. Nobby Clarke continued to chalk up the goals and Callender had made the green jersey his own after a long wait for a first team place. He had been kept in the reserves by Alderson and then by Bill Harper. But Callender was not as firmly established as everybody thought. Palace had overcome Kettering in the first round of the Cup in November 1928 and Mavin was so impressed that he bought up half the team including keeper Jimmy Imrie, who immediately took Callender's place.

Unfortunately, Arsenal beat Palace to the punch for Kettering's left back Eddie Hapgood, who went on to become England's captain and regular left-back – but centre-forward Peter Simpson, outside right George Charlesworth, inside left Andy Dunsire and centre-half George Barrie all joined Imrie at Selhurst Park. Sadly Mavin's judgement was awry. Only Simpson showed any real polish and none of the others made an impact as first teamers. Dunsire managed only two games, Barrie played six, Charlesworth five and Callender regained his place from Imrie after just 17 matches. Simpson by all accounts was one of the nicest men you could wish to meet. He was remembered with affection by Roy Peskett in the *Crystal Palace Story* and also on Cup Final day 1990 by comedian Roy Hudd, a lifelong Palace fan, who spoke of the childhood thrill of visiting Simpson's sweet shop. Peskett described Simpson as a "dynamic", but quietly spoken, Scot who was always appreciative of any interest shown in him.

"Of all the players of that or of any other era, I would think his autograph was requested the most, yet never did I see him show bad temper or a refusal to sign, unless in extreme emergency as on one occasion when he literally ran for a train. It was like the pied piper all over again as he dashed along Thornton Heath High Street with small boys, all clutching books of various shapes and

Hulton Deutsch

EVERTON GAIN THEIR REVENGE. F.A. Cup fourth round, January 1931. 38,000 Palace supporters witness a wonderful performance by Dixie Dean. Here, Dean forces the ball out of Jimmy Imrie's arms for the first of Everton's six goals.

sizes, running behind him in a long strung out gaggle.

But it was typical of the man that having ascertained that he had a couple of minutes in hand at the station before train time, he quickly made sure that all who had made the chase got what they were after."

Simpson began with Leith Amateurs in Edinburgh, turned professional with Scottish second division team St Bernard's and then joined Kettering. In his first season at Selhurst, he scored 36 goals in 34 games although he actually made his debut for Palace not as a striker but as a spinner. As the *Crystal Palace Story* pointed out at length, Palace in the early 30s tended to be about as good at cricket as they were at football and regularly took part in the *London Evening News*' Cricket Cup for Footballers which, wouldn't you know it, was dominated by Arsenal. We had the England and Surrey batsman Laurie Fishlock, but he was run out for two as Palace lost the final to the lucky Gunners by 152 runs.

At football, Simpson did not figure in the team until the fourth match of the season, but he wasted no time making his mark scoring against Norwich after 12 minutes. He got another in the second half and would have had a hat-trick had the Canaries' keeper Jarvis not been credited with an own goal trying to save his effort. It was the start of a record breaking career. Nobody has even approached his tally of 154 league goals for Palace, plus 12 more in the cup.

Fishlock followed Simpson into the team a week later. But the Palace half-back was always better at the summer game than the winter one and his appearances were relatively limited. Simpson, meanwhile, collected his first hat-trick for us against Merthyr just before Christmas. The Welsh club had three ex-Palace players in their line-up, including Jack Cross, who'd played 221 games for the Glaziers, but they were powerless to stop the Scots goal machine. But in the Cup, it was Palace who were on the receiving end. Leeds United, going well in the first division, proved too hot for us. Palace's cup record against supposedly better teams was an illustrious one. Newcastle, Man City, Spurs, Everton and Chelsea had all come to grief in the past, but, in the Elland Road snow, we were unable to cope with Leeds star forward Wainscoat who scored a hat-trick although, to be fair, the Glaziers' plans were upset early on when injured full back Tom Wetherby was forced onto the wing. The press concluded Palace would have lost anyway, but perhaps the margin would not have been so wide. However the *Advertiser* admitted: "It would be futile to suggest Palace were anything but outclassed." The one consolation was a superb goal by Simpson who met a cross from Laurie Fishlock after good work by Jack Butler, but by then Palace were three-down and within a minute Leeds restored their margin.

Palace's takings for the season established a club record of £30,765. But the good news was tempered by the death of chairman Sydney Bourne at the age of 77.

In 1930-31, we scored more than 100 league goals for the first time in our history. Simpson predictably was the main source, establishing another club record with 46 out of the grand total of 107. And in October, he set another record by scoring six successive goals at Mavin's old club Exeter. Palace romped home 7-2. Having crushed Exeter, we ran into problems. Mavin was taken ill and forced to retire, although he returned to football as manager of Gillingham. He was replaced by former West Ham and England player Jack Tresadern, who had been a member of the United team that played in the 1923 F.A. Cup Final, the first at Wembley. He obviously had a taste for teams who wore claret because he also played a season for Burnley before being appointed player-manager of Northampton, where his playing career ended with a broken leg. The managerial turnaround made no difference to Simpson, who was on top form. He scored a hat-trick against Coventry, got three more in the Cup against Taunton and, in the space of four days, grabbed four in the next round of the Cup against Newark before repeating the dose against Watford. The goal rush continued on Christmas Day, but with Palace on the receiving end of an 8-2 thrashing by Brentford. In the return the following day we gained revenge by scoring three times in the first five minutes while many of the crowd were still outside. We eventually won 5-1.

In the Cup, having seen off non-league Taunton and Newark with ease (both games ended 6-0) we overcame Reading in an epic. It went to extra time in the second replay at Stamford Bridge before Clarke and Simpson struck in the last five minutes to give us a 2-0 win. The reward for sticking with it was a visit from old Cup foes Everton the following weekend. It was a lucrative tie because, although Everton were now a second division team, they could still call upon several star names, including their legendary forward William "Dixie" Dean. On the morning of the match, an advert appeared in the national papers offering "Dixie Dean" football boots at 26/-. But Dean proved to be just as adept with his head.

Palace, with the memory of their victory of 1922 still fresh, were confident. And their optimism was fuelled when the visitors' England keeper Ted Sagar was ruled out. One Palace fan got quite carried away with the excitement and beerily staggered onto the pitch to offer stand-in keeper Coggins some advice on the finer points of guarding the net against Simpson, He was led away by "Old Bill" for his trouble. He didn't miss much.

Simpson was as much a spectator as the supporters as Dean turned on a super show, scoring a hat-trick of headers and hammering an unstoppable fourth past Imrie, who was standing in for the injured Callender. And so the Toffees gained exact revenge for the scoreline of nine years earlier. At least Palace could count the money from a 38,000 crowd.

Shortly after, Tresadern tried to strengthen his forward line, signing balding Brentford forward Jack Lane, the architect of the Bees' huge victory over Palace at Christmas. Lane was signed to replace the prolific Harry Havelock, but his four goals in 14 appearances added little to the already huge tally being accumulated by Simpson, Clarke and Butler. Only Pongo Waring of Aston Villa and England had scored more than Simpson, yet Palace still finished second, nine points behind Notts County.

Although the championship went to Meadow Lane, Palace still had cause to be pleased and looked forward to a fresh assault in 1931-32. Simpson scored four times on the opening day as Torquay were overwhelmed 7-0 in front of more than 18,000 supporters. He followed that with a hat-trick in a 3-1 victory at Clapton Orient as Palace looked set to carry on where they had left off the previous season. But we lost our rhythm when Bristol Rovers thrashed us 6-1 and, from then on, indifferent form dogged us. There was little satisfaction to be gained from many of the performances, although promotion chasing Fulham were held at Craven Cottage thanks to Callender's save from England man Albert Barrett's spot kick – his fifth penalty save of the season.

The most notable event of the year was the visit to Selhurst Park by Prince George, later the Duke of Kent – not for a Palace fixture but for a match between the British Army and the Belgian Army. Although erratic form let us down, Palace still finished fourth but a long way behind the leaders and never put together a really consistent spell of form. It was around this time that the team acquired the nicknames "Crystal Paralysis" or "Screaming Alice". The name "Screamers" certainly stuck and is still occasionally used by older supporters. It was an apt title for a team that could turn it on one week yet be unspeakable the next.

"Dire" was the only word to describe the F.A. Cup exit at Bath City on December 12. Simpson's goal gave us the lead but we lost it to two goals in the last quarter of an hour, the first a twice-taken penalty. The *Croydon Advertiser* said Palace were "desperately unlucky", but for the first time the F.A. Cup biters had been bit.

The 1932-33 season opened in tragic circumstances. Billy Callender was found hanging in the dressing room having taken his own life while overcome with grief over the death of his fiance Miss Eva Leslie. Palace supporter J. Coombes recalled that Miss Leslie was confined to a wheelchair and that Billy was regularly seen pushing her around Thornton Heath recreation ground. Mr Coombes said that the keeper's death at 26 "cast a gloom over the whole club for some considerable time". Palace turned to a former bandsman in the Dorsetshire Regiment to replace him. Ronnie Dunn had been spotted while playing in an army international and was snapped up immediately.

The season started with four wins, but it was clear that the Glaziers relied too heavily on Simpson and, when injuries and illness struck, their hopes went with him. The highlight of Simpson's season was a hat-trick at home to Cardiff. For the Welsh side it was harsh reward for a torrid journey to London which made them 45 minutes late as they later explained to the league:

"We have been trying since Friday morning to get away from Cardiff, but have been severely hampered by snow drifts and waterlogged lines. Finally we caught a train at 10.30 this morning and had a terrible journey as far as Swindon. The chief reason was the complete disorganisation of the the signalling apparatus, all the telegraph lines being out of order. It was all done by hand signalling and every time we reached a signal box, the guard exchanged a baton with one of the signalmen. We arrived at Paddington at 3.5, and changing in the coach did well to get to Selhurst in time for a 3.45 kick off."

And that was in the days before British Rail! The game attracted just 5,805 spectators. Cardiff deserved rather better luck than to meet

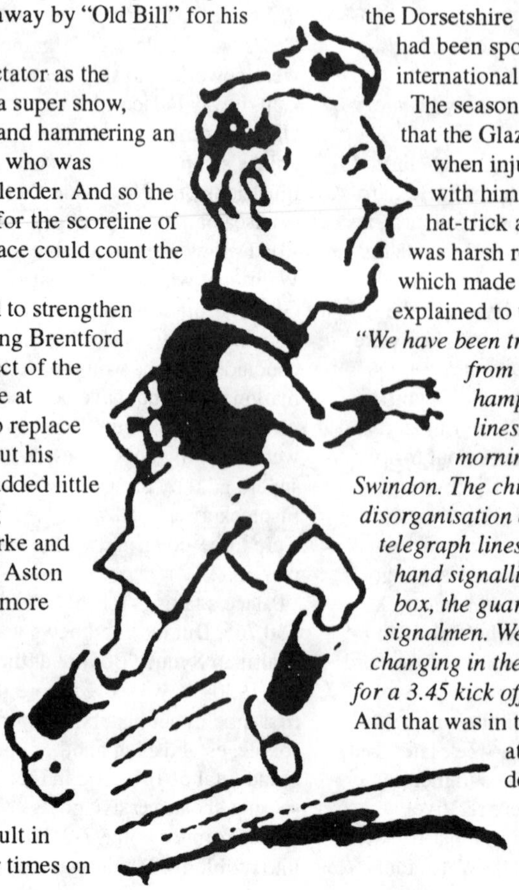

Peter Simpson, as seen by the *Croydon Advertiser*

Simpson on a good day. At least the league decided not to fine them for their late arrival.

On October 8, Palace lost at home for the first time in 32 matches, 3-0 to Watford. That undefeated run which stretched back to 14 February 1931 set a club record. At the end of the season, Edmund Goodman retired after almost 30 years' service. Before he left to open a butcher's shop in Anerley, he supervised the building of a gymnasium and a players recreation room which was "very well lighted, well ventilated and equipped with a first class billiards table and two whist tables".

The new season was marked, or marred, by the F.A. Cup visit to all-powerful Arsenal. Palace went down 7-0 in front of a fourth round crowd of 56,177. Ronnie Rooke, who was to lead Arsenal's front line in their championship season of 1947, made his debut for Palace in the 1-0 home defeat by Norwich. He had scored regularly for the reserves but struggled in the first team and Palace were destined to miss out on the lion's share of his prodigious scoring talents as Palace struggled to replace Simpson, who missed the last two months of the season with fluid on the knee.

Rooke later signed for Fulham where he made his name before joining Arsenal after the war. Meanwhile, Palace tried several players in the number nine shirt without satisfaction and their failure in front of goal was reflected by a final position of 12th.

The most remarkable match of the season involved the reserves, who led Portsmouth 5-1 at half-time in a Football Combination match at Selhurst. In typical Palace fashion, a 6-6 draw was only secured when Frank Manders, who played 23 times for the first team that year, including a couple of games in Simpson's position, equalised from the spot. Even then, he had to follow up with the rebound after the keeper had saved his first effort.

While Simpson's absence caused problems, the arrival of inside forward Albert Dawes from Northampton proved a great success. Dawes, who also played cricket for Northamptonshire, scored 16 times in 22 appearances and established himself as an outstanding prospect. In one spell, he scored seven times in three games including a brace in Palace's 3-2 victory over Gillingham at Selhurst and two more in the 5-0 return win in Kent. Sandwiched between that was a hat-trick against his home town club Aldershot. Manders added the other goal. Dawes' abilities as a cricketer also came in handy during the summer when Palace actually won a trophy – beating Fulham by 68 runs.

More important that summer, although not from England's point of view, was the first World Cup in Europe. It was won by the host nation Italy, much to the delight of their fascist leader Benito Mussolini. Fascism was on the rise all over Europe and an economically shattered Germany under the weak Weimar Government would shortly allow Adolf Hitler's National Socialists to wrest power. All this passed Britain by. What foreigners did was their own affair and this applied particularly to football. Everybody knew England were the true "World Champions" and we proved it by beating Italy in a brutal match at Highbury in November 1934. England's disagreement with FIFA meant it would be many years before we would have the opportunity to show what we could do in the World Cup. Meanwhile, Simpson was in his last season at Palace. One win in the first five matches was followed by some impressive results. Poor Cardiff were Palace's first victims – crushed 6-1 at Selhurst with Albert Dawes scoring five times to take his tally to seven in the opening three games. At least it wasn't snowing.

Preparations for matches were hampered when Tresadern broke his leg again and was forced to handle team affairs from home. His biggest headache concerned Simpson, who was not quite as sharp as he used to be. The thoughtful manager tried him in a more withdrawn role, as a decoy, but the Scotsman's best days appeared to be over and in the second half of the season he no longer appeared regularly in the team. Nevertheless, he still marked his final appearance with a goal in a 1-1 draw at Swindon.

The F.A. Cup brought the giant killers of old another taste of their own medicine, when we were knocked out in the first round by Yeovil and Petters by an embarrassing 3-0.

A note from the Palace v Watford programme of January 1935. "Good health," shouted the crowd when a certain footballer took a swig at the trainer's whisky bottle during the match. At first the trainer thought he wanted some iodine, but it was inward and not outward application which was required.

In the summer Simpson left, perhaps surprisingly moving

Hulton Deutsch

Palace prepared for their daunting cup tie at Highbury in 1934 by training in convivial surroundings at Brighton. The players also took the chance to relax on the sea front with a spot of putting. Pictured (left to right): Bill Turner; Tom Ward; Albert Harry; Jimmy Wilde, Bud Rossiter and Jimmy Earle.

BEHIND THE SCENES AT SELHURST, 1936.
Above: Palace skipper Fred Dawes, watched by centre-half Jimmy Wilde, congratulates new manager R.S. Moyes on his appointment Below: Palace in pre-season training. Notice the Holmesdale in full bloom.

In the first month of the season, chairman Louis Bellati died and no sooner had R.S. Flew taken his place than he passed away as well. The next incumbent Carey Burnett must have been a worried man for a while.

Performances were quite good and there were some impressive victories. Millwall were thumped 5-0 on November 2 in front of just under 20,000, although Palace undid the good work by getting walloped 8-1 by Coventry the following week. We swept five past Swindon, Luton, Bournemouth and Newport and chalked up sixes against Newport, again, and Bristol City. It added up to up 96 goals, 38 of which flowed from the boots of the irrepressible Albert Dawes, who was joined at Palace towards the end of the season by his younger brother Fred. Albert received some recognition of his abilities at the end of the season when he was invited to join the England party as a reserve for the showpiece international with Scotland at Wembley.

Left-back Fred gave equally valuable service to the club making 235 appearances and, after the war, he became joint manager after a spell as assistant to Ronnie Rooke.

Sixth place was respectable enough, but Palace suffered another indignity in the Cup, this time losing 3-1 at Margate in the second round. Again we took the lead but a dubious penalty swung the match away from us. The Supporters' Club had a good year announcing a profit of £126,13s,10d, of which £100 was given to the club as "an initial contribution towards the erection of covered accommodation at Selhurst Park". Exactly what the club did with the money is not clear, but nearly 60 years later Palace fans still huddle together getting soaked as a reward for their undying devotion to the team.

In November 1936, the Crystal Palace was destroyed by fire. Millions of people in south east England as far away as Brighton and Margate turned out to see the spectacular blaze and thousands of Londoners packed buses, trams and taxis to travel to see it. Many got so close that they risked death as the structure began to collapse, while the traffic from sightseers held up additional fire engines. A pilot of an Imperial Airways airliner reported he could see the glow of the flames from the English channel. Another tale concerned comedian Ted Ray, who was appearing at the Penge Empire for the first time when the entire audience got up and walked out. "I can't be that bad," said Ted, only to be told "Sorry mate, they're going to watch a better show. The Crystal Palace is burning down!"

In 1936 you could buy a pair of Mansfield Hotspur football boots for 18/9d or, if you preferred to watch rather than play, admission at Selhurst cost 1/- into the ground, 1/6d in the enclosure and 2/- and 3/- in the stands. Season tickets cost £3 or £2 for ladies and boys. And Palace began a merry-go-round of kit changes by trading their claret and sky blue to red shirts with blue sleeves. There were also some new rules to contend with. At the League AGM it was decided to introduce an arc on the edge of the 18 yard box to reduce incidences of encroachment at penalties. The goal kick rule was also changed so that full backs could not tip the ball to

up a division with West Ham. It was a time of great change. Albert Harry had already retired to run a pub in Staffordshire while new players such as Ernie Waldron and Jack Blackman were introduced. There was also a change of manager. Spurs had finished the 1934-35 season at the bottom of division one and turned to Jack Tresadern to rebuild their side. His move to White Hart Lane however was not a successful one.

Our new manager was another former England international, Tom Bromilow, who spent 11 seasons at Liverpool winning two championship medals and five international caps. After he retired, he went to coach in Holland before taking over at Burnley.

New scoreboards were installed so that half-times could be given out, the pitch was returfed and the ditch at the side of the cinder track was filled in to prevent the ball from rolling in the collected casual water. And, luxury of luxuries, a water tap was installed alongside the dugout so that the trainer could continually wet his magic sponge. What more could these namby pamby footballers want?

the keeper. All players had to be outside the area when the ball was kicked and it had to cross the line before it could be played again. But the most significant change from Palace's point of view was that a director, R.S. Moyes, took over team affairs after Bromilow resigned following a row with the board. Results under Moyes were poor and he incurred the displeasure of the supporters by selling Albert Dawes to promotion chasing Luton for a hefty fee. Moyes then signed Aston Villa's much travelled Jackie Palethorpe who in some circles was considered a lucky omen. During his spells at Stoke and Preston North End both clubs had won promotion to the first division and he had also collected a Cup winners' medal with Sheffield Wednesday when they beat West Brom 4-2 in the 1935 Cup Final. Palethorpe appeared to have lost none of his magic. He scored three times in his first two appearances, but it didn't help Moyes who reverted to scouting duties as Bromilow returned for a second spell in the new year. We immediately became tougher to beat, although more often than not had to settle for a draw. The best performance was again saved for Exeter. The Grecians were crushed 8-0 at Selhurst in front of an attendance that just topped 10,000.

In April, Palace acquired a classy half back from Torquay. Leslie Lievesley came from a large soccer family and, although he only played in the last game of the season, a 3-1 win at QPR, he was ever present in 1937-38. During the second world war Lievesley served in the Royal Air Force. He built a reputation as a trainer and, later went to Italy to coach Torino, the outstanding Italian side of their day. They won a string of championships with a team which featured outstanding internationals such as the legendary Valentino Mazzola. But returning from a trip to Portugal in 1949, their plane crashed at Superga and every one on board, including Lievesley, was wiped out. Ironically, Lievesley had survived an air crash while in the R.A.F.

Keeper Vince Blore, who had arrived from Exeter in 1936 started between the sticks, but was replaced after two games by Arthur Chesters, who had also been at Exeter. In fact, five of the team that drew the opening game with Aldershot had been replaced by the time Palace met Millwall in the third match. Only right-back Ted Owens returned to make any lasting impression on the rest of the campaign.

On a sunny day in January 1938, 33,000 people packed Selhurst Park to watch Palace take on Bromilow's old club Liverpool in the third round of the Cup. Palace had already beaten Kettering after a replay and followed that with a one goal win at Accrington Stanley in the second round. We fought hard against Liverpool but could not break the deadlock. In the replay at Anfield, we were beaten 3-1 after extra-time. But the Anfield management weren't content and wrote a scathing attack on what they perceived as Palace's rough house tactics stating that "it was remarkable that the Liverpool players escaped serious injury". They were not allowed to get away with such comments, though, and the F.A. Disciplinary Committee ordered a full retraction and apology in their next home programme. Later that month, Palace faced Peter Simpson, who had moved from West Ham to Reading. At half-time we led 2-1 but he showed his old touch with two second half goals to turn the tide against his old club. In a rather ordinary season, in which we finished seventh, Jack Blackman led the scorers with a modest 16. Ernie Waldron contributed 14 from his 23 games although he didn't play after mid-February. The Spanish Civil War, was raging with Franco's fascists fighting the nationalist government. Hitler's Germany was beginning to flex its new found muscles and the first clouds of war were gathering on the horizon. Back in Blighty, Palace's chairman Mr E.T. Truett spoke of Palace's ambitions for the future.

"I have often heard it said in the past that Palace have not tried, and that the management does not want promotion. People who talk on those lines talk from the backs of their heads. We, as a club, have but one ambition ... Promotion!"

Before the season started, Palace played Brighton in a Jubilee game to celebrate the 50th anniversary of the Football League, winning comfortably by five goals to nil with former Chelsea man Jack Horton and Albert Dawes, who had returned to the club after helping Luton take the third division south championship, getting the goals. The players did their utmost to provide the club with the much

Crap jokes of the Thirties

from Palace v Newport, April 1935

■ Household hint: to prevent cats from climbing through upstairs windows move into a bungalow

■ Financial hint: A good way to keep money in circulation is to stick a ten shilling note on a revolving door

■ A Scotsman wanted to travel but didn't like the expense so he just sat at home and let his mind wander

■ Softly Please! One of our readers whilst on holiday entered a small country garage and saw the following notice pinned to the wall: "No Smoking Aloud".

from Palace v Millwall, November 1935

■ Many tennis stars keep fit during the winter by sending the ball over the net for an hour at a time, we are told. So do a lot of footballers.

from Palace v Coventry City, October 1934

■ Small child: Please is this the baker's?
Assistant: No this isn't the baker's it is the dairy. What is it you want?
Child: A nice haddock

from Palace v Brighton, January 1935

■ Estate agent proposing: "Marry me darling! I've got a lovely flat, all modern conveniences, near station, two minutes from shops, cheerful situation and ..."
Modern Miss (derisively): "STOP! You make me go h. and c. all over!"

from Palace v Bournemouth & Boscombe Athletic, March 1935

■ Two young ladies who usually went to the cinema on a Saturday afternoon decided that by way of a change they would go to a football match. They saw the first half and then as the players reappeared on the field for the second half one girl said to her companion: "I think we had better go now, dear, this is where we came in."

talked about promotion, racing neck and neck with Newport for the championship as 1938-39, the last full season before the war, proved to be the club's best for some time.

After four games, we topped the table with seven points with just one goal against. The team was more settled and backed by good quality reserves such as Jack Lewis, signed as an 18 year old from West Bromwich Albion, and a local lad named Arthur Hudgell, also 18, who was being schooled in the second string alongside veteran campaigner Jimmy Wilde. We suffered only two defeats before Christmas, but the excitement was tempered by the increasing threat from Germany, a constant and nagging backdrop to national life. At the end of September, the Prime Minister Neville Chamberlain travelled to meet Hitler to decide, among other things, the fate of Czechoslovakia. War looked increasingly inevitable and in the programme for the home match with Orient on October 1, Palace printed the following message:

THE NATIONAL CRISIS

"The Directors desire to inform Supporters that Football will be continued until instructions have been received to the contrary from either H.M. Government or the Football Association. In these days, the words of the late Sir Maurice Greig, which were uttered by him at the time of another National Emergency are recalled: 'Everyone will be filled with anxiety, some with recrimination, and all with a sense of unrest. Anxiety is a disturbing emotion, and emotion interferes with right thinking and sound judgement. The greatest service we can do for our country and for ourselves is to control our feelings and our words, for quietitude is not weakness but great strength.' The National Anthem will be played immediately before the commencement of today's game."

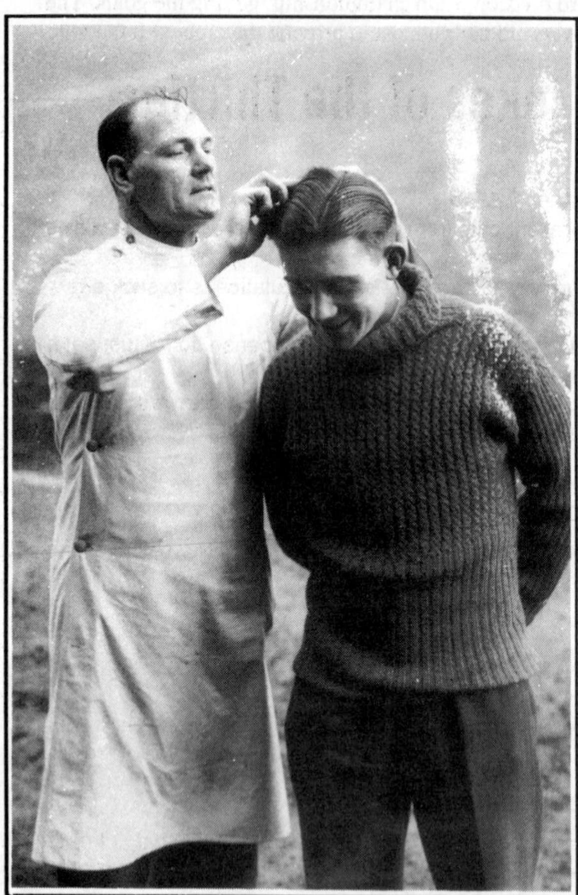

Hulton Deutsch

Trainer George Irwin inspects a head injury to winger Johnny Pritchard before the home draw with Bristol City in February 1938. Pritchard, who was equally at home on the right or left, was passed fit but a couple of weeks later he moved to Manchester City to help their fight against relegation from the first division. Irwin later became Palace manager and guided the club through the war years.

The notice was initialled "C.H.T.", those of vice-chairman C.H. Temple, who was the brother of the, then, Archbishop of Canterbury. It appeared however that the board's pessimism had been misplaced. Earlier in the week, Neville Chamberlain had returned to Keston clutching a document "signed by Mr Hitler" which proclaimed "peace for our time". A relieved crowd joined in with the chairman's request for three cheers for the Premier. The Crystal Palace band then struck up *God Save The King* before we completed a happy afternoon with a 4-2 victory which kept us top.

Our promotion hopes were severely hampered by a poor spell after Christmas, which coincided with the loss of our injured captain George Walker, who was ruled out for the season. We lost the lead to Newport and never regained it. But, although County were never less than three points in front, we kept up the chase right to the end.

Despite the four power summit in Munich, the war footing did not fade away. On October 21, Tom Bromilow, along with assistant manager George Stanbury, trainer Bobby Greener and 14 players, were sworn in as Metropolitan Police war reserve constables, while four of the younger players had already signed up for the Militia.

In the Cup, we went out to QPR after a replay, although we were consoled by the first round's biggest takings – £1,869 from a crowd of 33,276. Albert Dawes led the scorers with 12 goals from 29 games but towards the end of the season he was replaced, first by Robson and then Waldron. Durham born Robson, who finished second top scorer with 11 as the goals were more evenly shared around, was one whose peak coincided with the war years. He joined the ground staff in 1935 and signed professional the following year. He once scored a second half hat-trick in 15 minutes against Mansfield and in three war-time seasons scored regularly. On three occasions he scored four in a match – in a 5-2 win over Southend at Selhurst on Easter Saturday 1940, in the 10-1 win over Brighton and in the London War Cup against Fulham on March 1, 1941 when his centre-half opponent was the famous Wolves and England star Stan Cullis. Robson grabbed 36 goals in 40 matches in 1940-41.

But Bromilow had difficulties filling the centre forward position and Roy Peskett wrote: "How he must have sighed, as he desperately tried to fill this position, with the thought that he had left behind at Burnley, the club from which he joined Palace, a young man now revered as one of the all time great centre-forwards, Tommy Lawton."

During the season, Palace played in Brussels in an invitation match against the Diables Rouges, the Belgian National team when they weren't playing full internationals. They included Raymond Braine who had so impressed Highbury when he played for the Rest of Europe against England the previous year. The match was a reward for Palace's willingness to loan out Selhurst for Army matches. We played well but lost 5-4. The players' efforts during the season were rewarded by a share out of the permitted bonus of £165 – about £15 per player for the ever presents. The board had promised to make £20,000 available for ground improvements if promotion was secured, but sadly it remained unfulfilled.

During the close season, there was a managerial change.

CRYSTAL PALACE FC GOES TO SCHOOL.
The idea that players should prepare for life outside the game is not new. In November 1937, Palace offered an education scheme in conjunction with a former Selhurst Park amateur Mr Lockton, master in English and Mathematics of St Dunstan's College, Catford. Palace director C.H. Temple (standing) helps with instruction to players (in the foreground from left to right) Ian Gillespie, Leslie Lievesley, Bob Shanks and George Walker.

Tom Bromilow, who had become the third successive Palace manager to lead the club to the runners-up position, left to manage Leicester after a behind the scenes bust-up in which the directors placed George Walker on the transfer list. The exact reason for the bust up is unclear, but Walker was immensely popular and the *Crystal Palace Story* noted: "The directors did not wash their dirty linen in public." The rumour was that the board themselves had disagreed over the decision which was hotly disputed and as a result not only did Bromilow leave but president J.H. Nettlefold and vice-chairman C.H. Temple also resigned.

With the climate of international unrest adding to the gloom of internal wrangling, Palace turned to their former goalkeeper George Irwin, who'd made 16 appearances in the 20s, to sort things out. He brought in a new trainer, R.B. Wright, a former coach to first division Bolton Wanderers.

All players now had to be numbered and it was decreed that watering pitches would be allowed except during the winter months between November and February when it was assumed that the weather would do the job anyway.

Palace entered a new cup competition, the Southern and Northern Cup, which was to be played between the sides finishing in second and third place in the third divisions north and south. Having finished runners-up the season before, we were due to meet Brighton on October 15, with the victors going on to meet the northern section winners. The war ensured that the cup was never heard of again.

The Germans resisted the temptation to invade Poland just long enough to allow the football season to get under way.

Palace had begun each of the three previous campaigns with 1-1 draws, so it was definitely time for something different. By half time against Mansfield at Field Mill we were trailing 3-1, but fought back to win 5-4. Waldron grabbed a hat-trick, with Robson and former Millwall winger Ernie Steele adding the others. In the second match, at Elm Park, Reading trounced us 5-0 which left one more match before the inevitable intervention of Adolf and the lads.

By the time we met Bristol Rovers on September 2, 1939, the borders had been breached and the Nazis were advancing against the huge but outdated Polish army. Everyone knew Britain's guarantees to the Poles would have to be fulfilled. The new football season was about to become an early casualty of the war. These were the last players to represent Palace and Bristol Rovers in the inter-war period.
Palace: Tootill, Owens, Fred Dawes, Lievesley, Shanks, Reece, Steele, Smith, Robson, Waldron, Wilson.
Rovers: Nicholls, Forster, Feebery, Warren, McArthur, Whitfield, Butterworth, Fletcher, Iles, Buttery, Gardiner.

Palace won 3-0 which left them fourth, behind Reading, Exeter and Cardiff in the first, and last, table. On Sunday morning, September 3, 1939, Britain declared war. Eleven days later the players reported to Selhurst Park for instructions.

Secretary E.F. Burrell announced that all competition was cancelled and that the players' contracts were suspended. Meanwhile the Palace staff answered phone calls from season ticket holders asking for their money back on their cancelled tickets. But it was soon judged safe for a new football competition to commence.

Some of Palace's longest serving supporters gathered for an afternoon in Croydon to talk about the club they have followed all their lives

After a lifetime of supporting Crystal Palace, David and Olive Gowler's enthusiasm is undiminished. They are Lifeline members and still go to Selhurst Park.

Both were Civil Servants – Olive with the Board of Trade and David in the Ministry of Public Buildings and Works. Throughout their working lives and into retirement they've enjoyed many great moments with Crystal Palace the best of which, they agree, was the day promotion to division one was secured for the first time.

Olive's list of favourite players is endless and she punctuates an afternoon of memories with more and more names as she thinks of them: Vince Hilaire, Jim Cannon and Alan Whittle are all there, but her number one is Cliff Holton – "a wonderful player with a powerful shot, I liked him a lot". She used to watch Dulwich Hamlet – a team she first saw play when she was ten years old – but in 1955 she was converted to Palace by David. His Palace days go back much further. "My father was in the police and he was transferred to Dulwich just before the war in 1914 – so Palace became my local team. The ground in those days was at the Nest, just outside Selhurst station. We used to get the 3 bus and then the tram to the football. I can't remember much about the games, because I was so young – only about nine years old."

Tom Chippington on the other hand remembers the Nest quite vividly. He was born in 1905 – the year Palace were formed – and supported the Palace regularly at the little ground which they took over from Croydon Common just after the First World War. He had just started work as an apprentice tinsmith with the Croydon firm Hammond and Hussey.

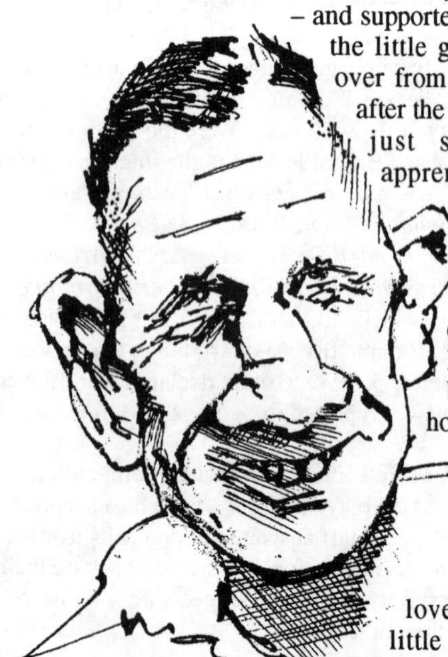

Palace were newly elected to the football league and Tom recalls being present at the first home league game in the third division – a goalless draw with Plymouth.

"The Nest was a lovely ground with a nice little stand. The railway ran along the back and you could see the signal box for Selhurst station. I stood on the terracing which was very low – the rest was cinders. It was quite difficult to see properly. "Me and my mates weren't very tall so we had to be there by a quarter-to-two in order to secure a place from which to get a decent view." It was very cramped and Tom recalls that the goal nets used to stand flush to the railings surrounding the pitch. The crowd and the keeper were so close they could touch each other.

Tom used to nip out from work on Friday afternoons to buy cakes for his colleagues which, on occasion, would give him the opportunity to meet the Palace players. "The team would often gather at the corner of George Street and North End waiting to be collected by coach to be taken to a hotel before away games. I made sure I got out to see them and chat to them. They were nice people."

Although most of the players of the time are now little more than memories – he remembers their names but not much else – he does recall that his favourites were the two wingers John Whibley and Albert Harry. "They were only in the third division, but when we were youngsters we thought they were marvellous players." Equally marvellous, Tom thought, was Selhurst Park, the new ground to which Palace moved in 1924. He was among the 25,000 at the first match – a second division fixture against The Wednesday. "In comparison to the Nest, it was wonderful." Like David, who also went to the game, Tom watched from the Park Road terracing opposite the main stand.

We'll support you

By the time Eric Bigg and Roy Davies started watching Palace, Tom and David had already seen the club fall back into the third division. Roy was also a civil servant – this time with Customs and Excise – while Eric, the brother of the 1930s Palace forward Bob Bigg, was an engineer. Both are from outside London. Eric moved to the capital in the early 30s from Larkhill, near Salisbury Plain, while Roy was born in Plymouth. His first memories of Crystal Palace are of watching them as visitors to Argyle in the third division south.

When Roy moved to London in 1934 he chose the Arsenal versus Palace F.A. Cup tie as his first match. But that wasn't where his affection for Palace began ... partly because they lost 7-0. Not surprisingly, he remembers the match as "very one sided" although many of the crowd were supporting Palace. Nobby Clarke in particular "received a special cheer each time he received the ball". Still with a noticeable West Country tinge to his accent, Roy says that he became a Selhurst regular later that year after a summer move south of the river.

Both Roy and Eric met the Palace players on occasion – Roy because his girlfriend lived where some of the players had digs and also through his connections with local club cricket. In the 1960s he played in the same Sunday cricket team as Ronnie

Left to right: Roy Davies, Eric Bigg, Tom Chippington, and Olive and David Gowler, Bottom left: Post war centre-forward Freddie Kurz
illustration by Jason Axell

evermore

Allen, against the likes of Johnny Byrne. Although Roy and David watched Palace regularly, they also had Saturday football commitments of their own. David recalls that after playing in the morning he would hurry off to Palace or Dulwich. "Many of the supporters used to cycle to the ground and would leave their bikes in the gardens in Whitehorse Lane. The people who lived there would charge tuppence or threepence for the privilege."

Roy has clear memories of many of the players of the time, such as the Dawes brothers, Cam Burgess and Bill Bassett. Burgess, who Palace signed from Chester, was a remarkable player. "He was the most unlikely centre-forward I ever saw," says Roy. "If he was playing today, the coaches would have a fit. He was a toe-kicker – I never saw him kick a ball with his instep. When he kicked the ball it would bobble and swerve all over the place. Just when the keeper thought he had it covered, it would suddenly move away." Burgess scored most of his goals from close range and Eric adds. "Cam never seemed to be more than a yard or two from goal."

Another memorable character was Fred Dawes' full back partner Roy Gregory who, Roy says, "had the biggest kick in the league".

"Dawes was the clever one, while Gregory could kick it from one penalty area to the other – a tremendous feat with a heavy leather ball. That was the thing in those days, you had two backs – one who did the rough stuff and one who was clever. It was the same with the wing halves – if the other side started getting dirty, you'd know you had someone who could get dirtier."

The leather ball would get gradually heavier in the rain and left muddy marks on anything it touched. "We had a bald centre-half called Bill Bassett and when it was raining the mud made it look like he had a full head of hair," laughs Roy. Then, of course, there was Palace's record scorer Peter Simpson. "The general opinion of Peter was that he was too clever for his own good," believes Roy. "As a result he was always liable to upset one of the backs or the centre-half and get his legs kicked from under him. That's what happened in the end, he got crocked."

Although he was rumoured to have attracted the interest of Sunderland, it seems strange that a player of Simpson's abilities stayed in the third division with Palace instead of joining one of the bigger clubs. "What was the point of his leaving? In those days players got seven quid maximum. If Palace were paying him and he was scoring lots of goals he was better off with them than with a struggling first division club on the same money but not scoring so many and not getting so much in bonuses." The maximum wage and the system of bonuses may explain why some clubs became known as "perpetual runners-up".

"It's probably being cynical," Roy continues, "but they used to reckon that there was a lot of teams in the second and third divisions that didn't want promotion. In those days there was only one-up and one-down and if you could finish second – preferably on goal difference – you could get the most out of the win bonuses. But if they went up to a tougher division they might not win so often and their income would drop. I remember Plymouth came second six seasons running in the 30s and it was an accusation often levelled at them."

Although the £7 maximum was far from generous considering the income the players generated for their clubs through the turnstiles, the players were by no means badly off. Eric's brother Bob was "considered a millionaire", earning £6 in winter and £4 in summer which compared favourably with Eric's £3.10s a week.

Some players supplemented their incomes with summer work – many of the Plymouth players, for example, used to work on the fishing fleet. Others were able to play summer sports as Eric recalls: "During the summer my brother used to go off on professional cricket tours. In fact Bob's only honour while with Palace was a medal he won in the *Evening News* Cricket Trophy for Footballers.

"Later, he broke his leg which slowed him down so he moved to Aldershot. But he kept playing until he was 45 for many different teams."

The atmosphere at Selhurst Park was quite different from today. "We were more fanatical but we were cleaner with it," claims Roy. "The size of the gates, especially after the war, was remarkable. Everybody would yell their heads off but they wouldn't punch the bloke next to them because he was cheering for the other side. That was the difference."

David says the crowd would shout and clap but there was little singing. "And you didn't see players jumping, cuddling or kissing when they scored. At most they would shake hands."

Another reason for the more relaxed atmosphere may have been the relatively limited presence of away supporters. Following Palace away from Selhurst was a rare occurrence. Even then trips were normally confined to London. Tom used to visit Fulham, QPR or Millwall but never went further afield.

From Roy's recollection the main rivals at the time were QPR and, to some extent, Millwall. But Palace's rivalry with Millwall was a friendly one. "Millwall was very nice, it wasn't rough – at least not compared to today,' says Tom.

Roy adds: "There was two ways of looking at the rivalry with Millwall. Lots of people watched Palace one week and Millwall the next and would support them both. It was only when they played each other that they would come down in favour of one team or the other. On Saturday afternoons you would see lots of people going up on the trains from West Croydon and Norwood Junction to New Cross Gate." Charlton weren't considered at all. "They were in the exalted heights of division one, so we didn't worry about them."

Roy says Palace and Chelsea were also on "friendly terms for many years", mainly he thought because of the regular to-ing and fro-ing of players between the two clubs.

In the days before war broke out, Palace enjoyed the services of two fine wing halves: Leslie Lievesley and Nick Collins. "Everybody said it was the best pair of half backs we'd ever had. Lievesley was the tough bloke and Collins was the clever one.

"Leslie was a good player in his own right though, he had a lot of talent, but when things started to get rough he sorted it out. Collins was the clever bloke ... he kicked the opposition when they weren't looking!"Another crowd favourite was Bernie Harrison, who had something of a cult image. "He was either 'good ol' Bernie' or 'Old Mother Harrison' depending on how well he was playing."

When war was declared, Tom stopped going and Eric was also away for much of the time. But David attended matches until he was called up by the Royal Engineers – later landing with his regiment at Caen on D-Day. As the Allies advanced across Europe, he was able to take a break to watch a wartime international in the Netherlands between Holland and England but that was his only taste of football until he was demobbed after the war.

But Roy's interest was undiminished: "We were very keen to watch football. It took our minds off the war and we often got gates of 10,000 or more. When it was raining we would stand on the terraces in our gas capes with the hood pulled over the top. With our wellingtons on as well we couldn't care less about the weather. We used to listen for doodlebugs [the V1 rockets] but the game wouldn't stop. It was only if the sound started coming straight at you that you'd get worried."

Towards the end of the war, Palace played Grimsby's Freddie Kurz under the guest system. "Kurz was an outside right for the Mariners, but played centre-forward for us," says Roy. "He was very popular and the fans petitioned the club to sign him. But he wasn't as good once he'd been transferred permanently." With London's clubs in regionalised competition there were chances to see some famous names in action, including Ted Drake. "A couple of games after, his career was over, but I remember the goal he headed against us. The ball went in quicker than most people could kick it."

Palace also had the famous Derby and England centre-forward Jack Stamps at their disposal for five matches. He made his mark with a couple of sweet goals. "He was a great player, a joy to watch," Eric recalls.

One of the club's darker days was the 4-2 defeat at home to Bishop Auckland in the F.A. Cup. "You'd have thought Palace were the amateurs and Bishops the professionals ... which they virtually were anyway," says Roy. "They had something like half-a-dozen amateur internationals in their side and they got good appearance money. They tore the Palace defence to ribbons. I don't mean they had continuous pressure, but when they attacked they knew what they were doing and caught us out of position."

"They had something like half a dozen amateur internationals in their side ... they tore the Palace defence to ribbons ... they knew what they were doing and caught Palace out of position."

F.A. Cup 1954-55
Palace 2, Bishop Auckland 4

This was one of a string of embarrassing defeats against non-league opposition at that time but Tom says there was little mickey-taking at work. "They didn't rub it in, it wasn't taken so seriously."

One of the most popular characters of the later 50s was Alf Noakes, who Roy described as "a little Cockney terrier – the sort of player who was after everything". Noakes' partner, Len Choules, had an unhappy start to his Palace career. "He was booed off the pitch after his first game, he was terribly nervous and downright hopeless. He was left back then, but when they moved him to centre-half he was outstanding. There was also a left-back – Harry MacDonald I think – who enjoyed a bit of a reputation. He used to like a drink before the game and in one match he got hit in the stomach and spewed all over the pitch. He made a name for himself in his first match – a 5-0 defeat by

Bournemouth – when he took a ball just inside his own half and cleared the goalkeeper with it for an own goal. "Some of my friends reckoned he drank a couple of pints before each match, but that was nothing compared to the rumours about Jardine at Millwall. They said he used to drink half a bottle of Scotch at half-time which was supposedly supplied by the directors!"

In the 60s Johnny Byrne was a great favourite. "I think he was a better player before he played for England. His greatest asset was that he could lose his marker. Palace attacks used to start with a throw from Vic Rouse and Byrne would wait by the touchline to receive the ball. Often he would be left on his own because the defender didn't know whether or not to come with him."

Like Budgie Byrne, Mike Deakin came through the ranks. "He worked very hard," says Roy. "We used to say he was the unluckiest forward ever. He got in some wonderful positions and either hit the post or the goalkeeper would make a great save – whatever he did he couldn't seem to get the ball in the net. Deakin's heading was good, he distributed the ball as well as anyone, he was good at flicks and would get up and nod the ball down to the inside forwards, but he just could not seem to score." Palace finally won promotion from division four with some sparkling football by Arthur Rowe's team. "He was a good footballing manager. His teams played very good stuff. But I knew one or two players at the time and they always said: 'It's no good. We play nice football but other teams kick us out of the game, and Arthur insists that there be no retaliation. We play football and that's it and the other teams come down and get stuck in and know that there's not going to be any comeback.' But Dick Graham was the opposite. He wanted them to get stuck in."

Roy says Palace owed a lot to George Petchey. "He was clever. Clever, but dirty with it. He kicked people accidentally on purpose."

One of the great highlights of the early 60s was the friendly with Real Madrid to unveil Palace's new floodlights. Tom thought it was a "marvellous spectacle" while Roy said: "We'd never seen anything like it before. The quality of the lighting was wonderful. The thing that stuck in my mind was the way the jerseys glowed and glittered in the lights. Normally in the dark of winter the colours didn't show up very well, but in the floodlights they seemed luminous."

Of Madrid themselves, Roy says the fans didn't know what to expect. "I suppose they were good, they certainly didn't need to break sweat. They did just enough to win and let Palace have some fun. It meant everyone was happy. If they'd humiliated us, they wouldn't be asked by other teams would they?" Roy also saw Arsenal play under lights when Palace centre-half Charlie Chase shut out the Gunners' new signing Charles. Dennis Compton, who had just returned from England's Ashes tour of Australia received a big hand. "Everyone wanted Dennis to score."

After Byrne had departed for West Ham, Palace

Under the turnstiles

I climbed in under the turnstile to see my first match at Selhurst Park. It was the days of Jack Stamps, Freddie Kurz, who had the sweetest left foot you could ever imagine, and "Bandy" Wilson. Money was short and until I was older and could afford to go, I used to wait outside until the gates were opened ten minutes from

Jim Lee, who now lives in Blandford in Dorset, is a Glazier in exile. He recalls some of the characters and strange incidents that stood out from his vantage point on the Holmesdale

the end and then sneak in. Later when I played football on Saturday's in the Thornton Heath League I used to run over with my team mates to see the last five minutes.

My favourite player was "Baldy" Bassett, the centre-half. "His favourite trick was to lean on the opposing centre-forward's shoulders to get more height and head the ball away, and more often than not he got away with it too. Fred Dawes was in the team at left-back, he was a really tough bloke. Johnny Rainford was a very clever inside forward and I don't know why he didn't go further in the game but Albert Mycock had a huge beer belly. Mike Deakin kept falling down but when he could stand up he would score goals.

Laurie Scott used to play Jack Edwards, a Welshman who wouldn't last five minutes in the game today, no prisoners taken with him. Laurie Scott was player-manager at left-back, he was still a great player, Ronnie Rooke could score a goal on a sixpence, Les Stevens would do nothing for most of the game and then suddenly pull out a shot which would hit the goal like it would collapse.

We always had a good laugh with the opposing supporters, no trouble. Everybody enjoyed going over there and it didn't really matter whether they won or not. You could have a good laugh. It was a different atmosphere to what I think it is now. We often moaned about the players, but we always went back although the facilities were terrible, it was a mud-bath most of the time.

I was called up in 1951 and didn't see any games for a couple of years. By the time I got back Cam Burgess was around as well. The main reason he scored goals was because he never left the penalty area.

The day I got married I still managed to get to Selhurst Park for a match in the afternoon. I used to live in Bungalow Road about ten seconds from the ground and always stood on the Holmesdale. We never went to away games, we didn't have the money. The exception to the rule was away games at Millwall, "only I was a coward and never let the Millwall crowd know I was a Palace supporter. You had to be careful with that lot!"

It's a wonder that Palace didn't do better, there were lots of stories about their drinking and that's probably why they didn't do so well. The main thing about Palace's training was ... straight out of the ground, nearest pub, have a few drinks and then back home. Although we were terrible in the league, I still think of them as good times. We still got good crowds. All I can put it down to was that they didn't train hard enough.

The first time I took my daughter was to see George Best play for Manchester United against Palace. George got hold of the ball on the touchline trying to throw it in and he was dilly dallying and some wag called him "Jesus Christ" and sent my daughter up the wall. She threatened to hit him and she was only about 14.

replaced him with the "busy little dribbler" Peter Burridge. Also in the line-up was Ronnie Allen, who was immensely popular. When Palace made it to division two, rumours circulated among fans that he and Cliff Holton would take over the managerial side from Dick Graham, who was under some pressure. Many believed that they is why they were allowed to leave.

Eventually it was Bert Head who led the club into the first division – unquestionably Tom's proudest moment. However, he missed most of the match against Fulham in which Palace finally made it to the top flight. "It was my daughter's wedding and I couldn't go. However, the reception was nearby and I managed to get away near the end. I arrived just in time to see the celebrations."

It's worth considering, as Palace yo-yo between the divisions just as they've always done, that supporting the club is a lifetime commitment. Tom, David, Olive, Roy and Eric have followed Palace at their lowest ebb, begging for a league place, through promotions and relegations and eventually to Wembley, in Tom's case after an 85 year wait. That is true loyalty which is to be admired – well worth remembering the next time Palace are bottom of the league and its raining.

Thanks to David and Olive Gowler, Roy Davies, Tom Chippington and Eric Bigg. The editors gratefully acknowledge the assistance of Jill Pritchard and her team from Age Concern, Croydon. Interview by Tony Matthews, Phil Huffer and Stuart Dunbar.

NEXT HOME MATCH:
NEXT SATURDAY, November 18th.
BARNSLEY
(League II.)
KICK-OFF, 2.45 p.m.

Crystal Palace F.C.
Official Programme
Price .... Twopence
Published under Authority by T. W. Morris Ltd. Advertising Agents 104 High Holborn W.C.1
No. 15
NOVEMBER 11th, 1922

At Home

The magnetic fascination of "Home"—its wonderful lure—after the day's work or play, is considerably enhanced by the standard of comfort provided by its Furnishing appointments—its invitingly restful atmosphere.

Smarts have made it possible for everyone to realize this "Home" ideal regardless of individual financial circumstances at the moment. Smarts' Simple System of Furnishing out-of-income provides for monthly or quarterly payments spread over a long or short period to suit your convenience.

Smarts' Free Fire and Life Insurance Policy—given with every order under our Simple System—cancels all payments due in respect of the Furniture in the event of the customer's death or the destruction of the Furniture by fire during the currency of the Agreement.

Write or call for Free Copy of Smarts' New Catalogue, No. C.P.I.

Smarts
SMART BROS LTD
Phone: Croydon 1746.
30 32 & 34, George Street,
CROYDON.

The Screaming Alice

By Ronald Spiers

I started supporting Palace in 1921 when I was about ten years old. My father was a fairly regular spectator although he was not a follower of the team he referred to as "Screaming Alice" – he was a Brentford supporter. Palace's team in cardinal and blue was usually Alderson in goal, Little and Rhodes at the back , McCracken and Jones (Greener came soon after) Bateman outside right, Conner and Menlove and Whibley on the left wing. After one great win against Fulham I recall the joke "Why is the Palace outside left the most popular man in football?" – "Because all Menlove Whibley."

I went to the first ever match at Selhurst Park but we lost to the Wednesday and were relegated to the third division where we stayed until long after the war. I stopped going for a number of years and when I returned the forward line was: Harry, Havelock, Simpson, Butler and Clarke. I saw Peter Simpson score six in one game against Exeter and it would have been seven if Butler hadn't helped a stunning free kick over the line.

Roy, Jack and Scotty

By Jack Saunders

Perhaps an old man's memories will not tie up with the authentic records, but to me they are very real.

My father served in Ireland in the "Troubles" after the First World War and it was only after he was demobilised in 1920-21 that he started to take me regularly to see Palace. In those days, regular supporters followed both the first team and the reserves in the London Combination, so every Saturday was occupied throughout the season.

One good reason for watching the reserves was that after the game a member of staff would appear at the players' exit and call out the result of the first eleven's away fixture, thus saving the expense of buying an evening paper. I assume he obtained this by telephone, you must realise that in the 20s very few of us had a wireless set on which to receive football results.

I still have an autograph book with about 20 players' signatures in it. Until recently I also had a Pinnacle collection of cigarette cards with about 30 Palace players grouped around the specially enlarged one of the captain Roy McCracken.

A couple of characters I should mention are Jack Jones, the trainer who preceded Bobby Greener. He was the only person I saw who regularly covered 100 yards in 10 seconds with his sponge and bag immediately a Palace player was even apparently injured. There was also "Scotty" a middle aged supporter who ran from one end of the enclosure to the other following the play throughout the match shouting quite unintelligible Scottish remarks non-stop.

ARSENAL
the root of all evil

Palace v Arsenal, good against evil

Back in my young day all we ever 'eard abaht woz bleedin' Arsenal. Gawd, they woz the most 'orrible, boring, lucky bunch of snivelling, brylcreemed gits yer could ever 'ave the misfortune ter meet. Arsenal woz ter the firties wot Liverpool woz ter the eighties, they woz barsterds.

So yer can imagine me 'orror when they started winning fings again a year or two back and, wot wiv selling young Wright to em, I dunno wot fings are comin' to. I tell yer, the rise of Arsenal woz abaht as welcome as Oswald bludy Moseley and 'is blackshirt mob and

Arsenal are historically horrible. Percy Palace explains why they are such complete gits.

wot a bunch er prawnz they woz. An' anuvver fing they only ever win fings when there's a recession on (Arsenal, not the Blackshirts). High unemployment and Arsenal go tergether like lamb chops an' mint sauce.

Anyway, it all started wiv this geezer called 'erbert Chapman although my old dad used ter sit me on 'is knee and tell me 'ow a Tory creep called Sir 'Enry Norris paid fer 'em to be put in the first division after the Great War. That's the sort of people yer dealing wiv at Arsenal. Now, this Chapman 'e woz a pretty good manager up at 'Uddersfield and no-one minded 'em winnin' fings cos they was up norf and so they didn't matter anyway. But course, bludy Arsenal couldn't keep their thievin' 'ands off 'im and the next fing yer know they was winnin' everyfink in sight by playing wiv more centre-arfs than 'itler ad bollocks. I 'ated 'em, we all 'ated 'em.

Now say wot yer like abaht that twerp 'itler but if there's one fing 'e did do wiv 'is war it was stop Arsenal winning fings, and when the bloomin Luftwaffe bombed 'ighbury, well, we all larfed down the Anderson shelter that night and mother broke out a small tin of tapioca we'd bin savin' for VE night ter celebrate. After the war, old Ronnie Rooke, oo we 'ad dahn at the Palace, won 'em a championship cos they couldn't do it on their own and then it was nice and quiet until that long 'aired lout Charlie George come on the scene. I remember when Palace nearly signed 'im. I wrote ter the club an I told em, if yer buy 'im tell 'im ter get 'is bloomin' 'air cut, it was bad enough with that gink Kember an' 'is sideboards.

I tell yer, yer don't wanna go watchin' Arsenal, no good'll come of it, stand on me. An if that young wotsit Wright knows what's good fer im e'll come back ter the Palace cos that norf London crowd don't know the first fing about proper football. Plastic fans? I ask yer, they used ter make em out o' bakelite in my day. An' worse than anyfink was when me little grandson Torquil got an Arsenal shirt fer Christmas. Cruelty ter children I call it, I told me daughter an that twerp of an 'usband I woz gonna report em to the Social Services fer trying ter bring up an Arsenal fan without a licence. Anyway Torquil was quite upset when I accidentally spilt two gallon o' creosote down it. So I promised ter buy im a smart new Palace one. Just as soon as the government gives me a pay rise on me pension. Cheerio then.

Ten reasons to hate Arsenal

1) Selling them Kenny Sansom
2) They come from north London
3) They always wear ridiculous away kits
4) Selling them Ian wright too cheaply
5) Coca Cola Cup 1993
6) Highbury, May 1993
7) Selling them Eddie McGoldrick (after what they did)
8) We never, ever beat them
9) Their pathetic support
10) Just because

Alan Greenhow

Jim Cannon's History of the Palace
PART 8
IN THE REPLAY THE GAME ENDED IN A BIT OF A BATTLE, MIND YOU MOST GAMES IN THOSE DAYS ENDED IN A BATTLE OR WAR...
PLAYERS WERE GETTING CUTS...
COULDN'T GET ANY ELASTOPLAST SEEMS THE PHARMACIST'S NOT OPEN FOR ANOTHER 672 YEARS
BRUISES...
...AND DECAPITATION ON A REGULAR BASIS.
HE'S RUNNING AROUND LIKE A HEADLESS CHICKEN!
ITS A DIRTY FOUL ACTUALLY!
ONE PARTICULAR GAME IN 1066 SAW A PALACE PLAYER HAVE HIS EYE POKED OUT
THAT'S THE LAST TIME I PLAY AS THE TARGET MAN!
AND YOU CAN RELIVE THESE AND MANY OTHER BLOODY FOOTY BATTLES WITH THE NEW VIDEO, VINNY JONES AND HIS FAVOURITE MEDIEVIL MARAUDERS AND MURDERERS.
Vinny Jones
VINNY JONES MARAUDERER
Medievil

PALACE: LIFE, THE UNIVERSE, EVERYTHING

Anyone who has ever watched them knows that Crystal Palace are heart breakers. Steve Crisp puts a lifetime of support into context

In May 1991 the girl I was living with left me and I cried. I swore then that I would never cry again. On May 8, 1993 at Highbury I broke my promise.

Life is good. I have a job I like, I go out a lot and generally I have a good time. So how is it that Crystal Palace take 90 minutes every Saturday to shape how I feel for the rest of the week?

It started on October 30, 1971. I was four years old and my mum and dad (a Spurs fan) had just split up. My mother remarried a Palace supporter and moved to Penge. And so, in an innocent, unquestioning way, my winter emotions were shaped. I should have seen what was coming, we lost 3-0 at home to West Ham.

Like most, if not all, Palace fans, I did not choose my team. I went because that's what my family or friends did and I was slowly but surely indoctrinated into thinking that here was the greatest team in Europe. It was just that nobody had realised it yet. Palace fans love their club, because it's theirs. Either their family of friends dragged them along or they just lived locally. This is both our strength and our weakness. When I was at school in south east London I was the only Palace fan. There were two Charlton fans, two Millwall fans and the rest. The rest, you will not be surprised to learn, supported Man United, Leeds, Liverpool and Arsenal.

Remember the 1976 Cup game at Elland Road? I do, it was the first time I'd ever taken the micky out of anyone. So while the rest made their clubs a fortune by getting daddy to buy the kit for them, I went to the match wearing my scarf and bobble hat with pride.

Crystal Palace is our club. We've all been through the trauma of people taking the piss and not being able to get our own back because "at least Arsenal are in the first division" and they don't care anyway. But we love our club in a way they will never understand.

I have seen Palace in every division except the fourth, my step-dad saw us re-elected three times, what the hell do Arsenal fans know about anything except 1-0 wins (4-0 if they're playing Palace) and brilliant offside manoeuvres. Did they feel untold delight at getting to the F.A. Cup Final? Or was it just relief because they had another stab at Europe?

I watched us get relegated to the third, then painstakingly build the Team of the Eighties to earn promotion back to the first. I missed only one home game in 1978/79 – against Burnley.

I'm not sure I've ever quite forgiven my mum and dad for booking a holiday in the South of France, but if you were in Montpelier that night you would have seen a British family huddled round a public phone box for 90 minutes and then hugging each other before retiring to a bar to enjoy a well earned bottle of Pomagne – having spent most of our holiday money on calls to my grandmother we couldn't afford the real thing.

We were back where we belonged. Or were we? Where do we belong? With most teams it would be easy to look at their form and decide in what part of the league they appear most comfortable. This doesn't work with Palace. In all but two of the 21 years I have followed the Eagles, we have either been fighting relegation or chasing promotion. Whatever division we are in we are not happy with it. I don't really think it matters. We love our club and don't give up because the team stops being successful. We give up because we can no longer stand watching the thing we love die in front of our eyes. When Palace fans stop going to Palace they stop going to football. People support those big clubs because they are successful. If they stop being successful, their *raison d'etre*, the supporters simply switch to another club that they nominally call their own. In London, for early 70s Leeds fans read late 70s Liverpool fans or 90s Arsenal fans.

With the demise of the Team of the Eighties, my dad tragically broke the habit of a lifetime and stopped going. I'd hit puberty and there were more interesting things than Tommy Langley and Paul Barron. From 1983 to 1987, I too gave up. In that time, I came very close to giving up on football completely.

Then came university. I was going to study in Londonderry for four years and I went through a phase of getting back to my roots. And the strongest and most beloved root in south east London lay at Selhurst Park. I went to as many games as possible and I was hooked again.

I sometimes think God was watching over me during this time. From January

Open to the elements: Palace supporters on the Holmesdale. One reason we are a breed apart.

of equal divisional status!

My abiding memory is of a group of 60 year olds, their hair grey, singing, chanting and crying. Even now when I think of that game it sends shivers down my spine.

I suppose it means different things to different people but to me it meant I supported a team that had made it, that had tasted recognisable glory. Like I said at the beginning, Palace fans don't choose their team.

I doubt if there was one red and blue heart at Villa Park who hadn't seen us lose to Shrewsbury or Swindon. We deserved our taste of the high life and it was so sweet. Ask an Arsenal fan how he felt on reaching Wembley and he'll tell you how happy he was. Ask a Palace fan and they'll do what I'm doing now – struggle. How do you explain what you feel about success when you don't really know what it is. I know why those life-long supporters cried when St Courtney blew the whistle. It was because in one half of their mind's eye they could see Wembley and in the other half they could see Blundell Park and the Manor Ground. If for most of your life you eat s***, when sweet success comes you will be overwhelmed.

The next season we finished third but we all knew it would be the following season which would make or break us. It did the latter.

And so to 1992-3, another relegation year (my fourth). I couldn't sleep after the draw against Man City and I wept at Highbury. After the game we walked back to the Flounder and Firkin in Holloway Road. Nearly everyone in there was a Palace fan and there was silence. After a while someone started singing, and everyone else joined in. With the tears barely dry, we belted out our love for the club. I looked around and saw 20 people (and some amazed Arsenal fans – those who had not slunk away) defiantly forcing out our grief.

We're not the sort of people who follow the tribe. Although everyone was singing *We Love You Palace* together. Every one of us meant it as an individual.

to October 1990 I was on placement in London and was able to do something I had only ever been able to dream about; I followed Palace to Wembley. Before I talk about April 8, 1990 I want to touch on the Final itself. To me, losing somehow didn't matter. I would have loved to have seen Palace lift the trophy and go on to play in Europe, but at least we got there. We don't expect Palace to get to finals. Not one person that I spoke to on the journey to Villa Park thought we would be going to Wembley. We were going to Villa Park because we were Palace fans and we wanted to cheer our team around the pitch for having done us proud.

I loved Wembley. I belted out the national anthem and *Abide With Me* not because I am particularly patriotic or religious but because I had a right to and I was proud of being able to. I nearly burst with pride. I've seen my team play for the world's premier sporting trophy and I'm going to bore my grandchildren crapless telling them about it.

April 8, 1990. What does it mean to us? It was a hell of a shock, but what a bloody game. At 5am I blearily groped around the bedroom to find some clothes. I set out for the mile walk to the station to get a train to Euston where the special was to leave at 8.15. But they were working on the track at Orpington and no-one had told me. The 6.30 train hadn't arrived and no-one was on duty until 7.30. When I finally met a member of the station staff they told me there would be no service until after 9am. It was 7.45 and I started to walk home. "We'll get tonked anyway and I can see it on the box."

One of the greatest days of my life and I nearly missed it. About 20 yards down the road, I realised what I was doing. This was the F.A. Cup semi-final and I had to be there. I phoned for a cab who reckoned we might make it if we were lucky.

"Fourteen quid mate."

"I'll give you 20 if we make it."

The driver, a Millwall fan, did 80 all the way from Bromley to Euston, we were followed by the police but lost them down some back roads. All lights were green – a good sign. On the train everyone said the only way we would win was if we sneaked one at the last. We were not wrong, but we were not right.

I took my place on the Holte End and the rest as they say is history. I lost my voice and everything out of my coat pockets and was hugged by complete strangers. Only they weren't strangers, they were fellow Palace supporters and even though we'd never met I'd known them all my life.

I stayed behind for 20 minutes to soak up the atmosphere. For us there will never be another day like it. We may reach Wembley again, but we'll never have that same feeling of shock about doing it. Seven months earlier we'd been hammered 9-0 by the team we'd beaten to get to Wembley. Outside bookmakers were offering 7-1 against a Palace victory – in a two-horse race with teams

Where do we come from?

David Crosier offers an insight into the genetic development of the Palace fan and outlines the role monkey nuts have played in Selhurst Park folklore

There are many theories to explain the phenomenon of Palace support. Among the most popular is the concept of some sort of "Palace gene". This rather peculiar gene may remain dormant in some families for generations before suddenly erupting to produce a new generation of die hard supporters.

On the other side of the theoretical divide are the social constructionists – those Palace-crazed families who think that by painting everything in their house red and blue, watching Palace videos all day long and taking their offspring to Selhurst Park from the age of six months somehow their own Palace fever will rub off on the next generation. Personally I wouldn't like to take sides in this debate, my own experience being inconclusive.

"The Palace gene may remain dormant in some families for generations before suddenly erupting to produce a new generation of die hard supporters."

I can't remember not being a Palace supporter but I've no idea if I experienced a natural childhood state or whether it was an indoctrinated one. My earliest memory of Palace is of being dragged by my grandad to a match against Portsmouth when I was about five years old. I can't remember much except that I was too short to have any view at all of the pitch. I was therefore more aware of the atmosphere of the game itself. In particular I remember being deafened by a very loud bell rung about five inches from my ear by an old codger who seemed to be a friend of my grandad's. Despite my requests to move to a more congenial part of the ground where I might be able to see what was going on and preserve my powers of hearing we stayed put. My complaining must have convinced my grandad that I was not the stuff of which Palace fans are made and he never took me to another match.

It was about five years later that my truly formative Palace experiences began. These were the years when Palace, having been promoted to the first division, struggled to stay up for a few years and then plummeted into the third division. At this time I could be found on the Whitehorse amid a hardy little crew that consisted of my younger brother, two other friends – also brothers – and one or other of our fathers.

My father wasn't too enthusiastic about spending his Saturday afternoons at the Palace, preferring his allotment shed, but occasionally out of a sense of paternal duty he'd take his turn. We would often meet up with a couple of school friends and their brothers and we'd sit on the Whitehorse wall.

For our little group the actual match was only a part of the entertainment. Indeed for certain among us, notably my brother and his mate, a whole match was often a bit too much and by twenty to five when the teleprinter would start spewing results onto our television screen they would be comfortably installed in front of the box. To this day, my brother has retained the habit of leaving a few minutes before the end of the match. Now his excuse is to avoid the traffic but the result is the same – the last minute goals and high tension are always missed.

Our entertainment at Selhurst wasn't always on the pitch, but it was real enough. The first part of the ritual consisted of getting the monkey nuts. These would be used during the afternoon as ammunition to lob at passing coppers and any baldies who passed underneath our wall. None of the victims could ever be sure who exactly had thrown the offending nut as we concealed them in our hands with faces the picture of innocence. Peanut-throwing, a particularly popular activity among our group was completely ignored by one person, the elder brother of one of my schoolmates. I've no idea what time he used to arrive but I guessed he was the first person inside the ground every time.

He was always in place by the time we turned up and gave the impression of being in some kind of deep trance. None of us would disturb him in this pre-match state for we feared it might be dangerous for him.

As he tended to be somewhat monosyllabic at the best of times his conversation wasn't much missed. However I did once ask him why he concentrated so hard on a patch of grass somewhere near the corner flag. I expected some answer such as an enlightenment into the ways of Zen Buddhism, but he actually said: "I'm counting the blades of grass on the pitch!"

Although our group eventually split up, I moved onto the Holmesdale with a different friend and the others moved away from London, there's no doubt that supporting Palace remains a fact of life for all of us. I now live abroad and only get to England two or three times a season so I rely on the World Service for the results and telephone calls to my brother for reports. On the first Saturday of 1992/93 the reports were lousy and only concerned with Alan Shearer's two goals for Blackburn.

I called for a more detailed and Palace biased version of the match. I should have known the answer when I asked for the details of our third goal. "Sorry Dave, missed that one. Had to beat the traffic you know."

The Forties ... Palace at War

When football took second place

As with the first world war, football competitions were regionalised at the outbreak of hostilities. Palace joined League South "A" Division alongside West Ham, Watford, Arsenal, Charlton, Clapton Orient, Southend, Norwich, Spurs and Millwall.

We started at Upton Park with an impressive 6-2 victory. The teams: *West Ham: Medhurst, Bicknell, Forde, Fenton, Walker, Cockroft, Small, Macauley, Foreman, Goulden, Foxall.*

Palace: Tootill, Gregory, F. Dawes, Collins, Millbanks, Hudgell, Robson, Trevor Smith, Blackman, Bark, Wilson

Blackman got a hat-trick while Bark, Robson and Gregory from the penalty spot completed the demolition job on the Irons. But Palace were soon on the receiving end themselves, going down 5-0 against Arsenal at White Hart Lane – Highbury had already been commandeered for military use.

Palace enjoyed only four more victories in that first wartime competition, all of which came in a short burst just before Christmas, but December was spoilt when the club got into trouble with the Football Association. Former director R.S. Moyes, who had managed the club for a short period in between Tom Bromilow's spells complained of "certain irregularities". Allegations were made that vouchers made out as "directors expenses" were in fact illegal inducements to players, thought to be Vincent Blore and Jackie Palethorpe. The League and F.A. held a joint enquiry and three directors were suspended sine die, two players were fined and the secretary was cautioned.

In January 1940, Selhurst hosted an England representative match against the Army. But even with the likes of Stan Cullis, Joe Mercer and Stan Matthews on show, the crowd was only 10,057.

The League South "A" was disrupted more by the way it was organised and the weather than by the war, and by mid-February, matters had been complicated by the establishment of another competition, League South "D", which was based on status rather than geography. The "A" division fixtures became of secondary importance and were finished off in dribs and drabs. Of Palace's last three "A" games, one was played in February, one in April and the last in May. The division was won by Arsenal and on Boxing Day they attracted the season's only crowd in excess of 10,000 to Selhurst Park. We lost 3-0.

Goalkeeper Alf Tootill, as seen by Mercer of the ***Croydon Advertiser***

League South "D" was more enjoyable from Palace's point of view, because we won it. However, most of the glamour teams weren't in it. In front of crowds which never exceeded 8,000, we fielded a reasonably settled side and enjoyed a number of big wins. Between March 22 and May 29, we won eight and drew one of nine matches, including a 7-1 win over Clapton and a crushing 10-0 victory over Brighton at Selhurst Park.

In the latter, Bark and Robson scored hat-tricks. Mee the regular Brighton keeper played on the wing in the first half while Clifford went in goal. Palace led 5-0 at half time and so Mee went back between the posts but Palace got five more anyway! In the football league war cup, Palace thumped Tottenham 4-1 at Selhurst in the first of a two legged tie, losing 2-1 at White Hart Lane in the return. Arsenal then beat us in both legs in the second round.

Having started late, the league didn't finish until June 8 when we won 3-1 at Norwich. The last three matches were all played outside London and attracted crowds of 500, 1,300 and 1,000 respectively. It is not hard to understand why. At that moment, the British Army was fighting a rearguard action at Dunkirk as an armada of small boats joined the Royal Navy in a desperate rescue attempt.

In the summer of 1940 Britain stood alone. France had fallen and the remnants of the British Expeditionary Force, which had proved so inadequate in the face of the Blitzkreig, had been lost. Invasion seemed imminent.

While Britain waited for the expected onslaught, the new football season commenced. Palace pounded Chelsea 6-3 on the opening day, August 31. The Battle of Britain was under way. We were one year into the war, yet Palace were still able to field a good side including captain Nick Collins, one of the best players of his generation, who in pre-war days had formed a pairing with Leslie Lievesley that was among the finest ever. Lievesley was one player Palace had lost. He would later be killed in tragic circumstances while Collins' career was ruined by the war – after playing regularly in the first three seasons, his appearances were restricted by his call-up to the Royal Navy where he was later decorated for his part in engaging and sinking an enemy submarine.

The need for football at the time was minimal, Palace played in the south regional league but crowds were tiny and there was little organisation. We finished top by virtue of having the best goal average even though, to illustrate what a mess everything was, we "lost" one match at Millwall when the game ended after 30 minutes with the home side leading 1-0. The result was allowed to stand and counted towards the final table. We achieved some big scores, twice hitting seven and adding to the thrashing of Chelsea by scoring six against Bournemouth and Clapton Orient. We also did well in the London War Cup, reaching the semi final before losing to eventual winners Reading. In the league war cup, we were beaten in both legs by QPR with only around three and a half thousand at each match.

Palace were gradually shorn of some key players due to military call-ups. Fred Gregory had joined the RAF as a PT instructor while Ted Owens and Trevor Smith were also in the air-force. Albert Wilson's appearances were limited and centre-half Joe Millbanks was in the Navy. Yet, in 1940-41 Irwin invited only two guest players – one of whom was Arsenal and England amateur Bernard Joy, who later wrote a column for the *Evening Standard*. This contrasts greatly with other clubs – on one occasion Fulham included ten guests in their side. There were numerous incidents of players playing against their own clubs. Ian Gillespie, for example, played for Orient against Palace on November 16, 1940 as did A.E. Waite an amateur on the Selhurst books. Gillespie scored in Orient's 4-2 win.

By the third season of war, the tide had started to turn against the Axis. The Luftwaffe had lost the Battle of Britain and concentrated on bombing London and other major cities. The Germans had abandoned Britain in order to attack the Soviet Union.

As Britain stepped back from the brink of defeat, Palace stepped back from the victories of the early years. Not that it mattered to anybody. Football was a release valve and the entertainment was of more importance. Palace certainly served up entertainment, often in bizarre circumstances. In March 1941 the visiting Brentford players disputed a Palace penalty and refused to continue. The referee then took all the players off the pitch where, after discussions with their officials, Brentford agreed to continue. Arthur Hudgell scored from the spot to complete a 5-0 victory. Later in the same season "a display of bad sportsmanship" by Rickett, the Southend goalkeeper marred our seven goal romp. We were already four up when Collins ran onto a through ball. Ricketts thought the linesman had flagged offside but the referee allowed Collins to go on to score. Ricketts then chased the referee and the linesman and as Southend players tried to marshall him away he walked off. Play was held up for ten minutes while the referee tried without success to convince the keeper to return. Eventually the exasperated official handed the green jersey to Southend's centre-forward Fielders. The Shrimpers, having already lost McLukie with a leg injury, were now down to nine men and Palace continued the rout unopposed.

The London League of 1941-42 was something of a unique venture. Before the season was under way, the capital's clubs announced that they were not prepared to accept the Football League's plans for a third year of war football and instead would form an independent league of their own which, they claimed, would benefit them by offering local games of interest to London supporters while removing the

SOUTH REGIONAL LEAGUE TABLE 1940-41

	P	W	D	L	F	A
Crystal Palace	27	16	4	7	86	44
West Ham	25	14	6	5	70	39
Coventry	10	5	3	2	28	16
Arsenal	19	10	5	4	66	38
Cardiff C	24	12	5	7	75	50
Reading	26	14	5	7	73	51
Norwich C	19	9	2	8	73	55
Watford	35	15	6	14	96	73
Portsmouth	31	16	2	13	92	71
Tottenham Hotspur	23	9	5	9	53	41
Millwall	31	16	5	10	73	57
Walsall	32	14	7	11	100	80
WBA	28	13	5	10	83	69
Leicester	33	17	5	11	87	73
Northampton	30	14	3	13	84	71
Bristol City	20	10	2	8	55	48
Mansfield	29	12	6	11	77	68
Charlton Ath	19	7	4	8	37	34
Aldershot	24	14	2	8	73	68
Brentford	23	9	3	11	51	51
Chelsea	23	10	4	9	57	58
Birmingham	16	7	1	8	38	43
Fulham	30	10	7	13	62	73
Luton	35	11	7	17	82	100
Stoke City	36	9	9	18	76	96
QPR	23	8	3	12	47	60
Brighton	25	8	7	10	51	75
Forest	25	7	3	15	50	77
Bournemouth	27	9	3	15	59	92
Notts County	21	8	3	10	42	66
Southend	29	12	4	13	64	101
Southampton	31	4	4	23	53	111
Swansea	10	2	1	7	12	33
Clapton Orient	15	1	3	11	19	66

Palace are champions of a masterpiece of improvisation

need to travel, which was increasingly difficult. The Football League responded in its usual adult manner by expelling the rebel clubs *en masse*.

Palace had made a profit of £400 on the previous season and with further attractive fixtures they could afford not to be worried. The league began with a home fixture against Millwall and we won a match marked by a minute's silence for Palace vice-chairman Bob Cornell, who had died during the week, with goals by Robson and Gillespie.

The highlight of the season was the 10-1 massacre of Brighton where, as one paper put it, "some of the crowd lost count". Robson scored four, with two each for Gillespie, Albert Dawes and Smith.

In the qualifying group for the London war cup, Palace finished fourth, which wouldn't have been too bad if it hadn't been for the fact that there were only four teams in it. Against Chelsea, Fulham and Portsmouth, we could muster just one draw.

After one season in "exile" Palace along with all the other London clubs plus Brighton, Watford, Reading and Aldershot returned to the League's fold in 1942-43, joining the Football League South. To keep travelling to a minimum, each of the 18 clubs missed three opponents. In Palace's case we did not meet Luton, Watford or Reading.

America had entered the war at the tail end of 1941 and their forces were now present in huge numbers. Although there is no evidence to suggest they were swelling the attendances at Selhurst Park (apparently, they were more concerned with chasing British women, chewing gum and complaining about our warm beer – at least if you watch old war films they did) they committed sacrilege by staging an Americans versus Canadians baseball match on the hallowed Selhurst turf.

Irwin still preferred to use Palace players rather than a mish-mash of guests – the only two strangers in the team which beat Spurs at White Hart Lane on the opening day were the Charlton keeper Hobbins and Roy Morris of Norwich. Spurs took the lead through Ludford but we replied with goals by Wilson and Robson, who beat Ted Ditchburn with a shot which squeezed just inside the post. Bark then hit the crossbar before Robson wrapped it up with a third with 20 minutes left.

The demands of the war soon forced a change of policy towards guests. No fewer than 21 were used as Irwin employed 45 players in the second half of the season. In total we used 70 players and only eight of those made more than 15 appearances. A 7-1 thrashing by Arsenal at Selhurst was the bitterest blow mainly because Reg Lewis, a Palace local boy, scored five times. But there was little relief for Brighton. In September we beat them 8-1 at the Goldstone Ground, allowing what few Brighton supporters there were to enjoy some attacking football for a change. But, after that, we didn't fare too well ourselves, finishing 15th in all. On February 6, we came in for another pasting at the hands of Arsenal, who beat us 9-0.

The make-do-and-mend policy was illustrated perfectly by Albert Dawes, who played in eight different outfield positions during the season and the following year he played in all ten! In the Football League Cup, South, we at last managed a win – 4-0 over Luton – but it wasn't enough to qualify for the semi-finals.

In the 1943-44 season, the Football League South continued, finishing for Palace on May 6, exactly one month before D-Day. We enjoyed a much better time of it with plenty of exciting matches and improved crowds as people felt able to relax just a little because the war was going our way. Big scores included a 5-4 victory at Craven Cottage, a 6-1 win at Clapton, a 5-0 home trouncing of Luton and the obligatory mauling of Brighton, this time 6-2 at the Goldstone Ground on Christmas Day. Before the season was out, there were further six goal hauls against Fulham and Aldershot and even Arsenal were restricted by an improved Palace. The Gunners only beat us 5-2.

Palace were determined to plan for the future and one of our brightest hopes was Jack Lewis, a youngster who had been signed before the war from West Brom. "By consistently good play," it was reported, "Lewis has established himself in the first team and made the right half back position his own."

It was his misfortune that the war had disrupted a promising career, but according to the *Croydon Advertiser* he was still "a good all round athlete with several years of good football in him, and providing he keeps free from injury should be wearing Palace colours for many years to come". But it wasn't all good news. As the Allied armies pressed on with their advance through Europe, it was reported that Howard Girling had sustained flesh wounds in both legs. Happily his injuries did not affect his career and he later returned to play for Palace.

In December 1944, the *Croydon Advertiser* reported that Palace had a keeper crisis: "For their match with Portsmouth at Selhurst Park on Saturday Crystal Palace have to find a goalkeeper owing to McFarlane suffering from influenza and Tootill going home for Christmas ..." Eventually a replacement called Brown was found and he played in both fixtures against Pompey. On December 23, Palace won 1-0, but on Boxing Day, he was beaten nine times at Fratton Park.

But on the field setbacks were nothing compared to the off the field shenanigans. The F.A. announced the permanent suspension of chairman Percy Harper from football, suspended director G.J. Ellis sine die and severely censured F.J Young. Harper refused to accept his punishment and the *Croydon Advertiser* reported that he intended to contest the decision in the High Courts.

The F.A. had taken offence at remarks made in an article in the Palace programme of September 30, 1944 which reflected on "the capabilities" of members of the F.A. Council and the management committee of the Football League. It had demanded a retraction and apology, but Palace had refused. The commission set up to look into the matter decided that the article was a direct incitement to clubs to break F.A. rules and was likely to bring the game into disrepute. Palace were ordered to pay costs to the commission and to publish its findings in three successive issues of the programme.

The following week, a letter appeared on the front page of the *Croydon Advertiser* from Palace director F. Broomfield under the heading "Palace F.C. financially sound". Broomfield said: "The late chairman may have made it appear that the club was financially in a bad way. To avoid any misconception, here are a few facts. The total liability of the club is £22,000 plus 10,000 £1 shares, all subscribed, a matter of £32,000. The value of the freehold ground, car park, stands, fittings etc, stands at £45,000 – plus value of players – and we have some very valuable young players. As soon as a new board is formed I intend to move that the £10,000 loan be paid off at once and I have no doubt that we shall be able to make arrangements to relieve Mr Harper of his guarantee at the bank, also any shares he may wish to dispose of. I feel sure we can sell as I have been made a firm offer for over £2,000 already."

Reading between the lines, it was apparent that Broomfield was glad to see the back of the autocratic Harper. But his determination to find a buyer was premature. On January 9, 1945, the *Advertiser* reported that Harper had successfully appealed for an injunction against the F.A. decision. He was reinstated and returned to the fold in time to see Palace beat Reading 4-1 on a snow covered pitch.

That wasn't the end of the story, though. Palace hit the front page once more: "The *Croydon Advertiser* learns that, following the reinstatement by the Football Association of Mr Percy Harper to the chairmanship of Crystal Palace Football Club, two of his fellow directors, Mr E.T. Truett of Sandilands, East Croydon and Mr F. Broomfield of Dagnal Park, Selhurst, have tendered their resignations which have been accepted."

In his letter of resignation, Broomfield stated: "... I find it impossible to work with the present Chairman". Truett was offered the presidency of the club in a telephone conversation with Harper, which followed the resignation of another director Sir Adam Maitland. He not only refused but chose to resign as well. It was left to George Irwin to write to both men accepting their resignations and to inform them that, at the AGM in June, they would be proposed as vice presidents of the club.

No sooner was that sorted out than there was another resignation, this time of the club's medical officer Dr J.C. Jones. But he was at pains to point out that his decision was not related to those of Broomfield and Truett. However Jones explained pointedly: "It is not in the best interests of football that directors with close business interests should monopolise the directorate." Harper's victory was later strengthened when the F.A. announced the cancellation of the censuring of F.J. Young.

As preparations began for football in the post war world, Palace announced that they had made a profit of £2,500 and that £2,000 would be put aside for "much needed repairs".

Towards the end of the war, the V1 flying bombs, Hitler's vengeance weapons, caused some damage around Selhurst Park, although, aside from some slight structural damage from blasts, the stadium itself did not suffer any direct hits. There had however been a lot of ordinary wear and tear and government restrictions had prevented clubs undertaking any repairs.

It wasn't only the ground that needed work. Palace took particular interest in signing and nurturing promising young professionals as we looked to rebuild for the future. The *Croydon Advertiser* was in confident mood: "With those whose abilities are already known on the club's books the Palace have every prospect of turning out a team composed of a majority of youngsters anxious to make their name and, by so doing, help the club to obtain the much desired second and first division status. The outlook at Selhurst Park is certainly bright."

Success was still elusive however. Palace finished second in their group in the league cup south failing to qualify for the semi-finals. But there was a rare sighting of a big name star in Palace colours. In the 3-0 win against Tottenham at Selhurst Park in October, we borrowed Arsenal and England's Leslie Compton to play at left-back.

By the start of the 1944-45 season, Palace's advances were almost as significant as those of the Allied armies. We scored seven against QPR in the first game with Freddie Kurz, a guest from Grimsby, scoring a hat-trick. Next it was four versus Watford and then five against poor old Brighton. However in typical contrary fashion, we then lost 8-2 to Chelsea and 6-2 to Fulham. Kurz played sporadically during the season and endeared himself greatly to the Palace crowd, not least because he scored the winner in a marvellous 4-3 victory over Arsenal at Selhurst Park.

The final fixtures of the war saw Palace involved in some highly entertaining affairs although fortunes were mixed. Brentford were beaten 6-1 in a canter which can partly be explained by their reduction to ten men for much of the game. The Bees goal came when Palace were also down to ten, Hudgell was off the pitch having a cut over his left eye stitched. Bob Ferrier, a guest from Oldham, scored a hat trick, with Kurz getting two and 18 year-old Eric Betts netting the other.

Against West Ham, it was Palace's turn to be reduced to ten when right back Ted Harding dislocated an ankle. Worse followed when Albert Dawes injured an arm in the second half. He continued gamely but later discovered he'd fractured a bone.

The *Croydon Advertiser* of May 11, 1945 was filled with joyous reports of the VE Day celebrations. The mood of the moment was captured by the report on Palace's last match of the war. The Glaziers had won 5-4 at Portsmouth in "a real

Albert Dawes. Initially signed as cover for Peter Simpson, he became a great favourite in his own right and in 1935-36 was the League's second top scorer with 38 goals. Illustration: Jason Axell

ding dong affair from start to finish, the football served up by both teams being so good that no sooner had one team scored than the other equalised".

The result was especially pleasing because Palace fielded three juniors. Almost on the stroke of full time, Palace won it. Gillespie attacked down the right wing and centred for Waldron, who drew the keeper and tucked the ball home. But the best goal was Palace's fourth – a scintillating three-man move involving Jackman, Gillespie and finally Kurz who drove the ball home with a first time shot. So Palace finished the war, as they had begun it, on a winning note. The team was: *E. Wilson, F. Dawes, Ferrier, Hudgell, Blair, C. Endicott, Gillespie, Jackman, Kurz, Blackman and A. Wilson.*

To celebrate the end of the war, it was announced that Palace would play two matches against a "well known league club" which turned out to be Leicester, who were under the guidance of former Glaziers' manager Tom Bromilow. The Filberts hosted Palace on May 19 when we won with a goal by Robson, but in the return it was Leicester who came out on top 4-1 to give Bromilow a happy send off. It was explained that he was shortly to "sever his connections with the City".

By the time the 1945-46 season began, the Japanese had also surrendered. All anybody cared about now was peace and returning to their homes to rebuild their lives. Football stood on the brink of a period of popularity such as it had never known.

The intention had been to resume the league programme with a repeat of the fixtures for the aborted 1939-40 season, but this found little favour with the third division clubs who were experiencing difficulties obtaining the services of many of their players, who were still in the forces. Therefore the "north and south of the Thames" plan was proposed and Palace, obviously, went into the latter grouping. As the season approached, Palace investigated ways to increase revenue. Although they had announced that £2,000 was available for ground improvements, it was estimated that at least five times as much was needed just to return it to 1939 standard.

Among the ideas put forward was a Crystal Palace cycle polo team and greyhound racing. In the *Advertiser's Sports Gossip* column of August 24, it was noted that Palace had undertaken a little decorating. "I had to stop, rub my eyes, and look again," said the paper's correspondent. "Over the main entrance to the stand and offices can now be seen in chocolate coloured letters on a primrose coloured-ground, the name of the club 'Crystal Palace F.C. Co Ltd'."

What possessed them to choose such a gaudy colour scheme is not clear, perhaps chocolate and primrose were the only colours available. But after the war years, when all signs and insignia had been painted out to avoid offering any help to the enemy, it must have been a lovely sight to see the club's name back - even in chocolate and primrose. As the *Advertiser* columnist said: "Though lost to sight, to memory dear." The opening matches were both with Aldershot. The first, at home, finished goalless, but in the second game Palace romped to a 5-2 victory.

The demolition of the Shots had the *Advertiser* purring about the "sparkle and keenness of the teamwork". Guests were still permitted and in this game, Matthewson of Bury enjoyed a "fine game" while another guest, Surtees of Forest, gave us the lead after a quarter of an hour. Although Sommerbee cancelled out the advantage when Ford got his hands to the ball but couldn't keep it out (the *Advertiser* felt he might have been deceived by a seeming change of speed as the ball approached him) Palace rallied and Albert Dawes scored twice to put us in control. The game was sealed by Kurz and Wilson's late fifth put the icing on the cake. Palace: *Ford, F, Dawes, Hudgell, Reece, Matthewson, J. Lewis, A. Dawes, Surtees, Kurz, Male and Wilson.*

We lost only four of our divisional matches and swamped Swindon 10-1 as the division, which was completed on December 29, was won at a canter. Around this time, the club came up with a bright idea to entertain the supporters. A signature tune was composed to be played by the Crystal Palace band before each match. It was written by Jack Morgan the musical director of the Croydon Empire and was appropriately entitled ...

The Crystal Palace March

Here we are together again
We hope to see the Palace win the game
Help them on their way
Make them bright and gay
If they win – should they lose – cheer them just the same
Here we are all merry and gay
We've come to cheer our favourite team today
So let's give them all a hearty welcome
With a HIP, HIP, HIP HOORAY

Okay so it wasn't up to Eurovision song contest standards, but perhaps it meant more if you could hear the tune. Nevertheless, the *Advertiser* reported: "From the reception the tune received on Saturday it was evident that it was popular with the supporters and the directors immediately decided to adopt it as their signature tune."

Not everything was a wizzard wheeze though. The programme requested: "We do earnestly appeal to our young team supporters not to 'barrack' the visiting goalkeeper when he is about to take a kick ..." Presumably an early version of the *You're s∗∗∗, aaarrrghhhh,* of the late 80s.

For the only time in history F.A. Cup ties were played over two legs. We totally dominated both games with QPR but could not score. A replay at Craven Cottage was needed where it was Rangers who got the only goal. After a draw at Loftus Road, the second leg at Selhurst Park only ended when it got too dark to continue. The idea was to play on until one side or the other scored in order to avoid replays if at all possible. The match, a rain swept affair, played in a gale force wind, actually lasted 117 minutes before the referee decided he'd seen enough.

When the players reported for the 1946-47 season and a return to league football, they were told they would be paid a maximum £10 in the winter and £7. 10s in the summer. This was an increase of £2 on 1939. Bonuses were also increased by £100 to £750. This lack of generosity put many players' backs up, but most had little option than to accept.

The fixtures for the season were the same as those originally intended for 1939-40 which meant Palace started at Mansfield, where they had originally won 5-4. Football couldn't have been more popular. A tour by Moscow Dynamo from Russia that year attracted huge crowds and when the Russians played Chelsea, thousands overran the turnstiles and clambered onto the roofs of the stands to see the game. Football was king and even the lowliest teams benefited.

The post-war general election had resulted in a landslide for Clement Attlee's Labour Party and the League's president Will Cuff feared that the new chancellor intended to bring football into line with other sports and impose Entertainment Tax, so he asked the clubs to bring in a maximum admission charge of 1/-3d. But the clubs wanted it to be 1/-6d, claiming they needed the money to fund ground improvements on stadia that had been neglected during the war. Eventually, a compromise was reached which ensured that clubs would set aside a reasonable part of the ground at the cheaper prices. Palace charged the full 1/-6d, but promised to put the extra 3d into a fund to buy players – a sort of prototype Lifeline. There was also a small section where 1/-3d was charged.

George Irwin made a number of personnel changes before the start of the season. Albert Wilson was transferred to his home town team Rotherham United – he had been born near the ground and Rotherham, with typical Yorkshire parochialism, were assembling a squad made up entirely of local players. For Palace, Fred Dawes, Tommy Reece, Bert Robson and Ernie Waldron still remained from the pre-war squad, although after a spell of ill-health the latter eventually returned to his native Aberdeen.

Rationing remained in force and Palace, like most, were in a pickle. Appeals were made to find accommodation for the players, some of whom were living as far away as Wolverhampton and Sheffield, and for clothing coupons to help get some kit. Supporters sent in over 100 coupons which were sufficient to acquire some shirts and socks, while the players wives chipped in from their meat and clothing ration to help their husbands.

We got off to a bad start, losing to Mansfield 3-1, and things got worse at Reading where we were hammered 10-2. Asked about the defeat by the *Croydon Advertiser,* Fred Dawes said: "Oh! Everything went right for them and everything went wrong for us." A slight understatement from Fred, there.

Despite the severity of the defeat there was little outcry. The *Advertiser* didn't even make it the main report, choosing to concentrate on the Mansfield reverse. But it was damning of Reece, the former Wolves player who had joined in September 1938. He was "completely useless on the right wing," the paper said, although just what a winger was supposed to do about conceding ten goals is questionable.

George Irwin was furious and made nine changes for the visit of Bristol Rovers the following Saturday. Goalkeeper Dick Graham, who had signed for Palace after appearing as a guest during the war, was replaced by Bob Lucas. But his exile lasted only three games before he was recalled to play in all but one of the rest of the season's matches.

Another initial casualty of the Reading debacle was centre-half Bill "Stopper" Bassett. The Palace programme editor thought a lot of him, as this profile shows. "By reason of his lack of hair, Bill Bassett is perhaps more easily identified on the field than any other Palace player … there are few players who can match paces with him. In addition his stamina is beyond question as he last the ninety minutes better than most." All of which makes you wonder what he was doing playing for a team at the bottom of division three south?

Bassett joined Palace from Cardiff in September 1942 having progressed through the Welsh club's junior ranks to become their captain. He served with the Welsh Guards but returned to Palace in time for the league cup qualifying competition in January 1946.

We continued to struggle although we never took another beating as severe as the one at Reading. Incidentally, we beat them in the return at Selhurst Park a couple of weeks later thanks to two goals by former Margate inside forward Lester Burrell. We could have paid Reading back in spades but Kurz hit the woodwork three times and a hatful of other chances were missed in addition to a couple of efforts which were ruled out for offside. Reading then had the cheek to

The *Croydon Advertiser's* impression of George Irwin, the man who steered Crystal Palace through the Second World War.

protest that the game should be replayed because the referee had blown five minutes early because of fading light. Bill Bark made his debut in that match but almost immediately changed his name by deed poll to Bill Naylor.

Fred Kurz, who was Palace's record signing, wasn't having the most fruitful of times, despite *Sports Gossip's* comment: "Palace now have a centre-forward who takes every opportunity presented to him and is capable of leading efficiently." Kurz, who relied on his pace to give him an edge, was first recommended to Grimsby by representatives of the YMCA.

He signed for the Mariners in 1936 and remained at Blundell Park until he joined the army at the beginning of the war, playing representative matches for the Army. He was included on a British Army XI tour of Scotland.

Kurz was an asset in other ways. He could play in both inside forward positions as well as in his more accustomed centre-forward role at a time when football positions were much more rigidly adhered to than they are today.

In November, Palace got into an argument with Portsmouth over the transfer of Jimmy Guthrie, who had led the south coast club to their F.A. Cup triumph over Wolves in 1939. The snag, predictably, was the fee – Palace didn't want to pay one, while Pompey wanted £1,250 for the Players' Union chairman.

The matter went to arbitration and the league ruled that the fee was in order only to have the F.A. overrule the decision by saying Palace could have him for nothing. Eventually Percy Harper and Portsmouth chairman Vernon Stokes met and came to an amicable agreement.

Guthrie, who had earned some notoriety for his commitment to the Player's Union, made his debut as player-coach in a 3-0 home defeat by league leaders Bristol City at Selhurst Park. His time at Palace was brief and, in his book *Soccer Rebel* (published by Pentagon Books in 1976), he dealt with the club only in passing. Yet what he wrote reveals more about life at Selhurst Park in the post war years than any number of hours of research would be able to uncover.

CRYSTAL PALACE

'On the recommendation of Freddie Forward, a former Pompey winger, I was appointed coach to Crystal Palace and acted as general dogsbody for the Union under the guidance of Sammy Crooks. Percy Harper, a bright boy, was chairman of Crystal Palace, George Irwin ex-Sheffield Wednesday goalkeeper, the manager, and Ralph Hann, ex-Derby County, the trainer, when I joined the Selhurst Club.

Harper, who had made a fortune out of automatic machines, told me how he had started by going around on a bicycle with a machine strapped on his back. He had big ideas for Palace and we often discussed his ideas over a noggin at his palatial Sanderstead home. He wanted to introduce speedway and greyhound racing at Selhurst, but the local residents petitioned against speedway because of the noise and the Football Association, although both Chelsea and Watford had dog tracks, refused to sanction the presence of greyhounds.

Harper hit the newspaper headlines with stories that Palace would spend a million pounds to get into the first division but there was little money put on the line. I sorted out a few players who would have helped but my recommendations were ignored. With the support of director George Ellis, husband of the last woman to be hanged, I suggested that the club should increase its share capital to get money for players, but Harper thought we should recruit from amateur clubs, as this would cost only £100 for each player and the club he left. The idea was sound but again there was no money. On occasion Harper would phone Irwin and say "Send Guthrie to sign Joe Soap." I would phone Harper back and tell him not to waste my time and the Club's money. If a player hit the news, irrespective of the writer, Harper assumed he was the answer to all Palace's playing problems.

I was also on the committee of the union and when travelling with Palace to away games I lost no chance of spreading the gospel. I wasn't welcome everywhere. The story that I was a communist began to go the rounds and, at times, I was threatened with mayhem. In the Manchester City board room I was told that I was going to be run out of the game, which proved to me that I was making some impact.

Meanwhile, Harper was selling off our best players. Arthur Hudgell, a very useful full back, was sold to Sunderland and after we had trounced Brentford 5-2 at Griffin Park, our left wing of Naylor and Girling went to the Bees for £7,000. The club was still £17,000 in the red."

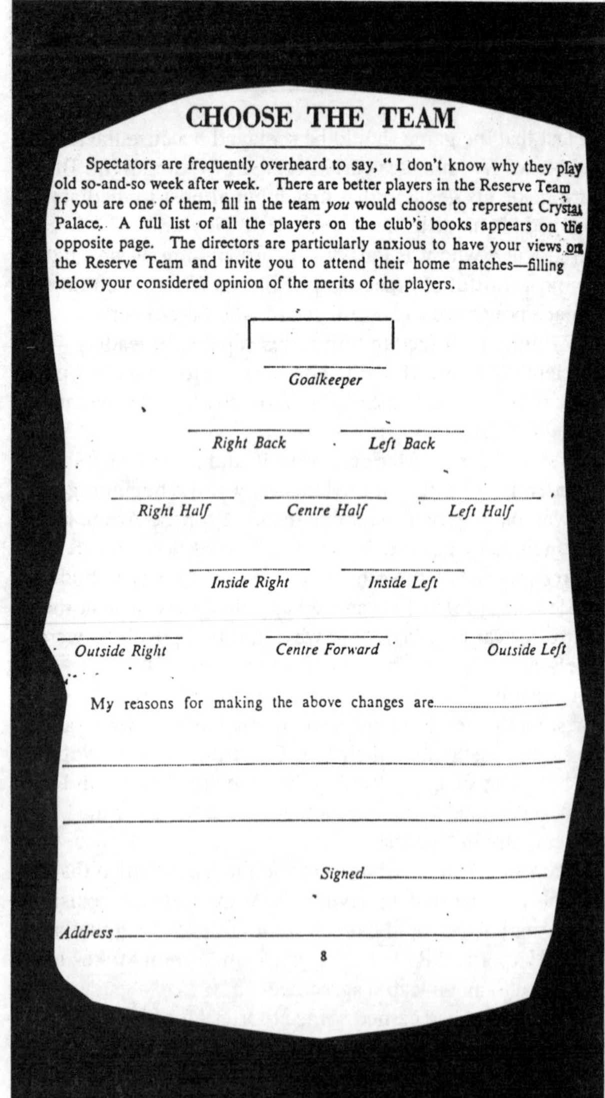

CHOOSE THE TEAM

Spectators are frequently overheard to say, "I don't know why they play old so-and-so week after week. There are better players in the Reserve Team If you are one of them, fill in the team *you* would choose to represent Crystal Palace. A full list of all the players on the club's books appears on the opposite page. The directors are particularly anxious to have your views on the Reserve Team and invite you to attend their home matches—filling below your considered opinion of the merits of the players.

Goalkeeper

Right Back *Left Back*

Right Half *Centre Half* *Left Half*

Inside Right *Inside Left*

Outside Right *Centre Forward* *Outside Left*

My reasons for making the above changes are.........

Signed.........

Address.........

8

In response to criticism of team selection, the programme for the Walsall match in April 1947 offered supporters a chance to let the club know what they thought of the team.

There had been only two real highlights in a long, cold and drab season. The first was a 6-1 defeat of Torquay United on Christmas day in which one of the United players, Bert Head, scored an own goal – an unhappy visit for the man who would one day return as Palace manager. We were helped when Phil Joslin the visitors' keeper was injured and replaced by their centre-forward

There was some good news when it was announced that Palace were exempted until the third round of the F.A. Cup. But we were then given the near impossible task of a visit to Newcastle. With our usual luck, we were the only London side to be drawn away in the third round. In front of 43,183, Newcastle, parading Len Shackleton, Roy Bentley, Charlie Wayman and Joe Harvey, forced us onto the defensive. But Palace held out for 36 minutes before collapsing. "Shack" opened the scoring and a minute later Wayman made it two. Bentley gave the Geordies a third on 39 minutes.

Palace recovered and 20 minutes into the second half Naylor pulled one back. That seemed to irritate Newcastle and they immediately got a fourth through George Stobbart. Shackleton completed his hat-trick before Naylor gave us the last word. It wasn't a bad performance but as Guthrie has explained it was to cost us the services of Arthur Hudgell. While playing at St. James's Park, he was spotted by Sunderland scouts (who presumably didn't advertise the fact they were there). They kept an eye on his progress and eventually came in with an offer that Harper couldn't refuse – a record fee for a third division player of £10,000. It was big money for a youngster who had walked into Selhurst Park and asked for a job, "any job, even clearing weeds, because I want to play for Crystal Palace".

Hysterical joke 1946-style

Visiting captain: "Not much grass on this ground old man."
Home captain: "May I remind you that you have come to play football not to graze."

Hulton Deutsch

Charlie Chase, Bill Bassett and Freddie Kurz in October 1948

Palace didn't finish the season until the end of May because of the winter freeze, one of the coldest on record. Some teams were still playing in June. Against Watford on February 15, groundsman Charlie Catlett recruited a number of German prisoners of war to help clear the snow from the pitch. The game eventually went ahead with the touchlines painted blue. Catlett was well known to the supporters and so was his horse, Kate, who pulled the pitch roller.

George Irwin's lack of success had cost him his job and he reverted to scouting duties as Palace brought in former Arsenal star Jack Butler, whose Highbury colleague Bob John came with him as trainer. Butler, "a pleasant kindly man" was very experienced, he had coached the Belgian national team, been trainer-coach of Leicester, manager of Torquay and coach to the Danish F.A. He and John had been members of the Arsenal side that lost the 1927 Cup Final to Cardiff. Bobby Greener, in his 26th year at Palace, was retained as a member of the training staff. Nevertheless the change was a sordid little affair as Jimmy Guthrie recalled in his memoirs:

"George, the chairman and I were having a drink at Selhurst one evening and parted the best of friends. Next morning the headlines read: "Crystal Palace manager sacked." I phoned George who couldn't believe that he was out. Harper had given no hint, only hours before, that he was going to make a change in the administration. I went to the ground where the new boss, Jack Butler, the ex-Arsenal centre-half, was already in possession.

He asked me into the office and informed me, by a hand-written letter, that he was giving me a month's notice. I told him he hadn't hired me and couldn't fire me. I called Harper on the telephone and told Butler to listen on the extension. I put the chairman in the picture. "You stay where you are Jimmy," replied Harper.

Such arrangements with the chairman and manager at cross purposes do no good for any club. In any event, I had a few weeks earlier succeeded Crooks as Players' Union chairman and the committee wanted me to quit coaching and devote all my efforts to the Union. I left Selhurst, after making my point with Butler, that morning."

Before the new season opened, the Palace supporters' club announced that it had a record 1,800 members including Alan George Knapp of Catford who had been enrolled by his father at one hour old. Poor little mite, all that misery in front of him. Wonder where he is now? Probably still on the Holmesdale cursing with the rest of us.

Although the National Emergency continued, the government relaxed some of the restrictions on football, permitting evening kick offs at the start and end of the season and afternoon kick offs on national holidays. But midweek games were not allowed. Many players were still returning from service abroad such as Roy Farringdon, who wrote to Butler asking for a trial.

He was immediately put into an "A" XI match and impressed so much that he was included in the first team for the match against Port Vale in the Cup. What's more, he scored from 30 yards. Unhappily for Farringdon, his career went no further. He played once more for the first team then left the club.

Jack Butler was a great believer in new ideas and before the Cup match at Bristol City, he took the team to Brighton for sea water baths, massages, a walk along the sea front and an afternoon matinee show. The change worked a treat, Palace won 1-0 in extra time (introduced in the first ties as an extra measure to try to cut down on replays). Having reached the third round, Palace were disappointing against Chester and lost 1-0 in front of 22,000.

In the league we conceded 49 goals, the second lowest in the division after Swindon's 46, but our forwards could do no better and we finished just below half-way. Kurz was top scorer with 18, including a hat-trick in a 4-0 win over Swansea, but the truth was that Palace weren't good enough and weren't getting any better.

In 1948-49 we reverted to claret and blue but the old saying "change your colours, change your luck" coincided with the worst season the club has ever known, marking our silver anniversary with our first application for re-election. We began with a 5-1 defeat by Reading at Elm Park and from there on, it got worse.

In the first home match against Swansea, Kurz failed from the penalty spot despite three attempts. He actually put the first one away, but the referee ruled that a Palace player had encroached. Then, the keeper saved but the referee ordered Kurz to take it again for the same reason and at the third time of asking the Glaziers centre-forward put the ball wide. Until we beat Bournemouth on January 20, there were only three wins. We won only eight times in all and had a goal average of 38 against 76 which showed just where the problems were – in attack and defence!

In both matches against champions-to-be Notts County, we lost 5-1. At Meadow Lane, County's star striker Tommy Lawton, who had cost them a British record transfer fee from Chelsea, did not play because he was in Copenhagen making his last appearance for England, but in the return, his presence drew a crowd of 30,925 and he headed a classic goal. Kurz again led our scorers with 12, but nobody else chipped in to any great effect.

Fred Dawes and Jack Lewis, two of the players upon whom Palace had pinned their post war hopes

Despite our poor form, Jack Lewis and Dick Graham were selected to play for a London XI in Brussels, and attendances actually increased. For first team home matches, there was a total increase of 23,000 while the reserves were watched by 16,602 more people than the year before. Palace increased total receipts by more than £4,000. Butler however handed in his resignation and despite the board's reluctance to accept it – it stayed on the table for a week – he left.

We had a bit of worrying to do over re-election. Normally league teams were voted back in on the nod. But this time, the Manchester United chairman Harold Hardman, with impeccably bad timing, made an attack on the "Old Pals' Act" which virtually ensured that existing members would be voted back.

Palace could at least point out that it was our first time at the bottom and we had the loyal support of large crowds. We needn't have worried though, Hardman's words were just hot air and all the league clubs got back as usual. The voting went: Bradford City 44, Aldershot 41, Southport 40, Palace 40, Shrewsbury 5, Gillingham 5, Worcester City 5, Scunthorpe 4, Merthyr 3, Yeovil 2 and North Shields, Wigan, South Liverpool and Peterborough none. What remains unexplained is how a diabolical team like Aldershot, who were supported by the proverbial one man and his dog, managed to get more votes than Palace.

Our new manager was Ronnie Rooke, who had been a young player at Selhurst before the war. His appointment was inspired by the success of Notts County's experiment with Lawton and the similar impact former Sunderland and England star Raich Carter had made with Hull.

Rooke had been the leading goalscorer in the league in 1947-48 with 33 goals and so his appointment was an ambitious one. His first signing was Jack Watson, an old club-mate from his Fulham days, who had played for Real Madrid. Rooke then moved for Wally Hanlon, a winger who had been at Brighton and Bournemouth.

Although we lost to Exeter by the odd goal in three on the first day, Rooke was not downhearted. "The ball doesn't come so accurately to you as in the first division," he said. "But the team played really well and I'm 100 per cent satisfied with their performance at Exeter. If they keep this up, we will win more games than we will lose."

Rooke was right. Palace did win more games, but only just, 15, against 14 draws and 13 defeats to finish in a vastly improved seventh place. Rooke scored his 100th league goal with the winner at home to Bristol Rovers, but blotted his copybook by becoming the first player-manager to be sent off in a bruising match with Millwall at the Den in which he had scored. He was subsequently suspended for 14 days and told that he was expected to exercise greater care that his actions on and off the field did not bring the game into disrepute.

Better news for Palace was the inclusion of Lewis in a London F.A. team to play the Belgian F.A. in Brussels. The *Daily Mail* said: "A particular pat on the back for Jack Lewis, the Crystal Palace centre-half, whose distribution and tackling was in keeping in such a setting and with such distinguished company. Here is a well built, quick and extremely intelligent player, who seems entirely fitted for first division football." High praise indeed, although the reporter was biased, he was Roy Peskett, a confirmed Palace fan. To show how much Peskett knew, Palace sold Lewis a couple of weeks' later for £7,500 to Bournemouth.

We made yet another disappointing Cup exit at the first hurdle, this time to Newport at Somerton Park. But in the league, Rooke led his men well. He also led the scorers with 21 goals from 39 games. Of the rest, only Kurz reached double figures, which makes one wonder how Palace would have fared without the arrival of Rookie.

One of the best performances was the 6-0 drubbing of Brighton, who included future Palace captain Johnny McNicholl. Rooke opened the scoring after eight minutes with a 25 yard shot. Kurz added to the lead before half time and Brighton's second half resistance ended when Rooke converted Blackwell's cross. Winger Ray Howells made it four and Rooke completed his hat-trick after Charlie Chase had grabbed the fifth.

The following week a 1-1 draw with Bournemouth proved to be Howells' last game – he broke his left leg in a tackle with Jack Lewis. He never played again.

We've got the worst team in the land

Bottom of Division Three South

	P	W	D	L	F	A	Pts
Bristol City	42	11	14	17	44	62	36
Watford	42	10	15	17	41	54	35
Southend	42	9	16	17	41	46	34
L. Orient	42	11	12	19	58	80	34
Northampton	42	12	9	21	51	62	33
Aldershot	42	11	11	20	48	59	33
Palace	42	8	11	23	38	76	27

The 1948-49 season and Crystal Palace are the worst team in the league. Bradford City who finished bottom of division three north had two points and 12 goals more than us.

Percy Palace proudly presents ...

The Glaziers: An A to Z

A is fer Albert. Albert Feebury was my 'ero when I woz a nipper. I once stood outside the Nest fer 36 hours waiting fer 'is autergraph and 'e sez: "Sod off." See, blokes knew 'ow ter treat kids proper in them days, none of this namby pamby mascot stuff.

B is fer Bleedin' Arsenal. Them sods was orrible, the most boring, lucky team ever. I remember a Jerry Zeppelin flyin' over 'em at a Cup Final once. We should've paid the Krauts ter bomb the buggers while we 'ad the chance.

C is fer Crap. Blimey, I've seen some crap dahn the Palace. When I fink of all the lolly I've chucked away watchin' that lot, cor luvvaduck!

D is fer Daisy. She was our Regimental goat out in the Western Desert in '42. I remember one day our mob captured this Jerry Hofficer and Daisy bit 'im on the arse and 'e woz gonna report us ter the Geneva Convention and I took me bayonet out and sez: "Shut yer face yer Bosche git." And der yer know wot? 'E woz Franz Beckenbauer's dad. Small weld innit?

E is fer Everton. They woz always bleedin' useless.

F is fer Fenwick. Gawd 'n' Bennett, when I fink 'ow good that young Sansom woz. Next fing yer know we've got Fenwick at left back, 'oofing the ball in the stand. When 'e got the ball the opposition never made a tackle they'd just run ter the sideline ready fer the frow-in.

G is fer Gilbert. 'E was my type 'er player. 'E could kick a bloke with both feet and dun great waist 'igh slidin' tackles. Luvverly! Not a bad footballer eever. G is also fer Glaziers which was our nickname before fancy pants Allison went an' mucked it abaht.

Haitch is fer 'arf backs. We 'ad some good 'uns dahn ere but I'm buggered if I can remember any of 'em.

I is fer Iris Shuttleworth. This ol' gel I used ter know, back in the war. I used ter knock 'er orf rahnd the back of the main stand while 'er 'usband was in the 'Ome Guard. But I'd better say no more coz old Alf's still alive.

J is fer Jacko. Cor, what a custodian. 'E should've played fer England but Sir Alf always picked Banks, I mean when did that Banks ever 'ave a good game fer England?

K is fer Kevin and Keef. They're not proper names. I mean young Kevin Mabbutt, 'e woz a good little player but 'e wanted ter get 'is air cut and 'e wanted ter get 'imself a proper name an all like Fred or Percy or Albert. Albert Mabbutt ... yeah that's got a nice ring ter it.

L is fer Liverpool. Gor what a right shower them Scousers are. An' them Beatles is a long 'aired bunch 'er louts an all, we should've locked 'em up when we 'ad the chance.

Rookie: They used ter call us the Rooke Regiment before all this Red 'n' Blue Army tripe. That's wot these 'ooligans need, get 'em in the army.

M is fer Malcolm. Look wot 'e dun fer Palace. Changed all the colours abaht, stopped calling us the Glaziers an' got us relegated twice and all them soppy kids loved 'im. I tell yer they don't know they're born some of 'em.

N is fer The Nest. All soot an' smoke an' magical. I remember I used ter pat Jack Alderson on the back ... and Billy Callender. A great place.

O is fer 'Orses. Ruddy great cart orses. Blimey we 'ad a few. Bill Bassett, 'e was yer original orse drawn centre-arf. Bald as a coot an all 'e woz.

P is fer Percy and Palace. I used ter like Percy Cherrett cos 'e ad the same name as me. An' Palace is me life. I only wish I could 'and it dahn in the family, but me daughter 'ates football and I s'pose that's why she lets 'er little Torquil support Arsenal. No son 'er mine would've bin allowed to support 'em. E'd ave gone in an 'ome first.

Q is fer Gerry Queen. I'll never forget 'is goal in the first ever match in div one it fair brought a tear ter me eye.

R is fer Johnny Rainford, 'e woz a good 'un, but we let im go somewhere awful like Cardiff. And of course fer Ronnie Rooke. Ol' Rookie an' 'is Regiment they used ter call us. 'E woz a ruff 'ouse barsterd. 'E got sent orf at Millwall once an' 'e woz offerin' these dockers ahtside as 'e walked.

S is fer Simpson. 'E was quite good ... fer a Jock.

T is fer ... er tea. The missus always stews me bludy char, Selhurst Park is the only place I can get a decent cuppa. It's also for "The" – it's "THE" Palace, not just Palace, and don't ferget it.

U is fer United. Every team in the world called United are sods. Colchester, Torquay, Southend, 'orrible mob they woz.

V is fer Tom Vansittart. I can't remember a soddin' fing abaht 'im but you try finkin' up stuff this far dahn the alphabet.

W is fer Wright and Wassock ... well its the same fing innit?

X is fer X-Ray Spex. I used ter be a bit of a musician in me young day and me and this ol' gel I knew called Polly played in a band called X-Ray Spex, very avant garde it was, but Vera Lynn and George Formby woz in the charts an' everyone said we made an awful racket so we packed it in.

Y is fer yeller kits. If yer turned up in yeller shorts in my day you'd get called a bloomin' poof.

Z is fer Zylerphone. We used ter 'ave a bloke play a bugle and some geezer 'ad an ARP bell 'e used ter ring when the team come out. But no-one tops old Fred Walker. Whenever The Palace used ter score, 'E would strike up wiv *Tuxedo Junction* on 'is Zylerphone.

Holmesdale productions presents

Escape to Defeat

An Eagle Eye film **X Certificate stuff!**

Starring
MICHAEL CAINE as a Midfield General
ARNOLD SCHWARZENEGGER as Nigel Martyn
DOLPH LUNDGREN as Jeff Hopkins
JEAN CLAUDE VAN DAMME as Alan Pardew
and DANNY DeVITO as Ron Noades

With Steve Coppell as himself

Also starring Andy Gray as the Scrounger, Kevin Mabbutt as the Poacher, Chris Armstrong as the Intelligence Officer, Dirk Bogarde as George Courtney, Richard Attenborough as Leading Seaman Higginbottom, David Seaman as Leading Seaman Seaman, Mick Jagger as Ned Kelly, Keith Richards as Mark Dennis and introducing Anne Bancroft as Novella Noades

France 1940. The British Expeditionary Force has been lifted off the beaches by an armada of small boats. Three hundred thousand men have escaped the clutches of the victorious German army.

Thousands more have not been so lucky and the prisoner of war columns stream pathetically away under the watchful eye of the Nazi stormtroopers.

With typical foresight, Palace have just sent a Club XI to play a friendly at Le Havre. The Palace team is captured and taken to Stalag Luft 5C in deepest Germany.

Almost immediately, Captain John Mills and Major Richard Attenborough form an escape committee and amuse themselves by jumping over fences, hiding in vans and generally irritating the Germans because it is the duty of every officer to try to escape.

Hidden in the hut of the escape committee is a smuggled radio receiver. Major Steve Coppell, manager of Crystal Palace, enters and salutes John Mills. "Permission to use the radio, sir?"

John Mills checks his script to see which war film he's making this week, realises its *Escape to Defeat* and says stiffly: "Permission granted."

He pulls out a makeshift ladder made of slats of wood taken from the bunk beds and leads Coppell up into the roof of the hut.

Coppell pulls the aerial out and tunes the radio in. "This is the BBC from London," says the announcer. "Here are some cryptic messages for the resistance, I bet you can't guess what we're talking about Fritz. The black cat is sitting under the Marmalade tree and my sister has run off with a pimply insurance underwriter from Shepton Mallet. Now here is the draw for the F.A. Cup third round. Gateshead will play the Arsenal, Brighton will play Crystal Palace … "

"Goons," whispers John Mills in a hurried voice. "Yes Brighton are complete goons," Coppell agrees. But that isn't what John Mills meant at all, he looks round to face the pointed gun barrels of the Nazi guards.

In the office of the Kommandant, Steve Coppell stands to attention. "Do not sink, ve do not know vy you ver listening to ze radio, Leutnant Koppell," the Kommandant says, polishing his monocle.

Coppell remains silent while the Kommandant continues: "You ver listening to ze F.A. Cup draw und Palace are avay to ze Zeaveeds. Do not make ze mistake of sinking zat you vill escape to fulfill zis fixture. Zere vill be no Cup for Crystal Pellis zis year."

Without Palace, the F.A. announce that Brighton will be given a bye into the next round if Palace are unable to escape in time.

When Coppell heard the news he threw the paper angrily to the ground and said: "By thunder we'll make that match if I have to bribe Adolf to do it."

In the Reichstag in Berlin, the Fuhrer Adolf Hitler, who only had one ball, Himmler, who had something similar, and Goebbels, who had no balls at all because he didn't like football (well you've got a filthy mind then) were discussing propaganda initiatives.

"Mein Fuhrer," interjected Himmler, who looked suspiciously like Donald

CRYSTAL PALACE EUROPEAN TOUR
Referee Benito Mussolini (Italy) introduces the two captains.

Palace versus the Third Reich. The two captains shake hands watched by the neutral referee Benito Mussolini of Italy

Pleasance (again). "Haf you seen zis notice in ze *London Times*?

"Ze 21st Panzergruppe captured ze Crystal Palace fussball team at Dunkirk. Zey are in Stalag Luft Funf C. Zey could be persuaded to play against a team from Greater Chermany and of course zey vould be thrashed.

"For a Pritish team to lose to Chermany at fussball vould be too great a humiliation. Both Vinston Churchill und Ron Noades vould haf to resign."

"Fantastisch," said the Fuhrer, combing his moustache with a toothbrush. "Zis vil be Deutschland's greatest triumph."

In the PoW camp, Steve Coppell held a training session. Conditions were difficult and the guards were losing patience because Lee Sinnott kept kicking the ball over the fence and then leaving the compound to get it back.

Coppell was kneeling down praying that the Germans would capture a decent left back when a pair of Jackboots arrived beside him.

Inside the Jackboots stood a very Aryan looking officer.

"Your team are krap, Herr Koppell," said the officer. He paused, expecting a reply but none was forthcoming.

"Do you not recognise me? Chermany versus England? Weltmeisterschaft? Mein name ist Hauptmann Karl-Heinz Rummenigge."

Coppell stood up. "I remember. It was 0-0 and Keegan missed a sitter."

"Ja, Ja," smiled Rummenigge. "He vos, how you say in Englisch, ein stupid tart! How vould you like to play again? Your Crystal Pellis against a team from Chermany?"

Coppell laughed a derisory laugh: "This lot versus Germany? You must be joking."

Hauptmann Rummenigge looked thoughtful. "Der Fuhrer expected you vould say nein. Zo he is prepared to make you an offer you cannot refuse.

"If you play and you vin, you vill be returned to England in time to play Brighton in ze Cup."

"I'd want special rations," said Coppell "and proper kit, in the old 1940s Crystal Palace colours, and big heavy boots and a leather ball that weighs a ton when it gets soaking wet ..."

Colonel Arnold Schwarzenegger was an American officer who had joined the RAF in 1939 because he liked wars. He wasn't very good at football but he was quite good at fighting and escaping. But despite being a huge German looking bloke with a German name and a pronounced German accent, every time he escaped he got caught. But Schwarzenegger wasn't prepared to give up.

The escape committee was in full session. Captain John Mills sat at the head of a table with some of the most noted British escapers of the war: Major Richard Attenborough, Colonel Dirk Bogarde and Lootenant Steve McQueen, a distant Scottish relative of Gerry Queen, who had added "Mc" to the front of his name to sound more American.

"Ah, come in Captain Coppell," said Attenborough. "This football match of yours ... we think you might need a few extra players in your team."

Coppell listened as the escape committee suggested a list of men who were important to the war effort and had to get back to England: Schwarzenegger, Michael Caine, Russell Osman, Kevin O'Callaghan, Pele and Mike Summerbee.

"I'm sorry," said Coppell. "I've already got a team and I can't take them all. But Michael Caine looks a useful midfielder and O'Callaghan is an Irish international winger, so I might be able to put him in goal. Does Pele fancy playing left back?"

Colonel Schwarzenegger was not satisfied. "You're going to need a trainer. I'm coming on the team as your fitness instructor. Whether you like it or not."

In the shadow of the machine gun towers, Palace trained for the match. Arnold Schwarzenegger built up the muscle on Simon Osborn until the 4'10" Palace midfielder was built like a brick outhouse.

The Germans were true to their word. Red Cross parcels full of essential supplies such as leather footballs, brylcreem and Bing Crosby records arrived and the team lived together and grew together.

Then, one fine day, two German trucks pulled in to take the team to Paris for the match. German propaganda planning had been meticulous except for one small point. They had chosen to play in front of a hostile French crowd in Paris rather than loyal German supporters in Berlin.

It was just the sort of silly mistake that ensured the Germans always came unstuck in war films. German radio would broadcast the match to the world and the Brighton supporters anxiously sat round their wireless sets, with their fake medical certificates exempting them from military service, eating black market food and smoking contraband cigarettes, waiting for news of their prospective opponents.

At the Stade Colombes in Paris, the German guard stood by the dressing door with his machine pistol pointing loosely at Eric the Ninja. The Ninja stared at the gun and then at the guard who hurriedly looked away. The Palace players pulled on their kit. "Now listen lads," said Coppell. "We're up against a team from Greater Germany, the whole of the Third Reich, that means they've got Lothar Mattheus and Feld Marschall Erwin Rommel in midfield.

"Don't be fooled that Rommel is an old man, he is a sly old fox – a bit like Peter Reid only without the grey hair. I want you to mark tightly but remember the ball is rock hard and you've got big boots on so if you give the ball an almighty thump it'll go miles. So we should be alright there."

Palace's players filed into the tunnel but suddenly an escape party from a neighbouring French tunnel broke through. "You seely Engleesh persons, you have ruined our tunnel," said an irate French escapee.

"I think you might be a bit off course," said a non-plussed Nigel Martyn, "'Ang on a mo ... aren't you Michel Platini, leader of the Free French Forces, famed Commando and captain of Juventus?"

The German guards bundled the other French escapees into lorries and took them back to the PoW camp, but quick thinking by the Palace goalie concealed the true identity of Platini and Coppell took the difficult decision to play his new acquisition instead of Simon Osborn. "Sorry Simon, but this is war."

Up in the commentary box, the German commentator, played by that chap who always plays the Germans even though nobody knows his name, although it could be Curt Jurgens or Anton Diffring, was ready to announce the teams. "Crystal Palace haf Nigel Martyn in goal, Michael Caine and Pele as full backs, Bobby Bowry as right half, Andy Thorn centre-half, Arnold Schwarzenegger at left half, Paul Williams outside right, Simon Rodger inside right, Chris Armstrong centre-forward, Michel Platini inside left and Wing commander Douglas Bader at outside left."

The Germans being the beasts they so obviously are didn't play our national anthem only playing their own so the French crowd gave Palace a rousing rendition of *Glad All Over* instead.

The Italian referee got the game under way with the Germans in brutish form. Jurgen Klinsmann took a dive and was immediately recruited by Admiral Doenitz for U-boat duty. He was replaced by Pierre Littbarski and the substitute scored a fine opening goal from the penalty spot after the Italian ref had penalised Douglas Bader for a wild kick at Andreas Brehme. "Well of course it was a wild kick," said Bader. "I've got tin legs haven't I?"

"Chermany 1 Crystal Pellis 0," crowed the excited commentator and the Free World groaned ... except for those who lived in Brighton.

The match continued in much the same vein. Every time Palace got the ball the referee would blow his whistle and order a free-kick to Jerry.

Back in Blighty, anxious Palace fans huddled round their wireless sets and cursed. "Drat, that's the 250th free-kick we've conceded and we're only 15 minutes into the game. The smart-arses on the *Guardian* and the *Independent* will call us 'Bully Boys', but we're not a dirty side. Honest we're not."

Just a note here to explain. One would not normally expect Palace fans to be huddled round a wireless when the lads are away from home. The vast majority of course would willingly travel to any away match. However, the ticket allocation for a match in occupied Europe is even worse than at Highbury so the fans had to stay at home.

Inevitably Andy Thorn was penalised on the edge of the penalty area. This time, even the few Palace fans who had managed to get tickets (most of whom were escaping airmen and undercover agents) had to admit: "Oh well, he did take the geezer's legs away, I suppose."

And so an Ipswich player pretending to be a German (perhaps Stuart Pearce would have been better cast in this role) stepped up and fired the second goal past the helpless Martyn. "Zwei-nil to Deutschland," crowed the commentator. Then another dodgy penalty put Palace drei-nil down at half-time.

"Oldham are vinning zo escape ist impossible," sneered the guard as the Palace players trooped wearily past.

"What do we do now?" asked Simon Rodger. "Are the French going to tunnel up through the swimming pool to get us out?"

Coppell shook his head. "No, its far more subtle than that. We boot the ball over the stand and whoever kicks it out volunteers to go and get it.

But, here's the clever bit, they don't come back. Eventually we will all be outside. Then we will make our way to the coast, sneak on board a Swedish tanker and sail back to Brighton. If you are stopped show these false papers Andy Gray swapped with the Feldwebel for some second hand tracksuits."

Rodger was a bright lad always asking questions and making thoughful, probing runs: "But won't Jerry get suspicious?"

"You stupid boy," said Coppell. "Every German expects an English team to boot the ball out of the ground at least a dozen times, that's how we play the game. They won't realise what we're up to until its too late."

But before Palace could put the plan into action the match took a strange turn. Palace were given a dubious penalty.

"I must say that looked a bit harsh ref," admitted Chris Armstrong after he'd banged it home.

"Si,' said the ref. "But I am Italian and I have changed sides. The Germans won't get any more help from me."

And so Palace fought back. Steve Coppell realised his team now had a

Chris Armstrong scores Palace's equaliser with a spectacular overhead kick.

great chance of actually winning the game and being allowed to return to England in comfort without any of this escape nonsense. But could Harry Hun be trusted?

Palace, with Michael Caine in top form, fought back despite being hampered by having all their best moves played in slow motion.

Laurie Sivell for Germany was given no chance with the second goal. At home the Palace fans were getting desperately excited and started making their "Brighton Here We Come" banners.

A second goal conjured up by a couple of players whose countries were actually neutral in the war had Palace buzzing.

Then a magical equaliser by Chris Armstrong with a slow motion overhead kick pulled the scores level, the crowd went wild.

They chanted *Victoire, Victoire*, which is French for victory, and invaded the pitch handing the Palace players hats coats and pairs of flared jeans as they stormed the stadium gates and completed the Eagles' escape.

The Palace players were taken to resistance cells in Paris and then helped via boats, planes, trains and automobiles to get back to England.

At the Goldstone Ground on third round day thousands of Palace fans waited excitedly as their team arrived by parachute. The Eagles had landed. But there was no sign of Brighton. "Where are they, are they so scared of us that they haven't turned up?" asked a mystified Coppell.

"No," said a Military Policeman, who came running into the stadium, which was deserted except for the Palace end. "By a remarkable coincidence, Winston Churchill was coming to watch the match. But somehow Hitler's intelligence operatives found out and a party of German paratroopers disguised as Polish soldiers under the command of Oberst Michael Caine (in his latest role) landed in an attempt to kidnap the Prime Minister."

The policeman explained how the plot had failed when a Brighton fan fell into the sea and one of the Germans dived in to rescue him.

"What, you mean his uniform came undone and somebody saw the German one underneath?" asked Coppell.

"No," said the MP, "Nobody but an imposter would have bothered to save a Brighton fan. Anyway, they've taken the Seaweed team and all their supporters prisoner and are holding them in a church. But its okay because the American Army under the command of Colonel J.R. Dallas from Ewing in Texas has got them surrounded."

As Coppell pondered on this amazing twist of fate, a man in a bowler hat and pin striped trousers arrived looking at his watch. "Good afternoon, I'm Kelly of the Football Association, I've just heard the terrible news about the Brighton team."

He looked at his watch. "It's half past three and under our rules that means they forfeit the game, you are the winners Mr Coppell and your team will go into the hat for the fourth round."

The Palace supporters cheered and made their way happily home.

And as for those unfortunate Brighton types? Well a German submarine party came ashore under cover of darkness and the paratroopers escaped with their prisoners back to Germany.

The Seaweeds spent the rest of the war trying to convince Himmler to allow them to play a match against Germany, but as the Nazi propaganda chief said: "Who would be interested in watching Brighton?"

And so everyone lived happily ever after except, of course, Hitler and the Seaweeds.

words and pictures by Tony Matthews

Rocking through the Fifties

Palace's worst decade

Despite finishing seventh in 1948-49, Palace were clearly not going anywhere. Tired of the endless failures and mishaps, a group of wealthy supporters sought to change things. As the *Crystal Palace Story* put it, "the club needed a blood transfusion and they were prepared to give it one".

In early 1950, Percy Harper told his directors that a "well known body of sportsmen" had approached him about the possibility of joining the board. Harper felt this would provide Palace with extra resources and strengthen the club.

The new men were: David Harris, J.R. Dunster, Victor Ercolani, Guy Robson, R. Shrager, Colonel J. Trevor and Arthur Wait. Harper explained: "They are prepared to purchase an equal number of shares and would jointly guarantee the club's bank overdraft." The directors immediately accepted and three; G.J. Ellis, L.A. Ward and E.A. Webber, resigned. Another director, R.E. Edwards, stated that he would only remain to help out until the Annual General Meeting.

After two meetings, the seven were accepted onto the board and Harris became the new chairman with Wait as vice-chairman.

The takeover soon became "public property". It turned out that the men met to dine at the Trocadero in Shaftesbury Avenue. All had some interest in Palace and apparently after one especially dire performance, Wait said: "You know what we ought to do? Buy this lot up." So each put in a cheque for £3,000 to purchase Crystal Palace FC.

The new board was not short of enthusiasm or grand ideas although Wait later admitted that it took them five years to live down their mistakes – and that was on top of the five years of living down the mistakes of the previous board!

On March 28, 1950 Harris wrote to Harper to "thank" him for his work. Harper then made a long speech at the AGM "criticising" the club's financial position after which the last remaining member was voted off the board. Palace could now make a fresh start. They didn't make a very good job of it ... the worst in the club's history in fact. The first lesson for the new men to learn was that financial clout of its own accord was not sufficient.

Having opted to retain the services of Ronnie Rooke and Fred Dawes, money was made available to strengthen the team. The new board decided £20,000 should be sufficient to secure promotion and Rookie certainly had no trouble spending it.

Our transfer record was smashed twice in the space of a couple of months, first when former Shamrock Rovers winger Noel Kelly was purchased from Arsenal for £6,500 and again when Les Stevens was signed from Bradford.

The influx of talent continued; Morris Jones arrived from Swindon for £4,000, Charles Rundle from Tottenham cost another four grand and a further £2,500 was laid out for George Smith of Southampton. Rooke finally topped the lot by laying out a staggering £10,000 for Bill Whittaker, a member of Charlton's Cup Final team of 1947.

The end result of all this spending was almost too predictable. Five defeats in the first six games and the crowing summation of the sports writers that "the Crystal Palace promotion plan is going haywire". As usual, Palace suffered a healthy slice of bad luck along the way. Rundle spent most of the opening game hobbling with an ankle injury and was sidelined for the next 14 matches while Jones' jaw was broken in the home game with Millwall, which put him out for the rest of the season. Although Rooke had officially retired, he returned to try to sort out the mess and actually finished as leading scorer with just five goals.

When Harris returned from a cruise – where he had been informed on the ship's telephone that there had been some heavy spending going on – even he was surprised by the amount of cash being thrown around. This little mess clearly had to be sorted out and it was hardly surprising when the manager paid the price. On November 29, Rooke was placed on "indefinite leave of absence" – a term designed to sound as if he was going to the electric chair. However, the board magnanimously said it was prepared to accept his resignation on terms agreeable to all parties.

The new management team was exactly that – a team. Fred Dawes stepped up from assistant manager, sharing the job with chief scout Charlie Slade.

Dawes, had been a distinguished Palace player and needed no introduction. But Slade, who had gained two F.A. Cup medals with Huddersfield in the 1920s, was something of an unknown quantity.

The two men faced a struggle to pull Palace out their nose-dive. The club was last with nine points from 15 games and had just been humiliated 4-1 at home by Millwall in the Cup. But the new boys soon had a win under their belts when 21 year-old Trevor Herbert scored the winner at home to Walsall. Unfortunately it was the briefest flash in the pan and there was to be no miracle cure. We won only three

---

"The true supporter is that rare thing, someone who regards his team as a gardener would his flowers, who looks upon their bad times as merely the Winter before the Spring and revels in the joys of success to a far greater degree than the ordinary man because, in his own small way, he has helped to sow the seeds of the flowers that have bloomed."

Gerald Williams,
Sports Editor Of The Croydon Advertiser
Writing In The Palace Year Book, 1950-51

---

games before the end of a season in which the lowest ebb was a record equalling 6-1 home defeat by champions-to-be Forest. It was time to beg for the help of those "old pals" once more.

Many of the problems stemmed from a failure to keep a settled side. Palace used four goalkeepers, which did little to ease the defensive uncertainty. We started the season with Dick Graham in his accustomed position but, when he was sidelined with a back injury, Charlie Bumstead took over. During October, Graham returned for what proved to be his last half-dozen games for the Glaziers. Sadly, his return coincided with a disastrous spell – he was beaten 21 times and Palace lost the lot. Graham's injury was more severe than first thought and although he returned to the treatment table he was eventually forced to retire.

Bumstead returned but fared no better. After a run of three defeats, starting with that 6-1 slump against Forest, he was replaced by Roy Bailey, who once distinguished himself by saving the same penalty three times in a reserve game. But he was one for the future and was wisely restricted to just two appearances. Billy Hughes, signed from Rochdale, took over but played only nine games before he was beaten five times at home by Norwich and Bumstead returned once more.

On March 10, we beat Exeter 2-1 at St James's Park to record the final win of the campaign – the next 12 matches brought six draws and six defeats. On Cup Final day, while Newcastle were beating Blackpool 2-0, Palace drew with fellow strugglers Watford to gain our final point of the campaign.

It was left to Norwich to complete the last rites, 3-1 at Carrow Road. By then a re-election appeal was certain. Palace, with 33 goals, set a record for the least number of goals in a division three south season. We lined up for re-election with Watford from the south and Accrington and New Brighton from the north.

The Americans were testing the first H-Bomb while, exactly 100 years after the Great Exhibition had spawned the original Crystal Palace, the King and Queen opened the Festival of Great Britain at which Foreign Secretary Herbert Morrison said the people were "giving themselves a pat on the back".

Palace didn't deserve a pat on the back, but the board and supporters must at least have hoped that some of the pickle had been sorted out. After the heavy spending, the club tried to cut its losses, but could salvage little from the reckless outlay. Stevens, Smith and Rundle, who were given free transfers, had collectively cost £23,500.

Morris Jones fetched a meagre £1,000 and although the sale of Noel Kelly to Forest showed a profit, the £7,000 received hardly made up for the loss of the one player to have lived up to his price tag.

It wasn't all outgoings, though. Palace recruited winger Les Devonshire from Chester and George McGeachie, a wing-half from Rochdale. McGeachie was made captain, although he lost the role before a third of the season had elapsed.

Palace began the 1951-52 season with their usual mindless optimism which was strengthened by a 2-1 win in the opening game against Exeter. But by October we had assumed the position at the foot of the table once more. Having just been re-elected, it was important that Palace didn't push their luck too far, so four successive defeats prompted Dawes and Slade to gamble. Upon the recommendation of Devonshire, they moved for the unorthodox Chester centre forward Cam Burgess, who made his debut against Bristol Rovers in front of an incredibly patient crowd of more than 10,000.

Although Burgess couldn't stop Palace sliding to their fifth

Hulton Deutsch

F.A. Cup, November 29, 1950.
The end of the road for Ronnie Rooke as bottom of the league Palace crash out at home to Millwall. Here Les Stevens is denied by Lions' keeper Hinton

defeat in a row, he did spark a revival when he scored a hat-trick at Leyton Orient as Palace surprised everybody, including themselves, with a 4-0 win. Those were Burgess's first strikes in a 47-game Selhurst Park career that would bring him 40 goals. But even he couldn't prevent another managerial change. Although, he scored five goals in his first three matches, Palace lost the next two. Dawes was told his services were no longer required while Slade reverted to scouting duties.

The new manager was another ex-Arsenal player, Laurie Scott, a classy full-back, who had played in 17 consecutive internationals for England in the late 40s. It was hoped that, as player-manager, he would bring some much needed know-how to Palace's overworked defence and his reign got off to a flying start – not that he had much to do with it.

Bob Anderson, our new keeper from Newcastle, had made a 437 mile round trip to make his debut at high flying Torquay, no doubt hoping to impress his new manager, only to find himself picking the ball out of the net within a minute. But after that Palace went on the rampage stunning their hosts 5-1. Burgess banged in a couple and so did Fred Evans while Devonshire got the other.

Scott's arrival certainly steadied the ship, although Burgess's goals were more significant in the short term. Had he been signed earlier, he may even have saved Dawes and Slade from the bullet, but he missed the home Cup game with Gillingham and Palace missed him, going down 1-0.

A couple of matches later, Palace's saviour surpassed himself by scoring in six successive games including three doubles. Yet, to demonstrate just what a bad team Palace were, we won just two of those games. The most remarkable match of the season was a 4-4 draw at Gillingham in February although the reserves went one better, 5-5 with Chelsea.

It was the year that King George VI died and Princess Elizabeth became Queen. Palace started the new "Elizabethan Age" with a six game unbeaten run, including four draws. The Prime Minister Winston Churchill had announced Britain's arrival as an atomic power with the news that the country not only possessed a bomb, but also the capability to produce more. But Palace's deadly strike force was laid up and, without Burgess, form tailed off badly. Only two more victories were recorded before the season drew to a close.

Burgess made just one appearance in the last two months, in Palace's final victory of the campaign, a 2-0 home defeat of Watford, but he still equalled Ronnie Rooke's post-war scoring record with 21 goals – a feat which took him just 22 games. It was enough to lift us from last to 19th – not what was hoped for at the start of the season, but a blessed relief because it kept us clear of the re-election places.

It wasn't all plain sailing though. Anderson, who looked a useful keeper, fractured a rib in the 2-0 home win over Norwich and was in and out of the team, first losing his place to Billy Hughes and finally the big Scotsman David MacDonald. Despite their woes, Palace could always draw comfort from the knowledge that the supporters were standing by them – 19,000 watched the win over Norwich and 20,000 plus crowds saw both Gillingham and Millwall – but the final game of the season on May 3, the day Newcastle retained the Cup by beating Arsenal, saw a meagre 7,214 turn out for an entertaining but meaningless 3-3 draw with Northampton.

Laurie Scott (sacked) has two years' pay to come

£2,500 A YEAR FOR NEW MANAGER? FANTASTIC!

Palace F.C. chairman denies reports

By GERALD WILLIAMS

Hulton Deutsch

The three Palace keepers sporting jumpers that most Indie bands would kill for are (left to right) Dave MacDonald, Ray Potter and Roy Bailey.

In the summer, while the sporting world was preoccupied with the Helsinki Olympics, Palace battled with financial problems. As a token of appreciation for the help that Arsenal manager Tom Whittaker had given in getting Laurie Scott to take over at Selhurst Park, the Palace directors gave him a silver cigarette case. Nevertheless, in typically generous Arsenal fashion, it had still taken a five figure sum to prise Scott from the Highbury clutches.

It was money Palace could ill-afford and it came as no surprise, when the annual report was issued, to find a loss of £22,858 "almost entirely due to the sums paid out for players".

And there was another problem. Entertainment tax was every bit as crippling as the clubs had feared and at the start of the 1952-53 season they raised the minimum price of entry from 1/-6d to 1/-9d. Not to follow suit would have cost Palace an estimated £3,000 per year. This is how it worked: if the entrance fee remained at 1/-6d, the tax was 1d which left the club with 1/-5d. But at 1/-9d, the tax was 3 1/2 d. So to make an extra ha'penny, Palace had to whack up prices by 3d.

For those Palace fans who followed cricket, there was plenty to smile about –

Surrey won the county championship for the first time since 1914. But the smile was soon wiped from their faces when the new football season began with a dismal 4-1 defeat at Brighton. In fact we won only one of the first 13 matches. Burgess, however, maintained his excellent form and Palace gradually improved. He wasn't quite as prolific as in his first season, but 19 goals in 25 appearances was still a remarkable ratio.

That's not to say Palace were brilliant. The *Croydon Advertiser* recounted this little tale of the time: "As Len Choules, a slim, fair-haired 21 year old product of Palace juniors, went for the ball in the Gillingham goal mouth during the second half of Saturday's match at Selhurst Park, a stentorian voice from the terraces shouted 'Shoot, Choules.'

"A Cockney wit, certainly quicker off the mark than the Palace team that day, rejoined: 'Why shoot Choules? Shoot some of the others!'"

Palace travelled to Swindon on November 1 without an away win since the end of March. There didn't seem much hope of changing things at the County Ground and another defeat looked on the cards when, within eight minutes, Palace's pressurised defence buckled and Owen put the Wiltshire club ahead. Against the run of the play, Devonshire equalised only for Owen to score a deserved second just before half-time to restore the home team's advantage.

Within five minutes of the restart, Palace were level again when a superb move involving Devonshire and Bob Thomas, who Scott had recently signed from Fulham, was finished off by Burgess. The Palace number 10 then supplied the pass for Thomas to set up Johnny Rainford.

Having taken the lead, Palace, sticklers for tradition, lost it immediately, but with 15 minutes to go, we simply swept them aside with a three-goal blitz in which Rainford completed his hat-trick and Burgess added two more. It was Burgess' third hat-trick in four games – a new club record.

Six goals away from home and two hat-tricks. Remarkable stuff indeed. But, if that was an enjoyable experience, the F.A. Cup was to provide one of Palace's most miserable moments. Twenty four thousand people were disappointed by our failure to beat Reading at home in the first round. But the team then surprised everyone by winning the replay at Elm Park. Had they any inkling of what was about to befall them, they would probably have surrendered to Reading and had done with it. Instead the possibility of a third round glamour tie hinged on an away match against Athenian League amateurs Finchley, who were having an exceptional season and were unbeaten in their league programme.

Palace had been in sparkling form in the weeks leading up to the match with four goals against QPR, the six at Swindon and three without reply at home to Aldershot. But we suffered a confidence shaking 4-2 defeat at Coventry just beforehand and were quite aware that it was going to be a tough afternoon. After 61 minutes, we trailed embarrassingly 3-1. But the good old British climate came to the rescue when the game was called off because of fog. It seemed we'd been let off the hook. But at the second attempt the embarrassment was just as acute. Again in foggy conditions, the game was replayed on the following Wednesday. Shortly before the kick-off Scott received a phone call from two players to say they were lost in the fog and couldn't find Finchley's ground. Forced to make urgent adjustments the manager turned to Bob Bishop who had arrived along with two other players who had not been selected and. Bishop was the only one who could get into the missing player's boots so he played. Finchley were a strong club and boasted one of the most exciting players of the day in George Robb, who had 12 amateur caps and was a target for many top sides. Robb, however, preferred to play for his local side while teaching at Finchley Grammar School rather than sign for Arsenal, Spurs, Derby, Leicester, Fulham, Brentford or the Italian club Padua, from which he could have taken his pick.

Even at Finchley his reputation preceded him. The Robb versus Scott contest was built up as the crucial one and there was no doubt that the amateur came out on top. To compound Palace's shame, Finchley also claimed that the last minute inclusion of Bishop contravened F.A. rules, pointing out that a list of players from which teams would be composed had to be submitted five days before the tie. Finchley claimed Bishop was not on it and was therefore ineligible. Scott denied this and said Bishop's name had been on the original list.

During the 1952-53 season, Roy Bailey began to realise his undoubted potential as a keeper and by March he had overtaken both David MacDonald and Bob Anderson, in the race to be Palace's number one.

Bailey played his first game of the season in a 1-1 draw at QPR and despite conceding five against Norwich shortly after he kept his place thus ending a long period of uncertainty over the position.

Palace even managed to conclude the season on a run of encouraging form, losing only one of their last six matches and finishing with two 1-0 home wins first when Colin Grimshaw, who Scott had signed from Arsenal, scored against Watford and then on the eve of the Cup Final when

Hulton Deutsch

Left to right: Ronnie Downs, Les Devonshire and Geoff Chilvers

FLOODLIT SOCCER? 17,082 FANS AGREE THAT IT IS GREAT STUFF

Palace versus Chelsea under the floodlights and the *Croydon Advertiser* declares the experiment a success

Bob Thomas's goal beat Bristol Rovers.

For those fans who had a television it was the chance to see if Stanley Matthews could finally gain a Cup winners medal in Blackpool's third final appearance, this time against Bolton Wanderers. Every wireless was tuned in. No wonder Palace played on the Friday – would anybody have gone to Selhurst Park otherwise?

The 1953-54 season began for the first and only time in history on a Thursday when Palace drew with Northampton at Selhurst. We followed up on the following Saturday by beating Southampton 4-3. It was a reasonable start, but the Glaziers soon began to collapse and the season ended with another appeal for re-election.

It was the year in which English football finally received the lesson which many had realised was coming. The national team's proud home record of never having been beaten by a foreign side was swept away by a famous Hungarian demonstration of skilful football and masterful tactics. The English side, which included George Robb who had since moved from Finchley to Spurs; Billy Wright; Alf Ramsey and Stan Matthews was mesmerised by Hidegkuti, Ferenc Puskas and Koscics. It was Robb's first cap. He never played for England again.

While we tried to come to terms with a new world footballing order (or, in some cases, went on blithely assuming the result to be a fluke and that nothing was wrong), Palace had weightier matters on their mind – those of survival. Although results were poor, Scott was still considered to have done a pretty good job. After all, he'd been forced to sell to balance the books and many good players had left, including forwards Johnny Rainford to Cardiff for £3,000 and Cam Burgess to York for £850 (Burgess had asked to leave for "personal reasons").

Replacements included the Chelsea forward Ernie Randall, who cost £1,000 down with the remaining £1,300 to be paid in October, and Jesse Willard from Brighton for £150. There were also a couple of direct swap deals: Ray Hancox went to Southend in exchange for Ray Woods and George Evans went to Rochdale in exchange for Bert Foulds. Shortly after, Scott decided to give up playing to concentrate solely on management. Meanwhile, the board decided to invest in a set of floodlights, which proved a great success when they were used in a couple of exhibition matches. After guarantees and expenses were paid, the first two games produced a useful profit of £14,000.

The inaugural match was a 1-1 draw against Chelsea on September 28. The games proved immensely popular and numerous friendlies were played although the match against the French team Stade Francais shortly after offered a taste of European diffidence. The visiting team began by presenting the Palace players with bottles of champagne, while the home team reciprocated with packets of 100 cigarettes.

That was where the generosity finished. In what was supposed to be a friendly the 6,598 crowd booed the teams off after it developed into a kicking match. Ernie Randall, the victim of rough treatment, had to be taken off to protect him from injury although he cheered up at the end when the Frenchmen gave him a beret.

Playing matters were soon in the shadows again when David Harris resigned as chairman to be replaced at the top of the table by Arthur Wait. Four days later, Colonel Trevor resigned as well. This, following the earlier resignation of Guy Shrager who'd gone to live in Mexico, left the board with just four members. Despite Palace's delicate financial position, we still made a surprisingly large bid of £8,000 for Jim Barrett of West Ham. Given the parlous state of finances and the club's record with big money signings it was perhaps just as well that the Hammers stuck to their valuation of £9,000 and the deal was scrapped.

In January, Palace lost five games in a row, including a 7-0 creaming by Exeter. The slump continued almost without respite and it was only the more dismal abilities of Colchester and Walsall that kept us safe from yet another round of begging letters. Even so, we didn't win any of our last nine games.

In the first round of the Cup there was further humiliation. Palace dominated Great Yarmouth but it was the non-league side who scored the only goal. The giant killers of old were well and truly getting a taste of their own medicine.

Palace, as was now expected, got off to an atrocious start in 1954-55. One win in the first 11 games included yet another depressing mauling this time at the hands of Watford. Former Chelsea centre half Jack Saunders hadn't played a competitive match so far for Palace but he was included at right half and lived to regret it. The team put in a "pathetic performance" conceding six goals from inside the six yard box as a "coloured" forward called Brown scored a hat-trick and gave Harry Briggs, hampered by two stitches in a cut knee, a torrid time. Watford scored five times in 15 minutes in the second half. Devonshire grabbed our inadequate reply.

Laurie Scott lasted for a couple more matches but, after three years of disappointing performances, his dismissal was inevitable. The *Croydon Advertiser* pointed out that there were two sides to every story, but the board was clearly influenced by the failures of both the first and reserve teams and, while admitting that Scott had limited resources with which to work, they had to do something.

Scott was noble in his departure, defending his

Thornton's view of Laurie Scott
courtesy of the *Croydon Advertiser*

coaches Jack Blackman and Tom Brolly, who had been "criticised from outside the club". The *Advertiser* also reported a stream of letters from supporters defending their manager.

Palace's statement

"Among the very many duties of directors they are sometimes called upon to take action which, from a personal angle, is very distasteful.

During the past few days, the directors have been subjected to a certain amount of criticism because they considered it time to make changes in the club. But it must be remembered that the Crystal Palace FC is greater than the individual at all times.

Should we consider that other changes are necessary to raise the club from it's present position these, too, will have to be made regardless of personal feeling.

More than ever the club is in need of the support its very many supporters have given it, and we hope that you will still rally round as in the past to share its fortunes or misfortunes.

The Board of Directors, in turn, will endeavour to do all in their power to improve the prospects of the club as quickly as possible."

Immediately after Scott's departure, Palace collected the season's second victory, 2-1 over Bournemouth and Boscombe Athletic, but it was achieved in front of our second lowest post-war league crowd of 6,165.

Scott's departure ran true to form. Palace have always chopped and changed managers with alarming regularity. This needs to be put into context. Even as late as the 70s, it wasn't unusual for a manager to stay with one club for years and years. Only the unstable switched every five minutes and Palace were certainly unstable. Even today, the club has one of the highest post-war managerial turnover rates in the country. The board moved for former Derby manager Harry Storer, who had retired from football, but were unable to persuade him to return to the game – and who could blame him? Rejected by Storer, they turned to the "quiet, scholarly" Cyril Spiers.

Like Laurie Scott, Spiers became joint manager and club secretary, although he later handed the secretarial responsibility on to his office secretary Margaret Montague, who thus became the first recognised female football club secretary. The 52 year-old Palace manager began his career in 1916 as a goalkeeper with Aston Villa. He went on to play for Spurs and Wolves despite an operation on a serious knee injury which at one point threatened his career. His managerial career started with Cardiff and then Norwich.

In an interview with Spiers, the former Palace goalkeeper Dick Graham wrote in the *Croydon Advertiser*: "My impression of Mr Spiers is that he is a sincere man who realises he has a tremendous job on his hands. He has a reputation of being a disciplinarian – but perhaps that is a good thing. Let us all give him as much support as possible."

Spiers watched his new charges concede a last minute equaliser at home to Reading, which is more than many of the crowd saw because they were already streaming home. Spiers could have been left in little doubt about the size of his task.

Around this time, Palace missed out on a rather good player thanks to a piece of poor advice from a scout. Arthur Wait and Charlie Slade went to Kidderminster to watch a centre-forward and decided to get a second opinion from another scout in an away game. The scout named "Jones" was not impressed. "The board was informed that Mr H. Jones was directed to watch this player against Hastings on Saturday, 30 October. His report was not very favourable and coincided with that given by the chairman. In consequence negotiations had been dropped."

It makes you wonder why chairmen kid themselves they know a good player when they see one. In this case the player was Gerry Hitchens, later an England forward, who represented his country at the 1962 World Cup and became one of the first big money exports to Italy.

Initially, Spiers could do little to inspire Palace. Victories were few and far between and, again, our cup luck was out … if you can call it unlucky to be drawn at home to a non-league team.

With so many clubs installing floodlights the F.A. agreed that, subject to mutual consent, Cup replays could be played under the lights. But Palace would not be needing their lights just yet because they had drawn Bishop Auckland, the premier amateur club of the day. Spiers controversially chose MacDonald in goal in preference to Bailey, but he had no chance as we were crushed 4-2 in front of 20,155 Selhurst supporters.

Towards the end of the season, Spiers announced drastic measures. "We have been losing £200 a week and have decided to go for quality and not quantity. Other clubs will have to follow. I am warning that many good players and club men will be left high and dry, and everyone in football should help them find other jobs in or out of the game," he said. His retained list, published in the programme before the home game with Brentford, did not make happy reading for many players. He fired half the playing staff and gave the rest a rise. There were changes behind the scenes too. Charlie Slade lost his job and Jesse Willard, described in a report to the board as "a fine coach, too good to lose", was promoted to coach and trainer of the juniors. Bobby Greener, who had been at the club since 1922, was also dispensed with. The minute noted: "R. Greener relieved of this office from 7 May, 1955." The only epitaph to a career of more than 30 years, it left a sour taste with many Palace followers.

The club however was at least preparing for a better future. Before the first game of the new season, Sir Stanley Rous,

Hulton Deutsch

Ernie Randall, a Palace recruit from Chelsea

THE SCRUFFY BUNCH.
The Palace players pose for the fashion press in August 1955.
Back row: (left to right) Roy Greenwood; Archie Andrews; Jack Saunders; Roy Bailey; Jack Edwards and Ron Moss.
Front row: (left to right) Peter Berry; Jimmy Belcher; Mike Deakin; Tommy Tilston; Harry Gunning.

the secretary of the Football Association, officially opened the new entrance hall and board room. Palace marked the occasion in fine style, losing 3-2 to Northampton. But the lowest point was a shambles at Leyton Orient on November 12. The Os were already two up when Bailey was injured and Len Choules took over the green jersey. Bailey, whose shoulder injury did not prevent him attempting to be of nuisance value at centre-forward returned to goal in the second half but we still went down 8-0.

Although Palace finished next to bottom, Cyril Spiers had at least begun the task of turning the club around. Increasing attention was placed on youth and players such as Mike Deakin, George Cooper, Jimmy Murray, Ron Brett and Barry Pierce were brought through the ranks.

Before the last home match of the season against Newport, Spiers elaborated further on the new financial reality at Crystal Palace: "During the season well over 200 youngsters have been given trials, eleven have been signed on professional forms and 58 on amateur forms.

"The total cost for the 11 professionals signed was £110, or in other words, just their £10 signing-on fee. Transfer fees paid: nil, as against several thousands of pounds each previous year. For once in a while our transfer budget shows a credit balance. This talk of finance may not mean anything to you, the supporter, but to the club it is a tremendous step in the right direction. I am hoping that by the end of our Financial Year we shall at least have paid our way. A very different picture to what it was at this time last year."

Spiers also said that instead of cutting wages – a move that had been forced on many other third division clubs – Palace gave them all a £2 per week rise which brought the standard up to that of the first division. "Two of our boys have also been paid full first team benefits of £500 each. No longer will any player of ours have to worry about receipts from a benefit game."

None of this however could compensate for another terrible season. On April 26, 1956, having just been hammered 4-0 at Walsall, Palace were 22nd, two points ahead of Millwall, who had a game in hand. Although we then beat Newport with a Jimmy Belcher goal, our last match at Shrewsbury ended in defeat. Millwall, meanwhile, suddenly hit form, scoring 11 goals without reply in winning their last three matches and so Palace joined Swindon in applying for re-election. Towards the end of the campaign, Arthur Wait stood down as chairman to be replaced by Victor Ercolani, to whom fell the task of writing a humble letter begging for the support of the other clubs as Palace faced another application for re-election.

"It is with regret that I have to confirm that my club finished second bottom of the Third Division South for the season ending 1955-56, and the object of this letter is to ask for your support at the Annual General Meeting of the Football League when we shall unfortunately be applying for re-election.

Although you may already know, I give below the following information regarding the club: One of the original members of the third division south on formation, gaining promotion to the second division at the first season, the club have always tried to uphold and maintain the prestige of football in this area with a population of over 500,000 people. The ground is the freehold property of the club and at the moment holds 55,000 people, 12,000 under cover. There is a car park, also owned by the club, for 1,000 cars.

Average gate attendances for the past five years has exceeded 12,000. In spite of adverse home results last year, the average gates were up by 700 per match. The reserve team gates were up by 900 per match and the team finished halfway up the Football Combination table comprising 32 clubs. I trust that I can rely on your club's support and look forward to meeting you at the League meeting."

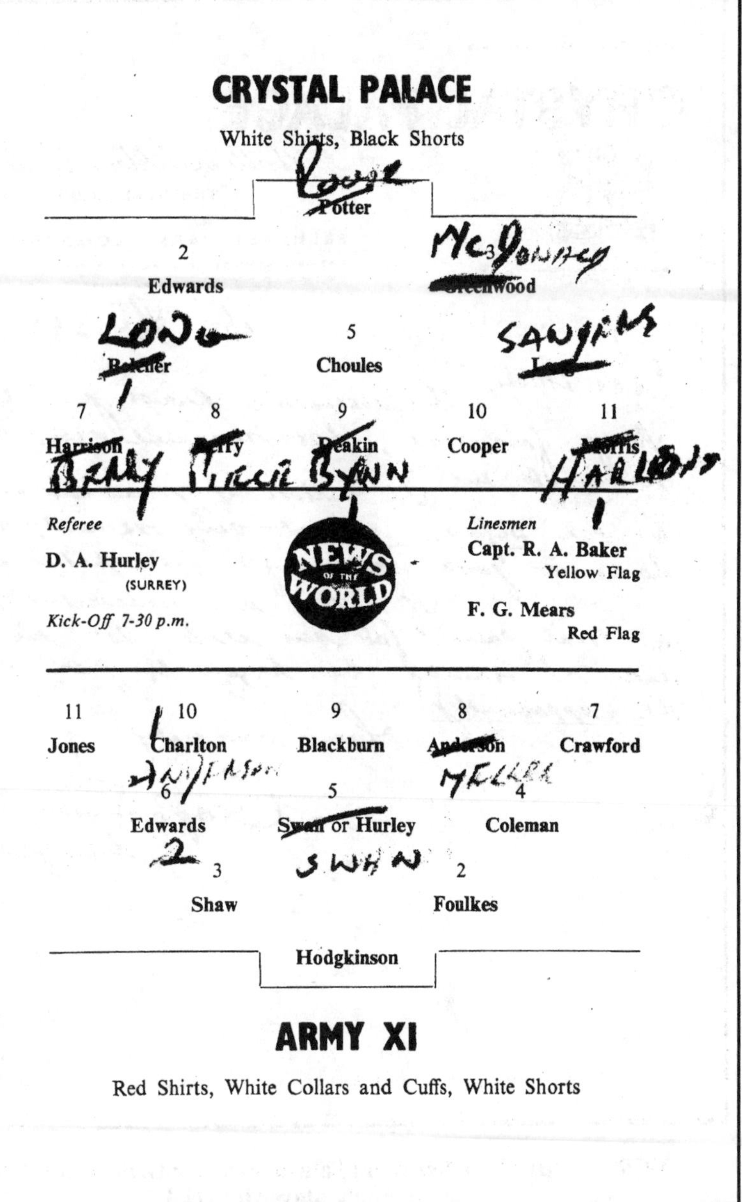

CRYSTAL PALACE

White Shirts, Black Shorts

Potter

2 Edwards — 3 Greenwood

Belcher — 5 Choules

7 Harrison — 8 Berry — 9 Deakin — 10 Cooper — 11 Morris

Referee D. A. Hurley (SURREY)

Kick-Off 7-30 p.m.

NEWS OF THE WORLD

Linesmen Capt. R. A. Baker, Yellow Flag; F. G. Mears, Red Flag

11 Jones — 10 Charlton — 9 Blackburn — 8 Anderson — 7 Crawford

6 Edwards — 5 Swan or Hurley — 4 Coleman

3 Shaw — 2 Foulkes

Hodgkinson

ARMY XI

Red Shirts, White Collars and Cuffs, White Shorts

October 1956, the teams from a match between Palace and the Army. National Service meant the forces often had an embarrassment of riches. From this team Alan Hodgkinson kept goal for England; Shaw played for England Under-23s; Coleman and Duncan Edwards were members of the Busby Babes, as was Bobby Charlton, who did not actually play in this match; Peter Swan played for Sheffield Wednesday and England; and Crawford had a Scottish Cup winners' medal with Hearts. Everyone in the Army team was in the first team at his club.

The faith that the other clubs showed was again, in all probability, never in doubt. They wouldn't have been too keen to vote out a club with as much potential as Palace although they were not to know that we were grooming a star who would soon help begin the task of hurtling up to the very top of the league.

Johnny Byrne, a talented young inside forward, arrived at Palace almost by accident when he turned up for a trial with another youngster. The only experience he could offer was that he had played for a youth club team, but Palace saw something and picked him out as a bright young talent. He signed professional forms just as our re-election for another term was confirmed. He was already a regular in the England youth set-up and Palace had just paid £100 for his mother and father to travel to Denmark to watch him play for his country.

Although Palace were returned on the nod at the League's AGM, there were calls for the establishment of a third and fourth division to replace the old "north and south" system. This would have been a disaster for us because we would have been forced to start in the fourth division. Fortunately, the first and second division clubs threw the idea out.

Spiers' spiel about "quality" began to look pretty silly as Palace finished the 1956-57 season in a lowly 20th place, but at least it meant no re-election scrounging, although things hadn't looked too good when we failed to win any of our first seven fixtures. There was never much relief for the Glaziers, although on October 13 there was the first glimpse of a better future when Spiers gave debuts to goalkeeper Vic Rouse and Byrne, in a 0-0 draw with Swindon. Rouse had started as an apprentice with Millwall and signed professional for them in 1953. A year later he began two years National Service and when he returned Millwall had a surplus of keepers so he joined Palace. By the end of the season both he and Byrne were established as first team regulars. Byrne's first goal for Palace helped earn a 3-3 draw

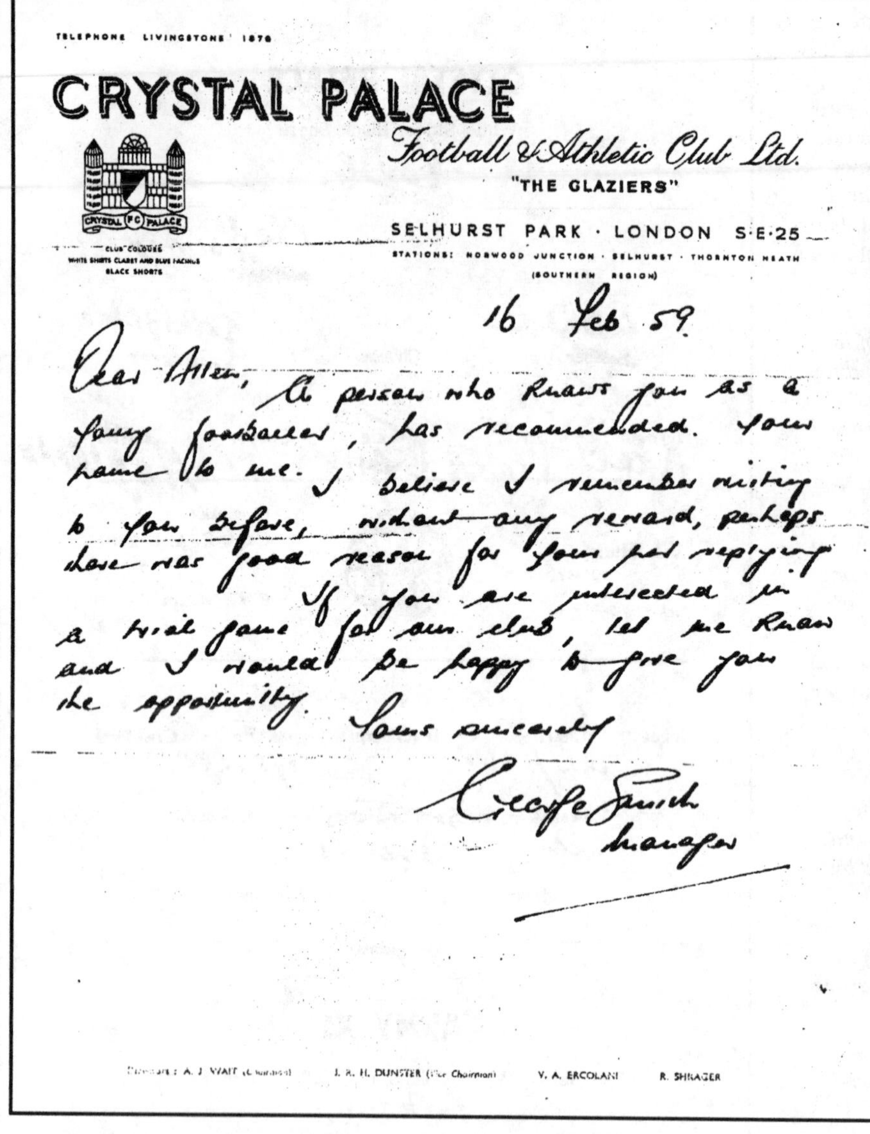

TELEPHONE LIVINGSTONE 1878

CRYSTAL PALACE
Football & Athletic Club Ltd.
"THE GLAZIERS"

CLUB COLOURS
WHITE SHIRTS CLARET AND BLUE FACINGS
BLACK SHORTS

SELHURST PARK · LONDON S·E·25
STATIONS: NORWOOD JUNCTION · SELHURST · THORNTON HEATH
(SOUTHERN REGION)

16 Feb 59.

Dear Allen,
A person who knows you as a young footballer, has recommended your name to me. I believe I remember writing to you before, without any reward, perhaps there was good reason for your not replying.
If you are interested in a trial game for our club, let me know and I would be happy to give you the opportunity.
Yours sincerely
George Smith
Manager

Directors: A. J. WAIT (Chairman) J. R. H. DUNSTER (Vice Chairman) V. A. ERCOLANI R. SHRAGER

1959: A copy of a letter from Palace manager George Smith inviting a young player for trial

at Coventry, a match which wouldn't have taken place at all if the Highfield Road floodlights hadn't failed in the first encounter two days before Christmas.

We were given another tricky non-league club in the cup, but this time we eased past Walthamstow Avenue – it was the first time Crystal Palace had appeared on television. We even reached the third round, but instead of a financially rewarding glamour tie with a big club … all we got was another visit to Millwall where we lost 2-0 in front of a crowd of 26,790.

The season finished on a high note though when 22,627 saw Torquay held to a 1-1 draw on Cup Final day. The result denied the Gulls promotion and meant Alf Ramsey's Ipswich went up instead.

The fear of having to become founder members of division four was soon looming large again as Palace scrambled to avoid the cut in 1957-58. The deal was simple, finish 11th or better or take up residence in the league's new basement.

Although Palace eventually missed the division three boat by three places, Spiers remained optimistic: "I can now say we have completed the first phase. We now have a fairly experienced first and second team made up of youngsters who have been carefully selected and groomed. They have had their baptism the hard way but it has been invaluable experience for them and their progress has been much more rapid than would have been the case had they gone through the normal procedure of the Reserve side for a couple of years or so. The next two years should be most interesting for those of you who have patiently followed our fortunes through the past two years."

The maximum wage for players was increased to £17 from £15 in the winter and from £12 to £14 in the summer and talent money also doubled. Cup talent money went up, the bonus for winning a league match was increased from £2 to £4, Television fees were introduced and the second spell benefit was increased from £750 to £1,000. Palace averaged 13,638 spectators for league matches as the team flirted with the prospect of retaining third division football. In the Cup, we broke Margate's attendance record when 8,200 turned up to see Mike Deakin's hat-trick edge us home in a five goal thriller. We then disposed of Southampton to set up a tie with Ipswich which we lost by one goal in front of 21,940 supporters at Selhurst Park.

Although Palace now faced life as a fourth division team, we could take comfort from the knowledge that Spiers was building a good side with Rouse now first choice in goal; Byrne, who had scored 7 goals in 28 games up front; and former Wycombe Wanderers full back Terry Long adding a sure touch to defence. Spiers had moved Len Choules to centre half where he settled brilliantly, while winger Ron Brett was successfully introduced towards the end of the season.

Choules had joined Palace as a 17 year-old amateur in 1949 and played "A" team matches for us in midweek, while turning out in the Athenian League for Sutton United at weekends. He signed professional in 1951 but was transferred abroad during his national service. He finally broke into the Palace team on his return and played in the last four matches of 1952-53. He played regularly in the following season usually at right back although he deputised as a centre-forward for a couple of matches in an attempt to improve the team's goal power. Although he scored in one of these against Gillingham. Palace still lost 2-1 and he reverted to defence.

In the close season, there was another bombshell when Cyril Spiers was sacked. Had the formation of the fourth division been suspended for a year, Palace would probably have avoided it, but football is full of ifs and buts and, although nobody could deny Spiers had done a fine job in keeping the wolf from the door and turning the club around, the ever grateful board of directors, made him pay for this failure to finish a couple of places higher up the league. He left Selhurst Park on June 30, 1958.

The year will be forever marked by the tragedy at Munich when an airliner carrying Manchester United's Busby Babes crashed killing half the team. The disaster also touched Crystal Palace, our winger Peter Berry was the brother of United's England international Johnny Berry who was killed in the crash.

Palace prepared for the fourth division, where they were to meet nine clubs for the first time: Barrow, Carlisle, Chester, Crewe, Darlington, Hartlepool, Southport, Workington and York, under a new manager. Compared to the gentle Spiers, George Smith was an altogether different kettle of fish. The former Charlton, Brentford and QPR player, who had appeared in three war time internationals, had been a PT instructor in the army, and was known as "the sergeant major" by some of the players he'd handled in the past.

Smith set himself a goal: "If I don't get promotion in two seasons, I'm off." It was going to be a tall order, but Palace started with a bang. On the first day of the season, Crewe were humbled 6-2, which unfortunately proved to be a misleading scoreline. Although the side was a good one, it wasn't ready to return to the third division.

Nevertheless, Byrne, nicknamed "Budgie" because of his incessant chatter, was developing into the player that would shortly terrorise international defences and Mike Deakin was enjoying his best season relishing the slightly lower quality football. However the team was erratic and lost too many silly games. Smith was livid after seeing seen his team brimming with potential stuffed 5-0 at Bradford and he set about toughening them up. His cause was helped by a generally settled side and, with greater discipline, it became a consistent unit.

In the Cup, Palace faced another potentially calamitous away match against non-league Ashford, but a Tony Collins goal saw the Glaziers scrape through. Three games were needed to dispose of Shrewsbury before Palace finally won 4-1 at neutral Molineux. Had we reached the fourth round, we would have enjoyed a relatively glamourous tie with fading Arsenal, however Sheffield United at Bramall Lane proved too great an obstacle and Palace went out tamely.

In the league, but a little more defensive stability was required. We had no trouble scoring goals, Deakin, ably assisted by Byrne, set a Palace post war record with 23 league goals and Roy Summersby's introduction from Millwall gave the forward line even more pep. The excitement helped increase attendances by 20 per cent to an average of around 15,000.

The defensive foundations took longer to come together before Smith settled on a regular back line of Rouse, with Terry Long, Alf Noakes, new signing from Brighton Johnny McNicholl and Choules. After being demobbed from the Navy, McNicholl was a part-timer at Newcastle where he trained to be an apprentice motor fitter in a local garage. He was never considered for the first team at Newcastle where the likes of Len Shackleton and Jackie Milburn made the Magpies one the biggest clubs of the fifties.

Brighton signed him for £5,000 and he stayed with them longer than was good for him until at 27 he moved to Chelsea where he linked up with Roy Bentley and Frank Blunstone in the team that won the league in 1955.

Before the end of the season Rouse became the first full international from the fourth division. He'd already made a couple of Welsh Under-23 appearances – the first in a trial match at Somerton Park on February 19 after which he was chosen for the match against Scotland at Edinburgh on December 10. His senior call came as a stand-in for Arsenal's Jack Kelsey in the Home International against Northern Ireland in Belfast. Rouse gave a defiant performance but a very good Irish side won 4-1. Nevertheless, the *Daily Mail* said: "Ireland's refreshing top speed, hell for leather football on a hard, dusty pitch gave Vic Rouse, the young Crystal Palace goalkeeper, one of the most testing international baptisms I've ever seen. It could have been a nightmare match for the first ever Fourth Division player to get a cap, but whatever mistakes he made through inexperience he more than made up for with his courage and brilliant interceptions.

"At times, only the luck of the brave stood between Rouse and a Welsh rout. The biggest cheer of the evening came nine minutes from the end when he cleanly held a sizzling header from William Cush, who stood six yards out unbelieving that the ball had not hit the net. At the end a sympathetic but highly delighted Irish crowd warmly cheered Rouse from the field."

The start of the new season brought Palace just one win in the first five matches, which severely hampered our promotion aspirations. Although we were never quite good enough to get up among the front runners, we remained in contention for long periods.

By way of compensation there were a couple of huge wins. In a frantically busy September, Watford's defence was given the run around by Byrne, Johnny Roche and Roy Colfar, all of whom scored twice. Johnny Gavin and Alf Noakes added to the Hornets' torment as Palace ran out 8-1 winners. One would have thought Palace would be buoyed by such a triumph, but we lost the next four league games before bouncing back with yet another enormous victory. This time it was Barrow's turn to feel the force as Summersby grabbed four goals in a record nine goal haul.

Smith had added the experience of West Ham's Dave Sexton, who had been signed in the summer. He added a quality touch to proceedings but his contribution was cut short by serious injury after he had scored 11 times in 27 appearances. Sexton's knee problem eventually forced him into retirement and he became one of the country's top coaches, leading Chelsea to their only Cup triumph in 1970 and coaching the England Under-21s.

In the Cup, Palace destroyed Chelmsford at Selhurst Park thanks to a hat-trick from Byrne. Then we brought Margate back to Selhurst where, on a muddy pitch, Roche and the balding Alan Woan ended the dreams of Almeric Hall's plucky team.

In the third round, we were disappointed to miss out on a big name club and even more so when we failed to make further progress against second division Scunthorpe at the Old Show Ground.

More disappointment was to follow in the promotion race. By mid-April, it was already certain that Walsall, Notts County and Torquay were going up which left five clubs scrambling for the last seat on the promotion express. On April 15, Millwall and Watford both had 48 points, Palace had 45 and Gillingham and Northampton were a point behind us.

But in the final run in, Palace came off worst, picking up only five more points and it was Watford, so soundly thrashed way back in September, who eventually took fourth place. True to his word, George Smith offered his resignation. It was an amicable but sad parting.

The 1950s were undoubtedly the blackest years for Crystal Palace, but by the end of the decade we were emerging from the dark and into the light. As the 1960s dawned it became apparent that the only way was up …

Who was there with me?

Barrie Greene's earliest memory of Palace was a match that the record books said couldn't have happened

I first started supporting Palace during the promotion year of 1969. I had just become engaged and as my teenage galavanting days were over I needed a new interest.

I had gone to watch Chelsea and Fulham on alternate Saturdays when I was at school although I was actually a Manchester United fan.

I often boasted that one of the first matches I ever went to was the famous match at Highbury when the Busby Babes beat Arsenal 5-4 just days before Munich.

My dad was an Arsenal fanatic and my bedtime stories were not of Snow White or the Three Bears but of the exploits of Alex James and Cliff Bastin and tales of the wonderful Gunners of the thirties.

For many years I had this faint memory of going to a match with my dad in the pouring rain at a place called Crystal Palace, though I recall the ground was Selhurst Park.

We saw Arsenal and they were playing this fourth division team.

We had arrived just after the kick off and had no chance of gaining a good position so my father had to lift me up on many occasions to see the play when it was going on directly below us.

The match was under floodlights and I remember standing on a grassy bank which was becoming muddier all the time. The ground was very noisy and there was a great atmosphere.

I must admit that I remained confused for years because history shows the match could never have been played in the league and Palace had not met Arsenal in the Cup. What was more confusing was that the ground was full.

It was only years later that the *Crystal Palace: A Complete Record* book solved the mystery.

The record shows that on April 27, 1959 Selhurst Park staged the final of the Southern Professional Cup when Palace were beaten 2-1, our goal being scored by Johnny Byrne. The attendance was over 32,000 so my recollection was spot on.

I'm sure this little story has bored most of you, but there might have been one or two other readers who were there with me that night so it is to them I dedicate my memory.

Childhood on the mud banks

Heroes: The 1953 Crystal Palace squad

IT STARTED for me in October 1957 when a friend, Brian Morris, asked if I wanted to go to see Palace. I jumped at the chance little realising that it would lead to a 35 year love affair with the Eagles, apart from a gap in the early 1980s when I did not set foot inside Selhurst Park for five years.

Brian said his dad would take us and we saw Palace beat Plymouth 3-0 to make the day special for a ten year old. We entered the ground via the Holmesdale terraces and stood and bought a tiny programme with a red, blue and green cover as well as a packet of Percy Dalton's peanuts.

We stood where the Holmesdale meets the Park Lane terracing. It was in the days when you could walk round the ground and both sets of supporters used to change ends at half time. The Arthur Wait stand had not been built and concrete terracing only reached half way up the Park Road side, from then on it was a mud bank, deadly in the middle of winter when you were struggling back from the tea bar with your OXO. We used to cluster around the wooden floodlight poles that were spaced along that side of the ground. They gave you something to hang onto if the terracing became a sea of mud. I was hooked and attended the next few games on my own. I was allowed to walk from my home in Anerley through the "bunny hole" up to the Goat House bridge and along Norwood High Street and up Whitworth Road. I ask myself whether I would allow a ten year-old to do this today.

Mike Deakin, Alfie "Pigeon Chest" Noakes, Vic Rouse, who played for Wales, and Johnny Byrne were my heroes.

The pitch was surrounded by a small metal railing and us youngsters used to leap over it at the end and run onto the pitch to pat the players on the back and if we were really lucky collect an autograph. Even then, the club officials did not look kindly on us running on the pitch and we were frequently warned off. Afterwards we waited at the main entrance at the back of the old stand for autographs from our heores and from the visiting team.

By Frank Glanz

Budgie Byrne, push and run and day trips to Torquay

Peter Butler was first taken to Selhurst Park after the war. He watched Palace decline to become the worst team in the league and then build slowly until they could compete with and beat the best

I think I first started going to Selhurst Park in the 1945-46 season. My father was a Palace fan and he dragged me over there, although I was quite willing. My father had the same name as one of the managers Jack Butler, but it was purely coincidental.

I was a keen Palace fan although I was about six years old. In those days we were known as the Lilywhites, because of our black and white colours. We used to go one week to the first team and the next to the reserves never missing a game.

My favourite player was Freddie Kurz who was a very lively centre-forward. He used to dart about and was a good goalscorer.

I also liked a bloke called Bill Bassett, who was bald as a coot but could head the ball from his own penalty area to the centre circle with no trouble – not a very cultured player, but in the third division south you didn't have to be.

Harry Briggs followed him as centre half. He once got his head cut open and they bandaged him up but he was soon caked in blood again. Being a very delicate child, I almost fainted at the sight.

I don't remember much skill, we were in with the dregs of the football league although we got 10,000 every match and the reserves used to get one or two thousand as well. The best thing was that the crowd was so small that you could hear every word and if you were playing someone like Arsenal they would often have first division players who were either dropped or recovering from injury. The wit of the crowd was often directed at these people. You could also hear the players swearing at each other, it was quite entertaining.

We really were a terrible side and in the early 50s had to apply for re-election although there was never any likelihood of us being thrown out because we had such good crowds.

I remember this bloke who was splay footed, his name, I think, was Sadler, although I've never been able to find any record of him since so he must have been a reserve. Even at ten years old I thought he's never going to make it as a footballer. At another match which I think was also probably a reserve game, the Palace captain Fred Dawes came out smoking a fag, and stubbed it out on the pitch as he ran out!

Palace have had some bad players, although every bad player has a redeeming feature from time to time and when they did something brilliant you'd think he's not so bad after all. Many bad players become good players, one such was Derek Jeffries who was a really cultured player but was played out of position for a while and looked useless.

Our keeper in the 40s was Dick Graham, an excellent goalkeeper and a hard man as he proved when he was manager. Palace were terrible, but they had a loyal band of supporters. They were the local team and I think in those days there was more loyalty to them. It was good fun even if the quality wasn't very high.

The ground was all open apart from the Old Stand and there were grass banks at the top. I always stood on the Park Lane side, sometimes wandering around behind the goal Palace were attacking in order to see the goals flooding in, the only trouble was they were usually going in at the other end.

The best football Palace have ever played was in the early 60s when Arthur Rowe brought a style and standard that was wonderful to watch. I enjoyed it better even than the Team of the 80s. The push and run game was all about space, you pushed it into an empty space and you knew someone would run onto it.

I belonged to the supporters club and

Random memories from 40 years at Selhurst

By Tony Halliday

■ Cliff Holton scoring with a shot from the half way line.

■ "Chopper" Greenwood who used to head everything above grass height

■ Beating Accrington 9-2 on the first day of the 1960-61 season and trips on the specials to Crewe, Shrewsbury, Gillingham and Aldershot.

■ Losing to Workington 1-0 with their goal being scored by a "utility" player.

■ Palace's manager George Smith (now sadly passed away) who was my ex-games teacher. My father "Doc" Halliday used to run the Addiscombe Boys Club and during George Smith's time they were invited to play against the Palace juniors at Selhurst Park.

■ Good times when you could discuss the match with a rival supporter, often running down your own team if they made a silly error and then joking about theirs.

■ Dave Swindlehurst's nickname. The people around me called him "Cinders" because he was always late for the ball and John Sewell was called "Shovel" because of his habit of hoisting the ball skywards on every occasion.

■ The struggle for survival in division one, and the really bad losses such as the 5-1 defeat by Arsenal.

■ The "goal that never was" by Clive Allen at Coventry. It was clearly recorded by the cameras and on slow motion. A good goal disallowed because it was too quick for anyone to see.

Johnny Byrne: a supreme talent

except we didn't like Southend who used be a particular enemy because they were just about the dirtiest side around. Even so, we stood on the terraces with opposing supporters and you could have an argument without any animosity.

There has always been rivalrly, hatred I suppose, with Millwall but the only time I ever saw violence in those days was when their fans were beating up Palace supporters.

I'd never seen it before and didn't understand what was happening. Charlton were also a slightly more aggressive mob.

The crowds were huge immediately after we were promoted, we had 28,000 for our first match back in the third division, its remarkable to think how many people would come along.

It was worth it just to see Johnny Byrne. His record speaks for itself, he was so skilful, a good finisher, although he could be a little bit selfish.

He was in a very good team. Roy Summersby helped him a lot although we had a real donkey called Dennis Uphill who the fans couldn't bear. He didn't look like a footballer and never should have been one, but he scored quite a few goals. His ball control was non-existent. I remember a brilliant goal Byrne scored against Wrexham on a muddy pitch. He beat about three players took it round the goalkeeper and had to scoop it out of the mud, he knocked it wide and had to get it back before taking it round the keeper again and knocking it into the empty net. He was so quick and could beat people, although he wasn't a great header of the ball. The only mistakes he made was when he was trying to be too clever. That was the best football, although I thought Malcolm Allison was brilliant, very charismatic, the team played good football under him as well. He had no chance of keeping

used to travel all over, to such wondrous places as Barnsley, Crewe Torquay and Mansfield, which was the worst ground in the country. We used to go by coach. The Torquay trip involved an overnight stop. We left Selhurst Park at midnight, arrived at about 7am, had breakfast in the hotel, walked around town, went to the match, went to the show on the pier in the evening and got back on the coach at midnight. We would finish back at Selhurst at about 7am on the Sunday morning.

At Barnsley when Byrne was playing for us, all the kids were waiting for us to get off the coach running up saying "Is Johnny Byrne playing?" There was no animosity just excitement. In fact I can't ever remember seeing Palace lose away except for my worst defeat and the only time I came close to crying. That was in the F.A. Cup at Aston Villa and we outplayed them throughout the match but Derek Dougan scored and in the last minute Vic Rouse left a cross slip through his hands to send us out 4-3. We were all devastated although the Aston Villa fans came up and patted us on the back and said: "You were unlucky." Unfortunately its a different atmosphere nowadays.

It was very friendly everywhere

us in the first division but we played football the way I like to see it played. I'd rather see good football in a lower division than awful stuff in the first.

However I was elated about promotion to the first division in 1969 even though I didn't feel the team had the necessary ability to survive.

Although we had a reputation for buying players we also had to improve the ground and a lot of money went on that rather than the squad, we didn't exactly buy quality. I had a season ticket and playing against Man United was wonderful although I remember it less than lots of other games of less importance.

I don't think the game was as dominated by money as it is now, you always expect to lose good players but I was devastated by Kenny Sansom going, more so than Ian Wright. When Kenny left it signalled the demise of a great team. The side that Wright played in doesn't even approach what the Team of the 80s could have achieved.

More recently the greatest moment was the semi final against Liverpool although the way they approached the Cup Final replay upset me. I've also been unhpapy with the style of football in recent years. If you're gonna go down at least go down in style.

My all time best team ...

Bill Glazier: He was the most consistent keeper. Even though I watched John Jackson throughout his career, I don't think Bill made as many mistakes. Jackson had a dodgy start at Palace and was blamed for a number of goals. He wasn't that popular when he started off.

I think Jackson suffered in the way Paul Hammond did in trying to follow a big favourite. Paul was on the verge of being a great keeper when he went. We've had very few bad goalkeepers.

Johnny McNicholl: Palace haven't had many good right backs. He was a two-footed player and could make good forward runs, he was good at overlapping and could beat people. He had a good shot on him.

Kenny Sansom: The other contenders were Harry McDonald, who played in the 40s, a brilliant player, and Don Townsend, the father of Andy. The other two didn't play in the first division and Kenny to my mind is the best player Palace ever had. He was a good tackler and a good attacker, he had everything. I'd like to think Kenny wouldn't have gone if he hadn't got into financial difficulties but when he went it started the break up.

Cliff Holton: Came to Palace as a centre forward towards the end of his career. He was very tall, good in the air, had a shot as hard as a bullet and, when he eventually moved back, ended up as a sort of second centre half, but he could still attack and score goals.

Ian Evans: He was very mobile. I thought Alan Stephenson was also very good and Len Choules, who was like a greyhound and had a tremendous stride. But Evans to me was supremely skillful and for sheer all round ability he was the best.

Peter Burridge: Came to us as a number 10, didn't perform too well and dropped back to number 6 and played like a Trojan. He was very left footed and had one of the best shots I've ever seen.

He was a powder puff up front but tackled like a tiger at wing-half. Apart from Jim Cannon's goal against Ipswich in 1979, the best goal I ever saw Palace score was a Burridge volley from about five yards outside the area after a Holton cross from the left touchline. It was pure perfection, those two together were tremendous

Peter Taylor: He beats Peter Berry and Vince Hilaire into my team. He was fast, tricky, accurate with his crosses and great with corners.

Taylor could beat people inside out with either foot and had everything a winger should have. I don't think the standard mattered, he just had natural ability.

Johnny Byrne: I've already said a lot about him. He was a trememndous player with supreme skill.

Ian Wright: He was a nice lad when he was with us. There are so many to choose from, I liked Freddie Kurz in the 1940s, Mike Deakin, Dave Swindlehurst, Rachid Harkouk and Jeff Bourne was brilliant but Wright was a cut above.

Ronnie Allen was a deep lying centre forward. He was a poacher but his great asset was that he laid on a lot of goals. Ian Wright would score 90 a season if he was playing with Allen.

Don Rogers: He could beat people. I remember being totally amazed once when he was in a one-to-one situation and the keeper saved it. I'd never seen him miss before.

The first time I saw him was on TV playing for Swindon in the League Cup final against Arsenal and he scored two goals.

That was enjoyable enough in itself but to have Rogers on one wing and Taylor on the other was tremendously exciting.

Son reined at Palace

By Anthony D. Powe

My first visit to Selhurst Park was in May 1957. I actually came not to see Palace but their division three (south) opponents Torquay United, who had to win what was the last match of the season in order to gain promotion to the second division. Torquay could only draw, Ipswich won and the Gulls stayed down.

My first experience of Palace as a supporter was on Spetember 12, 1959. It began an association which has lasted 32 years. Palace were in divison four at the time and beat Hartlepool 5-2. They then scored three against Stockport, eight against Watford, another three against Chester and finally nine against Barrow. Five matches and 28 goals in less than a month. I was hooked. However it didn't last and the season petered out with a final finish of only eighth.

The following season we began in fine style with a 9-2 win against Accrington Stanley. Palace scored 110 goals that year and failed to score in only six matches. Twice the attendance figure broke the fourth division record and five times there were more than 20,000. We were promoted to division three.

I watched many fine performance over the next nine seasons as Palace progressed from division four to division one.

In those early days as a supporter and a young father, I had to combine duties of watching Palace and looking after my young son. No problem. I bought him to Selhurst Park, tied one end of a long piece of rope to his walking reins and the other end to the bottom of the floodlight pylons. I saw the match and he was safe.

My favourite memory of watching Palace concerns the F.A. Cup quarter-final with Leeds in 1965. We were travelling to Selhurst in my mini-van when it got a puncture. There was no jack, so myself and five or six other supporters lifted the van up by hand and changed the wheel in about three minutes flat to make sure we got there. Last year, I received a new Palace shirt as a present and decided to wear it in one of my regular football matches. Unfortunately I finshed up with a broken ankle and when I came round in hospital, my mate insists the first thing I said was: "Is my Palace shirt okay?"

TELSTAR

Peter Winfield looks back on the Swinging Sixties and picks out some of the more unusual Palace moments

Telstar by the Tornados muffles through the PA while I slither and slide on the mud of the Whitehorse Lane end. The damp, autumn night air is thick with Old Holborn and the aroma of meat pies. A 2-2 draw with Shrewsbury and I go home on the 157 as happy as a sandboy.

With the wisdom of hindsight, the omens that night were crystal clear. An electronic dirge in celebration of a small sphere in orbit, followed by a distinctly uninspired performance against one of the less distinguished sides in the division.

Out of such ordinariness was born a lifelong allegiance. As an elver miraculously returns from the Sargasso Sea to the distant homeland of its mother, so a strange compulsion took hold. Thirty-one years on and from eighty miles distance I return with sons and daughter equally smitten.

Increasingly, small children (and not so small children) find instant favour and satisfaction with The Winner. Their allegiance begins and ends with a cup final victory or a championship clincher, viewed of course from the comfort of an armchair or even an executive box.

When Palace graced Wembley in 1990, my deep sense of pride was drawn from a myriad of memories – and not simply those concerning the result. The sentiment of the following recollections will, I hope, be recognised by all who love the club.

F.A. CUP second round at home to Mansfield Town, November 24, 1962. I take my dear old Auntie Lily to her first ever proper football match at the ripe old age of 75. We watch from the stand as Palace are less able than their opponents at mastering the swamp-like conditions. This doesn't stop us hollering and stamping our feet, willing a miracle. This arrives in the shape of a last minute penalty. Swarthy penalty king Ronnie Allen nervelessly converts. The Mansfield team takes great exception to the referee's late intervention. Rather than surround him with the more familiar finger wagging and howls of abuse, all eleven form two orderly lines either side of the players tunnel and slow handclap the referee all the way back to the dressing room which earns the whole lot a booking.

F.A. CUP second round replay away to Mansfield Town, November 26, 1962. Inspired by the referee's zeal, Mansfield win 7-2.

DIVISION THREE. Away to Colchester. March 21, 1964. A warm spring afternoon. Promotion in the air. Hard, uneven pitch. Several lost balls over the covered end. The score is 1-1 and an Act of God intervenes as in a period of no more than five minutes the pitch is transformed from the Sahara Desert into Norwood Lakes. Match abandoned. Back at the station, we check the timetable for Wednesday nights.

APRIL 15, 1964. Away to Colchester in the replay. Draw 1-1.

DERBY at the Baseball Ground in the second division. April 25, 1964. A cold, wet, grey afternoon, floodlights barely penetrating the gloom. One minute to three, we pant through the turnstiles, Burton Ale warm on our breath. We nip up the stairs. The Palace number 10 kicks off, dashes forward, receives the return and fires home from the edge of the box. (This takes six seconds to read – try it.) Charlie and I leap and embrace in joy and disbelief. "Oi," from below, "what the f*** are you two doing up there?" Then we realise we had seen it all from the half-time scoreboard gantry. An entry in the *Guinness Book of Records* for Keith Smith and we had the best view in the house.

JANUARY 22, 1966. Away to Carlisle

Did you know?

- It is not only Charlton and Wimbledon that have ground shared at Selhurst Park. Millwall also had a spell at Selhurst in 1945-46 when the Den was closed because of bomb damage.
- Selhurst Park hosted an England home match versus Wales in 1926 (better view than Wembley too!) and also staged two games in the 1948 Olympic Football tournament.
- Crystal Palace were the first fourth division side to win the *Evening Standard* London 5-a-Side Tournament at Wembley Arena. The tournament started in 1954 and in 1956 a decision was taken to invite all the London League Clubs. This was justified when Palace won it in 1959. On the way we beat Spurs 2-1 with goals by Budgie Byrne and Roy Summersby, then knocked out the other North London giant Arsenal with a single goal by Byrne and in the final thrashed Charlton 4-1 with a hat-trick for Byrne and another by Roy Colfar getting the crowd on its feet.

Harold Palmer wrote in the *Evening Standard*: "Arsenal and Spurs may have been the clubs with the most supporters at the Empire Pool Wembley on May 6th last, but I question whether any club had such enthusiastic, vociferous supporters as the Palace."

The win made up for a 1-0 defeat by Leyton Orient in the previous year's final.

Palace won the torunament again in 1969 but when it was relaunched in 1993 only 13 Palace supporters went and we were knocked out in the first round by Wimbledon on penalties. The Palace at least have the past to look back on in one of the few competitions in which we have a tradition of success.

Compiled by David London

in the F.A. Cup third round. We spill out of the coach at 6am into the Brunton Park mist, bleary eyed, stiff and hung over. Five hours of kick and rush in the adjacent municipal park sets us up a treat for opening time.

At two minutes to three, the home skipper places the revered mascot on the centre spot – a real stuffed fox. Big Tim, brylcreemed D.A. glistening in the pale winter sun leaps the hoarding and reaches the centre circle as the captains exchange pleasantries. Big Tim shakes each by the hand, a moment of warmth for all to savour. A Chelsea boot arcs deftly under the belly of the fox which loops the loop. Big Tim lumbers back to the anonymity of the terraces unpunished. Serves us right really. Stuffed fox, stuffed Palace, 3-0.

WOLVES away. September 7, 1966. Palace have started well, eight points out of ten. A chilly autumn evening. We check our team sheets: "At number eight for Crystal Palace, Steve Kember in place of David Burnside."

"At No 10 for Wolves David Burnside in place of ..." No printing errors here. A genuine transfer deal struck just hours before the game. Early in the match I'm puzzled by a rich Black Country voice describing every move. I look round.

There's something odd about four men in cloth caps and overcoats. The Black Country voice stands next to them. They are blind. Yet their expressions betray their passions for their beloved Wolves – their need to be there soaking it up. I doubt that these men are still alive but if they are they would undoubtedly still choose to stand in their preferred place.

The scorers in a 1-1 draw? Dave Burnside and Steve Kember.

WORKING for British Rail has its advantages, free rail travel for a start. March 5, 1969 and we're away to Derby in the second division. I wangle a dental appointment for 4pm, the train leaves St Pancras at 4.28. Charlie and the others get off work earlier and travel in style because Bob's got this Wolseley – as used by the constabulary in Ealing comedies.

Derby are riding high under Clough and Taylor – miles ahead at the top and invincible at home. We hover in midtable, despite a couple of recent wins.

Some of the great goals of the 60s and early 70s as seen by the *Croydon Advertiser*

The ball goes in the net five times – all efforts disallowed by a decidedly myopic referee. We play unbelievably well yet prepare ourselves for the sucker punch – which never comes. We net for the sixth time and, incredibly, it counts, 1-0.

A couple of celebratory pints means its too late to get across London from St Pancras. Luckily there's room in the Wolseley. We join the M1 and judder to a halt. Bob gets out, opens the door and – wallop! We look at each other. Bob closes the boot, climbs in, turns the engine and off we go.

Six miles later we judder to a halt. Bob orders Charlie out and joins him at the rear. Desperate remedies are required. Bob lifts the boot lid. This time Charlie is stuffed in the boot, hammer at the ready to clout the offending petrol pump. So the scene is set. We agree to stop at every service station so that we can each take a turn. At Watford Gap we pull up, two get out. One opens the boot, the stiff gets out and the other gets in, hammer at the ready. Boot closed, away we go.

Between service areas the engine shudders, but we hear the trusty dull thud, thud, thud and on we go. We get to Norbury by 3am. Bob, good bloke that he is, agrees to drive us home to Caterham in comfort in his works Escort van. He parks the Wolseley and gets in the van. The starter motor turns and turns ... and turns. Lights go on, curtains twitch. We push the thing and it fires ten yards from the Brighton Road. I get home at 4.15am and get up for work at 6.45 feeling a little stiff.

The following month Palace go into the penultimate game at home to Fulham having won five and drawn five since Derby. We need one point to clinch promotion and Fulham are already down. We trail 2-0 at half time. Deep in the dressing room Bert Head reaches for his hammer. We cruise the second half to win 3-2.

The Sixties ... swinging Palace

From division four to division one in less than ten years

In 1960 Accrington Stanley weren't long for this world and, on the first day of the season, Palace helped push the impoverished northerners a little further down the road to oblivion by thrashing them 9-2.

Our new signing from Millwall Ron Heckman marked his debut with two goals as 15,653 people were treated to a super show in which Johnny Byrne and Alan Woan scored hat-tricks. It was a grand opening for Arthur Rowe, the new Palace manager. Rowe had been Palace's first choice when they were looking for a replacement for Cyril Spiers. But he had been reluctant so George Smith was appointed with Rowe as assistant. After two unfulfilling seasons, Smith resigned and Rowe agreed to step up.

Rowe was first and foremost a Spurs man. He first signed for the Lilywhites in 1927 although his career was interrupted by the war. After he was demobbed in 1945 he became manager of Chelmsford and won the Southern League Cup for them before returning to White Hart Lane as manager at the beginning of the 1949-50 season. In his first season, he led Tottenham to the second division championship with his famous brand of "push and run" football. He followed that with the league championship in 1950-51 – the first in the club's history. The season after, Spurs were runners-up and Cup semi-finalists. But Rowe was plagued by ill-health and he left Spurs to work in the less stressful world of amateur football with the famous Pegasus. He was tempted back to the professional game as a scout for West Brom through his association with the Baggies' manager Vic Buckingham who was also a friend of Rowe's eventual successor at Palace, Dick Graham.

36,478! ENOUGH TO MAKE POOR OLD CHARLTON GO GREEN WITH ENVY

Although Palace had faded at the end of the previous campaign, the only real cloud on the horizon was a threatened strike by players over freedom of contract. Led by Fulham's veteran forward Jimmy Hill, the Professional Footballers' Association finally got what they wanted, including the lifting of the maximum wage restriction and the season went ahead as planned – which was just as well because it was a good one for Palace. After thrashing Accrington, we won our next three games including a 5-1 away success at Doncaster. To say the home side were outclassed was an understatement, the biggest threat came from the weather – the rain was so heavy that at one stage the referee had to take the players off the field.

Byrne got on the scoresheet in each of the first four matches and had nine goals to his credit. Alan Woan was hot on his heels with seven. Although there was a minor setback when Hartlepool held us to a 2-2 draw at Selhurst, we still led the table on goal average from Peterborough United, who were next to visit Selhurst Park. "The Posh", as they liked to be known, were the fourth division's new boys, having been voted in at Gateshead's expense on the strength of some stirling F.A. Cup performances.

The interest in the match was phenomenal and a fourth division record attendance of 36,478 was established. Unfortunately it was the visitors who took the points with two unanswered goals. The balance was restored the following week when Palace, despite being accused of "trying to walk the ball into the net", enjoyed a confidence boosting 2-1 win at fellow promotion hopefuls Wrexham. Peterborough lost at Mansfield.

And so it continued, with Palace and Peterborough running neck and neck for first place. Unfortunately, Palace's championship hopes were damaged relatively early on. In the return at Peterborough on September 12, we were well and truly pasted and the 4-1 scoreline was flattering in the extreme. Peterborough were three up at half time and by all accounts it could have been ten. In the end only the heroics of Vic Rouse prevented a rout. He saved a twice taken penalty and pulled off countless other saves as the home team threatened to run riot. Terry Bly scored a hat-trick as "the probing penetrative Posh attack cut Palace down to size".

That pushed us out of the promotion placings and it took us until the end of October to get back to the top again. After the chastening experience at London Road, Palace had struggled to regain their form and drew the next three games against Carlisle, Southport and Rochdale.

At Southport, we attracted a best of season attendance of 5,444 to Haig Avenue, while Carlisle's visit to Selhurst Park on September 17, brought the 100,000th supporter of the season through the Palace turnstiles. But 16,000 were left disappointed by a scraped 1-1 draw thanks to a Roy Summersby goal which Carlisle bitterly claimed was offside. After another draw, with Rochdale at Spotland, Byrne personally saw to it that Palace got back on the rails. Southport were the unlucky recipients of his four goal salvo in a 5-0 win. That performance, among others, tempted Arsenal to come sniffing round, but their manager George Swindin was soon put off by Rowe. "Johnny is going to play soccer in a higher division – with us," he said. "There is no question of selling him."

While he was still doing National Service, Byrne's schedule was hectic to say the least. He had travelled down from his base at Warwick to play in the Hitchin match, for example, then returned in time to play for the Army against Hearts on the following Monday. He was also attracting the interest of the England under-23 scouts and the *Croydon*

Advertiser proclaimed: "There is no question that when he is able to spend all his time with the club, those selectors will be there again. And the odds are on Byrne winning his chance." The *Advertiser* later pointed out that there was "74 shopping days until Christmas, 240 days before Private John Byrne becomes Mr Byrne again."

Although he was unquestionably the star of the show, Byrne was ably supported by the other forwards and in the next match Summersby grabbed three in a comfortable victory over Mansfield. But on the following Monday, we slumped to a surprise 5-2 defeat at Stockport, although there were vindicating circumstances. Byrne pulled up with thigh trouble which disappointed not only the Palace followers but a host of club scouts. Man United's Matt Busby was spotted at Edgeley Park along with representatives from Wolves, Blackpool, Sheffield Wednesday and Man City.

But there was still no budging Palace. Wait fully recognised the potential of the club's greatest asset: "If Byrne went our gates would drop by about 5,000." It was revenue the club could not afford to lose, even to the temptation of an immediate cash injection, although it was difficult to resist – the club accounts revealed a loss of £3,398, mainly because £8,011 had been spent on transfers. However gate receipts had increased from £53,813 to £55,839.

There were problems in the treatment room where Byrne joined a long list of casualties. Alf Noakes had pulled a muscle, Len Choules had only just returned to the side after six weeks on the sidelines with a broken collarbone, Roy Colfar had knee trouble, Bill Robson flu and Dave Sexton was a long term casualty with fluid on the knee, ruling him out for the rest of the season. Johnny Roche and Gwynne Evans, although back in training, weren't match fit.

Rowe decided to move into the transfer market. Dennis Uphill joined us on October 6 from Watford in time to make his debut at home to Barrow and he scored twice in a 4-2 success. Rowe knew all about Uphill – he had first signed him for Spurs in 1949.

Uphill was a member of Rowe's championship side of 1951 and remained at White Hart Lane until he was swapped for Reading's Johnny Brooks, the father of Palace's 1980's midfielder Shaun.

Away from the league, Palace were given a straight forward looking first round F.A. Cup tie at home to non-league Hitchin, who were managed by former Palace boss Laurie Scott. Hitchin were £800 in the red but their share of the gate money from the best crowd of the round, 21,118, cleared the debt. Just what the doctor ordered. What Hitchin's doctor did not order was a Budgie Byrne inspired 6-2 thrashing.

The bonfire night parties after Palace had disposed of Hitchin were happy affairs. It was our fifth successive win and goals were not in the least difficult to come by. But an upset was waiting. We lost a seven goal thriller at Oldham even though Heckman grabbed a couple for Palace. He followed that with another to add to Summersby's brace as Palace returned to winning ways against Workington.

With Byrne, Heckman and Summersby all finding the net regularly, we were set fair for promotion and our prospects were strengthened towards the end of November when former Palace keeper Dick Graham became Rowe's assistant manager. Graham, something of a disciplinarian, had had a varied career outside football including hairdressing, running a pub in Croydon and writing a sports column for the *Croydon Advertiser*. Most recently he had been assistant manager at WBA. At the end of the month, we made our Cup exit after a replay at Watford, who'd achieved a shut out in front of 33,699 at Selhurst. At least we could say we were going to concentrate on the league – and mean it.

December was a good month. Palace went unbeaten throughout, dropping just two points, one of which was a home draw with Exeter – particularly disappointing because we'd beaten the Grecians in the Boxing Day fixture at St James' Park the day before.

We soon made up for the lapse by whacking Doncaster 5-1 for the second time. But that was followed by a shock 3-0 reverse at Chester.

Three goal-filled performances followed. Hartlepool were beaten 4-2 at the Victoria Ground, Wrexham 3-2 at Selhurst and Chester punished for their earlier impudence with a 5-1 lesson in front of a relatively small 14,150 at Selhurst. But a long trip to Carlisle proved fruitless. It was a temporary aberration soon erased by four more wins. Palace were now approaching the final furlong.

Budgie Byrne had at last forced himself into the England reckoning. On March 1, he won his first representative honour – for Young England against Young Scotland. Although the Scots won 1-0, Byrne was praised for his performance. The *Daily Mirror* said: "In the first half, Brabrook received a superb service from centre forward Johnny Byrne. But in situations that screamed for a quick return pass to the Crystal Palace cockney, Brabrook too often blazed away over the bar or carried the ball too far. If Byrne had received anything like that sort of support himself from Crowe and Dobing it might have made a big difference."

Three days later, Byrne was on the scoresheet for Palace as we completed the "double" over Gillingham. Things were looking good when Palace suddenly got an attack of promotion jitters. The first of four successive defeats came at Bradford, where ex-QPR player George Petchey's goal was insufficient to answer three second-half strikes by the home team. It was especially disappointing because of the "four pointer" aspect – Bradford were one of the chasing pack.

The following week in another promotion shoot-out, this time at home to Northampton, we went down again. The near 21,000 crowd were stunned by a superb performance by Northampton's Barry Lines, who set up three goals with perfect crosses after Summersby had opened the scoring. It wasn't until Northampton had sealed the game that Heckman gave us hope. But it was too little too late. Northampton were beginning a meteoric rise that saw them climb in successive seasons to the first division. They sank back almost as quickly.

Byrne made his third England under-23 appearance against Germany and celebrated with a goal and all the plaudits in a 4-1 victory. "Glory for Johnny Byrne, the boy centre-forward from the Cinderella fourth division at White Hart Lane last night," said the *Daily Mirror*. "His intelligent passing and positioning stamps him as a great prospect for England's World Cup squad."

His goal was a peach too: "The kid from the football league wilderness took the pass in his stride ... went forward one, two, three, four steps and hammered a perfectly placed shot just under the crossbar." But while Byrne was able to take his mind off the promotion battle, Palace were struggling to get any rhythm going. The next slip was at the Recreation Ground where Petchey found the net after moving up front when Uphill was "pulled out of the attack". That was in the 85th minute which was too late because former Palace man Alan Woan had already given Aldershot a two goal advantage with a 69th minute strike under what the *Croydon Advertiser* called "the candlelight glow of the Hampshire club's floodlights".

Desperate to halt the slide, Rowe rang the changes for the Good Friday derby at home to Millwall. Geoff Truett came in for the increasingly unpopular Uphill, whose form had deserted him, and Heckman was left out against his old club, making way for Roy Colfar, who'd only made two appearances so far. But Palace were outplayed by determined opponents, still harbouring promotion ambitions of their own, in front of a new fourth division record crowd of 37,774. The change of Football League structure in 1991-92 guarantees it will never be broken.

With Rouse having a particularly unsteady game, Millwall ran the show. Peter Burridge rattled the crossbar before David Jones gave the Lions the lead. Burridge then stretched the advantage after 23 minutes when he latched onto a kick from keeper Reg Davis.

Palace had moved Byrne into an out-and-out centre-forward's role in place of Uphill with Petchey at inside left but it didn't work and one report said "Petchey looked utterly lost". On April Fools' Day, fine performances from Byrne and Choules helped us somewhat nervously overcome Oldham 2-1 in front of ITV's *Sports Special* cameras. The Latics could have snatched an undeserved draw if Branagan hadn't put an 85th minute penalty wide of Rouse's post. Nevertheless, the win took us to within touching distance of promotion. Playing with an injured right foot, Byrne took both goals with his weaker left. The *Daily Mirror* described it as "another international class performance".

Palace were revitalised and, on Easter Monday, gained revenge over Millwall in a match that drew a disappointing 15,502 to the Den, more than 20,000 down on the fixture of three days earlier. Millwall's Brady gave Palace the opportunity they were looking for with a silly mistake, allowing the restored Heckman to open the scoring. Heckman then turned provider, running along the line to set up Tom Barnett to grab the second. It was Millwall's turn to become rattled and in a bizarre incident, keeper Reg Davis lost his cool and chucked a clump of mud at left half Alan Anderson.

It was our first win at the Den for 11 seasons and edged us a little further along the promotion path. Only a couple more points were needed, but the bad news was that the injury list was mounting again. Byrne had an infected toe and Barnett was receiving treatment for a knock he collected against Millwall.

Just when it looked as if Palace had turned the corner, they misfired again, this time at Workington. The Cumbrians prolonged the agonising wait with a single goal at Borough Park. Our cause wasn't helped by losing Johnny Byrne to an army call. He was in Oran playing for the British Army against the French Army

We had a break from league action for a week and used the free time to entertain the Brazilian touring side Bangu in a friendly. Despite ecstatic reviews for the quality of the football, just over 12,000 saw the visitors achieve the only victory of their tour, 2-0. Meanwhile, Byrne's full England appearance moved a little closer when he was named in the Young England squad to play the full England team at Stamford Bridge. This was followed by the news that he had been selected to join the full squad's summer tour of Austria, Portugal and Italy.

The Squad:
Goalkeepers: Ron Springett (Sheff Wed) and Alan Hodgkinson (Sheff United), Full Backs: Jimmy Armfield (Blackpool), McNeill (Middlesbrough), Angus (Burnley). Half Backs: Bobby Robson (West Brom), Peter Swan (Sheff Wed), Miller (Burnley), Ron Flowers (Wolves) and Anderson (Sunderland). Forwards: Bryan Douglas (Blackburn), John Connelly (Burnley), Jimmy Greaves (Chelsea), George Eastham (Arsenal), Bobby Smith (Spurs), Gerry Hitchens (Villa), Johnny Haynes (Fulham), Johnny Byrne (Palace) and Bobby Charlton (Man United).

To celebrate, Palace made Byrne captain for the home game against Aldershot. We needed two points to secure promotion, but were understandably nervous. Meanwhile, the mid-table 'Shots tried to make life as awkward as possible. The tense crowd of nearly 20,000 were increasingly angered by the visitors' offside trap and their frustration was compounded when the unthinkable happened. Alan Woan, formerly of Palace, set up Carl Taylor to hit an angled drive over Rouse. Palace almost collapsed and Rouse was called upon to perform a damage limitation exercise. In one desperate scramble, Terry Long injured himself clearing a shot off the line and was reduced to a hobbling passenger limping on the wing attempting to be of nuisance value.

But finally it all came right. Having weathered the storm, Byrne set up the equaliser for Summersby and then Johnny

Super Palace

Just before they went onto the field to lick Bradford, Crystal Palace players were told by manager Arthur Rowe – "There are 15,000 people out there in the most wretched conditions we've had all season. Let's make it worth their while." And that's just what Palace did! If this is fourth division football then let's have four fourth divisions. It was superb and the 15,000 spectators were privileged to see the last minute goal of a lifetime by local hero Johnny Byrne. He fastened onto a loose ball in the middle of the field, took it out onto the wing and began to cut in. He dribbled his way twice round goalkeeper Gabbie and once each past the very good full backs Lawton and Lightowler and tapped the ball into the net."

From the Sunday Dispatch – October 23, 1960

McNicholl made a galloping run for Petchey to cross and Tom Barnett met the ball with a firm header.

"Palace go up" said the unimaginative headline in the *Daily Mirror*. The story was more quaint though. "Two captains and a cat clinched promotion in this fast and lively game." The captains were, of course, skipper-for-the-day Byrne and regular leader McNicholl. The cat was Tibby, "the coal black pet of Selhurst Park", who had wandered onto the pitch in the second half. Tibby was something of a lucky charm. He had strayed into the ground earlier in the season when a 5-0 victory over Southport had ended a bad run and been kept on as a lucky mascot. Lucky he proved again as Palace gained promotion for the first time since 1920-21. Although the *Mirror* made much of the cat's significance even they were forced to acknowledge the guiding role of "silver haired genius" Arthur Rowe.

On the following evening there was more good news when Peterborough were sunk by Bradford. Palace's championship hopes, seemingly killed off by those four defeats before Easter were still flickering. But the ball remained in Peterborough's court and on Tuesday, April 25, they went to Southport needing one more point. At one stage they trailed 3-1, but two goals from the irrepressible Bly, who set a fourth division scoring record with 52 goals, levelled the scores and Palace, barring a mathematical miracle, were forced to settle for second place.

We relaxed and avenged our earlier 5-2 defeat at Stockport. Byrne, who had pulled up with thigh trouble in the first match, made County pay in the second with "two flashes of individual brilliance that turned the game in Palace's favour". The reason the press got worked up came in the 63rd minute. "The young England star jinked past five defenders and fired in a shot which goalkeeper Smith could only parry to Roy Summersby, who netted," the *Daily Mirror* explained. As if that wasn't enough, he repeated the manoeuvre almost exactly for Summersby to crash in his second prompting the conclusion: "Byrne was brilliant."

In the final match of the season, Palace celebrated with a single goal victory over York when Summersby scored for the fourth consecutive game in front of 17,885. It was our 29th victory – a fourth division record. It was also our 110th league goal of the season. In their first league campaign, Peterborough took the championship and most of the praise but, from then on, it was Palace who made better progress.

While everybody basked in the glory of promotion, Rowe wasted no time strengthening his squad for the third division, buying six players. First in was John Cartwright from West Ham, who later coached Palace's F.A. Youth Cup winning teams of the 70s and managed the England Youth team. Andy Smillie had also played first division football for West Ham while Eddie Werge, a winger, was signed from Charlton where he'd found it difficult to hold down a first team place. Rowe also signed Roy Little from Brighton, who had played in both Manchester City's Cup Final sides of the 1950s collecting a winners' medal on his second visit.

But the most significant signings were from West Brom. No doubt encouraged by the links both Arthur Rowe and Dick Graham had with Albion, Palace moved for centre-forward Ronnie Allen and centre-half Brian Wood. At the time, Allen was Albion's all time record scorer with 206 league goals in 11 seasons with the Baggies. He had five full England caps, the last of which was against Wales in 1955.

"I was walking along Croydon High Street one morning when I met Gerry Williams, sports correspondent for the *Croydon Advertiser.* We got talking about the game. As I was watching Crystal Palace regularly, he suggested that maybe I would like to contribute a weekly column to the *Advertiser.* I was naturally delighted as this gave me a real interest in football – although I can't say I was always very kind in some of what I wrote about the Palace. Having been a player, I thought I knew a fair bit about the game and from time to time I used to give the club a bit of "stick". They got quite annoyed at me, which they were entitled to do. At that time I didn't appreciate the problems of running a club from the management side – although I have since learned."

DICK GRAHAM EXPLAINS HOW HE RETURNED TO THE FOOTBALL SCENE

Palace announced a new bonus scheme for their assault on division three. Each player would be given an additional £1 for every thousand spectators above 16,000 that they could attract while the reserves were to receive £1 for every spectator above 1,500. They would also receive the bonus again for the following week's away game. "Not much soccer slavery about those terms," observed the *Croydon Advertiser*.

Ronnie Allen immediately began to lead from the front and when the first tables were published, Palace were top on alphabetical order – with the same points and goal average as Reading.

Three wins were followed by two draws and another successful season looked in prospect but, after a late summer flowering, Palace began to wither. By October, we'd added just one more win and were out of the league cup, beaten 5-2 by QPR at Loftus Road.

Although we had little difficulty finding the net, it was the defence that was letting us down. The only respite was in the F.A. Cup where the visit of Portsmouth, who had just been relegated to division three and were on their way back up as champions, attracted a first round attendance of 30,000. Byrne and Heckman illustrated just what Palace were capable of, giving the visitors' defence a torrid time in an easy 3-0 victory.

We made further progress against non-league Bridgewater Town in the second round where Heckman got two more. This set up a third round tie at Villa Park in which Palace gave a superb performance to push their first division hosts all the way, only succumbing right at the death. Byrne served further notice of his ability to score at the highest level with two outstanding goals.

Villa took the lead after ten minutes through Harry Burrows but within seven minutes we were ahead courtesy of Byrne and Uphill. Before half-time Peter McParland had equalised but four minutes after the break Palace shocked Villa again, Heckman crossing for Byrne to head in. But we couldn't hold out and Derek Dougan put Villa back on terms. In the last minute, Villa literally fluked it. Burrows floated in a cross which eluded everybody including Rouse and sailed into the top corner.

In the league, Palace struggled, although an improved spell in November and December saw plenty of scoring including the best victory of the season – 7-2 over Torquay. But on the whole a team which boasted one of the most prodigious talents in English football and plenty of experience did itself little justice. On January 13, in a 4-3 victory over Halifax, the appropriately named Bill Glazier took over from Vic Rouse in goal. Glazier played 11 games before Rouse returned although Palace achieved only one victory as the young keeper failed to keep a single clean sheet. But it was clear he had something and the writing was on the wall for Rouse.

Our last victory of the season was against Shrewsbury and so began a run that lasted until we finally beat QPR on September 12, 1962 – a sequence of 20 matches without a win, still our worst ever. Glazier took his appearance total to 13 before the end of the campaign and it proved lucky when, in the last of these, he managed a shut-out against Port Vale. But the real responsibility for goals conceded lay not with the keepers but with the men in front of them.

Palace finished the 1961-62 season, almost inevitably, without Budgie Byrne. It had only been a matter of time and eventually it was West Ham who stumped up a British transfer record of £65,000 to take Palace's golden boy to Upton Park. The big clubs had watched and waited long enough. It was clear Byrne would be worth every penny and he went on to establish himself in the England side and collect an F.A. Cup winners' medal with the Hammers. His last Palace goal came in his final appearance – ironically a 4-1 defeat at Peterborough – which began a dismal run to end the season. Byrne's departure left both club and supporters with an almighty hangover.

Aside from the football, 1961-62 was also the season in which Crystal Palace received the honour of having a ship named after them. The Grimsby based trawler "Crystal Palace" joined Britain's deep sea fishing fleet. It served in two Cod Wars and, on one occasion, was the subject of an attempted ramming by an Icelandic gunboat.

There was even a reported superstition among the crew that a Palace victory would ensure a good trip. "Crystal Palace" was eventually scrapped in 1978 after a deal between Britain and Iceland over fishing rights effectively ended the reign of the big trawlers.

The post-Byrne gloom extended into the new season and

Sardines and tomato soup

Hulton Deutsch

November 4, '61. Gwynne Evans gets above the Portsmouth attackers as Palace ease into the second round of the Cup.

AS AN ardent away traveller of 30 years' standing, I always take sardine sandwiches and tomato soup to sustain me on the journey.

This tradition was established in 1962 when I was 14 years old and went on my first away 'special' to the memorable F.A. Cup third round tie at Aston Villa.

Dad and I got up in what seemed to be the middle of the night and, armed with a packed lunch Mum had made, we made our way to Penge West station.

As a youngster it seemed as if the whole of south London was on the train.

It was a freezing cold morning, but the camaraderie and joviality kept us warm. The journey seemed to take an eternity with long delays on the tracks just getting across London.

When we opened the packed lunch, Mum had done sardine sandwiches and tomato soup and included some of the remaining Christmas cake. I have never known anything taste so good. Villa Park seemed enormous. Why is it that the older we get the smaller grounds become?

The match was a well documented spectacular. Palace, who were in division three, did themselves proud, but lost 4-3.

After the game we walked the streets of a very cold Birmingham for an hour and a half because the train back was not due until 6.30pm. Everywhere was dark and closed and it seemed amazingly cold. We got home at midnight, very tired. Every match since, I have taken sardine sandwiches and tomato soup, but somehow it has never tasted the same as it did on that first away special.

Annette Legg

Palace got off to a dreadful start. By November, we were favourites to drop back into the fourth division. Millwall's Peter Burridge had been signed in the summer to replace Byrne but his arrival coincided with an opening in which we won just one of our first 16 games. Burridge had started with Athenian League Barnet, joined Orient in 1958 and then skippered Millwall to the fourth division title in 1962. He stayed with Palace until 1965 then moved to Charlton.

Palace combined dismal performances with more than their fair share of bad luck. At Hull on September 20 Stewart Imlach, a former Scotland international who had been a member of Nottingham Forest's F.A. Cup winning team of 1959, and George Petchey were both injured, yet we held out for a 0-0 draw with only nine fit men. Although Petchey rejoined the fray quite quickly, Imlach was out for more than a year. Then on October 20 at home to Notts County we lost Johnny McNicholl after only two minutes with a fractured cheekbone which brought down the curtain on his Palace career. The loss of these players allied to the post-Byrne blues did much to cause Palace's bad run.

But worse than all this was the death on Thursday August 30, 1962 of winger Ron Brett, who had returned to the club as part of the Byrne deal after a spell at West Ham, was killed in a car crash. This increased the gloom and so greatly affected Arthur Rowe that his health deteriorated. Soon after, doctors ordered him to retire leaving Dick Graham in charge, which was fitting because the assistant manager loved the club dearly and at one stage had even been chairman of the supporters' club. Rowe had always been

Beatlemania

All my friends at school were Beatle crazy. It was the 60s and new pop stars were appearing every day. Thousands of girls swooned to their heroes.

Me? I supported Palace.

No pop groups on my bedroom wall, it was full of posters of Palace players.

While others went to concerts I went to see the match. For me it was Johnny Byrne not John Lennon, George Petchey not George Harrison.

I would travel anywhere to see the skills of Cliff Holton, but not Cliff Richard. My parents, who incidentally had always wanted a boy, began to wonder if I was a normal girl.

All my pocket money went on Palace activities.

At school they were curious. I used to keep a small pocket book of pictures of Palace stars in my satchel.

On my way home from school one day it must have fallen out and was picked up by an elderly man, who must have been a Palace fan and kindly returned it to the school.

I was sent for by the headmistress. What was this book? She was unable to believe that any girl at her school would follow football. Luckily things have changed. Females at football are no longer an exception and now in the 90s those of us that go are no longer social outcasts. It wasn't always that way.

Annette Legg

Bertie: (Of Palace folklore heroes he's the best)

The following ditty should be sung (at the top of your voice, please) to the tune of the Benny Hill classic "Ernie"

You could see the wingers twitch as he raced across the pitch
And hear the screams of pain as they landed in the ditch
As he galloped up the touchline on his single minded quest
His name was Bertie Howe
Of Palace folklore heroes he's the best

Now Bert he loved the fullback role and wore his shirt with pride
And every week his man he'd seek with a forty-five yard slice
They said he wasn't good enough
He was clumsy, slow and dim
But Bertie left his autograph along their favoured limb.
They couldn't avoid old Bertie
(chorus: Bertie)
Of Palace folklore heroes he's the best.

Now Bert was what you'd call direct, he didn't beat about the bush
He got no fun from push and run, he preferred to run and push
Sky Blues' Ronnie Reece once got past him
With a clever swerve and touch
But, when he went to shoot, a dubbined boot
Connected with his crutch
You couldn't do that to old Bertie
(Chorus: Bertie)
Of Palace folklore heroes he's the best

I remember the game against
Coventry led by youthful Jimmy Hill
With an arkle grin and a prominent chin the size of Selsey Bill
He said our Bert was an animal
He preached a lot of s**t
When they (boo hiss) had George Curtis
Who was the hypocrite?
Certainly not Bertie

(chorus: Bertie)
Of Palace folklore heroes he's the best

Now Bertie had a rival
An evil looking man
The name 'Arry Cripps was on Millwall lips
He looked like Desperate Dan
At last there came a showdown
One reputation to shed
And when he saw the size of the geezer's thighs
It very near turned Bert's head
But they couldn't scare Bertie
(Chorus: Bertie)
Of Palace folklore heroes he's the best

Now both faced each other
And gave the hard case stare
And 'Arry waited for his chance
To kick Bert in the air
But Bertie was too quick for him
Things didn't go the way 'Arry planned
And a Mick McManus drop kick
Sent him spinning in the stand
That tickled old Bertie
(chorus Bertie)
Of Palace folklore heroes he's the best

But a manager's needs are manifold
And when Dick Graham had gone
Bullfrog Head, who managed instead,
Said it was time that Bert passed on.

Bertie was only fifty-two
But he didn't bitch or moan
Now I bet he's at ease
Cutting em off at the knees
At the Peckham Darby and Joan
We won't forget Bertie
(chorus: Bertie)
Of Palace folklore heroes he's the best
(chorus: diddle, diddle, dum)

By 'Baz'

quite easy going but Graham's contrasting style proved a shock. Some players were upset and reacted badly and performances suffered, culminating in a crushing 7-2 defeat at fourth division Mansfield in a Cup replay.

The players felt so strongly that a petition was made to the board for Graham's removal. But the board ignored the pleas and Palace moved into a more functional era. Results picked up however.

Graham knew his own mind and introduced the iron tackling of Bertie Howe at right back, while Burridge began to prosper under Palace's new style which became more direct and rugged. The long ball, far from being an invention of Graham Taylor and Dave Bassett in the 1980s, was employed with great accuracy and Graham's powerful new forward acquisitions, Cliff Holton from Watford and Dickie Dowsett from Bournemouth, began to prosper.

Bill Glazier, another in a generation of great English keepers. He was eventually transferred to Coventry for a world record fee for a goalie.
Illustration: Jason Axell

The first real signs of a revival came in the 3-0 drubbing of Millwall on an icy pitch on Boxing Day. The winter freeze then halted progress but Palace were rejuvenated. Bradford Park Avenue were slaughtered 6-0, Wrexham crushed 5-0 and Watford hammered 4-1 at Vicarage Road with Holton getting a hat-trick against his former club. Only the 1946-47 season finished later than the conclusion to 1962-63 when Palace went to South Yorkshire on May 22 and whipped Barnsley 4-0.

The battle for the keeper's shirt had been resolved with Glazier, who'd started the season as understudy, finally getting the nod over Rouse who moved to Oxford United, who were newly elected to the league.

Palace's improvement was due in no small part to the presence of Holton. The former Arsenal forward, whose physical presence alone caused problems for opposing defences, scored nine goals in 23 appearances which did much to haul Palace to the respectable, and unexpected, heights of 11th. Dowsett, meanwhile, grabbed 12 from the centre forward berth.

Having looked out for the count, Palace had lost only one of the last 15 games and served notice to the rest of the third division that a new force was about to take them by the scruff of the neck and rough them up. The onslaught was about to begin.

Even the normally unbiased BBC made it known that it was unimpressed by the Palace team which won back its second division place after an absence of 39 years. The *Sportsview Soccer Annual*, edited by Peter Dimmock, recounted a season in which Bill Shankly had led Liverpool to the championship in front of a Kop much given to singing Beatles numbers, West Ham and a certain Mr Byrne had lifted the F.A. Cup, after second division Preston had frightened everyone on their way to Wembley, and England began preparations to host the next World Cup. And tucked a little further back into the book was this:

"...the success story of the third division was the rise to power of Crystal Palace. Fifteen months earlier they were last but one and faced relegation. Dick Graham, their manager, could afford to scoff at those who criticised his team's enthusiastic style of play. Finesse and the subtleties of soccer have, unfortunately, little place in the Third Division.

Sometimes super-fitness and tactical ability must be a manager's prime consideration. Graham also gained maximum effort from his players and their reward was promotion.

Palace's promotion excited great interest in London, but their triumph was only a minor contribution to one of the most eventful seasons since the war."

Is it Real ... or is it our imagination

To mark the introduction of Palace's new floodlights, Crystal Palace played European Champions Real Madrid on April 18, 1962 in a friendly at Selhurst Park. It was Real's first visit to London and they were guaranteed £10,000 appearance money.

Although it rained heavily for 48 hours beforehand and Palace had had to put the prices up to cover the costs – the takings were £15,000 which secured the Glaziers a profit. A good crowd of 24,470 braved the cold to see Real, who fielded a full strength side, go two ahead in eight minutes. Heckman then scored from Palace's special guest Johnny Byrne's cross but, on the half hour, Ferenc Puskas hammered a 30 yarder to restore the two-goal advantage. It was 4-1 just before the break when Sanchez finished a move in which Puskas had combined with Alfredo Di Stefano. Palace responded after the interval with Andy Smillie scoring from close range and Terry Long hitting a 25 yarder to make it 4-3.

Palace: Rouse (Glazier), McNicholl, Little, Long, Wood, Petchey, Brett, Summersby, Byrne (West Ham), Smillie, Heckman (Lewis)
Real: Araquistain (Vicente) Casado, Miera, Sanchez (Ruiz), Santa-Maria (Marquitos), Pachin, Tejada, Del Sol (Pepillo), Di Stefano, Puskas, Gento.

Palace had signed Bobby Kellard a stocky midfield player from Southend. Although only 5'6" he still contributed extra power to the Palace side. But we began with a disastrous 5-1 thrashing at the hands of Jimmy Hill's Coventry City, who turned out to be the season's main rivals. Hill was new to management and had plenty to say for himself. And he chose to say most of it about Palace. Not for him the euphemisms of the BBC. Palace, in his book, were not "enthusiastic", they were dirty.

But Graham was not concerned with what Hill or the press thought. His team took a little while to get going but, like the steamroller they had become, once the momentum was built up it kept rolling and woe betide anyone who got in the way. A rich vein of form was struck which took us to the top and we led nearly all the way to the tape.

The defence, in direct contrast to the early days in division three, was now extremely tight. In one period between January 11 and March 18, when Walsall were shut out in a match hit by a first half snowstorm, Glazier kept eight successive home clean sheets. And in the away games during that period, no opponent scored more than once. Remarkably, Glazier's feat was not a record. That belongs to Millwall's George Lansdale who achieved 11 straight home clean sheets in 1920-21, the year Palace last won promotion to division two.

While the Selhurst fans had forgotten what it looked like to see an opposition goal, they certainly knew what to expect from the press. The *Daily Mirror* called Palace "experts of the snatch goal and dogged defence" and added "the football of these Dick Graham drilled men may not be entertaining but it certainly is effective".

In October, in response to two away defeats at Watford and Oldham, Graham signed John Sewell from Charlton who came into the side in place of Terry Long. But on February 22, after four minutes of the derby game with Millwall Sewell tore ligaments which kept him out for the rest of the season. Burridge settled the game for the ten men. It was the sort of gritty performance to please Graham but the papers kept up the sniping.

Our image was not helped by an unseemly brawl against QPR in which Brian Wood and Rangers' Stuart Leary were booked, the teams were called into the centre circle at the start of the second half and lectured about their behaviour. Both clubs were subsequently angered by referee Ted Jennings' decision to report all 22 players to the F.A. and to add a note to their record sheets to say that they had been spoken to by the referee.

Graham, using his best manager-speak – an art form which was in the early stages of development – said: "I think it most unfair for those players who are innocent. Things got a bit heated at times, but neither goalkeeper was involved. Unfortunately there is nothing we can do about it." Ronnie Allen settled the game in Palace's favour.

Although Bournemouth dented the defence's undefeated home stretch when they scored on March 28, Palace still came out on top which took us four points clear. At Fellows Park, we drew 2-2 in a game in which we were coasting thanks to goals by Holton

Hulton Deutsch

Top: Cliff Holton challenges the Oldham keeper Bottom: The championship has gone but the celebrations continue

'It is the best day in my life,' says chairman Arthur Wait

RYSTAL PALACE chairman Arthur Wait, who, as a young... watched Pala... Oldham Athletic in 1925...

Hulton Deutsch

and Whitehouse. But a carelessly conceded corner allowed Walsall to pull one back through Trevor Foster and then Alan Stevenson handled and the superbly named Granville Palin converted the penalty. How costly would that lost point be?

In a season in which Palace made as many friends as a skunk with a personal hygiene problem, there was more trouble when our tackling upset the crowd at Boothferry Park. An incensed "bearded youth" ran onto the pitch and struck Kellard. The arrested youth was taken into the Palace dressing room to apologise and Kellard said: "He did it so gracefully that we couldn't help feeling sorry for him. In no time we were wise-cracking." Graham added: "The lad was thrilled. He said he would be a confirmed Crystal Palace supporter from now on." Wonder if he still is?

The dropped point at Boothferry Park was bad news and things got worse when Barnsley, battling against the drop, won at Selhurst on April 11 with two goals from Eddie O'Hara. Although Brian Whitehouse replied, we were stuttering badly. It was our first home defeat of the season and it couldn't have come at a worse time. Graham observed: "Before our own fans the tension has been killing. You can even sense the tension in the crowd and it's affecting the players. They just can't relax."

The papers were full of the bribery scandal involving Sheffield Wednesday stars Bronco Lane, Peter Swan and Tony Kay that had rocked English football. But they still found room to criticise Palace. After the match at Colchester on March 21 which was abandoned after 57 minutes, the Layer Road club's chairman Bill Allen told waiting newsmen: "Palace didn't look worthy of the position they're in. They're not a good side, they're all rush. We had the measure of them."

He was proved partially correct when the match was replayed on April 15. It ended all square, mainly because Palace were suffering from promotion nerves. The *Daily Mirror* proclaimed: "Tough Palace grab a point," adding that we had "thundered and finally plundered another point along the rich promotion trail".

It took us a point clear of Coventry, although Harry Miller reported that tension showed in everything we did. Imlach gave us the lead with a tenth minute penalty after Duncan Forbes had brought down Burridge and Miller added: "We were entitled to see a little poise and polish from Palace after that. It never came." Instead Colchester equalised through Mike Grice on 37 minutes and that's the way it stayed.

Three games to go and Palace were nearly there. But with Coventry and Watford still hot on our heels it was clearly going to be a three-way battle to the last. Another tricky away visit to Peterborough brought us another point and the *Mirror* ventured: "Palace for promotion?"

Whether we achieved it or not, the paper was not offering any credit. "They have the strength to do it, but on this crude showing they won't take the same skill and poise into the second division as Coventry. Their crunching tackles won't gain them many friends if they make it." Graham was also showing signs of stress and was spoken to by the referee at London Road. Petchey collected a booking as Whitehouse's goal secured the point.

On the following Monday, Peterborough did us a favour by beating Coventry 2-0 and the following night Watford were held 2-2 by Brentford at Vicarage Road. Palace held all the cards and, in our third successive away match, we gained the point needed to secure promotion at Wrexham, who were heading in the opposite direction.

After the match the players surrounded Dick Graham and "roared" *For He's A Jolly Good Fellow*. Whitehouse, who had begun the season in Wrexham's reserves, opened the scoring with "a tremendous goal. A sizzling 30 yarder that left keeper Steve Fleet helpless." After Ernie Phythian had levelled the scores, Fleet grabbed Werge's ankles and Holton put us back in front from the spot. Had Palace held on, we would have been crowned champions there and then. Instead, Stevenson conceded a needless late penalty by elbowing Sammy McMillan in an off-the-ball incident and Ken Bonds kept the championship celebrations on ice ... at least until the following Saturday. Or so Palace thought.

Our form in the final straight – five draws and a defeat – had impressed no-one and Jimmy Hill was not about to become magnanimous now the battle was almost over: "Do they deserve it? I think part of the answer is in the crowd they attracted at Wrexham – 3,384," he whined, conveniently forgetting that the Welshmen were going down.

The last game was against Oldham, ironically the team that had sent us down from division two four decades earlier, and Palace were in party mood. The team presented Dick Graham with a silver tea set and did a lap of honour handing out bouquets of flowers to women supporters. The football became almost incidental and Latics' forward Bob Ledger cashed in with a second half hat-trick. Meanwhile, George Curtis scored the only goal of Coventry's match with Colchester and the championship was gone. Palace were barely concerned. "Going up is the important thing," said Ronnie Allen. "After a hard season of forty-six matches, you can't feel too upset about losing the last match."

Not even if it cost Crystal Palace a rare championship? The authors of this book were just toddlers at the time, some not even that, yet it still rankles. This club has won so little despite all its potential that even 30 years on the failure to add another piece of silver to the meagre collection is infuriating to say the least.

Palace rewarded the players with a club tour to Bermuda and Canada and returned to begin their first season in the second division since 1925 with three defeats, starting with a 3-2 home loss against Derby in front of 22,935. This was followed by away defeats at Swindon and Swansea as we struggled to find our feet.

But the Glaziers then stood everything on its head by reeling off five successive wins beginning with a 3-1 success over Swindon in the return followed by four victories all by the same 2-1 scoreline. At Derby in December, Keith Smith, who had joined from Peterborough a few weeks before, scored after just six seconds to record the fastest goal in history. And, at long last, there was a league cup win – over fourth division Tranmere – which set up a home tie with Southampton. The fragility of what was still a new competition can be gauged by the tiny crowd of 11,000 which saw us triumph 2-0. In the next round, we crashed out to eventual finalists Leicester City of the first division in a replay after the Filberts had held us goalless at Selhurst.

The F.A. Cup, however, was a glorious tale. Palace took advantage of exemption to the third round to beat Bury 5-1. Cliff Holton scored a fine hat-trick even though Brian Wood fractured his right leg while we led 3-1. The ten men were so superior that we added two more goals. In the fourth round Southampton were beaten in front of more than 26,000. Holton and Smith helped us through by the odd goal in three to set up a glamourous tussle with first division high flyers Nottingham Forest who included Alan Hinton and Ian Storey-Moore in their line-up. On a February afternoon in 1965 a record crowd of 41,667, undeterred by the snow on the ground, poured into Selhurst Park to see England centre-forward Frank Wignall equalise Dave Burnside's opener. But in the 64th minute Burridge volleyed past Peter Grummitt and instead of hanging on, we went for the throat. Holton scored to secure our place in the last eight for the first time since 1907.

The attendance record was smashed again a few weeks later when Palace entertained Don Revie's treble chasing Leeds in the quarter final. It was the tie of the round with much talk surrounding the enormous task that faced referee Jim Finney, who had been hand picked to officiate in what was seen as a potentially vicious encounter (at least according the the press). In the end there was no bother because Leeds were simply too good and cruised through 3-0. They were heading for disappointment, not only would Liverpool beat them at Wembley but they would trail in second to Man United in the championship.

Aside from all the Cup excitement, the biggest news at Selhurst was Coventry's decision to pay a world record fee for a goalkeeper of £35,000 to secure the services of Bill Glazier. It was an offer too good to refuse. Graham went straight to West Brom to buy Welsh international Tony Millington. But Millington didn't last long because Palace had a better keeper than either him, or Glazier, waiting in reserve; John Jackson.

We finished the season in seventh place – our highest ever in the league – but personnel changes were necessary as some of the stalwarts of third division days began to age. The heroic figures of Cliff Holton and Ronnie Allen had already gone, the latter to take over as manager of Wolves.

Allen took Palace's young defender John Holsgrove with him, while Peter Burridge, another striker reaching the end of his career, left for Charlton. Graham signed Ernie Yard from Bury and Jack Bannister from Scunthorpe, another player with West Brom connections. Another new face was that of former England international Derek Kevan, who had been the subject of a couple of big money transfer deals involving West Brom (naturally), Chelsea – where he failed to settle under Tommy Docherty – and Manchester City. But Kevan, who had the curious middle name of Tennyson, did not settle at Palace, scoring just five goals in 21 league appearances before being shipped off to Peterborough. Graham also signed Ian Lawson, a youth international who had previously been with Burnley and Leeds. But Lawson didn't settle particularly well either and the fans voiced their criticism.

In 1965-66 it was agreed that substitutes were to be allowed in league matches, but only for injured players. It wasn't long before managers were getting round this and the rule was relaxed the following season to allow them for any reason. Palace used 14 substitutes, the first of which was Keith Smith who came on for Lawson with ten minutes left of the 2-1 home win over Orient on August 28.

Our indifferent form, compounded by the high expectations after such a good first season, led to a predictable change in management. On January 3, 1966, the day of our disastrous 3-0 F.A. Cup third round defeat at Carlisle, Graham was dismissed with two years of his contract still to run, even though Palace, initially at least, weren't sure who they wanted as a replacement.

Some of the players had not exactly seen eye-to-eye with their disciplinarian manager and, in December, Graham and Alan Stephenson had had a public row on Euston station as the team prepared to travel to Carlisle for a league game. Stephenson was sent home.

Yet when Graham was sacked the 21 senior pros signed a letter thanking him for what he had done and telling him that they regretted his departure. How different to a couple of years before, when the signatures had been for his removal. It was equally surprising because Graham had not mellowed and several players were on the transfer list.

Arthur Rowe, who had been looking after the youth team, took over in a caretaker capacity and immediately vetoed any outgoings from Selhurst Park. It has to be said that under Rowe the side stagnated and it was a relief when Palace got their new man.

Bert Head's appointment was a tribute to the persistence of Arthur Wait. But the new manager's appointment from Bury was not without controversy. The Shakers resented Palace's approach and their chairman Bill Allen spoke out bitterly.

RONNIE ALLEN
Keeps you "In the Know"
DON'T MISS HIS WEEKLY COLUMN IN THE **CROYDON TIMES**

CRYSTAL PALACE (White)		DERBY COUNTY (Red)
1. W. GLAZIER	KICK-OFF 3.00 p.m.	1. R. MATTHEWS Transferred from Chelsea, 1961
2. T. LONG	Referee: J. LOWRY (Glamorgan)	2. G. BARROWCLIFFE League debut, 1951, at the age of 19
3. J. SEWELL		3. R. FERGUSON Formerly with Newcastle. Joined Derby 1962
4. A. HOWE		4. R. WEBSTER Local player, turned professional 1960
5. A. STEPHENSON	CROYDON TIMES	5. R. YOUNG A former England schoolboy
6. J. HOLSGROVE		6. J. PARRY Football League debut 1949, while only 17
7. E. WERGE		7. G. HUGHES Transferred from Newcastle
8. R. KELLARD	Linesmen: J. E. WITTS (Swindon) (Orange Flag)	8. M. CULLEN Previously with Luton Tn. & Grimsby Tn
9. C. HOLTON		9. I. BUXTON Part-time pro., also plays County cricket
10. B. WHITEHOUSE	E. F. M. MERCHANT (Colchester) (Cerise Flag)	10. A. DURBAN Welsh under 23 Internat'al., formerly Cardiff
11. R. ALLEN		11. J. BOWERS Part-time pro., signed in February, 1957

The teams from Palace's first match back in division two in 1964. Derby were one of the famous names glamour starved Palace were looking forward to meeting. "We are thoroughly delighted to be out of the third division. It has been a constricting influence," said the programme.

HEAD MASTER

Bert Head was the first manager to lead Palace into the first division. Laurie Dahl takes a look at the early days of his managerial career.

What was the most fabulous event of 1969? There can be no doubt about it. It was the year that Palace finally made it to the first division. So much for Neil Armstrong's lunar jaunt.

At the time, manager Bert Head's efforts were recognised as a minor miracle. It was an achievement he followed with a considerably greater feat – that of keeping the club in the first once they had arrived.

The three seasons in which Bert kept Palace afloat easily dwarfs any of the achievements of the much praised Terry Venables of ten years later. Head, who had been an unexceptional player, began his managerial career as assistant manager to Dave Russell at Bury. He stayed with the Gigg Lane club until 1957, when he moved into the manager's hot seat at Swindon Town in his native West Country. When he arrived at the County Ground, he immediately sacked 14 of the 25 players that he had inherited. The financial climate at the time was such that the main stand had been closed by the insurance company until major repairs were carried out and the club could not afford it, let alone replacement players.

Illustration by Jason Axell

Head's hands were tied as he later explained: "It was absolutely impossible to raise even £2,000 or £3,000 to buy any sort of player as this would mean the whole season's profit gone in one deal."

Instead, he made an important discovery. "Nobody has a monopoly on youth. No single club can corner the market. I proved this at Swindon, where we amassed some £400,000 worth of talent mainly drawn from an area in which people said they could not be found."

During the close season, Head had held practice sessions, playing his youngsters against the the older players. The youths won 7-1 and Head said: "I didn't know whether to laugh or cry. I went home a troubled man and decided to sleep on it."

In the end he concluded that another match was necessary to see if the scoreline was a fluke. It wasn't. The "elderly" lot were beaten 6-2 and Head was convinced. Many of his players, as young as 16 and 17, were plunged straight into Town's league campaign.

Head described the opening of the season: "As I watched from the trainers' bench, a very large set of players ran onto the field – the opposition. By contrast, my lads seemed to float out, they looked so young and fragile." The early matches were disastrous and Swindon were thrashed home and away. But, with experience, confidence grew and results improved greatly. Gates at the County Ground ranged from 6,000 to 20,000 as television appearances (those were the good old days when a third division match was not an uncommon sight on the box) projected the "wonder boys of the West" across the nation. Swindon's team featured many young names that would soon be of the household variety. Ernie Hunt, who played in the first division for Coventry, is immortalised by his astonishing free kick goal scored from Willie Carr's two footed flick against Everton, Mike Summerbee played for England and Manchester City, Rod Thomas (not the precocious Watford youngster of later days) became a Welsh international and Don Rogers and Cliff Jackson became first division heroes for Palace.

Head's policy was vindicated in the most emphatic way as Swindon won promotion to the second division.

His success made those at Selhurst Park sit up and take note. Dick Graham's limitations at the higher level finally proved his undoing and the appointment of the ageing Arthur Rowe was never more than a temporary measure. Head was appointed manager at Palace in April 1966, only a short time after he had returned to Lancashire to manage Bury. Within three years, he brought first division football to Selhurst Park.

Like Swindon, Palace had never performed at the highest level but, unlike Swindon, they had every ambition to do so. Chairman Arthur Wait, a lifelong Crystal Palace supporter, wanted the best for his club and his millionaire status gave him the financial clout to realise his dream.

Head soon discovered that it was not possible to place the same emphasis on youth at Palace. Results were wanted quickly. Instead he tapped another source of cheap talent – the Scottish League, where prices were less inflated.

Players such as John McCormick and later Gerry Queen came south to join bargain buys like Mark Lazarus and Mel Blyth. Palace and Bert Head were on the up.

Peanuts, pipe smoke and promotion

Brian Davis looks back on some eccentric Palace happenings

THE lady peanut seller who I think was Italian. She always seemed to be there ... and the piles of shells that filled the ground.

THE different aromas from the pipe tobacco smoked by the older gents when, as a boy, I used to stand at the Whitehorse End. I hate it now.

WHEN "hooliganism" was no more than pulling down the Union Flag at Carlisle Castle (a building of some kind anyway) and running up the Palace one. The local rag even included us on the front page under the heading "Palace fans invade town".

JOHN "Yogi" Hughes scoring against Sheffield United. He seemed to hit it just inside their half – the goalie didn't see it and neither did the *Match of the Day* cameras. All we saw was the ball in the net. We won 5-1.

LAUGHING my head off in an Arsenal dominated League Cup match at Highbury. Palace centre forward Gerry Queen was getting nowhere against the Arsenal centre-half, but continued to niggle him with pushes, ankle taps, elbows etc. The Arsenal berk got so frustrated by the whole business that he kicked Queen up in the air – inside the 18 yard box. Bobby Tambling despatched the penalty and we won.

THE ferocious shot of my hero Cliff Holton. He always seemed to hit the ball from very long range. I remember trying to copy him in a school match, but in my case the ball ended up closer to the corner flag than the goal.

He had the stature of an army colonel or, to my mind, would have been equally at home in a pin-striped suit and bowler hat. He ruined it for me one day by playing at Ipswich in yellow gloves.

I'M convinced to this day that on another occasion, in a cup game at Bury, he purposely missed a rather generous penalty and was consoled by the grateful keeper. He then scored a genuine hat-trick in a five goal win.

A STREAM of double decker buses lined up on the hard shoulder of the motorway – en route from Mansfield station to Field Mill. Well it was a long journey in the days of drink on trains.

MY early games sitting in the old stand with my dad (not about anymore I'm sorry to say) when *Telstar, Venus in Blue Jeans* and *Globetrotter* seemed to be the theme tunes.

THE old songs. *Daisy, Daisy* and *Maybe It's Because I'm A Londoner*, which always seemed to rub the opposition up the wrong way.

THE Fedora cup run, particularly the support at Leeds. Until that awful semi-final at Chelsea where we just didn't play. Total lack of atmosphere.

SOMEHOW managing to feel sick as a pig on the journey back from the Sunderland cup win, while the whole train was going beserk. I hadn't had a drink and the blame probably lies either with the spam sandwiches or from the tension of trying to get out of the ground alive.

THE flags, banners, rattles, characters, humour and togetherness of the Holmesdale terrace in previous years.

THE masochism of overnight coach trips to Carlisle and Plymouth, knowing that I didn't travel particularly well and was unlikely to get any sleep. I think we left at 11pm and arrived at 7am. And on the Saturday night, trying to get into the local flicks for a supposedly doubtful film – but being too young and innocent to understand what was going on anyway.

IN my early days of away travel, the small, funny group of regulars.

One, I recall, had a bugle and would sound the *Last Post* if things were going badly, or a charge a la Seventh Cavalry when we were pouring forward. They were a great bunch of "piss-artists", while I tagged along so as not to be stranded and invariably hid myself in the corner of a pub.

It never ceased to amaze me how, having travelled so far to watch a relatively short game, they would leave it to the last possible moment to leave the pub and risked missing the start of the game. These were the days of taking the micky out of Jimmy Hill's chin when he arrived in his sky blue Jaguar at Coventry City – but the car wouldn't have been damaged.

A HORRIBLE journey home on what I think was a Liverpool Bus Company hard seater coach after an Everton moron gave our Timpson's coach some extra ventilation.

AN ABANDONED game at Lincoln when we were winning – and another at Derby.

HAVING the gentle giant "D.W." to stand behind when the opposition indicated its intention to separate your head from its body. Witnessing the same in John Wayne/Wild West saloon action at Fratton Station when Pompey fans chose the wrong guy to pick on. I'm not attempting to justify this in any way.

Palace have never had, in my experience, a crowd intent on real trouble rather than seeing the game, having fun and maybe the odd bit of mischief. But it was useful to have someone who was a match for anyone when trouble, tame compared to recent problems, invariably found you.

STANDING at the top of the Whitehorse Lane grass bank and participating in the downhill slalom contest when it rained.

THE horrible gents behind the above. It's probably causing the damp smell problem in the town house now occupying the same position.

BEING locked in the Holly Bush pub at Crystal Palace on the 1979 promotion night. We paid the equivalent of 50p for about ten pints and several bags of crisps. I seem to remember the landlord being quite pleased that night.

Mark and Bobby

David Mearns recalls two men who were central characters in Palace's promotion to the first division in 1969

No supporters' record of Palace would be complete without mention of Mark Lazarus and Bobby Woodruff, who made such an enormous contribution to our first promotion to the highest division.

They could not have been more different; Mark was stocky, dark and pugnacious (with a boxer's nose to match); Bobby was tall, blond and handsome, every inch the athlete. Both were able footballers with an eye for goal and both were prepared to get stuck in, an essential requirement for Head's team that was to fulfil our wildest ambitions.

The *Complete Record* (thanks Mike Purkiss) shows that Mark joined the Palace from QPR in December 1967, scoring 17 goals in 70 league appearances before leaving for Orient, in October 1969. Bobby (an ex-Swindon player under Head) signed from Wolves in June 1966 and went west to Cardiff in November 1969 having scored 48 goals in 136 appearances.

Bobby was known for his very long throw which would arrive on the penalty spot like a driven cross. I recall Mel Blyth arriving to meet one with a volley into the Whitehorse Lane net although the identity of the opponents escapes me. Palace fans used to greet the winning of a throw-in in the opponents' half with chants of *Bobby, Bobby, Bobby* which didn't quite fit the tough, skinhead image of the emerging breed of fan but then Palace always were nice. Bobby also linked perfectly with Cliff Jackson (another former Head protege from Swindon) and the pair terrorised defences in the old Second Division. Bobby would also regularly belt home 25 yarders but the real dividend of his partnership with Jackson was Cliff's ability to place corners on to Bobby's head around the penalty spot. It was a real spectacle.

The Palace fans knew what was about to happen (as did the opposing defence) but six-footer Bobby was such an athlete that he would simply outjump the panic-stricken defenders before flexing his neck muscles and powering the ball into the roof of the net. Bobby was a great centre forward of the old style and will remain in my memory in the same league as David Swindlehurst and Mark Bright.

Lazarus was a tough, Jewish Eastender from a family renowned for its pugilistic skills. He made his name at QPR, scoring the winner in their 3-2 league cup final win over first division West Brom in 1967, when Wembley cup finals were still a special occasion.

I was so besotted with Mark that I began a scrap book devoted to him (which I still possess).

I spent all my pocket money on black and white photos of him from the club shop, resplendent in the claret shirt with the thin light blue stripes. Mark was a winger but his application was such that he was tigerish all over the pitch and his tricky wing play was complemented by fierce shooting and heading. Mark was a real wide boy in many senses. He would float around and through full backs with a shrug of the shoulders, arms dangling casually at his side, before delivering a pin point cross or cutting in to unleash a shot. Defenders didn't mess with *Marky, Marky, Marky Lazarus.* Those that were naive soon became mysteriously inert on the touchline when play was at the other end. Yet nobody knew what had happened. Such was my childish fascination at this new dimension that I cut out cartoons of brawling footballers and stuck them in my aptly named scrap book, crayoning claret and blue stripes and black hair on the most dangerous looking individual.

I revelled in the accounts of the match at Bury in August 1968 when football wasn't mentioned but there were descriptions of the altercation and punch that left six foot four inch Bury centre half Ben Anderson unconscious on the pitch for five minutes. Mark received his marching orders and a three week ban. I have many recollections of Mark but it's appropriate to recall a crucial promotion battle at the Den in November 1968. Palace and Millwall were slogging it out at the top (Millwall were first and unbeaten in eight games) and south London crackled all week before 28,000 saw a real battle. It was blood, thunder and constant stoppages as Mark thrashed home McCormick's flick from Jackson's corner in the 20th minute. In the 44th John Sewell overlapped to cross for Bobby to head home, 2-0 and Palace kept going on to promotion. "Palace Power Rocks Millwall" screamed that night's *Evening Standard.* Mark spent the second half nutmegging "Mr. Millwall" – the dockers' very own Harry Cripps. We had to concentrate hard to keep the smirks off our faces. Oh and Jacko saved a Keith Weller penalty, but that's another story. Mark and Bobby, you are not forgotten.

Six-nil, are you sure this is Palace?

The first match I saw was a strange affair. My brother took me to the game against Norwich City at home on April 16, 1968. I was eight years old.

Unbelievable, Palace won 6-0. I didn't know who the Palace players were but my copy of the *Complete Record* tells me that the scorers were Woodruff (2), Light, Lazarus and Vansittart (2).

Palace had played Norwich the day before and lost 2-1, so I assume it was Easter. I remember the glare of the floodlights and the noise of the crowd. Palace seemed to score every five minutes and I wondered if all matches were as good as this?

The strange thing was that it started my distrust of adults. A man spoke to my brother and I while we were queueing to get into the Holmedale and on being told that it was my first match he assumed the mantle of an expert. He informed me that Norwich were known as the Canaries because they played in yellow shirts.

This was fascinating to a young lad on his first pilgrimage to Selhurst Park. I knew nothing of club nicknames and colours nor of "away" strips. Imagine the disappointment on seeing Norwich come out of the tunnel wearing boring old white ... what a let down. That man was a lying bastard.

Anyway the game went past in a blur and at the final whistle, my brother being quite pleased with the 6-0 win, vowed to take me again, treating me like some lucky mascot.

All I could say was: "Are you sure Palace were in the claret and blue stripes?"

Donny the Beastie Boy

The big sky: Selhurst Park, a love affair

While everyone else bemoans the lack of cover at Selhurst Park Colin Readman offers an alternative view

I got off the number 75 with dad on a winter's afternoon. Across the road by the lights, down Park Road. Everyone is going our way, with dad and everyone else's dad, down the narrow road with big people, surrounded by big houses.

Past the parked cars on the left, grubby garage doors on the right, and there's a crossroads with a pair of dull corrugated gates to the left. A man in front of the gates is selling rosettes, badges and scarves. Can I have a rosette please, dad? Down the hill, on the left someone sells peanuts and other things closely resembling food. Dad pushes me into a little box with a metal bar across - money is handed over and the metal bar gives way letting me through. Out of the box, and into a different world - love at first sight.

Perhaps it was different for you, but I can remember the first sight of Selhurst from the top of the banking at the corner of Holmesdale and Park Road. Banking not terrace: this was the 60s before the Arthur Wait stand was built, when on sunny days you could sit on the grass at the top and watch the Palace play. But on a winter's day like this the wind whips up the bank from the south, where in the distance you can see the cranes building the mini-Manhattan of Croydon. On the immediate right is a tea bar, and the club shop - a wondrous cave of cheap goodies on which spotty herberts like me can waste their pocket money. I still have the pennant on my bedroom wall, but whatever happened to my flag?

My main memory is the view: a backdrop of the Surrey hills surrounding the Croydon basin; the sharp rise up to the parkland beyond the Whitehorse; the little shed down by the pitch which turned out to be a huge metal hanger close up; and most of all, the big, big sky.

I visited other grounds with my beloved Palace and occasionally without. I went to the ones on the telly every weekend: Upton Park, White Hart Lane, big grounds with big stands, ideal on a cold winter's day - but where was the sky? First to go were the grassy banks, then the Park Road terracing became the New Stand; our flagship for the first season in the top flight. Yet I began to realise that our lovely Selhurst was regarded with derision by others, non-believers, as being way behind the time - even Millwall's shabby ground had cover on all sides. And when the rain's coming down, and we're losing - not heavily, but enough to know we're outclassed - what would I have given for a roof over the Holmesdale.

Now I'm older (not wiser) and I watch another incompetent team cave in against a barely adequate side who can at least pass to the same colour shirt, and I think - why am I here? Kember, Jackson and Woodruff aren't playing - so why do I cheer? Dad doesn't bring me anymore - he's retired and moved out. It isn't even recognisably the same club - the colours differ from the claret & blue scarf that my mum knitted for me and we haven't been called the Glaziers for 20 years. But it's still Selhurst, the same ground I've been coming to for over 25 years now - slightly altered in every close season, heavily so in some, but the same unique atmosphere, a blend of loyalty, willing and desperation which can only be found at Palace. We have the passion that northern clubs are famous for, but our mix is unique to us, just as Barnsley's is to them.

If full-time professional football can survive the mugging being administered by the super-rich clubs, then probably one day Selhurst may be constructed to the same blueprint - four boxy stands huddled close around the pitch, with seats all round, giving little idea of the surrounding houses and hills. It must be difficult to stand on the centre-spot of the new grounds at Walsall and Scunthorpe and see an identifying landmark which pins down where you are. I hope there's a space for individuality in the next century; may Everton keep the church at the corner flag for ever. And most important of all to me, even when it rains, is that Selhurst keeps its big sky.

I'll see you at ten to three on the Holmesdale. Don't be late.

SONG SHEET

Presented with the compliments of 'CROYDON MIDWEEK'

1. **'COME ON THE PALACE'**
—to the tune of Colonel Bogey.

Palace, we've come from far and near
Palace, we've come to cheer and cheer,
Come on, come on the Palace
Let's show the world that
We are at the top.
Palace, our pride of Selhurst Park,
Palace, our team that's made its mark,
Come on, come on the Palace
Let's show the world that
We'll stay at the top.

2. **'WHILE WE'RE SUPPORTING THE PALACE'**
—to the tune of Marching through Georgia.

Hurrah, hurrah we'll sing the Palace song
Hurrah, hurrah as they go marching on
We'll sing this mighty chorus from Plymouth to Carlisle
While we're supporting the Palace.
Hurrah, hurrah we'll sing the Palace song
Hurrah, hurrah as they go marching on
We'll see them win the championship
We'll see them rise to fame
While we're supporting the Palace.

3. **'WE'VE GOT THEM ALL ON THE RUN'**
—to the tune of Bye Bye Blackbird.

We've got them all on the run
First division here we come
Bye bye Blackburn (Millwall etc.)
Crystal Palace rise to fame
To Highbury and Whitehart Lane,
Bye bye Blackburn.
While this song we are all singing
Crystal Palace they just go on winning
We've got them all on the run,
First division here we come
Blackburn bye bye.

4. **'AYE AYE AYE AYE'**
—to the same tune.

Aye aye aye aye
Jackson is better than Yashin
Woodruff is better than Eusebio
and ———— is in for a thrashing.

5. **'COME ON THE PALACE'**
—to the tune of Roll Out the Barrel.

Come on the Palace
We're here to cheer you along
Come on the Palace
So let us sing you this song
Get right stuck in lads
There's no team that you need to fear
Now's the time to come on Palace
For the Crowds all here.

6. **'ONWARD CRYSTAL PALACE'**
—to the tune of Onward Christian Soldiers.

Onward Crystal Palace
To division one
Goodbye Cardiff City, Charlton, [Rotherham.
Soon we shall be rising
Selhurst Park shall reign
As high as Arsenal's Highbury and Tottenham's Whitehart Lane.

7. **'ROLL ALONG CRYSTAL PALACE'**
—to the tune of Roll Along Covered Wagon.

Roll along Crystal Palace, roll along;
To the top of the league where you [belong;
If you go much further up,
You'll be winning League and Cup
Roll along Crystal Palace, roll along.

Sweet and sour at the Palace

On the last day of September 1967, Terry Long's goal beat QPR and took Palace to the top of the second division for the first time. It brought the archetypal cinderella club some overdue press recognition. Peter Gillman, a lifelong Palace fan, gave *Times* readers the lowdown.

Named after a Victorian glass extravaganza that was burnt down in 1936, just who are Crystal Palace anyway?

Hidden away in suburban South Norwood, London SE25, they went quite unheralded to the top of Division II two weeks ago, by quietly and efficiently beating the far more vaunted Queen's Park Rangers.

The match was watched by 38,000 people. "If you can get that many just for being top of the second division ..." ponders Bert Head, 50, the Palace manager. "Crowds could go up into the 40s and 50s. It's frightening. No it's not, it's thrilling."

Nicotine fingers and a slight tremble in his hands betray Head's occupational anxieties. But he says the 18 months since he joined the Palace have been the happiest of his career. "It's better to be worried at the top than at the bottom."

Heady times indeed, far from the days when Crystal Palace were one of the joke teams of the old third division south, with players like Mike Deakin, the best one-foot centre-forward in the division, Len Choules the centre-half who once scored an own goal from 40 yards, Carlo Nastri at 5ft 1in reputedly the smallest man ever to play league football, and Chopper Greenwood, the full–back with the longest sliding tackle in the business.

"We didn't seem to be going anywhere except down," says Terry Long, who joined the Palace over a decade ago and is still with them.

Crystal Palace finally started winning under Arthur Rowe, the former Spurs push–and-run manager. In two years they battled their way out of the new fourth division and in 1963-64 under Dick Graham out of the third into the second.

But nothing spectacular happened until Bert Head came across from Swindon in 1966. In his first season Head made seven first-team changes, and one of the newcomers at a cost of £45,000 was Johnny Byrne, the West Ham and England forward whom Crystal Palace had sold to West Ham for £65,000 five years before.

This season, until yesterday's game at Blackpool, Palace had dropped only four points in eleven games, scoring 21 goals against six.

"Last season we were in a process of bedding down and building up our talent," says Bert Head. "Now we're getting the results. Our football is based simply on the execution of a pass done quickly. We're trying to make our football attractive – the crowd like to see excitement, they like to see speed. Results and entertainment are what the supporters want. All the rest is frills."

The defence is pivoted on the tall England under-23 centre-half Alan Stephenson, the attack on Byrne at centre-forward, distributing the ball quickly and trying to wrong-foot defenders.

But the last four wins were achieved without either of these players. Against Queen's Park Rangers, there were four reserves in the side, and the winning goal was scored by Terry Long, normally a right-back, playing on the left-wing.

"We have the background now," says Head. "I was a bit worried with so many injuries. I have had to put in players who perhaps knew they would only be in for a few games. But suddenly everybody is playing for the club. There's no question of them playing just for themselves. This is something that's very difficult to obtain."

As Swindon's manager for nine years, Head built up one of the youngest sides ever to play in the league, and he is keen on bringing on young players at the Palace. Two of his best forwards, fast and skilful, are Steve Kember, 18, and Danny Light, 19.

Arthur Rowe, who is now the club's assistant manager, is mainly concerned with the youth teams. "Six of the first team players are local, and what's coming up is better than I've ever known." Relaxed now and distinguished with all white hair, he is enjoying the Palace's success. "Looking back it's mixed. There's the sweet and the sour – if you want to taste one you have to accept the other." He prefers to look ahead. "There's only one way to play football, pass the ball accurately then move, and that's what the Palace are doing."

Optimism about promotion varies from Terry Long's "It's gonna happen," to the greater caution of Bert Head: "It's a very hard division to win because the rewards at stake are so great."

Promotion would mean an immense amount to any club but Crystal Palace could really capitalise on the opportunities it would present.

The ground, Selhurst Park, is large – even with a 38,000 crowd there is plenty of room on the terraces – and the London borough it is in, Croydon, has a population of 250,000.

The nearest rival is Millwall, eight miles away to the north-east and attendances at the Palace this season already average over 22,000.

"We spent a lot on Johnny Byrne," says Bert Head. "But we might do it again. The directors are ambitious but not so much that they are petulant if we lose – as long as the whole set-up is making progress. We might even start getting the overdraft down."

"I had my doubts when I came back," says Johnny Byrne. "But there's a great spirit here, one of the best I have known. I'm more than hopeful. This could be one of the great clubs."

■ This article originally appeared in *The Times* in October 1967. The editors would like to thank Peter Gillman for permission to reproduce it.

✲✲✲ Psychedeaglia

Damp walls, dripping dark with mucus of indeterminate origin. At a small club tucked away in the suburbs of south London, thousands of bodies are tightly packed, breathing in a single pulse, waiting for the darlings of the underground. The noise is deafening.

Undiscovered by the hacks and hackettes of the football-fixated music press, there are no *NME* or *Melody Maker* scribes here to proclaim the next big thing. They may worship Suede and drop the names of Leeds United and Pompey but they are still searching for something that has always been there for all to see – the next big thing lives and breathes at Selhurst Park.

Fear is in the air. It's something intangible, but the hard core fans know that if they ever break into the mainstream they will lose something special. And that is why Palace will not, cannot, sell out. They don't play the big stadiums. They are at the nihilistic vanguard of the underground. Self destruction is better than the sugary glamour of Arsenal and Spurs. No future? Who knows. Certainly no future they can be certain of.

When Nico and the Velvet Underground – all die hard Eagles fans – penned *All Tomorrow's Parties* it was in the belief that those parties would never come. But they did come in the 1990 F.A. Cup semi final.

Palace have always eschewed the fleeting dandies that minced and skipped through London football in the late Sixties. While Osgood, Hudson, Marsh and George flounced in flower power shirts, the Palace avant garde remained aloof and unimpressed. Arsenal may have been wittering on about flowers in their hair, but Iggy and the Stooges were paying homage to John McCormick with *Raw Power*.

Iggy, stripped to the waist and bearing the scars of a death of a thousand cuts that every Palace fan knows so well writhed in self inflicted agony, his mind tortured by the three penalty misses against Brighton. Nirvana was denied. Devoted to the Selhurst cause, he later penned *The Passenger* to mark Alan Pardew's contribution to promotion. It's the sort of thing that the pop kids, all pimples and platforms shied away from, instead drawn to the false Pomp and Glam of Chelsea, Spurs and Arsenal. They were unable to penetrate through the dark shades of the Palace psyche. Palace walk on the wild side where doom despair and discord reign. Malcolm Allison tried to change the nature of the beast with his psychedelic imaginings, but while Palace jangled briefly it was to the words of Jim Morrison and the Doors that they always returned:

This is the end
Beautiful friend, the end
I know I'll never see that team again

Morrison was doomed the minute Palace failed to get past Chelsea in the third round of the Cup in 1971. It marked the end of a decade. The Sixties had been a rollercoaster in which Palace were on a magical trip, they just got higher and higher. Colin Noades, now on the board, remembers Big Brother and the Holding Company, there was the musings of Eric Young's Chocolate Head Band, the flash, power and technique of the Eddi McGoldrix Experience, whose tribute to eighties centre halves in *Foxy Lacy* and the managerial reign of Alan Mullery in *Trashman* are a seminal influence on many young bands, the Beatles with *Sergeant Glazier's Lonely Hearts Club Band* and the whimsy of the Andy McCulloch influenced *When I'm Sixty Four* and Simon Osborn's Small Faces who followed with *Itchycoo Parkin.*

The Doors loved Palace so much that Morrison could no longer live with the agony of a world in which the teleprinter was supreme. He became a recluse and eventually took his own life. Yet Palace was not the only haven of the underbelly of football.

Most of the 66,000 Charlatan Athletic fans became the Grateful Dead but they were replaced by a new breed and you could not dig them.

In the early 80s Palace were in the Joy Division, in fact they were top of it after Jim Cannon's stunning volley but heaven knows they became miserable and they moved into a more industrial format.

It was direct down the line no frills stuff, the fancy effects were eschewed by Perry Ubu, Einsturzende Neubarber and Nick Chatterton and the Bad Seeds. When Manchester suddenly went all baggy, Ian Wright took up the slack with a couple of blistering goals before he departed for the land of student squats and bohemian rhapsodies.

At Palace the scene has never been so healthy. Not since the days of the Pinkney Fairies and the Higginbottomhole Surfers have we seen such variety and vitality. The underground lives, psychedeaglia man.

By Danny Baker's Palace Supporting Auntie

Head seemed largely unaware of the furore, at least he said very little about it, but Wait's financial muscle won the day and Bury's chairman gave in: "We've lost and you've got the best manager in the business." Head had been at Gigg Lane as a manager for just under a season.

Head's reign at Selhurst began badly when we lost 1-0 at Southampton. With only three games left he had precious little time to do anything dramatic. Palace finished 11th which was steady but unspectacular and certainly not the sort of progress hoped for in the board room.

The Summer of 1966 was a glorious one for England. *Sunny Afternoon* by the Kinks and *Paperback Writer* by the Beatles were the anthems as some people on the pitch thought it was all over. Hurst made it 4-2 and English football was on top of the world. The Prime Minister Harold Wilson proclaimed England only won World Cups under a Labour government.

Palace toured Holland before the start of the season and beat DOS Utrecht 1-0 and Alkmaar 2-0 before losing the third game to Feyenoord 3-1.

The country went football mad ... why, even Carlisle could attract 11,000 to Selhurst Park on the first day, or perhaps everyone was still drunk after the parties following Hurst's third goal.

In scorching heat, two new boys Tom White, who'd arrived from Aberdeen with John McCormick, and Bobby Woodruff crowned their debuts with two goals each. Woodruff certainly expanded the range of Palace's forward options. He had played 73 times for Wolves and scored 18 goals for them, mostly in the second division. But with Peter Knowles and Alun Evans leading the Molineux revival, Woodruff was allowed to link up with his old Swindon supremo Bert Head.

In his first season at Selhurst, Woodruff hit 18 goals – the best by a Palace player in the second division. He was also known as the unofficial long-throw champion of England with a throw measured at somewhere around the 40 yards mark.

But not everybody had enjoyed such a wonderful time. After just 12 minutes of his very first game against Blackburn, McCormick, playing at number 11, suffered a serious injury. He played one more game that season – a 3-1 defeat at Birmingham. Palace were stretched by a series of unfortunate injuries. Sewell missed 13 games early on after breaking his collar bone in a 2-0 league cup defeat by Fulham. Ironically, the Saturday before, Tom White had broken his collar bone at Charlton.

To increase his defensive cover, Head signed Eddie Presland from West Ham and he played every game to the end of the season, establishing himself as the regular left back for the next season and a half.

In October, the qualities of Alan Stephenson were recognised with the first of three Under-23 caps. He wasn't exactly extended as England swamped Wales 8-0 at Molineux. Although this was good news, it predictably attracted the interest of the big clubs.

But first, Head delighted everyone with a romantic signing. Johnny Byrne had made 163 appearances for West Ham and scored 79 goals but was out of favour owing to the success of Geoff Hurst. He was persuaded to come back to Selhurst Park.

With both Palace and Leicester out of the Cup, a friendly was fixed up and the fans welcomed Byrne back by singing *Hello Johnny, Welcome Home Johnny* to the *Hello Dolly* tune. Byrne obliged with a goal.

Palace had had a decent season, Head had brought in some new faces and established a couple of young players. It wasn't only the 60s that were swinging. Under the least groovy manager the world had ever seen, we lost only one of our last eight games and Woodruff, prompted by the emerging talent of a new midfield wonder kid, Steve Kember, scored seven goals. The balance was almost right, as the last result of the season showed when Ronnie Allen brought his Wolves to Selhurst needing a point to go up as champions. Woodruff, who'd scored five goals in four games, got on the scoresheet again as Palace ripped them apart 4-1.

Kember had been introduced the previous season and was beginning to cause a real stir. Being a young groovy fellow, he had slightly longer hair than the proper haircut brigade led by John Sewell and was the closest Palace had to a "pop star" footballer, a type that was becoming all the rage especially at Old Trafford (George Best) and Stamford Bridge (Peter Osgood). A Croydon and Surrey schools player, Kember joined Palace in December 1963 and signed pro in December 1965. He made 11 England Youth appearances, the first of which was against a Palace Under-20 team at Selhurst on November 1, 1966. He was also in the England team which finished runners-up to Russia in the European Youth Championships. Kember made his league debut on January 1 against Bristol City, in Dick Graham's last match in charge.

Before the 1967-68 season, Palace lost 3-2 to first division Burnley in a pre-season friendly which marked the opening of new club offices, a boardroom and reception area. All the building work had been paid for through contributions by supporters in the Glaziers Club and Supporters Club, although there was no sign of a roof for the Holmesdale or the Whitehorse. Arthur Wait explained: "We have always felt it is inviting a sudden fall to better one's playing strength without improving the amenities at the same time. To be a successful second division side with aspirations of reaching the first division you have to make sure the administrative side is capable of dealing with the increased business this progress brings. In recent years while our playing record has improved our managerial and office staff have had to work in cramped, uncomfortable quarters 45 years old. No longer."

A more cosmetic change was made to the kit. Palace turned out in claret shirts with narrow light blue stripes, collar and cuffs, white shorts and light blue socks with a claret top.

We got off to a good start, beating Rotherham 3-0 at Millmoor and following up with a Woodruff header to beat Derby under their new manager Brian Clough. Aside from a 4-2 setback at Cardiff, our early season form was brilliant and when the much vaunted QPR, Rodney Marsh and all, were beaten by Terry Long's goal in front of a crowd of over 38,000, we went to the top for the first time ever.

We didn't stay there too long. Kember and Woodruff's goals beat Bristol City the following week but we were knocked off the top by Blackpool in a rain swept match at Broomfield Road. By the time we drew twice with Pompey at Christmas, we had dropped to sixth and by Easter, when Norwich were stuffed 6-0, we were down to 12th. We picked up a place to finish 11th with a 2-0 victory over Preston, but it was a disappointment after the season had promised so much.

Goals weren't easy to come by, despite the arrival of the much travelled Mark Lazarus from QPR. He'd managed only five goals while White had two in 18 games and Johnny Byrne had gone. On Saturday March 16, Palace were travelling back from a 2-1 defeat at Blackburn on the same train as first division strugglers Fulham, who'd been beaten 5-1 at Man City. It was transfer deadline day and the clubs completed the deal which took Byrne to Craven Cottage there and then.

A handful of younger players were introduced including Danny Light, Mike Cook, Jim Oliver and Phil Hoadley, whose appearance as a substitute at Burnden Park on April 27, 1968 at 16 years, four months, made him the youngest ever Palace first teamer. He was the only one to make a lasting impression though.

The development of young players was becoming increasingly important to clubs like Palace. Yet, we had never made much impact in the F.A. Youth Cup. Chelsea, on the other hand, enjoyed an envious reputation for getting the best young footballers in London from under the noses of their rivals. They had been winners on numerous occasions, which made our our quarter final victory at Stamford Bridge all the more special. We had led 3-1 but let it slip to 3-3 before two goals in the last two minutes gave us victory. Unfortunately we lost the semi-final to Coventry after a replay.

In the F.A. Cup itself, Palace suffered an exit at the hands of third division Walsall in a replay at Selhurst Park. Colin Taylor's thunderous free kick which had opened the scoring at Fellows Park attracted Bert Head's interest and, in May, he joined the Palace staff. The season also saw the start of John Jackson's unbroken run of 222 consecutive league matches with 32 cup ties thrown in for good measure. He'd already made more than a hundred appearances by that stage. Nobody was surprised when Palace sold captain Alan Stephenson to West Ham for a reported club record of £75,000, topping the previous best also by the Hammers for Byrne. It left the way open for John McCormick to take over the number five shirt alongside Jack Bannister.

The delight that elevation to the first division brought to Crystal Palace in 1969 was not tempered in the slightest by the lack of credit we were given for our achievement. "Unfashionable" has always been an easy, but sadly accurate, tag with which we have been saddled, except for a brief period in which all the glamour and glitz of the biggest clubs was brought to us by Malcolm Allison and his ability to appear in any number of tabloids dripping with jewellery, busty chicks, champers and cigars. But all that was still to come.

To say Palace were not among the fancied runners for 1969-70 was an understatement. In fact, the day after we'd won promotion, Brian Glanville wrote in *The Sunday Times*:

"It would be pleasant to be able to say that the manner of Palace's 3-2 win against poor, doomed Fulham encouraged hope for their assault on the first division. All it did however for those, like myself, who were at the game was to elicit admiration for their morale.

Palace, who responded just after half-time with a flurry of goals, still looked to me a dreadfully ordinary team, and not ordinary in the useful if negative sense of having an iron defence and no attack.

Their attack is banal, their defence far from

Interesting programme notes of the 60s

■ Brian Snowdon drives a Vauxhall Cresta and "cites Geoff Hurst as one of the best football players in English football today".

Palace v Oxford, February 1969

■ "The Woodruff's have a complete set of photographic equipment including two cameras (one still, one cine) a screen and projector.

Palace v Oxford, February 1969

■ "Here is an interesting little aid I was given the other day," wrote Roy Peskett, "to explain how decimal currency could be converted from old money. Write down the sum to be converted from old currency, for example ... it could be 2/1d.,6/5d. or 16/10d

If the pence value is between 0d and 2d leave it.
If the pence value is between 3d and 9d subtract 1
If the pence value is between 10d and 11d subtract 2
Which gives you either 2/1d, 6/4d or 16/8d
Rewrite this value omitting strokes and d signs

Divide this figure by two and the resulting values are the new Pence conversion of old currency ... ie 10 1/2p 32p or 84p"

Palace v Derby. FL Cup 1970., – fascinating stuff. At least it gave us something to take our minds off watching Palace.

■ "The meal cooked by Mrs Chatterton, Mrs Petchey, Mrs Honour and Mrs Head was served by the players and afterwards every guest received a Christmas 'box' consisting of a dozen eggs from chairman Mr Arthur Wait's farm and an autographed copy of the *Crystal Palace Story*."

Christmas dinner for the Thornton Heath Darby and Joan club – Palace v Liverpool 1970/71

■ Lynn Gibbons, a 17 year old secretary, "has successfully learned the intricacies of a 33-extension switchboard" ... "She progressed to Selhurst Park from Marks and Spencers and then selling kitchenware at Allders ..."
Palace v Newcastle October 1969

■ The Palace Dollies have arranged a halloween dance.

Palace v Blackpool 1969/70

Christmas 1968: Bobby Woodruff scores against Blackpool in icy conditions. The match was abandoned at half-time and Palace lost the replayed fixture 2-1. Note Woodruff's bumper boots for extra grip on the slippery surface and the skeleton of the New Stand being erected above the fans heads.

impermeable. Still, there's a whole summer for them to buy, as I hope they will. It would be good to see them stay up."

So how was it that such an apparently uninspired side could achieve first division status? We started the season with a bang. A 4-0 win at Ninian Park on the first day was followed by successive home wins over Huddersfield and Birmingham which meant that on August 17, 1968, we topped the first published tables. The season before, Palace's early form had proved to be a flash in the pan, so when we suffered a 4-0 battering in midweek at Middlesbrough, allowing the north-east club to take over at the top, similar fears arose. We then lost at Bury and despite crushing Carlisle 5-0 with Kember and Cliff Jackson scoring two apiece, our form was no more than reasonable.

The league cup proved to be a major distraction. Having knocked out Preston and Orient, we faced Leeds in the fourth round and in front of 26,000 ecstatic supporters we stunned the team that was going to win the league championship with a phenomenal display which prompted the *Croydon Advertiser* to call it our "finest hour". Cliff Jackson, settling down at last after his arrival from Plymouth a couple of seasons before, and Colin Taylor scored our goals. We met Burnley at Turf Moor in the fifth round and were hard done by when referee Jack Taylor gave the home side a dubious penalty. Palace lost concentration and conceded again. Bearing in mind that we had seemed somewhat distracted at times by the successes in the league cup, perhaps our F.A. Cup exit to Charlton in January was equally beneficial. Certainly until November, Palace's form was nothing more than indifferent.

But four straight wins gave the season some impetus which was undone by a home defeat by Derby and a loss at Hull. We kept in touch with the leaders without being considered to have serious promotion aspirations. Roger Hoy came into the defence alongside the ever-present McCormick as a solid backbone in front of John Jackson. The real turning point though was the bad winter.

There were three postponements in a row including important clashes with promotion rivals Millwall and Derby as well as Oxford on February 19. The interruption proved highly beneficial. After losing a rearranged game against Blackpool, we remained unbeaten to the end of the season.

PALACE—THE 99.99% CERTS!

AND FULHAM COULD BE THE CLINCHER

Frightened? 'Not us'

CRYSTAL PALACE, the 99.99 per cent ce[rts]

Almost there ... with Palace on the brink of promotion, the *Croydon Advertiser* stoked up the excitement

From being an outside bet, sixth placed Palace changed the picture within a week at the beginning of March. On the first of the month, second placed Cardiff, six points ahead, visited Selhurst and were sent away with a flea in their ear. Their strikers Brian Clark and John Toshack posed the biggest threat but sterling defensive work from the two Taylors, Tony and Colin, and Roger Hoy and goals for each of them left the Welshmen with all the headaches.

That was followed by a remarkable victory over leaders Derby, who were previously unbeaten at the Baseball Ground, and an equally valuable victory at St Andrews over another of the numerous hopefuls, Birmingham.

We were definitely in contention now and, after beating Bury, we moved into second place by thrashing fading Millwall 4-2. This match prompted some crowd trouble. Indeed, *Croydon Midweek* suggested that Selhurst Park could be closed while South Norwood traders openly said they hoped Palace would not get promotion because of the increased possibility of trouble in the first division. So they were probably pleased when Middlesbrough thrashed Hull 5-3 the following Saturday while we drew with Charlton which knocked us out of second spot.

During the season, the Palace Dollies were formed as a result of a suggestion that there should be a "ladies section" of the Supporters Club. Their primary function was to sell "first goal" tickets and the programme exhorted "listen for the *Hello Dolly* record and buy your first goal tickets NOW!" There was soon 30 of them and a waiting list of a couple of dozen more. The Dollies became a familiar sight in claret and blue shirts and mini skirts welcoming the team out although they suffered often intolerable abuse and are not remembered with the greatest respect by modern supporters, male or female. The best that can be said of the Dollies is that they were the well-meaning product of a bygone age.

Whether they proved particularly inspiring to the team is not clear but we beat Carlisle to go second again which set up a big promotion show down with Middlesbrough on Good Friday. A record crowd of 43,381 saw a disappointing goalless draw. At least we had a better goal average than 'Boro and stayed second. The following day we easily overcame Pompey, while Charlton beat 'Boro.

After a shaky draw at Huddersfield, we travelled to Preston. Although we only drew again, Middlesbrough surprisingly lost at home to struggling Bury and were now unable to catch us. That left Charlton four points behind with two matches left. We were mathematically promoted.

A week later Fulham made their first league visit for more than 30 years. It took them six minutes to score. Brian Dear beat John Jackson from Johnny Byrne's free kick to put the Cottagers ahead. Selhurst was silenced when Dear beat McCormick to set up Frank Large to make it 2-0, but a minute before half time Jack McClelland failed to hold Tony Taylor's shot and Kember finished the job. Palace's second half pressure paid off when Lazarus levelled the scores on the hour and four minutes later we were in front – Cliff Jackson putting the finishing touch to a scramble.

It was a fantastically exciting way to achieve promotion, although Charlton had lost anyway. More than 36,000 celebrated like never before. After 64 years, Crystal Palace were finally a first division team.

To round off a perfect day, both our South East Counties league teams got in on the act. In the first division Palace's youngsters scored six against QPR while West Ham were similarly on the receiving end in the second division. And down in the West Country, Bert Head's old team Swindon achieved promotion to division two with a couple of goals by a bloke called Don Rogers. We will hear more of him in due course.

At Ewood Park, the home team applauded Palace onto the pitch. Six points clear and uncatchable, our relaxed football could have made for a bigger win than 2-1. What did it matter? We were there at last. And now we really could sing *Bye, Bye Blackburn*.

Evening Standard London 5-a-side championships

Wednesday, April 23, 1969 at Wembley Pool (tickets cost £1)

First round
Tottenham 1 QPR 0
Arsenal 2 Crystal Palace 3 (scorers: Cliff Jackson, Sewell and Kember)
Chelsea 1 Fulham 2
West Ham 0 Millwall 1

Second round
Brentford 2 Charlton 0
Orient 0 Watford 0 (Watford won on penalties)
Tottenham 0 Crystal Palace 2 (Cliff Jackson, Sewell)
Fulham 1 Millwall 3

Semi-finals
Brentford 1 Watford 0
Palace 1 (scorer: Kember) Millwall 0

Final Brentford 0 Palace 2 (Payne, Sewell)

Palace team: J. Jackson, David Payne, John Sewell, Steve Kember, Cliff Jackson, sub Tony Taylor

UP WHERE WE BELONG

Crystal Palace had waited 64 years for this. On a late summer's afternoon the Glaziers faced Manchester United, Bobby Charlton, George Best, Denis Law and all. Bob Sinclair was among the record 48,000 crowd

Colorsport

Steve Kember and United's Tony Dunne in close combat

What Palace fan who is old enough could ever forget? It was 1969 and we'd finally made it to the first division. And the team against which it was ordained we make our debut could only have been the mighty Manchester United.

I remember walking up Whitehorse Lane to take my usual place in the old stand enclosure, a scrawny 19 year-old still trying to come to terms with it all. The excitement and anticipation were intense, we were in with the big boys with United and Leeds, Chelsea, Everton, Liverpool, Man City. How could we hope to compete with the likes of them?

Yet it had been only the previous season that we had beaten Leeds 2-1 in the league cup, the same Leeds who were to take the first division by storm with a record 67 points. So why should we fear anyone? We'd already beaten the best in the land.

Who did I think I was kidding? It sounded alright talking with your mates over a pint, but this was reality. We were about to play a legend. A team whose players were household names, who were known to people with only a passing interest in football – Charlton, Law, Kidd, Crerand, Morgan, Sadler and George Best. These were players of consummate skill whom I had marvelled at on television. What chance did we have?

But I was a Palace supporter through and through and as anyone will tell you we're nothing if not optimists (*we thought we were pessimists – eds*). So walking up Whitehorse Lane I had no doubt that we were going to win and establish ourselves as a first division force.

Our side contained two new players that Bert Head had bought during the summer; Gerry Queen a bargain buy from Kilmarnock and Roger Hynd, who had come from Glasgow Rangers. The rest of the team was; John Jackson, our best ever goalkeeper; John "skip" Sewell, our redoubtable captain; John Loughlan, another relative newcomer who had joined from Morton the previous season; Roger Hoy, a £20,000 buy from Spurs also during the previous season; John McCormick, a great defender who I will always remember for his goal against Sheffield United; Mark Lazarus, a much travelled player who made such a contribution to our promotion effort; Steve Kember our future captain and a skilful midfielder who I felt never quite reached his potential; Mel Blyth, who was vastly underrated; and, my favourite player of all time, Cliff Jackson our top scorer in the promotion year. As substitute we had Tony Taylor, who had come from Morton with Loughlan and who was to prove a terrific player in a variety of positions.

The crowd that day was some 48,000, a new record, beating the previous best of around 43,000 which we had attracted to a dour, hard fought 0-0 draw with promotion rivals Middlesbrough the previous season.

Even in those days, the Palace crowd was not exceptionally vocal, but I remember in the first half against United a veritable wall of sound cascading down from the terraces, or so it seems sitting here writing this 23 years later.

The game started as per script with Jacko making saves from Best and Brian Kidd, and John Sewell clearing a Morgan effort off the line in the first few minutes.

But the reds didn't have it all their own way and Hynd went close with a couple of efforts.

Then, ten minutes into the game, ten minutes into division one, Palace scored. It wasn't the greatest goal scored at Selhurst Park, but for me at the time it was the sweetest.

Roger Hoy took one of his long throws into the box, Roger Hynd went for the ball with United keeper Jimmy Rimmer and somehow managed to scramble it into the net off what appeared to be his chest. But it was Mel Blyth who was credited with the goal.

It might just as well have been a 25 yard blockbuster for all the crowd were concerned. We rose as one, more than 35,000 of us (for there were some reds' fans there as well) arms aloft saluting our heroes. In all my years of following Palace there are few occasions when the crowd went that wild – the 52,000 celebrating the first goal against Burnley in 1979, the second equaliser when we thought all was lost in the F.A. Cup semi final at Villa Park in 1990 and that first goal in division one.

When I was at Crystal Palace, I would on occasions look around the ground when everyone had gone home . I would imagine what a wonderful place it could be. In my mind's eye I could see new stands, a really magnificent stadium. I was determined to put that club in the first division. Alas, for me it was not to be, though when the club did eventually get promotion last year I was very pleased for them.

Former Palace Manager
Dick Graham

Needless to say, it didn't last and 15 minutes later Palace's defence did one of its formation statue routines and a cross from Willie Morgan reached Bobby Charlton, who thumped the ball into the net.

After that it was all United. We were lucky to still be on terms approaching half time. But Palace hadn't finished and it was the other half of the new Scottish connection that made his mark. Five minutes before the interval, we were hoping Palace could hang on. The previous half hour had been all United. Then a long pass from Kember (long in those days meant 20 yards) found Queen, who beat Sadler and hit a great shot past the keeper. It stayed 2-1 until the break.

Half time usually meant a cup of Bovril and a Mars bar (so nothing changes), but with the ground nearly full to capacity and everyone still buzzing about Gerry Queen's goal, nobody was moving.

Mind you that's not to say we couldn't have nipped out for a cuppa if we'd wanted to.

The old stand enclosure was the meeting spot for my friends and I. We used to stand by the half-way line. Palace regularly attracted big crowds so the trick of getting in and out of the enclosure was to get down the front and then walk along the bottom terrace which was always the least crowded.

Once level with the exit we went straight up. Non regulars were amazed how we could nip in and out and be back so quickly during the break.

United began the second half strongly and a great battle developed with Jackson making a terrific save, pushing a shot from Brian Kidd against the post. Palace looked dangerous on the break and Queen had one particular chance which Rimmer saved well. Then, after ten minutes, Denis Law pounced. Jackson could only push the ball to Morgan and he hammered it into the goal.

The rest of the game was a Palace rearguard action, although we continued to look dangerous on the break.

Tony Taylor came on for Mark Lazarus with a few minutes left and scurried about without reward. The match ended 2-2, but what a result. When the final whistle blew you'd have thought we'd won.

I suppose that truly was a moral victory. It certainly grabbed the newspaper headlines as nobody outside Palace had expected anything other than a runaway win for United.

Walking back to Thornton Heath station that afternoon we were full of pride for our team who had acquitted themselves with honour against one of the strongest teams in the country.

This was the springboard for our long term success in establishing ourselves as a first division club to be feared throughout England.

Well, as we know, things didn't quite work out that way, but nothing can take away from those of us lucky enough to have been at that first match in the first division great memories of the day.

August 9, 1969. 48,610. Crystal Palace 2 (Blyth, Queen) Manchester United 2 (Charlton, Morgan)
Palace: J. Jackson, Sewell, Loughlan, Hoy, McCormick, Hynd, Lazarus (Taylor), Kember, C. Jackson, Queen, Blyth.
M. United: Rimmer, Dunne, Burns, Crerand, Foulkes, Sadler, Morgan, Kidd, Charlton, Law, Best.

Wonderful life

Cliff Jackson was Palace's leading scorer in the promotion year of 1969. Phil Huffer and Tony Matthews asked him about life as a Palace star

Cliff Jackson is a neat man. He looks in as fine trim today as when he used to lead the Palace forward line nearly 25 years ago. The first thing you notice is that he is not tall. Sipping a lager in a pub in Victoria he is smartly, but casually dressed and looks as if he could easily give his younger interviewers the runaround on the football field. In fact, he still plays five-a-sides, although these days its strictly for pleasure. Football wasn't always like that.

"When you're brought up to be a footballer straight from school it's just a job," he says. "For fans it may be special but for a player it's just work. Once you're brought up with it and you live it, it's just a job. Not many footballers mix with the general public because, once they get to know you, all they want to talk about is football. Footballers don't talk about the game, they talk about anything else."

Football was all Cliff knew. He played for England schoolboys at 14 alongside Nobby Stiles, Bobby Tambling and Bob Wilson and joined his home town club Swindon – his Wiltshire accent is still prominent – straight from school.

"I think I was in a bingo hall one night when I got a message to go home. Bert Head, who had just become manager, was waiting and talked me into joining. I was the first signing he made for Swindon although I could have gone to any one of 15 different clubs. I started like everyone else cleaning boots, painting turnstiles and sweeping the terraces."

Head was busily assembling some quality youngsters including Ernie Hunt, Bobby Woodruff, John Trollope and Mike Summerbee while Don Rogers came two or three years later, when Cliff was 18 or 19. "Donald used to have a lazy stride. Bert once took us down to Bournemouth for a week under canvas and he threatened to send him home because he felt he wasn't putting enough effort into it. But it was only his lazy stride."

By the time Rogers appeared, Cliff, who made his first team debut at 17 and scored direct from a corner, was already established in the first team.

"Swindon used to have public trials in which they played the first team against the reserves. Most of us kids were reserves and we beat the first team something like 7-1 and it made the papers. They couldn't really believe it, so we had another game at the training ground and again we beat them about 6-2. So Bert put most of us in with a few older players."

It was 1958 and Swindon, like Palace, were in division three south. The league was about to change into four divisions and they qualified for the new third division by finishing in the top half of the table. The following year, with a bit more experience, they were promoted to the second division. Head's faith was vindicated although Jackson found him to be "a very raw character".

"I think he was fortunate at Swindon. He came down when the local youngsters were one of the top English schools sides, and he signed the majority of those players on. He was lucky to have a rich choice and he just played us."

But the older players didn't like Head. "I think the youngsters had more respect for him than they did. We used to train in the mud at Shrivenham Road and Bert wouldn't give in until his side were in the lead. We'd be out there for hours playing. Then it suddenly dawned on everybody that Bert's side had to win, so we'd let him get a few goals so we could go home."

By the time Head moved to Bury, Cliff was already away – at Plymouth. "The reason I left Swindon was that I didn't really like Bert. But Plymouth is the end of the world as far as football is concerned because there are so few other grounds around. I must have had about ten managers in my four years there, including Malcolm Allison."

Cliff remembers Allison's days at Home Park fondly. "He was a terrific coach, but not so hot on fitness. At one stage while he was at Plymouth we were top of the league and about six points clear at Christmas. But we didn't win another game until the last day of the season when we needed two points to stay up. Malcolm asked me what I thought we'd done wrong. And I told him it was because we never used to run. You've got to run to give you stamina and we didn't do any of that. But even in the early Sixties he made you feel good. He gave you confidence."

After four years, Cliff had the opportunity to move again and in so doing renew acquaintances with an old friend. "Plymouth in the winter is dead and in the summer it's packed and I'd had enough. By this time Bert Head was at Palace and when I met him one day I mentioned that I wanted to get away. I didn't think he'd be interested but I thought he might tell somebody else. But Bert wanted me to sign and at least he was the devil I knew."

Although Cliff wanted to get away, the rules in those days made it difficult to put in a transfer request. But rules were made to be bent slightly. "Bert came in for me, which meant I didn't forfeit my signing on fee by asking for a transfer. The next thing I knew I was on the train to London."

Was it a big step up joining Palace? "Not really. Plymouth were a good second division club and you could guarantee they'd be somewhere in the top eight. They'd get about 12,000 so they were quite a decent club."

Palace's reputation was built upon spirit and hard work. It may have been a team without stars but there was no doubting their fitness or application. "When I first joined, the other lads used to moan at the coach George Petchey because I wasn't around on Mondays because of travelling up from the West Country. I wondered what all the fuss was about until I discovered that Monday mornings used to be the hardest time for training. George would run us into the ground. Players used to be physically sick over the side afterwards. In those days the Palace ends behind the goals were just banks and we were up and down them like nobody's business. Sixty yards on a one-in-three bank – 'increased

Young autograph hunters greet Cliff and Sheila Jackson after Palace's first match in division one against Man United

demand' they called it. We'd start on the halfway line, jog to the corner, run across the back of the goal, run up the sideline to the halfway line, jog to the corner and so on round the pitch one lap and then back again. It was murder.

"Malcolm never did any of that, but you've got to have days like those because that's when you can call on your reserves. It wasn't only that either. There would be three or four separate exercises and that would be just one. Then Stuart Imlach would take us for quick steps on a horse, skipping and sprints.

"George Petchey did most of the coaching. I was playing in a practice one day and we were working on set free kicks. Everybody was in position when Bert came out swearing at George who just told him to settle down and watch. I then flicked it over the wall and Steve Kember smashed it in. It worked a treat and Bert didn't know what was going on. He was more for wielding the stick than for subtlety. But it worked.

Set pieces were also a speciality. "At Swindon, Bert used to say he could not understand how anybody taking a corner could put it behind the goal when there was 120 yards in which to put it. We had a lot of success with corners.

"Mike Summerbee used to drive them in and I'd pull away to the back post. I scored quite a few goals that way. I was once given a cigarette lighter for scoring a hat-trick with my head at Millwall like that."

As a new face, Cliff had a difficult time at Palace to start with. "When I was with England schoolboys I played inside left and I also played there with both Swindon and Plymouth. But Bert signed me for Palace as a left winger and there was no way I was ever a left winger. At Swindon and Plymouth I suppose I got a goal every three or four games, but now I was out of place."

His form slipped and he was replaced by Lenny Tomkins and was in and out of the side until the opening day of the 1968-69 season.

"I was twelfth man before the first game at Cardiff, but Bobby Woodruff, who was first choice centre-forward, went down with gastro-entoritis shortly before the game so I was called in as a makeshift and scored two goals."

And the match was memorable for another reason, too. Cliff tried a shot which a Cardiff defender cleared in the nick of time ... "As he got it away I kicked him by mistake and all hell broke loose. I went down, he went down, then a big crowd of players was around us. I felt a hand on my shoulder and ... whack. This chap had nutted me across the nose. He got sent off and I had a fat lip."

Cliff recovered in time to keep his place in the next game and, revelling in his new role, he began to score on a regular basis. "I suppose I was something of a playmaker. I'm not very big, not tall, and used to be referred to as the 'pale, frail Jackson', they played it in for me to lay off which is how Gerry Queen scored in the first game in division one against Man United after I'd laid it off for Steve Kember to pass through.

"It all came right and fortunately I scored a few goals and it went on and on., we just kept winning. We got promoted and I ended up top scorer."

Palace's form hardly faltered after an enforced break because of a bad winter and in the last home game they needed one more win to make sure of promotion.

"Johnny Byrne, an old Palace hero, had just been sold to Fulham and was playing against us. I was walking off at half time with him and we were losing 2-0 and he was going: ‘You ain’t got no chance, you ain’t gonna do it. I can’t see you going up, I can’t see you scoring three against us.’ He drove us mad. But we did score three and I was fortunate enough to get the third goal. The ball came through a crowd of players and it just sat up.”

Byrne was a chirpy character and his reputation for jokes and banter is well known. Cliff has one particular memory of the great man. “When Johnny first came back from West Ham, he was overweight, like a pudding, so George Petchey gave him a space suit made of plastic which they zipped up tight. They put cotton wool between the plastic and his body to make him sweat. We trained for about 15 minutes and he was gone. ‘George, I can’t go on,’ he said. ‘I can’t go on.’ And as they unzipped the bottoms of his trousers, the sweat just poured out like it was coming from a tap. I’d never seen anything like it, he was standing in a puddle.”

Without a first division appearance between them, Palace prepared to face the elite. “When you look at the fixtures to see who you’re playing that’s when it hits you,” says Cliff. “In the second division when we were doing well we got 20,000 but when you jump up to 50,000 or more … the supporters let you know who you’re playing. Where it would have been perhaps a thousand waiting for you to arrive, in the first division it would be five thousand. You’d be looking at an hour of signing autographs before the game.”

When Palace received a few good hidings early on was there a feeling among the players that it was all too much and they didn’t belong? “Not at all, we just saw it as a learning process. What you could get away with in the second division you couldn’t in the first. If you tried to pull away there would always be somebody there. It was difficult and we had to try something different.”

In the mid 60s, Palace had a big central defender called Alan Stephenson who went to West Ham for a record fee before the club was promoted. Ironically, Cliff found him to be one of the toughest opponents.

“The hardest thing to do was to take it around him because he had such long legs. You’d try to push it through and he’d bring you down. Jack Charlton was the same, he was like a giraffe. All the Leeds side were hard; Billy Bremner wasn’t very tall, but he was dirty.”

But who were the Palace players who would sort out the likes of Leeds. “Well, Roger Hynd was a nutter. He used to smack you in the ribs for the hell of it by way of a greeting. John Sewell was also very strong, a gentleman but tough with it, and John McCormick could wrap his legs around you. He was a very dry chap. We had a lot of Scotsmen at Palace at the time and would always have England versus Scotland in the five-a-sides.

> **“We saw promotion as a learning process. What you could get away with in the second division you couldn’t in the first. If you tried to pull away somebody would be there.”**
>
> – Cliff Jackson on Life In The Top Flight

“If you had a Scotsman in your side you never got the ball back. All they wanted to do was dribble. We all got on well, but when you’re successful you do. Yet even when we struggled in that first year the spirit was good.”

Just to survive in the first division was a tremendous achievement and Palace managed it by the skin of their teeth. What was the feeling when it was down to waiting for Sheffield Wednesday, who only needed to beat Man City to survive in Palace’s place?

“It was an anxious evening because it was out of our hands. I tried to phone John Sewell to find out the score but couldn’t get through because he was phoning me.”

The result went City’s way and Palace survived, but Cliff’s days at Selhurst were coming to an end.

“Palace already had Bobby Tambling, who’d had a spell on loan, and then they signed Alan Birchenall. When Bobby spent a couple of games with us earlier in the year it was the first time I’d played with him since I was 14. He was a Jehovah’s Witness and when he walked into the changing room on the first day, Roger Hynd came up menacingly and said: ‘If you’re gonna give us any of this crap about Jehovah, say it now, get it over with and we don’t want to hear no more about it.’ And Bobby just said: ‘I’m saying nothing.’ And he didn’t.”

Bert Head, who had been at Torquay in his playing days, always kept in contact with the seaside club and called Cliff in to tell him they wanted to sign him.

“I said I didn’t want to go, but Bert was keen on a deal. This continued for about a week and I spoke to A.J. Wait who told me to go down for a day out at the seaside and see what they had to offer.”

Cliff did, and so finished his playing days at Torquay, which he confesses he didn’t enjoy.

After that he became the manager of a sports centre in Essex from which he recently took early retirement. But did he never think of becoming a manager? “I did apply for a job at Cambridge, but it wasn’t really for me. You have to be a special character to be a manager, someone who can let things roll over you. Good managers bring people in and delegate because they can’t do everything.

“Brian Clough found that out at Hartlepool – he started by painting the gates and everything, but as he went higher up he changed and got other people to do the work. I didn’t want the hassle of management.”

Although Cliff says footballers don’t like to talk about “work”, he clearly has a lot of affection left for the game. But it’s Swindon, the local team where he made his name, who get first call when he checks the results.

“I still look out for Palace and we recently attended a vice-presidents dinner there. It’s nice to go back, but whatever era you play football in its great. You have exciting times and it’s brilliant. A wonderful life.”

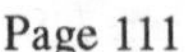

I married a footballer

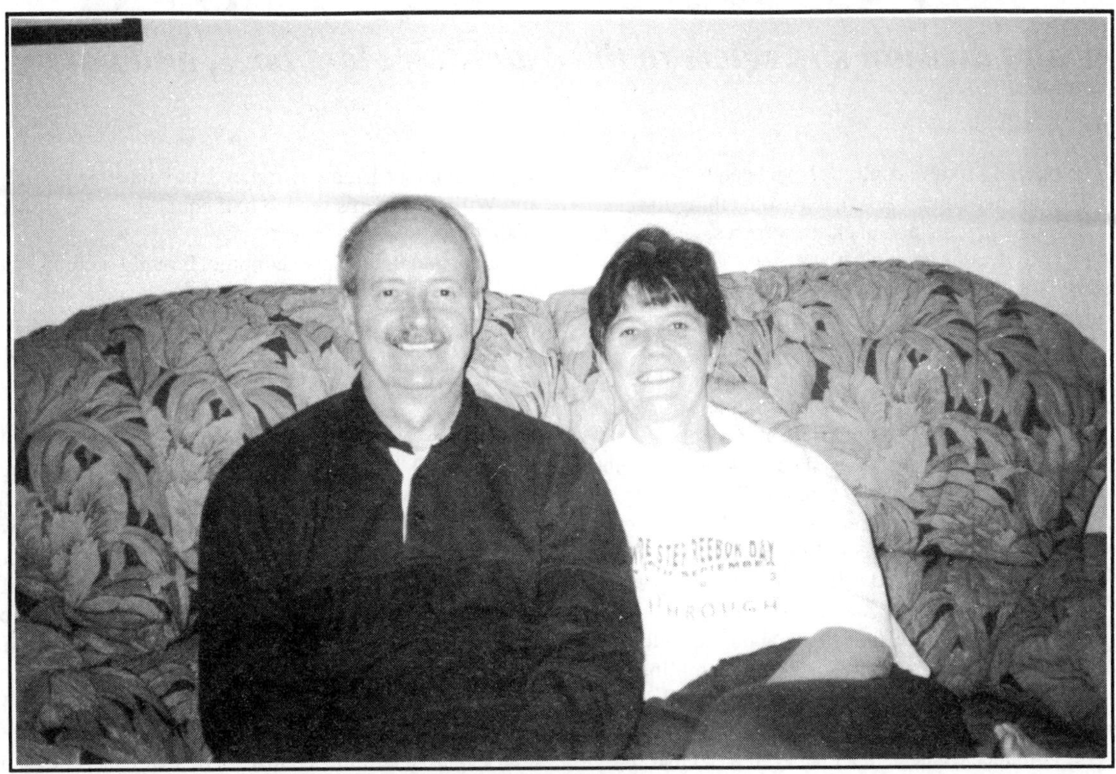

When Cliff Jackson first signed for Palace he used to travel to London from Plymouth, staying in digs with Barry Dyson. Eventually the Jacksons moved into a club house.

It was standard practice in those days; very few players could buy their own house. As Sheila Jackson points out, apart from anything else, building societies didn't like giving footballers mortgages because they were considered a high risk.

"We paid ten shillings a week for a three bedroomed house," says Cliff, who first met Sheila when she did some baby sitting at his home.

Sheila Jackson married Cliff when he was at Swindon. Although not a football fan, she has supported him throughout his career, sharing the good times and the bad.

"When Cliff told Bert he was getting married," she recalls, "Bert's first reaction was 'is she in the club?', then 'what are you getting married for?'." It wasn't unusual for football clubs to tacitly disapprove of wives and girlfriends, but Sheila feels Palace were different – the club lived up to its family reputation.

"At a lot of clubs if you're not in the first team you're not part of the crowd, but Palace wasn't like that. If you played for Palace you were part of the family. They were the first club to give Cliff a day off when I had a baby ... and they sent flowers. I can't remember that ever happening anywhere else."

Both Cliff and Sheila feel Palace's human face was due to Arthur Wait. "A.J. was a terrific bloke, who really made the club. It was a good club and like a family," says Cliff. "At the time they used to have table tennis tables in the ground. We used to nip down to the cafe on the corner and come back and hang around the club.

"My other clubs weren't as big as Palace who had a weight training room, we used to go in and play head tennis. It was a lovely atmosphere."

Like colleagues in any walk of life there was some socialising although the team didn't live in each other's pockets. "Mel Blyth lived on his own and he used to come round quite regularly and eat us out of house and home," recalls Sheila.

"We lived in Orpington and Bobby Woodruff lived 150 yards from us while Colin Taylor lived next door for a while, but it wasn't a particularly social thing.

But it was the other Jackson family, that of goalkeeper John, with whom they were closest, even sharing holidays with the children.

The happy atmosphere also spilled over into match days. "I used to take our two eldest children to the match when Cliff was playing. By half-time they would be getting restless and you used to be able to hand them down over the heads of the crowd onto the terrace where they could play without any trouble. At the end the crowd would hand them back.

"Palace was the only time I've hit another supporter, though. It was at a first division match and I was pregnant at the time and this man in front was telling a story about Cliff being seen in a gay pub, so I hit him with my handbag!"

Sheila was rarely alone in the stand. "Mark Lazarus's mum always went. She was a big lady who was rumoured to have had 17 children, while Steve Kember's mum used to get annoyed with anyone who dared criticise him."

But Sheila only left once because she could no longer stand it. "That was the day Cliff became the first player substituted for Palace.

"The crowd were booing and so I left the ground. But we had a good time and have no complaints. "Even the money was good. It's no comparison with today, but it was a good living."

The Seventies ... Palace go glam

From first division strugglers to third division glory boys, and back

The opening fixture couldn't have been better. Manchester United at home. Just the thing to set the pulses racing and pack the terraces.

United were in decline somewhat after their glory days of the late 60s. But although Matt Busby had gone and Wilf McGuinness was now in charge of their ageing side, United's name was still synonymous with glamour and success. Selhurst Park had never seen anything like it. Palace raced to complete their new stand, adding seats at the back – and creating a standing enclosure at the front.

Bert Head had a little money to spend and sought bargains north of the border. Roger Hynd a centre-half from Rangers cost £22,000, while Danish international Per Bartram from Morton and Gerry Queen, who cost £35,000 from Kilmarnock, were also tempted south. Alan Pinkney, was picked up cheaply from Exeter.

To celebrate promotion, a history book about the club was rush released. *The Crystal Palace Story* cost 15 shillings and for years remained the only written material about Palace apart from handbooks and programmes which rarely offered meaningful guidance to the club's history. It's sad that the gushing and 'loyal' emphasis of match programmes, which may be expedient to hide any embarrassments at the time of writing, have not served clubs well in the long term because, in many cases, it is difficult to discover the full story behind events. In programmes every player is good and whatever the result the team always play well.

The *Crystal Palace Story* was written by Roy Peskett, a respected *Daily Mail* journalist and long-time Palace fan. It had its faults, perhaps because of the haste in which it must have been written, but it also contained some genuinely interesting stories. Copies these days are rare but they do occasionally turn up in second hand book shops. If you see one, grab it while you can.

Palace announced their new ticket prices and it came as no surprise to discover that first division football was going to cost more. An old stand season ticket was £18.18s (no half price), while the old and new standing enclosures were £8 for adults and £4 for boys and OAPs.

In pre-season, we were given a taste of what was to come when Chelsea beat us 2-0 at the Crystal Palace sports centre. Two days later the Ghanaian touring team Asante Kotoko was defeated 3-1 and we followed that with a 1-1 draw at home to Morton.

The comparatively modest investment in players meant that the team which kicked off in front of another record attendance, this time 48,610, was more or less the same one that had won promotion. The match belonged to John Jackson, who denied George Best at point blank range and tipped a Brian Kidd header round the post as well as holding every cross United threw at him. Yet Palace scored first. And it was a defender's delight. From Roger Hoy's long throw, Mel Blyth met the ball with a header and although Roger Hynd followed it over the line the credit for our first ever top flight goal went to Blyth. The ecstatic crowd was quietened when Bobby Charlton equalised, but the feverish atmosphere was stoked up again when debutant Queen raced on to a through ball from Kember, beat David Sadler, and slipped it under Jimmy Rimmer. But Palace couldn't hold on and Willie Morgan's second half equaliser gave United a share of the spoils.

Our second match, also at home, brought a comfortable victory over Sunderland. The north-easterners were bound for relegation and, by all accounts, already looked doomed. The victory established a Palace record of 18 consecutive matches without defeat. Tony Taylor and Queen, again, scored the goals. The run ended in the first away match of the season – a tough proposition at Goodison Park. Palace went down 2-1 after Mel Blyth had opened the scoring. Although they had wilted under Evertonian pressure, the *Daily Mail* described Palace's performance as "stonewall". Later, Roy Peskett, writing in the programme for the match with Liverpool, suggested the name particularly suited John Jackson, who had played brilliantly so far, but would be called upon many more times in the coming years to live up to the "Stonewall Jackson" tag.

The Glaziers collected their first away point in a far from convincing goalless draw at Roker and were pilloried for their negative attitude against a side that had yet to score. Substitute Per Bartram had only been on the pitch 17 minutes when he served notice of his skills. "Bartram misses clincher" wrote the *Daily Sketch* after the Danish forward had fluffed an easy chance with a wild swing at the ball.

With the kind of moronic bias and blind lack of understanding you only get from programmes, the Palace tome proclaimed: "Never mind Per, there'll be many goals from you yet."

To emphasise such faith, Bert Head played him at centre-forward in the next four games. But the Dane didn't look remotely the part, even though he managed to get on the scoresheet in the last of these matches. His goal, past England's Gordon Banks, helped Palace beat Stoke 3-1.

Bartram also had difficulties off the pitch. The *Evening Standard* explained: "He has a work permit as an alien, but there are certain restrictions on his movements and he has to report to the police." A wise precaution, you could never tell when a second rate Danish footballer was about to make off with the nation's top secret defence plans, could you?

Palace had problems up front all season but Bartram was patently not the answer and, after a handful of dismal performances, he returned to Morton marked down by the fans as one of Palace's "little errors". He wasn't the only one who wasn't quite up to what was already proving to be a difficult season. Head began a clear out of some of his promotion squad. First to go was Colin Taylor, who returned to Walsall without making a first division appearance and, as Christmas approached, Mark Lazarus moved to Orient and Bobby Woodruff joined Cardiff City.

Palace struggled throughout, winning just six matches, but they developed a valuable knack of pinching unlikely draws and that is the main reason they survived. The heroes of the hour were undoubtedly John Jackson, John McCormick and Mel Blyth. But there was no escaping the fact that Palace lacked quality. Inevitably it meant there were one or two harsh lessons along the way, some of which were easier to take than others. In the draw at Chelsea, Palace were victims of Peter Osgood's famous "leave it John" call. Jackson was fooled and Ossie laughingly accepted the gift. Learning to expect ungentlemanly conduct from the swaggering Blues was one thing, but Palace could have done without refereeing inconsistencies at vital moments. In the 2-2 draw at Coventry, Pat Partridge gave City two dubious penalties and further angered Palace by ordering the second to be retaken. Kember's protests earned him a booking. On the train home, a narked Palace were further irritated by a "hooligan" element among their fans. According to *Croydon Midweek*, the communication cord was pulled six times and Head grumbled: "On the whole our fans have been well behind us but since getting to the first division there has been an element of support which is causing trouble and doing us no good at all." The childish behaviour caused a one and a half hour delay.

While the more sensible Palace fans savoured their first season in the top flight, they didn't have much to celebrate. A long season was not made easier by Chelsea and Arsenal, both of whom hammered five past us at Selhurst Park with the *Big Match* cameras making sure Palace's misery was plain for all to see.

In the first of these maulings, John Radford hit a hat-trick for Arsenal, while Bartram scored our scant consolation. A couple of months later, Chelsea turned up and gave everyone a severe case of deja vu. It was the fifth of six straight defeats for Palace and made it a miserable Christmas, we'd already been beaten at Spurs on Boxing Day.

Chelsea did help us out a little when, under the new loan transfer system, they lent us their record scorer Bobby Tambling. Although he didn't score in his three matches, he added a little zip up front and there was genuine disappointment when he returned to the Bridge, his fleeting appearance only serving to illustrate the shortcomings of our forward line.

The Arsenal and Chelsea fiascos were part of an appalling run which brought just three points in 25 games. Queen's consolation goal against Chelsea was the only one we recorded in five matches. Of greater consolation was another record busting attendance, 49,498. But record attendances counted for nothing in the table. It was the last match of the 60s. Palace had started the decade by being beaten 7-1 in division three south, so it was progress of a sort.

We went into the New Year third from bottom and matters took a turn for the worse when fellow strugglers West Brom

Bad day in Geordieland

Back in 1970, Andrew Fishleigh discovered what an unwelcoming place Newcastle can be

A letter to the Palace programme following the home game with Newcastle in 1970 complained: "Whilst returning home on Saturday from the Newcastle match I was disgusted to see a crowd of about forty louts wearing Palace colours attacking a man and his young son near Selhurst Station just because the boy was wearing a Newcastle rosette."

An unpleasant incident indicative of the times, but in Rail Travellers' News of 22 January 1977 Palace fan Andrew Fishleigh recounted a tale that showed Newcastle fans were hardly angelic themselves ...

Palace were due to play Newcastle United and, as usual, the coaches left Selhurst Park at about 11.30pm on the Friday night before the game.

Some of us wouldn't have noticed if the coach driver had set off for Cornwall owing to the amount of alcohol we had consumed beforehand.

When we arrived in Newcastle we were told to return to a pre-arranged pick up spot at 11pm that night, thus enabling everyone to stay in town to celebrate or drown our sorrows.

I was with a few friends and we were fed up with having to drown our sorrows after every match, so we decided to celebrate before the game.

We eventually left the pub and, after being chased through the scenic back alleyways by some friendly Geordies, we finally arrived at the ground only to see Palace go down by two goals to nil.

That was nothing. Two of us decided to escape the unwanted attentions of certain members of the Leazes End and in order to kill time we went to watch a film.

We eventually left to make our way to the pick up point at half past ten. Although we were in good time with fifteen minutes to spare, there was no sign of the coaches.

We later learned that the other Palace fans had been given a hearty send off by a load of Newcastle skinheads and the coach drivers had thought it prudent to leave while two of the coaches were still relatively intact, no doubt having nightmares about the send off we would have received had Palace won.

My friend and I were stranded, stony-broke and quite cold.

We decided to enlist the help of the Newcastle police, hoping they would prove more hospitable than the civilian inmates of that dark satanic dump. But they could not just lend us the fare home, oh no.

Instead they had to ring Norbury police to get them to phone both our parents homes and get them to pay our fares to them. Norbury police would then ring Newcastle to confirm payment. Meanwhile I was busily convincing myself that my parents would get their own back for being woken at one in the morning and would refuse to cough up.

Luckily they saw the "funny side of it", as they put it, – although we didn't – and we were at last able to catch the 2.15am train to London. We arrived home at ten o'clock on Sunday morning.

took both points in a 3-2 victory at Selhurst. It left Palace in the bottom two. Relegation looked more certain than ever. In January, as a brief respite from their struggles in the league, Palace took part in the BBC programme *Quiz Ball*. The team was: John Jackson, Alan Pinkney and Gerry Queen plus a celebrity. Queen had represented Kilmarnock the previous year and did so well that Head personally insisted he be included in the Palace team.

Palace couldn't have done worse at *Quiz Ball* than they did in the League Cup, going out after a replay to Derby, who were enjoying their elevation to division one rather more than us. The Rams finished us off in fine style at the Baseball Ground, 3-0. That left the F.A. Cup as Palace's last chance for glory. Third division Walsall were despatched 2-0 in the third round but when we were drawn at White Hart Lane, the chances of further progress looked limited in the extreme. Even the most optimistic couldn't have expected Palace to hold Jennings, Greaves, Gilzean and co. to a draw let alone to finish the job in the replay. The achievement was all the more remarkable because McCormick broke his nose after 20 minutes of the second game forcing a defensive reshuffle which might normally have prompted a collapse.

In front of 45,980, the decisive goal came in the 58th minute. Tony Taylor crossed for Queen to head home. It sparked wild scenes of jubilation and a lot of trouble behind the Tottenham goal. Spurs fans also caused trouble at Norwood Junction after the match, smashing up a train, but nothing could detract from Palace's victory and Geoffrey Green in *The Times* wrote: "If anybody was the King of Selhurst Park last night it was Queen."

It effectively finished Jimmy Greaves' career as a Spurs player – he was dropped for their next match along with Alan Gilzean, Cyril Knowles and Joe Kinnear.

As Chelsea had refused us permission to keep Tambling, Head considered signing Greaves for Palace. But it was West Ham who got him, which was probably just as well. By his own admission, Greaves was already reliant on the bottle. Now he was West Ham's problem, not Palace's – we had enough of our own.

Needing to reinforce the attack, Palace paid Newcastle £20,000 for former Hibs and Scotland international Jim Scott. He added some strength and height but failed to score in any of his 11 appearances which wasn't good enough, Palace needed goals. But Palace stuck to their task manfully and were rewarded with eyebrow raising draws at Wolves, Chelsea, Man United and Newcastle. There was also a fifth round cup tie crowd which fell short of another record by just 19 people. Chelsea were the visitors and, as usual, the result went emphatically their way. Roger Hoy's equaliser was never going to be enough and, inspired by Osgood, they scored four times. They had now put nine past us at Selhurst in the space of a couple of months. It was almost too much to bear, at least we could concentrate on the league.

No matter how we tried we couldn't seem to win and were now in a vicious spiral heading back towards division two. But just when it looked as if the game was up, we struck lucky. With three matches left, Manchester City, who had just beaten West Brom in the League Cup Final, threw us a lifeline by leaving out all the players who were presumably still hung over. Palace silenced Maine Road with a spirited performance, particularly from John Jackson and then plundered the points against City reserves with a Queen strike. Unbelievable! And it was immediately improved upon. A vital 2-0 win over Southampton set up a desperate last match of the season – against Man City.

The tension was unbearable, but Hoy grabbed the only goal and Palace clung on for dear life against a just about sobered up City – none of the City forward line who were listed in the programme played.

Six vital points. It put us in with a chance of the most unlikely escape since Harry Houdini cancelled his ticket for the Titanic. Our programme was now complete and it was up to Sunderland and Sheffield Wednesday, each with two games left, to try to catch us. Three points for either would send Palace down.

Sunderland faced Liverpool, but the greatest threat was from the Owls, who faced Man United at Old Trafford. When United cruised into a two-goal lead after eight minutes through Best and Charlton, south London rejoiced. But, while Sunderland conceded a goal two minutes from time to confirm their inevitable relegation, Wednesday staged a comeback. Coleman made it 2-1 just before half time and, when they equalised in the second half, the turnaround looked a certainty. They forced nine corners in the last ten minutes but, although George Best had a goal disallowed, the match finished level. Wednesday now needed to win their last game.

It didn't look good. Ironically Man City were the visitors to Hillsborough and, again, they were short staffed. They were not only unable to call upon star internationals Francis Lee, Colin Bell and keeper Joe Corrigan but had the added distraction of an impending European Cup Winners' Cup Final against Polish side Gornik.

Against Palace, such distractions had proved to be City's undoing, but this time they took the game to Wednesday and hit the post twice. Then they suffered a major blow when Mike Summerbee, one of their few remaining stars, was stretchered off. Ironically this turned out to be good news for Palace because, within three minutes of his arrival, substitute Ian Bowyer scored. City then missed a penalty – Peter Grummitt saving from Mike Doyle – and in the second half Coleman equalised. Forty-five thousand Wednesdayites, urged the home side to grab the goal which would keep them up and it looked to have arrived when Whitham netted … but he was ruled offside and with three minutes left Bowyer made sure for City, and Palace.

One season of first division football and we'd already set records: two points fewer than any club had ever needed to stay up, less wins than any club not to be relegated and fewest goals. Put that on the honours list.

Mysteriously, Sir Alf Ramsey declined to select any Palace players for his 1970 World Cup squad, but the Selhurst fans could at least watch the finest football feast in history happy in the knowledge that the players representing England in Mexico – arguably the best ever England team – would be parading their talents at Selhurst for at least one more season … although not in Palace colours. The relief throughout the club was summed up by John Sewell in the *Supporters' Club Official Handbook 1970-71* (price 2/-):

"We players expected a really tough struggle in our first season in the first division, but we did not expect it to be quite so desperate and nerve-wracking as it was.

"It was a terribly frustrating situation when we had put everything into our late fight to stay up but had to sit back waiting to see whether the other strugglers would send us down by finishing with two good results. I promise we won't let it happen again…"

During the close season, Bert Head finally did what many felt he should have done when Palace were first promoted.

He bought quality. The first "star name" to arrive was Chelsea striker Alan Birchenall, one of the earliest £100,000 footballers, who'd been unable to get into Dave Sexton's team. The fee was a joint one, included in the £140,000 Palace paid was Bobby Tambling, still Chelsea's record goalscorer. He was one of the real glamour boys of the 60s. Yet he was still only 29 and capable of doing a good job for Palace.

To strengthen the defence we moved for classy left-back Peter Wall from Liverpool, who were in a transitional phase after being humiliated by second division Watford in the F.A. Cup.

Meanwhile, some of the old guard moved out. Cliff Jackson joined Torquay, Roger Hynd went to Birmingham and Roger Hoy joined Luton.

Hoy was considered surplus to requirements because of the successful partnership between McCormick and Blyth and the emergence of Phil Hoadley. So Palace took the opportunity to recoup some of their outlay by releasing him.

The first match of the 1970-71 season was at the Hawthorns where West Brom included Jeff Astle. Poor Astle had been pilloried for a dreadful miss in England's 1-0 World Cup defeat against Brazil, even though he'd only been on the pitch a couple of minutes.

The Palace fans were not in a forgiving mood and were first to try out a new song:

He shot, he missed
*He must be f*****g pissed*
Jeffrey Astle, Jeffrey Astle

Astle and co. on home soil were no mugs though and Palace did well to come away with a point. Although the next game against Man City ended in defeat, it was the only reverse in the first eight games. The new men had settled well and Palace moved into third, behind Man City and Leeds. Some looked askance, but it was no fluke.

Birchenall was the leading light of a team transformed from the outclassed outfit of the season before. He scored his first goal for Palace in an impressive victory over Newcastle on his 25th birthday, but the best result of this golden autumn was undoubtedly the 1-1 draw at Anfield.

Bobby Graham gave the scousers the lead, following up on an Emlyn Hughes thunderbolt, but Peter Wall, skipper for the night against his old team, marshalled Palace superbly and we took the game to Liverpool. Ray Clemence was twice called upon to preserve the lead but even he had no chance with Queen's equaliser.

Perhaps it shouldn't have surprised anyone when this new found success went to Palace's head slightly. In September, while lying 4th in division one, a touch of complacency nearly allowed third division Rochdale to pull off a league cup upset at Selhurst Park. Palace started well enough, Birchenall putting us ahead, but Rochdale fought back and in the 23rd minute Norman Whitehead's 30-yarder took a deflection. Lacklustre Palace endured some harrowing moments before the visitors' leading scorer Reg Jenkins hit the back of the net at the wrong end to restore our lead. When David Payne made it three everybody assumed that was that. But Palace's complacency was punished in the last six minutes. Peter Cowans and then Jenkins scored to take us back to Spotland for a replay.

David Provan came in for the injured Birchenall in the return but this time Palace's attitude was better. After weathering an early Rochdale storm, Queen gave us the lead after 18 minutes and just after the break Scott made it 2-0. Rochdale hit back as Palace took their foot off the gas, but Queen knocked a cross down for Tony Taylor to finish the scoring.

Having reached the next round of the league cup and on the back of three wins in the row, Palace were in confident mood. The foundation of this early flourish was undoubtedly our defensive solidity. John Jackson had already kept six clean sheets, including four in a row. But a 3-0 defeat by Tottenham at Selhurst brought all the usual nightmares rushing back. Mike England lapped up all the thoughtless high balls and Spurs could have had rather more to show than Martin Chivers goal on the half hour. Alan Mullery clinched it in the 70th minute and Chivers got another at the end. Palace had been given a sharp lesson and a week later

Courtesy of Cliff and Sheila Jackson

Players, wives and girlfriends at the club dinner and dance at the Savoy Hotel before the 1970-71 season

Colorsport

1971: a Palace wall versus Tottenham.
Trying to get things organised are (left to right): Steve Kember, Jim Scott, Alan Birchenall and Bobby Tambling

Everton beat us 3-1– all the goals arriving before half time. Palace tightened up in the second half, but it was too late.

Those two defeats might have precipitated a collapse, but the team was made of sterner stuff and fought back with three inspiring victories. The first, against Southampton on October 3, proved unlucky for ten year-old Julian Turrell though. Tambling crashed a wayward shot into the crowd and broke the boy's right arm. The following week, Palace went to Old Trafford and spoilt Bobby Charlton's 500th appearance for United. Peter Wall broke down the left and crossed for Tambling to angle a low drive past Rimmer from the edge of the box. Tambling had, for the most part, turned provider for the Birchenall-Queen partnership and as a result Palace were finding it much easier to score than in 1969-70.

Another good performance brought a home win over West Brom and Palace lined up against struggling West Ham hoping to correct a disappointing failing. We had not beaten London first division opponents in the league so far. The struggling Hammers looked likely candidates to break the duck, but things didn't work out that way. Bobby Howe put United ahead after five minutes and although Queen had a goal ruled out, we struggled. It took until the 75th minute to get on terms but we couldn't conjure up a winner. It was considered a point lost and another two went missing the following week in a pathetic performance at bottom of the table Burnley.

On the evidence of Turf Moor, Coventry's warm welcome, in which their programme proclaimed: "Palace visit us today poised on the brink of a strong challenge for the First Division Championship," was just hot air. The truth was that the brief flowering of Crystal Palace as a first division force was nearly over.

There was still plenty of excitement though. We drew at home with league leaders Leeds in a match memorable for an absolutely farcical goal. Nearly 38,000 gasped in disbelief as Sewell sent an aimless lob goalwards which United's Welsh international keeper Gary Sprake, under no pressure, dropped into his own net for an unexpected equaliser. Sewell was credited with the goal, but Sprake was the real culprit and the *Big Match* reminded the growing band of London based Leeds fans of the moment in the opening titles for the rest of the season.

Sprake had a reputation for dopey mistakes. On one occasion he threw the ball into his own net and the season before he had allowed a soft shot slip from his grasp to give Chelsea an equaliser in the Cup Final.

Two days later, Palace went to Highbury in the fourth round of the League Cup and put up stern resistance in the face of wave after wave of Arsenal attacks. We then scored twice against the run of play to become the only team to beat the Gunners at home in their double year. Queen's opening goal and Tambling's penalty were the virtually only occasions in which we got out of our own half. Having knocked them out of the league cup, Palace returned for the league match, played in torrential rain, and put up another fine display. Radford opened the scoring for Arsenal but

Birchenall levelled almost immediately to secure a point.

Aside from that, Palace's record against London opposition remained the stuff of nightmares. To be fair, Chelsea, Arsenal, Spurs and West Ham, who at the time represented the capital alongside Palace in division one, were all tremendously powerful clubs, brimming with talent. It was hard to be a Palace fan. We couldn't hope to match the stars and the trophies of the other four. Against Charlie George, Peter Osgood, Bobby Moore, Geoff Hurst, Martin Peters, Alan Hudson and Alan Mullery, we had little answer, so this brief period near the top of the table was a rare moment in which to bask. It didn't last long. Just when things were going well, and we were celebrating Steve Kember's debut for England Under-23s against West Germany, the dark clouds arrived again.

Palace went out of the league cup at Old Trafford in a match which made the league result of a month before look like the mirage it was. We were missing Sewell and Tambling, while Birchenall was stretchered off after five minutes following a bad tackle. John Fitzpatrick put United ahead just before half-time and by the 52nd minute Kidd had added two more. Queen pulled one back but Charlton got a fourth before Tony Taylor made the scoreline respectable on the stroke of full time. Soon after, Tambling was ruled out for three months. His experience and class were greatly missed and he was joined in the treatment room by Payne and Queen, who had developed a useful understanding with Birchenall. It was unfortunate that they were interrupted. They never really regained the flow when they were reunited.

The effect on Palace's form and morale was startling – only five more wins during the rest of the season and a final placing of 18th, just two places higher than the season before. There were still some memorable moments though, including our first victory in 17 visits to Portman Road since Ipswich entered the League in 1938 and a home win over Liverpool with a goal by the recently restored Queen. But our Cup luck was out. The tie against Chelsea turned on a disallowed goal when we were 2-1 up and the visitors fought back to snatch a draw. Third round day was overshadowed by the Ibrox Park disaster in which 66 fans died following a late Rangers equaliser in the derby match with Celtic. The nation was stunned and there were calls for greater safety at football grounds. A week or two later the following note appeared in the Palace programme:

"Most of you who were here for our Cup match with Chelsea will have seen a 'disturbance' behind the Whitehorse Lane goal during the match. This was not as many people thought a fight amongst rival fans but a reinforced concrete crush barrier giving way. Fortunately no-one was hurt and the police quickly formed a human wedge into the crowd to prevent anyone from being crushed. A number of youngsters were helped onto the cinder track and transferred to the Holmesdale end of the ground.

As far as the barrier was concerned, this was erected in the summer of 1969 and was therefore only 18 months old. It had also been tested to withstand a great deal of pressure only a matter of weeks beforehand. These tests were made as a result of a Football Association directive earlier this season for all clubs to carry out stringent inspections as to the safety of grounds …

There is one important requirement for the safety of everyone at Selhurst Park and that is your co-operation. At the end of every game there is always a big rush for the exits. The police have particularly asked us to stress that crushes occur when everyone is in a hurry. Please therefore take your time when leaving the ground and WALK DON'T RUN. If you can wait for a few minutes at the end of a match please do so – it will help a great deal.

Here at Selhurst we have spent £400,000 on general ground improvements during the past two seasons but much of this as far as safety is concerned would be to no avail if we could not rely on your co-operation in leaving the ground in an orderly manner."

Palace Secretary Chris Hassell

Fortunately no-one was seriously hurt in the Palace-Chelsea incident but it serves to illustrate how long football safety rested on luck, even after Ibrox. There wasn't much to smile about when Chelsea comfortably overcame Palace in the replay, except this perhaps:

"Few clubs in modern football exist on more friendly terms than Crystal Palace and Chelsea, and next to Palace themselves no-one was more delighted than we were at their promotion to the first division in 1969 and their successful fight against relegation a year later.

We fancy we are revealing Palace's feelings as well as our own when we say how much we regret that our teams have been brought together so early in the Cup.

Hulton Deutsch

The hazy beauty of the old Whitehorse Lane end provides a fitting backdrop to Palace's F.A. Cup tie with holders Chelsea in January 1971. Gerry Queen beats David Webb to get in a header

Pity that one of us must lose interest after this third round; naturally, we hope it will not be us. But if that is the way it has to be, there is no club we would rather see go on at our expense than Crystal Palace."

Pass the sick bucket, please.

John Jackson was the main reason for living in the dark winter days of 1971. His inspired keeping and heroics beyond the call of duty eventually earned him a first representative honour. Sadly it was not for England but for the Football League against the Scottish League in Glasgow. Brian James of the *Daily Mail* wrote: "Jackson by his display joined a long and growing list of goalkeepers who have been thought good enough to represent their country. He gained his place with men like Banks, Shilton, Clemence, Stepney, Bonetti, Glazier, Montgomery, Rankin, Rimmer, Farmer and Corrigan around, at some level, internationals all."

Gordon Banks was in action at Selhurst Park shortly afterwards. Stoke had just been denied an F.A. Cup Final appearance by a last gasp equaliser for lucky Arsenal, so it was little surprise when they gave a tired display. Palace, gratefully, took full advantage.

We had signed Bolton's Terry Wharton in another feeble attempt to bolster the flagging goal tally. But his only striking contribution in 13 games was one that helped us beat Stoke. The match ended a disappointing spell of 15 matches in which the victories over Ipswich and Liverpool were the only bright spots.

Towards the end of the season, *The Big Match* cameras captured a sparkling performance from the much despised (at Selhurst Park anyway) Denis Law. He turned on the style as Man United came from two-down to beat Palace 5-3. We played our part to the full, but the United roadshow in full swing was too much even for the resistance of Birchenall, Tambling and Queen, all of whom got on the scoresheet together for the only time.

On the last day, after Palace had completed their home programme with a 2-0 win over Everton, there was a disgraceful showing at Southampton. The 6-0 battering brought the season to a shocking end. The Saints were considered whipping boys for most of the division and not the sort of side who should have been handing out six goal beatings, even to Palace. It left a sour taste to a season which had promised so much.

Birchenall had threatened rather more than the ten goals he delivered in the league but, with three more in the cups, he still finished leading scorer, one ahead of Queen. The end of the season marked the end of the road for John Sewell. After 255 games in claret and blue he almost inevitably joined Orient where he would be followed by numerous others in the 70s. The phrase "ex-Crystal Palace" would become very well worn indeed in east London as the decade progressed.

Meanwhile, the Crystal Palace Ladies football team reached the final of the Women's Southern Area Cup when they played a team called Willy Walker Wonders. Palace Ladies was run by Sue Head, the daughter of the Palace manager.

No new players arrived during the close season with Bert Head apparently satisfied that with a settled side we were good enough to compete, although this was contrary to the evidence of the second half of the 1970-71 season. The only new thing about Palace was the kit. The beautiful claret shirts with narrow blue stripes were replaced by an all-white kit with a claret and sky blue vertical band down the centre – clearly influenced by the Ajax number which had been worn with such distinction by Ari Haan, Johann Neeskens and Johann Cruyff as they strolled past Panathinaikos in the European Cup Final.

A similar kit was about the only link Palace had with Ajax. Although we beat Newcastle, who paraded their expensive new signing Malcolm MacDonald, 2-0 on the opening day at Selhurst, we barely looked a first division team let alone European Champions. We lost seven and drew one of the next eight.

Despite almost constant defeat, attendances held steady at around 30,000, not exceptional for the times when there were at least a dozen teams capable of attracting crowds in excess of 45,000, but a healthy figure particularly for a losing side. The Palace fans received plenty of praise for their fervour and devotion too.

For a glamour game against the London teams or Man United, gates would invariably swell above 40,000. In fact, the home draw with Forest was the only time the audience dropped below 18,000. Those that didn't turn up missed a bizarre incident when Palace were awarded a goal which clearly hadn't gone in. The Forest players went bananas and Steve Kember finally admitted to the referee that it was "no goal". His honesty won him the praise of the sports journalists and the condemnation of Arthur Wait, who would have appreciated the extra point rather more than the boost for Palace's sportsmanlike image.

There was an unusually small away attendance for the Leeds-Palace match. Only 18,715 saw the game because it was played at Leeds Road, home of newly promoted Huddersfield, who were kind enough to take one of the eventual relegation spots and thus keep Palace out of it.

The previous season, Leeds had lost the League Championship in controversial fashion when referee Ray Tinkler allowed an apparently offside West Brom goal to stand. The Leeds fans sportingly invaded the pitch in an attempt to reason with him (or kill him, whichever was easier). Elland Road, was closed for four matches and our game was moved to neutral Huddersfield. We were unable to take advantage and Don Revie's gentlemen won 2-0.

As our poor form continued, the board became increasingly concerned and encouraged Head to take action. It's unlikely that selling two of our best players was quite what they had in mind, but Chelsea's £150,000 offer for Kember broke the Palace transfer record. He was followed out of the door

David Payne
Illustration: Jason Axell

by Alan Birchenall, sold to Leicester for £100,000.

Also on the way out, in the first of several Stalinesque purges, were Jim Scott and Terry Wharton, both of whom could claim prominent places in the all-time hopeless Palace strikers list, and, more surprisingly, Phil Hoadley who was allowed to play his part in furthering Orient's reputation as the Palace graveyard.

Scott's last appearance ironically produced one of his few goals. Ross Jenkins added another as we beat Everton 2-1. The lanky Jenkins was not destined to make the grade at Selhurst although he would emerge as a first division star with Watford, but only after he'd spent a couple of years languishing in the fourth division waiting for the Hornets' brief rise to prominence.

Coming in were Airdrie's Sammy Goodwin, centre-half Bobby Bell from Blackburn and Blackpool's John Craven. Bell had started the season as an Ipswich player but after being swapped for Alan Hunter, he lasted only two weeks at Ewood Park before he joined Palace – he hadn't actually played for Rovers. The ink was barely dry on his contract when he was off again, for a three game spell on loan to Norwich.

With all respect Goodwin, Craven and Bell were not what the fans wanted at all. It would have been difficult to argue that any of them were adequate replacements for the departed and not even the return of Bobby Kellard for a second spell at the club was likely to set the pulses racing or silence the mumbles of discontent.

But old Bert hadn't finished. He moved for two big names, Celtic's Scottish international pair John Hughes and Willie Wallace, both of whom had genuine pedigree. Both had played in European Cup Finals for Celtic – Wallace in the 1967 triumph over Inter Milan and Hughes in the defeat by Feyenoord three years later.

Known as "Yogi Bear", Hughes became as much a cult figure with the Palace fans as he had been with the lads in the Parkhead jungle – he had scored 114 goals in 255 games for Celtic and earned seven full caps for Scotland. Not one to shirk a battle, he was one of four Celts sent off in the infamous "Battle of River Plate" against the Argentine champions Estudiantes in the 1968 World Club Championship. Hughes had started the season in the first team but lost his place to Lou Macari.

Willie Wallace was older and, it must be said, past his best. Like Hughes, he had also been displaced early in the season by an emerging star, Kenny Dalglish. But Wallace also had a wealth of experience, including eight caps for Scotland. He had scored 199 goals for Raith Rovers, Hearts and Celtic.

After the usual defeats by Arsenal and Chelsea, Palace pulled a cracking result out of the hat for the benefit of the *Match of the Day* cameras and it was Hughes who took the eye with two goals in a blasting performance. Highly rated Sheffield United, and their ever so fab and groovy Tony Currie, were ripped apart.

The blunting of the Blades (ha, ha) was followed by the second visit of the season to Leeds Road where we found Huddersfield rather easier meat than Leeds had been. Palace secured the two points with a goal by Tambling while the defence did a sterling job keeping Jimmy Lawson and the Terriers prize possession Frankie Worthington quiet. Head's policy of introducing new faces appeared to be paying off handsomely.

There was no mad rush up the table but, under Kellard's tigerish captaincy, safety was achieved more comfortably than third from bottom suggested. Forest had conveniently sold Ian Storey-Moore hampering their struggle for survival, while Huddersfield were dead in the water before Christmas and failed to win after November 13 except for a distracting Cup run. That left Palace four points clear. We could even afford the luxury of a disappointing goalless draw at home to Huddersfield in front of just over 18,000 on the last day.

Despite the relative comfort with which we secured our fourth season of first division soccer, the omens were not good. We'd won only once since the beginning of March against a Stoke side which had collapsed since lifting the league cup and who were without the Football Writers' Player of the Year Gordon Banks. Stoke's weaknesses helped us secure first division safety with second half goals by Kellard, who beat John Farmer with a penalty, and Queen.

Surely we could not afford to rest on our laurels, especially as the worry over goalscoring had become even more acute. Hughes and Wallace had not been a success. Yogi had been restricted to just 11 appearances because of injury while the diminutive Wallace had scored only three times in 27 matches. Bobby Tambling with eight and John Craven with seven led the league scorers, but Palace totalled just 39 goals.

Tambling had taken his tally for the season to 11 with three cup goals, including one in the league cup where we crashed out in a third round replay to third division champions-to-be Aston Villa. He scored from the spot and Craven was also on the scoresheet at Selhurst but Chico Hamilton and baldy

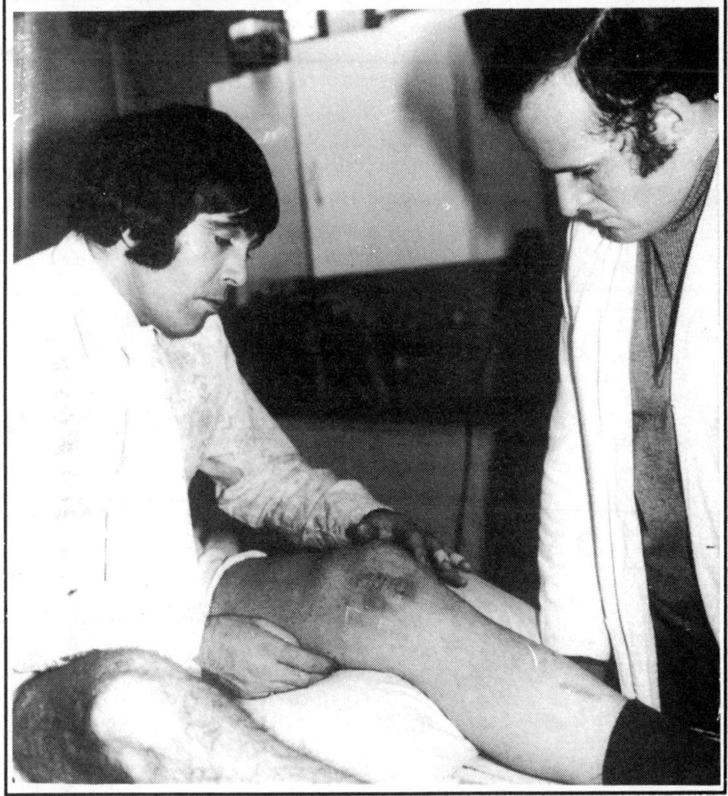
Hy Money

The inspirational Yogi Hughes inspects damage to his knee

Andy Lochhead lived up to their reputations to secure a draw. In the replay Lochhead again and Ray Graydon sent Villa through to meet Blackpool.

In the F.A. Cup Palace drew 2-2 in a fearsome clash with Everton which ended in a near blood bath and featured a rare pitch invasion at Selhurst Park. Yogi was sent off by referee Tommy Dawes and five other players were booked. Palace chairman Arthur Wait blamed the official for the scenes of disorder described in the *Rothmans Football Yearbook* as "scandalous". Wait claimed: "It was a diabolical game and Everton were the culprits. Dawes had a real stinker, at one stage I thought he was going to book the corner flag." Wee Willie Wallace scored twice for Palace, the first on the stroke of half-time and the second with a quarter of an hour to go, but within a minute of going 2-1 up, Colin Harvey equalised for Everton, whose tactics were initiated by an outrageous foul by Joe Royle on John Jackson which left the Palace keeper with a badly gashed leg. Everton have not been liked at Selhurst since. Despite a double from Tambling, there was no justice in the replay. Everton's goals were scored by Scott, Kenyon and Hurst. Hughes was later banned for 21 days for his part in the war.

> **"It was a diabolical game and Everton were the culprits. Dawes had a real stinker, at one stage I thought he was going to book the corner flag."**
>
> Arthur Wait on the Infamous Palace v Everton Cup Tie

It was obvious that Palace were still not good enough to compete, even with the division's more moderate outfits. It seemed only a matter of time before our fingertip hold on the top flight was broken – but not before a roller-coaster season in 1972-73.

Moustaches were all the rage at Selhurst Park. Huge bushy sideburns and long unkempt hair were also the in-thing as football fashion reach its nadir. The dandies such as Best, Marsh, Hudson and Worthington reigned supreme. But Palace were most influenced by the droopy hangdog 'taches popularised by Peter Wyngarde's character Jason King in the TV series *Department S* … and more were about to be imported from the Kings Road. Palace as usual were linked with plenty of good players but, also as usual, we didn't actually buy any of them. Our main priority was still a decent striker. Tambling had been a heroic figure at times but, as he grew older, he could not be relied upon to continue virtually alone. Support for his abilities had been sporadic. Queen popped up from time to time with valuable strikes but, like Wallace, he didn't score often enough and Hughes, who had been crocked in the Sheffield United massacre he'd done so much to inspire, was still not available. In the end, as expected by the cynics, Palace did sweet Fanny Adams or as close as they could get to it. Jenkins was given another chance alongside Wallace while Queen was relegated to substitute and Tambling could not get a look in at all. In fact, the biggest adjustment was to the kit. A white stripe was put down the middle of the claret and blue bands to make it look a little more balanced and a new badge was introduced.

To no-one's surprise we didn't start at all well – four draws but no wins in the first five games – and there was more bad news when Peter Wall broke his leg against his old club Liverpool in a tackle with Tommy Smith.

Things picked up a little with wins over Man City and Newcastle. The benevolent Mancunians were kind enough to score an own goal and miss a penalty, while the Newcastle match also featured a penalty which only Palace could have scored. To say it was harsh was an understatement, Wallace more or less fell over himself, but the referee pointed to the spot. As if that wasn't bad enough, the kick was a masterpiece of comedy. Kellard ran up, slipped and sent both the ball and a clump of earth slithering into the goal past a bemused Iam McFaul. At that stage, Palace looked as if they would be okay.

Although there was little to get really excited about, we were in a comfortable, if fortunate, tenth position. Then things, of course, went badly wrong starting with one of the all-time lame performances which produced a league cup exit against fourth division Stockport. Goalscoring was still a major problem and the only time we actually scored twice

How the *Croydon Advertiser* saw the victory over Stoke City. And another famous Palace fan to add to our collection; Kent and England cricketer Colin Cowdrey

in a match we conceded three. To make it worse, it was against Arsenal in John McCormick's last appearance at Selhurst Park. Paul Hammond, who'd made his debut in goal the week before at Wolves because Jacko had flu, pushed Charlie George's penalty onto a post, but the ref decided the ball had crossed the line. Craven equalised but Radford gave Arsenal the lead again. Craven equalised for the second time but Pat Rice finished the scoring. We then suffered a heavy defeat at Upton Park as our form against London opponents showed little sign of improvement. Head put in a £150,000 bid for Swindon's Don Rogers who, despite often brilliant performances, had remained out of the limelight at the County Ground. Rogers' arrival smashed our transfer record which had been set a short time before by the arrival of Dundee's midfielder Iain Philip who, apart from his record transfer status, remains memorable only for being one of the droopy-moustache brigade and spelling his first name oddly.

Much better was the signing of Chelsea's Irish international left-back Paddy Mulligan. His move across London prompted an outcry from his fellow Stamford Bridge players. Then there was the wing wizardry of Charlie Cooke, also from Chelsea, who, like Rogers and Philip, brought a handsome 'tache with him. Palace were acquiring real quality and no little glamour. Charlie Cooke ... what a player!

With McCormick replaced by Bobby Bell, the old guard was on the way out. Kellard put in a transfer request when Mulligan was made captain and he was replaced in midfield by Philip. Wallace and the ineffective Jenkins were also out.

The new look Palace roared off like a sleek new motor – or at least Rogers did. His injection of pace left Everton gasping as he scored a classic goal to give Palace two points at Selhurst. We now faced three extremely tricky away fixtures and gained highly creditable draws in each. The first was against Leeds, then their championship rivals Derby were denied a valuable point and then Chelsea were held on Mulligan's and Cooke's return to their old stamping ground. After a setback against Ipswich at Portman Road, Palace unleashed their version of the atom bomb on poor, shell-shocked Man United. Their manager Frank O'Farrell lost his job after a legendary Glaziers' performance.

Earlier in the week, Palace had signed Alan Whittle from Everton and he made a sparkling debut as the home team packed with star names and just as much verve, ripped United to shreds. It was Rogers' afternoon though and his skill and running terrorised the United defence. Mulligan scored the first two to give Palace an interval lead and Whittle's gorgeous curler was sandwiched between a pair for Rogers. That's not the whole story though, because Palace missed at least half a dozen chances which without exaggeration could have taken the score into double figures.

But it wasn't all plain sailing. Two days before Christmas, Palace lost to fellow strugglers Leicester at Filbert Street after referee Roy Capey gave City his Christmas present early. With Palace leading through Rogers, David Payne tackled Len Glover and was astounded when Capey pointed to the spot.

Payne told the press: "Glover tried to be too clever and fell over himself, I was stunned when the penalty was given." To add insult to injury, Jacko saved Worthington's penalty but was adjudged to have moved. Frankie Wortho made no mistake second time around and Alan Birchenall rubbed salt into the wound by heading the winner – his first goal of the season.

In the Cup we disposed of Southampton with a majestic performance. Goals from Cooke and Rogers followed up a three goal success against the same opposition on Boxing Day. It was a rare bright spot in a slough of despond. After Palace lost at Newcastle the *Sunday Mirror* reported: "In best stiff upper lip style, Palace boss Bert Head said after this one sided jaunt: 'We lacked aggression – but we won't go down.' It was rather like the captain of a stricken ship failing to notice that the water was lapping round his chest and that the crew had taken to the boats. The score suggests that it was a competitive match. In fact it was so one-sided in the second half that only Newcastle goalkeeper Iam McFaul failed to have a shot at Palace's goal."

In the fourth round of the cup we should have made further progress after earning a replay against second division Sheffield Wednesday. In the return, former Palace man John Holsgrove fouled our latest signing Derek Possee, the former Millwall forward, inside the 18 yard box, but the normally infallible Rogers missed from the spot. It seemed not to matter when Philip gave us the lead but Dave Sunley equalised in the last minute and, although Payne hit the post in a frantic finale, the tie moved to Villa Park where Payne gave us the lead. Brian Joicey equalised after the break only for Rogers to put us ahead again with 19 minutes left. But five minutes later Joicey equalised again and in the second period of extra time completed his hat-trick. Wednesday were in front for the first time and they stayed there.

The club was also in turmoil behind the scenes. Arthur Wait's long reign as chairman was over. Acting as front man for the club's purchasers, Matthews Holdings, Raymond Bloye was installed as vice-chairman and by November he'd taken over with Wait becoming president. It was from Bloye that the decision came to move Bert Head upstairs and bring in a new man.

Hy Money

Wee Willie Wallace takes a close look at Liverpool's starlet Kevin Keegan

THE ONES THAT GOT AWAY

In the early 70s, the Crystal Palace wanted list read like a who's who of British football. Neil Witheroe looks at the ones we signed and those who might have become Selhurst heroes

Colorsport

Palace's record signing from Dundee Iain Philip tussles for the ball with one of the few players we didn't try to buy, Derek Dougan of Wolves.

In our quest to make sense of the loss of Palace's Premier League status, one of the loudest criticisms of the club's management was that they did not buy. Fair comment, but 20 years ago Palace did nothing but spend to preserve a place in the top flight with the same result – relegation.

After many years under the penurious regime of Ron Noades, its hard to imagine Palace with a "power spending" reputation, but during our first spell in division one our purchasing grew more frenzied as we attempted to avoid the dreaded drop. This came to a head (pardon the pun) in the final season of that first tenure prior to which Matthews Holdings had taken control of the club with the promise of "unlimited funds" to strengthen the squad. While those players who actually did join Palace such as Alan Whittle, Derek Possee and Don Rogers have passed into Palace folklore, the list of players with whom we were linked but who never signed is surprisingly distinguished. Just before that fateful 1972-73 season kicked off, chairman Arthur Wait was quoted as saying: "We have been after 23 players and made offers of £100,000 or more in 80% of the cases."

The papers went into wild speculation about the identity of all 23. It is doubtful whether any of their guesses could be classed as informed opinion but the names of Stan Bowles (Carlisle), Alan Mullery (Spurs), Dennis Rofe (Orient) and John Hickton (Middlesbrough) appeared consistently. The only identities to be firmly established were Alan Gowling (Man United) and Derek Johnson (Everton) and only because they'd made it clear they wanted nothing to do with Palace. Whoever the others were it seemed their clubs had no interest in selling and so, in those days, that was that.

It was not only the players' identities that captured the imagination of the press. One bid was reckoned to be in excess of £250,000 which would have smashed the British transfer record. The identity of the player was subsidiary to the actual sum but reports managed to incorporate Southampton's Mick Channon, George Best, who was out of favour at Man United, and even Bournemouth's Ted MacDougall.

Palace started the season without any new stars although the team was obviously unsettled by the rumours. Results were indifferent but it was the league cup defeat by Stockport that finally unlocked the treasure chest – £120,000 was spent on on Iain Philip from Dundee following an impressive performance in a specifically arranged friendly against the Scottish club.

Palace recouped £70,000 by selling Gerry Queen to Orient which prompted more speculation. MacDougall once again topped the list followed by Arsenal's John Roberts and Colin Stein of Rangers.

One or two more astute observers noted that Head had made tentative enquiries with his old club Swindon which could only mean Don Rogers. Three days later the £65,000 purchase of Paddy Mulligan from Chelsea caught the papers cold. In an effort to repair their reputations a fresh round of rumours were launched: Brian Kidd (Man United) Sammy Chapman (Forest) and Charlie Cooke (Chelsea) were all linked with Palace. They were bound to get one right and Cooke signed for £85,000. With spending topping £250,000 further poor results prompted more talk; Joe Harper (Aberdeen) and Tony Brown of West Brom were mentioned although Albion boss Don Howe silenced further chatter about his striker. A possible double swoop for Everton's Alan Whittle and Jimmy Husband was mooted.

Palace mystery bid

£250,000

WAS IT BEST?

By KEN MONTGOMERY

In late October, events took a precipitous turn. Head finally signed Rogers for £150,000 after a month of delicate on-off dealings that had closely involved Arthur Wait, who then made the following statement: "All further transfer negotiations have been frozen until after a special board meeting."

The outcome was a bloodless coup. Ray Bloye, the managing director of Matthews Holdings became chairman while Wait was "kicked upstairs" to a life presidency. A fortnight later, as Bloye played down rumours that his appointment had been contrived at the time of the Matthews takeover, Wait sadly broke all ties with the club, saying: "If I go in future I will sit in the stand as an ordinary supporter. I don't want the backbiting and niggling."

In November the talk turned to our "overweight" squad with several displaced players demanding moves. Most disgruntled was Bobby Kellard, but Bobby Bell, Willie Wallace and Bobby Tambling were also actively seeking transfers. Wallace joined Dumbarton while both Kellard and Bell had been suggested as makeweights in exchange deals with Swindon and Bournemouth for Rogers and MacDougall respectively. Kellard eventually slipped anchor to Portsmouth for £10,000.

Head caused a stir on the eve of the home match with Everton by declaring his current spending was "peanuts" and the rumour-mongers were on the case again. Millwall's Derek Possee, it was almost universally agreed, was the likely target but Head signed Everton's Alan Whittle with £100,000, which raised a few eyebrows. Whittle had been at the centre of some unsavoury incidents the previous season when we played Everton. The press claimed Head was also after Tommy Baldwin (Chelsea) or perhaps Ernie Hunt, who he'd had at Swindon. But in January he went for the £115,000 Possee. With more than £650,000 spent the thought of more was considered too rich for most of the dailies to stomach although one could not resist a mention for Graham Paddon of Norwich.

The focus moved onto Head himself. Although Rogers was an undoubted gem, the team was still in trouble and speculation about the manager's future began to fill column inches.

Such was the gentlemanly nature of football reporting in those days that stories questioning the wisdom of Palace's entry into the Anglo-Italian Cup were taken to mean that all may not be well with the manager's position. Naming names before the present incumbent had lost his job was, on the whole, bad form.

The board started the ball rolling in mid-March while the team were in Bari playing an Anglo-Italian tie. They announced that Head would be promoted to general manager with Terry Long looking after the team on a caretaker basis. A replacement who would command a salary of £15,000 was sought and the press wasted no time listing their favourites. Gordon Jago of QPR was favourite but a "hands off" was issued by Rangers chairman Jim Gregory.

Other candidates included Jimmy Armfield (Bolton), Ron Saunders (Norwich), Bobby Robson (Ipswich) and former Palace coach George Petchey (Orient). But was Manchester City's Malcolm Allison on the list or not? Harry Miller of the *Daily Mirror* declared that Palace were definitely not interested in Allison, a view shared by Allison himself. Interviewed by the *Daily Express* he went on the record: "The Selhurst job doesn't interest me at all. I've nothing against the club – in fact I rather like their style. Unless the directors of Man City decide otherwise, I'm staying."

But when City's directors refused to back his display of loyalty, saying he was free to go if he wished, Mal went, joining us on March 30, 1973.

Although the transfer deadline had passed, the press linked Allison with the return to full-time football of George Best.

Allison had previously tried to sign Best for City but United had refused to part with their wayward star to their deadliest rivals. The story ran for several days with headlines such as "Best for Palace?" Rodney Marsh was also added to some reports as part of a joint swoop that would cost us in the region of £450,000.

Ambitious plans such as these melted away when we were relegated and reports turned from potential purchases to sales. Allison was forced to trim the staff. Although he was undismayed: "The cuts give me a more manageable staff, it was so big before that proper coaching was difficult." The truth behind the bravado was that the endless supply of money had dried up before Allison joined.

He had to sell before he could buy and Best and Marsh were out of the question. Philip was linked with Celtic but eventually returned to Dundee in October 1973. Craven joined Coventry in a £51,000 deal.

Mel Blyth was also a Coventry target and was linked with them in an exchange for Roy Barry, but a season later ended up at Southampton. Bell and Tambling went abroad while Rogers played for South African team Durban Celtic in the summer before returning to Palace for the new campaign.

In the close season the press picked up on stories of a different kind. Allison had a rather public row with his Bunny-girl girlfriend Serena Williams in the middle of a Mayfair Club and Rogers was joined by a "girlfriend" in Durban. The press revelled in the "horror" of their respective wives.

Amidst all this furore little notice was taken of a £35,000 golden handshake for Bert Head, who slipped quietly away from the club he'd managed for seven years, unable to conceal his sadness: "I feel like a kid who has built a sand castle and has had it knocked over."

One imagines Ron Noades and Steve Coppell felt much the same 20 years later.

Colorsport

Blyth spirit of Palace

One of only two players to survive the whole of Palace's first traumatic spell in the first division, Mel Blyth epitomised the 'never say die' attitude associated with the club. Barrie Greene remembers a great

Of the three Palace teams to have won promotion to the first division, the players who finished second in division two at the end of the 1968-69 season must have been the least likely to succeed. Yet it was only after four seasons of struggle and tumult that they finally succumbed to the drop.

When the Palace team returned to the second division in 1973, only two players survived from the promotion side of four years earlier: the great goalkeeper John Jackson, who was sold soon after, and the dependable and faithful defender Mel Blyth.

Mel joined Palace for a modest fee in the summer of 1968 from Scunthorpe United, having been spotted playing for Yarmouth. He was bought as a utility player, a term often used in the 60s for the type of player who can play in various positions.

With striking blond hair and good looks he was always a noticeable figure on the pitch. At first this was a disadvantage, because it was easy to see he was a pretty mediocre performer. But he seemed to command a regular place in midfield.

Mel was the first Palace player to score a first division goal when he headed in against Manchester United in a memorable opener to life in the top flight. That game ended 2-2, but, as the 1969-70 season wore on, immediate relegation back to division two looked a certainty. Mel, like the rest of the team, looked woefully out of his depth.

Parts of the crowd began to give him the sort of stick reserved for the likes of Alan Pardew in later years.

Roger Hynd (of the bow legs supreme) had been signed by manager Bert Head in the close season to give strength to the centre of defence. But he was having a worse time than many and so Mel was given the task of partnering craggy Scot John McCormick in an attempt to tighten up a defence that was the laughing stock of the media following five goal hidings at the hands of Arsenal and Chelsea among other lamentable performances.

This partnership, along with the heroics of Jackson in goal, proved the right formula to keep the Glaziers in the top flight for another season.

The first half of the 1970-1 season was a wonderful time for Palace fans. The arrival of quality players such as Bobby Tambling and Alan Birchenall from Chelsea and Liverpool's left-back Peter Wall gave the team sufficient class to perform well enough to stay in the top ten of the league – and they became the only side to beat Arsenal at Highbury in their double year.

The cornerstone of this brief successful period was the combination of Blyth and McCormick. Mel had finally come of age and found a position that suited his ever improving talent.

He began to add a confident air to his play, showing us he could mix it with the big names he found himself marking. He also developed a panache for back-passes. This amusingly became his trademark as he would endlessly gain possession and immediately look for the route back to Jackson's hands.

If ever records were kept for the most back-passes in a game, Mel would stake a claim to the top ten positions.

What stood out most of all, though, was the way he epitomised the new found spirit that coursed through the team.

Alas the good times were short lived. After finishing lower than they should have done, Palace found themselves by the following October firmly rooted to the foot of the table.

Frantic mid-season transfer activity saw players come and go. Mel was now one of the "old hands".

The new regime avoided relegation yet again, only to find themselves back in the same position the following season, when the flurry of activity included management changes, money injected into the club and more players bought and sold. Still ever faithful Mel remained.

This time he found himself alongside men who were really big names. Don Rogers, Charlie Cooke, and Paddy Mulligan all arrived to fight for the Palace cause.

In Rogers' first match, Palace beat Everton 1-0 and Mel was sent off along with The Toffees' Alan Whittle in a bad tempered incident. It was therefore something of a surprise when Whittle arrived at Selhurst Park shortly after.

For a few weeks, Crystal Palace were the talk of the town, winning games in style including the famous 5-0 drubbing of Manchester United, Denis Law and all. Mel was now playing his best football but, after three and half seasons, only John Jackson remained with him.

Despite the new power of the team, the euphoria was short lived. A disastrous run of defeats saw us slide back down the table almost as swiftly as we had risen up it.

Not even the arrival of the flamboyantly successful Manchester City coach Malcolm Allison as Bert Head's replacement could stop relegation.

It was ironic that Palace, after four years' hard labour against relegation, went down with their best team since gaining promotion.

Mel found himself back where he came from but carried on regardless. He was now as much a permanent fixture at Selhurst Park as the Old Stand. A Palace team was not a Palace team without his name.

He was also a vastly improved player and it must have been especially heartbreaking to see the team slide straight through the second division and into the third.

Once again players came and went. But he soldiered on, turning in solid performances while others around him gave up the ghost.

The 1974-75 season began with Mel, now 30 years old, playing third division football. Had the chance of real success eluded him?

It was Southampton who threw him a surprise lifeline when they paid £90,000 for him.

This figure was enough to show that his efforts had not gone unnoticed. The Selhurst faithful were sad to see him go but could not begrudge him a final fling in the top flight.

A year later, Allison and his young student Terry Venables had developed what was soon being hailed as the finest footballing team ever to grace the third division.

They were surging towards promotion and heading for a Cup semi-final. When the draw pitted Palace against Southampton, Mel, who had already been accepted by Saints' fans and was a pillar in their defence, was faced with the task of stopping Palace from reaching Wembley.

Palace put on a poor show while ever-consistent Mel not only reached Wembley but came away with a winners' medal as the second division team beat Man United. A fitting reward in the twilight of his career.

After more than 100 games for Southampton, Mel returned home in November 1977 for a loan spell. Palace were back in division two and were grooming the side that was to be hailed as "Team of the 80s".

But it was Millwall who wanted him on a permanent basis and that proved best for all parties. He made 75 appearance for the Lions and then drifted out of football.

Mel Blyth was to Palace what Jim Cannon became in later years. Dependable, reliable and almost a permanent fixture at Selhurst Park.

He embodied the spirit that often causes players to take the club to their hearts and with this spirit reach standards of play they may never have reached elsewhere.

Mel is still seen regularly around Selhurst Park, watching matches and always willing to take part in testimonials and charity games.

He is fondly remembered by the fans who watched him give his all for Palace in a career that lasted nine years.

The Man With No Name

Of all the famous players to have pulled on the Crystal Palace shirt, possibly the most mysterious was the taciturn San Jose striker known as the Man With No Name.

He made a remarkable debut one hot afternoon against the evil bandits of Brighton in a match that thousands of Palace fans still remember fondly.

The filthy Brighton defenders were lounging arrogantly around, looking mean and unshaven.

No Palace player dared look them in the eye, the Brighton villains did as they pleased.

Then, as the tumbleweed drifted down Holmesdale Road, a cloud of dust appeared on the horizon of Norwood Hill.

Through the heat haze, the Man With No Name rode into Selhurst Park. He had designer stubble and was smoking a dirty cee-gar and he looked the bees knees.

His hat was pulled down over his narrowed eyes and underneath his poncho was concealed a very fast gun. There was some atmospheric whistling and a bit of twangy guitar and these blokes going "Ooh, hah, hooh."

As he passed by, the Palace bench timidly ducked for cover. Ol' timer Ronaldo Noadez watched the Palace stranger with his beady eye.

"Prepare three coffins," said the Man With No Name dismounting and tethering his horse to the Palace dugout.

The drunken Brighton defenders who had been snoring loudly, stirred from their sleep.

They soon realised the stranger meant business and moved out to meet him. They stood in a line, their hands ready for a quick draw. The Man With No Name pulled back his poncho to reveal his Palace shirt. The Brighton defenders smiled an evil smile. Then he took out a Crystal Palace wristwatch (£5.99 from the club shop). It played a pretty chiming tune (*Glad All Over*). His eyes narrowed and he rolled his cigar round his mouth.

Before the chimes had finished and the Brighton scum could react, the stranger unleashed four lighting fast shots. When the smoke cleared, the defenders lay motionless in the dust of the goalmouth. The Man With No Name mounted up. "My mistake, make that four coffins," he said spitting his chaw of tobacco onto the head of a mangy mutt. "How dare you spit at me!" said the Brighton manager Alan Mullery.

"What'd d'you say your name was, pardner?" said Ronaldo as he handed the new Palace sharpshooter a fistful of dollars. "I didn't." said the stranger as he rode away.

Final score: Palace 4 Brighton 0.

By Tony Matthews

We are the boys who wear claret and blue

Football records have never had a very good image and aside from New Order's World Cup anthem *World in Motion* these days they are invariably unsuccessful.

But for the big clubs in the early 70s a Cup Final appearance effectively guaranteed a chart appearance which meant our innocent ears were subjected to horrors such as *Blue is the Colour* and *Nice One Cyril*.

One might have thought that Palace didn't have much to sing about in those days of struggle but you'd be wrong. Our record *Claret and Blue* was released in November 1972 to celebrate the fact that, against all the odds, we were still a division one side.

Among those who could be heard in fine voice on the disc were Bobby Bell, Mel Blyth, Alan Pinkney, John Jackson, John Craven and Tony Taylor. Professional singers Ray Davies (presumably not of the Kinks) and J. Edwards were recruited to keep the thing reasonably in tune.

It was quite a jolly sort of ditty not dissimilar to the sort of tune used to advertise hoovers and encourage people to do their housework.

The B side was perhaps the strangest record in football history because it didn't mention the game at all, preferring to concentrate on the aims of living peacefully together. It featured not only the players but their wives and was aptly entitled *Why Can't We All Live Together?* Nobody to our knowledge has ever managed to listen to the song all the way through. Anyway you want the words for *Claret and Blue* don't you? Ready, in the key of L, a-one a-two a-three a-four ...

We are the boys who wear Claret and Blue
And what we're doing, were doing for you
All our supporters are second to none
Three cheers for Palace of division one

So let us hear your voices roar
For when we do we are sure to score
When we are playing we always play the game
Home or away to us its all the same
We'll play it hard there's a job to be done
So three cheers for Palace of division one

So let us hear your voices roar
For when we do we are sure to score
We'll do our best and with luck we'll win through
And all your cheering will see our dream come true

Let's hear your voices and give it the gun
So three cheers for Palace
(hip hip) hooray
Three cheers for Palace
(hip hip) hooray
Three cheers for Palace of division one

PALACE (clap clap clap)
(four times)

The record was available from the social section for 50p but stunned the rock music world by failing to make it to number one.

Thanks to Rob Deeks

Born and bred in Folkestone I initially followed Millwall under my father's influence and in the face of the vogue for supporting the big teams.

While at school a new boy arrived. He wore a claret and blue scarf around his neck. He was football mad and actually went to Palace games, which made him the envy of many of his contemporaries.

We used to have a friendly rivalry and as 12 year-olds we went to see Palace play at home to Millwall in 1968. Palace won 4-2 and I was hooked on the club, the atmosphere and the style of football. My first away game was the F.A. Cup tie at Sheffield Wednesday, memorable for getting the ball in the face from a Peter Rodrigues hoof (I never did like that guy).

The boy in the claret and blue scarf

Phil Nicholson was a Millwall fan until a new lad arrived at his school

TAKING my sister to the 1976 F.A. Cup match at Leeds, the memory of the day was overshadowed by a brick coming through the bus window which just missed her (such good sports)

NICK Chatterton going in goal against Lincoln after Tony Burns had been injured in the warm-up.

WINNING 4-2 at Wrexham to set up a nail biting finish to the 1976-77 season. How could I sit by the radio on the following Saturday? I didn't I went back to Wrexham for their game against Mansfield. At Euston I met up with a few other Palace regulars and when we arrived at Wrexham we had a police escort to the ground. Once inside, we discovered about 150 Palace had turned up and after receiving some initial abuse we started cheering for Mansfield and very soon their supporters were chanting *Eagles*, converts all.

Wrexham had a lot of pressure but they couldn't find a way past Stags' keeper Jim Arnold. We were concerned when Billy Ashcroft clattered into him at the end of the first half. In the second half the tension was high, but when Ernie Moss put one away in the dying minutes we breathed a huge sigh of relief.

The Mansfield players saluted their supporters at the end and then came over to us, that's one team I've always liked. After the game we hung around the players entrance and spoke to Arnold who said that he did not remember anything of the second half because he had concussion.

Our first game of the 1977-78 season ironically was against Mansfield and there was quite a welcome for them and their followers.

IN THE Mansfield programme I placed a letter seeking to regain contact with my school chum of years before. Simon Watts was still a regular and we arranged to meet at the Fulham game. It was overshadowed by the injury to Ian Evans in that clash with George Best. I can still remember the sound of that tackle.

IN CANADA in 1978 I saw Vancouver play Dallas in the NASL. John Craven, Steve Kember and Derek Possee played for Vancouver while Jeff Bourne played for Dallas. Steve Kember had provided us with free tickets. I always did like him.

PALACE were 33-1 to win the second division in 1978-79 so I put on £20. Later with the odds reduced to 8-1 another tenner was prised from my grasp.

That Friday night against Burnley was more nail biting than ever bearing in mind what I stood to collect. When Ian Walsh scored the first it was like a great weight had been lifted from my shoulders. We adjourned to a pub in Croydon called the Grosvenor, I think, and spent the evening with Young's bitter and Tia Maria and Vodka chasers.

I worked on the railways and was supposed to be on duty at Dover station the next morning at 7am. My next recollection was waking up at East Croydon at 3am looking for "Hughey and Ralph". I made it to Dover somehow but was sent home again as I was in no state to face Joe Public.

CHATTING to Peter Nicholas while holidaying in Malta. He was there to play for Wales in a European Championship game. We were invited to watch the squad train. It was his full debut and he scored.

ROMANCE in the air brought my Selhurst days to an end with a 3-4 defeat and Vince Hilaire got sent off for pushing the ref over.

CLUB historian Nigel Sands, with whom I had developed a friendship, officiating at my wedding. We moved to Whitstable and I got involved with the local club, compiling and writing their programme.

In 1985-86 we played a Palace XI in a friendly and Ian Wright, Andy Gray and Kevin Taylor were included in the side. What happened to them, did they ever make the grade?

AFTER Whitstable I took up the ref's whistle in the Kent League. Through my association with Kent F.A. I got a ticket for the Cup Final. As the team passed me on Wembley way my mind flashed back to Aldershot, Halifax and Rotherham. I was so proud.

I queued for two and a half hours at Wembley for the replay ticket and they put the shutters up just as I got there.

ONE day I shall come back to Selhurst Park, I dream it will be in my referee's kit – a dubious penalty and I become the first referee ever to score for a Premier League club. I will be back.

Hulton Deutsch

MADE IN SCOTLAND FROM GIRDERS

John McCormick was always described as craggy. His features were appropriate for a man who, in the late 60s and early 70s stood like a rock at the heart of Palace's overworked defence. Keith Brody pays tribute

If anyone epitomised the Palace of the early 70s, those halcyon days in division one for the first time, it was John McCormick. Other fans will point you towards John Jackson, the lynchpin of our team, Steve Kember, our one superstar, or Gerry Queen, who scored most of our few goals. But John McCormick was what Crystal Palace were all about.

The trouble with Jackson and Kember, and even Queen to a point, was that in one way or another they were good footballers. John McCormick wasn't. But in a way he was better.

His angular figure, closely cropped, reddish hair and rolled up sleeves were the personification of what we were all about. Workmanlike, honest, committed and lion-hearted. Skillful? No. Classy? Never. Entertaining? In your dreams.

But when March came around and your backs were to the wall there was no-one else you'd rather find alongside you in the trenches than Big John.

The parade of excuses that passed through the Palace number five shirt after he left (Derek Jeffries, Stuart Jump take a bow) made us appreciate him all the more. And the thing about Big John is that every Saturday he was there, always battling, always in the thick of things and always doing what he did reliably. People like John McCormick were the reason why John Sewell's famous goal against Leeds was not, in reality, a fluke. If you pick up your lunch box and come prepared for a day's work every Saturday, sooner or later the breaks will go your way and, when they do, you'll deserve them.

It was Mel Blyth, who really set McCormick's qualities in bas relief; the perfectly contrasting duo. Blyth was younger – one of our first modern footballers – with styled, blond locks and cocky 70s demeanour. He was neither better nor worse than McCormick, but he could attract more attention because he was a man of his age. McCormick on the other hand had not a smidgeon of cockiness about him. He was an anachronism, not only a player of the sixties but of an era, perhaps, even before that. You got the impression that he was probably a wise old man at the age of 14, reared on oatmeal in the dour surroundings of a farm near Kilmarnock. My image of McCormick reinforces why I've never had any interest in actually meeting Palace players. If he turned out to be anything other than what I imagined I'd be disappointed.

With John Sewell, John Loughlan and Mel Blyth, McCormick played in the greatest defence ever to pull on the claret and blue. They were under siege week-in, week-out for almost 90 minutes a game and like a dam their sole function became to hold back the flood. They didn't need to play the ball out of the back intelligently because there was no-one worth playing it to. They simply had to stand there and absorb wave after wave of attack, saving the day any way they could.

Were they as talented as Hinshelwood, Sansom, Cannon and Gilbert? No. As successful as Humphrey, Shaw, Thorn and Young? No. How good they really were will remain a secret because they were four men in what amounted to a four-man team. They never had anyone around them to make their jobs easier so we could see what else, other than survive, they could do. But they were the best because they had the toughest job and in doing it they won the most respect.

When John left Selhurst Park I've no idea where he went. I think he played for a non-league team, but he might have played in a lower division. No matter. The thought of John in a shirt other than ours isn't really credible.

Some players and teams are interchangeable, but other players are the teams they play for. In the early 70s John McCormick was us.

I loved the over-rated Steve Kember because everyone did and that meant you had to. John Jackson was my hero because he was the best. But my enduring memory is this: a windswept Selhurst, the rain lightly falling against a grey south London sky, the masses of men in overcoats huddled together in the crowded stands. An opposition corner at the Holmesdale end ... the penalty area is muddy and packed with our shirts and theirs. Jacko is ready on the far post and everyone else is gesticulating frantically to get into position. And in the middle of it all, shirt tucked in, sleeves rolled up, bony face set in concentration, the imposing figure of John McCormick towering above it all.

Hy Money

John McCormick in relaxed mood

Don't talk to me about skill

When it came to fighting for Palace, Roger Hynd took no prisoners. Jim Chrystie's tribute is not for the squeamish

Whenever fans gather on balmy summer nights to talk of past skill, one person never comes to mind. They chat about Pele, Law or even Vince Hilaire, but one name never crosses their lips. He was the scourge of the 60s, the Alcatraz of the Alleyways, he was Roger Hynd.

It was not just lack of skill, finesse or any kind of ball control which bars our Roger from such discussions, but it is worth noting in passing that he was to skill what Gazza is to Alcoholics Anonymous and Eddie the Eagle is to space research.

There is another reason why Roger's name never crops up. It is the unspoken fear that he may return. For Hynd was the original role model for Freddie, Psycho and the Terminator. Mention his name three times within the hour and he could materialise before you in all his glory.

His speciality on the football field was the two-footed, shovel tackle. When Roger charged across the pitch to intercept a player rash enough to enter his pen, the Richter Scale went into overdrive. If the opponent was deaf and ignored the snorts, the moment of impact still troubles the minds of all who saw it. After one season of our Roger, Croydon Hospital changed its name to Mayday and both the BBC and ITV banned Palace matches until after the 9pm watershed.

Half time was busy then. While doctors collected the bits of mangled opponents from the stands and terraces in a vain attempt to mix and match, fans would pass the divots back down over their heads to the waiting bulldozers.

And the secret of Roger's appetite for the game (or its players)? It was his diet. Fed only on raw meat, even that ceased after Wednesday. From then on, all he was shown was the shirts of Saturday's opponents, dangled before his nostrils. The only time this failed was when one team changed their colours shortly before kick-off. Roger's confusion was woeful. He was last seen, horns lowered, charging towards an unsuspecting away fan who had been foolish enough to turn up in the original colours.

Normally, in such a friendly, adulatory pen portrait, one game would be singled out. In Roger's case, this does not apply, they all merged into one long, hard shovel.

His legacy lives on. Throughout south east London, parents and grandparents have found an infallible way to quieten their offspring. It never fails: "Shut up or Roger Hynd'll get yer." It has brought peace to many a Croydon household. The only musical mystery of the last ten years is that no-one has thought to do a *Hynd Rap*. But perhaps the three-time name-curse has quelled even the bravest rapper. The only mention in literature I have been able to find is in Shakespeare's original draft for *Henry V* before the Battle of Stamford Bridge:

And Crystal Palace fans shall not go forth
From this day on, until the ending of the Premier League
But he in it shall be remembered
This Hynd
This happy Hynd
This flaming nutcase

BIG MAC

Peter Gee followed John McCormick's career with admiration and was rewarded with an unexpected bonus when he attended the big centre half's testimonial

You've seen the advert on the telly, the one where the willing husband gets dragged round the shops, in and out of one boutique after another until he looks wistfully into space and says those immortal words: "I want a Big Mac!"

What exactly is this secret object of desire? Well, you know the feeling, one of hunger, and the need for a quick snack.

After having a Big Mac full of God knows what and tomato and slimy gherkin you probably wish you'd gone without.

When Palace went without their own Big Mac, they withered and were relegated in successive seasons. John McCormick played his last game for us at the age of 36 in a horrible 4-0 defeat at West Ham in October 1972. It makes you think when you realise that he is now 57.

But in my early Palace watching days, he was a real hero. In his brilliant book *Crystal Palace: A Biased Commentary,* Chris Winter selected Mac for his best ever Palace XI and few of us who saw him in action would disagree.

John McCormick always played as if he had claret and blue blood coursing through his veins, in fact I cannot imagine him playing in red and blue stripes.

He was signed from Aberdeen by Bert Head in a joint deal that involved forward Tom White.

White departed for Blackpool in February 1968 but Mac stayed to replace Alan Stephenson after our Under 23 international had departed for West Ham.

At this time, Selhurst was open on three sides and had grass topped terracing. As a new stand began to be built the team went on an unbeaten promotion push and Big Mac was ever present.

We came under great pressure in the top flight but he missed only one game. In a tense season, it often seemed that we were under permanent siege but with his able confederates Mel Blyth and John Jackson, John McCormick helped Palace survive.

Mac only missed 17 league games in the next two seasons because of a variety of bumps and knocks.

Bert Head introduced young Phil Hoadley into the fray alongside Blyth yet Mac remained first choice. He was also hard and fair and for a defender in the top flight he received remarkably few bookings.

In fact the only forward I can recall that ever had the edge on Mac was Mr Osgood from that nice Chelsea team of the time. I can still remember when to not be a Chelsea fan meant being an outcast.

Mac was ever-present for the first 12 matches of 1972-73 until that defeat at Upton Park. Bert Head had at last begun to sign players who were under 30 and not Scottish which signalled the end for Big Mac and an introduction to Bobby Bell. If you think Andy Thorn's methods can be crude on occasion you should have seen Bobby Bell. Not a pretty sight!

Mac scored three goals at the top level; a scrambled equaliser which gave us a vital point in a 1-1 home draw against Ipswich Town towards the end of our first season in the upper bracket, a scrambled equaliser in front of 42,123 against Chelsea in the F.A. Cup match at Selhurst Park in 1970-71 and his legendary left foot thunderbolt in the famous 5-1 thrashing of Sheffield United on the day of the Yogi Hughes one-man super show in 1972.

The smile on Mac's face after that goal was almost as much one of surprise as of enjoyment. All three goals were on television as well.

John McCormick appeared to truly relish the challenge of the top division and he played as if it was a privilege to be there.

If Phil Barber was Mr 110% then Big Mac must have been at least 150%.

He was awarded a testimonial in September 1974 when a 12,000 crowd turned out to pay their respects and saw a 1-1 draw with QPR.

They had a lucky programme draw that night and I won a trip to Canada! I was treated like a lord, met all the players and couldn't sleep with the excitement of it all.

Big Mac had a great night as well and few players deserved it more. He was true claret and blue and, like Chris Winter, he would definitely be in my all time greatest Palace line-up.

A really great Big Mac and not a gherkin in sight.

Ten things we all know about Palace circa 1971

1) Palace are struggling near the bottom (again)
2) Palace have not beaten a London club in the league
3) Other London clubs have glamourous stars, we have battlers
4) If Jacko gets injured we've really had it
5) John McCormick is not likely to come staggering out of a King's Road night club at three in the morning with Britt Ekland on one arm and Twiggy on the other
6) John Sewell has a proper gentleman's haircut
7) Every time the TV cameras turn up we're in for a humiliating afternoon
8) It's going to be a bad day at school on Monday
9) Jim Scott/Terry Wharton/Alan Pinkney is not the new Jimmy Greaves
10) Palace are a nice club with a family atmosphere and it would be nice to see them survive.

Shovel

John Sewell led Palace as we entered the first division for the very first time. Andrew Fishleigh recalls the influence of an "immaculate" player

There can be very few players in history who have made any impression on the watching public during their playing careers whose nickname fitted them so well as John Sewell's.

He acquired the tag of "Shovel" during the 1960s while playing at right back in the team that Bert Head would eventually take into the first division.

The difficulty with memories is that time can play all sorts of tricks. That said, there are a number of idiosyncrasies peculiar to John which the passing years have hopefully not impaired. John was never a media superstar. His background included a spell with Charlton where, by all accounts, he failed to set the world alight.

The record books show that he was well into his 20s when he joined Palace. However, he resembled a middle aged bank manager in appearance. His physique could never be described as "athletic" and he had a slightly corpulent midriff, rounded shoulders, accentuated by his habit of running with his head pointing downwards, and a boring short back and sides with never a hair out of place. He rarely seemed to perspire.

John was not blessed with any outstanding skill, was possibly one of the slowest players in the team and was ever so occasionally caught out of position. Lest you should wonder at this stage why the man was such an immovable object in the Palace right back spot for eight years an explanation is required. It is not easy to accurately and vividly portray the qualities possessed by John Sewell in mere words. Often the very mention of the name Shovel, uttered with the correct degree of angst and/or irony would give the Holmesdale more by way of instant merriment than was usually to be found on the pitch. Yet, despite all his shortcomings, or perhaps because of them, Captain Shovel was able to guide Palace through what were the headiest days of the club's history. In a vital promotion match against Portsmouth at Easter he showed nerves of steel to despatch a penalty under great pressure.

It was in the second division that he spent the majority of his career with Palace, digging the ball out of the mud and sending another hopeful punt upfield for Cliff Jackson, Bobby Woodruff or Steve Kember to chase.

Another penalty incident that sticks in the memory took place at Old Trafford in the season after promotion. It was rare for Palace to be given a spot kick and despite the usual protest from the ancient moaners, Shovel stepped up to purposefully convert the kick. He connected with the ball which proceeded at snail's pace towards the goal where Alex Stepney dived and got a despairing hand to the ball but failed to push it round the post. What happened next was even more incredible. Shovel actually beat all the other players to the ball to prod it home.

It was equally fitting that he should score the goal which could justifiably be called the most bizarre ever at Selhurst Park. Mighty Leeds led by one goal with barely a minute to go when Shovel received the ball on the edge of the penalty area and aimed a harmless hoof in the general direction of the goal. Harmless that is for any competent goalie. Fortunately Leeds achilles heel in those days of Elland Road glory was Gary Sprake. He missed it. There was a split second as the crowd gasped in bewilderment, unaccustomed to such negligence because they had the superb John Jackson at the other end, then uproar.

Shovel did not score many goals for Palace but when he did, the event, rather like the character involved, is well remembered. John Sewell offered moments of frustration, humour, bravery and sheer endeavour, all liberally intermingled over the years. He deserves more than a passing nod for his part in the club's ascent from relative obscurity.

THE DON

He moved like a blinding white flash. After years of struggle, Palace suddenly had a man who could terrorise first division defences. Peter Gee recalls the stir caused by the man from Swindon

Most of the "fans' favourites" over numerous seasons of supporting Palace have been men that have stayed for a number of years such as John Jackson and Jim Cannon. But there are some who have left an impression on us having played far fewer matches; Kevin Mabbutt (80 appearances) and Mike Elwiss (23 appearances) and the player who excited me most at Palace, Don Rogers.

Don made 76 appearances for Palace scoring 30 goals and gave us Selhurst regulars some memorable moments. Supporting Palace in the top division between 1969 and 1973 was both easy and difficult. Easy because we loved Palace and would always go whatever defeats came our way. Difficult because we simply could not beat any other London club and they all had line-ups peppered with star names; Osgood, Hudson, George, Hurst, Peters and Chivers. We had Jim Scott, Gerry Queen and Yogi Hughes. We loved them all, but they drove us round the bend. But they were real Palace.

The top flight at this time was one of great quality and Palace didn't have much of it. It was always hard work.

When we started throwing money around after a poor start in 1972-73 it seemed we were being linked with any player that moved. In typical fashion the two players we eventually signed from Chelsea – Paddy Mulligan and Charlie Cooke – were past their best and we blew a fortune on that household name Iain Phillip from Dundee.

Then, at the end of October, with Palace bottom, we signed Don Rogers. At last here was a player with the

A sense of anticipation

Martin Searle pays tribute to his first Palace hero

Don Rogers Illustration: Jason Axell

Many people have dissected dogfish in their biology studies at school. Some of them may have used a chalk mark to tell their dead fish apart from the others in the tank. I will be surprised if more than one fish ended up in full Palace colours with a number 11 on its back, being called Donna Dogfish (it was female). Such was the status of the great Don Rogers, my first true Palace hero.

I had been supporting Palace for three years when Don came to Selhurst in November 1972, and it's fair to say, although I loved the club, I had no particular heroes except perhaps for John Jackson. The team produced worthy commitment and effort rather than possessing any real stars. Tony Taylor, Willie Wallace, stars? I don't think so.

Integral to this was Bert Head's transfer policy, an addiction to buying elderly Scotsmen who nobody in England had ever heard of (I wonder how many had been heard of in Scotland). It was a major shock to the system when Bert shelled out the huge sum of £150,000 for a winger who had once even played at Wembley, famously humiliating Arsenal in the 1969 League Cup Final. He was known to be a great player at Swindon but it seemed he would never leave his native West Country.

Don made his debut against Everton and I remember the feeling of anticipation in the crowd. Could he perform in the first division? We didn't have long to wait. With what seemed his first touch of the ball he set off on a solo run down the right wing to score a great goal, the only one of the game. From that moment the Selhurst crowd was his for ever more.

If that had made Don a hero, the legendary 5-0 win against Man United a month later practically gave him God status. He scored two brilliant goals, very nearly scored an outrageous third with a cheeky chip and made two other goals. I have never quite forgiven the neighbour who took me to the game for making me leave at 4-0 "to beat the traffic" – I think I realised even then that opportunities to see Palace humiliate Man U might be a little sparse over the years. Mind you, my dad's feelings towards the couple whose wedding he had to attend that afternoon are best not recorded.

While Don was in the team we always felt there was a chance of a goal as long as the ball reached the figure with the sideburns and the Mexican bandit moustache. He was capable of dribbling past whole defences, down either wing or straight down the middle. Certainly every time he got the ball there was a palpable buzz around the ground. Sadly, the 15 goals he scored in each of the two full seasons he appeared for us were not enough to avoid two successive relegations. The third division came and he had to go, but he never really caught the imagination of the QPR crowd in the same way.

In many ways Don's career was wasted. He never played for England (no-one who played for Palace in those days had a chance) and his only major trophy was that Swindon League Cup. I just feel privileged to have seen him in Palace colours at his peak. I find it hard to believe that he only played at Selhurst for two years – Gary Stebbing was at Palace much longer but doesn't hold quite the same place in my affections.

As fate would have it, I now live in Wiltshire and my nearest team is Swindon. Don is still a well known figure in these parts. He opened a sports shop and then became involved with the Town again. In 1989, my seat at the play-off game against Swindon was directly behind the press-box where Don Rogers sat giving commentary for the local radio station GWR. Obviously he was on Swindon's side but there was no shortage of people my age wanting to shake his hand and thank him for the memories. I'm glad to say he still seemed to have a genuine affection for Palace.

potential to excite the fans. We were not to be disappointed. The big clubs had shied away from him, perhaps unsure whether he could step up to the top grade. We'd seen him on television on a number of occasions and he looked the business and we all remembered him racing across the Wembley mud scoring Swindon's third goal in the 1969 League Cup Final against Arsenal.

Rogers had seemed comfortable at Swindon and to step up at 28 appeared to be a couple of years too late. On the evidence of the first 20 minutes of his Palace debut against Everton it appeared our money had been misplaced. My dad was already moaning when it happened. Put away by John Craven, Rogers outpaced the Everton defence and, one-on-one against keeper David Lawson, calmly chipped home.

Cool finishing was Rogers' trademark along with blistering pace and two good feet. The papers were full of it as Rogers repeated the dose at champions Derby the following week in a 2-2 draw. It was the same score in a storming game with Leeds at Selhurst the week after that with John Craven scoring two Rogers' inspired goals.

Palace were on the verge of clicking into a fair side at last and somebody was going to get a hammering. The 5-0 thrashing of Man United is now part of Palace legend. And nowadays we can enjoy the goals on video over and over again. I can honestly say that I never tire of watching it. Rogers simply ran riot against poor United, laying on two first half goals for Paddy Mulligan before scoring two individual goals of the highest class with a debut goal by Alan Whittle in between.

To think my dad wanted to go home at 3-0 to avoid the traffic. If we knew then what we know now, perhaps we would have settled for four that afternoon and transferred the fifth goal through time to Wembley 1990.

It was not an isolated thrashing. Southampton were swept aside 3-0 in the next home game thanks to two more Rogers goals and the same opponents were beaten 2-0 in the third round of the Cup when Don inspired Palace to an open, attacking performance that began to draw huge crowds.

Rogers' performance against the less than saintly Saints prompted calls for an England call up. When previously, aside from Budgie Byrne, did Palace ever figure in England's plans?

As often happens at such times, the goals dried up and Palace couldn't pull themselves clear of the relegation dogfight. While we were winning at home, away points were difficult to come by and we couldn't make inroads into a terrible start of two wins in the first 15 games.

The fourth round cup ties with second division Sheffield Wednesday seemed to take something out of Palace. Wednesday went on to meet Chelsea while we were left to secure our top flight position.

A dismal defeat at Coventry was followed by four successive games against Birmingham, Wolves, Sheffield United and West Ham, which we thought would see us safely up the table. Two draws and two defeats later the writing was on the wall. Kellard, McCormick and Kember had all been used to struggle, Cooke, Mulligan and Whittle had not. Rogers fought valiantly up front but too much was expected of him.

Anxiety spread through the team, even affecting the immaculate Jacko. The imbalance of away fixtures was another worry. Malcolm Allison took over at the end of March and Chelsea became our first London league victims in 32 first division attempts. All looked well, but it wasn't.

Don gives Chelsea the jitters

"Don Rogers for England? Yes, it should happen! On this display nobody at present in the England side can match him as a potential match winner. And Ted Bates conceded after his team's defeat: 'He must be the best player in the country.'

SAM BARTRAM REPORTING ON PALACE'S 2-0 VICTORY OVER SOUTHAMPTON

Rogers was a marked man, Palace were still losing away and a last dismal home defeat against Leicester all but sealed our fate.

At Norwich, Rogers put us one up with a penalty but we lost both the match and our place in division one to a last minute header by Dave Stringer. Ironically we managed a second away win at Manchester City with two Rogers goals in the last match, but it was too late.

So he was lost to the first division after 26 appearances and 13 goals. Palace were finally relegated after four years of struggle and arguably with their best team. If only they had been together at the start of the season and ben able to play without pressure. They were a mid-table outfit at the least, or so we thought, so with Big Mal at the helm we knew we'd only be in division two for one season. We were right about the last bit.

The new season opened with a typical Rogers effort. One-up at home to Notts County. The new red and blue stripes were rampant but Notts didn't read the script properly and replied with four goals.

By the time Don scored his eighth and Palace's 14th goal of the season, 18 matches had passed and Palace were adrift at the foot of division two with just one win. Jacko and David Payne had gone and the club was in turmoil as Mal tried all options to get a winning blend.

The crowd now had a new hero in Peter Taylor with Rogers somewhat in the background. But Don could still inspire and on New Year's day 1974 he raced away to score one of his specials against West Brom. Palace won eight and drew three of the next 13 to haul themselves clear only to blow it at Easter.

During the revival, Don was rampant again although not with the spark of the previous year. Mal had the idea of converting Don into a midfielder and it plainly did not work. Against Millwall at home he even started in a sort of left back role, ridiculous but a telltale sign of the awful season of 1973-74. Palace were relegated on a dreadful night in Cardiff. Taylor was now definitely the new star with Rogers taken for granted by the Palace faithful.

After just two appearances in the third division, he was traded to QPR for Terry Venables and Ian Evans. The move suited all parties. We'd seen the best of Don Rogers and Venables and Evans were more suited to a third division campaign.

When Don Rogers joined Palace he made the kind of impact, and brought the sort of winning flair, we had not seen previously. He was a bit of a luxury, but the type of player who pulled punters through the turnstiles.

When the boringly predictable wing play of Andy Sinton and Lee Sharpe can now win England caps you realise how high the standards were in the early 1970s when Rogers was starring for Palace. How he never played for England is a mystery but the same can be said of Stan Bowles, Tony Currie, Keith Weller and Frank Worthington, all of whom had minimal England careers. I wish we had a player like Don now. I was privileged to see him at his Palace peak.

FORZA GLAZIERS

The 1970s saw the brief flowering of a number of small cup competitions; the Anglo-Scottish Cup, the Watney Cup, the Texaco Cup and, best of all, the Anglo-Italian Cup. Palace left their mark on the latter as Neil Witherow reveals.

Imagine a competition in which Crystal Palace play against the cream of the Italian League. Think of the glamour of meetings with Internazionale, Fiorentina and Lazio.

In the early 70s it was more than wild imaginings, our modest Glaziers did indeed do battle with such opponents. The Anglo-Italian Inter League Clubs' Competition lasted four seasons between 1970 and 1973 and Palace took part first in 1971 and again in the final year.

The tournament emerged because clubs in both countries found themselves faced with enlarged wage bills caused by the extension of the close season to accommodate the 1970 Mexico World Cup. It was a tournament of, not always successful, experimentation although the first competition produced tidy profits for all competitors, sufficient to make sure it would become a regular fixture. Played at the end of the season because it was considered too difficult to incorporate into the hectic regular season schedules, the tournament featured a number of revolutionary rules which lent it a real international flavour, including squad numbering, a choice of two from five named substitutes, a penalty shoot-out to settle drawn finals and, most radical of all, a league point for each goal scored. An additional benefit was the international experience gained by the referees in each league.

The contingent of English clubs in the first year included Swindon, Middlesbrough, Sunderland and Sheffield Wednesday from division two alongside first division Wolves and West Brom. The Italian half comprised Napoli, Fiorentina, Lazio, Juventus, Roma and Lanerossi Vicenza.The grouping and league system was complex. The clubs were divided into three groups, each containing two from each country. Each English team met its respective Italian opponent on a two-legged home and away basis, but the two clubs from the same country did not meet. After four games the records were combined and divided back into English and Italian sections. The winners of each country's table then contested the final. Still with me? Good.

In the first tournament, Swindon topped the English and met Napoli in the final. The clubs had already played twice having been drawn in the same group. The final in Naples was marred by politically motivated crowd trouble and was abandoned after 79 minutes with Swindon, somewhat remarkably, leading 3-0. Thus the Wiltshire side became the first winners of the trophy.

They returned to defend their title the following year – the only other survivors from the first tournament were Roma and WBA. Italy now wheeled in their big guns. New champions Inter and the team they succeeded, Cagliari, accompanied Bologna, Hellas Verona and Sampdoria. England meanwhile fielded five first division sides, although Blackpool had just been relegated. Stoke City, Huddersfield Town and Palace completed the deputation.

Typically, we were drawn in the tough group along with West Brom, Inter and Cagliari. However, the record shows we acquitted ourselves admirably getting off to a flying start by beating Cagliari, who included the legendary Luigi Riva, star of Italy's World Cup Final side of 1970.

BOLOGNA
CAGLIARI
HELLAS VERONA
INTERNAZIONALE
ROMA
SAMPDORIA
BLACKPOOL
CRYSTAL PALACE
HUDDERSFIELD TOWN
STOKE CITY
SWINDON TOWN
WEST BROMWICH ALBION
FOOTBALL LEAGUE
F.I.G.C.
LEGA NAZIONALE
MAY 26th to JUNE 12th 1971
OFFICIAL SOUVENIR HANDBOOK
PRICE
10p
150 lire
THE ANGLO-ITALIAN INTER-LEAGUE CLUBS COMPETITION 1971

In front of a Selhurst crowd of 19,326, Bobby Tambling scored the only goal of an entertaining game. Three days later on

May 29, 1971, we entertained mighty Inter which attracted the *Match of the Day* cameras to Selhurst.

Palace's determination from the off upset the blue blooded Italians and when Cella under hit a back pass, Alan Birchenall was on-hand to blast past Bordon before the keeper could react to the danger. Palace were inspired – although some of our tackling was not to the liking of referee Angonese. However Tambling, Queen and Birchenall all failed with good opportunities.

Inter came back. Boninsegna, another World Cup star, scored a superb solo goal, rounding the back four before shooting under the advancing Jackson. They now took a vice-like grip on the game and there was no further scoring.

Palace were nonetheless delighted and Bert Head claimed: "We should have won it in the first half. This game today would have made a great final." Palace travelled to Italy at the beginning of June to play the return with Cagliari – a very different affair from the match in London six days earlier. Roared on by 30,000 Sardinians, Cagliari took full revenge for their shock defeat with Riva, who retains God-like status on the Mediterranean island, scoring both goals in the 2-0 win. Because of the goal scoring ruling, this effectively ended Palace's interest in the competition. But we put up a good show against a team that boasted four of Riva's World Cup colleagues. Because of their defeat at Selhurst Park, Cagliari also failed to qualify for the final.

Palace moved on to the San Siro where Inter had not lost since the previous November. And we turned in a remarkable performance. Inter Milan 1 Palace 2 amazed everyone. "Bobby Tambling kept a promise here tonight when he gunned in two great goals and lifted Crystal Palace to a stunning two-goal victory over Italian champions Inter Milan," wrote Norman Giller in the *Daily Express*.

Tambling had a point to prove, having been written off not only by Chelsea but by sections of the press, who had upset him by misquoting his age. The striker protested that, at 29, he was not yet at the veteran stage. Giller agreed and said the Palace man looked like a "coltish thoroughbred" as he lashed one goal with his right foot and another with his left. But the writer was surely overstating the case when he said: "By the time the final shots were fired Palace had built themselves a reputation of greatness that will live long in the memory of this Soccer-mad city."

It was nothing compared to Spurs' first European triumph or those of Celtic and Man United. But for Palace this was a rare moment to bask in the glory many others took for granted. And the merit was all the greater because of the stomach bug that had affected Steve Kember and the fact that Alan Birchenall was not fully fit.

Tambling opened the scoring on the quarter hour, squeezing a right foot shot from Kember's free kick inside the post. Burgnich equalised four minutes into the second half and Jackson was called on to pull off a string of "incredible" saves, but it was Tambling's rising 25 yarder that silenced the San Siro.

Unfortunately, the victories over Inter and Cagliari were not rewarded as they should have been. The other English clubs, with easier matches, had scored more goals and Palace finished fifth out of six, a placing described by Harry Miller in the *Daily Mirror* as "a tragedy". Head was equally disappointed. "I feel sorry for my players that they are not in the final," he said "They deserve to be there."

It had been a magnificent tournament and we had the consolation of a £20,000 profit from the two home matches – the Milan match had established a record for an English staged game in the tournament.

It was Blackpool who won the cup. Six points ahead of Palace for bigger but less impressive victories, the Tangerines put a miserable league season behind them to defeat Bologna 2-1 in the final. We wouldn't have swapped places with them though, having already won the bigger battle for survival. Attendances for the tournament exceeded 395,000 – more than 30% up on the first year – evidence that the cup was growing in popularity.

Palace did not take part in 1972 when, once again, Blackpool made the final on the back of a 10-0 thrashing of Lanerossi Vicenza which, under the tournament rules, netted them 12 points from one game. Roma, the Italian ever-presents, made it through by virtue of one "goal point" from Atalanta and won the trophy for Italy by triumphing 3-1 in the final.

In 1973, Palace returned for what

GROUP 2 GRUPPO

TEAM SQUADS

No.	W. B. ALBION	No.	CRYSTAL PALACE
1	J. Cumbes	1	J. Jackson
2	L. Hughes	2	J. Sewell
3	A. Merrick	3	D. Payne
4	G. Lovett	4	P. Hoadley
5	J. Wile	5	J. McCormick
6	J. Kaye	6	M. Blyth
7	C. Suggett	7	B. Tambling
8	A. Brown	8	S. Kember
9	J. Astle	9	A. Birchenall
10	R. Hope	10	G. Queen
11	R. Hartford	11	T. Taylor
12	L. Cantello	12	J. Scott
13	R. Wilson	13	T. Wharton
14	J. Talbut	14	J. Loughlin
15	J. Osborne	15	A. Pinkney
16	A. Robertson	16	M. Brown
17	H. Reed	17	B. Goldthorpe
18	R. Minton	18	S. Wooldridge
19	A. Glover	19	R. Jenkins
20	H. MacLean	20	G. Humphreys

No.	CAGLIARI	No.	INTER
1	E. Albertosi	1	I. Bordon
2	M. Martiradonna	2	M. Bellugi
3	E. Mancin	3	G. Facchetti
4	P. L. Cera	4	G. Bedin
5	C. Niccolai	5	M. Giubertoni
6	G. Tomasini	6	T. Burgnich
7	A. Domenghini	7	Jair Da Costa
8	O. Nene	8	M. Bertini
9	S. Gori	9	R. Boninsegna
10	R. Greatti	10	A. Mazzola
11	L. Riva	11	M. Corso
12	A. Reginato	12	M. Cacciatori
13	C. Nastasio	13	M. Frustalupi
14	C. Poli	14	B. Fabbian
15	M. Brugnera	15	G. Cella
16	R. De Petri	16	A. Reif
17		17	
18		18	
19		19	
20		20	

WEST BROMWICH ALBION

CRYSTAL PALACE

CAGLIARI

INTERNAZIONALE

PROGRAMME OF MATCHES

26th May 1971	RESULTS
CRYSTAL PALACE	1
CAGLIARI	0
WEST BROMWICH ALBION	1
INTERNAZIONALE	1
29th May 1971	
CRYSTAL PALACE	1
INTERNAZIONALE	1
WEST BROMWICH ALBION	1
CAGLIARI	2
1st June 1971	
CAGLIARI	2
CRYSTAL PALACE	0
INTERNAZIONALE	1
WEST BROMWICH ALBION	0
4th June 1971	
CAGLIARI	1
WEST BROMWICH ALBION	0
INTERNAZIONALE	1
CRYSTAL PALACE	2

TABLES

TEAMS	PTS.
CRYSTAL PALACE	3
INTER MILAN	2
W.B.A.	2
CAGLIARI	0
TEAMS	PTS.
CRYSTAL PALACE	5
CAGLIARI	4
INTER MILAN	4
W.B.A	3
TEAMS	PTS.
CAGLIARI	8
INTER MILAN	7
CRYSTAL PALACE	5
W.B.A.	3
TEAMS	PTS.
CAGLIARI	11
CRYSTAL PALACE	9
INTER MILAN	8
W.BA.	3

FINAL GROUP TABLE

CAGLIARI	11
CRYSTAL P.	9
INTER MILAN	8
W.B.A.	3

turned out to be the last year of the Anglo-Italian Cup until it was resurrected in a different, second-rate format in 1992. The tournament bore no resemblance to the one Palace had played so well in two years earlier. Gone was the points for goals rule, presumably in the wake of Blackpool's qualification via one huge victory, and it had now branched out to include eight clubs per country while the group structures were reviewed. There was now just one game against the Italians in the same group and venues were drawn so that each club had two home and two away games.

The motives for these changes are not clear, but it would seem that the alarming drop in attendances in 1972 played a part. But the biggest change was the transfer of games from the season's end into the middle of the campaign – a move that drew sharp criticism from the English press. Palace in particular were singled out for admonishment as it was thought that the Anglo-Italian games would prove a distraction from the annual relegation dogfight.

It may also have had something to do with the fact that certain journalists had strongly tipped Palace to lift the F.A. Cup on the strength of their 5-0 wrecking of Man United and the later Anglo-Italian ties were scheduled within a week of the latter stages of the Cup.

One criticism of the English was that, compared to the Italian sides, they tended not to field their biggest names. In 1973 this changed with the entry of Newcastle, who had won the Inter-Cities Fairs Cup in 1969, and Manchester United, who were engaged in a relegation battle and to all intents and purposes a spent force. But they still needed no introduction. The rest were a motley crew and Fulham, Blackpool, Hull, Oxford and Luton were hardly likely to set Italian mouths watering. Their representation came from regulars Roma, Fiorentina, Hellas Verona and Bologna, while Lazio, Como, Bari and Torino were all new entrants.

In spite of major surgery, the patient continued to flounder. Even the pulling power of Manchester United faded when their performances matched their league efforts. Palace were also affected by the downward spiral. A total of just 13,510 people turned out to see the two home games compared to 44,800 for the 1971 matches.

On a February night at Selhurst, we wiped the floor with Verona in front of only 7,436 taking the opportunity to give debuts to Bill Roffey, Martin Hinshelwood, Jim Cannon, Nicky Chatterton and David Swindlehurst.

It was Hinshelwood who opened the scoring after six minutes. Following a neat one-two with Derek Possee, the Palace youngster shot low under keeper Giacomi. After that, Don Rogers and John Craven both had chances to extend the lead, but we had to wait until just before the interval for Bobby Bell to sweep in Rogers' corner. We were so dominant in midfield that it was an embarrassment, but Cazzi reduced the deficit after 63 minutes. Finally, Alan Whittle rose to head home Rogers' free kick and with five minutes left he made the most of a defensive error to slot the ball into an empty net for his second.

Palace's next match, away to Bari, was a flowing game, we were considered fortunate to come away with a win. Spimi, the Bari captain, gave an outstanding display, as did the acrobatic keeper Colombo, whose handling was exemplary. It was unfortunate for him that Palace's winner came when Possee, unmarked at the far post, headed home. At the end of an attractive and sporting contest, both sides were given a standing ovation by a comparatively large crowd of 10,682.

Palace were on a high after beating Chelsea, yet only 6,074 turned up for the match with Lazio. Those who dragged themselves away from the telly or the pub witnessed Craven make Anglo-Italian history by becoming the first player to score a hat-trick. It put Palace within a point of the semi-finals. Those who had shelled out to watch were not happy with new manager Malcolm Allison's decision to assess the depth of his squad. Palace's team makes interesting reading, mainly for the players who didn't quite make it at Selhurst.

Palace: Towse, Roffey, Prince, Chatterton, Parker, Brown, Pain, Mann, Craven, Martin Hinshelwood, Thomas.

Only three had any previous league experience.

Lazio, who fielded only four regulars themselves, scored first, former Swansea striker Giorgio Chinaglia driving past third choice keeper Garry Towse but within four minutes Craven pulled us level, drilling home Hinshelwood's cross. Lazio held out until the 70th minute when Craven bicycle-kicked Roffey's free-kick past amazed Mioriggi. Then a challenge by Valera on Thomas gave Craven the chance to convert number three from the spot.

Palace visited Florence to complete their group games against Fiorentina. It was a deflated team that travelled to Italy, we had finally succumbed to relegation. However, we only needed a point to qualify for the semis and we got it thanks to two goals by Possee.

Newcastle had been one of the few sides that Palace had enjoyed playing against in their brief sojourn in the first division. But the one-off semi-final at St James's Park proved too much and the Anglo-Italian dream ended on English soil. Jim Cannon scored Palace's consolation as Newcastle ran riot 5-1.

The Magpies went on to win the trophy while we were left with the memory of nine matches against Italian clubs whose names in many cases have gained lustre while most of the English are now some way from the top class.

Nevertheless, the next time you watch *Football Italia* on Channel 4, just consider that someone in the San Siro might remember the day Bobby Tambling and co. humbled Inter in their own back yard. Dream on.

■ This article is a reprise of one that appeared in the Palace fanzine *So Glad You're Mine*. Additional material supplied by Robert Deeks, Peter Gee and Tony Matthews.

The Anglo-Italian Inter-League Clubs' Competition

PALACE'S FULL RECORD
P 9 W5 D2 L2 F15 A13

THE OPPONENTS:

1971
PALACE 1 CAGLIARI 0
CAGLIARI 2 PALACE 0
PALACE 1 INTERNAZIONALE 1
INTERNAZIONALE 1 PALACE 2

1973
PALACE 4 HELLAS VERONA 1
BARI 0 PALACE 1
PALACE 3 LAZIO 1
FIORENTINA 2 PALACE 2
SF: NEWCASTLE UTD 5 PALACE 1

CRYSTAL PALACE
ANGLO-ITALIAN SCORERS

3 GOALS: BOBBY TAMBLING, JOHN CRAVEN, DEREK POSSEE

2 GOALS: ALAN WHITTLE

1 GOAL: ALAN BIRCHENALL, MARTIN HINSHELWOOD, BOBBY BELL, JIM CANNON

Hulton Deutsch

December 16, 1972: Palace 5 Manchester United 0. Aside from Alex Stepney fishing the ball out of the net, Ian Storey-Moore was virtually the only other United player to touch it

Man City had been one of the success stories of the late 60s. Under Joe Mercer they had collected all three major domestic trophies and the European Cup Winners Cup. Mercer had been assisted in these conquests by the brash, young, former West Ham wing half Malcolm Allison. It was to Allison that Palace turned to complete the job of making them great. Things would never be dull again.

The loyal Bert Head and Terry Long introduced Allison before the match with Chelsea and, although the new man could have had little to do with it, it seemed as if the Messiah had arrived when Palace won 2-0. Teenage centre-half Jim Cannon not only kept Osgood quiet but marked his debut with a goal, and a booking. The victory brought fresh hope of escape but Palace failed to win until the last day of the season – ironically against Man City – when it was too late.

On April 1, 1973 Edward Heath's government introduced Value Added Tax. This was levied on entertainment as well as consumer goods and the programme carried the following notice: "The Directors have decided not to increase admission prices for the remaining matches this season at Selhurst Park. This decision will involve the club in a VAT liability of several thousand pounds, but the board have been pleased to accept this as a means of saying thank you for the wonderful support the club has received this season."

"Here comes Rogers ... this could be their greatest afternoon. Is this gonna be five? It's gonna be five ... IT IS FIVE!"

Brian Moore – ITV's *The Big Match*, Crystal Palace 5 Man United 0

The thank you was appropriate. Palace have never been supported by so many people as in 1972-73. The last home match of the season on Friday, April 20 was a typically dreadful 1-0 home defeat by Leicester which all but confirmed relegation, yet Head was able to write in the programme: "The national trend is still down but we at Crystal Palace have reversed it and are in fact ahead of last season's figures. Not by many, but in a season where things have not gone as well as we hoped a remarkable tribute to the loyalty of our fans. This is the last game of the season and a crowd of around the 33,000 mark to see us play Leicester will give us an average of almost exactly 30,000 which I believe puts us tenth in the first division."

Unlikely as it seemed the fans did turn out – 36,817 to watch Leicester on a Friday evening, those really were the golden days. Head added: "We seldom get the nastiness on the terraces associated with certain other clubs, so much so that we now get supporters coming in from many miles away because they like the atmosphere. At nearly every home game we have ten to a dozen coachloads coming in from the West Country, whereas in the old days a day out in London and a soccer match usually ended at Highbury or Stamford Bridge." But the result was nothing short of a

Malcolm Allison joins Crystal Palace

Big Mal's first day as Palace manager: Here he chats to Charlie Cooke (right) and Paddy Mulligan about flowery shirts and dodgy tank tops

THE *Evening News* carried the details: "Palace Shock – Head Moves Up."

"Bert Head's seven-year reign as manager of Crystal Palace is over," it began. Head had been moved upstairs to the position of General Manager while new Palace chairman Ray Bloye announced the club wanted a "track-suit manager".

"We are prepared to pay big money for the right type who can help us get success." Terry Long took over playing matters while Bloye assured: "There is no question of Bert being kicked upstairs." Shortly after, Palace got their man. The former Manchester City coach Malcolm Allison was not short of confidence. Shortly after his arrival at Selhurst Park he announced: "In two years – possibly less – I will be competing again with the giants of English football ... with Leeds, Arsenal and Manchester City. This is why I'm now facing a solid month's ordeal in the battle for Crystal Palace's survival as a First Division team."

"Palace chairman Raymond Bloye has a vision of Selhurst Park as a super stadium of the future. I believe I can give him a super side to go with it. The potential is staggering. A huge slice of London awaits real football success. Already there are players of high skill and character at the club. This was proved to me in Saturday's defeat of Chelsea. I have two years to get Palace into a striking position for honours. That was my experience at Manchester City.

"We can do it more quickly than that ... but obviously the relegation issue is crucial and it is likely to be in the balance right up to the last kick of the season."

disaster. Prior to the game, Palace were clear of the relegation places if only on goal difference from West Brom and Norwich – all three clubs had 28 points while Leicester were four points above us. We needed the victory desperately because we had three away games to come all of which were tricky. Irony has always reigned supreme at Selhurst Park and on this night John Jackson, the man who had done so much to put Palace in the first division and keep them there made the crucial error that lost us the match. Defeat left Palace with an uphill struggle. We'd seen the impossible achieved before, now we needed a miracle.

The penultimate match was against Norwich at Carrow Road. We went ahead after 27 minutes through Rogers but Colin Suggett's diving header levelled things before half time and in second half injury time Dave Stringer slammed home a free kick. Palace were down.

We had the makings of a great team in 1973, gained more points than in 1971 or 1972, but were still relegated. But Allison, despite his earlier assertion that survival was the first step on the road to producing a team to challenge the best, was far from despondent.

There were no imports in the summer but there were plenty of other changes. Allison began to reduce the club's wage bill with Craven among the notable departures. Behind the scenes, Alan Leather took over as secretary from Chris Hassell who joined Everton. Leather's career began in football administration with Spurs in 1957, where he was assistant secretary. After that he left for Coventry and later

Hulton Deutsch

A different perspective on the pre-season team photograph: Big Mal (right) selects an appropriate nickname

Brighton. He also helped to organise the South East Counties League in the early 50s.

Allison decided to jazz up Palace's rather staid image, dispensing with claret and blue in favour of elegant red and blue striped shirts and blue shorts – the idea was rumoured to be based on Spanish giants Barcelona. The club also looked to Europe for a new nickname, apparently taking their Eagles title from Portuguese giants Benfica. The new badge depicted an Eagle astride a stylised version of the Crystal Palace and was worn in the centre of the shirt (Manchester City-style) and small numbers were added to the sleeves. The programme was well worth having for the list of nicknames alone. It cost 8p and in it Allison offered his thoughts on the forthcoming campaign.

Although there were no new arrivals he said there was money available if he felt the need to spend it. But he preferred to give youth its head. As part of this policy, Jackson was discarded for the opening games and Paul Hammond given his chance, much to the chagrin of the supporters.

The fact that Jackson continued his career with other clubs rankled with many as Palace suffered goalkeeping problems. Also in the starting line-up for the clash with County was 18 year-old Nicky Chatterton, the son of groundsman Len, who'd been on Palace's books as a junior in the 40s, and 19 year-old striker Dave Swindlehurst. Jim Cannon was on the bench.

Allison told the fans: "We are going to play more professionally than we did last year. We gave away far too many goals. In training our object has been to reduce the opposition's scoring

Those nicknames

Before the opening home game against Notts County, the Palace team sheet on the back of the programme included a nickname for each player. This is how Palace lined up:
1. Paul Hammond (The Cage); 2. Paddy Mulligan (The Dealer); 3. Tony Taylor (The Road Runner); 4. Nick Chatterton (Interceptor); 5. Bobby Bell (Blockbuster); 6. Mel Blyth (Masterpieces); 7. Derek Possee (The Sheriff); 8. Charlie Cooke (The Card Shuffler); 9. Alan Whittle (The Hustler); 10. Dave Swindlehurst (The Problem); 11. Don Rogers (Troublemaker). Substitute Bill Roffey.

Apparently being left on the sub's bench meant having to do without a nickname. The shame of it must have been almost too much to bear. Anyway, Roffey actually made the starting line-up even without a pseudonym – although he could perhaps have borrowed Paddy Mulligan's. Twenty years later, it was pointed out in *Eagle Eye*, that Bill Roffey would have his own day as a sort of rhyming slang for coffee.

Hulton Deutsch

April 1974: Alan Whittle (9) and Derek Possee (8) celebrate Palace's goal but Cardiff snatched a draw to save themselves and condemn us to a second consecutive relegation

opportunities whilst increasing our own." Palace lost 4-1.

The promise that really stuck though was the one he made to get Palace out of the second division. True to his word, he took us into the third. It was a joke we were still living down at the end of the 80s. Palace's "achievement" in being relegated for the second successive year was founded upon five defeats and a draw in the first six games.

Hammond, blamed by many fans for the County debacle and the ensuing defeat by West Brom, was replaced by Jackson who, in turn, lasted just five games before he was blamed by the management for two Cardiff goals and Hammond was recalled. It was the end of a long and proud Palace career for Jackson, who joined Orient where he proved he had plenty of mileage left. His name stands high among the league's all-time appearance makers, but it will always be more firmly placed in the hearts of Palace supporters.

In the next six matches we collected two more points, both from draws. Hammond was beaten four times by Sheffield Wednesday on his return but although Rogers managed to score in three successive matches we only got one point.

"A day is a long time in football. The last result, that is all. If Palace win on Saturday they will feel great. Now if you had asked them at the start of the season how they would feel if they won a game making it five points adrift, they would have been speechless. Probably not able to envisage how awful they would feel. But if they win on Saturday they will feel great. One win and you are away. The dream is on again and off you go.

EAMONN DUNPHY – *ONLY A GAME?*

The promotion dream was in tatters and Allison had little option but to get his cheque book out. Derek Jeffries, one of his Maine Road proteges, arrived to strengthen the defence, as did the experienced Roy Barry from Coventry. Their arrival looked likely to signal the end of the last link with the promotion team of 1969, Mel Blyth. But Mel fought his way back into the team later in the season. Others on the way out were Iain Philip and Bobby Bell, who was bound for South Africa.

On November 10, we finally got that elusive first victory when Whittle grabbed the only goal against Bristol City at Ashton Gate. It may not have been spectacular but it sparked a mini-revival. More than 30,000 turned up to see Millwall held 1-1, followed by another point at Fratton Park – always a happy hunting ground for Palace – Rogers scored twice. The second win was a 4-2 thrashing of Swindon – marked by the first goal for a new arrival, Peter Taylor from Southend.

Taylor had first been brought to Palace by Arthur Rowe for a trial four years earlier but Palace weren't interested in him at the time. Southend snapped him up after spotting him playing for a local side in Essex in which he scored once in a 28-0 win.

Taylor had struggled to get into Southend's team owing to a run of poor form but at Palace he was a revelation. His promptings inspired those around him and his crosses were a vital ingredient in a team that offered pretty, scientific football but which lacked the final ball. Nevertheless, Allison's proclamation that Taylor would play for England drew weary comment from the Palace faithful. But, for once, he got it right. If you make enough wild claims, one is bound to come true eventually. To put the fans' cynicism in context, not much had been going right lately.

But we were not entirely out of the mire. On Boxing Day, a team of Palace rejects disguised as Orient thrashed us 3-0 at Brisbane Road. The Eagles remained bottom.

The new year brought an upturn. Rogers gave us victory over West Brom at the Hawthorns, we got a point from a goalless draw with Bolton followed by three straight victories; 3-1 at Meadow Lane in our first ever Sunday match when Ben Anderson a centre-half who had arrived from Cape Town was converted to emergency centre-forward and had a hand in two of our goals, and home wins over Bobby Charlton's Preston in which Taylor well and truly announced his arrival with a dazzling run from the half-way line to make it 2-0, and Oxford.

The 2-1 defeat at promotion chasing Luton was only to be expected and, following a draw with promotion chasing Orient when John Jackson was given a standing ovation on his return to Selhurst Park, Rogers floored F.A. Cup holders Sunderland with two goals in a 3-0 win. The surprise package was Carlisle who with the outrageously-moustached Bob Hatton knocking in goals for them denied Orient a first division place at the last. Palace's recovery wasn't enough to deliver the goods at Brunton Park, but three wins and a draw from the next four matches and Possee's rediscovery of his shooting boots meant Palace were pulling clear. For the first time, the league introduced three-up, three-down which made Palace's struggles more difficult … but we'd done it, we'd collected 19 points from a possible 26. Having been miles adrift, survival looked assured. But just when things looked good, the Eagles crashed to bitter defeats against Millwall, Fulham and Hull. Taylor got the great escape back into gear with the winner at Swindon and that meant, depending on Sheffield Wednesday's result, we needed to win by two goals at Ninian Park. Stuart Jump scored for Palace, but Cardiff equalised through Tony Villiers and down we went. Such was the occasional quality of our football, despite Mal's wacky permutations, and the abundant talent at the club that neither Allison (nor the press) had any doubts that we would storm back. But they had been wrong before.

Only Derek Possee, who had been a grave disappointment, departed in the summer. Allison still had a good squad but we started with a defeat at Brighton who were under the other Peter Taylor's guidance following the departure of Brian Clough for his ten minute flirtation with Leeds. Although the Eagles beat Tranmere at Selhurst in the opening home game with a late winner from substitute Swindlehurst there was a nightmare reverse to Halifax Town at the Shay.

After the bright lights of Old Trafford and Anfield, it was agony. But things brightened up, as they always do. Swindon were washed away in a sea of goals – five in twelve first half minutes and *Grandstand* reported that "Palace went mad at Selhurst Park." We eventually settled for six. The following week Chatterton, replacing the out of favour Rogers, scored the only goal of the game with Southend.

Despite losing 2-0 at Edgar Street to Hereford United, who were on a roll following their election to the league and promotion from division four, Palace won the next four matches finishing with a 3-0 win over Grimsby which took us briefly to the top from where we fell spectacularly, 4-1 at home to Chesterfield.

Taylor took the first steps towards fulfilling the faith Allison had in him when he helped draw an unusually large crowd to Selhurst for the England Under-23s' match with Czechoslovakia. He scored after three minutes in the first match at any level of Don Revie's reign as national manager. Among Taylor's team mates were Brian Greenhoff, Steve Perryman and Mike Lyons.

Taylor scored in all his four matches at this level, finishing at Palace a year later against Portugal. Duncan Thompson was among the Palace fans who turned up. "I remember the long and dreary Portuguese national anthem. It was interminably long and I could see everybody in the stand about to sit down thinking it was thankfully over, only for the band to start up again!"

At Port Vale, we were trailing 2-0 when Tony Burns was injured in a collision with Keith Chadwick. Cannon pulled on the green jersey and kept the home forwards at bay for the rest of the first half and all of the second. We even reduced the arrears in the last minute with a Taylor shot from Whittle's free-kick, but it was too late for any further fight back.

Draws were a rarity and we became a pools punter's nightmare. Aside from

Campaign for Palace

The Campaign for Palace was set up in 1974 with the board's support aiming to raise funds and develop assets on behalf of Crystal Palace by means of sponsorship, collections, etc. The chairman was John Macdonald who led a committee comprising finance, promotions and supporters' liaison. The campaign sought to "mobilise the goodwill and skills of football's finest fans".

One of the first ideas was "Bring a Pal to Palace" in which fans were asked to bring a friend with them under the basis that if everyone brought one person then the ground would be filled. This was supported by show business personalities such as Ronnie Corbett, who brought his comedy partner Ronnie Barker, and ventriloquist Roger de Courcy, who presumably brought Nookie Bear.

Box Offices were opened at Debenhams in Croydon and Medhurst of Bromley to make ticket buying easier and the campaign formed separate committees charged with looking into enhancing the image and success of the club. Local school groups were invited to attend training sessions and a committee was set up to try to attract sponsors. There was also a supporters' liaison committee. Supporters also undertook maintenance work around the ground and Palace fan Stanley Mann recalls that at one stage when the police had threatened to close the Holmesdale Road end because of the rubble laying around, the Campaign organised a clear up.

the stalemate that brought Watford back to Selhurst Park for a league cup replay, the first draw of the season didn't arrive until November 2, when Taylor found the net for the third successive game at Peterborough. Typically, once Palace discovered what a draw was, they couldn't stop. Six of the next eight ended level, which was every bit as frustrating. Although Watford were crushed 5-1 in the league cup, our interest ended with a disastrous 4-1 reverse at home to Bristol City.

Early in the season, Mel Blyth left for Southampton, while Rogers was traded to QPR for centre-half Ian Evans and ageing campaigner Terry Venables. It didn't look much of a coup for Palace, but Venables, who waddled about in midfield to no great effect, was to become one of the most important names in Palace history, while Evans, who Allison felt was better in the air than Blyth, became one of the finest central defenders we've ever had. Still among the leaders, Palace looked little more than an outside bet for promotion and the introduction of Venables did little to change that. He was also in part responsible for our F.A. Cup exit.

One of the less pleasant facts of relegation to division three is going into the first round draw of the F.A. Cup. There were sighs of relief when the potential embarrassment of defeat by the respected non-leaguers of Tooting and Mitcham United was avoided – no thanks to Whittle who missed a penalty. But Palace got no further than round two. At Home Park, fellow promotion hopefuls Plymouth knocked us out in front of 17,473 with Venners missing a last minute penalty. Dave Swindlehurst, who had come into the side the previous season for sporadic games but had not found the net, replied for Palace.

Early in 1975, the Palace players were sent to see films and lectures looking at the psychological aspect of the game. Allison said: "It is vital that players should be made aware of the mental pressures which can affect them and be prepared to combat them." Paddy Mulligan was sent to see an American sporting psychology film *The Second Effort*. He explained: "The most valuable application of second effort thinking comes when things go wrong, when you have obtained the initial objective only to lose it … this film underlined to me how wrong my thinking was when I lost my place earlier in the season. I now realise that I lost three-months because my attitude to this setback was wrong."

We were out of the Cup but there was still a big tie at Selhurst when 46,000 watched the Wimbledon versus Leeds replay. The Wombles had captured the imagination of the nation with a heroic display at Elland Road in which Dickie Guy had saved Peter Lorimer's penalty.

The receipts from the replay, when Dave Bassett scored an own goal to put Leeds through, wiped out Wimbledon's overdraft in one fell swoop. "They made the right decision in switching the replay to Selhurst Park," said Allison. "I have always maintained that the crowd potential here at Palace is second to none and on Monday we had an opportunity to confirm my assessment." Cup glory earned Wimbledon the attention necessary to help make a successful application for league status.

Meanwhile, struggling QPR needed a new manager. But although they had their beady eye on Venables, Big Mal was already aware of Tel's qualities and moved swiftly to quell the rumours. In the programme for the match against Chesterfield, he wrote: "There has been a lot of speculation with regard to the future of Terry Venables at Crystal Palace. The newspapers hinted that Terry might be heading to QPR, after Gordon Jago's resignation, as coach, player-coach or player-manager. Terry has been to see me about this and has made it clear that he sees his future at Crystal Palace." And so the former Chelsea, Tottenham and England midfielder remained at Selhurst and began to learn the ropes of football management under Big Mal. After a period of almost constant decline, Palace had made the move which would help change their fortunes.

It was not only Palace that was on the brink of major change. Football was confronted with a new reality. The 60s were now all but forgotten and Britain was in economic decline. As Big Mal pointed out in his programme notes: "I can see some clubs charging 75p to stand and watch matches next season. They would prefer to keep prices down. They would like to make football an even cheaper means of entertainment in comparison with other branches of the industry. But they cannot."

Yet, despite rising prices and static football, Palace's support remained remarkably loyal. We were easily the best supported club in the division although that counted for nothing when the team lacked the goalscorer necessary to help us out of the third division. Dixie McNeill of Hereford, Billy Rafferty at Plymouth and Swindon's Peter Eastoe led the divisional scorers, while Palace had no-one up to the task.

Even towards the end of our second season as the

Palace in the NASL

THE North American Soccer League attracted a great deal of interest in the mid-70s. American teams with glamourous sounding names such as Los Angeles Aztecs, New York Cosmos and Tampa Bay Rowdies were buying up the world's stars for soccer extravaganzas complete with artificial pitches and shoot-outs for drawn matches.

It was not unusual to see kids in schools and on the street sporting the white shirts and green and yellow sleeves of Tampa Bay, whose most famous Englishman remains Rodney Marsh or the green tops of the Cosmos who included Pele, Gerd Muller and Franz Beckenbauer.

There was also a steady stream of players heading across the Atlantic to pick up big wages in the summer.

During the summer of 1975 three Palace players; goalkeeper Paul Hammond Stewart Jump and Mark Lindsay went to play for Tampa Bay Rowdies and helped them to win the championship and cup final

As Palace approached the end of the 1977-78 season, no less than five players were preparing to head for the good ol' U.S of A.

Among big name Palace talent on the way was Jeff Bourne and Stuart Jump again, whose arrival on the NASL bandwagon, brought Palace £45,000 in transfer fees.

Peter Wall also joined Bourne and Jump on a permanent basis while Tony Burns and youngster Neil Smillie were loaned out.

The income from America was immediately spent on John Burridge a £40,000 goalkeeper from Aston Villa who had lost his place to the experienced Jimmy Rimmer.

The Top of Division Three 1974-75

	P	W	D	L	F	A	Pts
Blackburn	46	22	16	8	68	45	60
Plymouth	46	24	11	11	79	58	59
Charlton	46	22	11	13	76	61	55
Swindon	46	21	11	14	64	58	53
Palace	46	18	15	13	66	57	51
Port Vale	46	18	15	13	61	54	51

Eagles,there were still those who resisted the death of the Glaziers. One correspondent in the programme wrote: "Chanting *Eagles, Eagles* to the dying chords of *Hey Jude*, I find very uninspiring. How about using a similar sort of song with a heavy beat? My suggestion is John Lennon's *Power to the People* using the words *Power to the Palace* in the right place."

Could this have been the man who provided the inspiration for one of football's greatest ever tunes?

Palace took the ageing Welsh international Wyn Davies on loan from Blackpool for three games. He had previously played under Allison at Manchester City.

But the manager's search for a striker ended with the purchase of Mick Hill from Ipswich. In April, Grimsby beat us 2-1 in a stormy match when referee Jack Hough sent off three players, prompting the Palace boss to say: "This was the most incredible game I have ever witnessed. We will report the referee and get him banned for life." We didn't.

The story of the season was perfectly summed up in the last six matches. We had two four-goal home wins, over Bournemouth and Gillingham, and four away defeats. Our last away victory had been in the last week of February with a single goal by Swindlehurst, and that wasn't promotion form.We finished 1974-75 in fifth place after a 2-0 defeat at Tranmere in which a 17 year old left back called Kenny Sansom made a highly impressive debut along with a young striker from Slough called David Kemp. It had been a rather drab season, punctuated by occasional high spots, and even Big Mal could not lift our spirits. Palace, the great under achievers, had let us down again.What we needed was excitement. Roll on 1975-76.

Continued on Page 178

Crystal Palace F.C. - F.A. Cup Squad 1976
Peter Taylor
Standing
Jeffrey Johnson, Ian Evans, David Swindlehurst, Paul Hammond, Stewart Jump, Derek Jeffries,
Jim Cannon, Malcolm Allison.
Seated
Alan Whittle, David Kemp, Martin Hinshelwood, Nick Chatterton, Phil Holder, Peter Wall.
CRYSTAL PALACE F.C.
produced by the Croydon Advertiser

The Croydon Advertiser marked Palace's achievement in reaching the F.A. Cup semi-finals whilst still a third division side with a gift to the supporters. Note Big Mal's (ahem) tasteful tie

THE SPIRIT OF '76

For many Palace supporters their *annus mirabilis* was 1976. Even the triumphs of 1979 and the early 90s pale into insignificance when compared to the glamour and glory of that season. Contributions from Barrie Greene, Nick Crivich and Neil Wensley

In yonder years, when the divisions of the Football League were numbered from one to four and everyone knew that being in "one" meant being the best, Palace found themselves the first victims of "three-up, three-down" and went tumbling out of the second and into the third. A complete bloody disaster you younger ones may think. Not a bit of it. In our first season of third division football, under the guidance of Malcolm Allison, we averaged crowds of 17,000 at home and regularly gave other sides their best home gate of the season, such was the size and fanaticism of our away support.

In 1974-75 we visited and won at places such as Southend, Watford and Huddersfield and lost at Halifax, Hereford and Walsall. The team contained Spud Taylor, Jimbo and Taff Evans. We lost our opening game against the Sussex swine, put three past them at home, went out of the Cup at Plymouth, trounced Swindon 6-2, gave Kenny Sansom his debut in the last game at Tranmere and finished fifth. So what?

The point is this. The results never seemed to matter. We were Palace; respected, revered and feared, the biggest fish in the third division pond. We had the most fans, the best ground and the greatest press coverage. We made them raise their game against us. It was their cup final when Palace were around. It was a special kind of feeling to turn up at Bury and poke fun at the locals who had never been outside the confines of their own town, unless it was a day excursion to Blackpool to see Auntie Maud on her birthday. They certainly never came to Selhurst.

Never had we had a more exciting, emotion-filled and ultimately frustrating and disappointing season than 1975-76.

In the early stages, Palace played the finest football of any side ever to represent the club and, by winning their first five league matches outright, they set a new club record.

The influence of Allison at Selhurst lingers on. Every time the chant of *Eagles, Eagles* rumbles around the ground let us remember that it was this flamboyant manager who transformed almost 70 years of tradition. It was he who changed the club badge to an Eagle sitting proudly upon the old glass Palace and the traditional colours of claret and blue to the red and blue stripes we still use today.

However he should be remembered for far more. He brought glamour and excitement to Selhurst, even in the third division, and gave Palace fans reason to be proud. A pride that reached its peak in the great Cup run of 1976.

Being labelled "Team of the Eighties" has proved to be a mighty embarrassment to Palace, but when we were labelled "the best team ever to play in the third division", many accepted it to be true and it still holds.

At Man City, Allison had helped Joe Mercer build a fine side. One feels he only joined a struggling club to prove that his ideas could work whatever the size of club. He was determined to experiment with the continental approach and even relegation in two consecutive seasons did not deter him from applying his principles.

Gradually he assembled a team to fulfil his ambitions, acquiring the perfect player; Peter Taylor from Southend United, a brilliant winger who was good enough to make the full England team as a third division player.

Allison built his talented team around this star and bought players to fit his jigsaw rather than for individual talent. The apparently unglamorous, such as Stewart Jump and Derek Jeffries, along with the giraffe-like Ian Evans proved they were good footballers.

The sweeper system was still looked upon as an innovation, yet, in the depths of the third division, Palace played that way before many top teams dared. The role was assigned to a classy full-back, Peter Wall, who had been plagued by injury while Palace struggled.

Meanwhile, Jeff Johnson and Phil Holder battled for the midfield ball-winner's role and up front Dave Swindlehurst came of age while David Kemp, a delightful player, arrived from non-league Slough to score an avalanche of goals. Early season success also spurred Alan Whittle to his best form for the club and Martin Hinshelwood joined Nicky Chatterton who, on his day, looked a great player to complete the midfield. Jim Cannon at left back was evolving into the great player that would serve Palace so well and between the posts Paul Hammond was first choice after Tony Burns had played in the opening three games.

Whether Allison truly gained the recognition he so dearly wanted from the footballing fraternity is still not cer-

Average attendances for 1975-76

Third Division Home	
1) Crystal Palace	20,123
2) Brighton	15,343
3) Cardiff City	11,702
4) Sheff Wednesday	11,219
5) Hereford United	8,273

Third Division Away	
1) Crystal Palace	10,437
2) Hereford United	8,917
3) Millwall	8,575
4) Brighton	8,476
5) Sheff Wednesday	8,123

tain because the success that grew out of those two relegations only really began when he acquired Venables from QPR.

If Allison purchased Venables for any reason other than that he saw him as a perfect purveyor of his ideals on the pitch, it quickly became apparent that here was a man who mirrored his ideas and possessed the potential to become an even greater coach. All of which brought about a sort of father and son relationship that was to ignite Selhurst Park for a golden season.

By the start of the campaign, Venables had retired and was officially Palace coach. The summer had been very dry and this continued into autumn.

It provided pitches that suited good football and Palace raced to the top with five straight wins, remaining unbeaten away from home until December 20. It was a time for fervour and passion and electric performances etched into every Palace memory.

At that time, we were still regarded as something of a joke. We'd made no discernible impact in four years in division one and then, under the media's favourite glamour boy, plunged into division three. Allison was outspoken and his comments often brought ridicule.

The Palace haters and professional mockers loved it. The penchant for champagne and a love of London's top nightspots didn't help, but Allison had another side. He stuck to his guns and relaid the foundations most notably with his development of the youth team.

Palace were installed as bookies' favourites for the third division crown at the start of 1975-76.

Had the bookmakers witnessed the uninspired pre-season friendlies against Millwall and Epsom & Ewell they may have revised their odds, but once the season was under way their judgement couldn't have been more correct. Palace played breathtaking football that was a joy to watch.

The chief architect was Peter Taylor. When he got going he was nothing short of masterful. Every time he got the ball an air of expectancy hung over the crowd. What magic would he produce? A dazzling run down the wing? A deft cut inside for a shot? Or perhaps a penetrating ball for Kemp or Swindlehurst to latch onto?

The *Croydon Advertiser* hailed the 3-0 victory over Colchester in the League Cup with "Brilliant Palace". It was, said the paper, "one of the finest displays in years". Kemp scored his third goal in two games and followed with another at Chesterfield on the following Saturday when Phil Holder's 35-yard screamer stole the show and clinched the points.

Goals came from everywhere; Ian Evans popped up with a hat-trick – the first ever by a Palace defender – in a comfortable win also over Colchester at the end of August.

Allison's belief in tactics established the Eagles as a team that could and would use set plays effectively. These were often cunningly planned and involved all sorts of signals which as much as anything upset and frightened already wary opponents.

At Cardiff the 100 per cent league record was preserved when Kemp popped up for a last minute winner. The most controversial moment was the referee's failure to send Holder off for a wild yet not misplaced kick on Tony Villiers – the man whose goal sent Palace crashing into division three in 1974.

A league cup defeat at Doncaster produced a few adverse headlines, but the 2-0 win over Rotherham the following Saturday restored spirits and left Palace as the last club in the league with a perfect record. It lasted three days until we dropped a point at Walsall although it could have been worse, Ian Evans saved the day with a last minute goal.

At Shrewsbury Palace turned on a super show scoring three in 30 minutes in a 4-2 victory. Everyone was asking, "who can stop Palace?"

The short answer was Brighton. The visitors took an early lead and although Palace produced their usual brilliant football and put them under continuous pressure 25,600 people screamed as a hatful of chances just would not go in.

Stamford Bridge party

TAFFY Williams taught maths with a little explanation, a lot of threat and a liberal use of the slipper.

He believed his slipper was a magic "cure-all" for tardy schoolboys who indulged in "soccer yobbery".

He was an ex-Welsh rugby international and, in his eyes,

Chelsea v Palace was more than a Cup match. It was war. Matthew Simmonds was a frightened 13 year old

supporting Palace was akin to soccer yobbery. Saturday afternoons, Taffy believed, should be spent either playing rugby for the school or cheering on the hallowed XV.

Saturday, February 14, 1976 was a day that couldn't come soon enough. It was F.A. Cup fifth round day and Palace were away to Chelsea. The programme described it as "the match the whole of south London is talking about". I was a big boy and went to the game on my own – or to be precise I was 13 and went with a group of schoolmates. We took the bus from south Croydon to Chelsea and arrived a couple of hours before kick-off. There was already expectation in the air – a sense that something big was about to go off.

We walked up the slope towards the "away supporters" gates and joined the long queue. It cost around £1.50 of hard earned pocket money to get in and we nudged our way across the concrete slope of the away end until we found a spot to the left of the goal.

I opened my packed lunch, but no sooner had I started to nibble at its contents than I was submerged by people flooding over me. We staggered up and joined the flow. In a second or two everybody was trotting back and straining to look up at the back of the terrace.

A couple of police helmets were visible – moving into the crowd – but the surge happened again.

It was clear that a group of Chelsea nutters had infiltrated the Palace end intent on trouble. And trouble they made.

By kick-off the ground was jam packed. Fifty-five thousand partisan souls. I could move my head but that was about all.

The noise from the Shed was spellbinding. When we started singing my eyes filled. It was emotional, it was a passion play, it was almost religious.

Palace's form since beating Leeds in the previous round had been patchy. But the media coverage of Big Mal and his troops had been immense. Finally they were to be put to the test. To my amazement, we began superbly. Peter Taylor crashed a vicious drive against the underside of the bar and Nick Chatterton reacted quicker than Peter Bonetti to bundle the loose ball home. Before Chelsea had settled, Taylor struck again. Palace conjured a neat move on the edge of the box and he bent a low left footer past Bonetti's outstretched right hand and into the bottom corner. Shortly after, we jumped for another reason. The

a day of terror and triumph

fighting had flared again and this time it was worse and seemed to be in more than one spot. I got separated from my mates and sought them anxiously. As the second half began a massive surge carried me to the front of the terrace where I felt like I was in a moat. People were panicking, pushing, calling out.

I was squashed between a police horse and a wall and was concentrating on getting out in one piece. I'd lost interest in the game. Someone came hurtling through the crowd with blood streaming from his face. A couple of blokes were after him and the police were after them.

As I tried to take stock Chelsea, attacking the Shed, scored. A wave of sound battered my senses and I was carried by another surge towards a wall. I'd had enough and decided to leave. A policeman led me around the side of the pitch towards the tunnel. I felt dwarfed by the huge stand. There was trouble inside it. The policeman turned to watch, while I turned towards the game continuing not more than a couple of feet in front of me.

I could see the sweat dripping from the players faces. The Palace players looked shaken and exhausted.

"Take care son," said the Plod as he directed me out of Stamford Bridge. As I walked down the tunnel Chelsea scored again. I turned for a last peep. The Shed was a seething cauldron and the roar almost lifted me off my feet. Once outside the stadium I felt as if I'd returned to the real world.

As I jumped on the bus home, I heard a muted roar and I wondered. Later, back in Croydon I saw a Chelsea fan and asked him the score. As he told me, a bolt of joy shot through my whole frame. In response to his dejection, I tried to keep a straight face. That night the game was featured on *Match of the Day.* Taylor's work was stunning for the opening goals but Jimmy Hill made a point of discussing the violence and even showed some action replays drawing attention to a "kung-fu" kick.

What he didn't address was why a large group of Chelsea fans had been allowed in the Palace end to cause mayhem for a couple of hours. Back to the football. As play drifted to the far side I noticed two figures on the cinder track. The camera panned in. Unmistakably it was Plod and me. The "babbling chin" made mention of a young hooligan being escorted from the ground by the long arm ... etc etc. I sat transfixed, he meant me.

A free kick 25 yards out, Butch Wilkins organised the Chelsea wall. Taylor stepped up and the flight of the ball took it high into the net. Not in the top corner, just high in the net. Thank you Bonetti. The Cat? Ha Ha!

At school on Monday morning all the talk was about the match. I took lots of stick for letting on I'd left early so I shut up and wondered who Palace would get in the quarter final. Mr Williams passed me in the corridor: "Good win for Palace in the Cup."

"Yes sir," I answered brightly.

"I saw the match on TV," he continued. "And there was a lot of soccer yobbery."

He fixed me with glinting eye. We all know Taffy Williams' cure for that don't we?

It was at this game that the rivalry between Palace and Brighton really developed.

The atmosphere was tense and highly charged and there was fighting on the terraces, no doubt a continuation of a riot that had taken place at the Goldstone Ground the previous season.

Thankfully this was the only major outbreak of violence at Selhurst Park during the season.

Alerted to the excitement at Selhurst, the *Match of the Day* cameras were present for the home match with Sheffield Wednesday, sharing the bill with the Mersey derby. The result was a tired 1-1 draw, followed by an equally lacklustre goalless affair at Port Vale. But Palace were still top and there was no indication that they were about to relinquish the position in a hurry.

Indeed, we reinforced our dominance with a 3-0 win over a physical Grimsby, who had four men booked and seemed intent on continuing the war of the previous season when three had been sent off and four booked.

Palace's "finest result of the season so far" was how the *Advertiser* described the goalless draw with Preston who until that day had won all their matches at Deepdale and had scored in every home game for a year.

It was a good performance but it soon became the lot of Palace themselves at Selhurst. Lesser teams, terrified of what would happen to them if they attempted to take us on, settled for containment.

What should have been easy victories over Hereford, Southend and Peterborough finished with only a share of the spoils.

Superb victories on the road at Halifax by three goals to one and Swindon kept Allison's bandwagon rolling and another 100 per cent home record, this time Wrexham's, was shattered by a superb 3-1 victory. Swindlehurst scored a couple and Kemp added the other. Taylor again was the magician that mesmerised the Welsh.

The F.A. Cup first round paired Palace with non-league Walton and Hersham, famed for their 4-0 destruction of Brian Clough's Brighton a year or two before, and once again Palace's home malaise continued, but we scraped through 1-0. Swindlehurst scored the best goal of the season when Mansfield were trounced 4-1 and Palace were seemingly back on the straight and narrow when a solitary goal by Kemp at Bury took us seven points clear of the pack.

Our record at that stage was:

P20 W12 D7 L1

An envious league looked on. Millwall's programme summed it up: "Palace are currently romping away with the championship of the third division and only a sensational slump in form will prevent them returning to the second." We were a first division quality side in third rate company but at least we joined the big clubs in the third round of the Cup thanks to a Kemp goal and a twice-taken Taylor penalty at the Den.

The words of the Millwall programme were not only prophetic but the Lions helped to make them come true. Over the Christmas period Palace's form was diabolical.

Four days after the Cup win, Millwall reversed the scoreline at the Den and then Aldershot, Gillingham and Walsall all scored single goal victories to halt our run. The last of these was a terrible showing made worse by a referee who chose not to give Palace a penalty for a blatant handball.

Four points clear but whether it was a surplus of Christmas pudding or something worse there was something very wrong. Both the team and supporters developed a nervous edge which spoilt matches. But as league form turned sour, the Cup run began to take shape and the see-saw emotions began to tear at us.

Given Palace's form at the time, the third round tie at Scarborough had all the makings of an upset, but with the TV cameras present Palace rose to the occasion and put in a thoroughly professional performance that contained and eventually over-ran the non-leaguers.

Allison's flashy fedora hat, which he had borrowed to keep the sun out of his

CHELSEA
FOOTBALL AND
ATHLETIC CO. LTD.

SATURDAY
APRIL 3rd
1976

ADMIT TO
GROUND

This portion to be
given up at
Entrance to Grounds
by **Britannia Gate**
C
See map on reverse

CHELSEA
FOOTBALL & ATHLETIC CO. LTD.

F.A.Challenge Cup 1975-76 Semi-Final
SOUTHAMPTON
V.
CRYSTAL PALACE
SATURDAY **3rd APRIL** 1976
KICK-OFF 3 p.m.
You are advised to take up your position by 2.30 p.m.
ADMIT TO GROUND **£1.50**
inc. VAT
THIS PORTION TO BE RETAINED
C NORTH TERRACE
Ealoroker
Secretary, The Football Association

Top: the Palace team take a break from training to tune in for the draw. Above: A ticket for the semi final complete with its stub. It belongs to Donny the Beastie Boy of the Addiscombe Eagles who was supposed to sell it on behalf of a friend who couldn't go, but he was unable to do so because he says he was too drunk

eyes, attracted more interest from the press than the match.

He denied that Cup matches were adversely affecting his side and predicted "we could do well in the Cup this year and surprise a lot of people," although "the side I fancy to win the trophy outright is Leeds United".

The following Monday, Palace were drawn away to Leeds in the fourth round. Although it was an exciting prospect, we didn't really believe that we could get a favourable result. In the meantime, we hoped the Scarborough performance would lift the team's league form and when Colchester were whipped 3-0, this time at Layer Road, with Alan Whittle the fans' favourite back for the off form Kemp, we seemed to be back on the right track. But against Shrewsbury it was the same old story. One goal ahead, Palace enjoyed 80 per cent of the play and laid siege to the Town goal only to concede a late, soft equaliser. It was like being hit in the stomach with a baseball bat. We left the ground feeling as if we had been beaten.

The see-saw season continued brought into sharp relief by the plum away draw at Leeds. The first division leaders were considered the best team in Europe and the previous season had been unfortunate to finish runners up in the European Cup.

Nobody expected Palace to win, except Big Mal. Revelling in the media attention, he was overjoyed to find himself in the limelight and made headlines by absurdly boasting that Palace were going to give Leeds the fright of their lives. Back page photos of the increasingly famous fur coat, big cigar and fedora helped swell his image.

An improvement in league form gave the team a boost prior to the big match but by twenty-to-five on January 24, 1976 it was generally assumed that Palace would have been given a football lesson. In fact, the reverse happened and it stunned the football world. It was the finest achievement by any post-war Palace team and the manner in which they outplayed Leeds must have astonished even Allison.

The 1-0 scoreline, achieved with a Swindlehurst header from a Taylor free kick, does nothing to underline the superiority of Palace that day. The quality of their football belonged to the first division and it was from here that they earned that tag of the finest team ever to play in the third. Palace's name was on everybody's lips although Allison later revealed that he would have played coach Terry Venables at Leeds in order to add some experience to his youngsters, but couldn't get him fit in time.

That incredible result rekindled the buzz at the club and restored the belief that, despite all the setbacks, this was going to be a season of glory. It lifted the team for the visit to second placed Hereford the following week where we gained a valuable 1-1 draw. But then came disaster, Palace lost 4-1 at Rotherham and had Cannon, Taylor and Jeffries sent off.

As if impending suspensions for the trio weren't bad enough, another calamity followed. Palace savaged relegation battlers Swindon in front of the *Big Match* cameras. The 3-1 lead could so easily have been 10-1, but two late goals cost us another point.

The supporters just couldn't believe it and had Swindon not missed a penalty it could have been worse. For the first time all season, Palace were no longer in first place.

The Cup became a welcome distraction and the fifth round visit to Chelsea was not only the talk of London but the biggest tie in the country.

Nobody dared forecast the outcome but the press featured it throughout the week almost as if it were the Final itself. The media turned the spotlight on the players, particularly Chelsea's teenage skipper Ray Wilkins and Palace's dazzling winger Peter Taylor, who was playing the best football of his career.

Comparisons were made between Taylor and his Palace predecessor Johnny Byrne, who had played for England while in division three – the last player from the third division to do so. *Match of the Day* captured Malcolm in his now trademark fedora taunting the Chelsea fans with his pre-match prediction and then 54,000 saw Palace in a flashy new white kit with a red and blue diagonal sash win a classic.

Chelsea fielded Butch Wilkins, Steve Wicks – who both scored – and Teddy Maybank along with former Palace player Charlie Cooke, while Micky Droy, a Palace player of the future, was replaced by David Hay after he broke an elbow. We soaked up early home pressure and then went two-up, but Chelsea fought back before a classic Taylor free-kick took us into the quarter finals.

BBC TV pundit Jimmy Hill, however, spent longer analysing the slow motion replays of the Kung Fu talents of the notorious North Stand than the free kick that won the game.

By now Ian Evans was firmly established in the Welsh side and Martin Hinshelwood was touted as a candidate for young player of the year.

If Palace had once more risen to the big occasion they immediately plummed the depths in their bread and butter duties against lesser teams. Wrexham drew 1-1 at Selhurst Park and Brighton and Peterborough both beat us 2-0.

After the Wrexham game, the *Advertiser* echoed the feelings of everyone when it commented: "It is almost criminal that a side that was once seven points clear at the top of the table should have dropped to fifth."

Had it not been for the Cup run, the fans might have been baying for blood. Instead Allison insisted that it was the Cup that was keeping the players attuned.

Phil Holder said: "It's difficult to put a finger on it. Lady Luck has definitely played a part in some teams taking points at Selhurst Park that they didn't deserve." But the barren patch ended on February 27 with a 2-1 win at Southend.

In a strange game, Peter Wall scored from a cross and Taylor won it with a penalty after Southend had made the miss of the season. Hammond dropped a cross a yard from goal but, presented with a tap in, one Southend striker kicked the ground and fell over the ball and another following up missed his kick completely.

After Taylor had given Palace a match winning lead the Southend supporters showed their displeasure by throwing cushions onto the pitch!

It was just the tonic for the daunting trip to Roker Park for the sixth round. Palace had once again been drawn away.

Big Mal's traditional pre-match stroll onto the pitch to show the thumbs down to the Sunderland supporters resulted in a warning from the police to stop inciting the crowd, but his prediction rang true.

Another miraculous performance was capped by Whittle's late winner to end an unbeaten home record going back to when God was an embryo. Wembley was in our sights. Palace were in the F.A. Cup semi finals for the first time.

Cup fever swept south London. At home to Port Vale there were 23,000 and the players received a heroes reception. Palace repaid them with a goal after just four minutes but succumbed

Aside on Southampton '76

As an exiled Palace supporter living near Southampton I keep having a recurring nightmare that we are continuously beaten by the Scummers (Hampshire slang for Southampton, which originated in Portsmouth).

Ever since the semi-final in 1976 I have been regarded as the village idiot because of my allegiance to Palace.

I used to live a few doors down from David Peach and one day while walking my dog, he emerged from his front gate with his dog.

Upon seeing me, his dog's sixth sense obviously told him I was a Palace supporter and it sank its teeth into my arse. I told Peachy what I thought to which he replied and I quote: "My dog's not an animal, you know."

You could have knocked me down with an inflatable banana. I felt the weight of the world lift from my shoulders. It wasn't me who was the village idiot, it was David Peach.

Now, every time I wake up in a sweat, screaming: "No Richard don't pass it back to Nigel," my wife soothes my brow and reminds me about the teeth marks on my bum. Soon I'm asleep again, safe in the knowledge that the Scummers couldn't even beat us when we'd given them a goal start.

Paul Baker.

to a predictable late equaliser.

"A team that Palace should have gobbled up joined the long list of visitors generously rewarded at Selhurst Park for their feeble efforts," said the *Advertiser*.

At least Palace followed up with a better spell. Wins over Grimsby, Preston and Bury and draws with Mansfield – where probably the last decent gesture instigated by the club saw four train loads of fans travel at a price of £1 each due to the late arrival of many at Roker – and Millwall put us back in the promotion places and in the right frame of mind to face Southampton in the F.A. Cup semi final at Stamford Bridge.

If Palace were to have any inkling that it wasn't to be their day in the semi-final, then surely the alarm bells would have been ringing after comments by "The General" on the *Palace Guard* page of the programme for the match with Preston.

Apart from statements such as: "I wouldn't like to forecast the scoreline of our semi-final but I cannot honestly see us losing" – a red rag to a superstitious bull if ever there was one – the General also pointed out that Palace had met Lawrie McMenemy's side twice in the Cup and won both times. Surely third time lucky for Southampton?

Not if the general had anything to do with it. He further tempted fate by stating: "Stamford Bridge is something of a bogey ground for the Saints as far as semi-finals go. They've played there three times before and have yet to win!" What better time and what better opponents for Southampton to lay their ghosts?

Trouble loomed when Martin Hinshelwood entered hospital for a cartilage operation and was ruled out for the rest of the season. Allison said: "He is unquestionably the most intelligent player I have ever worked with, a player whose attitude to the game is 100 per cent right. He took on Billy Bremner and Brian [Pop] Robson on their own parks – and played them off the park."

Seat and ground tickets went on sale on Sunday, March 21 at Selhurst Park. One ticket per person for season ticket holders, Glaziers Club members, Social Club members, including the coach travel section, Palace Bingo agents and Rail Travel Club members.

Tickets for the ground only went on general sale the following Sunday. Palace had the North Bank, Southampton the Shed.

While the first team had reached the semi-finals of the F.A. Cup, the juniors had reached the same stage of the Youth Cup having beaten Oldham in front of 2,407 people at the end of February.

The team included Kenny Sansom, Neil Smillie, Billy Gilbert, Peter Nicholas, Steve Brennan, Ian Walsh, Vince Hilaire, Jerry Murphy and Steve Leahy.

Whatever happened at Stamford Bridge, a new order was waiting in the wings. The youth team was still a little on the young side, however, and was beaten over two legs by West Brom, who also boasted a number of emerging youngsters.

As it turned out, the promotion battle against Millwall probably did the team more harm than good. In a tense and emotional battle in front of 38,000 people Taylor put a penalty yards over the bar and at the end there were some visibly weary players on the pitch.

The atmosphere for the semi final was indescribable. On paper, this was the easiest game since Scarborough, and Palace had avoided the admirable Derby County and Tommy Docherty's Manchester United. We also had the advantage of being on familiar territory; a London ground where we had already won in the competition.

But Southampton gave a thoroughly evil performance and two disgraceful fouls in the first ten minutes by Rodrigues crippled Taylor, who never really got into the match.

But the harsh truth was that the Eagles never produced the form of the earlier rounds. All that mattered were the goals, the first was a stupid one

Adore a fedora

Palace cash in on Allison hat-trick

FEDORA fever is sweeping South London. Copies of Malcolm Allison's hat are being snapped up by Crystal Palace fans as fast as a Southend firm can produce them.

Palace have sold 3,500 of the red and blue fedoras so far during their FA Cup run. 'As soon as we get a supply in, we sell out,' said commercial manager Tony Shaw.

'We sell them for £1 each and they're made of felt. We got the idea going after Malcolm wore one at Scarborough

'I was watching television with the sound turned down when I saw him and I thought it was John Wayne or someone.

'It created such interest that when I saw him a couple of days later, we decided to get some

'American gangsters used to wear them in the 20s and 30s. Now they are identified with our Cup run.'

The manufacturers are hoping that Palace beat Southampton on Saturday. A Palace spokesman said: 'If we lose, it's the end of a good gimmick. If we win, we'll be in business and there will be 25,000 of them at Wembley.'

Palace have also sold 15,000 scarves during their Cup run

NOTE: The fedora wasn't an American invention. The name comes from Princess Fedora Romanoff, a character portrayed by Fanny Davenport who wore the hat in a play produced in this country in 1883.

Daily Mail

During the Cup run, I worked for the Crystal Palace Commercial Department at the time of Malcolm Allison's fedora mania.

The hats were manufactured at a small factory in Southend and such was the demand after our sixth round victory over Sunderland that they couldn't keep pace. On one occasion, I was taken off my normal duties in order to drive the little old claret and blue mini van (it remained claret and blue even though the club's colours had changed) which was my company vehicle to Southend to collect a consignment of fedoras that the company were unable to deliver themselves.

On returning to Selhurst I was literally mobbed by a queue of people desperate to buy one of these felt hats.

We had a home match on the Tuesday before the semi-final and the *Daily Mail* wanted a picture so I had to get a couple of assistants from the club shop and a couple of passing fans to pose.

Driving the old minivan was an experience in itself. You'd get plenty of thumbs up signs and hoots and people would give way for you which made me feel quite important. On other occasions, as you can imagine, I'd get the V-sign, get cut up, sworn at etc. I just had to take it and sit there and smile.

Richard Gribble

from Palace's point of view defensively and we were killed off by a penalty that television proved should never have been. That put paid to Wembley.

Confronted by their greatest disappointment, supporters sat on the terraces weeping openly.

In the dressing room too there were tears. Palace were not going to be able to brush this off like a minor inconvenience. Brave words about concentrating on promotion had a hollow ring.

We'd always believed without doubt that we would win, so to lose was a devastating blow to both team and supporters.

To rub salt into our wounds we lost our next two league matches and were out of the promotion places. In the second of these, a home game with promotion rivals Cardiff, 25,000 turned up. We dominated once more only to lose to a late goal. How many more times could it happen? The situation was desperate. It was almost inconceivable that after so much promise we might end with nothing.

But it was fast becoming reality. John Matthews wrote in the *Croydon Advertiser*: "The sparkle and zest that so typified their play have evaporated and unless they can restore them for the last four games all of the season's good work will be undone. Indeed if they cannot beat Aldershot at home they hardly deserve to go up ... even though they reached the F.A. Cup semi-final, if they fail to win a second division place then they will have won nothing."

Against a Shots side that had the worst away record in the third division, Palace put on a dreadful performance and drew 0-0. The same happened the following week at home to Chesterfield when another huge crowd, praying we might still do it, watched in dismay as Palace couldn't break through. And that was that. We'd played first division football with international class footballers in a first division ground, attracted first division attendances and reached the last four of the Cup. But week-in week-out, we couldn't beat third division opponents. The nightmare continued with a 1-1 home draw with Halifax, whose very name was a stark reminder that, whatever heights we had aspired to, we were still a third division club.

Somehow we kept in touch with a 2-1 win at Gillingham, but that was it. There were no more victories and the season finished in front of a meagre 6,702 at Chester where Taylor's penalty was insufficient to salvage anything from the match or the season.

"I could be like my old man. He thinks the best days were applying for re-election in 1956!"

NEIL WENSLEY

It was the end of an era. Allison, broken by failure, parted company with the club for whom he had brought glamour and glory, but not success.

These were the days when the Whitehorse Lane was called the Whitehorse Lane and when you could stand in the Old Stand and drink during the game. Time plays tricks but it was enormously enjoyable.

Any fan wants Palace to succeed at the highest level but were these the best days of our lives? Was David Price fat? Does everyone hate Arsenal? Have things been the same since Jim Cannon left? Is Chris Armstrong the new messiah?

Hy Money

Not only the story of a semi-final. Hy Money's picture captures the story of the 1975-76 season. It is five o'clock at Stamford Bridge and Terry Venables contemplates defeat

THE GLORY, GLORY TRAIL

Jim Cannon's guide to the '76 Cup run

In 1976, Palace's F.A. Cup exploits captured the imagination of the nation. Jonathan Scarlett and Laurie Dahl asked Jim Cannon for his version of events

First Round
Palace v. Walton and Hersham
Selhurst Park
Saturday, November 22, 1975
Won 1-0. Scorer: David Kemp
Attendance: 16,241

JC: Pass. Don't remember that one. I thought the first one we played was against Tooting and Mitcham

Second Round
Millwall v. Palace
The Den
Saturday, December 13, 1975
Drew 1-1
Scorer: Dave Swindlehurst
Attendance: 14,920

Replay: Selhurst Park
Tuesday, December 16, 1975
Won 2-1
Scorers: David Kemp and Peter Taylor
Attendance: 18,284

JC: Nope, I don't remember playing Millwall in that cup run either.

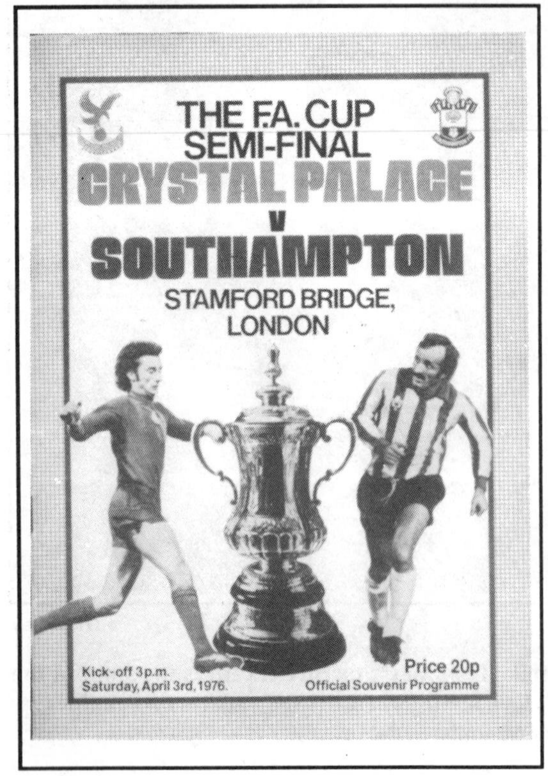

THE F.A. CUP
SEMI-FINAL
CRYSTAL PALACE
v
SOUTHAMPTON
STAMFORD BRIDGE,
LONDON
Kick-off 3p.m.
Saturday, April 3rd, 1976.
Price 20p
Official Souvenir Programme

Third Round
Scarborough v. Palace
Scarborough
Saturday, January 3, 1976
Won 2-1
Scorers: Peter Taylor and Ian Evans
Attendance: 8,001

JC: That was a hard game. I'll always remember it because it was on the telly. They had quite a good record there and I think any pro team going to a non-league club is on a hiding to nothing.

Fourth Round
Leeds United v. Palace
Saturday, January 24, 1976
Won 1-0
Scorer: Dave Swindlehurst
Attendance: 43,116

JC: We were just going up there for the ride, but in all fairness we should have come away with a four or five-nil win. It was so one-sided it was untrue. We missed a lot of chances and I just don't think they could believe it.

Malcolm had brought in this tactical game where he let the two full backs push on – I was at left back. They all use it now, they call it a diamond shape these days, but Malcolm was the first to use it during that Cup run. Using a sweeper with two centre halves was not unusual but using two full backs was. Normally if a team played with a sweeper they had four at the back. Peter Wall was the sweeper and I remember I was playing against Peter Lorimer and Malcolm said if you run all day long he'll be chasing you and I thought to myself that won't be the case, but that's how it worked out. Lorimer chased me up and down that line all afternoon, which was great. Leeds had such a good record at the time and were a quality team with so many household names but we really gave them a good hiding. When you set out on any cup run you feel confident and obviously we had nothing to lose.

When you're a third division side and you're going to Leeds you expect to lose and the onus is on them.

They probably thought we were going to be an easy touch but we were a good team because we were about ten points clear in the third division and on song. I think they were surprised at the quality of our football.

Nevertheless it was always going to be hard for us and we played really well that day – all the Cup run we played well until the last game.

The Leeds players were good about it, and offered us their congratulations although you could see they were totally gutted.

Fifth Round
Chelsea v. Palace
Stamford Bridge
Saturday, February 14, 1976
Won 3-2
Scorers: Nick Chatterton and Peter Taylor (2)
Attendance: 54,407

JC: They came back from the dead. Nicky Chatterton got the first one. It came off the bar and he just touched it in. Peter Taylor set about them and we were cruising at 2-0.

Then they took Micky Droy off and brought Davie Hay on, which we didn't want. Steve Wicks pulled one back and all of a sudden it was a hard game.

Then it was two-all and finally Peter Taylor conjured up a majestic goal. It was a great game.

I thought we played well, but we just sat back a little bit and they came back into it. I think being a London derby there was massive pride involved.

Malcolm really set it all off and I think that the police started getting a bit fidgety with him because his behaviour was inciting the crowd. There's no way he would be allowed to do it these days.

I don't think anybody expected us to win that one either. Malcolm just made

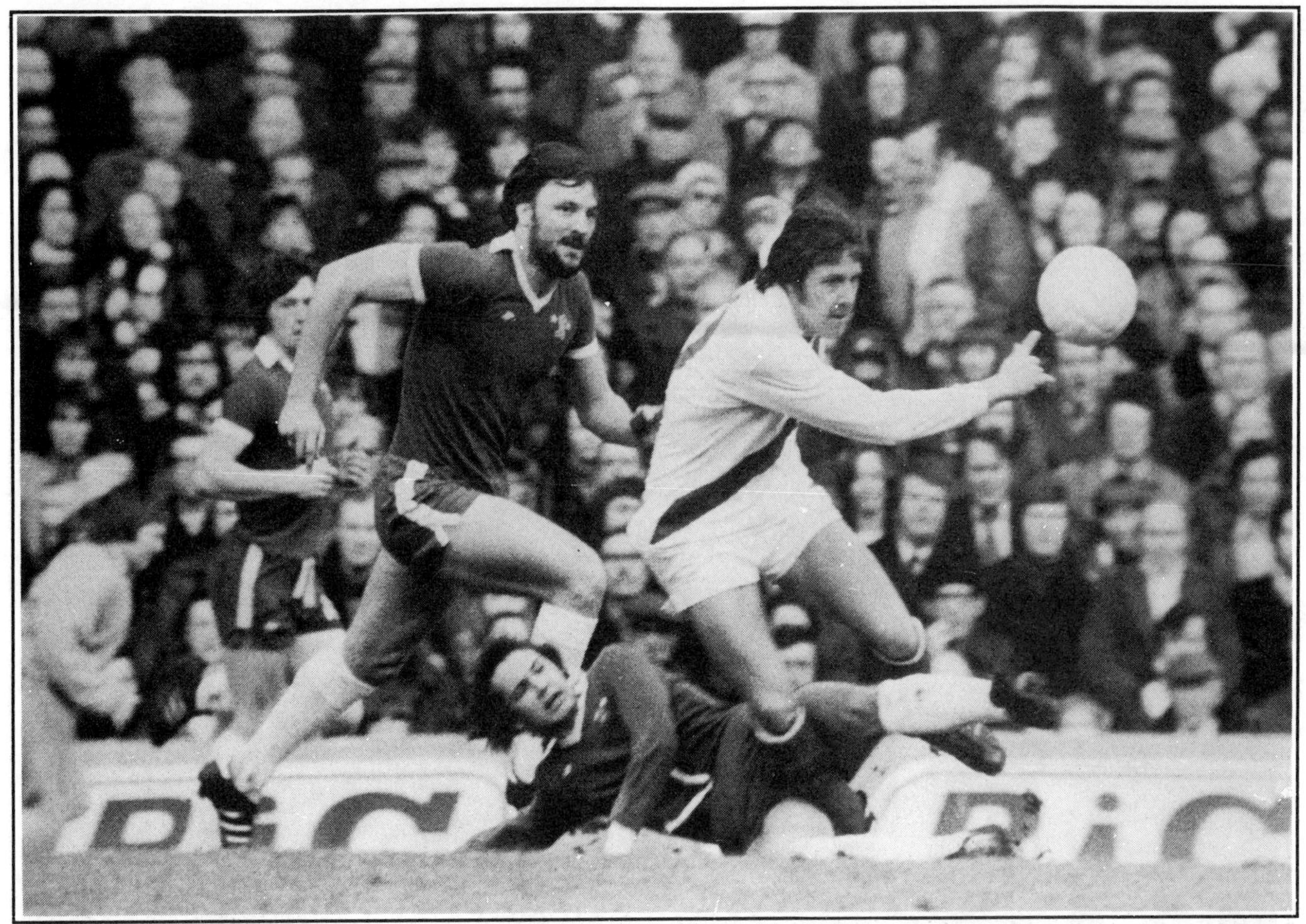

Colorsport

Stamford Bridge 1976. Dave Swindlehurst evades the attentions of Chelsea's Micky Droy and Butch Wilkins

us believe that we were gonna win. He gave us so much confidence.

He basically said we were a first division team playing in the third division.

Quarter Final
Sunderland v. Palace
Roker Park
Saturday, March 6, 1976
Won 1-0
Scorer: Alan Whittle
Attendance: 50,850

JC: We had a terrible, terrible wind against us in the first half and for about 35 minutes we couldn't seem to get out of our 18-yard box.

Sunderland hit the bar and did everything but score. I thought if they get one they might get two or three because they'd played 19 games at home won 18 and drawn one, or something like that.

But we rode our luck and in the second half it was completely the opposite. The wind dropped a little bit but they didn't have a shot after the break.

We were always going to be the team ... we were certainly going to get a draw out of it. Alan Whittle got the winner.

Once we'd got the lead it was just like the Alamo.

Semi Final
Southampton v. Palace
Stamford Bridge
Saturday, April 3, 1976
Lost 0-2
Attendance: 52,810

JC: You certainly think you can win the Cup once you get to the semi-finals. The disappointment lasted the rest of the season and we bombed out on promotion. For me, personally, it was hard.

I think every player wants to play in an F.A. Cup Final and not just people from England; although certainly people who play in the English league want to play at Wembley. So many players don't play there, its nice if you get there and in the back of your mind as you start out every year you think about it.

You know the odds are stacked against you really but being 90 minutes away from it was certainly the biggest disappointment I've felt and as a team we just didn't recover from it.

It was the whole day, the weather ... it was a sunny sort of day and the pitch didn't look right. Sometimes you walk out and everything looks right and other days you walk out and there's a little bit of a breeze and and I thought, hmm, things aren't the same as when we played Chelsea. But saying that, I was talking to Mick Channon and he was saying: "I'll see you at Highbury for a replay on Tuesday."

All of a sudden they got a goal from a throw in. It was a silly bit of marking from somebody in the middle of the park, he got away and it was a longish shot and it was in the back of the net and I thought that's the end of it.

Players were crying their eyes out. Malcolm was very upset. I think perhaps as the manager of the team you want to get to the F.A. Cup Final more than the players.

He didn't look happy, but he was geeing the players up saying we'd got the third division to play for. But we hardly won a game after that. We lost a couple of silly games. Peter Taylor missed a penalty against Millwall which I think went out of the ground and, at the time, they were just a couple of points behind us.

That switched the whole thing round. They went up and we missed out. It backfired on us not just in the F.A. Cup but in the league. But although the league's your bread and butter I think if you're in the third division you would swap the chance of playing in a Cup Final for promotion – certainly for one more year.

THE ORIGINAL SUPA-AL

Colorsport

'A quarter of an hour to go now. Is this going to be a problem for Crystal Palace? It's not because Hammond is there. And look at that for a good throw ... straight into the path of Peter Taylor. Whittle is up with him as well. Taylor taking on Bolton. Moncur, getting in behind Bolton, and he needs to. Taylor going past Moncur as well, here's the cross. Whittle ... a goal ... Alan Whittle.'

Brian Moore, The Big Match

Sunderland v Crystal Palace, F.A. Cup 6th Round 1976

Brian Moore's television commentary on March 6, 1976 at windy Roker Park captured the moment Alan Whittle fired Palace into the F.A. Cup semi finals with, as it turned out, his last goal for the club. What a day – one that suited Alan Whittle. A big match, the perfect stage for him to prance and perform his little flicks to grand effect. But how good was he?

Not everything Alan Whittle did was successful, but it was always exciting. By Peter Gee.

The records say he made 103 league appearances, with five more as substitute, and scored 19 goals. But that tells you nothing. Alan was something of an enigma, he loved the big occasion, but you felt that he should have done better considering the talent he possessed. At Everton, he had gone on a scoring spree in the late part of the 1969-70 season that had clinched the championship for the Toffees. But two seasons of frustration followed before he moved to Palace. We wondered if he was a flash in the pan.

When I first heard we'd signed him, my reaction was: "Why have we bought that horrible little so and so?" A few weeks beforehand, playing for Everton, Whittle got Mel Blyth sent off and we were in no mood to forgive and forget. But he soon won us over.

John Craven had looked set to become the regular number nine for the Glaziers but it was Whittle who captured the imagination with a memorable debut against Manchester United, setting up a beauty for Don Rogers, before scoring the fourth himself with an extravagant chip into the top of the net. But he also missed a couple of chances which were easier, and that was what dogged him throughout his Palace career. Between December 1972 and March 1973, Alan scored quite regularly for us but he needed a big front man alongside him and didn't get one. Instead he got Don Rogers and Derek Possee – neither really members of the heavy mob.

Whittle suffered with everybody else during 1973-74 as Palace slumped into division three in a team bamboozled by Big Mal's tactics. But the blond striker eventually found his feet the next season contributing to some super football as Palace tried to attack their way out of division three.

However, he still didn't get enough goals although two in the last match of the season, a 4-0 victory over Gillingham, saw him chaired off the pitch by excited young fans. One of the goals was an exaggerated placed shot into the far corner of the net. Typical Whittle. Never do the easy thing, always play the showman.

At the start of the following season, the more predictable David Kemp kept Alan out of the team. Kemp offered guaranteed goals, and his combination with Dave Swindlehurst up to Christmas was a revelation. But when Kemp's form deserted him, and he got injured, Whittle returned and scored against Colchester as a prelude to one of Palace's greatest days; Leeds United 0 Palace 1. Whittle was back and playing really well, but still wasn't scoring.

The next round was away to Chelsea and Peter Taylor's brace and Nick Chatterton saw Palace through 3-2. Still there were no further Whittle goals ... until Roker.

The trains were late arriving. What a long way it was from Seaburn station at 2.50pm. Then, we went into the wrong stand and couldn't find our seats. Eventually we managed to sort ourselves out and watched Palace performing with their backs to the wall.

Then with approximately 15 minutes to go it happened ... I can still picture the goal as if it was yesterday. Ask me about any of Tommy Langley's goals and I wouldn't have a clue, but Alan Whittle's at Sunderland leaves me with Palace, Palace, Palace on my mind.

We fluffed our promotion chance and froze at Stamford Bridge in the semi final and Alan was on his way shortly after Big Mal left.

I loved Alan Whittle, I called my first car the Whittlemobile! But in the cold light of day, you have to question his goals return against his undoubted potential. His habit of being over elaborate could frustrate both team-mates and fans.

He had an aggravating charisma that left you feeling that he was yet another great player who didn't quite make it. "We want Whittle," the crowd would chant as he sat on the sub's bench while we were struggling goalless against Halifax or whoever. He could brighten up any match, but often without end result.

Alan Whittle will always be remembered by Palace fans with affection which is more than can be said for some others who were, perhaps, better players. I will always think of him as the man who fired us into our first semi-final and gave a very happy 20 year-old a delirious trip home on the train.

How good was he? I'm afraid we'll never know.

Hy Money

Alan Whittle receives a smacker at the Glaziers Club player of the year do

Colorsport

MR PALACE

Jim Cannon made a record 653 appearances for Crystal Palace. In conversation with Jonathan Scarlett and Laurie Dahl, he looks back and offers an insight into the life of a professional footballer.

As a young Glaswegian in the 60s Jim Cannon only had eyes for Celtic. Yet, although he idolised Tommy Gemmell and Billy McNeill, it was not the Celts but a rather unglamorous outfit from south London who won his signature.

"When I first signed for Palace in 1970, one of my mates said to me:

'I didn't know they played football down there!'

'Oh yeah,' I said. 'They've got a couple of leagues.'

'Well what's Crystal Palace?'

Cannon wasn't too sure himself. "I knew nothing of them, although I had seen them on the television. They'd just got promoted and I remember the kit was claret and thin blue stripes."

By the time he was catapulted into the big time by Malcolm Allison, Palace were not only wearing a different kit but were on their way down the league. Jim made an eventful debut in a televised encounter with Chelsea, earning a booking and then scoring the goal that sealed Palace's first ever top flight win over London opposition. An exciting start, but he soon lost his place as Allison tried five different players in the number six shirt in the last five games.

"Before that I think I was sub at West Brom but I didn't come on," he explains, his Glasgow accent still difficult to make out despite so many years in London. "My first away game was at Sheffield United and we played quite well even though we lost, I think Tony Currie scored. It was a nice stadium and there was a big crowd. It was very different from playing at home because everything was against you. It was all new and enjoyable though, the overnight stay, everything."

The big time didn't last long. Palace's win over Chelsea was their swan song and, despite Mal's promises, they were relegated.

One might have thought this would have a damaging psychological effect, but Jim didn't feel any real pressure. "I didn't know any different. I'd only had two or three games in the first and the rest was a struggle. It might have been different if I'd been playing for five years and doing well. I suppose at the time I just thought that's the way it is."

Cannon developed in the lower divisions and worked his way up to become captain. How did he perceive his role changing? "When you're young you're trying to make your way in the game. But you get to a stage where you think I wouldn't mind being skipper.

"I think everybody knows their own temperament and I felt it was a job I would eventually do because I was always a bit loud and arrogant and what have you. When Ian Evans was injured against Fulham I had an inkling and Terry Venables just came up.

"Being skipper of a football club is different from being a captain in other sports. You're not above the players. In cricket a captain is a lot bigger than the players and picks the team, in football that's not so. Apart from the name and what you do on the park there's not a great deal to it. I always tried to work hard, even if I wasn't playing well, and encourage the others. But some skippers don't say a word. Look at Bobby Moore, he was such a quiet lad that he probably never opened his mouth on the pitch. But you only had to watch him play. Others scream and shout and moan all the time."

Football is not just about Saturday afternoons, though. Throughout the season the players work to make sure that the 90 minutes goes just right. "With Malcolm and Terry on a Monday we used to go to the Crystal Palace Sports Centre and do a 25 minute warm up and then sprints. Everything was against the clock. There would be about half a dozen 100 yard sprints flat out. Although we had a little breather, players were always sick with the effort. Then we'd go into the indoor five-a-side court. Monday was always hard. Other managers did different things – under Steve Coppell we did a lot of cross country – but no-one made us work as hard as Terry and that was just for the one day. On Tuesday we'd do ball work, pressurised stuff, maybe eight against eight or seven against eight."

Did the players hold back in case of injury? "No. If you don't do it to him, he'll do it to you, so you wouldn't pull out of anything although on Fridays it would be easier. Tuesday was different because you had four days to recover."

Wednesday was normally a day off while Thursday was reserved for tactical training. "It would be on the ground, ball work, thinking about how you're playing, shape and formations, a lot of shadow play with no opposition, seeing how smoothly you could get the ball from the back up to the front and a little bit of movement.

"We used to do crossing and shooting sessions on Thursdays, while Fridays would be free-kicks for about an hour and corners. That was one of Terry's fortes, Malcolm as well. Players used to stay out to do free-kicks. We also worked on throw-ins. Venners used to give us a little book with all the diagrams and drawings for both sides of the park, right from the back up to the front on free-kicks and corners and used to test us on it. He'd get us in a group and say: 'Right, what's number one for the throw in on the left hand side defending?' It was like being at school, and I used to think I hope he doesn't ask me because I can't remember any of them.

"We always finished Fridays with five-a-side and it was much the same for weeks with away games, except on Friday at about two o'clock we'd travel up by coach to the hotel. There was a lot of ball work in those days, more than I can remember in the last four or five years I played."

Cannon's matchday routine tended to follow a set pattern. "At home games, some managers made us come in about 12 o'clock. We'd meet at the Holiday Inn in Croydon, have a pre-match meal, watch telly then wander back to the ground. We'd start getting changed about two o'clock although some lads changed at half-one and would be sitting about. Others would watch the telly for a bit of racing.

"I used to take my time and get ready about half past two and then go and warm up in one of the gyms we used for knocking the ball about. Sometimes I'd go on the pitch, sometimes I didn't. Some managers would make you go out and warm up, others didn't bother. It's really mental preparation. You just concentrate on the job and whoever you're marking. I used to lock myself away for five minutes and tell myself over and over 'Today I'm gonna win every header, today I'm gonna win every tackle.' You just get your mind clear on what is at hand."

Jim wasn't superstitious but others had strange routines to help them through. "George Wood used to touch every door in the building. Other players used to sip whisky. Tony Burns did and Vince Hilaire used to have a little dram, because his stomach used to go. I think sometimes he had too much!

"You get to a certain stage where you think I wouldn't mind being skipper. I think everybody knows their own temperament and I felt it was a job I would eventually do."

JIM CANNON ON CAPTAINCY

"Some had rituals with their gear, shorts would be the last thing to go on, or socks. I never really took any notice. Some used to make themselves sick before a game. John Burridge used to go to the toilet about 900 times and would go red trying to squeeze out the last drop of whatever was in there. He was terrible. They did their own little thing. It's hard to explain why. There's a lot of tension. But when you're concentrating on yourself you tend not to take any notice of the others. You just get on with what you've gotta do. I suppose, as the years went on, I got more relaxed and felt I didn't need to prepare as much. But as a youngster you're very aware of who you're playing against. Later on I wouldn't know half of them. But the first four or five years, you're aware of your opponent and what you had to do.

"I always got butterflies ten minutes before we went out and the hairs on the back of my neck would stand up as I went onto the pitch. It never went. When we'd been doing well and there were big crowds there – and in the third division with Malcolm we were getting bigger crowds than many in the first division or even today in the Premier League – it was a great feeling. It made you feel ten feet tall."

As with any profession there are always people whose approach to life lightens the load. "Tony Burns and John Burridge, famous for his warm up routines and exaggerated muscle development exercises, were hilarious. We had a good two or three years with

Pictured opposite: Jim lays into Mel Eves and Kenny Hibbitt of Wolves after an incident in which the Eagles' loan keeper Terry Gennoe was flattened. The Palace captain always found Wolves to be difficult opponents and considered Molineux to be something of a jinx ground

Hy Money

Jim Cannon has just scored a brilliant goal to put Palace 4-1 up against Ipswich. Kenny Sansom offers his congratulations. It took us to the top of the first division.

Tony. He was a very dry lad especially when he'd had a drink and everybody knows what John Burridge was like – a complete nutter. Kenny Sansom was always mimicking and Ian Evans was a good story teller. Peter Taylor was the 'Steve Harrison' of his day.

"Peter's favourite trick was to walk into a packed hotel – and they were very grand then, not Trust House Forte jobs – storm into the restaurant, trip himself up and go flying all over the place.

"We'd run to pick him up and he'd be saying 'It's alright lads, I'm okay.' He liked to have the biggest pudding ever, piled high and he'd suddenly fall face first into it and come up screaming 'who done that' and everybody would be looking. He was carried in on a stretcher and once went in wearing an old guy's mask in a wheelchair. Some people fell for it, but we never did."

One of the more eccentric moments of the Allison era involved porn queen Fiona Richmond. Was Jim involved?

"I certainly was. I can tell you something but I'm not going to name names because some of my mates' wives might be reading this. There was a picture of Derek Jeffries, myself, Fiona Richmond, and Phil Holder in the bath and that's all you could see. But I promise you there were four other people underneath the water all holding their breath because they didn't want the cameras to see them.

"She just turned up. We were training at Langley Park and Malcolm arrived in his big fur coat and fedora with this girl. We didn't know who it was but somebody said it was Fiona Richmond and a few who read *Men Only* knew her. Malcolm hadn't even taken the training session – Frank Lord was doing the coaching – and he just said he wanted a photograph at the end. We were playing five-a-side and it was really muddy and she went in goal. Paul Hammond was the keeper and I remember him diving on top of her and pulling her top off. She had her boobs hanging out, she was so brazen about it, it didn't make any difference.

"In the end he was rubbing mud all over her and the cameras were taking pictures and then she got in a group with the whole team and that was it ... so we thought.

"We went back to the ground and got into the bath – in the old dressing rooms at the time – and we were sitting there with the coaches changing up in the referees room. All of a sudden she walked in with this guy. She was only wearing a white robe which she took off and jumped in and I thought ... well, I ain't getting out!

"We didn't hear any more until ... I was sitting in bed on a Sunday morning and the missus used to get up and make a cup of tea – we didn't have any kids at the time – and she came back with the papers. And I'm sitting there reading the *People* and all of a sudden I felt the biggest slap across the face ... and there it was, front page of the *News of the World*. I think my reply was: 'Well it's the only time I can get my picture in the paper. I can't get in by scoring goals.' And that was it. It was a very innocent thing but a few of the wives didn't like it. Some of them were saying 'my husband doesn't get involved in that sort of thing'. But it was very innocent."

Nevertheless the interest of the more sleazy tabloids was stirred and Jim recalls: "All of a sudden there were reporters there after games, not nice reporters but the garbage from the *News of the World*. Football reporters are a different breed. They're not into all that – they're just there to report on the football and find out what's going on. But these guys were not nice. You could see them a mile away. They'd show up in their white coats with the collars turned up and it got a bit silly for a few months. The F.A. was saying this ain't right and all from a completely innocent thing. But Malcolm could get away with anything.

Was it exciting because of Malcolm? "Even in the third division, if you'd asked any player of any club to come to Palace I think he would have come. The money differential wasn't as big as it is now and so the difference between a third division club and a first was closer. Palace I think, having come down from the first, were still paying relatively good wages so players would have come just for Malcolm. He put us on the map. Unfortunately, he got us relegated two years on the trot and any other manager would have been sacked but, being Malcolm, there was an aura about him."He was a good coach but I think he went too far. He really needed an international squad, then I think he would have been great. He used to say to us, right, this is the way West Germany play and Frank Lord would say 'these players aren't German. This is Jim Cannon not Gunter Netzer. He can't do what Netzer does', which was true.

"Frank Lord knew we weren't Holland or Barcelona or Ajax, we were Crystal Palace. The sad thing about Malcolm was that he didn't work with the England team. I think he would have been ideal for that – the F.A. wouldn't have handled him of course and he would never have got the job in a million years, he had more chance of going to the moon – but that sort of job was right for him. I can only speak highly of him because he looked after me and we got on well together. He played me at left back and that's how I got in the team, until Kenny Sansom came along.

"And we were in the papers every day. One day we turned up thinking we were just doing another training session and there were all these Rolls Royces in the car park – we used to change at the ground and go on to wherever we were training – and we went out and the comedian Jimmy Tarbuck was there shouting 'come on lads' and there were all these other celebrities we'd never seen before. There was a coach laid on for us after the session and we were taken to the 21 Club next door to the Hilton. We came out of there at seven or eight o'clock at night all pissed out of our brains and that was the sort of thing Malcolm would do. He'd say we'll go for a recording session next week. He was brilliant."

Allison's attention to detail touched every part of the club. Even the kits received an overhaul. "One I remember was orange with a blue stripe and white shorts. It put an extra stone on you, it was horrible. Malcolm had all the strips redesigned. I don't think anyone had bothered before, but it's important that players feel right. Shorts need to fit and we kept changing them until we got the ones we were happy with. Players like to wear nice kits. I used to like the blue and red striped one. Our best kits were the away strips, we had a nice yellow one with black shorts and an all blue one."

After relegation in 1973, Malcolm was at his bubbly best. "The champagne that was drunk that night, I could see some fellers wondering, but Malcolm was saying don't worry, we'll come back."

Although the roller coaster continued for a couple more seasons, it wasn't until Terry Venables arrived that Palace began to recover. By the end of Venables' first season in charge, our promotion hopes were in the balance. "We were something like seven points adrift but we had to play games in hand including promotion rivals Wrexham twice. They walked all over us at home but we beat them 2-1. Then we went up there knowing we had to win by two clear goals and hope they couldn't find a win on the Saturday. We were two-up and cruising, nice and relaxed and everyone was playing well. Then out of nothing they got a couple of goals and it looked all over." But Wrexham collapsed in an amazing last 90 seconds. "I'll always remember their centre half, I don't know his name, but he was never a ball player in his life and twice he tried to run with it from the back and twice in the last 90 seconds we'd taken it off him and scored. It was unbelievable. It was as if we'd won the championship, that's how we treated it. I vividly remember the stick their players and the manager were giving this centre-half. It was something he would never do in a

"She walked in with this guy. She was only wearing a white robe which she took off and jumped in and I thought ... well, I ain't gettin' out."

JIM CANNON ON THE INFAMOUS FIONA RICHMOND INCIDENT

Hy Money

Paul Hammond provides Fiona Richmond with some handy hints on the rudiments of goalkeeping. This is one of the more demure photographs. A bit of innocent fun that got out of hand said Jim Cannon.

million years – 2-2 and he should have been kicking it anywhere. He threw us a lifeline. That's the lovely game of football."

After that Palace's rise continued and Jim returned to the top flight for the first time since he was a teenager. It meant more glamourous and tougher opponents. Who did Jim have most trouble with and where did he like to play? "I hated Wolves. I always had a nightmare there and might as well have said to the manager don't play me today. There were always players I hated playing and Wolves' Andy Gray was the worst – he was a nutter in those days – I could never play him.

"Little guys were a pain in the neck to play against as well. There were places which you'd think you wouldn't like but they'd be fine. Barnsley was hard but it was a nice place to go. They always looked after you and the pitch was good. But sometimes we'd go to real holes. Hartlepool was a dump, we lost 2-1 there in the Cup."

And in order to get that extra edge there were often attempts to wind the opposition up and very personal things were said. "Its part and parcel of the game. I remember one young striker saying to me: 'How the f*** have you played 500 games, you're s***!' It got to me sometimes, others used to laugh it off. Other times it was quite good and you'd have a nice chat while the game was up the other end. You'd be talking about where you were going that night or see you in the bar after for a beer."

So how far does a professional take the need to win? "Most times you'd make a genuine attempt for the ball. Even if you weren't going to get it because you'd been beaten. You'd still try because the guy might slow up or lose control. Its changed a bit now because if you're the last man and you pull a guy down you're off and that's not a bad rule.

"I've gone for the ball many times and know I've conceded a penalty immediately. You can't do anything about it. I didn't give a lot of penalties away though and I didn't give many handballs. I was very disciplined in the box.

"You see some guys and they handball it or bring players down who are moving away from the ball and it's a needless penalty. I hate idiots who stick their hand out. You shouldn't be playing if you do things like that."

The pressures of the game are not confined to the pitch either. Managers, trainers and even substitutes react to the tension in different ways. "Dave Ewing, the trainer under Bert Head, was very loud and forever being told to shut up. Some people are quiet and prefer to sort it out at half time. I can't remember Malcolm being on the bench. As a manager at Dulwich I've tried it myself and I've got to be down on the bench bellowing.

"At half time the activity in the dressing room can be frenetic. It's either 'well done lads you're having a good game' or 'you're a bunch of f*****g w*****s'. It's very black and white. If you're having a bad time they'd gee you up, but so much goes on in the ten minutes that you tend to forget it. They tried to cram a lot into you. I remember thinking when I became a manager I'd never go on too much and would try to sort it out quickly. But it goes that quick, you would have to digest everything that was said very quickly."

What about Burnley in 1979? "At half time, as I remember, it was very relaxed, as it was the whole week leading up to the match. I'm sure there must have been a lot of tension at the time. We could have been three up but it was still 0-0 and at the back of our minds there was a niggle that if they scored on the break we'd have to battle. At half time it was a case of 'don't go daft and don't do anything stupid'. Terry didn't put any pressure on us. I think we had a couple of days off and just enjoyed ourselves. We didn't need to train because it was the last game of the season.'

Jim lifted the championship for Palace and within a few months led the club to the top of the first division. And it was a thunderous Cannon effort, one of 34 goals he scored in his career, that lifted the Eagles to the top.

Which leaves one regret. "I wish the TV cameras had seen that goal against Ipswich because it was the best scored at Selhurst Park in the last 50 years. A brilliant move from start to finish."

Hy Money

Paul Wright/NUDA

Jim Cannon, then and now: (fourth left of the back row) in the Youth Team of 1971-72 and (right) as manager of Dulwich Hamlet FC in 1992

MALCOLM

The best thing about Malcolm Allison's reign at Selhurst was that he gave our club what it needed; an image. And if you want an image – good or bad – there's no better place to get one than from someone like Malcolm.

The episodes of prat-like behaviour that littered Big Mal's reign can be easily enumerated. His treatment of John Jackson (which I often go on about at length) was prattishness of the worst kind. His bathing session with Fiona Richmond was prattishness of the highly intelligent kind. His changing of our name from Glaziers to Eagles was pratttishness of the ignorant variety. Widening the pitch to give our speedy wingers room to work, then narrowing it back after we'd lost four on the trot was prattishness of the optimistic variety. Making us wear stupid shirts with crests on the sleeves was simply prattishness of the prat-like variety. No doubt about it; Big Mal was a prat.

But the mark Big Mal left at Selhurst Park was bloody huge. It says it all about the complexities of the man that he took over a side in the first division and left them in the third in a lot better shape than on the day he was hired.

For possibly the only extended period in the past 25 years, Palace under Mal were truly a football team. And this, of course, is why they never went anywhere.

Under Mal, Palace just played. Everyone eulogised his tactical acumen but he had nothing of the sort. What Mal understood was that if you had fun doing it, chances are you'd do your job at a higher level than your capabilities, organised or not.

Mal's mediocre team had fun, played to a high level and entertained us in the process. They never actually went anywhere but then that wouldn't have been Mal ... it needed a marriage of Venables' organisation and the higher quality young players Mal had signed to take us to the next level.

The Cup run was proof of this. We read endless pages in the papers about Allison the awesome tactician whose sweeper system had thwarted Leeds. Rubbish. We beat Leeds because Mal convinced the players they couldn't lose. That was his gift. Sure, the sweeper idea was a good one, but it was the players' self confidence, not the idea in itself, that made it work.

Mal believed in his players and they, in turn, believed in themselves. He could, as the saying goes, have sold ice cream in Alaska.

Mal's teams continually reflected the truth of this assertion in other ways, too. They scored a lot of goals and almost always entertained. They also lost matches they shouldn't have lost and they rarely handled pressure well, crumbling in March and April each year.

Teams who have fun rarely know how to react when the pressure heats up and March and April are no time for fun if you're in a race at either end of the table.

But in August and September every year, with the sun on our backs, grass on the pitch and the world to play for, Mal's lads were absolutely unbeatable. That's why, even with Palace in the third division the TV cameras were at Selhurst Park almost every month.

The style is also why Mal was so successful at Manchester City. What Mal brought to Maine Road was prattishness, allied to organisation from Joe Mercer. It was a combination that worked. Mal was the ultimate assistant manager if the right man was in charge.

If it could've happened, Mal would have made the perfect assistant for Terry Venables, not the other way round. With that combo, Palace might really have been the Team of the 80s.

After relegation in 1973, they also went straight through division two without missing a beat. After relegation and with a rapidly changing team we needed consolidation and rebuilding.

But men like Mal don't waste time consolidating because they don't know how. They go for it all today. That's why Mal was always making promises he couldn't keep. It was the only thing he knew. Whether or not he had a team capable of achieving his goals was secondary to the fact.

Mal's days, if it's not obvious by now, were the antithesis of Palace under Steve Coppell.

Where Stevie talked through pursed lips, Mal babbled away to anyone who'd listen. Where Stevie's teams probe for a break Mal's teams just went for the jugular and bugger it if they missed. If commitment epitomises Stevie's teams, the word for Mal's teams was explosive.

I don't know if I'd want to trade in what we've got now for a place in the third division and a side that plays Allison-style football. Human nature is to be greedy and you can't play Liverpool with style if you're not in the same division as Liverpool in the first place. However, I do know this. If someone could have held Stevie down and injected him with a dose of Mal-ishness we'd have enjoyed instead of endured our Saturday afternoons once again.

There's nothing sadder than seeing a manager go through 42 matches and not once having a smile on his face. And you can be sure that if the boss isn't enjoying it the players aren't either.

Big Mal proved that a prat is not necessarily a bad thing and once a week it can even come in handy. If only he'd treated John Jackson better ...

Nobody provokes such contrasting opinion as Malcolm Allison. But he, more than anybody, is responsible for what Crystal Palace Football Club is today. Keith Brody ponders whether Big Mal was a football genius or just a prat in a hat

Hy Money

Bert Head out, Big Head in

Nick Booth casts a jaundiced eye over his support for Palace and compares the different styles and characters of the two men who managed us in our first spell at the top

Hy Money

Two classic photos by Hy Money. Left: Malcolm Allison – film star looks and expensive tastes. Above: Chairman Raymond Bloye (left) and Bert Head welcome Big Mal to Selhurst Park in 1973

Unfashionable as Palace are now, they are regular Kate Mosses compared to the pioneers who brought first division football to Selhurst Park in 1969. Bert Head (or Bert Head out, as he became known when push came to shove) was the man behind this enormous feat. Malcolm Allison took us in the opposite direction, two seasons in a row, and yet I know who I'd sooner see back at Palace.

Considering the players he had at his disposal (and let's face it, disposal was the best thing for most of them) Head's achievement was miraculous. Although I was only nine years old and in only my second season, I knew it wasn't just our ludicrous kit and open air terracing that needed fixing (covering the Holmesdale was a moot point even in 1970). Why did John "Shovel" Sewell execute that curious sideways back-peddle every time a winger (wingers – remember them?) threatened to take him on? Even milk turned quicker than Sewell. He was forced to start swivelling at least five minutes before his opponent made his move. Invariably Shovel would guess wrong and John Jackson would have to bail us out again. Jackson played once for the Football League, although he'd have been an automatic choice for England if he'd played for one of the big clubs who dictate the running (down) of English football. Jackson wouldn't have lost the World Cup for England the way Peter Bonetti did. And that one handed save by Gordon Banks from Pele … ha! Jackson would have cut out the cross in the first place. I'd have loved to have seen Sewell facing Jairzinho though.

Despite his international credentials, Jackson spent almost his entire career with Palace. Can you imagine that today? Nowadays, as soon as a player gets picked for his country, he's off on a lucrative subs' bench warming contract with Liverpool or Arsenal before you can say "Mel Stein". Will Eddie McGoldrick get picked for Arsenal? Only if he puts on two stone and grows a foot taller. What a waste of talent.

Talking of which, remember our one other real talent? Steve Kember, the local boy made good. He played for England Under-23s, was bought by Chelsea and ended up achieving nothing much with Leicester. I think he was overshadowed by Alan Hudson, you obviously didn't drink enough, Steve.

Like Jackson and Kember, Phil Hoadley was a product of our youth policy and a useful player too. Which probably explains why Bert replaced him with Peter Wall, a free transfer from Liverpool.

At Palace, Head was not a great believer in youth, presumably because no-one could tempt an ambitious England schoolboy to Palace without placing a large wedge on the table. As numerous *Sunday People* exposes told us, this was not only what all the big clubs were up to, but it was highly illegal. Bert Head, damn him, was far too principled to break the rules. Funnily enough, Malcolm Allison would persuade schoolboy internationals like Ian Walsh, Kenny Sansom and Vince Hilaire to join a club that was plummeting towards the third division. I wonder how he managed that?

Since Head couldn't or wouldn't dip into the reserve team (makes you wonder why we bothered having one) he was forced into the transfer market. When speculating, managers tend to fall into two categories; those who can afford to play safe by forking out millions to strengthen their squads (stand up Kenny Dalglish and Graham Souness) and those who have a knack of spotting potential internationals in the lower leagues such as Bobby Gould

> **"We won't just get promotion, we'll win the second division championship."**
>
> BIG MAL AFTER PALACE HAD LOST 4-1 TO NOTTS COUNTY

and Dave Bassett. Bert fell into neither category, reaching an unhappy compromise. Like Souness and Dalglish he went for experienced players from the first division, but unlike them he couldn't or wouldn't spend money. The upshot was that nine times out of ten, as the *Croydon Advertiser* announced our latest signing, it turned out to be some grizzled old Scotsman with a wealth of first division experience – the Scottish first division, which is not the same thing at all. Remember John McCormick, Tony Taylor, Willie Wallace, John Hughes and Roger Hynd? Scotland was not our only source of "new" talent. Per Bartram and Borge Thorup were Danish internationals – the Danes have come a long way since then.

The one player Head signed who really quickened the pulse was Don Rogers. Head described Rogers as "poetry in motion". Managers were just learning to be quotable then and Brian Clough's media career was in its infancy. For once Bert had actually splashed out on a player who not only had class but his own hair and teeth.

On his debut against Everton, Rogers actually outpaced an opposition defender before scoring. Great as he was, even he could do nothing about Palace's disastrous record in first division London derbies.

Brian Moore (whose head looks uncannily like London Planetarium) loved it. Whenever Palace were on the *Big Match* losing to Arsenal or Chelsea, Moore would engage in the sort of hysterics that makes Capital Gold's Jonathan Pearce seem placid. When Palace scored Moore treated it with polite enthusiasm, but when an Arsenal player got near goal ... Armstrong! Brilliant cross! To Radford! Is he going to try one? Yes! A goal! ...

Hulton Deutsch

Crystal Palace FC in August 1973 with their new manager Malcolm Allison to the fore. Big Mal moulded the club in his own image. Note the new red and blue striped kit with badges in the middle and numbers on the sleeves.

and that was just the warm up.

Whenever we lost a London derby, which was at least eight times a season, all the local creeps would come out of the woodwork. The "I-support-whoever's-just-won-the-league-crowd" loved to crow when they'd beaten us. I always wonder about these types; what sort of satisfaction do they get from their temporary heroes if they win? If you live in Croydon and Palace win it's great because it's your team.

But how can Man United or Arsenal mean anything to you? I have a theory that if we'd lost the Battle of Britain 50 years ago and the Nazis were marching down Whitehall, they'd be the people saying "Hitler's not such a bad bloke you know. He can't be because he's a Bayern Munich fan like me!"

Not that fascism's been eliminated from football. Palace still have a few. It must have pissed them off when Wright and Bright were at their best. If they don't like the fact that Martyn, Young, Thorn and Armstrong can all play for the same team they should f*** off. Its not as if this cretinism makes any sense. They drone on about patriotism and then adopt the philosophy of some deranged dictator who tried to crush Britain. They are sad, ugly creatures and yet they purport to be examples of white supremacy. Some master race they'd make.

About 20 years ago, one of these brain donors painted some graffiti on a wall in Holmesdale Road, no more than a brick's throw from the NF's Pawsons Road headquarters and centre for literitchur ... well, written stuff. The message, still visible today, said: "Cones out". Pathetic, laughable even, but he (let's assume it was a "he" rather than an "it") also painted the word "Palace" elsewhere on the wall, which isn't so amusing.

I digress. It was Ray Bloye who saw our first manager of the 70s off. Yes, Bert finally headed out. If the *Croydon Advertiser* had a sense of humour they could have put "Bert Heads Out", needless to say they didn't.

Bloye was one of a new breed of chairman; young, ambitious, thrusting ("young" seemed to apply to any chairman not confined to a bath chair). Compared to Arthur Wait, he was indeed young and pushy, then again so was the Queen Mother. We have Bloye to thank for bringing Big Mal to Palace, for which we should be eternally grateful. Later, according to Ron Noades, we had Bloye to thank for the huge debts Palace had amassed but, hell, nobody's perfect.

Within 24-hours, our man Allison had managed to end the jinx London teams had over us and injected some youthful exuberance into the side. Eighteen year old Scotland youth international Jim Cannon scored on his debut as Palace routed, yes routed, Chelsea. After this morale boosting win it was unthinkable that we should go down. But we did.

Allison inspires enormous loyalty among Palace fans, which is odd considering he took us down two divisions, whereas Terry Venables, who took us in the opposite direction doesn't seem to.

Another contradiction is that Palace had far bigger crowds when they were passing through the second division *en route* to the third than they do now. In 1975-76 the crowd for a third division home match with Chesterfield was 27,892. We wouldn't get that now if we were to play Man United (not that we're going to anyway). Why were so many fools like me prepared to watch Palace home and away yet only make the occasional visit now? Has it got something to do with the price of admission? In 1979, it cost £1 to stand and £1.70 for a seat in the New Stand. In other words prices have increased by more than 900%.

It can't be down to the team. We've just had our most successful period ever (apart from last season, of course). We actually won a cup, at Wembley, and still we didn't get the same home gates against Arsenal that Port Vale used to attract (though that probably tells you more about Arsenal than anything). God knows what our gates will be next season.

I think it was because Allison knew more about marketing than a whole smarm (that's the collective noun for chairmen) of Ron Noadeses.

Who was more effective in attracting the fans to Selhurst? Remember the Palace Dollies? Remember Bring a Pal to Palace? Both pathetic attempts by the chairmen and marketing people (who assured us that they really new how to run a business) to lure back the lost fans.

When Malcolm hopped in a bath with Fiona Richmond, the resultant publicity probably had far more impact on the fans. It was Allison's youth policy that laid the foundations on which Venables and George Graham would build a great team (two of our senior players turned managers, whatever happened to them?)

On reaching the first division the papers would proclaim them "Team of the 80s" and when the chips were down the very people who coined the phrase would sneeringly describe them as "the so-called Team of the 80s".

Crystal Palace? Well, someone's got to support them. I'm afraid it's us.

Big Mal and the curse of Romark

IN the 1970s a publicity seeking psychic called Romark publicly fell out with Malcolm Allison and placed a curse on him and Crystal Palace.

Before long the club had fallen from the first division to the third and lost an F.A. Cup semi final.

There's plenty of evidence that the curse lingers still – though Romark doesn't, he was killed while attempting to prove his psychic powers by driving a car blindfolded!

Whenever I try to remember it I still get butterflies in my stomach – my first game as a six or seven year old was at Craven Cottage on Good Friday 1974. The weather was cold but bright and clear and I was in my claret and blue scarf and bobble hat that my gran had knitted me. We had chicken and chips in a pub lunch and I drank coca cola out of a pint glass to be like my dad.

Even before we reached the ground I was physically sick with the excitement.

The crowd was enormous and he bought me a programme and lifted me over the turnstiles after arguing with the man on the gate who wanted him to pay for me.

I was dragged through a forest of knees and Dad then hauled me up so I could see the floodlights which excited me even more. I watched the match perched on a crush barrier with my dad's hand on me to steady me so I did not fall.

Two things stay with me, the deafening noise when we scored, which I thought would carry me away and then the ball being kicked into the river – if I remember rightly a bloke in a coracle paddled after it does anyone remember the coracle and could it be seen from the away end?

My day was not complete, Palace won and I refused to take off my hat gloves and scarf and slept a happy child that night.

Alan Dunlop

THE BLOKE IN THE NUMBER 11 SHIRT

Hy Money

The 1975-76 season was a memorable one for Crystal Palace as they strode majestically to the top of the third division. They won six of their first seven games before losing 1-0 at home to Brighton in front of a bumper 25,600 crowd. After that they continued until a second defeat at Millwall in December. This signalled a mini-disaster for Malcolm Allison's Eagles as they lost four on the trot.

Progress however was made in the F.A. Cup and remarkably, not only because they were in the third division but because after a 1-0 home victory over Walton and Hersham they were drawn away from home in all the subsequent rounds, Palace's exploits brought crowds flocking in. Attendances in excess of 20,000 were recorded at no less than ten home league games including a 38,000 lock out against Millwall.

After relegation in 1973, we kept right on sliding. At such times you need something to live for, somebody to believe in. That somebody was Peter Taylor. By Norman Grimes

In the Cup they played in front of more than 50,000 on three occasions. But Palace lost to Southampton in the semi final and also to Millwall in the battle for promotion, Nevertheless these were heady days and the dynamic duo of Malcolm Allison and Terry Venables filled the air with cigar smoke and champagne corks. The crowd wore fedoras and warmed to the stars in red and blue; Ian Evans, Jim Cannon, Alan Whittle and of course the bloke in the number 11 shirt.

Eyebrows were raised when Allison

paid out £100,000 for an unknown Southend winger in October 1973, but over the next two seasons it became clear that, in Peter Taylor, he had unearthed a real gem. Taylor became the catalyst for Crystal Palace's transformation, creating and scoring goals while bringing out the best in the players around him. His skill in turning defenders and sending in pin point crosses was a joy to watch and he was a superb showman.

An example of this came during one match in which he was giving the visiting right back a real roasting. The defender resorted to the only method left in his repertoire for preventing Taylor getting away from him. Following one such tussle Peter still escaped the defender's clutches and set off down the line. Having completed the move he ran over to the defender and, to rapturous applause, took off his shirt and handed it to the defender.

Such incidents, combined with his great skill, gave Taylor a special place in the hearts of the Palace fans. His fine individual performances played a significant part in the cup wins at Leeds, Chelsea and Sunderland for which he will be best remembered. He was involved in the winning goals in each of these matches, including scoring one of them. The cup run brought him national acclaim and the attention of the national manager. He had in fact already been approached by international selectors earlier in his time at Palace. Due to parental qualification, he attracted the interest of the Dutch and might well have finished playing in the 1974 World Cup finals for Holland. Allison however persuaded him to wait for England recognition which arrived with two Under 23 games against Czechoslovakia and two more against Portugal. He scored in every game, the first at Selhurst Park, making him one of the most successful England players at that level and earned him a place in the full squad.

He made his full England bow in the centenary game against Wales on March 24, 1976 as a substitute for Mick Channon and in so doing became the first and, to date, the last third division player to be picked for England since Johnny Byrne, also of Crystal Palace, in 1961. Taylor netted the winner prompting Kevin Keegan, who captained the side for the first time that night, to describe the Palace man as a positive, skillful asset to the team. Taylor kept his place for the next game, also against Wales, and again scored the winner, this time with a superb 20 yarder. His Wembley debut came in the 4-0 defeat of Northern Ireland and he made his final appearance in the defeat against Scotland at Hampden. By this time he had moved to White Hart Lane in the wake of Palace's eventual failure in both league and cup. He played in all but one of Spurs' matches as they were promoted back to division one at the first attempt. He moved onto Orient after the arrival at White Hart Lane of Osvaldo Ardiles and Ricardo Villa from Argentina and from Brisbane Road joined Maidstone in the Alliance, where he won a championship medal and three England non-league international caps. He is the only full England player ever to do so. He became player manager of Dartford via Exeter City, Chelmsford and Heybridge Swifts.

As a Dartford fan I was at a match in which he played against Slough. One of their supporters came up to me and said: "I don't mind losing today, cos we lost to a better side and do you know what makes you a better side? The bloke in the number 11 shirt."

■ This article is abridged from one that appeared in the first issue of the Dartford fanzine *Light At the End of the Tunnel* at a time when Peter Taylor was player manager at Watling Street.

Norman Grimes

Opposite page: Hy Money's study of Peter Taylor in full flight. Above: Dartford FC parade the Kent Senior Cup. Peter Taylor is at the left of the front row. Jim Cannon is on the extreme left and Paul Hinshelwood in the middle of the back row

LOVE AT FIRST SIGHT

Andy Gilbert's first visit to Selhurst Park was such a traumatic experience that he nearly fell in with the wrong crowd – Chelsea's crowd

My first trip to Selhurst Park was on an autumn day in 1970. I was eight years old and didn't really support a team, although Chelsea and Arsenal were my favourites from TV and radio.

Despite having always lived in South Norwood, I never really thought of Palace as my local team. This was because my dad didn't like football.

All I knew about Palace was that they were always rooted to the bottom of the table and other London sides always thrashed them. Palace fans were a distinct rarity at school. Nevertheless, my dad was taking me to "the match" against the famous Spurs.

That Saturday afternoon, we set out with our next door neighbour Les and his son Kevin to walk the mile or so to Selhurst. The trudge along Tennison Road seemed to last an eternity, but my anticipation was heightened by the thickening stream of bodies heading towards the ground.

I'd never seen so many people. Nor apparently had my dad. He made some excuse about having forgotten something and before I could protest he was gone. It took me years to realise this was pre-planned and I am afraid that I never really forgave him. The mounting terror of a small boy in a big crowd without his dad was heightened by the shattering experience of finding a separate under-16s' entrance. How would we find Les again on the other side?

Even to an eight year old the turnstiles seemed horribly narrow. I could think of all sorts of reasons not to go through, but it was too late to back out. I emerged at the top of the Holmesdale and was swallowed by the millions (well, 45,000). I was on the verge of panic when the reassuring figure of my neighbour appeared.

I don't remember much except that Alan Mullery scored in a 3-0 win for Tottenham. We stood high on the Holmesdale. The players below seemed impossibly far away and I could only catch brief glimpses of them through the crowd. It just didn't seem as real as watching on TV, but even so it was obvious that Palace were outclassed. Strangely, I don't recall any away fans nor much crowd noise, only an eerie silence when a goal was scored and the persistent grumbling of one old Palace fan next to us.

By the time the third goal went in I was cold, tired and miserable and wanted to go home. I was sure that I was not a Palace fan. To my eternal shame, I tied my colours to Chelsea's mast. The great advantage was that nobody was going to take me to the Bridge.

If Palace had even managed one goal then the celebrations might have got me hooked. As it was, I soon lost interest in Chelsea and my football experience was at Croydon amateurs until I discovered teenage rebellion. It took the 1976 Cup run and Malcolm Allison's showmanship to bring me home to Palace and the 1978-79 promotion season to make me a regular. Since then, I've hardly missed a home game and seen the team on 40-odd away grounds. I'm glad I came to my senses in time, it's been far more enjoyable supporting and suffering with Palace than any big five club (or Chelsea). But never believe in love at first sight.

Thrashing about

Why don't Palace thrash anybody? The reality is that Palace have rarely been prolific in front of goal. But the start of the 1974-75 season produced successive games where Palace actually scored 11 goals.

The first five came against Watford in the league cup replay when Alan Whittle scored twice in a supremely one sided exhibition. We went home bemused. After two relegation seasons we actually had cause for optimism.

It was the first time we'd scored five since we whacked Man United.

But the next home game was even better. Swindon had been relegated with us the season before and arrived at Selhurst on a sunny afternoon unprepared for their fate. After 20 minutes of fairly even play we came alive. One minute it was 0-0, 12 minutes later it was 5-0 – all in front of a delirious Holmesdale.

Stuart Jump started it while two each from Whittle and Swindlehurst made the game safe by half-time. Peter Taylor ran John Trollope ragged.

We were the only side in the league to score in every home match that season. It was organised chaos but no less entertaining for that.

Peter Gee

No. 18 May 1974

AllisonWonderland

ALLISON LOOKED ABOUT him as he fell down the well. First Division, Second Division – would it never end? He came down, splash! into a pool of salt water – the tears of thousands of men who appeared to be attendants at a vast palace made of glass at the water's edge. As he emerged from the water he spied a bottle labelled "Drink me!", so he did – and at once shrank to a height of six inches. Facing him was a door marked "Bored Room". He went in.

Inside was a large table at which the March Hare and the Mad Grocer were having a tea-party; a Dormouse was asleep between them. The Grocer wore a top-hat with a ticket in it saying "Shop at Bloye's". The March Hare was saying: "I represent the Supporters' Club."

"He must be even madder than I thought," said the Grocer.

"That's right," said the Dormouse, "club the supporters!. . ."

"We'll support the club through sick and sin," cried the Hare.

"You mean 'thick and thin' " said Allison.

"I know what I mean," said the Hare.

"Come, my dear fellow," interrupted the Grocer, "have one of my best biscuits." Allison took a bite.

"Look," said the March Hare, "his head's even bigger than it was before!" And so it was. Then suddenly a loud voice behind him called: "Off with his head!"

"Who are you?"

"I am the Queen. This is *the palace, isn't it? Off with his head!"*

"He certainly won't miss that," said the Grocer.

"No," said the Queen, "I have a better idea. Shall we dance?"

"Yes," said the Grocer, "Let's line up all the players and have a Transfer Quadrille."

So they danced solemnly round singing:

" 'Will you play a little harder?' said the trainer to his men,

" 'Or we'll put you on the transfer-list at twenty-two pounds ten.'

" 'Will you, won't you, will you, won't you, will you join the Orient? . . .' "

NO Minister

John Fraser has been Norwood's MP since 1966 and a Palace fan for much longer than that. Here he recalls a ministerial treat for a West Ham fan.

I'VE been a Palace fan for 33 years since I moved to Norwood (I became its Member or Parliament in 1966) and now have children and granchildren as supporters, and not just casuals at that.

My proudest memories are of course those of beating Liverpool at Villa Park in the F.A. Cup semi final in 1990 and the occasion on which we just scraped into the old first division via the play-offs.

But I do recall one moment of embarrassment over Palace (only one?)

In 1976, when I was Minister of State in the last Labour government, Palace were due to play Millwall at the end of the season.

I offered to take my government driver to a game (Ministers get a car and a chauffeur, so I decided to ring the changes and drive him to a match). He didn't think it was that much of a favour. "Yes Minister," he said. "That's all very well, but I'm a West Ham supporter. I'd think twice about going even to a second division match." Palace were then in the third.

Anyway I drummed up enough enthusiasm and drove my driver to Selhurst Park. It was a midweek match and we were held up in traffic. Almost 35,000 other people went and we were locked out. The driver thought it infra-dig to go to a third division match, let alone be locked out of one. I offered him the compensation of a drink in my regular matchday pub. But as Millwall were playing we got locked out of the pub, too.

The final insult came when walking back to my car we saw a fellow minister (the MP for Bermondsey) being driven in late for a seat in the directors' box.

The next time I invited my driver to a match it was: "No Minister." Incidentally he missed an exciting 0-0 draw.

Palace: a life

Bob Sinclair looks back at some of the incidents that have stuck in his mind from a lifetime of supporting Crystal Palace

Neil Everitt

Big John

John McCormick's goal against Sheffield United

John was the UK's first real Big Mac. A tall, gangly Scot who was a stalwart in our defence. He was brilliant with his head but when it came to dealing with the ball at his feet the hefty boot up field was his speciality – we definitely had a long ball game in those days.

John used to go forward for the corners but other than that you never saw him put a foot in the opposition's half.

So you can imagine the amazement when he decided to do this Franz Beckenbauer impression and went storming forward. He hit the ball like a bullet straight into the top corner of the net with the keeper nowhere.

I have seen many goals at Selhurst some good, some bad, some lucky, some brilliant and I wouldn't claim this one to be the best or worst but after all these years it still sticks in my mind.

Stamford Bridge

The 1976 Cup Run. When I read or hear anyone talk abut that year it is invariably about the great games, the great wins ... about Leeds, Chelsea and Sunderland.

For me though the lasting memory of that Cup Run is a piece of concrete that forms the terrace at Stamford Bridge, the same piece that I spent ten minutes staring at after we'd lost to Southampton.

Everything had gone right up to that day, the results had gone our way, we'd got the semi-final draw we'd all been hoping for, we could now look forward to stuffing the red filth in the final.

What could go wrong? My first doubts started to creep in when we arrived at the ground only to discover that we hadn't got the Shed End. A bad omen to my mind.

I don't remember much about the game itself except that we didn't play very well. All I can really remember is a numb feeling at the final whistle ... the disbelief that we had fallen at the final hurdle to one of the worst teams we had played.

So near yet so far. My memory of the '76 Cup run is still a piece of concrete in Fulham.

The new nickname

I have many memories of Malcolm Allison, almost all good, and am definitely in the camp of those who thoroughly enjoyed his time.

Who remembers the quirky things he did like widening the pitch a couple of yards during the close season "to give more room for our skillful players to operate in"? He simply forgot or didn't believe that at the time most of our opponents were more skillful than us and he was giving them more room in which to operate.

One of the first things he did was to change our colours and introduce a new nickname. What a brilliant stroke that was. You didn't hear too many calls of *Glaziers, Glaziers* in those days – we went from being a club with a really naff identity to one that stood out from the pack (even if the results didn't).

Unsporting Chelsea

John Craven was a good old fashioned centre forward, stockily built but not the quickest of players. It was at Stamford Bridge against Chelsea, who at that time seemed to be Palace's bete noir, that a pass was pushed through for John to chase. But it was too long and went behind for a goal kick.

Everyone knows there is half a mile of space behind the goals at Chelsea but John, being a good sportsman, ran and got the ball and threw it to Peter Bonetti.

The keeper did not wait for John to get back on the pitch but took a very quick goal kick catching the retreating Palace players out. Chelsea scored and won the game.

To me that sort of incident helped to drive sportsmanship out of football and made the game the lesser for it. Just what you'd expect from Chelsea.

A worrying experience

The precise year escapes me but I seem to recall that it was 1979.

Gary, Peter, Martin and myself set off for the league game at the Gallstone. We went early as we thought we'd have a look around town and find time for a bevy or two.

The pub looked an attractive proposition and a couple turned into several which turned into a lot and, before we realised, it was ten to three.

A mad dash got us there just before

kick-off and as we went in there were chants of *Eagles, Eagles* reverberating around the terraces. We made our way to the top of the terraces joining in at the top of our voices: *Eagles Eagles*.

Then I noticed there was something different about the scarves being held above the heads of the throng in front of us. The difference was that they were blue and white and it dawned on us that what we heard was *Seagulls, Seagulls*.

In our haste and under the affluence of incahol we'd gone in the wrong end. I'm sure I don't need to describe the horror, our scarves went into our pockets very quickly and we got as far to the side of the terracing as we could where we were pleased to see a policeman to whom we explained our predicament.

He spent the rest of the match standing with us. It was the closest shave I've ever had at football and one that taught me a lesson I have never forgotten.

Villa Park: the semi final

I doubt many fans, in their heart of hearts, believed it would happen. My most memorable moment is not Pembo's great run or Supa Al's winner but the second equaliser. That was the moment I knew we were going to win; that, for once, fate was with us. We have never been a "comeback team" and after the cruel blow of the penalty I could see another 1976 looming.

Nigel at Spurs

The game towards the end of 1991-92 did not have anything riding on it but pride.

Spurs had an appalling home record and our away form wasn't half bad, if somewhat erratic, so it was no surprise that Eddie McGoldrick's goal gave us a deserved win. But the highlight was in the second half when Nigel made one of the greatest saves I have ever seen.

People still talk about the save Gordon Banks made from Pele in the 1970 World Cup and I believe this was in the same class.

The ball was crossed in low from the right and Gary Lineker moved onto it right in front of goal, no more than five yards out. The groan was already in my throat; England's top striker could not miss. Lineker hit the ball first time, low along the ground catching it really well.

Nigel's anticipation and reaction were astonishing not only did he get down fast enough to stop the ball he somehow managed to hold onto it not even giving Lineker a whiff of a rebound. A great save by the best keeper in the country.

Diary of an Eagle

One or two Palace inspired memories from Ben Roxby

Chelsea v Palace, F.A. Cup 1976

On observing the "disturbances" my uncle proposes a draconian but effective solution: "Turn the 'ot 'oses on 'em, burn their noses off!" ID Cards? Who needs them?

Palace v Ipswich, September 1979

Overheard in the Arthur Wait from a bloke behind me on observing the rotund Mike Flanagan trundling up the pitch ..."Bleeding hell, he's running with the ball, get yer f*****g paint brushes out."

What did he mean by this? Was Flanagan a decorator in the afternoons? Did he help the world's most famous groundsman Len Chatterton mark the pitch out? Had he helped respray the Flatterer (a VW Beetle with a roller on each wheel?

Nowadays this would be the cue to introduce a weird decorating cult with everyone on the Holmesdale waving brushes, ladders and cans of Dulux when the team comes out, beats inflatables any day. Can anyone explain this phrase to me, its been bothering me for years?

■ Eds' note: We think Flanagan may have worked as a decorator while he was in dispute with Charlton. Pity he didn't keep it up.

Arsenal v Palace, 1980

My uncle and I escape with our lives after we spend the afternoon in their main stand. Uncle spent the entire second half berating Willie Young: "E's an animal but they all love 'im up 'ere!"

Joyce

She goes everywhere to support Palace. "Go on Palace, give us a goal to warm us up." Another is "Come on Palace, attack!"– usually in the face of the Nottingham Forest tide which continually engulfs us. Whatever the situation she never gives up and is always positive. She never gets on anyone's back.

Slightly soiled

I found an envelope with some dust and dried grass in it. This was a piece of hallowed Selhurst turf I took as a souvenir at the end of the Burnley game and have kept all this time. I cannot account for this behaviour other than everyone was doing it. My choice of entrenching tool was a ten pence piece, I think.

Anti-Social Section

Some clubs have Supporters' Clubs or a place where you can go to get a drink and something to eat prior to matches. Palace had a club house at the back of the Old Stand in the 70s but it wasn't called a supporters club or even something imaginative like "The Eyrie".

It was called The Crystal Palace Football Club Social Section. What was the "Social Section"? Was it user friendly? No. Could you take kids in? No. Everyone had to be over 18. So there you go everyone called Palace "the family club" but you couldn't take your kids to the club house unless they were over 18. Could you bring a friend? No. You couldn't even bring him in if you signed your watch over as a guarantee of good behaviour.

But it was a good place to watch the racing before the match.

Hereford Reserves

Remember those epic matches when we celebrated promotion? Fulham, Burnley, Blackburn, Hereford reserves ... Hereford reserves? Duncan Thompson was there.

No need to be despondent. Feeling bad about relegation? Well, of course we are but think how much fun we'll have when we bounce back and we always do (eventually). Who will ever forget the victory over Blackburn; or winning the second division against Burnley in front of 52,000; or the string of successes in the 1960s that culminated in overturning a 2-0 deficit to beat Fulham and reach the first division for the first time. Great days.

Sometimes however, the occasion is not quite what it should be. Who was at Selhurst Park on May 4, 1977 to see Palace reserves beat Hereford reserves 4-0 in the Football Combination? The first team weren't playing except for a handful who turned out for the reserves in what was the final match of our frustrating spell in the third division. Meanwhile champions Mansfield (yes, really they were) beat Wrexham 1-0. It deprived Wrexham of promotion and sent us up instead.

The first teamers, led by Dave Swindlehurst appeared in the directors' box and we had quite a party. The 4,000 of us that were there congregated and a picture of us celebrating was used on the front of the programme for the following season. There had been even more the previous night when 14,000 turned out to see us beat Everton in the F.A. Youth Cup with a goal by Terry Fenwick, a feat he was to repeat the following season against Aston Villa.

It had been an odd season, marred by inconsistency and rather an anti-climax after the break up of Big Mal's side that had reached the Cup semi final with such style. We always seemed to be just too far adrift, somewhere around eighth. Perhaps it helped that the pressure was off for a change and there were no cup distractions after nearly 43,000 saw us bow out in a third round replay to Liverpool.

In the league we'd get a couple of wins and think we were in with a chance of promotion only to suffer a defeat in the next game and you knew we weren't up to it. I remember coming back from champions Mansfield (yes, really) in March, having lost 1-0, cursing George Graham's last minute header which was finger tipped over the bar.

Graham arrived in November in a straight swap for David Kemp and missed the new year's day victory over Walsall because he thought the match was an evening kick-off. He was sitting at home when the half-time score came through (imagine how he would react if one of his Arsenal mob missed a game). When Graham remembered to turn up on time, he was a steadying influence in what had been a somewhat brittle midfield.

The defeat against Mansfield followed a midweek defeat against Lincoln and all looked lost. We bounced back in front of 29,000 to beat Alan Mullery's Brighton 3-1 (this was the year of the embittered three-game cup contest) only to lose 0-3 at Northampton the following Tuesday.

Then followed eight games without defeat and a hatful of goals mostly from our new signing from Derby Jeff Bourne and the infamous Rachid Harkouk. It culminated in the 4-0 thrashing of Sheffield Wednesday, who were also on the fringe of promotion, in the only game I've ever known to be held up by a hailstorm. We were back in contention. But, oh so typically, we went down 4-1 at Port Vale where Graham was sent off (I hope he was fined). Victory at Chesterfield left us four points behind Wrexham, who had a game in hand, with three games to play.

Interestingly, we had still to play Wrexham twice. On Tuesday, May 3, they came to Palace knowing that we couldn't catch them if they won and that even a draw meant we could only catch them on goal average, and even then their tally was superior to ours.

Wrexham took the lead after two minutes and our hearts sank but Paul Hinshelwood equalised from the penalty spot and Dave Swindlehurst grabbed the winner.

We thumped Lincoln 4-1 on the Saturday with Paul Hinshelwood scoring twice from the spot after Nick Chatterton played in goal because of an injury to Tony Burns. Wrexham could only draw.

Then came the return at Wrexham the following Wednesday. The mathematics were dreadfully complicated. Wrexham needed a draw to go up while if we won by one goal they would only need a draw at home to Mansfield on the Saturday. A margin of two goals for us meant they would have to win in their last outing.

Having been pegged back from two-up, our 4-2 win meant we were amazingly still in with a chance. But the biggest frustration was that our fate was in someone else's hands.

Wrexham failed to beat champions Mansfield (and they really were) while there was an outside chance for Rotherham if they could beat Port Vale by six goals at Vale Park. Fortunately they "only" won 4-1.

Other than go to Wrexham to support the Stags, Selhurst Park seemed the only place to be. Ian Evans, Jim Cannon, Phil Holder, Rachid Harkouk and Dave Swindlehurst turned out against Hereford's second string and Harkouk scored twice. One of the youth team, Neil Smillie, got another and Phil Holder rounded it off with a thumping shot from outside the box.

Rash the Smash had his own private war with Hereford's lumbering centre-half (and it doesn't take much imagination to imagine just how lumbering a Hereford reserve centre-half can be). After Harkouk was brought crashing down for the umpteenth time the referee gave a penalty. On a hat-trick, Rash stuck two fingers up at his opponent in derision, got booked and then missed the penalty.

We huddled in eerie silence around anyone with a radio, waiting for news from the Racecourse Ground. They waffled on and on about Liverpool winning the league, again, then came the news we wanted. Wrexham had lost and we went mad.

So next time someone gets misty eyed about Blackburn, Burnley and Fulham, don't forget Hereford reserves 1977.

What's in a NAME?

Peter Sheeran believes Palace names should be short and crisp like their football.

Let's face it, if you're a Palace fan, sooner or later you're going to have to accept that you're uncool. From the very earliest days, the club has been associated with all that's naff. For example:

We had The Nest – they had the Den
We had stripey, pastel coloured shirts – they had flame red
We had Bert Head – they had Shanks
Our Holmesdale was inaudible – their covered stands were a wall of sound
And so on ...

As a young boy in the late 60s, I was desperate for anything which would imbue Palace with the media glamour of other teams. For me it wasn't a question of results or attendances; it was all in the names and the headlines. While I cringed over "Queen is a skivvy at the Palace" (the *Sun*, 1971), my younger brother crowed over "Six of the Best". This lousy state of affairs continued for a couple of years (culminating in Alan Leather's "headline-setting plane dash" to sign Mick Hill) until the incredible happened. We got Big Mal.

The most glamourous manager in football, a man with a genius for publicity. Forget the relegations, all seemed set for a glorious future. Forget the Glaziers, we were the Eagles and, at last, we had a chant of our own. Gates went up and interest was high. Allison's Eagles scarves sold like hot cakes (it had never occurred to anyone to exploit the marketing potential of Bert Head's Glaziers).

But I knew early on that all was doomed to failure. The Hinshelwoods, Stewart Jump – crazy names for second rate footballers. Great footballers have great names – Best, Law, Cruyff, Pele, names that commentators pronounce with relish. They also have short, crisp sounds; Pele recognised this early on. Still, Palace staggered on through the early 70s – "Perky Perrin peps Palace" (*Evening Standard*, 1975) – with Big Mal bearing all the weight of our expectations on his padded shoulders. His name at least helped us get through to the FA Cup semis:

"Allison Wonderland" (Leeds 1-0)
"Allison Sunderland" (Chelsea 3-2)
and, sadly, "Allison Blunderland" (Southampton 0-2)

After that, we knew he had to go but the spirit was still there:

*Gorn and lost the f****** Cup*
We're not even going up
We're no good, in fact we're bad
We are the Palace, we're mad
(Chester 1976)

While Venables settled in, news filtered through of a startling upsurge of talent in the youth team. Although sceptical at first, I was converted as soon as I saw the team sheet for the F.A. Youth Cup semi final against West Brom. Hilaire, Nicholas, Walsh, Sansom, Fenwick – now we're talking! Before we knew it, we were the Team of the 80s and all seemed possible. Chelsea fans were jealous and sick of hearing about us.

We made the top of division two and bought players with brilliant names like Elwiss, we made the top of division one, we ...

I knew early on that it was all doomed to failure. Principles were abandoned and suddenly we had Flanagan and Allen playing up front. No wonder Terry left.

Of course, it wasn't all down to nomenclature. The scene is the directors' lounge:

Faceless moron 1: What we need is a dynamic new manager to restore us to the heights. Any ideas?
Faceless moron 2: Hmm ... do you remember an F.A. Cup tie v Brighton a few years ago? Sharp young manager there, what was his name? Anyway, we beat 'em 1-0 and this bloke comes charging over to us, starts shouting and screaming, takes out a pile of fivers, tears 'em up, throws 'em down and starts jumping on 'em!
Faceless moron 1: Sounds like just the man for us.

So Mullery came and we got McCullochs and Strongs and gawd knows whats and a period of utter despair. The media lost interest.

Then came the King. He understood. He introduced short names. Wright, Bright, Gray, Young, Shaw, Salako, Thorn and times were wonderful. Promotion, Wembley, 3rd in the league, fans chanting again ...

I knew it was doomed to failure early on. Out went Wright, in came Gabbiadini ... some things never change do they?

Poetry Please

Taylor Made

Prince of wingers,
England star Peter Taylor,
Til he joined Spurs
And old Terry Naylor,
A penalty, he struck it,
In the Holmesdale, he stuck it,
And Millwall all cheered
at his failure.

Silk Cut

Head of curls, socks rolled down,
flying wingman,
Of that ilk there's only one
Barry Silkman,
He'd skip down the line,
Deliver crosses on time,
He'd have probably made
a good milkman.

By Matthew Simmonds

PETER AND JACKO

Hy Money

What ended with John Jackson, began again with Peter Taylor. No less lovable, perhaps, but very different and lovable in a different way.

When you're a boy, especially one who plays up front, you tend to love goalscorers. For Palace fans in the early 70s that didn't give you many options because, when it came to goalscorers, we didn't have any. John Hughes had his five minutes, literally, of fame (all five against Sheffield United), Gerry Queen bumbled around courageously for a couple of years, scoring occasionally when the law of averages was applied to the sheer volume of chances he had, and Don Rogers put a few in the back of the net although, to me, he was never a genuine 20 goals-a-season man.

So who would your favourite player be? Per Bartram was not the antecedent of today's stylish Scandinavian imports, being closer in fact, to Glen Toran than Glenn Hysen. Tony Taylor ran and ran (all the way to Canada at one point), but never to any great effect, John McCormick was reasonably lovable, but not stylish, a sort of clever Jeff Hopkins, Mel Blyth might have been close, but he was a centre-half. I always thought John Sewell was ugly, even though I later found out he was well dressed. It doesn't help when you're looking for fans in the nine year old ranks. So who did that leave? John Jackson who, even for a forward like myself,

John Jackson and Peter Taylor. Two very different players, two very different positions. The link? Both were the outstanding heroes in their respective teams. Keith Brody offers an appraisal.

begged idolisation. What made Jackson unique in the context of the Palace team of the early 70s is that he was a biological anomaly, the backbone in an amoeba. Now that's not entirely fair, I know. If nothing else, the side had plenty of spirit, but spirit should not be confused with spine. "Stonewall" Jackson had both.

Jackson was, as the apocryphal phrase goes, "the greatest player of my generation never to play for England". The excuse for that is that Gordon Banks and Peter Shilton, the two greatest keepers in the world, were in front of him – to which I say rubbish. The real reason is that then, like now, England managers don't pick Palace players if there's anything else cooking at a temperature of vaguely 98.5 degrees to be had. Jacko could have, and should have, played for England.

For us, during our first four years in division one, he was pure class. In an age where style supplanted substance, people were lining up to buy the likes of Steve Kember, our greatest player ... but leaving our real superstar where he belonged, at Selhurst. There are so many details about Jackson's string of great performances that I'm not sure I can remember a single individual moment of brilliance. In every game during that four year spell, we could leave Selhurst secure in the knowledge that he had played a blinder – win, lose or draw. It was simply one great save after another. Without Jacko, Blyth and McCormick might actually have looked bad enough to sell to the Arse.

When Jacko left us, it marked the end of an era, culturally as well as football-wise. It is oddly fitting that he was swept away with the same disrespect that has come to symbolise the generation that replaced his ilk. Even though we have plenty to thank Big Mal for, his treatment of our hero means it should always be done through clenched teeth. It would have been offensive if a loyal, but crap, goalkeeper had been replaced by Paul Hammond and Tony Burns, but to do it to Jacko was unthinkable. Watching the ineffective Hammond for three long years after the joys of Jackson was almost unbearable. Every game was spent pondering on the value of what we'd given away. I'll go out on a limb here and question whether we ever really replaced big John until Nige arrived. Budgie had his moments, but he was always a nutter and never likely to provide long term stability. George Wood was, well, Scottish for a start, and Perry was sort of like Pembo – you could idolise just about everything about him, but his ability.

It's an interesting question to ponder, who would you pick in your all-time Palace team, Jacko or "the big Cornishman"? For sentimental reasons, I'd go with Jacko, but either are among the best players ever to wear a Palace jersey. Imagine if they had been here together!

Jacko's team, in a matter of years, became Peter Taylor's team. Spud (who knows how he got that nickname?) became probably the first real celebrity to play for Palace in my years of following the team. He was a player with a genuine national reputation. He played for England when he was in the third division, which helped, and scored every time he played for them, which helped even more. About the only thing he didn't do, as far as I can remember was get in the bath with Big Mal and Fiona Richmond, probably not for the want of trying!

Spud was also the idol of Brian Moore, or so it seemed. He was a comic talent who'd go on the *Big Match* (versus Hereford was a "big match" back then) and do Max Wall impressions that were really funny.

He even hosted the *Big Match Christmas Show* with a couple of less funny, and therefore forgettable, professionals. Mostly, it was the usual footballer to footballer banter: "I fink he's done good, Brian, specially when the ball's come to him." It was left to Spud to liven the proceedings with his antics.

On the pitch, albeit against crap opposition, he was good. The fact that he sunk without trace at Spurs suggests the quality of the opposition may have had something to do with it, but at Palace he was the best player to watch. He would run at defenders, take them on, beat them, shoot on sight, pass intelligently, do almost everything you could expect not to see in the old third division.

I don't know if he was really skilful, but he was powerful and could knock it forward and run over, rather than around, the defender. How he got by the defender didn't really matter. He was a like a train, building momentum as he moved down the pitch, then exploding a shot toward goal. He had a presence for the big occasion. Who can forget his England Under-23 debut at Selhurst, a stunning goal minutes into the game.

Spud was not a big name when he came, proving Malcolm's eye for talent and he ceased to be a big name almost as soon as he left.

He was a player that only Palace got the best out of. I suspect that he was only an average player whose purple patch coincided with his stay at Selhurst. It's a happy coincidence, no more, no less.

The story of Jacko and Spud is a lot more than just two players who wore different colour shirts. It's the story of two different eras that collided and the two different styles that emerged. The Taylor era produced excitement and Spud embodied it. Jacko's era produced a more visceral experience, but one which lasts longer in this fan's memory.

Opposite page: John Jackson (right) with his 1980s successor Perry Suckling.
Illustration on this page by Jason Axell

The prophecies of NOSTRADAMUS

The army of the Lion shall venture forward to do battle ... obviously a reference to Millwall aggro in 1988

Football League Management committee perish in third world war

War between Palace and Stockport

The Pope gets on the end of Salako's cross to score the goal that sends Arsenal into the second division

Michel de Nostradamus, famed 16th century prophet and historian, has shaken the world with his uncanny predictions.

He's a fantical Palace fan and, sitting cross-legged on the sofa in his 1970s replica shirt, he is in relaxed mood. "People have got me all wrong. Everyone seems to think I predicted the end of the world, but it was just a laugh. Most of my predictions were made in the pub after a few beers and all of them were about football, not politics or war. Sod the future of the world, I don't care when it ends as long as I can see the Eagles win a trophy first. Whether or not they will is anybody's guess."

But why Palace, especially as he was born in Paris 400 years before the club was formed? "I had a speech defect as a kid and when the other kids asked who I supported I meant to say Paris, but it came out Pallis. They all took the mickey and said Steve Kember couldn't play for toffee. I felt sorry for Palace so I decided to stick up for them, it stemmed from there." But surely if he can see into the future why didn't he pick a team that would win, at least sometimes. "Well Malcolm Allison said Palace were going to dominate football, how was I to know they'd be so unpredictable?"

So what of Nostradamus's own predictions? "Well I foresaw the rise and fall of France as a world power. Just look at the World Cups of the mid-80s, I was right on that one – and with the Germans' rise to power."

As far as Palace are concerned, Nostradamus says that Mabus (or Mabbutt) would save the legions of the Eagle. "Again I was misquoted. Everyone thought it was Saddam spelt backwards or a combination of Major and Bush and meant doom for the world.

There has been a lot of misinterpretation of his work. For example there was the recent belief that the reference to Michael the Marked, supposedly the next Anti-Christ, referred to Mikhail Gorbachev, who has that famous birthmark on his bonce. "Nah, that's not what I meant. I was referring to Michael the 'un' marked – Mickey Thomas who scored the goal that won Arsenal the league title at Anfield in 1989. But it was just one lot of evil reds replacing another.

"They are both criminal empires and I hope one day they will be crushed. By the way the Anti-Christ is, of course, Lee Dixon."

How does Nostardamus see Palace? "I think we've got a bright future. But there will be trouble for others in south London. I've been quoted as saying the Pope will die in Lyon. But what I meant was 'Pop' Robson will sign for the Lions. It's desperate days ahead for Millwall I'm afraid."

Will Palace win the Cup? "Sadly not. There's more chance of England being attacked by Moslem submarines while the US Army and its Hungarian allies try to rescue the King of Spain after Italy has been invaded by South Yemen."

Mrs Minchella the peanut seller

In the very late 60s, throughout the 70s there was one ever present at Selhurst Park who no-one who has ever stood on the Holmedale is ever likely to forget.

Donny the Beastie Boy of the Addiscome Eagles recalls a famous Selhurst character

Her name was Mrs Minchella the peanut seller.

Nobody knew her first name but she was famous for selling Percy Dalton's monkey nuts along with a small army of urchins that would have graced any Charles Dickens novel of downtrodden Victorian waifs and strays. Mrs Minchella resembled an old gypsy; gold earring, red bandana, the lot.

She had skin as tough as an elephant's hide and no wonder, the abuse she was given would have made a Millwall docker blush. Hers was an unenviable task, trying to sell nuts to football fans although her offer was not always easy to refuse.

To this day I can still remember the sound of crunching shells and people munching nuts. There was also more crunching of shells under foot when we celebrated a goal with the immortal Palace anthem *Knees Up Mother Brown*. How apprentices and ground staff must have hated that old woman whose empty shells and paper bags had to be swept up on Sunday mornings. Perhaps she was also responsible for one of the saddest chants ever heard at a football match: *One, two, three, four ... listen to the Charlton roar: peanuts for sixpence!*

The old lady did not confine her sales to the football season. She could also be found selling her wares at school sports days in the summer (Duppas Hill, Purley Way and Croydon Arena).

She may not have had much to do with the fortunes of Crystal Palace but I'm sure she'll always be rememberd by those of us who misspent our childhood and adolescence on the famous Holmesdale terrace.

Terry Venables: a new era for Crystal Palace

There could only be one successor. One school of thought already suggested Terry Venables was the true power behind the Allison throne anyway and had been for some time. It meant continuity at least. The young manager didn't make too many changes. Palace already had good players and he had no pressing need for team rebuilding. What changes there were concerned departing personnel. Neil Martin, something of a disaster, was released to play in Ireland. Martin Hinshelwood returned for the big kick-off while 18 year-old Kenny Sansom, who had made a startling debut at Tranmere at the dog end of the previous season, took the left back position allowing Jim Cannon to move into central defence alongside Ian Evans. Peter Johnson, who had played in the final two games of the previous season, went to Bournemouth while Dave Swindlehurst renewed his partnership with David Kemp.

Apart from that, it was pretty much Malcolm's team that took the field against York. After some of the huge crowds of the previous season it was an unattractive start and only 14,426 hauled themselves along to watch Taylor win it for Palace. But there was not quite the same swagger or arrogance about Palace. The disappointments of the last few seasons had bred an insecurity that lingers today – although subsequent events have fuelled it greatly. What Palace most needed was a convincing start and they successfully built on their opening day success when Kemp scored the only goal at Grimsby. But the old erratic ways struck again with stupid defeats at Tranmere and at home to Chester where the attendance slipped further to 12,390. By this time we were already out of the League Cup.

Having beaten Portsmouth over two legs in the first round, we lost 3-1 at home to Watford on the last day of August. League results also continued to disappoint and infuriate although we remained in touch with the leaders – just about. The good news was that big Dave Swindlehurst began to find the target with some regularity and his physical presence was an asset even though Kemp never recaptured his form of the early part of the previous season. Venables soon lost patience. In November, Kemp joined Portsmouth and Steve Perrin was given an extended run in the number nine shirt, but goalscoring didn't come easy for the Eagles.

Another early faller was Martin Hinshelwood. In the first defeat of the season at Prenton Park he broke down again and was replaced by his brother Paul. After having to do without him at the end of the 1975-6 season – a major reason in the view of many for Palace's eventual demise – this was a bitter blow. Paul was given a run in Martin's number eight shirt but the difference was plain to see. The real hammer blow though was the loss of Peter Taylor. The inevitability of his move to Tottenham did nothing to ease the disappointment. Nor were Palace in such a healthy position financially that they could afford to go out and blow the £200,000 they received for him. After a dozen or so games, Venables tried a tactical switch which was to prove of real value to Palace, moving Paul Hinshelwood to right back and replacing him in midfield with an experienced but cheap signing, George "Stroller" Graham.

Graham had been around a bit. He was at Chelsea under Tommy Docherty, played in Arsenal's double winning team of 1971 and had a spell with Manchester United. His arrival from Portsmouth, where everybody had assumed he was down and going, raised a few eyebrows but he added toughness and experience to the midfield where Paul Hinshelwood had been found wanting. Palace were in the middle of a three-match battle with Brighton in the first round of the F.A. Cup. Not only did we win, we proved that our capacity for hitting the back page headlines was not entirely lost with the Allison era.

Just under 30,000 packed the Goldstone Ground for the first match in which Palace backed by massive travelling support were saved by Rachid Harkouk's brilliant late equaliser. On the following Tuesday another near 30,000 crowd saw the former Feltham striker score again as the match once more ended in stalemate. And so the drama shifted to Stamford Bridge, where appalling conditions (the weather, not the ground) kept the crowd down to 14,000. It was a controversial match in which referee Ron Challis awarded Brighton a penalty from which they scored. Challis was not satisfied and made them retake it only for Hammond to save. Brighton also had a goal disallowed and so former Tottenham midfielder Phil Holder's goal for Palace proved to be the winner. After the game, miffed Brighton boss Alan Mullery, Venables' team mate from their Spurs days, let the Palace fans know what he thought of them. Until that moment the relationship with Brighton was none too clever. After, it was one of pure hatred.

Palace's reward for beating Brighton was an away match with highly rated non-leaguers Enfield. The match was switched to Selhurst and Palace, wearing their away kit, played in red and blue stripes for the last time at Selhurst for a few years. The preferred kit was now all white with a red and blue diagonal sash, the one which had been omnipresent in the previous year's cup run. Swindlehurst's brace, accompanied goals by Barry Silkman and Paul Hinshelwood ensured a smooth passage.

With memories of Cup glory still fresh, Palace produced an equally satisfying, though not victorious, result at Liverpool. We not only held the league champions who, with the inspirational Kevin Keegan, were heading for another championship and European Cup victory, but outplayed our illustrious hosts.

Anfield was heaving and 44,000 Scousers offered Palace a hostile welcome. The home supporters belied their sporting reputation with savage attacks upon Palace fans both inside and outside the ground and even the Palace players were greeted by a hail of detritus. But our lads were far from overawed. The 0-0 scoreline flattered the home side rather than the Eagles and Kenny Sansom gave an immaculate display.

We looked as if we might finish the job in the replay, where the attendance almost matched the Anfield one of

Dodgy joke from the 70s

A racehorse asked Alan Mullery for a trial. The Brighton manager was desperate as usual so he agreed. The horse was given his chance in a practice match and showed remarkable ball control and heading ability. The Seaweed boss said: "Okay I'll put you in the first team, and I want you to run down the wing. The opposition will never catch you."

"I'm sorry but I can't run," said the horse. "If I could run did you think I'd be playing for Brighton?"

three days earlier. Paul Hinshelwood gave us an early lead with a thunderous shot, but Liverpool, stung by the insult, scored three times before Graham made the score respectable. After that, Liverpool were guilty of some outrageous time wasting – a frustrating compliment to their third division opponents.

Palace lost nearly 30,000 fans between the replay and the appearance of Grimsby the following Saturday. The visitors, confused by yet another Palace change of colours, ended up wearing Palace's red and blue striped away strip while the *Big Match* captured the moment when their keeper Nigel Batch hit a pigeon with a goal kick. Aside from these magic moments the match was far from exceptional but Palace eased to a 2-1 win with goals by Nick Chatterton and Barry Silkman. Although we kept in touch with the leaders, promotion looked as if it might be tantalisingly out of reach. But towards the end of March things changed. First there was a humbling at Northampton. Peter Hurn was among the away support and recalls a bizarre incident. "It was Tuesday evening and we lost 3-0 in one of those travesties of justice we'd got used to in the mid-70s. One of their goals was a penalty scored by John Gregory who went on to play for the Old Enemy and England. The penalty was well struck and gave Tony Burns no chance. It rebounded from the net back out to Gregory who belted it back in and to rub salt into the wounds ruffled Burns' immaculate hair. Our Tone was not impressed and gave chase. The celebrating Gregory sprinted to the half way line with Burns in hot pursuit at which point, the ageing keeper conceded defeat. That remains the only time I have collapsed laughing after Palace have let a goal in."

Results were far from spectacular but the steady gathering of points while others faltered kept us in or around fifth place. Perrin and a new signing from Derby, Jeff Bourne, provided single goal victories over Oxford and Preston respectively and, in the first match of April, Harkouk earned us a point from fellow promotion challengers Rotherham at Millmoor. Gillingham and Swindon were well beaten at Selhurst while draws were gained at Fratton Park and Gay Meadow. But there was still little indication of how the season would pan out. Aside from the pleasure of seeing Palace put third rate teams such as Swindon to flight there was the goal difference to consider. Nobody was yet aware of just how important the five goals against the Robins and a further four against fallen giants Sheffield Wednesday would prove. Another youth team player, Jerry Murphy, made the breakthrough as a substitute for Graham against Wednesday. Murphy had joined Palace straight from school in June 1975 and signed apprentice forms in May 1976. He was the second of Allison's proteges to break into the first team. Venables was beginning to reap the benefits of his old mate's belief in bringing the best young players to Selhurst.

It was spring and the scent of promotion hung in the air. In 1975-76 we had fallen away away. In 1976-77 the story was quite different. We appeared unlikely contenders unless we could produce a really outstanding spell. Thus, on Saturday April 2, 1977 with ten games left to play, the table appeared thus:

Brighton	36	20	8	8	68	32	48
Rotherham	35	17	14	4	54	31	48
Mansfield	36	20	7	9	60	36	47
Wrexham	35	19	7	9	64	41	45
Preston NE	36	17	10	9	55	34	44
Palace	36	16	11	9	42	30	43

In a two week period which included Easter, Palace's position held steady, although we were now fifth because Preston had dropped out of the running. Rotherham had slipped from second to fourth because of three defeats and although they had scored more, their goal difference was the same as ours. The following Saturday, April 23, three of the top five clubs won, while Mansfield and Rotherham drew. On the Tuesday after, Palace lost 4-1 at Port Vale in farcical circumstances and three Palace players were sent off.

With only four games left, we had little hope of overhauling any of the top three clubs but for the fact that we were still to play one of them, Wrexham, twice. Moreover, two of Wrexham's other remaining games were against Brighton and Mansfield, both likely to be tough battles although Wrexham were at home in both.

If Palace still had a slim chance of promotion then so had Rotherham (level on points with us but with a game in hand); but they were not due to meet any of the top clubs and so, in effect, their hopes rested on Palace doing their dirty work for them and then pipping us at the post. On Saturday, April 30 Wrexham and Brighton drew 0-0 while the other three clubs all won away. On May 3, we strengthened our position slightly with a fortunate 2-1 home victory over Wrexham. Rotherham lost by the same margin at home to Reading. Victories for Mansfield and Brighton assured both clubs of promotion and now it was a fight for third place between Wrexham, Palace and, at a pinch, Rotherham. Goal difference could yet settle the issue.

The results on Saturday, May 7 went Palace's way. We whacked Lincoln 4-1, despite losing Tony Burns in the warm up and having to play midfielder Nick Chatterton in goal for the entire game. Rotherham also won by the only goal while the best Wrexham, who were beginning to feel the pressure, could manage was a draw. The position was now clear. Our last game was at Wrexham. Anything less than victory would finish us off and, as our goal difference was three worse than theirs, even a single goal margin would leave us short of target and would mean Wrexham would only need a point from their last match at home to Mansfield. Rotherham were nearly out of it, not only needing Palace to win and Mansfield to draw at Wrexham but also to come up with two big victories themselves to make up their goal difference.

It was May 11, 1977. Tony Burns was still injured and so

Season Tickets

Old Stand	centre	£37
	wing	£32
New Stand	centre	£32
	outer centre	£28
	wing	£24
enclosures	adults	£17
	jnrs/OAPs	£8.50
Matchday		
Old Stand	centre	£2
	wing	£1.60
New Stand		£1.50
Enclosures		£1
Terraces	adults	90p
	jnrs/OAPs	50p

Palace finish with a fling

They hit two in last 90 seconds

Wrexham 2 C. Palace 4 : By DERICK ALLSOP

Palace's youngsters started the year by knocking Fulham out of the F.A. Youth Cup, 4-1 after a replay. They took two replays to sort out Arsenal's youngsters before whipping four unanswered goals past them at Tooting and Mitcham's Sandy Lane. Then Chelsea were beaten 3-2. There was no doubt that the new Palace generation were special.

In 1976, the emerging talents of West Brom had been too strong for our kids, but the extra year had made all the difference. We cruised past Albion 3-0 at Selhurst before an increasingly interested crowd and savaged Tottenham 6-0 in the second leg of the semi at White Hart Lane for an 8-0 aggregate. The final was staged over two legs, starting at Goodison Park where Everton were shut out. Palace had done a good job and in the second leg on May 13 lifted the trophy for the first time – the winning goal coming from Terry Fenwick. To cap the year, Kenny Sansom, at the tender age of 18, was voted PFA third division player of the year.

Palace began the 1977-78 season back in division two with an old score to settle with Millwall. On the opening day the Den was bathed in brilliant sunshine – the perfect setting in which to give the hosts a lesson. Caswell, who had played just one league match – the victory over Wrexham – started in goal and had an afternoon off as Palace ran riot. Another youngster, Vince Hilaire, who'd made only three substitute appearances, was given his full debut and scored the second goal. But it was the third that really iced the cake. A sweeping move from the Palace penalty area finished with Chatterton stroking the ball into the corner of Nicky Johns' goal. None of the demoralised Millwall players had come remotely close to touching it. In five passes Palace had cut

Palace gave a debut to Peter Caswell in goal. We took a two-goal lead through Swindlehurst and Perrin. But Wrexham fought back and pulled the scores level. With two minutes left that's how it remained. Wrexham were just about there. Then Palace pulled a dramatic finish out of the bag with two goals in the last two minutes. First Harkouk's overhead kick flew into the top corner and while the fans were still screaming with joy, Bourne raced clear to drive in number four. People were laying, falling and leaping almost insane with joy. It was as if we'd won the league. Now we had to wait. Rotherham had beaten Reading 3-0, making the calculations simple. Wrexham needed to win to go back above us. Rotherham could also do it, but only if they won by six clear goals at Port Vale.

That Saturday, Mansfield held Wrexham until the last minute then scored the goal that silenced the Racecourse. Rotherham, chasing goals, could only win 4-1. It was enough to give us promotion.

Neil Everitt

Two of Palace's celebrity supporters. Ronnie Corbett (left) and Roger de Courcy (minus Nookie Bear) in discussion at the Stoke City match in 1978

Mark Moylan/Allsport

Peter Nicholas advances against Brighton in October 1978

their rivals to ribbons. In the next match Mansfield were given a hearty welcome to Selhurst after the favour they had done us at the Racecourse on the final day, but the third division champions were shown that it was the team who'd only just scraped up with their help who were the class act. Two goals by Rash the Smash and a welcome strike by Martin Hinshelwood (making his comeback, again) cheered a 19,000 crowd. Hinshelwood however was substituted and returned to the treatment table not to be seen again for three months.

In September, Kenny Sansom, living up to every ounce of his potential, made his debut for England under-21s versus Denmark. He was clearly the jewel in the Palace crown, a shining example of a brilliant youth system, and there were plenty more where he came from.

After the excitement of those early wins, the season settled into one of transition and consolidation. The youngsters who had won the F.A. Youth Cup were outstanding and by the end of the season many were on the verge of first team status if not already there.

Centre-half Billy Gilbert made his debut in place of Ian Evans after a bad tackle by Fulham's George Best had broken the Welsh international's leg in Palace's 3-2 defeat at the beginning of October. Those who were present still wince at the thought of the audible crack of the bone.

It was clear that the recovery process would be a long one. Peter Wall took over in the centre of defence for a short while and there was even the welcome return of Mel Blyth, on loan from Southampton as Venables tried a few options including using another junior Peter Nicholas who, in the absence of Paul Hinshelwood, had made his debut on the opening day at right back. Eventually Gilbert was given a further chance to establish himself alongside Cannon, now skippering the side, and the youngster took it.

Terry Fenwick made his league bow in the 2-0 home win over Notts County on December 10; Murphy, who'd two substitute appearances to his name, got a full outing at Eastville, where Palace crashed 3-0 to Bristol Rovers; Neil Smillie came on as substitute for Bourne at home to Burnley and keeper David Fry was given an easy debut on the last day of the season when a Swindlehurst hat-trick demolished Blackburn 5-0. Fry's appearance was an isolated one. After Burns had returned in place of Caswell for the third match, he kept goal until Venables moved for Villa's experienced and athletic John Burridge.

Burridge began, as all Palace keepers should, with a clean sheet against Brighton, who were now chasing their second consecutive promotion.

Meanwhile Jeff Bourne, whose goals had helped Palace to promotion, made nothing like the same impact on second division defences and by February, after just one goal in 17 matches, he left for Dallas Tornado. This gave another young player, Ian Walsh, a chance to stake his claim alongside Swindlehurst. But the goals had dried up.

Despite finishing with that flourish against Blackburn, we had not made any significant impact on the division, although ninth wasn't bad. But, after the glories of recent years, there was some pride to be swallowed when we suffered a dismal defeat at Hartlepool in the F.A. Cup.

Overall progress was more than satisfactory and Venables had good reason to be optimistic. The juniors had retained the Youth Cup, outclassing all who stood before them. In the third round, having already seen off Fulham, they thrashed Chelsea 3-0. The Palace team makes interesting reading:

Palace's teenage starlet Vince Hilaire brings the ball under control

David Fry, Chris Sparks, Kevin Dare, Terry Fenwick, Billy Gilbert, Peter Nicholas, Les Carter, Steve MacKenzie, Steve Lovell, Jerry Murphy, Vince Hilaire, sub Tony Paul

Murphy scored twice with Fenwick netted the other. Only Sparks and MacKenzie failed to make a first team appearance for Palace and the latter was only denied his chance by the intervention of Malcolm Allison's cheque book.

In the fourth round, Palace beat Leeds with a Steve Lovell goal and then overcame Port Vale in the quarter finals. Steve Leahy replaced MacKenzie in this match while Neil Banfield was substitute. Both would eventually graduate to the first team although neither would make a serious impact.

West Brom's youngsters were undoubtedly Palace's closest rivals at the time and the semi-final proved to be an epic. It finished 1-1 on aggregate after the two legs and the first replay at the Hawthorns ended 2-2. Finally on home soil Palace cruised through with three unanswered goals and in the final the young Eagles secured a 1-0 win over Villa in a one-off final at Highbury with another Fenwick goal.

Palace prepared for 1978-79 with high hopes and Terry Venables trying to keep everybody's feet on the ground. Blackburn's opportunity to avenge their 5-0 hammering came swiftly, but at Ewood Park on the opening day their arch-tormentor Swindlehurst secured a point. The big forward was also on the mark in the 3-1 win over Luton at Selhurst with Hilaire and Murphy scoring the others.

Venables had used 29 players the previous season, trying out numerous permutations and introducing young players. Now he knew what his best line-up was. There had been surprise when Rachid Harkouk was allowed to go to QPR in the close-season, but the manager clearly had a settled side in mind.

Palace in fact kept an unchanged side for the first nine matches; a side that supporters of the period still recite with affection:

John Burridge, Paul Hinshelwood, Kenny Sansom, Peter Nicholas, Jim Cannon, Billy Gilbert, Nicky Chatterton, Jerry Murphy, Dave Swindlehurst, Micky Elwiss and Vince Hilaire.

Hy Money

Selhurst Park, Friday, May 11, 1979. Hy Money captures the unprecedented scenes as almost 52,000

Even substitutes were unnecessary on six occasions.

The most notable acquisition of the summer was Mike Elwiss, bought from Preston with the money from the Harkouk deal. There was something about Elwiss, he just looked and sounded right. The fans took to him almost immediately and although he was unfortunate at times in front of goal it was obviously going to come right and with the team doing so well we could afford to be patient.

While the team stayed together they remained unbeaten, a tremendous feat in a fiercely competitive division. All the teams Palace faced in those early days of the season had reputations to protect but none were able to get the better of a virtually impregnable defence.

If Millwall had recovered from their 3-0 drubbing of the previous season they soon had more scars to bear. Palace repeated the dose on September 16 with another sublime footballing display.

As we showed our promotion credentials, the rest of the division began to sort itself out. Our main rivals were Stoke, who'd bought experienced campaigners such as Mike Doyle and Howard Kendall to help them regain the first division place they'd lost in 1977, newly relegated West Ham, Sunderland and Mullery's slime balls from the South Coast.

There was an early test at Stoke. With Palace trailing, Venables sought to make a change: "I was considering taking off Jerry Murphy when he scored our equaliser. He took it well – I could say superbly – and all I can do is repeat that if he wants to make me look a fool like that with a similar effort again I will pat him on the back."

In early October, Brighton who, much to the delight of all at Selhurst Park, had missed out on promotion by a hair's breadth to Tottenham the previous year, came to south London nursing ambitions to get it right at the second time of asking. They were sent home with their tails between their legs. After a goalless first half Palace scored three quick goals including two from the livewire Hilaire.

The following week, Preston became the first team to score twice against us but were undone by their old boy. The North End programme noted that Elwiss had "not yet settled to his true scoring form and has netted only once for his new club". Jim Golden was among the travelling support: "Preston were third from bottom and having seen Palace crush the Seaweeds the week before we were confident of at least a draw. But, being Palace, this was not as easy as it seemed. Preston scored and it began to look like a wasted day. We started a few nice little moves but when Preston surged forward, bang, they were two up. Christmas had come early for the North End fans and they wanted to let us know it. Despite this the 200 or so Palace fans just kept on singing. Preston though were having a great time and dishing out a lot of stick to Mike Elwiss. Soon after the second Preston goal, Ian Walsh managed to pull one back but it seemed like it wasn't going to be our day. The minutes began to tick away and with the home fans chanting *2-1,2-1,*

Budgie

What a character, what a goalie, what a steal at £40,000. People talk of the great back four of Kenny, Jimbo, Billy and Doris, but John Burridge was the rock upon which that defence was built. Remember his penalty save at Aston Villa in the league cup? Or his heroics at Old Trafford when only a 97th minute equaliser from Joe Jordan beat him? No coincidence that goodbye Budgie, hello Barron signalled the beginning of the end.

If you never saw Palace in 79 with John Burridge marshalling our rearguard you never saw the best back five ever to grace Selhurst Park.

Matthew Simmonds

people celebrate promotion to the first division. Note the goal posts submerged by the supporters.

2-1 Walsh sneaked in to stab the ball past Tunks, the Preston keeper. We went barmy, screaming and shouting and jumping up and down and while we were still celebrating, up sprang Elwiss to hammer home a beautiful left foot shot that left the defence standing. We went over the edge, with people who had just been calming down after the equaliser going stark staring mad. Blokes were climbing the fenced enclosure like monkeys. Fifteen years on I still grin when I think of it. Palace are never dead until the whistle sounds for time."

Walsh had only been included for the missing Swindlehurst and was left out the following week when Palace shut out Wrexham, who'd finally managed to win promotion to division two. Our unbeaten march to the top attracted *Match of the Day* to come and see what all the fuss was about. Palace, of course, waited for the cameras to arrive before serving up a poor performance against Fulham. In a bizarre match, the referee blew up five minutes early, realised his error and called the teams back out to complete the game with many of the crowd on their way home, but we couldn't make the most of the reprieve and slid to a 1-0 defeat.

There was more woe the following week – Chatterton's penalty at Turf Moor was insufficient to prevent us going down at Burnley. It was the last thing Chatterton would do for Palace, the following week he joined Millwall to be replaced by a familiar figure. After a spell in Canada with Vancouver Whitecaps, Steve Kember was brought home by Venables to steady his young team. Kember's experience would prove vital.

After fielding an unchanged team for ten matches, we were suddenly hit by a spate of injuries. Swindlehurst dislocated a shoulder, Cannon twisted an ankle and "Doris" Hinshelwood had to undergo a cartilage operation after catching his studs in the pitch against Wrexham. He was replaced at right back by Fenwick. It was a double blow because Martin Hinshelwood had finally been forced to admit defeat in his battle for fitness, announcing his retirement at the age of 24.

In the run up to Christmas, Palace began to see the best of Elwiss. He scored in four successive matches – the home wins over Sheffield United and Newcastle and away draws with West Ham and Cardiff – while Swindlehurst also scored at Ninian Park as Cardiff became the third, and last, side in 1978-79 to beat Burridge twice. After a 0-0 draw at Notts County, Elwiss added to his tally as we beat Leicester 3-1. But a disaster for club and player was looming. At Cambridge the stretcher was called on and that was the last we ever saw of a player who would have graced the first division and may well have made the story of the "Team of the 80s" very different indeed.

Elwiss's progress was followed closely by Palace fans for a couple of years as he struggled for fitness. Every now and then a note in the programme or local papers would give faint hope but it was all over ... Micky Elwiss, now there was a player.

Elwiss's number ten shirt went all over the place from that point on. Walsh, Smillie and Tony Sealy, a speedy acquisition from Southampton, all wore it for a while but the goals dried up again. We were beaten at home on Boxing Day in a disappointing performance against Bristol Rovers and dropped further home points against Orient, Millwall and promotion rivals Stoke in successive matches.We then scraped goalless draws at Brighton and at home to Preston. One wonders what difference a razor sharp Elwiss would have made?

Most championship teams go through a bad spell at some stage of the season and Christmas was Palace's. Even then it was draws rather than defeats that spoilt the look of the record books. The goals never flowed quite so smoothly after the loss of Elwiss, but at the other end our defence could not be breached. When we were drawn away to first

Above: Crazy, crazy night. Hy Money captures the mixture of joy and relief as Ian Walsh celebrates the goal that won the championship for Crystal Palace. He is pursued by Peter Nicholas and Jerry Murphy. Opposite page: Terry Venables celebrates. Walsh and Swindlehurst, the men who sank Burnley prepare to sink some bubbly. (All photographs by Hy Money)

Burnley 1979 – a fan's tale

In a funny way there's not much to say about the match against Burnley. It was a huge crowd and the celebrations afterwards were magnificent. But, unlike the two F.A. Cup semi-finals the odds were not stacked against us (quite the opposite in fact). Unlike the promotion game against Blackburn there was not the unpredictability, this team was too good for that. But this is not to belittle or underestimate the importance of the match. The short contribution by Peter Gee which follows is not especially exceptional but it captures the experience of probably 95 per cent of the people who were present ...

"We'd gained an excellent win at Orient on a sunny Saturday to set up a grand finale.

The *Sun* set the scene in the morning when it stated that: 'Crystal Palace will emerge as football's team of the 80s at jam packed Selhurst Park tonight.' It was right about Selhurst being jam packed – 51,801 in the crowd. How did they all get in? I took my usual spot in the lovely old stand enclosure at 6pm. Kick off time seemed to take an age and by the time it arrived there was nowhere to move in the ground. It's a haze now but at one of the most important and famous games in Palace's history I'm proud to say I was there."

Peter Gee

division Middlesbrough in January 1979 we established an F.A. Cup record. No side had previously been drawn away ten successive times (and that doesn't include the semi-final against Southampton which was played on neutral territory). Those who subscribe to the theory that Palace are naturally unlucky will not be surprised to discover that we hold this record. It made little difference, we were too hot for 'Boro. Wolves awaited us in round four.

It was now a four way battle for promotion with Brighton, Stoke and Sunderland. West Ham were a little off the pace. Every match was watched with ears pressed to transistors; every goal against our rivals greeted with cheers of joy. Defeat for any of them was as good as a Palace win, defeat for Brighton was as good as a pools win.

Since Christmas, our form hadn't been too clever. We hadn't lost, but we hadn't won very often either. Ironically what shook us up was a defeat. Although we responded to our failure at Newcastle with yet another draw we suddenly turned on the power to set up a storming finish to the season. Ian Walsh scored the only goal in the last minute at Eastville to keep the pressure up, then 30,000 saw an equally precious strike by Murphy beat Charlton and, at Leicester, Paul Hinshelwood popped up with a last gasp equaliser as we moved towards the tape. Swindlehurst and Murphy saw off Notts County and "Swindle" again secured two points at Orient on the last day of the season proper. That was a tricky match against a club not averse to causing upsets. It was such a delicate moment and we stood the test brilliantly. There are those who claim that, ten years after he had helped Palace into division one himself, John Jackson in the Orient

Hy Money

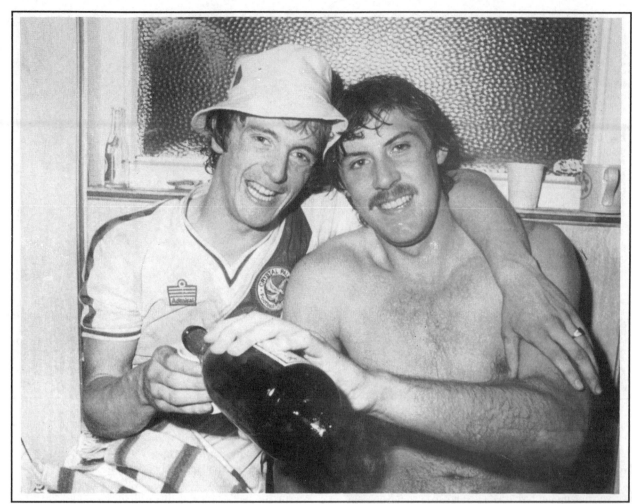

goal turned round after conceding and smiled at the Palace fans. But Palace were such a class act that, for once, there seemed no room for fate or luck. We were within touching distance of the prize and it was in our own hands.

The other clubs had all completed their fixtures, while we had one match to come. We were fourth but a draw would ease us beyond Sunderland and into division one, a victory would secure the championship as well, denying Brighton in the process.

On the Friday before the Cup Final between Arsenal and Manchester United, the talk was of a 40,000 crowd. The statistics don't tell the whole story. That there were 51,801 inside is well documented – the figure was well above capacity – but that takes no account of the thousands locked outside an hour before. Mid-table Burnley, prompted by the wise, but bald, head of Peter Noble, were plucky but overwhelmed, although you couldn't tell that to the tightly packed fans who lived on their nerves until Walsh's bullet header from Hilaire's cross beat Alan Stevenson.

Swindlehurst finished the scoring and Brighton were denied the championship by a far better team.

Palace: Burridge, Hinshelwood, Sansom, Kember, Cannon, Gilbert, Nicholas, Murphy, Swindlehurst, Walsh, Hilaire, sub Fenwick.

Burnley: Stevenson, Scott, Brennan, Noble, Thomson, Robinson, Jakub, Ingham, Morley, Kindon, James.

It was agony for the Rokerites who had travelled down to support Burnley. Their manager watched from the stand as the Selhurst pitch disappeared under the celebrating

Hy Money

Kentish Times

The second division champions acknowledge the acclaim of their supporters

multitude. "I'm sorry for Billy Elliot of Sunderland," said Venables. "Its been a difficult week for both of us but Palace were in a position to do something about it. I'm pleased we've gone up but I've tried all along to keep the pressure off my players by saying we were aiming for the top group rather than promotion itself." Elliott was gracious, admitting Palace were not only the best but had proved it.

The team set off for a short tour of North America where they met Memphis Rogues in the Liberty Bowl stadium in front of just 3,500 people. Those who turned up witnessed the end of George Graham's career. He broke his leg as Palace won 3-1. In the second match, against Fort Lauderdale Strikers, Palace renewed acquaintance with an old foe; George Best. The Strikers also had the legendary German striker Gerd Muller and Hector Cubillas of Peru playing out the last days of their careers but Palace cruised to a 2-0 win

Our credentials for the first division had already been tested during the promotion season with victories over Bristol City and Middlesbrough in the F.A. Cup and Bristol City again in the league cup. Although we hadn't done ourselves justice against Wolves in the fourth round, Villa had needed three goes to knock us out of the league cup mainly thanks to an incredible penalty save by Burridge at Villa Park.

Unlike the 1969 vintage, few thought this side lacked class. There was Kenny Sansom for a start, now a full England international – impressing everyone with his performance against Wales in the end-of-season Home International.

Gilbert, Hinshelwood, Hilaire, Walsh and Nicholas all had under-21 caps, Murphy was knocking on the door of the Republic of Ireland squad and there was an experienced backbone with Burridge, Cannon, Kember and Swindlehurst. Overseeing the whole show there was the hottest young managerial property in England, Terry Venables. What could possibly go wrong?

What the team lacked was first division experience and Venables sought to remedy this with the exciting £400,000 acquisition of QPR's former England captain Gerry Francis. He followed that with a club record £650,000 for Mike Flanagan, a prolific goalscorer who had fallen out with his club Charlton. Arsenal were interested but Palace secured his services strengthening the impression that the balance of power in London football was shifting. With Swindlehurst and the emerging Walsh also competing for places, that seemed likely to cure any deficiency in front of goal.

We had arrived. Those boasts by Malcolm Allison, that Palace would dominate London football within a decade were on the verge of reality. The Palace fans celebrated at Plough Lane in a pre-season friendly with fourth division Wimbledon, greeting the team with chants of *Champions* which assuming, not unreasonably, that the supporters of 1921 didn't sing it, was the first time any Palace team had been welcomed in such a fashion.

The home support was bolstered by a smattering of Chelsea fans and the large Palace contingent taunted *Palace Up, Chelsea Down* in salute to the Stamford Bridge club's demotion to the second division.

Chelsea were more numerous the following Saturday when Selhurst Park's championship welcome was spoilt by their thugs on the Holmesdale. Palace took their retribution on the pitch with more than 11,000 celebrating goals by Flanagan, Cannon, Murphy, Walsh and Francis in a five goal rout.

Chelsea fielded a number of players who would become only too familiar to Palace supporters during the next decade: Gary Locke, Micky Droy, Tommy Langley and Trevor Aylott. But we weren't to know that and the immediate future seemed to promise nothing but blue skies for the Team of the 80s.

Palace memories of a south London

GAS HEAD

Palace are Chris Scargill's local team but his true allegiance is to Bristol Rovers

All things bright and beautiful

All creatures great and small

Rovers won the championship

And City won F* All (AGAIN!)**

You may well be wondering what a Bristol Rovers fan is doing reliving memories of watching Palace in the early 70s.

To be quite honest, I should really be a Palace fan.

I've lived in West Wickham, a staunch Palace stronghold, for 28 years, a fact that my Palace friends remind me of whenever we meet. But I must have been born with blue and white quartered blood in my veins. Being a lifelong supporter of "the Gas" has had its highs and lows (more lows than highs if you must know) but this article is not about Rovers but about my years spent on the Holmesdale.

It was m father who first suggested we should go to a match and Palace being nearest got the vote. And so began a love-hate relationship that remains with me.

The match versus Oxford was played on a Sunday afternoon because of the energy crisis of the time when many London matches had to be staggered because of the drain on energy reserves of using all those floodlights.

I don't remember much except for the sight of the peanut lady and two Oxford fans who stood behind us wearing silk scarves. There was that distinctive smell of onions coming from the hot dog van outside. It's a smell I always associate with Selhurst Park.

As most of my friends supported Palace it was only natural that I should join them on a regular basis. Palace were getting crowds of 15,000 or more for third division stuff, but how I loved it. Bury, Chesterfield and Wrexham were the visitors and I even went to a Combination game where I got my first glimpse of Tommy Langley, who was playing for Chelsea.

In 1976 it was cup run time and luckily I lived close to the London Transport Sports Ground at Langley Park where Palace trained.

Every day during the school holidays we would watch the lads, often acting as ball boys, fetching and carrying, just to be near our heroes.

Peter Taylor was my personal favourite especially when he treated us to his famous Norman Wisdom impression.

Taylor was a regular at my Dad's local, the White Hart and once came in without a shirt. The female customers loved it but Jack the governor told him if he wasn't properly attired he wouldn't be served.

The team at that time was my favourite Palace side ever; Paul Hammond, Peter Wall, Stewart Jump and the brilliant Alan Whittle. When he was sub, he was serenaded by the Holmesdale with *We Want Whittle!* ... and we got him as well.

The fifth round cup match at Stamford Bridge introduced me to something I'd never previously been involved with; football violence. I'd heard of crowd trouble of course and Chelsea and Man United were renowned as the worst fans but I'd never seen it at close quarters.

On television that night a great deal of attention was paid to the disturbances. One particularly intelligent chap was shown in slow motion attempting a Kung Fu kick. It was bloody frightening to say the least.

By this time a rivalry had developed with Brighton and when they came to Selhurst for an away game I'd never seen an away following like it. They had the whole of the Whitehorse Lane end and appeared to be doing some kind of *You'll Never Walk Alone* impression.

After the match there were running fights all the way back to East Croydon.

Later, in 1978, I recall some Brighton fans running towards the Holmesdale only to be met by a fat skinhead who kicked one up the arse and chased them all the way back, much to the amusement of the massed ranks of Eagles. In 1979, a bloke was running with the Palace fans after the game only for his Brighton scarf to fall out of his jacket. I really felt for him, the kicking he took was terrible.

In the return at the Goldstone Ground, there was an almighty fight in the park outside and one of my friends was asked where he came from. "Bromley," he replied and was promptly smacked in the face. Fortunately he was our only casualty as we made our escape back to Hove station.

On another occasion against Aldershot, I was walking past the Robin Hood at Anerley when some Shots fans ran out shouting "scarves". I threw my beloved red and blue one to the ground and ran for my life. About 200 yards later there was no-one to be seen.

In the first division, I saw some ugly scenes. Spurs fans took loads of bamboo sticks from the allotments behind the Whitehorse to attack Palace fans with and against Liverpool, a character ran up with a black hood with a zip where his mouth was, shouted "Liverpool" at us and ran off.

Later, someone told me he'd had his tongue zipped up by one of the more violent Palace fans.

But it's not all been violence. The coach trip to Anfield in 1991 with the balloons at the start is a cherished memory as is the trip to Wembley in the Zenith Data Systems final against Everton when my friend and I wore our Bristol Rovers shirts and were made most welcome.

A Rovers shirt at a Palace final? Well, you can't change the habit of a lifetime can you?

SPIDER

Malcolm had promised we would win the Cup and we believed him. The depression that followed failure engulfed Selhurst Park. Then, out of the mists to lift the gloom, came Rash the Smash. By Barrie Greene

TWO Crystal Palace stars were under arrest at a London police station today.

Rachid Harkouk and Barry Silkman were detained last night by Scotland Yard detectives investigating a forged currency racket.

By JEFF EDWARDS

Harkouk, 22, was arrested at his home in Stamford Brook Avenue, Chiswick. Silkman was arrested at an address in Kingsland Road, Hackney.

Goals

Police said thousands of American dollar bills were seized and taken away for examination.

Both players spent the night in the cells at Dalston police station.

Today they were being questioned further by senior Yard officers and were later expected to be charged with possessing counterfeit currency.

Harouk, rate at £300,000 on the transfer market, was born in Chelsea and privately educated in Kensington. He has an Algerian father and an English mother.

Sickness

He was discovered by Palace while playing for amateurs Feltham.

So far this season, he is the Football League's joint second top scorer, with nine league and cup goals.

Last season his 13 goals helped Palace win promotion from Division Three [illegible] of their key players in and the club sees him as one of their key players in their push this season to get into the First Division.

The striker is the darling of the Selhurst Park crowd. His last goal was against Fulham at home on Saturday.

It was his second in the game but Palace went down 2—3. He was expected to play against Stoke City at Stoke tomorrow.

Silkman, 24, joined Palace last year on a free transfer from Hereford.

But this season sickness and injury have kept him out of the side.

Called

Crystal Palace Chairman Ray Bloye said: "The first I knew of this was when Terry Venables called me and said the players had been arrested.

"I know nothing apart from that. Terry and I will meet to talk later if we can find out any more."

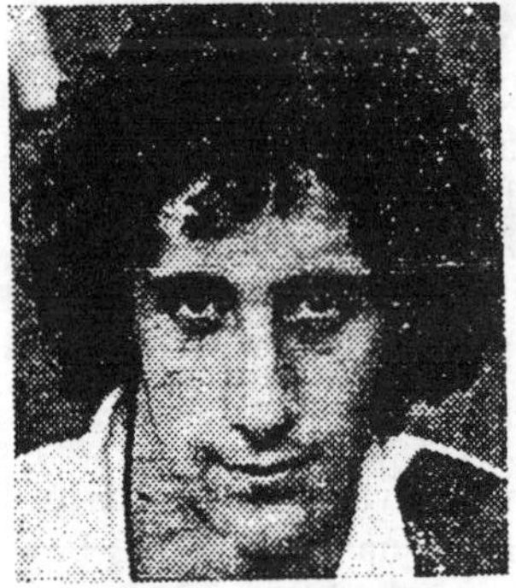

RACHID HARKOUK

Labelled the finest team ever to play in the third division, we had led the table by miles in December and beaten three top teams in the F.A. Cup – all away from home – to reach a semi-final we were odds on to win.

Malcolm Allison's flamboyance and Terry Venables' coaching had players queueing up to sign for us. We drew huge crowds, attracted even greater media attention and, in Peter Taylor, had only the second player from the third division to play for England – the first was Palace's Johnny Byrne in the 60s.

Within a few short weeks, we had lost to Southampton in the Cup, missed out on promotion after the semi had proved too great a distraction, seen Allison admit failure and finally walk out on Selhurst Park and sold Taylor to Spurs.

The new season had begun in low key fashion and third division football looked as if it was about to become a permanent status. What the fans needed was a new hero.

In the close season, Terry Venables had signed an odd-looking chap from non-league Feltham with an Arabic name.

Rachid Harkouk first appeared as a substitute in our first home game of the season and amazed the fans.

Who was this anaemic, shaggy haired, beanpole with long arms and legs?

Rachid was born in Chelsea of Algerian parents and had a reputation for being something of a wild boy. In the opening stages of the season he made only four appearances, even though he showed in those brief moments that he had genuine flair. It was only puzzling why he should have been held back for so long.

On November 20, Palace travelled to Brighton in the F.A. Cup and Rachid stormed off the bench to hit the headlines with a stunning equaliser. In the replay he scored again.

The Palace fans liked what they saw. He had a great shot and was not afraid to take opponents on.

More than that, his gangly appearance and explosive temperament marked him out as a "character". Before long the nickname "Spider" was ringing around the terraces.

By the turn of the year Rash was a free-scoring regular and, as his confidence grew, so the entertainer within was revealed.

His goals were often spectacular. In

the 5-0 romp over Swindon, Tony Burns' clearance up field bounced high into open space ten yards beyond the half way line. Spider moved onto it and, as it dropped, volleyed it from more than 35 yards to leave the Swindon goalie dumbfounded.

In the early games, Palace had struggled to score but with Harkouk in the side the attacking flair increased.

Venables bolstered the forward line with Jeff Bourne of Derby County while a youthful Dave Swindlehurst kept chipping in as Palace raced up the table to clinch promotion in the very last match. Rachid scored one of the goals in the legendary 4-2 victory over Wrexham.

His Jack-the-Lad reputation increased when the papers got hold of a story which involved Rash and his bosom buddy Barry Silkman, a classy but infuriating midfield player.

Rash and Barry were stopped by police with a car boot full of cash. The pair told the police they were doing an "errand" for Mr Venables although nothing more was ever heard on the subject.

The 1977-78 season began with Harkouk proving that higher grade football was no problem for him. He scored nine goals in the first 12 games, culminating in a double against Fulham on the day Ian Evans had his leg broken by George Best.

The big clubs watched Rash closely but made no move, perhaps put off by his wild ways.

After that, injury disrupted his season and by the time he was fully restored to the team in April, the youngsters had won the F.A. Youth Cup and were being groomed to form the nucleus of the squad for the following season. Venables knew that Rash was ready for the first division anyway.

The tall striker joined QPR for £100,000 in the summer and Palace said goodbye to a hero whose reign had been brief. He had scored 26 goals in 56 full appearances with a couple as a sub.

Rachid failed to do himself justice at Loftus Road and, surprisingly, moved to lowly Notts County. It seemed he was bound for the football scrap heap. But thoughts of a terminal decline were premature. County gained promotion to division one, albeit briefly.

Rash then amazingly reappeared in full view of the whole world as his native Algeria competed in the World Cup Finals. He played in midfield but little of his old magnetism was evident.

Like Mark Lazarus and Don Rogers before him, and Vince Hilaire after, Rachid Harkouk provoked a buzz of anticipation whenever the ball came his way.

The sight of Spider picking up the ball out on the right, sidestepping two defenders and drawing the keeper before slipping the ball home for the first of a brace against Mansfield in September 1977 will stay among my favourite Palace memories for a very long time.

The Palace Chart of the 1970s

1) My Harkouk a Choo – Alvin Stardust
2) You're So Vain – Carly Simon (for Big Mal)
3) Bert's Head Soup – Rolling Stones
4) Whittleloo – Abba
5) Kung Fu Fighting (Stamford Bridge 1976) – Carl Douglas
6) Mulligan of Kintyre – Wings
7) Get Dancin' – Disco Tex and the Heppolettes
8) Tubular Bobby Bells – Mike Oldfield
9) T. Rexham 2 Palace 4
10) Glass of Champagne – Sailor

Quote ... Unquote

(a taste of the 1970s)

"The toast in the pubs of south London last night was simply: 'Jacko.' All that bitter was pouring down 100 throats for John Jackson, Crystal Palace's long serving goalkeeper."
Sunday Mirror, Palace 1 Man City 0, 1970

"Palace might well prove a worthwhile F.A. Cup bet after Christmas if they can put aside league worries. And that's the first time in years I've honestly rated Palace a good bet for anything."
Reg Drury, Palace 5 Man Utd 0, 1972

"The side that Terry Venables has moulded into a professional footballing force and guided to the brink of the first division is clearly years ahead of their time."
The Sun heralding the Team of the 80s

"I don't think it's going to stop with industry just sponsoring the odd match. It will increase over the years and, eventually, I believe that in the future there are going to be manufacturers actually owning clubs ... and why not? Because it's becoming increasingly obvious that today's soccer is too expensive for any individual to back out of his own pocket."
Malcolm Allison, 1975

" ... our development at youth level convinces me that in two or three years time we are going to have an exceptional side here at Selhurst – not only a team capable of getting into the first division but one which will stay there and be a power."
Terry Venables, April 1977

" ... no less than justice was done in the victory of Palace's ball playing artists over the untutored thuggery of Southampton. The brave, skillful and handsome Palace side went ahead ..."
Peter Dobereiner (a Palace fan) reporting on Palace 2 Southampton 0, 1970

DORIS

Paul Hinshelwood took a long time to win over the fans. But as Palace rose and fell, his commitment and loyalty changed the meaning of his mocking nickname "Doris" into a term of respect. By Colin Readman.

Why Doris? Why not Edna or Agnes or Freda? I mean, Paul Hinshelwood never looked anything like my mum, she's nowhere near as tall as him for a start.

But Doris he became and Doris he will always be wherever two or more Palace fans are gathered in his name.

The facts, according to the *Rothmans Football Year Book*, are that he was born in Bristol, he was 5ft 11in, weight 11st 8lb, a forward, brother of Martin Hinshelwood (also Palace). Ah, say the cynics, that's why he plays for Palace. Buy one Hinshelwood, get one free. Martin was the talented one they said, with his deft little touches in the middle of the park – pity about his legs. And Paul? Well consider the championship team of 1979, you know the one, the

Team of the Eig ... well, the team of 1979 anyway.

It really was the team of all the talents; the uninhibited youth led by Kenny Sansom, Vince Hilaire, Peter Nicholas and all; the granite personified by Jim Cannon and John Burridge. Oh yes, and Paul Hinshelwood.

It really was embarrassing at times seeing this lanky fellow, who hadn't been much good as a forward, being given the run around by the opposition's international winger. He really did stick out like a sore thumb. In the midst of a team of eagles, he was a duck.

"Gawd, he's only got Doris to beat, come and get it Budgie" or "Don't pass to Doris, he won't know what to do with it." Some of the phrases from the 1980 copy of the English-Palace dictionary. I'm afraid the nickname Doris was used with venom and pity in those days; we all knew that as soon as Venables bought a class player for the number 2 spot it would be goodbye Doris.

But it didn't happen like that. The record books say that Palace were in the first division in 1980-81, though many of us profess to have no knowledge of that particular year ... the mind can erase the cruel and painful memories. Yet, for me, there is one abiding memory of that season. No, not the goal that never was at Coventry, though God knows how many times I've cringed as it is wheeled out for another showing on the "what happened next" round of *A Question of Sport*. No, the main memory is seeing some of our so-called class players (and managers) looking for a quick way out, making damn sure they didn't go down with the ship.

Some didn't care tuppence but others kept battling on, even though the club was the butt of every cruel joke in that terrible winter. One of the few was Doris.

"Our Doris" he was now – the name a badge bestowed from the terraces to be worn with pride. And on into the second division and Dario Gradi, Brian Bason and Trevor Aylott, but Doris was always there to keep the team steady, a real trier through and through. He is one of the Palace greats. Perhaps not in innate skill, but in character. Doris was one of the best after all.

Main picture: Paul Hinshelwood, his face a picture of determination, gets ahead of Liverpool's Kenny Dalglish. Opposite below: An early shot of Hinshelwood on the left in the white shirt with other members of the palace Youth team in July 1972

Doris and the drag back tackle

Paul Hinshelwood ... master of the drag-back tackle
aaarghh!
HINSH.
wraps his feet around an onrushing forward
leaves his victim grounded and away on another Eagles attack
by matthew simmonds

Doris bags a corker

I have many fond memories of Paul Hinshelwood. In my view he was, for the 1978-79 season at least, one of the finest right-backs around.

But my sweetest memory of him comes from the 1977 third round F.A. Cup replay against Liverpool.

Although I had seen Palace in the first division I was really too young to appreciate it and so I cut my Selhurst teeth watching the Eagles play the likes of Lincoln and Port Vale.

The visit of mighty Liverpool – and in my eyes they really were mighty then – was an event not to be missed. I stood as usual in the Arthur Wait enclosure close to the half-way line.

In the first half Palace attacked the Whitehorse Lane End in the days when we had an end and not a supermarket.

Doris collected the ball. He was near half way and everyone was stunned by his stupidity when he just hit it. The groan from the crowd was audible: "Bloody hell Doris what are you playing at? You're never going to beat Ray Clemence from there." Then I noticed Clemence was in a bit of trouble. The ball seemed to be floating over him – the term "grasping at thin air" came to mind.

The Liverpool keeper fell backwards as the ball went in the top left hand corner. Everything stopped and a stunned silence fell over Selhurst Park. People looked at one another and then back at the ball nestling in the goal.

Not only had Palace taken the lead against the Red Machine but Doris had achieved it with a 40-yard screamer. The place erupted. Doris went berserk and set off on a marvellous celebratory run. The players went berserk and the crowd went absolutely potty.

The dream didn't last long. Those were the days when Liverpool really were at their most dangerous when they were behind. They scored three times before George Graham pulled a goal back for us.

I rushed home to see Doris' goal on TV only to be told that a camera had broken down in the first half and so I don't think there is any record of the goal.

I gave up watching football from 1982 until 1987, but in 1984 I did go to Selhurst for Paul Hinshelwood's testimonial against QPR. There were so few people there that only the Sainsbury's End and possibly a small bit of the Old Stand were open.

Even then the Sainsbury's was not exactly packed. It's the only Palace testimonial I've ever been to, but I had to pay my respects to the man who starred in the best Palace game I saw until a sunny April day 13 years later.

Stephen Crisp

EASTER RISING

A sweltering hot day at Eastville in 1979 and Matthew Simmonds pays tribute to an unlikely man of the match

When season's done and stored away, the final game looms large in the accumulations of the football brain. This is natural. Anyone asks you about Palace in such and such a year and I'll wager your answer is coloured by that last game. Promotion, relegation, cups, mid-table obscurity, you take your cue from the concluding 90 minutes of nine months worth of action.

Think of 1979. Those were the days, second division champions, Venables brightest young manager in the league, Sansom, Nicholas, Walsh and Murphy were fledgling senior internationals; Hilaire and Gilbert close behind; Burridge, Cannon, Hinshelwood and Swindlehurst ready to test themselves against the best. It was mouth watering.

The Friday night finale with Burnley surpassed every dream. As theatre, it had it all, what a crowd, what a sea of emotion, with 52,000 including a couple of thousand Rokerites to cheer for Burnley.

It's a Selhurst scene from a bygone age. You can't imagine the like again. Somebody says 1979, you say: "Ah, Burnley." But I say: "Ah, Bristol Rovers."

Easter Saturday 1979 and Palace were at Eastville. Rovers were eighth bottom, casting nervous glances behind them. Palace were third, a point behind Stoke and two behind Brighton. Sunderland were level with us, while West Ham were five behind but with two games in hand.

Palace travelled to Bristol on the back of two disappointing draws and a rare away defeat at Newcastle. Rovers had the boost of having beaten us at Selhurst during our traditional Yuletide dip in form. We were in need of a good Easter.

The weather was phenomenal. I sweated and squirmed on the plastic covered seat of my cousin's van all the way down the M4. At the services I was aware of arch-rival Seagull fans heading for Cardiff.

The sun turned Dave's old van into a tin oven. Two well done south London steaks finally arrived in sun drenched Bristol. We parked close to the ground and sauntered into the away end. Eastville didn't look so clever. It couldn't make up its mind whether it was a football ground or a greyhound stadium.

Palace took the field in blinding sunlight to a strangely muted welcome from the travelling throng. It was too hot to get excited and the team appeared to feel the same.

The heat dulled the brain, inducing torpor. Alcoholic heads stewed to oblivion, pink flesh sizzled like morning bacon spitting fat.

"No Hilaire." As the teams were announced I mimed along to the PA: Burridge, Hinshelwood, Sansom, Kember, Cannon, Gilbert, Nicholas, Murphy, Swindlehurst, Sealy, Walsh, sub: Fenwick. Palace were defending the goal in front of us and most of the first half action centred around Burridge's area. Bristol seemed sharper, quicker to react and Steve White spurned a couple of early chances. By contrast Palace couldn't seem to get their passing game going.

Burridge was doing a lot of shouting and Sealy a lot of running but that was about it. We gave the ball away with unusual frequency. Basking on the concrete steps, we barely managed a decent chorus of *Eagles* all half. Suddenly excitement. A car on the flyover practically above the left side of our end jettisoned some builders rubble in the general direction of our dozing left flank. Such a quaint West Country custom.

Half time and goalless. I wished I'd brought a sunhat and sunglasses. I sipped and wished, wished and sipped. Suddenly, even more excitement. Two locals, doubtless bored, announced their true affiliation from within our midst. Thump, thump, fizz and plod led the miscreants away. A mini outbreak of *We Are Palace,* then back to silence. Baking, morose, silence.

Fenwick replaced Swindlehurst which meant reorganising the rampant attacking machine that wasn't Palace. Rovers looked content with a draw. The seagulls wheeled off, seeking something more interesting elsewhere. I gazed around the stadium, taking in the detail and comparing it to my television-shaped impressions of the place. God it was hot.

The concrete was hot, everything was hot. Everyone was sitting down, squinting through the glare at a game designed for mud, rain and cold.

Palace were keeping their shape, Rovers were keeping their shape and we were keeping ours, motionless, huddled, sweat drippingly quiet.

We followed the mirage of blue and white quarters jousting white with red and blue diagonal sash on the green baize yonder.

A figure pulled himself unsteadily to his feet and swayed momentarily. "Come on you bastards, you want 'em to go up," he beerily implored. The man deserved a medal. "Get up you f*****s and sing for the Palace!" What a motivator, a leader of men, a drinker of ale. But it worked. It bloody worked. To a person, the silent thousand and a bit rose and sang.

Eagles, ad infinitum drifted up and across the pitch. Incredibly the players seemed to respond, as though they actually thought the game could be won. Palace were more urgent now, pressing. We won a throw. Sansom delivered the ball long and swift to Ian Walsh on the edge of the box.

He shielded cleverly, then spun across his marker to drill the ball low into the corner past Martin Thomas's outstretched left hand. Delirium. Last minute, last gasp, at the death we'd won it. *Going up, going up, going up* ... voices cracked hoarsely as vocal chords protested after such a long lay off.

Back in the boiling van I smiled at Dave's sunburned features, pink and comical. I would have laughed at anything, so great was the elation and relief.

The radio crackled the news that Brighton had won 3-1 at Ninian Park. Damn! How did Brighton score so freely?

Still, we'd scraped two points as well and made ground over the others. Promotion beckoned ever stronger.

Well done that man who raised the rallying cry. Your deed goes unrecorded in the match facts and league table but you won us that game as much as Walsh's right boot.

You say ah Burnley, I say "ah, Bristol Rovers."

NO GOING BACK

the secret diary of a Palace fan aged 30 and three quarters

From appendicitis to Arsenal ... Paris based Palace fan Kester Lovelace charts his support for the Eagles spanning more than 20 years.

April 1970. This is where it all begins ... we move house nearer to Selhurst Park. Farewell Coulsdon, hello Purley.

MAY 1970. A little known government law stipulates that youngsters under eight years must support their local professional league team. I pledge a lifetime allegiance to Palace. Chelsea win the F.A. Cup, the law is suddenly and universally ignored and subsequently abolished. Too late for me though. There's no going back. Man City beat Sheffield Wednesday to keep us in the first division. City become my second favourite team.

SEPTEMBER 1970. Three days before my eighth birthday, my first match. Crikey, John Jackson looks just like my dad (he's not though). Palace crush Forest 2-0 (difficult to believe these days).

A week later on my first day of a new primary school, the bully takes me aside immediately and asks what team I support. On the verge of tears (the first time I cry over Palace), I croak my reply. A hearty slap on the back reveals that I said the right thing. There really is no going back now.

SEPTEMBER 1971. Returning home after the 3-1 defeat by Man United, my mum has stuck painful reminders on the gate and front door such as "We hate Law", "Down with Charlton" etc. Funny way of showing sympathy. It gets worse. I am inconsolable when Steve Kember is transferred to Chelsea.

DECEMBER 1971. I dream of Palace beating someone 5-1; the next evening I am allowed to watch *Match of the Day*, a rare treat. An even rarer treat, Palace are on. And guess what? They beat Sheff Utd 5-1.

Yogi Hughes' son joins our school. I don't know what I'll say to him ... probably something like: "Good goals your dad scored."

MAY 1973. I'm hospitalised for three weeks. I receive a surprise telegram from "the players and staff of CPFC". Apparently my grandmother, who used to work with Malcolm Allison's mother, wrote to Big Mal saying Palace's greatest fan was in hospital ... well, I'm ten, have seen eight matches and haven't even stood on the Holmesdale yet. Nevertheless, I make a miraculous recovery ... unlike the team whose failure to win at Norwich means the end of division one. Shame at school, tears as well, but there's no going back now.

APRIL 1974. My debut on the Holmesdale. I can't see sweet F.A., but fortunately it ends 0-0. Another relegation, more shame. I start secondary school in September, what am I going to tell them? Too late to change though.

SEPTEMBER 1974. First in a long line of famous victories over Swindon, 6-2, the day before my birthday. The class bully is a Palace fan, again.

MARCH 1975. Wimbledon replace City as my second team after I see them lose narrowly to horrible Leeds at Selhurst Park in the Cup. My first victory over Brighton, 3-0, and goals by Taylor, Swindlehurst and Johnson.

SEPTEMBER 1975. My first defeat against Brighton, 1-0.

WINTER/SPRING 1976. The Cup run. I can hold my head up at school at last. I hate Southampton and David Peach. Lose in the semi, miss out on promotion, sell Peter Taylor, swap David Kemp for George Graham. Head down again.

JANUARY 1977. My mum's first ever match. We see Palace nearly beat Liverpool in the Cup. Kenny Sansom marks Kevin Keegan out of the game. I predict he will play for England (oh, and Keegan will probably play for them too).

APRIL 1977. Statutory victory over Swindon, only 5-0 this time. Start watching the Youth Team, the "team of the late 70s" or what?

MAY 1977. I creep downstairs to glimpse the result on Sportsnight. Wrexham 2 (oh no), Palace 4 (yeeesssssssss!). Joy and rapture.

Two nights later on Friday, 14,000 of us turn up to witness the clinching of the F.A. Youth Cup. The next afternoon, 4,000 of us are back to see most of the first team play in the reserves against Hereford.

Rachid Harkouk misses a penalty and his hat-trick because, like the rest of us, he was trying to listen to a scoreflash from Wrexham v Mansfield.

Orgasmic rapture, cartwheels on the pitch, we're promoted. I chuck my old claret and blue bobble hat into the directors' box, saying goodbye to childhood. Kenny catches it, the pride, the pride.

1977-78. Can no longer count the number of Palace matches I've seen on two hands, so I start writing a list. I could've been a train spotter I suppose, but there's no going back.

Adolescent anger; George Best may have wrecked Ian Evans' career with a dubious tackle, but I am more incensed at David Peach hacking down Rachid. My "bring back Ricky Heppolette" cries get a laugh or two on the Holmesdale, after inept displays all season by Chatterton and Perrin.

SEPTEMBER 1978. Two days after my 16th birthday, I tot up 50 Palace matches. They rise to the occasion with a frustrating 1-1 home draw with Sunderland.

DECEMBER 1978. A friend's uncle has been taking us to matches recently. After Mike Elwiss's superb strike against Leicester, he screams out adoringly "Elwiss the Pelvis!" ... I think I'll go on my own from now on.

GPO GREETINGS TELEGRAM

46 GTG 12.41 CROYDON T 22 GREETING =

KESTER LOVELACE WARD CW2 MAYDAY HOSPITAL THORNTONHEATH =

: GOOD WISHES GET WELL SOON = FROM

PLAYERS AND STAFF OF CRYSTAL PALACE FOOTBALL CLUB +

· CW2 TS 634

Above: a get well telegram from the club. I wrote a belated "thank you" letter saying something like: "My mum and gran have been nagging me to write ..." When my gran found out she made me write again to apologise for my stupid remark!

JANUARY 1979. Stuff first division Bristol City, 3-0, and they have Ritchie and Norman Hunter sent off. But why not Gerry Gow, one of the dirtiest players I've ever seen ...

APRIL 1979. 100th Palace goal (that I've seen), Jerry Murphy v Notts County. Mike Elwiss hasn't played since December.

MAY 11, 1979. Last lesson at school, packing my bag discreetly under the desk, ready to rush home, gulp down some tea and zoom off to Selhurst Park for "the match". Just my luck, the teacher gives us a class detention: it's probably a Chelsea fan who is to blame. Just as panic is creeping in and things look critical, time wise, the teacher caves in and lets us go. The teacher's name is Mr Morton, he'll probably become a football referee.

Remember the 190 bus? At 5.30 it is packed with red and blue scarves all the way from Old Coulsdon.

The sun sets slowly over the Holmesdale and no-one can breathe (in either sense) from 6pm until ten minutes from time when Vince crosses and Walsh rises. What about that back pass from Billy Gilbert? I couldn't see the goal let alone Burridge. We've blown it ... but no, Burridge appears, ball at his feet. We're champions.

SEPTEMBER 1979. Jim Cannon's goal v Ipswich. Still the best ever. Top of the league.

DECEMBER 1979. Match 99, 0-3 at Brighton ... match 100, 1-2 at home to Middlesbrough. But there's no going back.

AUGUST 1980. Kenny leaves (too cynical to cry this time), Burridge leaves, Hilaire-ious sending off, things still going wrong and Elwiss still hasn't recovered.

SEPTEMBER 1980. I forsake Palace away at Coventry for Surrey in the Gilette Cup Final at Lord's.

Not only do Surrey get creamed, but Clive Allen has "that goal" disallowed. Things are getting embarrassing. Murphy and Hoddle sent off in the League Cup looking more like two ballet dancers doing a pas de deux. Hysterical.

1981. Too painful for words. Relegation, again. I should be revising for my A-levels. Elation of 1979 turns to feelings of betrayal and cynicism. I'm leaving the south and going to study in Manchester. Is there any going back?

1981-85. I enter the wilderness years. I see 27 games and get 21 goals. United, not City, become my second team and average crowds of 50,000 at Old Trafford warm my soul when I should be watching Langley and Lovell. Elwiss still not fit but worse is that Kevin Mabbutt is struck by the same curse. Will we ever score goals again?

FEBRUARY 1985. The nadir, the slough of despond, a bummer. On a rare trip south I take in a home match, 0-5 v Wimbledon. I'm thinking of moving to France.

DECEMBER 1985. Nine months later. My 150th match and a Boxing Day present, 1-3 at home to Wimbledon. I'm definitely off to France for a very, very long time.

SEPTEMBER – DECEMBER 1986. I've always liked Stevie Coppell. Things begin to look good from over here in Paris ... 6-0 at Birmingham, the goals going in. I'm back at Christmas and we beat Brighton ... who is this team we call the Palace?

OCTOBER 1987. Another short trip over to see Wright 'n' Bright sink Swindon of course. These two look useful, helping to counter the loss of Elwiss. I start saving for the play-offs.

MAY 1988. Down (well, not promoted anyway) and out in Paris as Millwall cock it up for us. Decide to end my exile, come back and help the lads get back into division one.

OCTOBER 1988. Commutin' from Tootin', 100th match from the Holmesdale and Swindon lose ... again.

MAY 1989. I finally see Mark 'n' Ian score and miss in the penalty farce v Brighton. Keeping promotion alive at Maine Road, what an atmosphere. And my 250th Palace goal v Birmingham, so near to promotion. Not to worry, Wright 'n' Bright sink "you know who" from Wiltshire and ten years on, we beat another Lancashire club beginning with "B" to get back where we belong. Mission completed, I return where I belong, to Paris.

1989-93. Only seven matches in four seasons but still the passion remains.

SEPTEMBER 1989. I phone my ex-pat pal in Paris (a Swindon supporter) to see if he knows the Liverpool-Palace result. He has a strange sense of humour. He says we lost 9-0.

APRIL 1990. I listen to the quarter-final v Cambridge on a crackling walkman in west France while playing tennis. I'm convinced we will draw Liverpool in the semi.

I lost at tennis as well. I manage to find a friend with cable TV who agrees to let her flat out to me and Monsieur Swindon for a raucous afternoon. The most unbelievable thing is not Pardew netting the winner, but the fact that my friend cheered with me all the way. My Palace scarf goes with me everywhere including on stage when I perform Nigel in *The Secret Diary of Adrian Mole* to baffled French schools' audiences.

MAY 1990. No chance of tickets for exiles like me. But I come over anyway for the atmopshere of Cup Final day in a darkened living room.

I fly over on Saturday and back on Sunday only to discover that French TV have shown "le Cup Final" live for the first time ever.

Oh well, I'll be able to watch the replay. Holed up in a hotel room on tour in Rheims with my tennis partner (a lapsed Palace fan). We go to drown our sorrows in a bar and bump into another Palace fan. He gets drunk first. My first article published in *Eagle Eye*, a vitriolic attack on David Peach.

DECEMBER 1990. Home at Christmas and another first, my name is called out on the tannoy, during the 1-0 win over Liverpool.

MAY 1991. Just as I predicted our downfall following the departures of Venables, Sansom and Burridge in 1980, I have similar bad vibes when we are not allowed into the UEFA Cup at the end of the season. Where will the club go? Will Ian Wright leave? Oh, Palace!

1991-92. My worst season as a spectator. One match, one goal (an own goal).

1992-93. It's hard to celebrate the Liverpool and Chelsea wins at such a distance on my own. It's easier to stomach the Hartlepool and Arsenal disappointments in relative anonymity. But it's the 0-4 v Wimbledon that does it for me.

I wouldn't do a lap of honour after the Ipswich game chaps. Mathematically I've worked it out, we might need a point at Highbury. The worst comes to the worst. I don't believe it though, hearing the results on a crackling World Service at 6.15pm French time. I thought there was no going back.

MAY 1993. And even worse still, Swindon take our place.

Hmmm. Swindon: they borrow our chaplain, the Rev Nigel Sands, from time to time, they even bought David Peach once, but it seems they have the last word.

However, I'm not sorry I'm not coming back to England. Not for Alan Smith, not for Ricky Heppolette, not for Mike Elwiss, not for no-one.

There really is no going back.

Games to really remember

Maybe I'm getting old and cynical but 1991-92 was a season without any "Greatest games" that I will look back on.

But I can nevertheless recall fondly some epics from a bygone era.

Let's not forget when looking back with rose coloured glasses (to match the tank top and loon pants) that the team in those days was pretty useless and if it wasn't for the superb Jacko we would have been relegated by Christmas 1969.

Indeed, I remember one newspaper article saying that the Palace defence was making progress and that the opposition was now being forced to shoot from outside the goal area!

Yes, there were rather a lot of Crystal Palace 0 Coventry 3 (or West Brom, or Newcastle) type results but there was also the 5-1 over Sheffield United and an epic 2-2 with Arseanl in an evening game after being 0-2 down before we'd got off the train. And we scored a penalty and Bob Wilson played a blinder, can you believe it?

For me though, the real epics were the F.A. Cup fourth round replay against Spurs when after a goalless draw at White Hart Lane, with Jimmy Greaves putting the ball over the bar from an inch, there was a really high adrenaline evening with Palace going through thanks to a Gerry Queen header from a free kick.

The *That's the Way* played after each win in those days sounded extra special.

I think, in fact, that brought about the end of the Greaves era at Spurs and Bill Nicholson had a big clearout right after – pity ITV don't do the same.

The other epic was the final game of the season when, although we were finishing before Sunderland and Sheffield Wednesday, everybody knew we had to beat Manchester City to have any chance.

Once again an intensely atmospheric evening game ensued. Roger Hoy scored in a scramble after 25 minutes and from then on it was desperate defending all the way to the final whistle with the crowd screaming for full time from the moment they came out for the second half!

John Jackson made three impossible saves including diving up to his left to catch a ball already past him, amazing stuff.

Some people could not watch when City had the ball.

When the dust settled both Sheffield Wednesday and Sunderland only managed two points from their last games and Palace survived with 27 points to suffer another three seasons.

Keith Marriage

NAN

WHO is responsible for Palace's success of the last few seasons? Steve Coppell most of you say. Some might even give Ron Noades a share of the credit, not to mention Ian Wright, Mark Bright, Geoff Thomas or Andy Gray.

Worthy though their efforts have been they all fade into insignificance when compared to my dear old Nan.

Nan had never been to Selhurst Park, in fact she'd never seen a football match during her long life.

This woman born in an Oxfordshire village seven years before Palace were founded had no reason to be interested in the fortunes of the club even having lived in the area since the 1920s.

What sparked her influence was my continuing optimism through the early 1980s and her mild enquiry in August 1984, "Off to the Palace again?"

Its got to be better now Mullery's gone I told her and I told her to keep her fingers crossed. Nan crossed her fingers.

For the next seven seasons this old lady spent Saturday afternoons with the fingers of both hands crossed tightly – extremely awkward for a woman whose hobby was doing jigsaws while peeling potatoes was out of the question.

Under Nan's inflence Palace's results improved dramatically although there was the odd blip when her fingers slipped but any statistician would see that it worked more often than not.

Can anyone who was at Villa Park that Sunday afternoon deny that mysterious forces were at work?

Sadly, midweek games were different – the 9-0 debacle at Anfield was surely down to nan turning in at nine o'clock. The penalty outside the box incident happened, by my calculations, exactly at the moment she dozed off.

Nan has since passed on and the 1992-93 season kicked off without her influence though Simon Osborn's last minute goal suggests she's still around somewhere.

So those of you who are grandmothers take heed. No matter how great a manger Steve Coppell may be, he cannot stand alone against the forces of evil. Are there any double jointed volunteers out there?

Andy Gilbert.

Norwegian Eagles

What makes a Norwegian support Crystal Palace? Bjarne Johansen explains and recounts the sorry tale of "Don Rogers" and the Everton shirt

It was 1972 and because of some TV company arrangement nearly all live English matches came from the Midlands.

Stoke were televised quite a lot and built a following among my friends. The danger of this was local stump-nosed Mike Pejics performing ruthless tackles week-in, week-out.

As an individualist, I wasn't able to find a team to support, fed up with Wolves, Stoke, Aston Villa, Birmingham and Derby as I was.

In late December the cameras were at Selhurst Park and I witnessed a lively Palace beat Man United 5-0. At last I had a team as well.

My best friend was a Stoke supporter and had a grandpa who travelled a lot. From one of his journeys abroad he brought back a Stoke shirt for his grandson.

Realising that I would never own a Palace kit, I did some serious thinking. When my mother gave me a new white T-shirt the answer became obvious: make my own.

It was an outstanding idea which I knew wouldn't make my mother too happy.

I went upstairs and carefully painted one blue stripe and one claret stripe, topping it off with "C.P." in a circle on the right side of the chest. Satisfied with my creativity I rushed to the football pitch and insisted on being called Don Rogers. I wished I had a moustache.

Well into the first half and while "Don Rogers" was having a magnificent match, it started to rain and Mr Rogers realised that the colours on his shirt were far from water resistant. The result was the transformation from Crystal Palace star to psychedelic mutant football hippie.

Needless to say, my team mates found this very funny, my mother did not. She had no interest in my talk about the "authentic game" and I was suspended and my shirt re-coloured dark blue, very-Everton, but I was not persuaded to change teams.

In 1980, the first Norwegian Palace supporters club was founded. It lasted about three years and then died in perfect synchronised fashion with the Team of the 80s. It has now been replaced with a newer model.

The man responsible for this is Tor Øystein Vaaland. In 1969, this young man from Stavanger met a guy from Croydon who was a Palace supporter. The Croydoner introduced Vaaland to the dubious ways of Palace supporting.

Anyway, Mr Vaaland grew up, followed Palace and in 1991, as a radio journalist with access to both printing processes and the publishing package Word Perfect, he decided to start the Norwegian Friends of CPFC.

An important part of this great idea was a "news zine" where club members air their views, trade videos, pick up the latest news and be very rude to anyone who deserves it.

The idea of Norwegian supporters clubs for British teams is not a new one. The Norwegian branch of Man United supporters boasts 4,500 members and our Palace club has now grown to the fantastic size of about 40, and is still growing.

Our aim is to reach 100, which with a little understanding from relatives, friends and partners is possible.

Our main problem is arranging meetings because the members come from all over Norway, Sweden and Denmark.

It is hard to tell why these 40 people have decided to support Palace. But the Team of the 80s was an influence, as was the match which for us oldies ranks high as an answer to questions like "why Palace?"

The game was in December 1972 and was shown live on Norwegian television: Palace 5 Man United 0. That's where I came in.

But most of all, it is important for Norwegian Palace supporters to do it our own way.

I WANNA BE EJECTED

Trevor Edwards recalls a couple of unsavoury incidents while following Palace

Over the years, I have seen more than the odd bit of trouble particularly in the 70s. Although I have never been one for trouble, never thrown a punch and indeed in the mid-70s actually retired to the New Stand to be out of the way, I have been involved in two incidents.

The first was in February 1974. A tall, well-built lad of 12, I was a regular at home games sporting flared jeans and white imitation fur-lined jacket. I'd missed the last three matches because of an appendix operation.

My mates and I stood regularly at the front of the Holmesdale just to the right of the goal. Here we enjoyed ourselves annoying passing Bobbies by draping our home-knitted claret and blue scarves over the advertising boards only to be told to pull them back.

Anyway, half way through the first half against Huddersfield we went to join "the Holmesdale" where we sang our hearts out for the Glaziers. In those days certain bobbies used to stand "in the crowd" in order to prevent surges and other tomfoolery. One particular Bobby stood about ten steps in front of me watching the crowds and the game. I started to get bored and stuffed myself with chewing gum. It then occurred to me how I could show off and become one of "the lads". I started to screw up pieces of paper and flick them at this copper's helmet much to the delight of those around me.

I did this several times making the policeman, who became gradually angrier and angrier, turn round. Encouraged by the laughter around me, this only persuaded me to carry on. I didn't notice another copper coming up behind me. He pulled me out of the crowd (to the accompaniment of groaning from the others) and into the white police box that used to stand at the back of the Holmesdale.

I was crapping myself as a sergeant asked me for my name, date of birth and school, but funnily enough not my address. He told me to turn out my pockets and raised his eyebrows when he worked out my age. When I turned out an empty leather wallet he obviously thought he had caught a pickpocket.

Perhaps he was convinced by my innocent rendition that it had been used to keep my holiday money in last summer. I was then marched to the turnstiles. I pleaded that I couldn't climb over because I had recently had my stitches out but to no avail and had to endure the obstacle.

My parents were surprised to see me home early and were initially angry with the police but eventually decided that it was "good corrective treatment".

When I got to school on Monday word had got round and I was a hero – the first person in Sylvan High School to be thrown out of Palace. A hooligan at twelve and a quarter! Needless to say, I didn't go in the Holmesdale again but ventured into the New Stand enclosure where I had many a good day.

I used to stand near the group who sang *We're the New Stand, we're the New Stand, we're the New Stand Selhurst Park*, and would join in. They were the first to throw paper up in the air and even used to applaud Fenwick.

After Bristol Rovers in 1979 we arrived at Paddington and my mate Mark discovered he'd left his scarf on the train. We went back to retrieve it but couldn't find it so we rejoined our other friends. All this meant we became separated from the main body of Palace fans.

As we made our way along one of the tunnels to the tube a couple of blokes crossed back across my friends and started walking towards me.

The next minute, there was an almighty thud against my right ear and I remember turning around in a daze to see this bloke with my scarf in his hand staring at me from about 20 yards away. He must have been a complete nutter because he was foaming at the mouth!

We made our way to the platform where we caught up with the other fans. Word got round that I'd been "got at" by Spurs fans.

I was just desperate to get home, but the tube took ages to come and then to leave. I remember cries of "West Ham have just pulled in" and calls for volunteers to provide them with a reception committee. I remember the ring leaders stirring up real brain dead troopers with cries like "Come on Dave, you hate West Ham!"

You may feel that as a 15 year-old this experience would have a profound psychological effect on me and you'd be right. For years after I refused to go to potentially troublesome games and used to be in a state of near panic when coming out of games for fear of trouble. To this day I have never worn a scarf (although I do now wear a shirt).

The man who knew Palace were going to win

Palace 2 Wolves 1, February 1970. In those halcyon days I went to most home games and took my brother Howard as well. We were going through a lean spell (between September and April!) and had not won for ages. On this particular morning I woke up just knowing we were going to win, really knowing, even more than in the play-off game against Blackburn or Liverpool in the semi-final. I knew some sacrifice was required which took the form of forsaking the familiar faces in the Holmesdale to join the motley crew in the Whitehorse Lane End. After five minutes I wondered whether it was all worth it when John Sewell sliced the ball into his own net. I tore the programme in half and threw it on the floor – then picked it up again quickly so as not to lose the spell. The game then chugged along fairly evenly with Palace equalising through Trevor Dawkins. Then, after about 72 minutes, he scored again with an outrageous banana shot that left the goalie diving completely the wrong way. I don't recall any deflection (he probably stubbed his toe on shooting or something) but we didn't care it was a vital goal. A victory and two precious points towards our goal of avoiding the drop. There was dancing in the streets of Croydon after that.

I was originally going to muse on why the Glaziers couldn't beat any London clubs when, on winding the brain cell back, I remembered it was worse than that. It was actually all TV games. We used to roll up Holmesdale Road and if you could see the TV vans, deep down you knew you might as well go home there and then or another afternoon of torture would await. Luckily LWT tended to show only London derbies or we'd have been relegated even sooner. I can still hear Brian Moore signing off with: "We leave you then from Selhurst Park with the final score: Crystal Palace a token 1, the Opposition lots!"

Keith Marriage

Didn't we have a lovely time, the night we went to Lincoln

It was not often in the third division in the mid-70s that Palace fans were outnumbered, but Donny the Beastie Boy recalls a rearranged fixture at Lincoln where the odds were stacked against the travelling band

About 20 Palace fans went to the rearranged fixture with Lincoln after the original match had been abandoned because of a heavy snowfall. Ricky Heppolette scored his only goal in that game.

We met at Selhurst at about 2pm and set off on the one and only coach going to Lincoln. I hadn't been to the Saturday game but had heard that there was a lot of trouble before, during and after the match. I was travelling with two friends, Steve and Colin, and when we boarded the coach we found most of the usual lads on it. The journey was very boring – this was long before toilets, videos and other modern conveniences and we consoled ourselves by smoking and drinking.

As we approached the outskirts of Lincoln a couple of police motorcycles pulled us over and two Darth Vader style coppers got on the coach. "Is that all you've brought?" asked one, while the other chipped in: "There was a lot of trouble here last time." One of the wags at the back answered: "That's why we're here!"

At that moment, I knew this trip was a mistake. The police informed us that they were going to escort us to the ground and a stop-off at a pub was out of the question. We were dropped off and made our way to the so called visitors' turnstile beside a canal. We'd lost about ten of our number who had tickets for the seats. Inside we found ourselves in a corner section with covered terrace to our right which was obviously the Lincoln end. To our left was uncovered terrace running the length of the pitch, not unlike the Gallstone Ground. There wasn't a programme seller or a refreshment hut so we were left to watch the Lincoln fans arrive. The uncovered side terrace filled quite quickly, populated with 12-16 year olds in rolled up jeans, Doctor Martens and those appalling football jumpers (red cardigans with two white stripes on either sleeve. Northerners liked them rather a lot I seem to remember). These brats welcomed us well travelled die hards with *You're Gonna Get Your f****** Head Kicked In*. Charming, I thought, but they looked harmless in a schoolkid sort of way.

About ten minutes before kick off the covered end began to fill as the pubs began to empty. The older fans looked a different proposition altogether. There is something disconcerting about grown men staring at you as if you've just landed from Venus. During the 70s Londoners seemed to have that effect on opposing fans. The teams came out and a stifled cry of *Eagles* came from the disinterested Palace fans, we were more concerned about how we were going to get out of Sincil Bank unscathed. The Lincoln fans were captivated by the ten Cockneys and looked at nothing else.

> **"There was nowhere to go. Thoughts of jumping the fence were met by howling youngsters who would readily have killed us if we were mad enough to attempt it."**

Palace looked quite good, but my thoughts were elsewhere. We moved *en masse* to the back of the terrace against the fence where the brats were housed. When I say fence, it was more like a scaffold pole at shoulder height offering little protection. The brats were baying and taunting. It was going to be one of those games. A policeman, sensing there might be trouble, came and stood among us which made us feel a little better. Meanwhile Palace scored through Swindlehurst and the chants of *We Hate Cockneys* echoed around the ground.

More disturbing was the apparent movement of people from the covered end towards us. After about ten minutes it was quite obvious that about 20 rather big Lincoln fans had surrounded us not more than ten yards away. The policeman seemed not to notice. Palace then did what they always do in these situations, they scored. "Oh s**t," was chorused by one-and-all. At last the inept policeman noticed something was wrong. He radioed to his control centre a message I will always remember: "It's getting a little cold up here, Sarge." As he spoke, this Neanderthal man standing just below us turned and threw a cup of boiling hot tea over three of us, before wading in like an out of control windmill. Suffice to say an almighty punch-up ensued, about 30 Lincoln versus ten Palace. There was nowhere to go. Thoughts of jumping the fence were met by howling youngsters who would readily have killed us if we were mad enough to attempt it. A Palace fan informed Steve and I that "it's alright, I'm bladed up", which did little to allay my extreme anxiety, especially as the policemna had disappeared into thin air.

Luckily he was returning up the terrace with reinforcements. We were getting a good old fashioned hiding. The police restored order and surrounded us. I can't remember if half time had been and gone, but Lincoln had pulled one back during the melee. No arrests were made and the Lincoln thugs just stood in front slagging us off. They got another goal and the whole ground went mad.

At least a point would do. No such luck, Lincoln got a winner and you'd have thought they'd won the F.A. Cup the way their fans reacted. By now the police had had enough and frog marched us out of the ground, passing the thugs on the way. "You're going in the canal, Cockney," was their good-natured farewell. A couple still wanted to remonstrate with Neanderthal man but didn't take much persuading to return to reality. We got back on the coach with everyone seemingly okay. The fans in the seats had been moved out as well so with a police escort we made a fast drive out of Lincoln. The talk on the coach was centred on the great escape. How had we got out of there virtually unscathed? We agreed we would never go to Lincoln again.

But I would go to Lincoln again, although I would definitely get a seat. We got back to Selhurst at about 2.30am after one of those traumatic nights when only Palace fans would venture north with hope in their hearts.

Why do we do it?

Allsport

Special K

Kenny Sansom was the player of all the talents. Steve Crisp recalls a real football genius

Losing Ian Wright was a grievous blow to Palace, but in my opinion it was nothing to the loss of Kenny Sansom. Kenny was never able to taunt us by scoring against us because he was in the wrong division, he was a defender and he was a defender at Arsenal. When Ian left he hurt us and we were eventually dragged down. When Kenny left, the cornerstone of the Team of the 80s went with him. All but a couple of our players went and Palace collapsed, never able to recover. I know we got promoted again but I do not feel that we got the waking nightmare that was the early 80s out of our system.

Kenny was not just a very good player, he was special. To me he could have been one of the best players ever seen in England, but unfortunately it was Arsenal that got him.

I saw Kenny's first home game, but I cannot remember it. I can remember coming out of Selhurst after an evening match in the third division and ranting onto my step dad and Brian (who used to give us a lift) about how Phil Holder was my favourite player. On asking them who they claimed as their favourite player, they both said Kenny Sansom. From then on I kept an eye out for this chubby 17 year old with short hair.

The second climb from the third to the first was the happiest times for Palace fans and standing as I did, right in front of the Arthur Wait on the half way line, one of the most exciting sights was Kenny streaking down the left to the opposition by-line.

He was not just an outstanding left back, he was a talented winger and a good midfielder. I can remember Dave Sexton talking about him after an England Under-21 match and saying that you could stick him in goal and he would have a good game. In a way he epitomised all that was good about the Team of the 80s. He was young, supremely talented and he was going to the top of the first division.

At the time it was between Kenny and Derek Statham of West Brom as to who was going to be the England left back of the future.

There was never any doubt in my mind and when he came on against Wales I knew he was going to be there for years. By the time he'd made the England place his own, however, he'd come under the influence of Don Howe and instead of terrorising opposition defenders he just stopped their attackers.

It was well known that Kenny had one major problem and that was gambling which eventually forced him to leave Palace. He even bought his own shop. How many bookmakers do you know that lose money ? It was a tragedy for us that Kenny was one of them. He needed money and Arsenal could give it to him with a fat signing on fee and higher wages than Bloye was prepared to offer.

It was football's tragedy that it was Arsenal that came in for him. Who knows, Liverpool at that time might have made him into a football legend; Arsenal made him into a boring left back. They had bought a defender and Howe knew that defenders did not pass the half way line.

I hate Arsenal for many reasons but destroying Kenny is in the top three. Kenny was a good left back for Arsenal, he could snuff out the best wingers in the country but it did not occur to the negative north Londoners that his talent comes but rarely. He was and should have been so much more.

Neil Everitt

EUROPEAN TOUR

Steve Carleton, Stanley Mann and David Hynes look back upon their participation on Palace's overseas jaunts in the 70s and 80s.

Calais, 1982, is the stuff of legend. The *Sun* carried a back page story of an English hooligan incident in which Palace fans tied the home goalkeeper to the goal post with a Union Jack.

This story is wildly exaggerated says Steve Carleton: "He wasn't tied to a post, someone just dragged the flag in front of him. We played Gravelines (just outside Calais) at a place called St Phillipe fort on the Wednesday and there was about eight of us over there. We won quite easily, then we went to Calais. We stayed three days and got pretty bored. On the Saturday we realised there was something strange. The Palace fans had divided up, so south Croydon was in one bar, Addington in another, Norwood in another, all told there were about 150 there.

"The thing was that we didn't play Calais in Calais. They had a perfect ground two miles east of the town, but we had to catch a bus to Guines. We only knew this becasue I'd lived in France so I was able to speak the language.

"We turned up at midday with no police around. Guines were playing Calais' second side. Then Palace played Calais. We won 2-0 and Kevin Mabbutt and Jim Cannon scored. At the end a few Palace kids next to a fence started throwing stuff at the French fans. After the game it got quite serious because some of the French got quite annoyed and came across. All I remember is running across, dipping under a barrier and getting kicked in the chin. Someone else got hit by a bottle, another by an iron bar and another by a baseball bat. I met a guy from Crawley who was hit by a bottle and was stitched up by the Palace physiotherapist.

"We eventually got a lift back on the team coach and were dropped back at Calais. But if the game had been held in Calais everything would have been fine. On a lighter note, we heard one person completed the journey across the channel three times because he dropped off to sleep on the ferry!"

Steve was already a hardened traveller and took the role of unofficial fans' organiser for several of Palace's European jaunts. The first tour game he went to was an Interail trip to Sweden in 1974 when we got relegated to division three.

"We turned up at Helsingborg after a 30-hour journey and slept in customs," he says. "Palace played Helsingborg the following day. Then we went to Lyndkoping and stayed in a tent in the middle of a car park. Everyone else had campers. We beat IF Saab, 2-1 and Mark Lindsay was in the team. The Swedish girls had never seen a black man. Malcolm Allison was manager and he told us we'd sold Derek Possee, we were the first fans to hear about it. In the final game we played Norkkoping, which is south of Stockholm, and drew 2-2. Paddy Mulligan got sent off and after the match we weren't allowed into a pub in Stockholm, not because we had Palace scarves but because our hair was too long.

Stanley Mann's first tour was to Holland and Germany in 1976. "Steve organised it. We decided not to get an Interail and opted for Trans-Alpino because it was based just around Holland. We travelled by train to Arnhem with a straight return ticket so when we were travelling elsewhere we made out we were going back to the boat and had got the wrong train by mistake.

It was the Summer of '76 which was really hot. We all met in Scamps disco in Croydon which had the cheapest beer. In most places it was about 30p a pint but in Scamps you could get it for 25p and they used to have strippers as well, but best of all it was lovely and cool in there. Then we moved on to the Hole in the Wall in the Strand but all the city types got a bit fed up with us because we had all our bags with us. We got on the boat train. And as we approached Harwich Steve, who always manages to fall over, tripped on a bag and cut his head open. He looked a bit like Terry Butcher in Sweden.

Steve adds: "I then went into the next carriage along and did the same thing again!" The others said he'd better get it stitched up but he realised that would mean missing the ferry and the first game and so they all got on the ferry!

"We headed for Arnhem where Palace were going to be based," says Stanley. "At the time we didn't have much money and the pound was very weak, so it didn't go very far. We thought we'd go there and try to get a lift to the German game at Aachen. When we arrived, the Dutch started panicking because they thought we were the team and we'd arrived early. When the team arrived we weren't there to hero worship them so much as ponce a lift to Germany.

"When the team got off the coach they all had suits and ties except Phil Holder. He was an amazing sight in shorts and had a beer gut concealed by a Worthington E T-shirt. He saw us and said "Oh look it's the quality street gang," and brought our new signing Mark Nightingale from Norwich over to meet us. "We hadn't bothered about accommodation and slept rough in a big sports centre.

"Barcelona, who'd just signed Johan Cruyff, were due to come for pre-season training a week later. There were two other teams, Sparta Rotterdam and a team from Guyana. We borrowed one of their footballs for a kick about."

Palace lost 3-2 to Alemania Aachen. "We hoped we might get in for nothing, but games in Germany were about two or three times as much as we were used to paying in England. Anyway this guy came out who spoke very good English and, as far as I could make out he owned the club and said 'come in and sit with us'.

"The stadium was terraced all round with covering on one side and cushions to sit on in the equivalent of the directors box. Anyway, we were making a lot of noise and acting silly shouting things like 'Hitler' and spending too much money at the bar and the guy's wife came in and sat down. She had her hair done up in a bun like Emily Bishop used to have in Coronation Street. Simon Wisdom, known to everyone as "Wiz", jumped up and was yelling and waving the Union Jack. I think this guy was beginning to regret bringing us in

Down and out in Germany

Geoff Haywood recalls the Germany tour of 1976

After originally planning to make it a biking holiday, Neil Everitt and I went by train. The first game was on a Saturday against the German side Alemania Aachen. It had originally due to be played in the evening but kicked off in the afternoon but fortunately a message had been left for us at Aachen station.

It was a historic occasion marking Terry Venables' first match as manager although the game was totally forgettable. We lost 3-2 with Aachen's winner coming three minutes form time after Nick Chatterton had equalised seven minutes earlier. David Kemp had given us the lead after only two minutes. For our sins we all had our photo taken with Venables after the match. The after match celebration in the supporters' club bar went on for a few hours and we ended up sleeping on waste land back over the border in Holland as we were too late/tired/pissed to find anywhere to stay.

That was the German leg of the tour over. The next day we travelled to Arnhem which was near to where the team were staying. We met up with the other six Palace fans there and there were a few Cardiff City fans there as well. I don't think Cardiff were playing, they were just on a boozy holiday. That afternoon we went to see Vitesse Arnhem play Feyenoord in a Dutch league game.

Palace's second match was against S.C. Heracles '74 who played in Almelo. This was played on the Wednesday evening which resulted in a 2-0 win to us. Kemp and Chatterton scored again. Heracles were a reasonable team but Palace were too good for them. On the Thursday we travelled to Leiden near the coast for a match on the Friday against a team who were in the Dutch amateur second division called Rijnsburgse Boys. Outside the ground, which was basically a pitch with a metal pole barrier, I can remember the hundreds of bicycle stands. As the buses to the ground were not very frequent it was the only way to travel. During the game, a couple of Palace fans wandered onto the pitch while the game was in progress. This led to Phil Holder shouting out to them "oi, get your f***ing mates off the pitch." Palace strolled to a 6-0 win (Swindlehurst, Walsh, P. Hinshelwood, Silkman 2, Holder) and a few of the Palace officials came over a chat in the club house.

On the Saturday, we took a trip to Deventer to see Go Ahead eagles play Schalke 04, which the German visitors won 4-1. Our final match was on the Sunday against W.V.V. Wageningen. This place was a fair walk from the local station and for some reason we got to the ground at about 11am for a 3pm kick off. The ground was nowhere near a bar and so an exciting time was had by all. In the most difficult of the four games, Palace won 2-1 through Evans and Swindlehurst. In hindsight I think the opposition was of quite a poor standard but nevertheless it was an enjoyable ten days or so, seeing Palace play in places they are not likely to go to again. It obviously did us some good as we were promoted at the end of the season. Having gone to Jersey the following year to see Palace play two games and then in 1980 to the last two of four games in Sweden, this 1976 was a sort of apprenticeship in european travel watching our beloved team.

and his wife turned round and said: 'Mein Herr, I do not like it,' and Wiz quick as flash said 'We don't like your f****** hair either, why did you get it done that way you stupid cow!'

"We got back to Arnhem and there was a guy called Harry Elsdon, who used to run the old supporters club, a real gentleman, and he gave us some money because he knew we were short although it didn't look like it the way we were drinking! Phil Holder said there was no need to sleep rough and told us to meet him at midnight.

"He took us into the sports hall. There were some rooms but they were ready for Barcelona so he said well we'd better not go in there. He put us up in his chalet which he was sharing with Jim Cannon, Peter Wall and Ian Evans. The other three were out and he just said 'bed down in here', and then he went out again. Anyway, about three in the morning the others came back and all I can remember is Jim Cannon's Scottish drawl going 'Och, the stench.'

"We told them Phil Holder said we could stay and they went off and found him and told him to clear us out 'cos we stank of beer and then we went and found these other rooms. Holder said whatever you do don't use the sheets but we ended up sleeping in rooms reserved for Barcelona. Early in the morning about five o'clock he knocked us up to tell us to get out and we climbed out of the window."

The next game was against Heracles and Palace won 2-0. "Nicky Chatterton was brilliant and all the Dutch thought he was Peter Taylor! We stayed in a youth hostel and met up with some Welsh blokes. Next we went to Leiden for a match which was being covered by ITV, who were doing a documentary on Vince Hilaire. They did two films, one on Palace and one on Vince. We were winning 6-0 and at the time Palace had never won away by more than six goals. Wiz was messing around with some Dutch kids and they ran on the pitch, not meaning anything, just as Dave Swindlehurst had a shot which was going in. It hit one of them and deflected wide. Phil Holder was going mad because it would have been Palace's biggest away victory.

Stanley says the most memorable games were the other matches, involving Go Ahead Deventer and Schalke 04. Go Ahead were one of the top sides in Holland at the time. Schalke won 4-1 and it was an amazing game of football. "I actually watched it as opposed to Palace when I just used to mess around. Terry Venables said to us after there was an amazing lack of throw ins. The other game was Vitesse Arnhem and Feyenoord and there were loads of Feyenoord fans."

At the time the Palace Rail Travellers club had started and we had some cards made up with "Crystal Palace Rail Travellers Club Piss Artists Society". We had the Welsh lads with us and we showed the piss artists cards to the Dutch at the ground and they let us through. A little later Venables turned up with his boys and said 'we're Crystal Palace' and the Dutch didn't believe them because we were already inside and they all had to play to get in!"

The following year Palace played a couple of matches in Jersey. "A guy called Jim Kirk went," says Stanley. "Four of us met at East Croydon in a pub called the Railway and he said he would meet us at the airport for the flight over. When we got there, Jim was looking a bit sheepish. He had his wife with him. We came over and said hello and he said to his her: "Oh, didn't I tell you, Palace are playing over there as well!" He was always pulling strokes, I don't think it went down too well.

Steve recalls: "We landed at Jersey and had to check in straight away to get to a game they'd added which was a 2-0 win over Jersey under-21s. We had to go a day earlier to get this match in."

The second match turned out to be a farce says Stan. "It ended up 9-3 and we missed two penalties, so we still didn't get to see the seven goal away victory."

Coming back there was some bad weather. "We ended up bunking on a plane with the Palace players, they had reservations and we didn't but we managed to get through and sat next to George Graham, who had a blinding hangover which, given his modern disciplinarian image, is quite funny. I thought he was a tasty player although he was past his best.

Later, in 1982 just after Alan Mullery had been appointed manager, Palace played in Germany. David Hynes takes up the story: "Only three people went, myslef and Steve and another chap we met over there. Steve worked for the airline and could get a free trip, while I was a fare paying passenger. He had all the details of the games and everything. I sat on the plane, five minutes before we were due to leave a stewardess came up and said: 'Are you Dave?' I said yes and she said: 'Steve can't make it, he'll see you tomorrow!' With that the the doors shut and the plane took off! I landed in Hamburg with this telex, never having been to Germany in my life and wondering how I was going to get to the hotel.

"When I was at the airport, German guys kept coming up to me asking if I was a British builder who'd come out to work. I managed to find the hotel and Steve arrived at 7am the following morning, which just as well because I didn't have a clue where any of the games were.

"We got to the ground for the first match and there was about ten Germans in a club house drinking and playing cards. We said: "Crystal Palace." And they told us the game had been moved about 200 kilometres away. Both Palace and the Croydon Advertiser knew about this in advance but had assumed no-one was going, so they didn't bother to tell anyone. The Germans didn't want to laugh, but they did. Such is their sense of humour.

We were playing three times in three days and so when we saw Palace secretary Alan Leather the next day we told him what we thought in no uncertain terms. He just seemed to me like he was in a daze. Nevertheless the Germans were pleased to see them. "In one game I kept getting people hassling me to swap my shirt. We played SV Larup and even the chairman of the club wanted my shirt to hang on the wall, he wanted to get the players to autograph it. But I had nothing else to wear, so I was understandably reluctant. The German fans really liked us. 'We've bought you a beer now you must come and sing with us, they kept saying. They were like German bikers."

Less welcoming was Ron Noades. "I was walking round the pitch after the match and, although I didn't know him, I said: 'Hello Ron.' And he just said: 'What the hell are you doing here?' and not in a nice way. I was really disappointed with that.

"Alan Mullery, I have to say, was a very agreeable man. Obviously we were not greatly enamoured with him but he was really good.

"We went to the party afterwards and there were some really nice flags with wooden bases. I thought I'm having those as a souvenir. And Alan Leather came up and was saying 'put them back', I thought he was going to give me the 'you're ambassadors for your country' line. Then the German chairman saw us and came up and was saying I could take them, so I just put them in my bag and smiled at Leather.

"Later in the evening, I was trying to impress these gorgeous Germans girls by telling them that I was a player. But this girl said: 'How come the others are in suits and you're in jeans and a Crystal Palace shirt?' I replied that I didn't have time to get changed. The standard of the opposition wasn't very high – the equivalent of our third division. In the second game Dave recalls, the main stand was a disused train carriage."

The Germans had some strange attitudes. "Two guys came up to us in England shirts, they loved everything English. One was saying "The greatest rock band ever is English, Barclay James Harvest! And I like your Kim Wilde too!"

When the team were leaving, Alan Mullery came up to us and said: 'How are you getting back to Hamburg lads?' We told him we were getting the train and he said: 'No problem, come on the coach with us. It was all really luxurious. I was sitting next to Steve Galliers, who was nicknamed 'inch high private eye' by the others, and opposite Henry Hughton and Kevin Mabbutt.

Mullery got on and the whole team were going 'Al, Al where's the beers? And he got off and got them.' In the first game of the season, his first match, I remember reading his manager's notes which said the team has been ill disciplined but they now wear suits and 'call me boss'. I burst out laughing."

Palace in St Vincent, Italy 1990

Palace set out for the real European Cup, the Pier Cesare Baretti Memorial Tournament, a four-way Makita-esque competition featuring Sampdoria (Mikhailichenko, Mancini, Vialli), Fiorentina (Lacatus, Dunga), Torino (Martin Vazquez, Muller) and of course Palace (Barber, Pardew, Hedman).

Visions of a multi-storey, San Siro stadium soon disappeared. We were to play in a sub-non-league ground compensated for by the fantastic Italian Alps.

In the first match we met Fiorentina while across the Valley in Aosta the local favourites Torino faced Sampdoria.The coach arrived early on Wednesday and I awoke to the south London vernacular infiltrating the campsite which until then had been filled with a combination of middle aged, sun stained flab and youthful enthusiasts from Fiorentina and Torino.

Once the red and blue hordes (50 of them) had tracked down accommodation, an ant infested campsite for some, the back seat of the coach for others and hotels for the wealthy, we settled down to breakfast in the bar.

The Carabinieri waddled around like John Wayne. But a few hours of our friendly demeanour persuaded them to drop their guard. As another £2 lager sank bellywards we noticed two poseur Italians strolling along the road. Slick hair, £100 shades, fashionable shorts. Only these two style gurus were in fact Gary O'Reilly and Jeff Hopkins. Jolly friendly they were too. The rest shufled past not knowing how to take us. Fiorentina's followers nervously introduced themselves and were submerged with offers of ski-hats, shirts and scarves. If you ever wondered where multi-coloured swap shop went here was the answer. Matches were set up and Plaace drew 9-9 with Italy.

The stand was draped in Palace flags but the match was nothing to write home about until we took the lead through O'Reilly. Then Lacatus, golden boy of Romanian football, dived over Nigel's arm. One-all from the spot kick and a defensive mix-up after a Thomas miscue sent Palace to defeat.

It was a poor performance and we drowned our sorrows with beers and spaghetti al pomodori while Torino took Sampdoria to the cleaners. There was a distance between players and fans. The thin line between bowling up and saying: "Hello Steve, I think you saved our souls and what about this season's tactics, I've got this great idea for a free-kick," was too much to cross. The next day it was the Matterhorn for some, more beer for others and an audience at a Palace training session.

We completed our footballing defeat of the Italian fans, 6-4 under the gaze of assistant manager Ian Branfoot, Spike the kit man and some snow-haired, white shoed bloke called Ron something.

Much beer was supped in our case with Italian fans – a strange lot, wearing Union Jack T-shirts with "ICF" on them, they declared their love of Liverpool because of their rabid rivalry with Juventus who they called "merde" the Italian word for Brighton.

They sang a song about the size of Dunga's manhood to the tune of the *Can Can* and asked if they could come to Palace v Liverpool to fight. But they were very friendly. It didn't make sense. They were equally non-plussed when we told them that we didn't rate violence. We exchanged scrawled notes of songs and said ciao setting of for the third-place play-off with Sampdoria.The Fiorentina fans watched from the road overlooking the ground singing *Eagles Eagles* and *La Viola* alternately.

On one memorable occasion the Palace fans gave a perfect rendition of *Chi No Salta, Doria?* Which roughly translated means if you're not jumping you must be Sampdoria. The faces of the opponents at this English cheek were changed by the conga performed for their benefit and happily mixed with us at half-time although few of us had anything left to swap.

After another uninspiring first half in which Palace fell behind, the second period was a great improvement. Glynn "Anne Robinson haircut" Hodges scored a cracking goal and it went to penalties. Barber, Wright and Gray all scored before Thomas relived his Anfield nightmare. But Suckling saved one and Doria missed anohter. It was all down to Rudi Hedman. What's Italian for delirious? Most of the contingent set off for home. I was left to make my own way.

Laurie Dahl

CHAPTER ON VERSE

A selection of Palace poems

Exit at Leicester

The fourth of January, ninety-two
The FA Cup third round
Where Palace got a tricky draw
To Leicester we were bound

Stevie Coppell's Red n Blue Army
Before the game we sang
It sounded so impressive
As right round the ground it rang

We nearly had the lead
It would hvae been so fine
Two minutes gone when Marco's shot
Was cleared right off the line

It then went down the other end
The back four screamed "offside"
So Tommy Wright went racing clear
But screwed his shot just wide

With almost half an hour gone
Big Eric lost his head
The bastard ref saw elbowing
The card he showed was red

So we were lucky at half-time
To go in at nought-nought
Though Leicester had the extra man
The ball was in their court

Now Palace in the second half
Made no attempt to score
'Twas obvious that Stevie tried
To hold on for a draw

But as we all know Leicester scored
With almost the last kick
To come so close and lose it all
It really makes you sick

Arron Trevor

Perry

Perry Suckling we were told
England class, not very old
A future star to grace our game
Our goals against he was to tame

We all thought at last a chance
To lead division two a dance
And with excitement and a notion
We at last could gain promotion
To division one where we belong
And prove those doubting critics wrong

Perry started in our team
To us a goalkeeper supreme
With lightning saves and quick reaction
A joy to see the man in action
Until that fateful day did come
When Perry kicked, his thigh was numb
An injury robbed us of
The man we all thought so much of

About ten games had then passed by
But the man to make the Eagles fly
Was struggling to regain his place
To get the team back in the race
To gain the pace with the elite
And get the club back on its feet

He then retuned to claim his right
And helped the club to scrap and fight
To nearly grab a promotion place
But play-off games we had to face
The play-off games were hard and
tough
Emotion high and fairly rough

The save from Garner was just great
And saved us from a sickening fate
But home clean sheets did see us
through
And Palace fans a dream come true
We'd made it to division one
With help from Perry, our number one

An injured hand was diagnosed
But only us true fans could know
They cannot take us for a ride
What most was hurt was Perry's pride

To us Perry there will always be
A place in Palace history
A man who held his head so high
And made the Palace Eagle fly
So Perry now we say goodbye
No more to hear that welcome cry

One Perry Suckling, there's only one
Perry Suckling

Martin Huckle

Paradise Regained

Saturday's here, its time for the game
Down to Selhurst, glad I came
What a performance, oh what skill
With such a start it could be fifteen-nil
Palace, Palace you've nothing to fear
You fought your way up to the first last
year
Two goals here, three goals there
Our defence is tight, shots taken with
care
Coppell's colts have always vowed
To give of their best and make us proud
When our line-up includes Thomas,
Gray or Bright
We know we can win, everything's right
Football is such that there's joy and pain
But Palace we'll watch again and again
I'll give of my money, I'll give of my time
For watching the Eagles is a feeling
divine

Eagle in Beds' Mum

Palace mania...a girlie's guide to getting hooked

First game:
Crystal who?
In love and eager to please
I prepare to be bored.
Bee-striped red and blue,
We swarmed towards the ground.
So many men!
A brotherhood praising Palace;
The hum of the rhythmic chant
Rose to engulf me.
Eagles! Eagles!
Eighteen thousand people became one,
With one thought, one dream...
They drew,
They booed the referee.
"He only did his best," I said.
Uncomprehending looks followed.
I did not belong,
Yet.

Fifth game:
Palace today.
Wearing the new shirt,
I lean over the rail
And I'm Glad All Over,
As Martyn salutes me.
Eagles' enthusiasm consumes.
Stevie Coppell's Red and Blue Army –
Stevie Coppell's Red and Blue Army...
I agree with the crowd's remarks –
Their sympathy for the injured:
("Bring him a body bag")
Admiration for the opposition:
("You can't read, you can't write,
But you can drive a tractor")
Guilt for insulting the referee:
("God that feels better")
Respect for the linesman's decision:
("Do you want to use that flag as a
suppository?")
Understanding difficulties in tackling:
("You tart, Humphrey")
And fluently expressed frustration:
("Oh ...cking...ck...")
I cheer my team
As they trudge off the field.
We lost.
"But then we always lose to Norwich,"
I say to him.
He smiles, knowing I'm converted.

Faye Harvey, October 1991

Spirit of Charlton

The day Charlton returned to the Valley
I read that Lennie Lawrence had said:
"John Humphrey was the spirit of
Charlton."
He was sorry he sold him, he said.

If he wasn't playing for Palace we
heard
He'd have gone to the Valley that day
But low and behold he was on the pitch
And on the programme cover display

Perhaps he caught the Palace spirit
For the Gods must have blessed his
feet
A we triumphed in our first home win
His performance was a treat

Every time he touched the ball
He created more good chances
His passing spot-on and creative
No minuses in play, just advances

I've always had a soft spot
For John, who has taken some stick
But today he was working for Palace
I bet the moaners felt sick

I always felt he had some style
But that he wasn't part of the team
But the day the singing returned to
Selhurst
The spirit of Charlton played like a
dream.

Gill Walsh

Eddie

(to the *Beverly Hillbillies* theme)
Come and listen to my story about a
man named Ed
He once made a tackle before the
Chelsea shed
The Chelsea fans were singing
something rude
The Palace fans said the buggers are
crude

The next thing you know they came to
Selhurst Park
For a league cup match
It was pouring, cold and dark
George Ndah went skipping through
the rain
And the Chelsea fans got a taste of
league cup pain

Now its time to say goodbye
To Eddie cos he went
He's gone to Highbury as a force he's
nearly spent
But he's invited back next year
To this locality
Where he'll be on the receiving end
Of Selhurst hospitality (hostility that is)

I'm living in a box, I'm living in a cardboard box

Peter Hurn recalls a toe curling experience for the Palace fans at Cambridge

Five or six of the faithful travelled to the Fens on a miserable day and sought solace at a pub near Ware. After several pints of the local brew we resumed our journey. As we approached the Abbey we recalled that we hadn't paid for our meals and vowed to call in on the way home.

After parking we made our way across a field that could only be described as a bog. My dictionary calls a fen a bog. Near the ground, everybody was stopped and searched and those wearing anything that looked like Dr Martens were instructed to remove them, causing great mirth among the half-sozzled trainer wearing fraternity. One stroy recalls people being made to wear cardboard boxes, but I don't remember that.

The game was mind-numbingly dull, memorable only for the last appearance in a first team shirt of Mike Elwiss, a fine player, who hobbled off after ten minutes never to be seen again. Now there was a good player.

The score was 0-0, we lost only two away games that season at Burnley and Newcastle. Vaguely I recall the much touted Cambridge winger Derek Christie being completely obliterated by our left back, whose name escapes me.

Digging out the programme revealed the following trivia. Cambridge's manager was John Docherty, later of Millwall, Dave Stringer, who sent us down in 1973, wore number four and the Rod Stewart clone Alan Biley was in the number 11 shirt. The great Bill Garner was an unused sub.

We had "natural midfielder" Fenwick in place of "stocky, young" Murph with the indescribable Vince Hilaire on the bench although, of course, h played for 80 minutes or so.

Palace at the time were proudly atop division two with 28 points from games, two points clear of Stoke. Sixteen of the 24 goals had been con ed already. Leading scorer in the division was Pop Robson with 16 whil Dave Swindlehurst had ten and was listed between Flanagan (11 Crooks (9) a position not to be recommended.

The next game saw Palace lose to Bristol Rovers in one of our gre ing day performances while appearing at the Cambridge Arts Th *Mother Goose* was none other than Christopher Biggins and Geo ton, irresistable Christmas Fayre. The editorial felt that, thanks to T ables, it appeared that "the future of the club is in safe hands years to come". Spot on. And on the way home we forgot to go b pub. We've had a guilty conscience ever since.

HOLMESDALE

For a small boy, Selhurst Park in the late 1970s was a tumultuous place. Alex Warner relives a childhood of dreams and nightmares

I never bother to read the feature on Palace in away programmes anymore.The customary opening remark "these are heady days at Selhurst Park," irritates me because it is so grossly inaccurate.

Okay, we are established in the top flight and have pulled off a few impressive results in the past few seasons. Nonetheless, I am sure most Eagles fans over the age of 20 would agree that the balmy years at the club were those of the late 70s.

Those were the days when the roasted peanut seller enjoyed prosperity; the old Whitehorse Lane was packed tight with visiting supporters; the Seaweed manager, that man who made frequent pilgrimages to Rome, had an unbeatable pair of sunglasses for all occasions and Ronnie Corbett regularly parked his blue mini outside the main stand on match days.

The very thought of Palace in the late seventies warms my insides with a nostalgic yearning to be taken back to the era when my sister excitedly bought *Roy of the Rovers* for the page six pin ups of Rachid Harkouk and Nick Chatterton.

Those were the seemingly endless days when the sun never stopped shining, Ian Walsh's goals never dried up, Steve Leahy paid regular visits to the hairdresser and Dad had flared trousers.

Who can forget the atmosphere that existed on Saturday afternoons as the team rolled out onto the pitch to be greeted by the sound of that remarkable record *We're Flying High* and the Holmesdale Roar? When I was a child of six or seven, Selhurst Park was a compelling place in which sheer pandemonium and hysteria reigned.

The whole ground seemed to lack the rder and placidity that I had been aught to acquire at school. Laxly nforced segregation meant that sticuffs occurred with the same rapidi- as John Burridge's inexplicable venres beyond the six yard box.

ut the essence of the late seventies s demonstrated by proceedings on Holmesdale. As a vulnerable infant, sight of that huge expanse of terracing filled with ruffians was a daunting experience. It seemed as if the entire criminal fraternity of south London converged on those steps every fortnight.

My distant glances towards the Holmesdale educated me in a way that Johnny Ball's *Think of a Number* programme had failed to do.

I could have done an 'o' level in Sociology at the age of seven. Punks, hippies, mods, grannybashers, pregnant teenagers, Leo Sayer fans, you name it and I tell you they were there on that very bank in SE25.

Our family stood in the new stand enclosure, as far from the Holmesdale as possible.

Dad had warned my elder brother about standing behind the goal. It was no place for kids, he constantly told us.

Many an innocent child had been trapped in this inferno of deceit, seduction and immorality.

Our fears were heightened by the cover of the programme which showed an orgy of boisterous disorder taking place with hordes of unshaven men sporting shaggy hairstyles and ghastly pullovers and relentlessly proclaiming their undying affection for Palace.

It seemed that the club officially supported the antics of the Holmesdale army. The pushing and shoving, the scuffles and raw blooded passion.

Standing where we did, however, was never dull. What fun it was to bang on the advertising boards whenever Kenny Sansom was about to take a throw in, or to giggle remorselessly at the balding Teddy Boy with NHS specs and a bugle. Every time the opposition got a free kick he would melodically inform us that "the referee is biased".

Indeed, habitual tendencies thrived in the football atmosphere of the late seventies. Families were shunned if they didn't sup their Bovril from a flask at half time.

Parents were deemed uncaring if their offspring was not clad in those endearing bobble hats. If we were lucky we could be freed from the restraining arm of Mum or Dad by sitting on the stewards bench, which was just one yard closer to our heroes — although I nearly abused this privilege by trying to touch Jeff Bourne's back after he scored the second against Cardiff in 1978.

A visit to Selhurst, though, was not just about the 90 minutes of action that occurred on the pitch. It was the whole experience, from the time we got in the Cortina until we arrived home four hours later.

The pre-match anticipation was heightened by the question of whether the game would be televised. The thrill as we walked down Park Road and saw the London Weekend Television crane was one of sheer excitement.

I felt a sense of importance that I could tell the kids at school that I had been at a match that they had only seen from the comfort of their own homes.

The after match routine set the adrenalin flowing as we tried to get from the ground without being mobbed and attacked.

For a child, the ten minutes that ensued as soon as we left the enclosure was an experience every bit as frightening as witnessing Simon Groom's *Blue Peter* initiation test — abseiling off Tower Bridge — or seeing *Hong Kong Fooey* dice with death.

More often than not there would be an almighty brawl outside Norwood Junction station.

After one game against Spurs in 1979, the scrapping was of such intensity that I had nightmares for weeks to come.

Once we had passed the station, in the presence of opposing fans, unscathed I would break into a frivolous cry of 'Eagles'.

My rebellious instincts satisfied, I would settle into the back seat of the

---

"Crystal Palace. That's where all the bike gangs used to go, the greasers, they supported the Eagles."

DAVID ROBINS
WE HATE HUMANS (PENGUIN BOOKS)

---

car and study the programme. These were the glory days when the club historian Rev Nigel Sands' picture marked him down as a true seventies fashion victim and when a page every week featured the Palace Guard.

Unfortunately, the habit of reading the programme on the journey home was disrupted after the events of 1979, when our family got pelted with toilet rolls by, once again, Spurs yobs. The thought of lavatory utensils being used for this purpose filled me with the sort of trauma not felt since Brian Cant's departure from *Play School*. Dad had decided that enough was enough and that we must, in future, remain in the ground until the very last person had left.

There we would stand every fortnight in a deserted stadium, reading our programme, hoping that the groundsman would suffer from hunger pangs and decide to go home for tea.

After Dad had decided that there was no other person within a five mile radius of Selhurst Park, Mum would line us up against the perimeter fencing and search us for anything that would suggest to rival fans that we had, sometime in our lives, held the slightest affection for Crystal Palace Football Club.

Eventually, my duffel coat was banished to the wardrobe on matchdays, because the claret toggles suggested that I was a closet supporter. However, Dad's caution eventually paid dividends. In one match against Fulham, the referee blew for full time five minutes early. When he realised his error, he took the players back onto the pitch to finish the game. We witnessed Palace fail to make a last ditch effort to equalise.

The climax to this balmy period occurred in May 1979, when Palace drew a record crowd as they clinched promotion. Clutching my teddy bear, dressed in Palace kit, in one hand and Dad's arm in the other, we raced onto the pitch. It was possibly the greatest experience of my life. The feeling of sheer unbridled elation and delirious joy as Dad lifted me above the thousands of fans to witness the players celebrating in the directors' box, will remain vivid forever.

The memories ... Ian Walsh's diving header and Dave Swindlehurst's goal that sparked off an impromptu surge onto the turf; clutching the grass as a souvenir after the match and listening to car horns piercing the south London air. Everything symptomatic of the late seventies atmosphere was in evidence on that unforgettable night.

Sadly though, May 11, 1979 was both the climax and end of an era. The happiness shared by so many at the full time whistle was one of utter innocence. We deluded ourselves into believing that that those ecstatic days could continue and the coming of first division football to Selhurst would bring further success to the club.

Despite one enjoyable season, the late seventies football experience became tame and finally expired. It is hard to pinpoint when and how it started, but somehow a visit to Palace was no longer an occasion for the family.

Proposed supermarkets, players departing for exorbitant fees, inflated admission prices, sophisticated policing and a lack of vocal support was what Palace in the early eighties was all about. It wasn't what we wanted to be part of.

The strange man with his bugle was replaced by a dodgy family that smelt and swore and drank to excess, the fighting outside became all too sinister and, most of all, the players lost their desire to play for the club with any conviction.

A sense of alienation filled the supporters. My Mum stopped going, my sister stayed home and washed her hair and when Dad suggested we went less often I didn't put up the slightest argument.

The spirit of the 70s was lost forever and with it a momentous part of my childhood.

Sideburns

We don't know his name, we rarely hear him speak apart from his shout of "programmes". Yet his very existence is infamous. He is the immortal programme seller "sideburns", whose robust physique, brown attire and distinct orange vest are the component parts of a celebrated figure. Ever since I bought my first programme from him to receive the statutory nod of approval he has been a vital element in the complicated task of supporting Palace.

Instead of conforming to the usual characteristics of a programme seller; post-pubescent acne, greasy flat top, an inability to give you the correct change from a fiver and an over enthusiastic attempt at selling programmes, sideburns remains ice cool and conducts his business professionally. By his blue container of glossy programmes he stares into the Holmesdale, he will sell you a programme without delay, offering no small talk about how Noades is going to Wimbledon, and giving you your change in an immaculate and spontaneous manner that would make any market stall holder proud. He is in control of the programme situation. While other sellers melt unseen into the crowd unable to remain level-headed or stocked up, sideburns conducts irregular journeys around the ground with unnerving sophistication and temperament, seldom chanting "programmes". It is his almost eerie presence that has anxiously induced suspicion in us. We must always keep an eye out because spotting him can cause ecstasy.

From the smeggy Holmesdale end, often the sight of a half eaten hamburger, coupled with the sweet aroma of hot dog burps provides more entertainment than the scuffles on the pitch. People spotting is a common pastime. The result has been "hunt the sideburns". An extremely difficult job because, rumour has it, he habitates the top right hand corner of the Arthur Wait stand, which limits our sightings of him. Many a 1-0 home defeat has been sideburns and excitement free. But ocasionally we catch a glimpse of him strolling behind the goal, fag in mouth, half heartedly acknowledging the football. Immediate relief from the tedium ensues. A swift move, some delicate and delightful football and Palace prod in a scrappy goal – but at least its a goal. For a split second the crowd is plunged into euphoria, moody and mundane people leap about with joyful expressions as they celebrate an offering of football excellence for south London. Even the rotting Holmesdale end somehow manages to elicit some sort of atmosphere and all because the messiah sideburns has appeared and conveyed our desperate pleas to those on the park admirably. As the celebrations become muted he is nowhere to be seen. As if by magic he has slipped out of sight.

Sometime in 1987-88 sideburns was christened fatty voodoo (when sanity had been completely lost). Why? because he's not slim and he's a voodoo charm. Long may he sell programmes at Palace.

Matty Davis

FAMILY CLUB

In the flashy Seventies, the first lesson for Ed Barrett was to come to terms with what a bunch of softies Palace fans were.

Every small kid carries around his own particular set of misconceptions and delusions until one by one they are shattered by harsh reality. For years, I happily believed the "consolation toffees" given to runners-up on *Crackerjack* were a real brand and pestered my mum to get me a tin. It was equally obvious to me that the teams on *University Challenge* sat in a double decker arrangement, one above the other. For reasons that remain unclear to this day, I thought the Beatles all lived in the same house and wore false moustaches during their *Sergeant Pepper* period. And, of course, I naturally assumed that the pint-sized Man United, Millwall, Chelsea, Charlton and West Ham fans at school used to rush down the front of their respective terraces and bang the advertising boards before the game, to give a thunderous greeting to their heroes.

I can still recall the pitying looks at school. "What do you mean 'banging the boards'? You're f*****g mad, you are!" Well, I thought everyone did it. On my first visit to Palace, I took a ridiculously large rattle that knocked a passing copper's helmet off and nearly wrenched my arm out of its socket. But before long I was down at the front of what was then the Arthur Wait enclosure, banging the boards in time to *Glad All Over* and trying to work out which one of Bert Head's latest useless purchases was which.

It wasn't until I started going to away games that I realised how unusual Palace was. In contrast to the people you saw at other grounds, the Glaziers' clientele was peculiar to say the least. There were four sorts of Palace fan. One lot wore car coats and smoked "slim" panatellas. Another lot wore anoraks and black framed NHS bins with manky bits of sticking plaster holding them together. Then there was the "me" and all the other little kids who squeaked "Pa-LISSS, Pa-LISSS!" like a primary school full of recorders being blown too hard, and banged the boards. Finally, there was a small bunch of lads towards the back of the Holmesdale who waved scarves and sang, much to the derision of the vast away crews that casually "took" both ends.

In the early 1970s, a "self-confessed" football hooligan wrote a guide to the fighting capabilities of the various crews and firms that followed each club, awarding marks for size, hardness, etc. Palace merited just one withering sentence: "Take the family."

It wasn't until I started going to away games that I realised how unusual Palace was. In contrast to the people you saw at other grounds, the Glaziers' clientele was peculiar to say the least.

Ah yes, Crystal Palace, the family club. But it was a funny sort of family. Like those villages whose entire young male population was wiped out during one day at the Somme, there seemed to be a lost generation. Between the squealing hordes and the thermos brigade that filled the rest of the ground to bursting point stood ... nothing. Close scrutiny of archive footage confirms this strange phenomenon: there are practically no teenagers in crowds of 40,000 plus.

The few that did attend bore little resemblance to the "yobs" who dominated the newspapers of that nervous decade. Aside from the inevitable parka (that's as in Tufty Club, not mods down at Brighton) their distinguishing characteristic was a tendency to wear slightly flared "slacks" that reached to just above the ankle revealing a grey or fawn ribbed sock woven from man-made fabrics. White nylon school shirts were popular, and would cling damply to vests, which were tucked into Y-fronts worn "high" to show off the waistband.

It couldn't last forever. By the early eighties, the demographic shifts were having a significant effect upon Palace's image and today our away support is as good as most other top clubs.

Personally, I'd say you haven't really lived until you've seen a Palace fan at Highbury, face screwed up in purple rage screaming "F*****g NORTHERNERS!" at the Arsenal fans. Even the school parties at Selhurst no longer simply shout "Ten, nine, eight ..." in time with the electronic scoreboard to remind the ref that it's full time and we're a goal down.

These days they trill ditties like "the referee's a w****r" and hurl abuse at the world and his wife to the amusement of jaded thirty-somethings like myself.

Sometimes I think back to the days of Rogers and Taylor, Hilaire and Sansom, when I had a season ticket in the Old Stand. I sat behind a middle-aged couple who remained motionless throughout each game. They were always there when I arrived and never seemed to leave at the end. Perhaps they were dummies, placed there like the Highbury mural to "enhance the crowd". I once tested them out by tying partly sucked polo mints in the woman's hair, while a spider weaved a web between her left ear and the shoulder of her husband's sheepskin jacket. I managed to get five in place before she twitched very slightly and that was probably from a gust of wind.

As the memories come flooding back, a warm nostalgic glow overwhelms me. Then I remember the bloke in the cloth cap who used to shout "Give 'im a hanky!" every few minutes, regardless of what was actually going on in the game, and the warm feeling stops abruptly.

Strange Fascination

Understanding why some poeple get a kick out of fighting is difficult. 'Guesty' explains the attraction.

While not violent myself, I have been a voyeur of hooliganism over the years. Close to the action, never involved.

Let me explain how I became fascinated with disturbances at Palace. My first game was against Fulham in 1969. But as an 11 year old, it was not the clinical finishing of Lazarus, Jackson and Kember that stayed in my mind but the unruly hordes among the 36,000 who invaded the pitch and cavorted wildly on the hallowed turf.

The following two or three seasons I witnessed punch ups in the Holmesdale against our more illustrious first division London rivals. These were of the shaven-headed, rolled-up Levis and Doc Marten boot variety. The Palace contingent always "got done", but from a distance I formed an emotional alliance to them. After all, they supported my team and I felt there was an heroically romantic aura about them because they were outnumbered and fighting a lost cause.

This affinity was endorsed when I attended Palace v Middlesbrough at the beginning of 1973-74 with my mate Alan and his father Alf, a respectable pillar of society, insurance salesman. Boro fans had infiltrated the Holmesdale and a brawl broke out. To my astonishment (and glee) I watched Alf urging the Palace fans on and decrying the Boro fans by screaming "Let 'em 'ave it Palace, bloody hooligans shouldn't be in this end anyway!" I was hooked. If a respectable adult took an interest, why shouldn't I?

I witnessed many skirmishes, the highlight of which was seeing the Palace leader (yes in the early 70s the Palace fans had a leader whose name I cannot mention for fear of retribution, though I gather he's mellowed nowadays) ripping off a full length silk claret and blue smoking jacket from a Villa supporter outside the Whitehorse. That season I saw my first away game, the last match of the season at Cardiff. We had to win to stay up, drew 1-1 and were relegated. Before the game a Cardiff fan ran on the pitch displaying a Welsh flag. A Palace fan followed, kicked him in and unfurled a Union Jack. After the game during an almighty punch-up outside the station, I witnessed a Palace fan deposit a full Watney's Party Seven (7 pint beer can) on the bridge of a Cardiff fan's nose. The following season took us to Brighton (the start of the rivalry) in which myself and around 8,000 others "took their North Stand". The 1975-76 season heralded my coming of age. Almost 18, I attended the Leeds Cup tie. Believe it or not, we ran Leeds everywhere after the match. This was big time. Then down to earth with a bump!

Next was Chelsea away. We had at least 20,000 in a crowd of 54,000 in a very hostile atmosphere. The *Eagles* chant was sung by thousands at every chorus to which Chelsea fans took exception. There were outbreaks of furious fighting in the North Stand and enclosure throughout the match. At one point the game was interrupted while police on horseback galloped across the pitch to restore order. *Match of the Day* freeze framed pictures of fighting Palace fans with the chilling message: "if anybody out there are parents of these louts, contact the police immediately". Possibly the most sh** bricking 90 minutes of my life, but I thought our boys acquitted themselves well. It's the old romanticism again - outnumbered once more, Chelsea thugs clearly the aggressors specialising in lethal kung-fu kicks, but Palace attempting to stand their ground.

There was a notorious hardcore gang called the Northwood. The name originated from a side streets close to Selhurst which was the scene of pre-planned orgies of after match violence. Whether this is true or just folklore I cannot say. I do know their members were "recognised men" in their 20s, who me and my fellow teenfans looked up to. They had wonderfully descriptive nicknames such as Mad Monty, Mooncrater, Tufty and Basco and often teamed up with the Addo, a gang from New Addington.

A friend came to me at the start of the 1977-78 season and suggested it was time to form our own firm. We were nearly 20 - no longer boys. He had a name - AERO (Addiscombe Eagles Rule Okay). Faced with such elitism and a formidable name to boot, I had no option but to agree. I became a fully fledged passive member of the 70s equivalent to ICF and Bushwhackers.

Incredibly, it escalated and we soon had 30+ "men", many with our own names such as Mad Simms from Croydon, Eddie the Viking (26 football convictions in four seasons) and Hardman Holeman. This group were not so much perpetrators of violence as perpetrators of minor skirmishes, surging, verbal abuse and occasional blackouts due to excess drinking.

But our reputation grew and was being whispered among younger fans. I became a 'face', after my one and only uncharacteristic bout of violence at Preston. We were greeted at the station by the police. Overcome by the effects of a Party Seven, consumed on the train and in the middle of a chanting Palace throng, I was overcome by nausea and puked over the head of a policeman standing below. This delighted my fellow Palace fans, and was met with rapturous applause as I unleashed the old Sex Pistols punk refrain "and we don't like ya!". Someone in the crowd said: "He's AERO". I was a star.

The following season was our 'piece de resistance'. We were at home to Millwall, a club not blessed with high intellect within the ranks, they've never been able to fathom out how they can hear *Eagles* humming around the ground, without seeing any Palace fans mouths moving. Anyway AERO was in full flight. A couple of dozen of us met early in the pub beforehand and talked enthusiastically about 'standing our ground'.

At 2:30pm we arrived, fuelled by twice as much drink as was necessary to stand by our convictions. As we reached the crossroads of Selhurst Road/Holmesdale Road we met a similar number of Millwall fans. My immediate thought was "oh no!" but Mad Simms, Eddie the Viking and others responded with a charge and to my amazement Millwall fled. We marched onto the Holmesdale chanting "there's only one Crystal Palace", arms aloft and into the Millwall throng gathered behind the goal. A punch or two may have been exchanged but for certain Millwall ran. We sang enthusiastically. More and more Palace fans, pleasantly surprised to see us making ourselves known, tagged on. This was the only time I can remember that we formed a vocal crew against the 'Wall. By the time kick off arrived, there was a 'thin blue line' segregating us from them. This was shortly after a BBC documentary on Millwall fans had named Harry the Dog as their leader. I take personal pride in instigating the immortal chant of that day: *We all agree, Harry the dog is a poodle.*

Afterwards we were run everywhere and the following season versus West Ham our spirits were matched by Hammers fans with flick knives which forced us into early retirement.

TRAVEL MAGAZINES

The inspiration for this book came from the success of the Palace fanzine *Eagle Eye*. But the present mob weren't the first supporters to use that name as Joe Grech explains.

Crystal Palace Supporters Club has been in existence for several decades. But, to my knowledge, has only been involved in organising travel to away games, trains, coaches and end of season dances. It has never attempted to exert political influence in the way that the recently formed Palace Independent Supporters Association hopes to do.

Like thousands of others I have benefited from their work, through my frequent use of coach one in which to travel to away games. Since 1976 I have collected numerous copies of both the Supporters' Club's magazines *Rail Club News* and *Rail Travellers' News*.

Rail Club News was more professional and reflected our pride in the Palace of the mid-Seventies. We had first division gates and top class players with Malcolm Allison and Terry Venables constantly in demand for television work. Yet we were a third division team and played at Halifax, Aldershot and Chester among others. Looking back, the atmosphere was pure magic, the Cup run of 1975/76 hasn't been touched since, although it's a pity we couldn't tag our 1990 semi-final victory onto the end of the '76 run and perhaps wipe out Mark Hughes late equaliser at Wembley.

Back in the 70s, home gates topped 20,000 and our away support was at its height regularly exceeding 1,000 even on long distances, while the F.A. Cup and more local games would see us take 5,000 or more (or perhaps I have a vivid imagination).

When Terry Venables succeeded Big Mal in 1976-77 the support dwindled slightly, although it was well up on the modern day Premier League, and looking at the prices for travel and other football related expenses it's not hard to see why. It seems football's prices have massively outstripped inflation.

There were many highlights: the goalless draw at Anfield in the third round of the Cup in 1977; the second round, second replay against Brighton at Stamford Bridge where Alan Mullery lit the blue touch paper on an already smouldering rivalry between the clubs by giving us the Harvey Smith 'V' sign after the Seagulls' unfortunate defeat; our epic last gasp win at Wrexham which kept alive Palace's promotion hopes (a coach party of Palace fans revisited the ground a few days later to see Mansfield become third division champs and ensure we went up and the Welsh stayed down). That was my initial season as a proper "home and away fan" and it was the most exciting.

The following season, the Supporters' Club produced *Eagles Away* and gave it out free to rail and coach fans alike. The editorial in the first edition of October 1977 stated its aim to be monthly but, in the end, just four copies were produced that year and five were issued in the promotion year of 1979.

It was rather bland in comparison with the earlier *Rail Travel* efforts which was a shame because, although we didn't realise it at the time, it covered the high point of Palace's history, at least until Mr Wright and his buddies appeared more than a decade later. *Eagles Away* finished on a high note because its last issue appeared at the first game back in division one at Manchester City in August 1979.

It was at this time that I turned my Frank Spencer-like talents to producing a newsletter myself. Palace fans have always preferred rail travel I believe because of the often ridiculously early starting times of the coaches, which sometimes set off the night before.

The narrow seats made life uncomfortable and the high point was listening to a Monty Python tape on the coach hi-fi or hoping someone had brought a tape player or radio. *Strangers in the Night*, the old Frank Sinatra number, was the coach one "anthem" – an apt choice as we sped down the M1 late at night heading home from another third division outpost. They surely didn't come any stranger than the special breed of nutter that used to frequent the back seats in those far off days. Many was the time some poor soul would spend the journey searching for lost shoes, socks or trousers that had been wrested from him in moments of madness.

There were regular barrages of rolled up pieces of paper and discarded food and, in more sombre moments, there would be pauses for reflection on the day's match, past journeys, old players and all manner of memories treasured by those Palace connoisseurs. All this seemed to come to an abrupt end at the same time that *Eagles Away* finished. At the same time, a more sober family-type atmosphere prevailed.

It's hard to relate the sense of fun of those coach one trips, and I doubt that it matters much as far as the history of Crystal Palace F.C. is concerned, but the regulars on coach one at that time had a real sense of identity, although maybe it seemed a bit "closed-shop" if you were an outsider.

The Hurley family, Lisa, Neil, Guy and Audrey, was a focal point, as was Dave Cox, a giant of a man at 6ft,7in. and weighing in at 20 stone. He was literally a gentle giant and always the centre of fun, organising bingo, raffles and fun nights out away from football.

Choice cuts from the early fan mags

Michael's Coaches of Croydon terminated their contract to carry Palace supporters after they found one beer can in the rubbish bag after the Carlisle trip in 1985. They also claimed the coffee machine on that trip was short by 20p.
The police were contacted but they felt that one beer can hardly constituted an offence. Our
stewards Robbie Tobin and Dave Cox had already signed an agreement with the company to refund any difference in takings for tea and coffee sold, so a complaint of holding back 20p they quite rightly took as an offence.

December 7, 1985 report in of F.A. Youth Cup match in which Palace were beaten 7-3 at Southampton."One boy that really stood out was John Salako, who looked very composed when running towards goal ... we may be seeing a lot more of him in the future"

1981, for China was the year of the Cock, for Palace it was the year of the Cock Up said the first edition of 1982

January 2, 1982 shows the hatred of QPR with the following jokes:

A QPR fan, sick of seeing his team beaten by Chelsea, nailed his season ticket to a tree in disgust. When he came back the following morning he found someone had stolen the nail

Did you hear about the QPR fan who thought mint condition programmes were the ones with holes in them?

Thieves broke into QPR's ground and the police were called. When the law asked if any cups had been stolen, the Rangers boss said: "No they didn't get as far as the canteen."

Comments on the Whitehorse singing in the F.A. Cup at home to Swansea: "There were great vocal arrangements on the terraces that night and we were treated to *Dream, Dream, Dream, The Bonnie Bonnie Banks of Loch Lomond, Bring on the Fog, There's Only One Ivor Engine* and others a bit rude to say the least ...

There were many characters, young and old, who were all out for fun regardless of the score. These people gave their name to the early editions of my newsletter *The Hurley Burley Club News and Views*. They are largely unintelligible unless you were in on the humour and much of it was taken from daft running jokes between 15 or 16 people at most.

Later editions ran under the heading *Loon Away Notes* where my schoolboy sense of humour (I had just left school) spoke for itself. I must admit that I was more concerned with putting across my view of the latest outing or event than recording Palace's record or what the fans were doing at the time.

My first attempt at producing a mag for all Palace fans as opposed to a few friends came at Christmas 1981. I enlisted the help of Palace's club photographer Neil Everitt, who contributed the satirical piece *Christmas on the Great White Telephone* – a piss-take of Palace's information line, which in those days was an ordinary answerphone which cost no more than the local rate. Clubcall was still seven or eight years off.

The magazine was modelled on *Private Eye* but was such an effort to type up and letraset that after incurring a huge loss on printing costs on the first issue I decided to knock it on the head. Copies remained on sale in the away travel cabin for several weeks after the Enfield Cup match for which it was originally produced.

I suppose I was too much of a loner to make a real go of it, or enlist the help of other fans, but I also had regular work to contend with. That's my excuse anyway. Three and a half years later I hit upon the ingenious idea of buying a photocopier, although I think I got ripped off buying it, and that enabled me to have another stab with *Eagle Eye*.

The first effort was for the match at Shrewsbury on August 10, 1985 and it was my favourite. Once again it took ages to type up and, after selling the 50 or so copies, I decided to do a smaller version for sale at a "nominal" price that barely covered the cost of the copy paper. After deciding it was too much effort to collate enough material for each away trip, I scaled it down to an A4 newsletter featuring coach one's favourite game "top tipster" a sort of predict-a-score with a winner take all jackpot.

It was only intended for coach one's regulars and when I read the first edition of the current fanzine *Eagle Eye*, I realised my dream had come true and I donated my copier to Capital Radio's Helpline and put away the letraset and typewriter.

Team of the 80s

Terry's terrors in verse by Matthew Simmonds

Billy's boots

Billy Gilbert stood shaggy and tall
Pleading "Ref, I went for the ball!"
When shipped off to Pompey
He played like a donkey
Booting all creatures great and small

Can't Wyn 'Em All

Now Walshie of Wales could sing
Of daffodils, leeks and such things
'Pon crosses he fed
He'd score with his head
And fly like he had dragon's
wings

Vincent

Hilaire, he of magical feet,
Full backs he could tease and then
beat
He'd let them recover
Have one chance, then another
To tackle and make them retreat

Great Rock 'n' Roll Swindle

Swindle was built like a truck
At free kicks he'd oft try his luck
With his right he'd let fly
F*** me! went the cry
And the back of the Whitehorse
would duck

So big and so strong was Dave
Swindle
Like a barrel on legs, not a spindle
When he missed he got boos
Choice foul language he'd use
And his fan club would wither and
dwindle

Poor Dave had his critics of course
Though he played with some style
And such force
A dead ball he'd blast
He could run bloody fast
And kick like a drayman's cart horse

Jerry Can

Jerry Murphy but flattered to deceive
He could dribble any ball he'd receive
A lovely first touch
But he didn't run much
Pretty patterns with his left leg he'd
weave

Nasty Nick

In the midfield so clogged and so tight
Peter Nick would battle and fight
He'd put it about with a shove
and a clout
When things got tasty he'd bite

Sansom for ransom

Kenny Sansom just simply oozed
class
Til we swapped him for Allen What a
farce
We got Barron in the deal
Well done Terry Neil
You shafted us right up the ... Khyber!

Kenny, they said, would go far
With his signing on fee and flash
car
Ne'er heeded the boss
Like a Vince Hilaire cross
Just went straight out and over the bar

Palace Trivia

■ In the film *My Beatiful Laundrette*, the lead character played by Daniel Day Lewis claims to have switched allegiance from Palace to Millwall.

■ In Fyodor Dostoyevsky's novel *Crime and Punishment*, the hero Raskolnikov goes for a drink in a bar called The Crystal Palace.

Snippets from Gerry Simpson

Al, Al Supa Al, Supa erm ... Alamo

General Santa Anna led his huge Mexican army towards the Alamo. Inside, the 350 besieged Texan rebels, including Davy Crockett and Jim Bowie, stood firm. Wave after wave of Mexican troops stormed the fort but with each attack they were repelled. The Palace fans were gathered in a corner of the fort singing *Stevie Coppell's Red 'n' Blue Army*. Before the final assault the women and children were allowed to leave, then the Texans fought to the last man. The Palace fans didn't stop singing throughout the battle. Even though the defenders had been massacred the Palace fans boarded their coaches for south London knowing it was, somehow, a moral victory. *Tony Matthews*

Silly songs etc

Jingle bells
Jingle bells, jingle bells
Jingled by a gnome
Oh how long must we wait
To see Palace win at home?

Palace science-fiction chart
1) George NDahlek
2) CPFC3PO
3) Zaphod Eaglebrox
4) Don Rogers in the 25th Century
5) Perry Suc-klingon
6) Red n Blue Dwarf (Steve Galliers)
7) Dilithium Crystal Palace
8) Nigel Martian
9) Moon Base Supa Al-pha
10) Robocoppell

Andy Thorn
Andy Thorn, Carshalton born
He doesn't mince
He doesn't fawn
He clatters forwards from behind
He makes them writhe, but never mind
He's been sent off several times
But he's Palace so we don't mind
And when he flattened snide Mark Ward
He entertained the Palace hordes
And though Thorny remains unsung
He's as great a hero as Eric Young

Novello's Lament
I've watched in the east and watched
in the west
I've seen Mark Bright in his vest
I've seen Ian Wright change his shorts
I've seen Big Trev get a string of
noughts
I've seen Kevin Mabbutt save the day
I've caught a ball on the Holmesdale
from Andy Gray
I've sworn at the linesman
And Brighton toads
But I'll never sing "I love Ron Noades".

Alan
I beg your Pardew
I never promised you a rose gardew
Along with the sunshine
There's got to be a little rubbish
sometime
(with apologies to Lynn Anderson)

I heard it through the Holte End
Oh I bet you're wondering how I knew
Bout that man called Alan Pardew
With some other team he played
before
Yeovil Town even paid him more

It took us by surprise we must say
When he scored that April day
Oh I saw him score in extra time
I saw it cross the goal line

Within SPITTING *distance of Selhurst Park*

Were you ever plagued by annoying little sods at the footie who were in need of a jolly good hiding? Chances are it was John Pateman and his gang

I'm not one of those boring trainspotter-type fans who can remember every moment of every game. In fact my memory is so bad that I can't recall any match details at all. But I can cast my mind back to when I first watched Palace as a kid.

I always lived in Orpington, south London and so Palace was my local team. The only other rival geographically was Charlton yet many of my mates had the annoying habit of supporting other London teams such as Arsenal, Spurs and West Ham.

I used to visit all the other London grounds, especially Chelsea. The crazy thing was it was often quicker to get to a ground like Stamford Bridge or Highbury than to Selhurst. It took 20 minutes on a fast train into London followed by another 20 minutes on the tube. To get to Palace, however, involved either a train to Beckenham, change for Crystal Palace and again for Norwood or a train to Penge and a bus to Selhurst. Either way it took over an hour.

To make sure we got there on time we used to leave absurdly early, like 9am. We were usually at the ground by 11 and as there was no queue and nothing to do we used to hang around the local shops, one of which sold football programmes. The trick was to enter the shop *en masse* and stuff as many programmes up our jumpers and down our trousers as possible when the shop keeper wasn't looking. One day Geoff, our leader, was caught red handed and ran from the shop with his coat bulging with programmes. Unfortunately he went sprawling straight into a copper and ended up on the path with programmes everywhere. He got off with a severe telling off, we were only about 12 years old.

When we were eventually allowed in the ground at 1pm we made a dash for the wall on the Whitehorse to establish our place and wait for kick off. We passed the time by holding spitting contests such as who could produce the greenest gob. Sometimes this degenerated into fights and we would end up covered in spittle looking like front row spectators at an early Clash concert. It's a wonder we never contracted TB, it certainly made our throats sore.

Another trick was to buy bags of monkey nuts and flick them at the coppers as they walked past. One of my mates was caught doing this and thrown out of the ground. Another of my friends turned up at Palace v Wolves with his school cap on. The colours were black and gold and he was told to take it off because he was "inciting the home supporters".

We were never hooligans, but we did have brushes with rival fans. On getting on the train at Orpington one Saturday, we saw this skinhead with a blue and white scarf sitting alone in a carriage. One of my mates said in a deliberately loud voice: "Look at that Chelsea w*****. The six of us laughed and we got into the next carriage. Seconds later the door flew open and this Chelsea skin stood there resplendent in steel toe-capped Doctor Martens, crombie overcoat, Levi jeans, Ben Sherman shirt and braces. He shouted: "If you weren't so young [he was at least twice our age], I'd kick all your f****** ..." at this point the train pulled away. We all shouted abuse to him out of the window and then the train stopped at some lights. He sprinted up the platform towards us but we were saved by a green light.

A favourite trick was to unscrew train light bulbs and throw them out of the window or we'd steal the toilet roll from the station bog to throw on the pitch. One day a ticket inspector got on and I had a light bulb in one hand and a toilet roll in the other. I pocketed the light bulb and put the toilet roll behind my back and deftly dropped it out of the window while he checked my ticket. As the train left the station it trailed down the track. It was that horrible shiny medicated stuff that skidded off your arse. It gave you GBH of the bum and should have been banned from football grounds as an offensive weapon.

Cannon's Burnley Burns night

Twas Burnley at home what a sight
52,000 crammed in on the night
Jim led the team
All Scottish and mean
No goals try hard as he might

Come half time 0-0, stay the fight
All Palace ...
Could Burnley? They might
Vince crossed, Walsh jumped
His header he thumped
Top corner, promotion, delight.

Toothless and roofless

Following Palace for years I have noted
The hope when we got promoted
On the Holmesdale no roof
Incontrovertible proof
That eventually we'll get demoted

But a roof to protect us we ask
Under cover we'd sing and we'd bask
To spare us a soaking
You've got to be joking
Says Ron, an impossible task

Mr Noades of course sits in the stand
Ignoring our courteous demand
The fans on the terrace
He views as a menace
"I'm chairman, Big Boss, in command!"

Only a cover, kind Sir, we beg
A little something for over our heads
Wife Novella from Neath
Ask your Ron to bequeath
No executive box, just a shed

By Matthew Simmonds

STRIKING MEMORIES

As a member of the Team of the 80s, Ian Walsh scored 28 goals in 131 appearances for Palace. Matthew Simmonds talked to him about the glory days and what went wrong

Hulton Deutsch

A behind the scenes look at Crystal Palace. Ian Walsh relaxes with friends after a training session.

I recognised Ian Walsh instantly although he is slightly broader of beam and with a shorter haircut than in his heyday.

In a quiet Cardiff hostelry we sat amid some old programmes I'd brought, where a rather spiffing crowd was listening to a posh Welsh voice banging on about her wine tasting society, "the only rule is that one must always swallow".

Ian Walsh is now a financial and insurance advisor and summarises for BBC Wales' radio soccer commentary team. His football is limited to a few 5-a-sides with his BBC colleagues though he plays golf with the sort of passion and touch with which he led the Palace and Wales line just over a decade ago.

"I joined Palace at 15 years-old. Palace paid parents substantial amounts to get the boys they wanted. Malcolm Allison wanted to attract all the good young players, nurture them, have a team to be proud of and take them from strength to strength. I was offered £1,000 to sign Schoolboy terms, £3,000 to sign apprentice and £6,000 to sign pro. I got the first lot, but they reneged on the other two payments. It was happening at all the clubs but that's how Palace got their youth team. Allison didn't want to stay in division three."

Obviously Walsh's time under Allison was limited, but what was his perception? "He was great on the coaching side, but in a man-to-man situation he couldn't handle it. He wasn't prepared to talk to you on a personal basis about your problems."

Walsh's greatest early influence at Selhurst Park was Ernie Walley. "I had so much respect for him and learnt a great deal of discipline from him. He had this high pitched squeaky North Walian accent, but he was a big man, you wouldn't dare look at him the wrong way. Walley formed a good combination with Alan Harris and John Cartwright. They were all fine footballing coaches and their philosophy was to get the ball down and pass, pass, pass."

With Walley, Cartwright and Harris, Palace had one of the finest youth teams ever. At one point they were almost

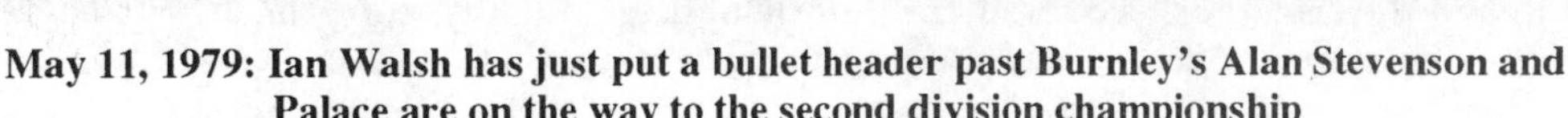

May 11, 1979: Ian Walsh has just put a bullet header past Burnley's Alan Stevenson and Palace are on the way to the second division championship

unstoppable. "I remember we beat Tottenham 6-0 away in the FA Youth Cup. I'd scored two goals and we were five up. Billy Gilbert wanted to get on the scoresheet. He beat two or three players and knocked it into me. All I had to do was knock it back for him to stick in the net but I turned and slotted it in myself. Billy called me all the bastards under the sun. He never forgave me for that."

Another team-mate was Kenny Sansom, still many people's choice as Palace's best ever player. "In his early days he was unbelievable," says Walsh. "We played well together. As a full back, he liked to drop it in to the strikers. I was the sort who could take a defender away and make myself space so that as soon as Kenny looked up I'd be there. He attacked so well because he was confident that Jim and Billy would fill in the space behind him. He was a great attacker as well as a defender. When Billy got the ball Kenny would go knowing Billy could put it over the top on a sixpence for him to run onto. Kenny put in crosses as a left winger."

Walsh also played against Sansom. "In internationals he was absolutely brilliant". The solution was obvious: "I used to kick him and he didn't like that. But we always got on well and shook hands after the game."

By the time Walsh collected his FA Youth Cup medal in 1977, he had already broken into the first team. The main strikers were Dave Swindlehurst with whom he formed his most notable partnership and Rachid Harkouk. He has different perceptions of them. "Harkouk was a bit of a flash in the pan. He had the ability to excite crowds and was one of the best strikers of a dead ball but he wasn't the most disciplined player because he came into the game late. You just had to let him go on the field. He was a fine man.

"Swindlehurst helped me a lot. We helped each other with our style of play. Off the field we played golf regularly. We had to borrow old tweed jackets from the groundsman to get into the bar. I remember playing at Walton Heath with Swindly and Jim Cannon. I had an impossible shot at the 2nd and stuck it two or three inches from the cup. Swindly shouted from the other side of the green, and remember its a very posh club, "Walshie, you should have been a f****** golfer!"

With Terry Venables as manager, Palace were on the move. Walsh recognises his influence and the value of the individual coaching he received. "Venners was such a funny guy. But he was serious about approaching things the right way. He would always tell you to enjoy it, do your best and that's all you could do. But you couldn't just go out and enjoy yourself. You had to win the battle."

When he first started, Walsh described himself as "excellent" in training. "Peter Nicholas, John Burridge and I always hit the front on runs. It was great competition for everybody." But he admits his attitude changed. "I would always give 100 per cent on match day. But the older you get the more you try to pull the young boys back."

Finishing was practised every day. "We used to put the ball on the centre circle, spread it wide with one striker darting to the near post, another pulling off at the back, and crossing in from both sides. Six balls on the 18-yard box, and a beacon five yards away. Touch the beacon, back in and hit it. Left foot, right foot. Everyone knows the kind of finishing, but you can't look to that for the real thing when there's so much pressure on you."

The supplies came mainly from Vince Hilaire and Jerry Murphy. "Vince was brilliant at getting by his man, but not perhaps the best with the final ball. Neil Smillie's pace took him into great positions but for culture and quality Jerry Murphy had a great left peg."

By Christmas 1978 the team started to consider the possibility of division one. "We got together and had meetings where we said that we had a chance if we kept doing the same things. We knew with the defence we had that we weren't going to concede and therefore we wouldn't lose too many games. The only thing was that it was surprising we didn't score more goals because all the players were excellent strikers of the ball."

That assessment was spot on. Palace never faltered although the lack of goals meant that the championship had to be won on the last game. "I had my family up from West Wales. We went out and there was this massive crowd. At half time it was 0-0 and I remember Leighton James, who I knew well from the Welsh international set-up, telling me: 'Walshie, if we go 1-0 up you'll shit yourself!'.''

But Walsh scored with a spectacular header to set us on the way. "I always get confused over who played the ball in, Vince Hilaire or Terry Fenwick. I just remember flying through the air. It was right on the button, straight in the top corner. I'll never forget it although I've never seen it on tape. I think someone's got it on video. It was the most incredible moment, I have a picture somewhere of me running to the bench with Kenny Sansom, Jerry Murphy, Peter Nicholas and Stevie Kember chasing me. It was my best goal for Palace and made doubly so by the occasion. Kevin Keegan said on television that it was one of the best headers he'd ever seen."

Walsh recalls a great spirit among the team. Not surprisingly, his best friends were the other Welsh lads, Peter Nicholas, Steve Lovell and Terry Boyle but the whole team socialised. "We all used to go out on Thursday night, same pub, have a couple of pints. The camaraderie was there. The manager wouldn't admit it but if you are successful, going out on a Thursday night becomes a habit. I don't think anybody wanted to change that.

"On Friday morning we'd have five-a-sides and it would be a heck of a battle, a good sweat. That's what we used to enjoy. Venners would join in and he was brilliant. We came in ready to do the job on the Saturday."

It was a glorious time to be a Palace player and Walsh recalls that the club treated its stars "as though we were the most important people at the club". Sometimes before home games, the team would dine at the Savoy before heading for Selhurst. The money wasn't bad either. There was a simple incentive scheme. The higher up the league they went the more they earned.

As Palace prepared for division one they strengthened the team with two big money names, Gerry Francis and Mike Flanagan, the latter a direct threat to the partnership between Walsh and Swindlehurst. How did Ian see Flanagan's arrival? "I understood we had to strengthen the squad. Even though he paid a lot of money, there was no guaranteed place for him. I had to fight for my place and I felt I had a good attitude. I was never as good a goalscorer as Mike Flanagan, or Mike Elwiss for that matter, but I think I was a better player overall. A better team player." There was a competitive edge. In November, *Match of the Day* covered the return of Big Mal to Selhurst as Man City boss. "I scored the first in a 2-0 win and Swindly scored the second. As I went to congratulate him he said: 'Walshie, who's Venners gonna f****** drop now?'."

Another memorable moment was the defeat of European Champions Nottingham Forest when Walsh scored. But it wasn't what you would call a cracker. "It was unbelievable. Peter Shilton said if I'd struck it well he would have saved it. Because I mis-hit it, it trickled through his legs and he had egg on his face. It was very embarrassing."

At the other end of the field was John Burridge who rumour had it modelled himself on Shilton. "He's an utter nutcase. He lives and breathes football. He'd go to bed Thursday all day, train Friday morning and go back to bed. His poor wife cooked him meals and took them to the bedroom. When I signed for Barnsley I lived with John for six months. He used to give me an orange while we were watching telly and tell me to throw it at him. Good for reflexes! We'd be watching a film and all of a sudden I'd sling this orange at him. He'd see it out of the corner of his eye and just pluck it out of the air. 'That's why I'm number one goalie,' he'd say. At least he used to think he was ... no-one else ever thought so!

"He'd always win the pre-season cross-country runs, it was the competitive instinct in him. Win, win, win. He'd drag me back in the afternoons to practice his stopping and my finishing. He couldn't live without football."

Leading the team on and off the field was Jim Cannon. "It was diabolical he never got a Scottish cap, he would have fitted into any Scotland side no problem. Jim was a good players' player and as club captain if we had a problem he would always steam into the manager's office to sort it out."

Yet despite all this, Palace began to collapse. The cracks appeared at Anfield in December 1979. "Swindlehurst and I were totally isolated. I can't honestly remember having more than two or three touches. They murdered us and it really knocked the confidence out of us."

It didn't happen overnight, but slowly the rot set in. "The togetherness we had as a team began to go out of the window when we started going down. We bought players who perhaps didn't fit and the cameraderie was lost. Then Venners went."

It was cataclysmic and Walsh regrets the fact that the board didn't back Venables. "We had such a high regard for him, he was a father figure. I remember when we couldn't come to terms over my new contract. We were both stubborn but he said: 'If you move along Walshie then we'll shake hands on it like men.' That's the way he was. But he left before I did and that was it for Palace. If we could have kept him I've no doubt we would have stayed in the first division. It's just that he wanted to achieve things in life that he couldn't achieve with Palace, so he went. As soon as someone like that goes it knocks the stuffing out of the players."

It wasn't long before Walsh also left. "The club was my life for seven or eight years from when I left home at 14. I can go back ... in fact I did with Barnsley and also with Grimsby when I scored in a 3-0 win."

But he regrets not having scored more goals for the club and feels his commitment to the team rather than a striker's selfishness was in part responsible. "If I'd been a lazy bastard I'd have scored more. Someone like Clive Allen wouldn't care where the ball was was until it was in the box. He would be ready for the chance, fresh. I worked hard for Palace and was more conscientious. Perhaps if I'd taken that away from my game I'd have scored more goals."

WHY PALACE?

Charles Bake's introduction to Palace was a goalless draw, it hasn't got much better since then

It was a horrible mistake. Good Friday 1969 and I was a happy Spurs supporting teenager. I'd never been to a real match and I'd been nagging my dad to take me to see Spurs play West Ham on Good Friday. Unfortunately, the Glaziers were in the running for promotion and the neighbours, even those who'd never had a good word to say for "Croydon's team", seemed keen to see the crunch match against Middlesbrough. So, extremely reluctantly, I was taken along from Norbury to Selhurst Park. There was no way I was going to enjoy the game and I wondered whether I ought to show my loyalty to Spurs by standing with my eyes closed for the 90 minutes.

Looking back now, it's a blur – the bright, sunlit morning, the smell of onions and cigarette smoke, the huge banks of supporters, 'Boro in white with McMordie looking dangerous, Palace playing a tight game, not having many chances, being right next to the pitch and seeing the players close up.

No goals, typical, but I was hooked and was there the next day to see Palace play Portsmouth with their beanpole number nine Ray Hiron and have the pleasure of watching it all again on TV on the Sunday. After that, it was the clincher against Fulham and the wonderful, hot summer of '69, looking forward to first division football. There it was, a footballing life mapped out for me.

I CAN'T remember the opposition, one of those forgettable home games in the early 70s, and as usual we were getting stuffed by all and sundry. During the second half, John Sewell attempting to pick up a clearance from "their" defence. The ball dropped down in front of him and he landed again wondering where the ball was.

JOHN SEWELL again I'm afraid took a penalty in the game against Portsmouth in '69. I'm not sure whether he kicked the ball or merely stumbled into it. In my mind's eye, I see the ball bobbling apologetically into the Holmesdale end goal with the Pompey goalkeeper leaping like a salmon in entirely the wrong direction.

MICKY DROY, the only centre half who could outjump opposing forwards without leaving the ground

PER BARTRAM and Borge Thorup, enough said!

FEBRUARY 1970, Chelsea in the Cup. One down from a first half goal and then Roger Hoy scored with a downward header at the Holmesdale end. I jumped, not a good idea as, at the time, I was in the middle of the Whitehorse surrounded by a solid phalanx of Chelsea fans. I got several "wait 'til after the game, matey" looks and started to wonder whether it would be Croydon General or Mayday. Luckily for me, Osgood, Hutchinson and co turned on the power and blew us away 4-1. The Chelsea fans were too delirious to care and, having politely applauded each goal "well done Blues, another good goal", I slipped away before the whistle and set off for home looking over my shoulder all the way.

IN A different way, the atmosphere in a '72 home cup tie against Everton was the ugliest I've ever experienced. Everton kicked Willie Wallace and Yogi Bear all over the place with hardly any action from the referee. That day I really hated the Toffees and wanted us to kill them. We drew 2-2, I've never liked Everton since.

PETER TAYLOR worked non-stop. He could turn a match single handed and scored some wonderful solo goals. As a side, the Team of the 80s was unbeatable – skilful, confident, not frightened to play the ball around until an opening came and only lacking one player – a deadly and consistent goalscorer. In that respect, I always admired Jeff Bourne. For me it was his clinical finishing that did more than anything to get us out of division three.

MOVING the floodlights in 1970 and the shadow across the pitch caused by the Arthur Wait stand.

BUYING the newspaper colour souvenir team and score charts for Palace in the 1970s and starting to fill them in religiously after each game (team names, half-time scores, attendance, league position) then getting fed up as the Palace scores kept repeating "0" and the league position was "20-something".

AFTER the Burnley game, walking off the pitch listening to an Elton John single and watching the fans salute the new champions and looking up at the lights of an airliner and hoping it was the Brighton team just learning that their holiday had been spoilt by us. We went up as champions, they went up as second best.

MARCH 11, 1970. Kneeling in front of the TV at the end of *News at Ten* and paying homage to the scoreline Manchester City 0 Crystal Palace 1 (Gerry Queen). The unbelievable lifeline to our ultimate first division survival.

THE ROCHDALE player with white boots who tormented us all evening in a September 1970 league cup match that ended 3-3.

BOBBY Tambling's outrageous goal scored from somewhere near the left corner flag in an otherwise forgettable friendly against some foreign team.

DECEMBER 4, 1971 making my way to the home game against Sheffield United when we were in deep trouble and United, Dearden, Woodward, Currie and all, had thrashed Ipswich 7-0 the previous week ... meeting a small boy who said "Palace'll lose today" and agreeing with him. Result: Palace 5 Blades 1.

IN OUR early division one days, seeing the TV cameras and knowing that their malevolent presence would ensure we lost.

THE DREADFUL feeling during the 1990 Cup Final just before Hughes scored when I said: "We've stopped running and tackling."

THE EVEN more dreadful climax of the Cup Final replay.

THE UTTERLY horrendous moment when I put on my Eagle Eye t-shirt and realised it looked like a Texaco petrol advert.

Palace versus Brighton: a case history

US AND THEM

I said, "I hate Brighton. I think there's a kind of wisdom in that – the British person, or even the foreigner, who says simply I hate Brighton. What's there to like here? It's a mess.'
Paul Theroux – The Kingdom by the Sea

I hate Brighton. Not for me the some time rivalries with Chelsea, Man United or the Arse. I will always hate the Seaweed from the South Coast. Their isolated position means that no-one else could give a monkeys about them – they are "our" rivals. The Johnny come latelys at Palace have difficulty understanding the hate generated with what they see as mediocre nobodies with a crap ground from just south of nowhere. They've had little opportunity to experience the passion of a bank holiday encounter in recent years. The odd friendly and a Zenith Cup victory may have done little to fire the imagination, but this is the real enemy even though they've been easily overcome on the last three occasions, twice, it must be said, with sub-standard performances on our part.

It's not much, but it's ours. Others are puzzled by the Palace - Brighton rivalry while Charlton can only look on jealously. Neil Witheroe tells the tale of the modern antipathy and looks back for its origins

Neil Everitt

Seaweeds v Palace 1984. Andy McCulloch loses out in a duel to a certain Mr E. Young

When it all began is not an easy question to answer when applied to rivalries. As the seeds of hooliganism grew in the mid-60s the only fights to be found on Brighton's seafront were of the Mods and Rockers variety. There were no Palace-Brighton encounters in that period and it's difficult to trace anything that could be called "rivalry" prior to the mid-70s "Mullery-at-the-Bridge" incident. Then, the Brighton manager waved a fiver under our noses and told us "You're not worth that, Palace." The reason for his outburst was that Brighton had just lost a second F.A. Cup replay at neutral Stamford Bridge on a "dodgy decision". His exaggerated protestations brought forth the rather original *Mullery is a Muppet* riposte from the Eagles faithful.

Even in the Southern League, Brighton used to attract larger crowds to Palace than usual. The reasons are lost with the passage of time and are probably only geographical, I have uncovered no evidence of a "special" relationship despite unconfirmed rumours of incidents on the seafront between rival supporters as early as 1936.

Our early record against the Rockmakers, as they were then known, was fairly even: seven wins, seven draws and six defeats. Our first double was achieved in 1907-08, the first Boxing Day encounter was in 1910 when we won 2-0 away from home.

We joined the league together and in the first season we were pormoted while they finished 18th. After relegation in 1925 we faced each other in every season up to the war.

As war broke out, we'd been due to play in the North and South Cup for those who'd finished second and third in the two third divisions. It took the format of a knock-out semi final in which the winners would have played either Bradford or Doncaster on a neutral ground for gold medals. Hitler's mob saw to it that the games never took place.

The first match at Selhurst after the declaraton of war was a friendly against Brighton on October 7, which was drawn 2-2 and attracted 3,500 – just under half the number who had attended our first and last home league game of the season. The war was most notable for two occasions in which we chalked up ten goals against the men from the Goldstone.

After 1945, the clubs met for 12 league seasons. We only finished above Brighton twice, in 1947-48 when they finished bottom and had to apply for re-election and in 1949-50 when we were separated for seventh place by our better goal average. We'd beaten them 6-0 at home.

In 1957-58 Brighton won the division while we became founder members of the fourth. We did not meet again until 1962-63 when we drew at home and won 2-1 at the Goldstone as Brighton slipped into division four. By the time they crawled out two seasons later, we were up again.

The modern story of Palace and Brighton begins in 1974 just after Big Mal's Eagles had been relegated to division three. New nicknames for the first game of the season "the Dolphins" versus "the Eagles" and we suffered a 1-0 defeat in front of a crowd of 26,235, the largest to watch Palace home or away that season. The following March, revenge was extracted with a 3-0 drubbing. This did little to boost our flagging promotion campaign while Brighton only just managed to avoid the drop. The following season we were undefeated in seven games and were top of the division, until Brighton. Even a 1-0 defeat couldn't stop our inexorable march – we didn't lose again in the league until just before Christmas, by which time we were seven points clear. The away game came when we were in the middle of our epic cup run and we went down 2-0. Brighton finished fourth, one place above us on goal average.

It was 1976-77 when it really happened. Hooliganism was at its height and the clubs met five times, three of which were to decide an F.A. Cup tie. The "x" factor in the smouldering rivalry was that new Palace boss Terry Venables and Alan Mullery didn't see eye-to-eye. Running the Brighton boys to Hove station and across the park became an integral part of the away days.

Palace took the upper hand on the pitch as well, remaining undefeated with three draws and two wins. We could now rightly call them "the enemy". Although both sides were promoted, it rankled that Palace, if truth be known, were lucky to get there and Brighton finished above us – but not as champions.

"[Mullery] was asked about his two-fingered gesture and he replied: 'I did that to the Palace supporters' He then threw five £1 notes on the ground and added 'They are not worth that.'"

EVENING NEWS
PALACE 1 BRIGHTON 0 F.A. CUP 1977

Mullery's outspoken views fanned the flames. Some thought he was motivated by jealousy, having coveted the Palace job himself. Whatever, his comments added spice to a well seasoned dish – he changed their nickname to the Seagulls, about as close to Eagles as you can get. What he was trying to achieve is unclear but the Palace fans deftly altered it to Seaweeds which, I would venture, was neither anticipated nor welcomed. It has now reached the ears of fans all over the country and Brighton are thus forever labelled.

Palace had the better of them on the pitch. On a glorious Indian summer's day Vince Hilaire stole the show. The *Sunday People* said: "they lost him in the shadow of the stand". The victory was all the sweeter for being on the *Big Match*. Brighton had failed to reach division one on goal difference in their first season and there was now a battle royale between us, them, Stoke and Sunderland. Although our three rivals had provisionally claimed the promotion places, we had the trump card of a game in hand against Burnley. We won 2-0 and 51,801 saw us snatch first place from Mullery's grasping paws. What better way to clinch a championship?

To cope with division one crowds, Brighton erected a temporary grandstand which was immediately coined "legoland" by the Palace fans, appropriate to go with the Goldstone's Subbuteo floodlights. Palace were riding high while Brighton limped along at the bottom. But fate decreed that the clubs should not meet until Boxing Day. There was no Christmas cheer for us, we lost 3-0 when they scored from our corner on a break away. An Easter draw did little to restore our pride and we eventually finished 13th, three places above Brighton, who'd spent heavily to lift themselves out of the mire. Our woeful sequence of results agianst the Seaweeds had begun.

By the time the 1980 Christmas fixture at the Gallstone came around, we were on our third manager, Malcolm Allison, and anchored to the bottom. We lost 3-2 in controversial circumstances and Mike Robinson, who Allison had signed for a hefty sum while at Man City and then sold, reacted to rejection by scoring twice and then giving Mal a a couple of fingers to let him know the score.

By Easter, we were already down and Brighton arrived at Selhurst in danger of joining us. Our lads did not seem keen on taking our rivals with them and we meekly surrendered 3-0. Brighton escaped for a couple more seasons.

The procession of Palace managers continued. Gradi, then Kember, then, in a staggeringly unpopular move, Noades appointed the Beast of Brighton himself. Alan Mullery MBE (Massive Bullshit Excreter). In a deal of which only Dr Faustus would have approved, the muppett had finally landed the job he'd always craved. Dismayed fans drifted away in numbers, me among them.

In the second year of the Hell Hound's managerial reign, we renewed acquaintance with the lame brains from England's edge. The white dancing shoes of that geriatric swinger Jimmy Melia had been unable to manoeuvre them out of the relegation places although, to our horror, they reached the F.A. Cup Final. They came close in the first game but one of their supporters made a grave mistake. The misguided fool took a banner along bearing the legend: "The REAL team of the 80s". When the TV cameras picked it out, the Palace fans began to smirk. Only misguided Brighton fools could curse themselves on their biggest day. We all knew that "Smith wouldn't score". Man United sealed their fate with a 4-0 replay stroll which left Eagles everywhere baying for double figures when the game was over as a contest by half time.

Mullery stuck the dagger further into Palace hearts by allowing the Seaweeds to escape with maximum points from the following season's proceedings. These were the darkest moments of recent Palace history and the fierce fighting that followed the April trip to the Gallstone, only served to underline this.

Steve Coppell's first south coast encounter brought no reward although Trevor Aylott stopped the rot in the home game, earning us a deserved draw. The match was marred when Palace's Henry Hughton was sent off for a late tackle on Gerry Ryan, whose leg was broken. Brighton's non-entity of a manger Chris Cattlin claimed it was the worst tackle he'd ever seen but Ryan tellingly refused to condemn Hughton. It was embarrassing though because it was not Palace's style. We'd always left the spite to the likes of Brian Horton and Andy Rollings.

The smallest crowd in Palace-Brighton history was for the Full Member's Cup when 2,207 saw our reserve keeper Ken Hughes concede a first minute goal in his only Palace first team appearance. On New Year's Day we lost 2-0 away in a match remembered for Terry Connor's outrageous swallow dive to earn a penalty from which they scored their second goal.

In March, Paul Brush's free-kick gave us the result we'd waited seven years to see. It maintained our modest promotion push. We finished fifth, comfortably ahead of mid-table Brighton who had reappointed Lucifer's lapdog Mullery as manager.

It was just like the good old days. Palace played their part to perfection with a 2-0 stroll on Boxing Day, but Mullery didn't make it to the Easter match, Barry Lloyd was now at the helm of the rickety old boat, but Palace hoping for play-off points put in their worst performance for a couple of years. The team came over to applaud the huge away following and were sent away with a flea in their ear, which if nothing else let them know just what a Palace-Brighton match meant to us.

Some of the worst violence between the two sets of supporters erupted with about ten minutes left as the Eagles fans stormed out of the terraces where they had been tightly packed to confront Brighton in their own end. I have vivid memories of the running battles across the park opposite the home end.

Brighton were relegated only to turn up like a bad penny (or a bad Steve Penney) a year later. We now had Wright, Bright and Thomas, but on Boxing Day the team turned in another dreadful performance, going down 3-1. The return at Easter holds a place in the record books as referee Kelvin Morton added an extra something to the rivalry. He awarded five penalties, four to Palace who managed to miss three of them. Brighton had always amused us with their propsensity for fielding players with ridiculous names that nobody had ever heard of, Giles Stille, John Crumplin and Richard Tiltman being prime examples, but Mike Trusson (wonder if he did have his truss on?) took the biscuit. Before we could take a good look he was sent off. Despite playing against ten men we only won 2-1 and missed a golden opportunity to inflict a defeat of biblical proportions on the old enemy. Early in the game, Ian Wright scored the goal he claimed was the best of his Palace career, but Johnny Pemberton stole the show with his spot kick rocket up and almost over the Holmesdale which reduced both sets of fans to hysterics. It is perhaps fitting that this, to date, is our last league meeting with them. Nothing will ever beat it for utter farce. We earned our deserved promotion while Brighton also got what they deserved – they finished 19th.

"Do you know what is impossible to see from the worst pressbox in the league? It's impossible to see how such a sub-standard side as Brighton have climbed off the bottom, where they and their ground belong.'

MIKE LANGLEY OF THE *SUNDAY PEOPLE*, 1980

TELLING IT LIKE IT IS

The 1990 Cup Final brought to an end the only thing the Seaweeds ever had on us. No longer could they taunt "You'll never get to Wembley." Such was our success and the abject mess into which they had fallen it looked as if we might never meet again. Indeed *Eagle Eye* ran a spoof notice of termination of rivalry. The joke nearly back-fired when the Zenith Cup took us back for an unexpected visit to the tangle of rubble and rusty poles that is the Gallstone Ground. Brighton's league form mysteriously picked up and they earned a replay after a draw with Liverpool in the F.A. Cup. Rumours circulated that Barry Lloyd had pinned up the offending back page in the dressing room to wind up his players.

Despite the IRA bombing of Victoria earlier in the day, some 2,000 Palace fans went south to an ice bound away terrace. Brighton forced extra time before two goals in two minutes by Bright and Wright. Both clubs made Wembley that year; Palace in the Zenith and Brighton in the play-offs where they were crushed by Notts County.

The following season with money troubles mounting Brighton did get out of division two, they went down to division three. But thanks to the creation of the new Premier League, they would still compete in division two. Trust Brighton to get relegated but stay in the same division.

August 1992 saw injury hit Palace deliver a below par friendly performance which we won 1-0 thanks to Eric Young, who silenced the "Brighton reject" chants by powering home a corner. The game was played on the Friday night – perhaps the only "friendly" ever to have been moved on police advice!

After the game, Palace fans were subjected to a CS gas attack at Hove station. Apparently some Brighton fans had been taunting them and then, true to form, ran away. Palace gave chase only to be met with a supermarket trolley carrying the gas cannister. The police and their helicopter arrived too late.

At the friendly in August 1993 some Palace fans were subjected to another tear gas attack this time during a prematch drink. Just for once, we turned on the style even though Chris Armstrong and Simon Rodger were absent. A 2,000 contingent of Palace fans in a 4,000 crowd enjoyed a 3-0 demolition with goals by Simon Osborn, Bobby Bowry and Gareth Southgate. Given the massive financial problems that beset the Seaweeds it was ironic to see a perimeter advert proclaiming the benefits of Brighton and Hove Albion Financial Services!

Their debts are crippling, their ground tumbledown, they have trouble paying players' wages and the Inland Revenue are baying at the door. It's not beyond the realms of possibility that this may go down as the last clash between the two clubs.

That's the story of a rivalry and its ours, Palace or Seaweeds we like it that way. Now ere comes the abuse. If you want my opinion their fans are spotty-faced, train spotting, pre-pubescents who haven't a clue what following their local team is about. Why do so many of them wear Milan tops or Arsenal-style managers coats? Perhaps its because they look so ridiculous in their tesco carrier bag, Chewitts sweet wrapper kits. If there's one thing they hate more than Palace it has to be their kit designer. Their hooligan activity, reprehensible at the best of times (as is ours) is of the schoolboy mentality, witness the coin throwing sessions of the early 80s. They have three famous fans; David Lacey, Desmond Lynam and Attila the Stockbroker. The first is the *Guardian's* chief soccer writer with a penchant for using his position to run Palace down. Lynam presents BBC Sport and once laid into Palace for the crime of finishing fifth in division two something along the lines of: "It's been a nothing season for Palace and their manager Steve Coppell." This was after he had turned the club around after four years of relegation battles.

Attila, a little known punk poet, entitled an album of his work *Donkey's Years* attributing it in part to gripes about Palace's successes in the 90s. We've got Carter the Unstoppable Sex Machine they've got Attila. Life's like that when you follow Brighton.

The town's major attraction is its pier entitled would you believe the Palace Pier. And they've got the club itself. What can you say? Their finest moment is only remembered because their manager wore white shoes, a list of their greatest players takes 20 seconds: Horton, Ward, Foster, McNab, Perry Digweed, Jasper, Walker, Connor, Pates and Crumplin. Brian Clough once managed them and was beaten 8-2 at home by Bristol Rovers and knocked out of the F.A. Cup 4-0 by Walton and Hersham so he took himself off to Forest

Now they are on the verge of extinction. Yet, I really don't want to see them wound up. Freddie Mercury once sang about needing someone to love. The opposite is equally true and Brighton fill the role.

So it's long live Brighton, long may they be infested by donkeys.

Even friendlies have meaning sometimes

"Do you fancy going to Brighton versus Palace?" I casually asked my friend in Hove. "Why not?" he replied. Well, there was the thunderstorm for a start, or the fact that the wheelchair section is in the corner of the pitch away from the action, or the fact that Brighton police insisted on getting their (s)wanky new helicopter out to strafe local residents. The closest thing I saw to subversion all night was the upside down union jack with "Palace" scrawled all over it. We wormed our way round the ground, lured by the all pervading smell of Bovril and were dutifully let in by the steward on the gate. On the pitch a small group of youngsters eagerly awaited Geoff Thomas' autograph. Geoff looked understandably reluctant to sign anything, after all one of the children might have been a midget agent from Blackburn Rovers' sugar daddy Jack Walker, or Arsenal boss George Graham.

It was Gary Chivers' testimonial match, apparently, and he was presented with a small trophy for still being alive. Meanwhile, Palace skulked furtively by the stand as far away from us as possible. That proved no help in identifying the 11 mystery men who turned out. No Brighty, no Johnny Salad, no Eddie Scissorfeet and the programme was no help. I thought there might have been a little clue courtsesy of the tannoy, but it stuck to a staple diet of eight year old pop records that were too bad even for local radio to play. What did happen to Howard Jones?

Brighton, who seemed to have a small boy playing in goal for them also had a bloke with a headband. Steve Foster was playing left back. Laugh? I nearly did. Pretty boring in the first half really. Stuart Massey, the £25,000 sigining from Sutton, looked pretty good. Foster made such a bad tackle that he injured himself and was awarded a sympathy free kick. Brighton fans shouted "Seagulls", Palace fans shouted "Seaweeds" and that was that.

Then it started raining. Then it thundered and really started raining. Paradoxically this livened up the match. The ball flashed across the Palace goal a few times, but luckily the Brighton manager Barry Lloyd had sold all their strikers and their youthful enthusiasm was no match for the big Cornishman – sorry about that, I developed a spot of "Motson amnesia" a strange ailment where you can remember every jot of tittle tattle about a player, except his name. Alan Shearer, for example, suddenly becomes: "the 3.6 million pound, 21 year-old son of a sheet metal worker from Newcastle". Goodness knows how Motson would manage to describe Clive Allen. Anyway, after much pfaffing about, Eric the Ninja saved the day with a 68th minute header for the only goal. Five minutes latter he was nearly sent off for arguing with the referee. That sums everything up nicely.

Geoff Thomas was substituted much to the Brighton fans' delight. Obviously Palace didn't want the rain to affect his new haircut.

Oddly enough, the Brighton fans did not resort to their normal taunt of "you're worse than Crystal Palace" – perhaps because their team really are worse, much, worse. They preferred "what a waste of carrots". I expect you can buy a lot of carrots with £3 million. Then we trundle off through the gates the potholes, the squalls and police searchlights to the pub to reflect on our lack of target man and what the Ninja would do to "wor Alan" next Saturday. Don't you just love football?

Steven Chapman

Victory is ours

Living in Brighton but supporting Palace is not a unique experience, but the few Seaweed fans at College were telling me by how many goals they would win our Zenith Cup tie at the Goldstone Ground.

Palace hadn't won at the Gallstone for years so the 'Weeds thought they had a pretty good chance.

I tried to contact Heinz, a Palace fan of 13 years and the man who first got me hooked, but he was already on the way to Brighton's rubbish tip.

With time running out I got a bus to the town centre, but in Brighton all the public transport is either late or cancelled so I jumped into the nearest taxi and shouted Goldstone Ground. As we sped through the back streets the driver revealed he was an Everton supporting Scouser and we talked until arrival where I dashed inside. With five minutes to kick off the terraces were full and I relished the familiar faces and discussion of the outcome.

I spotted Heinz and we watched as the game drifted along with a makeshift Palace – Thomas at centre back because of injuries. Lanky Seaweed Mike Small hit the bar with Martyn beaten. For the first time I was worried. But Palace survived into extra-time when Wright and Bright injected some life into proceedings. Mark opened the scoring and then Ian Wright tucked away a glorious second. The Palace fans were ecstatic and a pitch invasion was a prelude to a mega party. Heinz and I danced and sang until the final whistle. After the match we were kept behind while dejected Seaweeds were allowed to catch the last buses.

Stuck in Hove with no transport home, we didn't care and strolled through the deserted Brighton Streets happily anticipating the Brighton faces at college the next day.

Guy Woodford

The Eighties ... gloom and glory

From Team of the Eighties to the Coppell revolution

Hy Money

Our £400,000 signing Gerry Francis rises to a header with Jerry Murphy and Dave Swindlehurst in attendance

Back in 1969, Palace were given a romantic opening fixture against Man United. Ten years on romanticism was still the order of the day as Terry Venables' exuberant Eagles returned to the top flight. We were asked to visit Manchester's better half. City were now back under the guidance of Malcolm Allison, the man who had created the young Palace, and it was Big Mal who added further spice to the occasion by making an outrageous swoop for one of Selhurst's teenage starlets shortly before the big kick off.

At 17 years old, Steve McKenzie had yet to make a first team appearance, but City were prepared to offer £250,000 for him and Palace, needing to recoup some of their outlay on Francis and Flanagan, took the bait.

Match of the Day was there to see Palace in their much hated yellow and black Admiral strip (the one with black bits on the shoulders) take the field. Forty thousand people weren't exactly given their money's worth but a goalless draw was good enough for the Eagles.

On the following Tuesday a goalless draw was less welcome. Try as they might, Palace could not break down a thoroughly negative Southampton, who amassed somewhere in the region of 35 back passes in the second half. Such was the tedium they inspired that the 31,756 crowd who had raucously welcomed top flight football back to Selhurst were reduced to counting each back pass out loud by the end.

Dave Swindlehurst broke Palace's duck with our goal in another draw at Ayresome Park but we were just as satisfied with our fourth draw at Stockport in the league cup. Finally, the flood gates opened. Declining Derby were crushed 4-0 with two-goal Mike Flanagan prematurely hailed in one Sunday paper as "King of the Palace". We followed that with seven in the second leg against Stockport, who were hampered by an injury to their former Everton keeper David Lawson. Flanagan cashed in with a couple, so did Ian Walsh, while Gerry Francis scored his first goal for the club.

With Flanagan leading the way and Walsh, who had not been included in the opening league games, popping up with important goals, Venables had welcome competition for the strikers' positions. For the moment, Swindlehurst was still first choice. But things would soon come to a head.

Hulton Deutsch

Palace, Palace top of the league! Paul Hinshelwood heads over Paul Cooper in the 4-1 mauling of Ipswich and the Eagles are heading for top spot and unprecedented critical acclaim.

Palace continued with their rich vein of form. Jerry Murphy, now a full Irish international, scored twice as Villa were beaten in an ill-tempered encounter, which prompted much Villa whingeing in the press, then a peach from Vince Hilaire enchanted *Match of the Day's* viewers as Palace won at Stoke.

We were now third on goal difference behind European Champions Forest and Man United. Our next visitors were Ipswich, a side brimming with quality and international reputations. Bobby Robson's men were taken apart by a dazzling Palace display. It was all over before half time thanks to Swindlehurst, Hinshelwood and a twice-taken penalty from Francis, who put the first one over the bar. We reached the top of the table when Jim Cannon, appropriately, scored a fabulous goal. The move was untouchable, the shot unstoppable. Ipswich were wrecked and Palace were hailed as a team capable of emulating Forest's performance of two seasons before by following promotion with the league championship. "The Eagles Have Landed", "Team of the Eighties", "every member of the team is capable of scoring". No praise was high enough. The autumn sun shone on Palace and every team below them was in the shade.

> **"We don't have to fear any team in the first division. We have the equipment and the talent to be capable of beating any of them."**
>
> – Terry Venables, April 1980

Just prior to Ipswich, we had been dumped out of the league cup by Wolves in front of more than 30,000 on a Tuesday night at Selhurst. It seemed little more than a hiccup – we'd never liked that competition anyway. We were still unbeaten in the league and entertained Spurs. *Match of the Day* came to sunny Selhurst and so did 45,296 paying customers to see the battle between Palace's form and Spurs' pedigree. Within the opening minutes it was the visitors who drew first blood with a long range dipping shot from Ricky Villa which dumbfounded the normally reliable Burridge. The young players faced a test of character and passed convincingly. Substitute Ian Walsh saved a point with a piece of quality opportunism, but we couldn't find a winner and the draw wasn't enough to keep us at the top of the tree. Few who made their way home that afternoon wanted to believe that, 15 years later, Palace would still not have repeated the feat of that autumn afternoon against Ipswich.

Our first league defeat came as a bitter surprise. The 4-1 margin was almost unbelievable bearing in mind what a dire, dour side Southampton had seemed only six weeks before. It heralded a bad October, we were rocked at Goodison and dropped silly points against Bristol City and Bolton, both of whom were struggling.

It took *Match of the Day's* interest to spark a return to winning ways. Big Mal returned to Selhurst for the first time since the glory days of 1976 but it was Venables' day and Walsh and Swindlehurst grabbed unanswered goals in a compelling victory. Swindlehurst led the line brilliantly, his power and finishing had eclipsed Flanagan, who had only

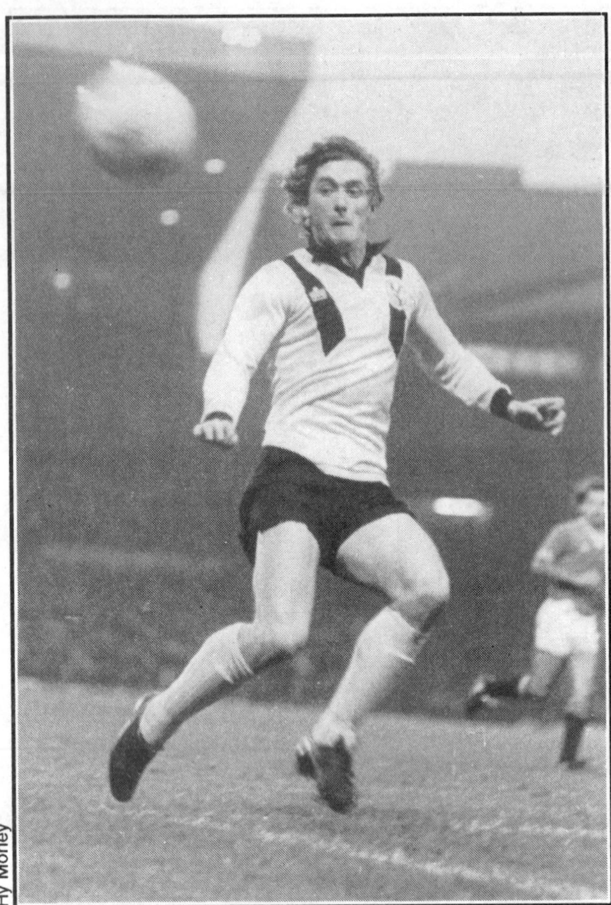

Hy Money

Crystal Palace at the peak of their powers. Ian Walsh in action during the 1-1 draw with Manchester United at Old Trafford.

managed one consolation goal since his premature proclamation as a Selhurst monarch.

Swindlehurst scored with a fluke to beat Arsenal with nearly 43,000 celebrating our first ever league triumph over the Gunners. Arsenal had been involved in a gruelling European match in midweek which gave them an excuse to adopt their traditional tactics – defending in depth and leaving only Frank Stapleton up front. The result was a dour, untidy match which came to life towards the end of the first half when we scored a messy goal. Under Cannon's challenge, Pat Jennings flapped at the ball and it came out to Nicholas who hit it against Swindlehurst. The deflection took it past the Arsenal keeper. The north Londoners applied pressure in the second half but Burridge would not be beaten, even heading the ball away on one occasion. Budgie's best save was a one-on-one with Brian Talbot. Palace also had a couple of chances to extend their lead but on each occasion Hilaire and Walsh could not outwit Jennings.

The first really big away test was at Old Trafford. Man United, as usual, were among the favourites to take the title, but Palace played brilliantly and led through a 78th minute Swindlehurst goal until well into the twilight hours that the referee felt obliged to add on for "stoppages". United stole an undeserved equaliser and the Palace fans returning to London were left to ponder how many minutes a football match was supposed to last.

Despite the outlay on Flanagan, our biggest problem was still goals. Swindlehurst's strike at Old Trafford was to be his last for the club even though the ex-Charlton forward never looked like he was going to hit the target. Walsh did quite well but he needed help, although he scored a fluke through the legs of Forest's Peter Shilton in front of the *Big Match* cameras to keep us riding high and maintain the illusion that all was well. The barren patch continued over Christmas though. Liverpool softened us up with a 3-0 thrashing before we travelled to meet the old enemy at the Goldstone on Boxing Day. It didn't occur to most of us as we packed the road to Brighton with red and blue scarves that Mullery's strugglers had much hope of beating us, but Palace were in strangely lethargic mood while the home side were determined and committed. The magnitude of the defeat was a shock and so was the home defeat by a very ordinary Middlesbrough three days later. The bubble hadn't burst, but the air was leaking out of it at an alarming rate.

We picked up slightly, drawing with Norwich in a icy bore at home, then beating Derby at the Baseball Ground with two Walsh goals. Flanagan ended his "goal drought" with the only strike against Wolves but we then lost an 89th minute 2-0 lead in the rearranged game against West Brom. The original fixture had been postponed because of heavy snow before the festive season.

SOME PEOPLE think Terry Venables has only to keep breathing for a few years to lead England to future glories.

He's the whizz-kid with the fat salary who writes books and buys pubs as well as managing Palace to the greatest season in their history.

Well, Terry boy has a lot more managing to do now. He's got his first real crisis.

And how far he can calm the sweaty fears of his little boys lost will be the true measure of his ability. Santa's come and gone without leaving so much as a tatty old toy for these sad Palace kids.

Three defeats in a row. Only two goals in six games. A debt of around £2 million. Who dares wish them a Happy New Year?

Venables said: "Our approach annoyed me more than anything. If only we can play a ... match as we did

By DAVID BARNES

Crystal Pal. 1 Boro 2

sighed: "No complaints."

Palace started badly even before the ref whipped the coin from his pocket. The announcer got Boro midfield...

he explaine... I'd have a... time I sc...

Hilaire... player, ... back ... Keep... him ... him...

After that, we really went to pot picking up just two wins (over the weaklings of the division Bristol City and Bolton) in the next 12 matches. The disturbing thing was that we were beginning to get hammered. We had sold Swindlehurst to Derby for £400,000 even though he was our leading scorer with seven goals. Terrace rumour had it that he was the cause of a certain amount of dressing room bickering. It was a sad moment after the glory years and even if he hadn't been prolific he would probably have got us more goals that any of his successors until Mark Bright arrived on the scene.

Neither Walsh nor Flanagan scored after March 1 and Palace managed just five goals in the last ten matches. We were also knocked out of the F.A. Cup by John Toshack's Swansea after three

Hulton Deutsch

July 14, 1980 and the Palace players begin pre-season training at their Mitcham training ground

thunderous ties. We drew 2-2 at the Vetch and 3-3 after extra time at Selhurst having trailed 2-0 in the first five minutes thanks to some rank bad goalkeeping by Burridge. In the second replay at Ninian Park we went out 2-1 which left us to plod through a disappointingly empty season.

The final two matches offered both a glimpse of what Palace could achieve, and more tellingly, of what was to come. Our last home game was a goalless draw in which we played our best stuff for some time although Liverpool held us to a 0-0 draw. It was our biggest crowd of the season, 45,583, topping both the attendances for Arsenal and Spurs, and it helped make Palace the sixth best supported club in the country with an average nudging 30,000. But the season closed in dismal circumstances. We were thrashed 4-0 by Nottingham Forest at the City Ground and Kenny Sansom was unfortunate enough to make the tackle that crippled Trevor Francis and ruled him out of England's summer European Championship campaign in Italy. Sansom was now firmly established as England's first choice at left back. He played in all three matches in the Home Internationals including a 4-1 defeat by Wales in which Ian Walsh belied his league form for us by scoring twice. Sansom then played against Italy and Belgium as England were swiftly eliminated in front of their rioting fans. The pleasure of seeing our most talented player representing his country was tempered by the mounting speculation that Arsenal, who could never resist buying defenders, were after him. We became increasingly resigned to his departure.

The most pressing need was still for a quality striker. We were linked with Steve Archibald of Aberdeen at a fee of £925,000 but almost as soon as Spurs expressed an interest we dropped out leaving Keith Burkinshaw with a clear field. Arsenal meanwhile paid £1 million for QPR's highly rated 19 year-old striker Clive Allen. So that was another option closed to Palace.

The transfer merry-go-round took on ridiculous proportions with clubs lashing out millions on ordinary players. Manchester City's Malcolm Allison attracted most attention with his spending spree but he wasn't the only one and Palace soon became involved themselves. Arsenal made their interest in Sansom official and Venables, resigned to losing his prize asset, asked for one of their three strikers Alan Sunderland, Frank Stapleton or Clive Allen in exchange. Surprisingly, Terry Neil was prepared to part with Allen in a direct swap estimated at £800,000 nett. In addition, Venables paid £400,000 for goalkeeper Paul Barron in order to solve a mini goalkeeping crisis caused by Burridge's pay dispute at Selhurst. Barron was highly rated although his track record didn't bear close scrutiny. The supporters, loyal to Burridge, were not impressed.

Palace opened the season at Anfield and fared no better than they had the season before. Allen and Francis had chances but we were always on a hiding to nothing. As well as the team changes, Palace were also undertaking major work on Selhurst Park. Sainsbury's supermarket chain had purchased one end of the ground for a reported £2 million. The Whitehorse Lane was demolished to be replaced by a smaller end with a supermarket behind it. The regulars were unceremoniously chucked out to find new spots or stay away altogether. Away fans were moved to the corner section between the Holmesdale and the Arthur Wait, thus driving a wedge into the Palace fans. With the Whitehorse closed the atmosphere was muted and the boards placed up behind the goal only served to detract from home matches. Only 27,000 saw us lose a seven goal thriller to Spurs on August 19. We had trailed 3-1 but fought our way back and looked likely to rescue the situation until Vince Hilaire lost his cool and pushed the referee over earning himself an early bath. It made everyone laugh but probably cost us a point.

The bad start was rectified by a storming second half on the following Saturday when Middlesbrough's hard earned interval lead was washed away by a spectacular Allen hat-trick rounded off with a gorgeous curler into the right hand corner of the Boro goal. Goals for: 7, goals against: 9, a lively start and if Allen maintained that form we would have a decent campaign. We didn't bargain for seven straight defeats at the end of which we would have no manager and would be the laughing stock of English football. The oldest joke doing the rounds was: What's the difference between a triangle? The answer being that a triangle has three points.

This was actually grossly unfair. We were genuinely unfortunate to lose to Wolves at Molineux, we were robbed by identical goals at identical times in successive weeks at home to Villa and West Brom, where Fenwick's limitations in Sansom's left back berth were cruelly exposed, and most ludicrous of all, we were denied at Coventry where *Match of the Day* confirmed that Clive Allen's brilliant strike didn't count only because the referee hadn't seen it. The fates, it seemed, were against us.

QPR meanwhile were having an equally dismal time in the

second division and were looking for a saviour.

They had made a private approach to Palace for Terry Venables during the summer and been rebuffed. But the turmoil at Selhurst Park persuaded them to try again. Would he stay or would he go?

Venables departure couldn't have come at a worse time. The circumstances which surround his departure remain unclear even today, it depends on who you wish to believe. Either the board refused to back their manager, opting to make his position virtually untenable, or, alternatively, he brought it upon himself and simply deserted the sinking ship. For many years, if you'd asked most Palace supporters you would certainly have expected to find them believing the latter. More recently there has been a mellowing towards the young man who led us from the third to the first division yet his integrity has been called into question by recent revelations made by the Tottenham Hotspur board and the BBC TV programme *Panorama*.

Whatever your opinion, it was a bad moment for Palace's youngsters to lose the man they considered to be their guiding light. Venables' coaching ability was not in question and Palace needed to play their way out of trouble.

While he settled into his new office at Loftus Road, Palace turned to Ernie Walley, a crop haired disciplinarian from North Wales, who had looked after many of the players when they were in the youth team.

In a caretaker capacity, Walley set about instilling some backbone into the team. It produced immediate results with a spirited 2-1 win over fellow strugglers Leicester and a miraculous fight back against Southampton in which the somewhat rotund Flanagan left his detractors gasping with a breath taking hat-trick. After an unlucky defeat at Leeds, our fourth 1-0 loss in six matches, Walley dropped a bombshell by leaving out Allen and Hilaire for the visit to Carrow Road. It worked though, we picked up our first away point of the season. Asked about Allen and Hilaire by BBC's *Football Focus*, the taciturn Walley repeated monosyllabically: "We got a point at Norwich." It may have been an expedient move in order to secure an away point but it gave him a problem for the match with Manchester United at Selhurst. He opted to keep an unchanged side with no place for his talented front runners. Yet, again, it worked. Nicholas, near the by-line in front of the Arthur Wait, floated in a long cross-cum-shot which sailed over Gary Bailey to give us both points. But that's where the revival ended.

Tony Duffy/Allsport

Clive Allen celebrates his hat-trick against Middlesbrough. It was a rare moment of joy for the young striker who was dropped by Ernie Walley and eventually sold back to QPR

> **"I would have liked Terry to stay, but I believe that if a person, for whatever reason, wants to go, there is no point in trying to keep him ... We want a young man with a progressive outlook, for Crystal Palace are the progressive organisation. We are one of the leading clubs in Britain and it is the intention of the Board of Directors that we stay that way."**
>
> – Raymond Bloye, October 18, 1980

We played well enough but the results just wouldn't go our way. Hilaire was recalled but we now had a million pound teenager sulking in the reserves. As Christmas approached, the Palace board decided to add an element of farce to our struggles.

Malcolm Allison's departure from Maine Road had been inevitable. Bewildered by his tactics, his misfit collection of million pound players were having almost as bad a time of it as Palace. With Mal back in the job market, Bloye decided to sling Walley out.

Allison, attired in mackintosh rather than fur coat and fedora was given a warm but guarded reception by the crowd before the restored Allen banged two goals past Norwich to help us chalk up our best win of the season, 4-1. The messiah was back.

Not for long. We were on the receiving end of four goals ourselves in an open match at the Dell before collecting a fortuitous point at home to Arsenal on Boxing Day when their fans taunted us with *there's only one Kenny Sansom*. We could hardly reply with *there's only one Clive Allen,* could we? Sansom at least had the decency to score the own goal which knocked Arsenal out of the F.A. Cup at Everton a week later. But our interest in the Cup was equally short lived. With the sort of irony that only the F.A. Cup can provide, Allison took his team to Maine Road to face a City team revitalised by John Bond. City were the subject of a year long documentary by BBC's *Nationwide* which meant Palace's misery was captured for all to see after we collapsed to a 4-0 defeat.

The home match with rough house Stoke summed up our luck. Despite an early goal by our Welsh centre-half Terry Boyle, the visitors kicked their way to a point. The clogging started with a foul by Paul Richardson on Francis. Ray Evans was then booked before Richardson chopped Francis again. The Palace player was carried off while the City player received his marching orders. We continued with ten men until Francis returned in the second half with his knee heavily strapped. Eventually he limped off and Palace, who'd already brought on Smillie for Hilaire, joined Stoke on ten men. Mike Doyle earned the fourth Stoke booking but also scored an undeserved last minute equaliser. A farcical one it was too. Gilbert, under no pressure, lifted a back pass over the stranded loan keeper Terry Gennoe to leave the Stoke man with a tap-in in front of a cursing Holmesdale.

Allison had the highest regard for Francis although the midfielder was unhappy with the sweeper role the manager wanted him to play. Nevertheless, Francis was quite superb adding elegance to the side. But we kept losing.

At Manchester City we lost 3-2 and then were well thrashed by Forest, 3-0 at the City Ground. The situation looked hopeless.

By the time Palace returned to Selhurst Park for the next home match, we not only had another manager but a new board as well. After weeks of speculation, with several different bidders rumoured to be interested, Palace came under the control of a consortium led by former Wimbledon chairman Ron Noades. It didn't take the new board long to dispense with Allison's services. Mal's second reign at Selhurst had lasted six matches – his only victory had been that first one against Norwich and his only other contribution had been to sell John Burridge, Terry Fenwick and Mike Flanagan to Terry Venables for £100,000 apiece. This he declared was 'good business' for Crystal Palace while everyone else wondered if that wasn't a little on the cheap side and whether Mal's friendship with Venables had anything to do with it.

Palace announced that their new manager would be Dario Gradi, the Wimbledon manager who had once been Chelsea's youth coach. Gradi at least achieved continuity. We were getting beaten before he arrived and we kept getting beaten. After two away defeats, the manager watched his new charges go three down to Coventry before half time. Anybody still hoping for a miraculous late escape had their illusions shattered. Indeed Noades and Gradi had already conceded defeat even though, mathematically, Palace were still in with a real chance of survival. They decided that the club was in too big a mess to be able to resurrect it other than in the second division. It was no good looking at the tables. We weren't that far behind, but we didn't have the morale necessary for a relegation battle.

Gradi's biggest problem was trying to placate the disgruntled stars. Allen was still in a strop, Nicholas was thinking about his international future and asked if he could go when relegation came. To make matters worse, the new manager had seven straight defeats under his belt.

Transfer deadline day arrived and Selhurst Park resembled Waterloo station in the rush hour. In came Tommy Langley from QPR in a deal involving cash and Tony Sealy, David Price arrived from Arsenal plus a half a million quid for Peter Nicholas, while Brian Bason joined from Plymouth. Langley and Bason had been with Gradi at Chelsea and the manager explained: "I tried to buy Brian Bason almost as soon as I arrived here, because he can play in three or four positions and I felt he would be a useful member of the squad. Plymouth wanted more than we were prepared to pay until the day before the deadline. That deal agreed, I arrived at Selhurst Park on the day of the deadline anticipating a quiet day. Arsenal were already on the phone offering £500,000 for Peter Nicholas. I had wanted Peter to stay at least until the end of the season when I had agreed to discuss a possible transfer to a first division club if we were relegated. However, Arsenal offered David Price at £80,000 and I did not think I would be any better off waiting until the end of the season."

Gradi got his first point at Leicester with a Price goal followed by the last two 1-0 defeats of the season, the second of which at Old Trafford confirmed that we would be playing second division football in 1981-82. We had been beaten by the odd goal on less than 17 occasions.

"I believe Palace has a catchment area nearly as good as Arsenal or Tottenham. It's certainly in the top four of the London clubs. We should be in Europe and the top half of the first division. It's a fantastic club. It's in a bloody mess."

New Palace Chairman
Ron Noades, February 1981

Once the dirty deed had been done, Palace relaxed and, ignoring the taunts of *who the f****** hell are you?* from sections of the Holmesdale, Gradi's new boys gave him his first victory as Palace manager, 3-1 over Birmingham.

It was left to Nottingham Forest to apply the coup de grace to a dreadful season with a 3-1 stroll at Selhurst Park in which the visitors were so superior that the home fans were reduced to cheering for the opposition, in any case we hardly felt loyal to the strangers in the red and blue sashes. We got a point from Manchester City on the last day with a Walsh goal which took our points tally to 19, a record low for a first division season (although it has since been beaten by Stoke).

Few thought, a year before, that Palace would be back in division two by August 1981. In the ensuing period, everything that could go wrong had gone wrong. The club was under new management which few supporters trusted while the team, shorn of its best players, was under the guidance of a man whose track record was far from encouraging. It was pointed out that when Gradi left Wimbledon they were 13th in division four with 28 points from 27 games but they eventually won promotion. Nevertheless the sun came out for the home match against Cambridge and Hinshelwood scored the Football League's very first goal of the season stroking a first minute penalty past Malcolm Webster. The irony that Palace should be the first team on the scoresheet in 1981-82 will not be lost on any supporter who witnessed the shambles which followed. Against Cambridge, we played better than the 2-1 win suggested and although the team was an unfamiliar one we left Selhurst Park hopeful that the forthcoming campaign would be a good one. The Palace line up:
Barron, Hinshelwood, Dare, Price, Cannon, Gilbert, Smillie, Murphy, Walsh, Langley, Hilaire, sub Hughes.

After Cambridge, Palace faced two difficult away trips to potential promotion rivals. It was the same old story. Both games ended in 1-0 defeats and it was already apparent that defending stoutly wasn't enough. The imports were not up to the standard we had come to expect and the goal scoring problems that had dogged Palace seemingly throughout eternity were no nearer solution. Even two thunderous strikes by Walsh which gave us a 2-0 win over Charlton could not paper over the cracks. The game was notable for possibly the worst miss in Selhurst history, Derek Hales managing to hit the stranded Barron with an open goal at his mercy. If that provided a little light relief, we were soon asked to swallow another bitter pill. Terry Venables and his collection of ex-Palace players awaited.

On QPR's unfamiliar and much derided plastic pitch Palace played well enough, but the result went against us thanks to a scrappy goal by John Gregory. The supporters' simmering resentment against Venables was developing into full-blown hatred.

In late September, Palace played Orient before which the Archbishop of Canterbury presented club president Stanley Stephenson with a cheque for £210,000 from the Football Grounds Improvement Trust for Palace to carry out safety work. It was the first time Runcie had visited Palace even though, as the programme pointed out, we are the only league club in the Diocese of Canterbury. After Hilaire had taken on Orient almost on his own – scoring and then being sent off for fighting in front of our Holy visitor – Palace began their nightmare sequence against Shrewsbury. The Shrews shattered our 100% home record in a soggy match and although things picked up with our first away point at Leicester and two wins, first at home to Rotherham and then at Wrexham – the first on our travels since Bristol City on March 1, 1980 – we were already out of the reckoning for promotion. At home to Derby, the bad luck continued. Troubled by a fierce wind we ran Derby ragged only to lose to a John Robertson cross that was blown past Barron by an untimely gust.

Luton were early season pace-setters and they beat us at Kenilworth Road with another single goal. Patience with Gradi, not in the most plentiful supply, was wearing thin not only on the terraces but in the boardroom as well. After Blackburn collected maximum points at Selhurst Park in front of a meagre 9,452 a year after Nicholas's goal had beaten Man United in front of more than 31,000, Gradi was dismissed. It's cruel, but the general reaction was one of delight. He had never won the fans over. It wasn't his fault that he was forced to preside over the sale of some of our major assets and perhaps only a miracle worker could have rescued us from relegation, but the fans could see for themselves that Langley, Bason, Hughes and Price were hopelesssly inept. And they were Gradi's fault. Palace appointed youth coach Steve Kember, a far more popular figure, as caretaker manager.

Although most supporters agreed with the decision to remove Gradi, they were not impressed that the club were back in the market for another manager. Allied to concern over the loss of star players, dwindling crowds and bad results, criticism of Noades mounted. But the chairman pointed the finger elsewhere. In the programme before the Grimsby match, Steve Kember's manager's notes were elbowed into touch for a a lengthy rant:

> *"I am continually asked by certain supporters to resign because of the way I am running the club, together of course with the Board of Directors."*
>
> *"Personally I am sick to death of being criticised and being kicked in the teeth by all and sundry because I have not had any choice in how the club is run over the past 15 months. I have had a continual battle to keep the creditors at bay, and to continue playing football, and our supporters should realise that so far the directors have managed to stop the club going the same way of Bristol City. I think you all have a perfect right to be critical of some decisions, but you also have to understand that a great many of them have been dictated by other circumstances affecting the club behind the scenes."*

A point from a goalless draw at Oldham, followed by victories over Norwich – in which Kevin Mabbutt scored twice – and Bolton, thanks to an own goal by Paul Jones, signalled a false dawn. Mabbutt had been Gradi's last throw of the dice, arriving from Bristol City in exchange for Terry Boyle and a cash adjustement of £100,000. The impish little striker had taken time to settle but after the change of management he enjoyed a more productive spell.

Another change saw Ian Walsh swapped for Swansea's Kevin Keegan-lookalike winger David Gile, who had been brilliant in the Swans' F.A. Cup defeat of Palace in 1980 but failed to live up to expectations during his spell at Selhurst. Giles must be considered as another erroneous signing.

Not that Kember had much leeway. There was no money and although our £700,000 signing Steve Wicks, who had been the bait in the deal which took the unhappy Allen back to Loftus Road, returned from injury having played only four games thus far, it wasn't defensive cover that was needed. Wicks scored in the defeat at Sheffield United – one of only two Palace goals in seven matches (the other was by Shaun Brooks in a 2-1 defeat by Charlton at the Valley). Langley, with only one league goal to his name all season, scored in our 3-1 League Cup exit at home to West Brom in December. Had we beaten Albion it would have been perfectly acceptable to call it a "giant-killing" such was the pitiful position in which we found ourselves. Rumours circulated of a Venables plan to offer £200,000 plus Bob Hazell in a £400,000 swoop for Wicks and also to give us

1 BARON
2 HINCHLEWOOD
3 BOLTER
4 MURPHY
5 WICKS
6 CANNON
7 LEVELL
8 SMILEY
9 WALSH
10 MABBUTT
11 HILAIRE
12

Referee

Keren P. Barratt, (Coventry) Commenced refereeing in 1968 and progressed via the West Midlands League to the Football League List. Has refereed various local Cup Finals, including the West Midland League Premier Cup Final in 1980.

A married man with two daughters, he is a machine tool fitter. For six years was Secretary of Coventry Referees' Association and was also an amateur goalkeeper with Coventry City.

Linesmen

K. Miller (Essex) Red Flag
R.G. Smith (Oxon) Yellow Flag.

Matchball Sponsors

Tonights Matchball Sponsors are ABBEY ACTION

We're the famous Crystal Palace. Well, not if this Cambridge programme is anything to go by. In the pen pics they also managed to put "Vice" Hilaire!

back John Burridge plus £20,000 for Barron. Speculation it may have been, but the constant worry that more of what remained of our star team was heading for west London only served to anger and alienate more fans. It hurt that almost every time one opened a newspaper there was another player on the transfer list or more speculation of unhappiness and financial difficulties behind the scenes. It was little wonder that the supporters were deserting in droves.

Little more than a fortnight after our League Cup exit, we faced another tricky cup-tie; away to Enfield in the F.A. Cup third round. It was a game that many predicted would be a giant-killing formality – it would be a miracle if Palace survived. We were never more pessimistic and for a week beforehand we had to endure the taunts of Enfield's manager Eddie McClusky who told the press: "Palace are the smallest big time club I've ever seen." Once again it was the heroic figure of Vince Hilaire who came to the rescue. His brace and another by David Price – a rare useful contribution from the ex-Arsenal man – gave us a slender 3-2 victory to spared our blushes. Big mouth McClusky was silenced and we heaved a sigh of relief.

Our progress in the Cup was steady if unspectacular. Cannon's penalty edged us past Bolton after a visiting defender had been harshly penalised for handball. Then, after Orient held us to a goalless draw in the fifth round, Smillie produced a brilliant shot in the replay to set up a date with destiny on the detested QPR plastic.

Sandwiched in between was a controversial outing to Charlton, after which Kember was reported to the F.A. for remarks made to referee Brian Daniels about certain "inconsistencies" in his handling of the game. Murphy was sent off for dissent in the last minute, having reportedly called the linesman "a cheat" following a disagreement over whether or not the ball was out of play. The Palace midfielder had not been so much as warned and, typical of Palace's luck, Charlton snatched an undeserved injury time winner.

The Rangers match was a nightmare. All that mattered was to win. There was more than a semi-final place at stake and, if anything, the Cup was almost incidental. All we wanted was to beat Venables and his Palace rejects but after Hilaire had been the victim of an unpunished professional foul, by Glenn Roeder, Allen knocked in the winner with his knee with 30 seconds left. It was another undeserved defeat but no less predictable for that. Wicks summed it up afterwards. "This club is always getting kicked in the teeth." Not that he needed to worry, by the end of the month he was wearing blue and white hoops again. Another less than successful signing, Wicks' return to Loftus Road a little more than half a season after he'd arrived, brought in an estimated £325,000 – money desperately needed to keep the wolf from the door. Venables must have known about Palace's parlous financial state. At the time he was involved in legal proceedings against the club for monies still owed to him.

"The Board of Directors of Crystal Palace Football Club have decided with regret to terminate the contract of team manager Dario Gradi. The club's coach Steve Kember has been appointed manager on a caretaker basis. The directors recognise the difficult circumstances under which Mr Gradi had to work since coming to the club at the beginning of this year. They appreciate that he has laid the foundations of a successful long term youth policy which should produce positive results in the years to come. They believe however that they must take account of the team's current performance and the effect that team results have on the level of support at the turnstiles."

TUESDAY, NOVEMBER 10, 1981

Despite all the crises and disasters that had befallen Palace in the last 18 months it wasn't until we achieved our next victory that most of us began to come to terms with our staggering decline. Twenty four and a half thousand had packed Loftus Road for the quarter-final and it is no exaggeration to say at least half were Palace. Yet three days later it was Cardiff in the pissing rain and a depressed 6,526 watching Langley score the only goal – his second and last of the season. While we huddled on the Holmesdale, soaked to the skin, he roared off to salute his strike. A week later, the programme, desperate for good news, carried a photo of him, arms aloft, in front of row upon row of empty seats in the Old Stand.

All that was left was a battle against relegation. More salt was rubbed into the wounds by Dave Swindlehurst, who scored one of Derby's four goals at the Baseball Ground, although the gloom was lifted by an inspired performance from Murphy at Stamford Bridge the following Wednesday. He joined Mabbutt on the scoresheet to earn what remains our last victory at Stamford Bridge to date. One of the few comforts of those dark days was that Chelsea were in just as big a mess as us.

An attendance of just over 13,000 even for a midweek match between the clubs at the Bridge would surely have been unthinkable had either side been halfway decent. It was the first time Palace had scored two goals in a league match for almost four months.

The following Saturday, we produced a performance of rare style and courage to hold promotion fancies Luton at Selhurst in far and away the most entertaining match of the season. As one Holmesdale wag put it: "Six goals – and we've got three of them." The revival was soon over. Chelsea exacted revenge for their earlier defeat with a goal by the awful Alan Mayes on the day Britain imposed its 200-mile exclusion zone around the Falklands. Palace were as deep in the mire as the Argentinian forces and for many there was now an exclusion zone around Selhurst Park.

We were in need of a miracle and for some unexpected reason we got it. Oldham kindly laid down and died in the April sunshine. Hilaire and Mabbutt took advantage to chalk up a 4-0 victory, our biggest for a very long time. Kember had been saying for weeks that Palace were going to give someone "a hiding" but few of us believed him. It was huge, 4-0 to Palace was the equivalent of 12-0 to anyone else.

Not only but also … on the following Tuesday we came away from Grimsby with maximum points, thanks to another Hilaire goal, and a point at Bolton gave us a great chance of escape.

Watford, playing a new style of direct football under Graham Taylor, had surprised everyone and arrived at Selhurst Park looking to clinch promotion. For many Palace fans it was a first encounter with "the long-ball game" and we didn't like it. But it was effective. Watford impressed no-one but they won comfortably and their tiny band of supporters, who barely influenced a larger than usual 12,355 crowd, celebrated elevation to the top-flight while the disgruntled Palace fans moaned their way home again.

Alan Mullery, who struggled to keep Palace afloat in the face of crippling debts. He was still the Brighton antichrist, though. Illustration by Jason Axell

As the season drew to a nerve wracking close, two incidents summed up our fortunes. Against Barnsley, Mabbutt's shot hit the bar and bounced down seemingly over the line. The referee waved play on. Three days later, a Shrewsbury shot hit the Palace bar and bounced down and a goal was given. We lost both games on those decisions, causing more anxious glances over our shoulders until, in a desperate match at Ninian Park, where we had come to grief eight years earlier, Mabbutt – rapidly acquiring cult status – grabbed the only goal to pull us a little further away from the drop.

To make certain of safety we had to beat Wrexham. After three appearances as substitute, a gangly youngster called Paul Wilkins was elevated to first choice number nine and delivered two goals to Wrexham's one. And so Palace could afford a celebration in the last game at home to Newcastle where Murphy's strike at least looked set to finish the campaign on a winning note. But two Newcastle goals in the last two minutes summed it all up. A final placing of 15th belied a season of massive disappointment. We scored just 34 league goals, the lowest total in the division; five less than Orient who finished bottom, yet we were not that bad a team. Cannon, Gilbert and Hinshelwood remained from the back four that won promotion two years earlier while Murphy, Hilaire and Mabbutt were all gifted individuals who had played at the highest level and were capable of doing so again. The nucleus of a good team was in place and the fans liked the manager. If we could solve our scoring problems there was no reason why we shouldn't do much better.

Off the field, the club were making progress and making a big song and dance about it at the same time. "Strikers" restaurant opened in February 1982 and the club installed executive boxes and partially completed the car park. There was also a banqueting suite at the back of the Whitehorse, more executive boxes and further work on the car park. Noades explained the position: "As you well know the Club has had serious financial problems and a great number of things have had to be done just to keep us in business. We didn't refuse to pay the away gates – we just didn't have the money."

There weren't too many fans who cared much for ground development. We wanted results first and foremost, but in June, to the dismay of almost everyone, Steve Kember, who had done enough to be given the manager's job on a permanent basis in February, was dismissed. Noades, apparently overlooking the fine job he had done in keeping Gradi's moribund team out of division three and the bonus he had produced by taking the club to the quarter-finals of

Loyal Supporters

In an early episode of *Only Fools and Horses*, a Crystal Palace scarf can be seen hanging in Del Boy's hall. However in later episodes both Del and Rodney make occasional mention of supporting Chelsea and Millwall.

Did You Know?

On 4 May 1982 Former Palace keeper Vic Rouse returned to Selhurst Park as manager of the Metropolitan Police team which faced the RUC in the British Police Cup Final

Did You Know?

In late 1982, Palace were involved with a paper called the *South London Eagle* which, it was grandly claimed, would have a readership of 250,000 with coverage of Palace and other entertainment in south London. It died a death.

the Cup, horrified everyone by appointing former Brighton manager Alan Mullery.

Mullery had resigned from Brighton in June 1981 but was back in management less than three weeks later with Charlton. But after a spectacularly unsuccessful season, he'd parted company with them, and Noades snapped him up. Mullery had a good reputation, having taken a third rate club into the first division, but he was hated by the Palace fans. For many it marked the end of supporting Palace. If further reason was needed they would not follow a team belonging to the man they referred to as "the antichrist".

A little wheeler-dealing took Neil Smillie to Brighton for one of Mullery's old hands, left back Gary Williams. Former Wales striker Ian Edwards arrived on a free transfer as did Orient's enthusiastic midfielder Henry Hughton. It brought about what the programme incessantly described as "a unique blood link" between Palace and Tottenham with regard to the Hughtons and Mabbutts – they had Chris and Gary, we had Henry and Kevin – this was a feeble attempt to bask in the reflected glory of Spurs' cup winning teams of the time.

Mullery made some back room changes bringing in former Chelsea manager Ken Shellito as his coach.

Bason, who subsequently featured in many fans' all time worst Palace line-ups submitted to the fanzine *Eagle Eye*, went to Reading on a free transfer, even though Portsmouth had reputedly offered £60,000 for him and Price only months before. Steve Galliers, for whom Gradi had paid £70,000 returned to Wimbledon. The diminutive Galliers was a tigerish midfielder for the Dons but completely hopeless for Palace. We recouped just £17,000 of the original outlay.

The club announced that the new Whitehorse terrace would be ready by Christmas taking the capacity of Selhurst Park back above 40,000

A bright and breezy opening draw with Barnsley was followed by a 2-2 draw at Rotherham where Hinshelwood and Mabbutt pulled back a two-goal deficit to earn a point. After Shrewsbury were convincingly beaten it looked as if we were set for a good season. But another comfortable victory at home to Blackburn was followed by a disaster at Brunton Park, where former Brighton player Malcolm Poskett scored all four Carlisle goals. But we resumed our good form with a 3-0 drubbing of relegated Middlesbrough where Mabbutt took his tally to five in six games. Even a tricky visit to QPR produced a point thanks to some excellent keeping by Barron, who achieved his third clean sheet in four games. And so we moved into the top six, having also eliminated third division Portsmouth from the league cup.

Then we suddenly ran into trouble. Two successive visits to Lancashire ended in defeat, first at Bolton and then at Burnley. We seemed to have some sort of unique deal with Lancashire clubs; we won down here they won up there. As if to prove the point we gained an unexceptional 1-0 win at home to Oldham – unexceptional except for Barron hitting the post with a drop kick. Although Mabbutt's goals were valuable, they brought only two victories in 11 matches as we went off the boil. In the last of these, a 4-3 defeat by Wolves at Selhurst, the nippy striker was injured and forced out for four months.

The Wolves match was a minor classic. The *Match of the Day* cameras no doubt had come to see the Midland club's title challenge rather than the silky skills of Langley, Giles and Lovell, but it was Palace that started with a bang. First

Personality plus

For any fan who hates to be patronised, programmes have always been something of a bugbear. John Ellis looks at all those player profiles

YOU always find them in programmes. A chance to discover the personality behind the player. But why are player profiles always so depressingly similar?

It sounds like a good idea, but if some of the answers are anything to go by, the players either don't have a personality or the profiles fail woefully to fulfil their function. How we would love to imagine that the players lead exciting, mysterious lives away from football, to think that they read all the great novels, write poetry and watch the right programmes on Channel 4.

Let's pick a year. Let's whizz back in time to 1983, back to the days of Ronald Reagan's star wars dream, of Greenham Common women, of another Thatcher election triumph and Billy Joel singing *Uptown Girl*. What were the players thinking about? What insights could we get?

Well almost every player liked golf and tennis. There is supposed to be a good reason for this. It's called insurance. If you are a footballer you are not supposed to take part in potentially dangerous sports such as skiing. Instead it's endless rounds of golf and tennis which are only dangerous to the mind. After-match routines are also very similar. A drink or a meal with the wife or girlfriend, steak and chips and half a lager. No heads down no-nonsense mindless boogie in a rock club or even a night at the opera. It's always back home in time for *That's Life!* and *Match of the Day*.

One area I am always intrigued by is music. Why does everyone like "soul"? And why does soul always manifest itself as Diana Ross, Michael Jackson and Lionel Ritchie? The occasional oddity among this sea of blandness is to be treasured.

What about Gary Locke's favourite film, *The Texas Chainsaw Massacre*. Having seen him play, perhaps it isn't so surprising. Everyone else seemed to be fed on a diet of *Rocky* and Clint Eastwood. And while they all wanted to play for their country (fat chance with that Palace team) John Lacy was, perhaps, more down to earth about his abilities. He wanted to meet a member of the Royal Family.

The worst aspect of these personality breakdowns has to be the nicknames: Vince Hilaire – "Vinny"; Peter Nicholas – "Nicko"; Gary Locke – "Lockey" and Gary Stebbing – "Stebbo". About as inspiring as the football they played. But there was one who was different; Tony Evans was known as "Shergar".

Why? Perhaps it was prophetic for the man who finished leading scorer that season without ever being seen at Selhurst – scoring that is. Perhaps it was he and not Lord Lucan who rode away on Shergar ... into obscurity.

Cannon and then new signing Chris Jones, a free transfer from Man City, scored in the opening two minutes. But by half time Wolves were 3-2 ahead, helped on their way by some abysmal goalkeeping. Barron somehow contrived to drop one header onto his knee and then lay prostrate as the ball bounced over the line.

In the second half, Doris Hinshelwood epitomised the old Palace spirit with a brilliant performance topped off by a rasping drive beyond John Burridge. But it wasn't enough to prevent us going down 4-3. If only we'd had a striker of the calibre of Wolves' Andy Gray.

Four more were conceded at Grimsby the following week in a performance that sent Mullery up the wall, the rot had set in. In the league cup, we were beaten at home by an efficient but uninspiring Sheffield Wednesday even though substitute Langley suddenly achieved cult status among the terrace humourists. There was little reason for the fans to take the ex-Chelsea starlet to their hearts. Nothing more than the fact that he tried hard, although he achieved little. Nevertheless, the raucous cries of "go on Tom" (often followed by derisive laughter) seemed to inspire him and he came within an ace of forcing a comeback from two down. Palace earned applause for entertainment value but still went out. In the league, Wednesday were not so fortunate. Not only did Langley score, but Palace enjoyed the rare luxury of a two goal winning margin. The ever reliable Hinshelwood got the other goal. A draw at fellow strugglers Derby caused Mullery to blow another fuse. The number of chances Palace missed was scandalous and although Langley scored again he could easily have had six. Jones, now partnering the ever enthusiastic Tom in the absence of long term injury victim Mabbutt, scored the Christmas goal that sent most of the 17,966 crowd against Charlton – the biggest of the season – home relatively happy. It was a rare strike by the balding ex-Spurs man. In fact, his third and last goal for Palace was a consolation in a 3-1 defeat at Barnsley two weeks later.

Our form was poor but the fervour generated by the home clash against Venables' promotion chasing QPR meant that stood for little. Once more we had most of the game but, against the run of play, Clive Allen silenced the Selhurst hate campaign with two spectacular strikes.

Palace were in a mess and Mullery had no answers. Even if he had the answers there was no money. And there was more bad news to come:

"The club has decided to concentrate the efforts of our youth development and coaching staff to establishing a new and exciting programme for the apprentices. To that end we have withdrawn from the South East Counties League to 'go it alone'. Many of our apprentices have already graduated to reserve team level and that is a measure of the strength of Palace's youngsters. Palace will concentrate all effort and energy on bringing through the players from the 14 year-old age group."

This announcement prompted complaints from fans. Whatever the club claimed, it looked like another cost cutting exercise and with memories of the proud youth tradition still fresh, it was considered both an insult and foolhardy. The club issued what it thought was a reassurance.

"Contrary to recent reports the Crystal Palace youth system is alive and well. We have withdrawn from the South East Counties League but the latest news is that, if the new youth policy produces the expected results, Palace should return to the league in two years. If the club had decided to stay in the league we would have had to sign six further apprentice professionals. The fact that only one of our youngsters reached the required standard meant that Palace would have been in a position of having to offer professional terms to five youngsters who we considered had no future at Selhurst Park.

This action, merely to keep a place in the South East Counties league would have been a disservice in the long run both to the players and to Crystal Palace FC.

Now the total resources of the club's youth network are being concentrated on the development of the lower age group which is currently full of quality youngsters. They will form the nucleus of the youth, reserve and we hope senior side in the near future. The emphasis is therefore on quality rather than quantity ... It is not and never has been the intention of the club to dispense with a youth policy. The measure of withdrawal from the SE Counties is one which may prove more and more common as clubs seek the readjustments made necessary by the present economic climate.

The last sentence gave it away. So much for the "successful long term youth policy" Dario Gradi was supposed to have put in place. The club had hocked its future. It would be more than six years before Palace would again be able to introduce players who had progressed through the ranks.

We won on New Year's day at Leicester but after that, right through to April, there were some shocking displays and only one win – a 3-0 success on a freezing February night at home to Bolton. Midfielder Shaun Brooks, for once, fulfiled his promise with a sparkling display, but Bolton were absolutely diabolical.

The following week we travelled to Oldham and received a hostile reception from the natives as Palace fan Gary Chapman recalls: "The Oldham fans were attacking any Palace supporters they could find. There were about six of us walking down the road and somewhere in the region of 50 Oldham hooligans chased us. We were saved by a hearse. The driver pulled up and told us to get in and he drove us to the police and told them what was happening. The team was travelling home on the same train as the supporters and the club physio was actually fixing up people's injuries after our fans were

Jerry Murphy: "When he plays, Palace play," said Alan Mullery
illustration: Jason Axell

attacked at the station."

Fulham, managed by Malcolm MacDonald, were chasing promotion. Our visit to Craven Cottage in March summed up the difference between the two sides – decent strikers and luck. We matched the Cottagers in every department (except up front) yet they went ahead from a free-kick they shouldn't have had in a mysteriously extended first half. Near the end, Chris Jones (some of the more witty fans had taken to pronouncing his name in the same way that Leonard Rossiter's character Rigsby from *Rising Damp* said: "Miss Jones") hit the post, but Palace succumbed 1-0. There seemed little doubt that we were going down again. The following week we met Chelsea in what must go down as one of the worst football matches in history – 0-0 flattered both teams and in any other sport there would have been an inquiry. It was Palace's fourth successive match without a goal, a sequence which was broken at long last by Murphy's penalty at Elland Road, we still lost.

Mullery sought to strengthen his attack by bringing in another free transfer, West Brom's 35 year-old veteran Ally Brown, who had been an effective finisher in his day, which was some considerable time ago. What Palace got was a thin, pink bloke, who looked a bit like the lead singer in the Hollies. He had no pace and less desire but at least had enough of the old sparkle to find the net against Charlton. To no avail, Palace hit the bottom of the table for the first time.

There seemed no way back. Indeed, there would have been no way back had it not been for the injection of enthusiasm provided by Mabbutt's return – for which every Palace fan should remain eternally grateful. His entrance into a traditionally drab afternoon at the Valley was greeted by the biggest roar of the day. He then chased everything that moved.

Although by no means fit, the impish striker unsettled Carlisle sufficiently the following week to force Dave Rushbury into conceding an own goal. Brown then grabbed a vital winner.

Although we were hammered at Blackburn we gained two more valuable points by beating Grimsby, the great escape was on. The match marked the opening of the new Sainsbury's superstore and with it the restored Whitehorse Lane terracing which, from its former glory, had been reduced to a pitiful 5,000 capacity. Palace offered free admission to school children on the new terrace and Noades told *BBC2 News*: "The Norman Chester report tells us that we should be allowed to keep our home gates. If that proposal comes into being we can experiment by letting in for free other members of the community." The club then announced the experiment would be repeated for the home game with Derby. At Molineux, the TV cameras revealed to the nation exactly what Palace fans had been saying for two seasons, somebody up there hated us. We outclassed promotion chasing Wolves only for Andy Gray to break his goal drought to send us home empty handed. But Palace gave a performance of equal brilliance the following week, slamming Derby 4-1 with two goals for Mabbutt and one each for Nebbeling and Hughton. Billy Gilbert celebrated his 200th appearance in fine style with an own goal. We now had a fighting chance of escaping the drop. The situation was still desperate though and away defeats at 'Boro and Wednesday left things nail bitingly poised.

Back in January, we'd reached the fifth round of the cup after an Edwards' goal had "giant-killed" first division Birmingham. But our home tie against Burnley in front of 15,000 brought another mind-numbing display of inept finishing. The replay was another of those travesties of justice Palace so loved to provide for their supporters.

We dominated from start to finish, hitting everything but the back of the net. On one occasion Jones miscued from four feet with the goal at his mercy. Then, Burnley, with their only attack of the match, were awarded a penalty. David Fry – who had replaced Paul Barron, sold to West Brom for a much needed £65,000 – watched the Burnley player shoot wide, only for the referee to order a retake. Mullery bought champagne for his beaten players on the way home but it couldn't wash away the bitter taste of defeat.

But the robbery wasn't quite complete. Burnley had to come to Selhurst for the final match of the season and win. If they did, we would go down in their place. A draw would be enough to ensure our survival. The tantalising prospect of swift and ultimate revenge attracted 22,714 fans and com-

Top Score

"There's no doubt about it – Top Score, the nation's new 6 from 49 pool, is going to be football's last chance for financial survival," declared the Palace programme of August 24, 1985.

Ron Noades was a prime mover behind the competition he believed would inject much needed cash into the sport – football had missed out on the opportunity to cash in on the pools years before. A total of 86 clubs entered a joint venture to put 100% of the profit after prize money and expenses into football. But public interest was minimal not least because the rules were fairly incomprehensible. Although Palace's shirts carried sponsorship by Top Score this only served to further identify it as a failure and link it to Noades' popularity rating. Despite the Palace chairman's protests about lack of support, Top Score sank without trace unmourned.

I WOULD LIKE TO TAKE THIS OPPORTUNITY TO APOLOGISE TO ALL CRYSTAL PALACE SUPPORTERS FOR THE PERFORMANCE AT PETERBOROUGH UNITED DURING THE SECOND LEG OF OUR MILK CUP FIRST ROUND MATCH ON WEDNESDAY, SEPTEMBER 14th.

THE PLAYERS ARE KINDLY DONATING THEIR WIN BONUSES FROM THE FIRST LEG MATCH AND THE AWAY BONUS FROM THE MATCH AT PETERBOROUGH TO LEN CHATTERTON'S FUND FOR THE ANNUAL HANDICAPPED CHILDREN'S PARTY.

Did You Know?

In 1984, Andy McCulloch's training kit was sponsored by Dorothy and Sally Antiques ... probably trying to tell him something.

parisons were inevitably drawn with a May night four years earlier when we had roared the Eagles into division one. The match itself was dull and, had the stakes not been so high, it would have defied description. But Edwards' late goal won it for Palace and Selhurst went mad. We'd finished 15th again.

Although this was a closer shave than the previous year, the overall effect of appointing Mullery was that everyone was a year older and nothing had changed. The manager promised there would be no repeat performance but deep down we knew his words were hollow, Palace were treading water.

During the summer the Conservative government was returned at the General Election. It was business as usual for Britain and little had changed at Selhurst either – we lost at home to Man City on the opening day and had Henry Hughton sent off.

Mullery boasted that he had acquired a "million pound player for nothing" after tempting striker Stan Cummins south on a free transfer from Sunderland. The Roker club had offered the diminutive forward a reduced contract and under league regulations he had the option of a free transfer. The only other notable change was to the kit. After seven years in all white with a red and blue sash, we returned to red and blue stripes. The strip, supplied by adidas, carried a sponsor's name for the first time – Red Rose supermarkets. Five matches into the season Palace were still in the market for their first win. While Newcastle were full of themselves over the signing of Kevin Keegan, Tony Evans was more our speed. Another free transfer, this time from Birmingham, he scored his first goal at St James's Park where we lost 3-1. Evans would finish the season with a remarkable record as one of the few leading scorers never to score on his home ground – all seven of his goals were scored away from home.

Palace were at a low ebb, having been dumped out of the league cup by fourth division Peterborough in shameful circumstances at London Road. Two goals from Hilaire and a Shaun Brooks penalty had given us a first leg cushion in front of a post-war low crowd of 3,975. But the second leg was an unmitigated disaster and we were beaten 3-0 ourselves before going out 4-2 on penalties.

Mullery went spare. He printed an apology to the supporters in the programme and fined the players a week's wages. It was the second and last match that future Wimbledon and England star John Fashanu played for us. Still very much in the shadow of his million pound brother Justin, he had been on loan from Norwich with a view to a permanent deal. But the Canaries wanted a fee which Mullery was reluctant to pay so he joined Lincoln instead and from there moved to Millwall and then Wimbledon. He was rubbish for us anyway.

After a hefty kick up the backside, Palace produced three excellent victories; first at home to newly promoted Portsmouth, where the visitors' centre-forward Mark Hateley headed a fabulous own goal – he couldn't have finished it better if he'd been trying – followed by two successive 3-1 away wins, first at Middlesbrough and then at Cambridge. Hilaire, of course, was instrumental in all three.

Palace still lacked firepower but suddenly it appeared there was money available. The papers carried stories that Mullery was after both Frank Worthington who, although he was getting on a bit, had immense class and glamour, and old Palace favourite Dave Swindlehurst. According to the press Palace were prepared to spend £150,000 on their former striker. As luck would have it, Derby were next to visit Selhurst, by which time negotiations were supposedly at an advanced stage, so much so that Swindlehurst was virtually a Palace player again. Many Eagles fans cheered when he scored what proved to be the only goal of the game. We went home less disappointed than usual believing Swindlehurst would soon be doing it in Palace colours again. But Noades decided after a board meeting that Palace didn't have the funds to make the deal. Even allowing for the excesses of the press, it is difficult to understand why things had been allowed to go so far when we didn't actually have the money. All it achieved was to alienate more supporters and make the disappointments to come more acute. Swindlehurst later returned to London with West Ham. While Palace continued to struggle he helped the Hammers out of division two and enjoyed a successful spell among the leading scorers in division one.

We did restore one member of the "Team of the 80s" to the ranks. Peter Nicholas, out of favour at Arsenal, returned on loan with a view to a permanent move. He pulled on a Palace shirt once again for the 2-0 defeat at Grimsby. His services were clearly going to be needed. While the Welsh international added extra bite to the midfield, nothing had been done to address the lack of goals. We struggled on with a £5,000 signing from Sheffield Wednesday, Andy McCulloch, labouring under the serious handicap of old age.

McCulloch was the perfect illustration of all that was wrong with Palace. In the 1978 league cup, he had played in the Brentford team destroyed 5-1 by Palace's precocious youngsters. Five years later he was playing for us.

The match of the season was at Stamford Bridge where, against all odds we took a 2-0 lead against Chelsea, who had spent heavily to acquire Kerry Dixon, David Speedie and Pat Nevin. Their investment had paid off, they were on their

Interesting programme notes of the 80s

■ Tommy Langley part owns a two year old gelding, Annsome Boy, named after his wife Ann. He bought it for £3,800 and it ran its first race at Leicester on March 31, 1981 finishing fourth in a large field.
Palace v Birmingham, April 1981

■ Gary O'Reilly has a hobby "others consider a chore", he is decorating his West Sussex home and enjoying every minute of it.

■ Alan Pardew hates smokers and training bibs

■ Steve Galliers' nickname at Wimbledon was "Mushroom Head" - *Palace v Derby October 1981.*

■ Kit manager Maurice Drewitt's geraniums are "bang on target for next summer" ... "They will start to flower in late February-early March and when they do I'll have trouble getting some of them through the door," explains Maurice. *Palace v Rotherham. January 1983*

■ A handy holiday hint. "Tie a coloured ribbon to each item of your luggage. The unusual case that you paid a lot of hard-earned cash for will appear in the airport baggage collect hall with numerous similar cases belonging to fellow travellers and, of course, ... eat foreign food in moderation and use the cheap, bottled water." – *Palace v Blackburn, February 1987.*

■ Palace's first goal in the League Cup was scored by Andy Smillie in 1961, the 100th goal was scored by Andy Gray in 1985. The fact they were both scored by Andys is "a remarkable coincidence".
Palace v Man United. FL Cup, 1986

■ Vince Hilaire has bought a rosewood cabinet for his TV and video and it looks "terrific".
Palace v Man United. November 1981

way to the championship. Palace on the other hand were in such dire straits that we fielded centre-half John Lacy – another of Mullery's misguided free transfer bargains – at number 10. Another free transfer, Gary Locke, gave Palace, wearing boring red shirts and black shorts, which made us look like Charlton, the lead against his old club with a 35-yard pile driver. It was a remarkable effort – the sort of goal that Palace just didn't score. When Evans headed a second, Palace's tiny band of supporters went into a frenzy. But John Hollins' first goal since returning to Stamford Bridge reduced the arrears and Chelsea eventually grabbed a draw. The following Saturday, we did our beloved neighbours a big favour. Leaders Sheffield Wednesday arrived at Selhurst protecting their 17 game unbeaten start to the season. But we sent the Owls crashing with a brilliant Giles goal.

Such fine performances against the top two teams in the division proved to be a springboard ... for five defeats. The last two of these, on Boxing Day and December 27 respectively, were at home to Brighton, where Neil Smillie scored one of the Seaweeds' goals, and away to Charlton. Palace always did know how to ruin Christmas for their supporters.

On the last day of 1983, a rare product from the youth ranks, Gary Stebbing, scored to secure a draw with Shrewsbury which was enough to give everyone a reason to get plastered. Hogmanay? Happy New Year? Palace got a point at home to Shrewsbury. Trebles all round!

For the second year running, we joined the ranks of F.A. Cup third round "giant killers", and this time the press meant it. Our name was added to one Sunday paper's "roll of honour". And which footballing great had we beaten to deserve this accolade? Leicester. That's right, Leicester. Well they did have Gary Lineker, although he wasn't as famous as Steve Lynex at the time.

The goal was suitably bizarre. The Palace keeper George Wood, yet another free transfer, took a drop kick that would have gone straight in if Mark Wallington hadn't tipped it over the bar. Leicester were just thinking how embarrassing it would have been when Gilbert materialised at the corner to head home. Our reward was a money-spinning home tie with West Ham. We'd just achieved a remarkable home victory over promotion chasing Newcastle and there was a rare air of confidence about the club. The Geordies, playing in revolting shiny grey, fielded Peter Beardsley, Kevin Keegan and Chris Waddle but Palace amazed themselves, their supporters and their opponents by going in at half time 3-0 up. McCulloch, the restored Mabbutt and Gilbert scored the goals. We enjoyed a stress-free half time on the Holmesdale for the first time since about 1976 and speculated on the possibility of further scoring and, God forbid, even five in a match. Instead, Waddle scored a beauty and our defence had to be at its best to make sure that there was no way back for the Geordies. The away fans took it well, chucking light bulbs out of the train at the Palace fans waiting at Thornton Heath station – all six of us – and threatening to "kick our f****** heads in" if we tried to get on the train. So sod off Geordies, may your team rot in hell.

Palace took record receipts from the 27,590 crowd which attended the West Ham match (Noades, throughout his time as chairman, has maintained a remarkable knack of taking record receipts with ever decreasing attendances), but a large proportion were Hammers' fans. The bubble blowers had the centre section of the Holmesdale as well as the normal away allocation and were just about everywhere else as well.

We took the lead with a McCulloch effort which went in off the bar and then, against an impressive array of talent including former Palace junior Alan Devonshire and England's cultured Trevor Brooking, we fought a superb rearguard action. Devonshire, who had been discarded in the days when our youth policy provided an embarrassment of riches, spent the first half of the 80s making sure we all knew what we had missed. Having to watch the likes of Sansom, Allen, Swindlehurst, Devonshire and even Fenwick enjoy success elsewhere made the "dark ages" even more difficult to bear. Not that we begrudged them, its just that they could and should have been doing it for Palace.

Bobby Barnes was tormentor-in-chief but our defence held firm until, just when all looked lost for West Ham, up popped Swindlehurst. Seven minutes left. We swallowed hard as the Holmesdale rang to the sound of *I'm Forever Blowing Bubbles*. Three days later at Upton Park, Palace, backed by noisy support of their own, put up another spirited show but were overrun and West Ham eased through, 2-0.

We could comfort ourselves that our brave performance had surely tempted some of the lost support to stick with us. Well not quite ... in fact just 4,819 watched in amazement as referee Brian T. Stevens from Stonehouse in Gloucestershire sent off mild mannered Mabbutt for a second innocuous tackle and, inevitably, "suspension King" Billy Gilbert for arguing about it. While we were still booing, the ref fell for one of Hilaire's outlandish dives and Nicholas despatched the penalty to give the nine men an unlikely victory. Palace chose to wear their red and white kit again at Fulham which probably confused anybody who'd had a couple of drinks. Many of us thought we were on drugs as well when McCulloch popped up with a header four minutes from time to save a precious point. Another point at Barnsley with a Nicholas goal edged us closer to safety, but every silver cloud has a black lining and once more it cast its shadow over the injury-prone Mabbutt, who was ruled out after doing his dodgy knee no good on Fulham's bog of a pitch.

We had been trailing a hot-shot 17-year old from non-league Aylesbury. The fight for Phil Barber's signature had come down to a straight duel between us and Man United. Obviously there was only going to be one winner and we stumped up the phenomenal sum of £7,000 for the youngster's services. This signing was totally out of character for Mullery. For a start, Barber had cost money and, secondly, he wasn't half way to his bus pass. Our manager declared that his protege was one for the future but was forced to use him immediately. Barber scored in only his second game at Boundary Park but we still lost 3-2.

It never seems to matter how we are doing, we always have an Indian sign over Portsmouth and this year was no exception as we chalked up an unlikely "double" thanks to a goal by Evans at Fratton Park. Inspiration was not forthcoming however. The home game with Cambridge, who were rapidly acquiring the tag of "worst team in all Christendom", was declared "Ladies Day" when women supporters were let in for half price ... and more fool them. The Us were in the process of establishing a record 30 game stretch without a victory, so there was two ways of looking at this encounter:

a) Palace would lose, or

b) Cambridge would have a man sent off but still get a draw.

This time, the answer was "b" and the 29 Cambridge fans who made the trip, delighted with anything less than defeat, spent the afternoon singing *we're gonna win division three next year* (such optimism – they actually went down again). It put the Palace pessimists firmly in their place. We hadn't quite reached the insanity stage yet, but we were well on the way.

Continued on page 267

THE MAN BEHIND THE MIKE

John Henty is known to all as the matchday announcer at Selhurst Park. He talks to Neil Witheroe about *Glad All Over*, Hospital Radio, Brighton and Hove Albion and Holly Johnson's *Americanos*

John Henty's voice is familiar to generations of Palace fans. The pre-match DJ has followed the club for more than 40 years and his association has spanned the most exciting moments of the club's history.

"As a Croydonian, I have always supported Palace and my father actually played one game for the club in the early 1920s, although I'm not sure if it was a full first team appearance. My father was an amateur with a club called Brookside, which was based in the Pollards Hill area, but never signed on professionally with Palace. I still have the programme somewhere recording the appearance of L. Henty.

"He used to take me to Selhurst and I remember being lifted over the the turnstiles in the Wing Stand (now the left hand side of the Members' Stand, near the present PA room) which was where we normally sat. I saw my first game around 1947."

Obviously there was some soccer talent to be inherited, did John never try to follow in his father's footsteps and try to make the grade with Palace? "Unfortunately in that respect I went to Whitgift, a rugby playing school, so my opportunity to participate in competitive football was practically nil. I was however known as the 'Cam Burgess' of the playground, where endless rounds of that most noble of games 'tennis ball footie' took place. Due to my bulk I also earned the less flattering title of the 'flying plum pudding'."

When John was old enough to go to Palace without his father he used to dread being forced to play rugby for the school on Saturdays. "I hoped the rugby would kick off early so that I had a fighting chance of getting a 68 bus to Selhurst for just after kick-off."

Those were the days of the "rather autocratic" chairman Percy Harper, who never had any problems keeping Palace at the forefront of press attention. "Of the players, I held in some esteem were the likes of Ronnie Rooke, a left winger called Jimmy Clough, a Belgian Marcel Gaillard, the Dawes brothers and Freddie Kurz. This list is by no means definitive."

Most people at the time rarely considered travelling away from home to watch Palace although there was the odd London derby. "I did see a number of away games during my National Service, in particular at Walsall, which backed onto the laundry."

At home games, John found Palace the ideal place to bring his latest girlfriend. "It could be quite romantic, particularly on the Holmesdale during a cold, windy evening game and it probably explains why most of my girlfriends of the time lived in the Thornton Heath area. I didn't meet my wife there although she is a lifelong Palace fan and attended the Lady Edridge school which stood where the executive car park is now."

John's first association with the club came when he joined the *Croydon Advertiser* as a reporter in the early 1960s. "I got to know a number of players as they attended functions I was covering and then Roy Preston of Croydon Hospital Broadcasting approached the paper to publicise their service which offered live match commentaries to patients at the Mayday and Croydon General Hospitals. I signed up with a couple of colleagues as a commentator and literally within hours was sitting at the rear of the Old Stand with a microphone and socket in which to plug it."

In the early days the service was fraught with problems. "There was no two-way communication with the hospital and the often biased commentary was met with ridicule by those seated around us, especially if they were away supporters."

The biggest match, John covered was Palace versus Real Madrid. "It was the first time I'd encountered foreign names and there was a period in the second half when Real were constantly bringing on substitutes whose numbers seemed to bear little relation to those in the programme. I could barely see the numbers anyway. Palace may have been

> **"There is no one game I can point to, although surprisingly few records work that well over the tannoy. *Glad All Over* is marvellous and probably for that reason alone I kept playing it. Thus, I suppose I am responsible for it becoming the club song."**

Power to the Palace

We play the game like it always ought to be
You've just got to come along and
join with me-e-e-e-e-e
Banners swinging, voices singing
Goals will come you'll see

All Power to the Palace
At home and away
All Power to the Palace
Bring a friend to watch us play-ay-ay
Bring a Pal to the Palace today

Now when our players take the field we shout out
loud
We're the fans in the Crystal Palace crowd
Banners swinging, voices singing
Eagles do us proud

(Chorus)

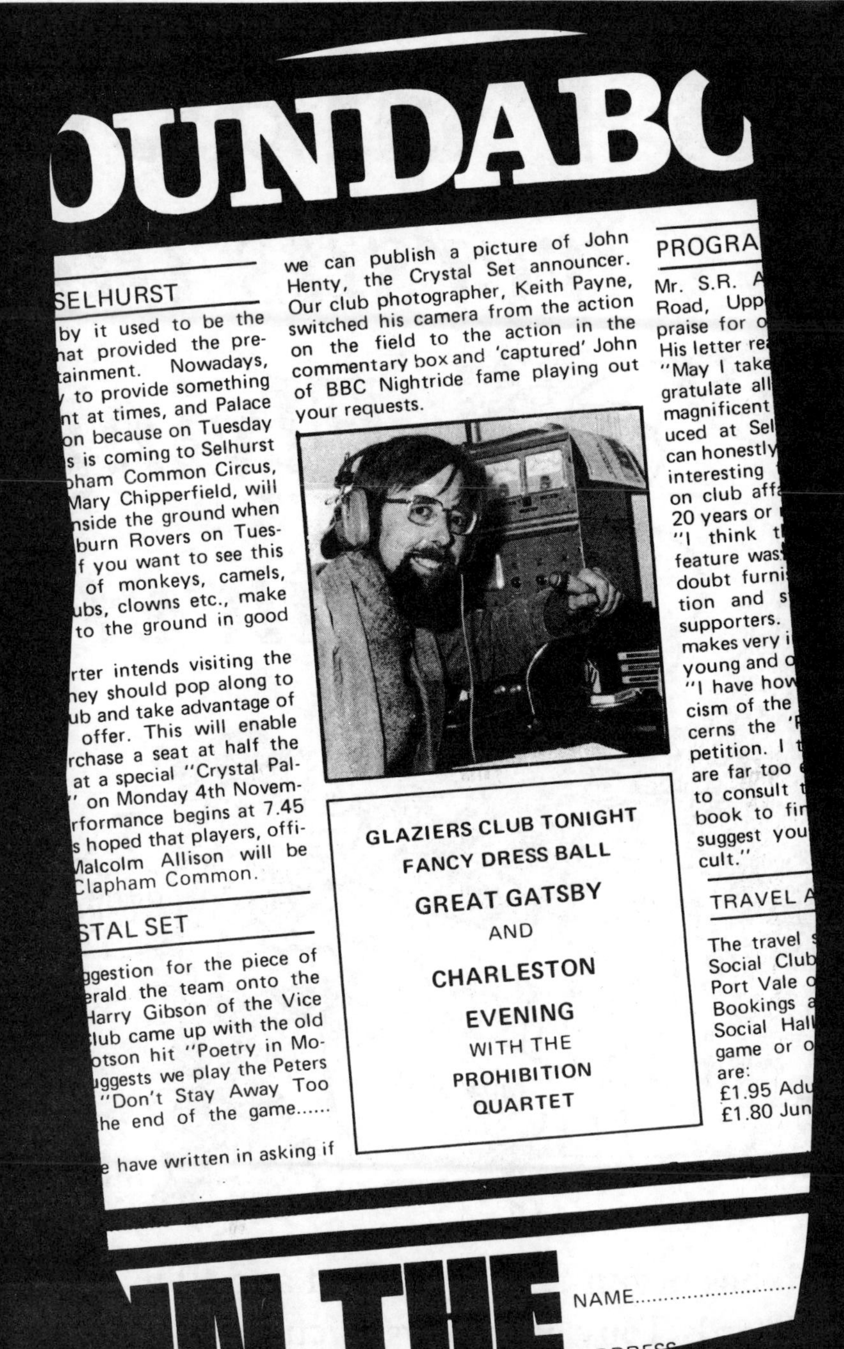

OUNDABO

SELHURST

by it used to be the
hat provided the pre-
tainment. Nowadays,
to provide something
nt at times, and Palace
on because on Tuesday
s is coming to Selhurst
pham Common Circus,
Mary Chipperfield, will
nside the ground when
burn Rovers on Tues-
f you want to see this
of monkeys, camels,
ubs, clowns etc., make
to the ground in good

rter intends visiting the
ney should pop along to
ub and take advantage of
offer. This will enable
rchase a seat at half the
at a special "Crystal Pal-
" on Monday 4th Novem-
rformance begins at 7.45
s hoped that players, offi-
Malcolm Allison will be
Clapham Common.

STAL SET

ggestion for the piece of
erald the team onto the
Harry Gibson of the Vice
lub came up with the old
otson hit "Poetry in Mo-
uggests we play the Peters
"Don't Stay Away Too
he end of the game......

e have written in asking if

we can publish a picture of John
Henty, the Crystal Set announcer.
Our club photographer, Keith Payne,
switched his camera from the action
on the field to the action in the
commentary box and 'captured' John
of BBC Nightride fame playing out
your requests.

GLAZIERS CLUB TONIGHT
FANCY DRESS BALL
GREAT GATSBY
AND
CHARLESTON
EVENING
WITH THE
PROHIBITION
QUARTET

PROGRA

Mr. S.R. A
Road, Upp
praise for o
His letter re
"May I take
gratulate all
magnificent
uced at Sel
can honestly
interesting
on club affa
20 years or
"I think t
feature was
doubt furni
tion and s
supporters.
makes very i
young and o
"I have how
cism of the
cerns the 'F
petition. I t
are far too
to consult t
book to fir
suggest you
cult."

TRAVEL A

The travel s
Social Club
Port Vale o
Bookings a
Social Hall
game or o
are:
£1.95 Adu
£1.80 Jun

IN THE

NAME..............................

celebrating the opening of their new floodlights but it was pitch dark where I was sitting."

From hospital commentaries, John moved onto matchday announcements for the club. "In the early days we took it in turns. Strangely, I have no recollection of the PA System before I started doing it.

"It isn't the easiest of jobs because you are very exposed. Things do not happen in a routine way which makes the job very stressful and that's as true today as its ever been.

"By the mid-60s I was doing the job solely with the help of Sylvia. I was also contributing to the programme with *Henty's Viewpoint*."

Somewhere during that time, the Dave Clark Five's *Glad All Over* became a Palace anthem. Henty has no idea how or why it happened. "There is no one game I can point to. Surprisingly few records work that well over the tannoy but *Glad All Over* is marvellous and probably for that reason alone I kept playing it. Thus, I suppose, I am responsible for it becoming the club song."

At one stage, Ron Noades wanted Bobby McFerrin's *Don't Worry Be Happy* played as the team came out and there have been other challengers too. "Herb Alpert in the late Sixties was very popular. I still kick off with him although few people hear it of course because they don't arrive that early. We also had a spell of playing the Beatles' *Hey Jude* and Bert Head wanted *Hello Dolly* because, in his mind, it tied in with the return of Johnny Byrne to the club – 'Well hello Johnny, it's so nice to have you back where you belong ...' And Malcolm Allison wanted crowd noise broadcast during the game."

Henty's experience with Palace stood him in good stead because in 1968, directly as a result of his work at Selhurst, he was offered the position of Sports producer at one of the first of the

In the late 1980s I alternated between Palace and Brighton which led to the Brighton fanzines calling for my head on a plate

BBC's new local radio stations, Radio Brighton. From there he became involved with Brighton and Hove Albion FC although he points out that his relationship was "purely professional".

"As part of my *Saturday Session* we used to do a live broadcast from the Goldstone Ground called the *Goldstone Sound* between 2-3pm. It doubled as their pre-match PA and included the usual news, weather and travel, together with sports interviews.

"We once interviewed the referee Roger Kirkpatrick during his pitch inspection – it was innovative stuff. There was also a chap called Des Lynam working on that programme. In the late 1980s I alternated between Palace and Brighton which led to the Brighton fanzines calling for my head on a plate!"

Wherever Henty's work has taken him he still regards Selhurst Park as the one stabilising influence in his life. "I have always returned even during what I consider to be the dark days of Malcolm Allison when my interest in the club fell to its lowest ebb.

"I'm proud to have been associated with the club in each of its promotion seasons to the first division, but it was the Burnley game of 1979 that stands out.

"It was a crazy evening. We had new cars circling the pitch before kick off, how they got there I don't know, I remember the biggest St Bernard dog I had ever seen wearing a Palace hat and scarf alongside the thousands of people packed in. It was a hysterical, historical night, if you missed that, well ..."

Crystal Palace *versus the Flying Saucers*

2 BIG BURGERS
WILKIN'S?
OH NO THEY'RE USING A RAY!
NO THANKCHRIST!

The battle to save the earth has begun ... can the Red and Blue Army halt the Martian invasion? Words Tony Matthews. Pictures Jason Axell

The newspaper boys hung on Steve Coppell's every word. The Palace boss dealt with them patiently and then stunned them all: "Gentlemen, I have something important to tell you. We are about to be invaded by aliens."

That's how it started. Just six weeks ago the earth stood on the edge of an abyss. The end of the world was nigh. This is the story of how Stevie Coppell's Red 'n' Blue Army saved the earth from slavery by Martians.

The pressmen phoned in their reports: "Invasion by Martians" screamed the *Daily Mail*, "Massacre the Little Green Bastards" said *The Sun*, "Geoff Thomas isn't good enough for England," trumpeted *The Guardian*.

But the invasion took an unexpected twist. The Martians were not as black as they had been painted (nor as green). In fact, although their intention was to seize control of our planet and enslave us all, they had a sense of fair play. "Greetings earthlings," said their leader as their technology interrupted every TV and radio transmission in the world. "We are superior beings who are going to rule the universe, and you will be our slaves. But we are a sporting planet and are prepared to offer you a chance. We are football mad and believe it is the greatest sport in all the galaxies. We therefore challenge you to a match. We have assembled a team from the best players of our galactic empire. If you can beat us, you may live in peace. If we win, your ass belongs to us."

At FIFA headquarters, important decisions were being taken. "So, goal posts will now be made of rubber and the ball will be oval and made of sheet steel," said Joao Havelange, president of the whole game. "Now it's item 12 on the agenda – the Martian Intergalactic All Star XI versus Planet Earth. What are we to do?"

They discussed the match carefully and many fine teams were considered including Milan, Barcelona, and Marseille, but finally it was agreed that the squad would be selected from the world's greatest players.

The next day, a space pod belonging to the chief executive of the Martian Soccer Federation pulled up outside the Football Association headquarters at Lancaster Gate. The F.A. officials waited to greet him. "Greetings Mr Mar-

tian," said Graham Kelly, chief executive of the F.A. "May I say I never dreamt that one day I would come face to face with someone from another planet."

"Have you tried looking in the mirror?" replied the Martian.

The Alien V.I.P. was shown into the sumptuous banqueting suite where the F.A. chefs had prepared a traditional Martian meal: brown rats and tree frogs garnished with piquant juice of spiders.

"I am empowered by FIFA to tell you," began Kelly, "that we agree to a match against the Martian Intergalactic All Star XI at football, with the ownership of the earth as the prize. The game will be held at Wembley Stadium and I assure you that we will field the greatest team the world has ever seen."

The Martian agreed and they shook hands (and tentacles) then settled back to enjoy a rather super lunch. "For your entertainment we have assembled video highlights of the best of English football," said Kelly proudly.

"Well that shouldn't take long," said the Martian, as Kelly switched on the television and pressed "play" on the video. First up was Crystal Palace's Cup semi-final against Liverpool; an exciting and tense affair. The Martian was impressed. "I must say I admire your Earthling football supporters tremendously," he said. "But I'm afraid my mastery of your language is poor. What are they singing? *Crystal Palace FC?* Then what's the next line?" A Martian aide offered a translation of the Palace song: *By far the greatest team the world has ever seen!*

"Ah, so this team in red and blue shirts will be earth's representatives for the big match? That will be splendid. They are passionate but not very skillful and I'm sure we shall beat them easily."

Kelly nearly choked on his Minestrone. "C-C-C-Crystal Palace, our representatives? Oh no, no, no, you've got it all wrong."

"Well I don't think so," said the Martian. "You said the greatest team the world has ever seen and that is what those earthlings are singing. My F.A., planet and people accept the challenge. In one month we shall defeat Crystal Palace and the earth will be ours!"

Word spread like wildfire. What had those bunglers at the F.A. done? The whole future of planet earth depended on Palace. The world's press was aghast. In Italy *La Gazzetta Dello Sport* said: "Who is this Crystal Palace? They will win nothing," the *New York Times* suggested that the Jets or the Giants should take Palace's place and crush the Martians into the dust while the *Guardian* claimed the Martians would win because Palace played the long ball and the earth therefore deserved its fate.

But Palace remained confident. Steve Coppell addressed his players at their morning training session. "Lads, it's quite a big match," he mumbled.

Palace chairman Ron Noades wrote to the Football League: "Dear Sir," he began, "considering Palace's unique position in representing the entire planet earth, we would like permission to postpone our league matches against Coventry, Luton and Notts County and the Zenith Cup match versus Oxford United ... " The League wrote back: "We have considered your request and have decided you must play, if you do not field a full strength team you will be fined ..."

Panic spread throughout the world. Surely Palace had no chance. In a desperate bid to escape the feared Martian onslaught, millions fled to the hills – except in Holland where they haven't got any hills.

Steve Coppell was quietly pleased with his preparations. His players were determined, their training schedules were tightened. They were sleek, finely muscled and had excellent hair-styles. Palace were ready.

On the night before the match the world waited. Most people (the ones with any sense) spent it in bed screwing anybody they could find. Others watched the BBC preview programme *Who'll Win The Planet?* Jimmy Hill agonised over team selections. The Martians were impressive, he concluded, but Palace had their stars.

But anchor man Desmond Lynam pointed out that the Eagles had spent just £1 million on their goalkeeper which wasn't enough to buy a twiddly red handle for a Martian death cannon.

On the big day, the fans poured into Wembley. Stevie Coppell's Red and Blue Army was enormous. London was full of Eagles souvenirs and even the Brighton fans wanted them to win. They needn't have bothered though, the Martians didn't have the Seaweeds down as members of the human race so they were in no danger anyway.

Every human being tuned in to watch the global broadcast, except for a handful of Hooray Henries in Sloane Square who were miffed that the Martians didn't like rugger. John Motson was the commentator: "And, oh I say, well, ha, ha, he's a great chap, Andy Gray, and the Martians with all their experience of other worlds, the Beetelgeuse grub monster at number 6 has taken my eye and he once played in a corresponding fixture against the Venutians which Mars won 1-0 with a disputed penalty and remarkably enough that was the day Andy Thorn had gone to the Chemists to buy some corn plasters and there were 37,152 there and ..."

Motson had been so busy talking that he didn't notice the Martian mothership hovering over Wembley. An exasperated, metallic alien voice screamed: "Will you shut up, for cryin' out loud? Your monotonous drivel is interfering with our computers." A plasma torpedo hit the commentator amidships leaving a globule of steaming purple jelly where he had been sitting.

The Wembley roar was deafening, the atmosphere electric. The teams took the field. Geoff Thomas led Palace out in their new Wembley kit, sponsored by Virgin. "Fly Virgin to Alpha Centauri," it said. The Martians wore all green.

They lined up for the national anthems, starting with the Visitors. "Bleep, Bleep, Bleep," it went to whistles and boos all around the ground. Palace were presented to HRH the Duchess of Kent.

Referee George Courtney tossed the coin and Thomas called heads. The Martian called heads as well. "You can't have two heads," said the ref, but realised his mistake when he looked at the Martian captain.

Palace kicked off and Andy Gray smashed the ball straight into the stand. The Palace fans cheered, the rest of the world held its head in its hands and wept. The throw-in was taken by the five-handed hair monster from Alpha Centauri. This was it. Could Palace, facing the might of an intergalactic empire, achieve the impossible?

The hair monster dribbled upfield with Mark Bright chasing back to tackle it. The loose ball was picked up by a thousand-legged thing which sped forward, each football boot trundling over the lush Wembley pitch.

It raced into the 18-yard box where Gareth Southgate, who had no experience of playing this quality of opposition, caught the hideous creature's 997th leg. Courtney had no hesitation. Penalty!

The Tauron Smog Beast stepped up to blast the ball at warp factor five past the helpless Nigel Martyn in the Palace goal. 1-0 to the Martians.

Meanwhile, in a Dublin registry office, Republic of Ireland boss Jack Charlton was scouring the records to see if he could find the vital piece of paper that would prove that the Tauron Smog Beast had an Irish great grandmother.

Palace attacked. John Salako had a shot kicked off the line by the 623rd foot of the thousand legged thing and the Martians counter attacked. Their Petulan international winger crossed. There was no apparent danger. No alien was in the Palace half as Martyn came out to make the catch. But suddenly the creature-with-a-57-yard-neck stretched to head past the dumbfounded keeper.

The future for planet earth looked bleak indeed and things got worse when a reptile with the power to de-materialise, re-materialised in the Palace six yard box to make it 3-0. "Where was the marking?" cried Steve Coppell. "We were ball watching."

"Not so much ball watching," said assistant manager Alan Smith, "as orb watching." He pointed to a silver sphere, which glowed and hummed as it gently hovered above the pitch. The Palace players stood transfixed. A beam of light appeared from the orb and a pink, wrinkled creature with pointy ears was placed onto the pitch. "The Martians are bringing on a substitute and he looks like ET," said another Palace fan.

The new player was without doubt the most skilful in the known universe. His balance and spiritual grace allowed him to ghost past Richard Shaw, who was assigned a man-to-man marking job.

The ET-type thing set up goal after goal. The Wembley scoreboard could hardly keep pace: 4-0, 5-0, 6-0, then a seventh goal and an eighth and, right on the stroke of half time, a ninth. Palace 0, The Martian Intergalactic All Star XI 9. It was all over bar the shouting.

BBC analyst and Arsenal fan Bob Wilson sat smugly in the TV studio with QPR's Ray Wilkins. "Ray, the Martians are the finest team the universe has ever seen, they're 9-0 up and Palace are crap. I want you to convince the peoples of the earth that it might be possible for Palace to get back into the game." Wilkins gave a knowing half smile. "I can't see it Bob, the ET-like creature has been absolutely majestic."

As the second half began, the 80,000 Palace fans decided that, as this was the last game they would see before they were transported to distant colonies to be used as slaves in the mines, they might as well have a massive party. *Stevie Coppell's Red 'n' Blue Army* echoed endlessly round the ground. The Palace players, inspired by the rousing chorus, attacked. Bright met a perfect Simon Rodger cross with a downward header. The crowd went wild, but the anti-matter force field in goal for the Martians dissolved the ball just as it was about to cross the line.

The Palace fans roared, the whole planet roared, everyone in China roared and caused such a violent wind that it blew down Hong Kong. Wembley had never known noise like it. But the Martians regained their composure. The five-handed hair monster had a golden opportunity to score after Martyn could only parry a shot from the thousand legged thing. But, fortunately for Palace, he tripped on a tuft of hair and missed his shot.

"Aaarrrghhh," the Palace fans yelled defying of one of the creatures that would shortly enslave them: "What a stupid haircut, what a stupid haircut." The five-handed hair monster was mortified. He was a superior being and had

... AND I MUST SAY THE BEETL-GEUSE GRUB HAS TAKEN MY EYE!...
BBC

never had the piss taken out of him before. His game went to pieces. Palace won a corner and the distressed hair monster headed an own goal. The anti-matter force field was so surprised that it forgot to dissolve the ball. Nine-one. Palace were back in it. But there were only 15 minutes left.

The Palace fans didn't care. They celebrated the goal and mocked the Martian goalie. "What's it like to have no hands?" they crowed at the force-field, which had no shape but just floated about hazily. The keeper too, was stunned at being mocked. It fumbled an Andy Gray cross and Salako was on hand to turn home the second goal. The whole planet went crazy-ape-bonkers. Nine-two now, and Palace were in storming form.

At the University of Johannesburg, professor Nebbeling had completed his tests. "Its a gamble, but worth a try. Get me the telephone." He dialled Wembley. "I have discovered the Martians' weakness," he said in an outrageous South African accent. "They don't like being mocked. So tell the crowd to insult them. They will not be able to play their natural game."

The scoreboards flashed the vital message. The tannoys made announcements. "Attention. Attention. Take the piss out of the Martians, sing up Palace. Wind them up and put them off."

Unfortunately for the Martians, they'd fallen foul of the wittiest supporters in the world. The aliens were taunted mercilessly until they were on the verge of tears. Palace took advantage of the distressed visitors, pegging back goal after goal, 9-6, 9-7, 9-8 ... But the ET-type creature was still playing beautifully. He was the danger man (er, thing) and the fans were stuck as he caused havoc.

Then a young fan began chanting: *Are you Beardsley? Are you Beardsley? Are you Beardsley in disguise?* The rest of the crowd joined in until all 80,000 were singing at him. The ET-type thing was crestfallen at such a grievous insult and spontaneously combusted. The Martian substitute, a two-ton-orange-crested-vole-monster, was called a "fat ginger bastard" making him slice a clearance straight to the feet of Chris Armstrong, who struck the equaliser.

Nine-all with a minute to go. Simon Rodger ran at the crumbling Martian defence and was tripped. A free-kick to Palace. Andy Gray spoke to his captain: "Geoff, I'm going to blast it in the top corner. It can't fail, I can win it for us." Thomas agreed to the subtle and original plan and Gray lined up to take the kick.

At that moment, on board the Martian mothership which hovered menacingly over Wembley, a grand council of war had assembled. "Fellow Martians," began the Imperial leader. "Palace are giving our lads the run around. We have waited too long to surrender our prize on the outcome of a football match. We must send for our war-saucers and batter the earth into submission." The council agreed: "We shall destroy the earth ..."

Andy Gray took a huge run up and let fly with every ounce of his strength. The ball flew like a rocket over the Martian wall, over the crossbar, over the ducking heads of the massed Palace fans behind the goal (who were ready for it), out of the stadium and up into the sky. It hit the mother ship like a speeding train.

"What in the name of buggery was that?" screamed the Imperial leader as his saucer sank faster than a Brighton promotion campaign and crashed among startled shoppers in Wembley High Street.

The Martian Fleet in disarray without its mother ship lost heart and direction and retreated in ragged defeat.

Just to sew things up, George Courtney ordered the free-kick to be retaken because the wall had not retreated the full ten yards. Gray stepped up, and smashed a fierce drive beyond the force-field and into the net.

WE ARE PALACE

Neil Everitt

Five Palace fans identify what the club means to them and recall some of the more interesting moments

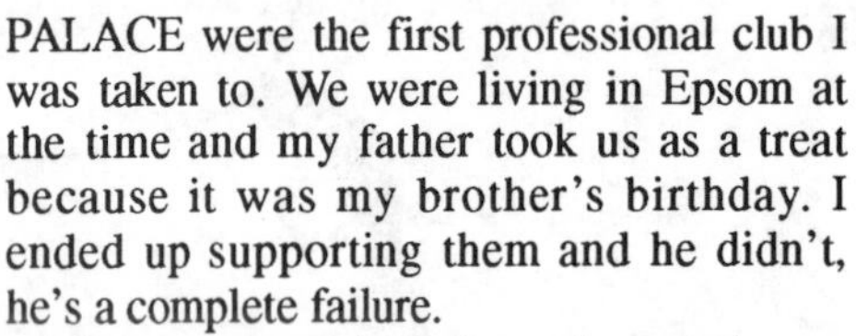

Palace 2 England 0

by Chris Beale

PALACE were the first professional club I was taken to. We were living in Epsom at the time and my father took us as a treat because it was my brother's birthday. I ended up supporting them and he didn't, he's a complete failure.

All I can remember about the match was having a banana boat beforehand in the Wimpy. It was about 1973 when we had Derek Possee playing for us and Palace were abysmal. They lost to Leicester 1-0.

It wasn't until my second match when we played Preston North End that I knew that I supported Palace. Preston played in England's colours, I was only about six or seven and I thought we were playing against England. Preston could have been England. And I thought no way would Palace beat England, but we did. We beat them 2-0. And my friend came from Preston and we made a bet afterwards that Palace would always beat Preston North End or end up higher and we always have but he never paid me.

Soon after that, my family moved to Brussels to live. I remember one afternoon my mother came in and told me she had bad news and that Palace had been relegated. She is a Birmingham City supporter and she understood what I was going through. We both supported rubbish. My Dad supported Man United, my older brothers supported Liverpool and Tottenham so they were no help. But my mum and I were both in the same boat.

As far as I'm concerned, Big Mal is a major reason why I support Palace. The team played good football but, in his words, it was more important what was happening in their minds. He was like Brezhnev in charge of Russia. The USSR was on its last legs but to hear Brezhnev and the Politburo you'd never have believed it – and Big Mal was the same about Palace. It was total madness.

I loved all the stories about Fiona Richmond and all the other girls, rumour had it that there were at least two or three involved, in the changing rooms and in the bath and holding the players knees. Anybody who came into contact with Big Mal immediately became beautiful – forget Jim Morrison, forget Jimi Hendrix, Big Mal is beautiful. His autobiography is enshrined in a special grotto in my house.

Neil Everitt

The cost of tea bags

by Steve Smith

SEVENTY pence for a pot of tea at Newport Pagnell. How much does a tea bag cost? Tuppence?

Exchanging pleasantries with 20 coachloads of Leeds, Leeds, Leeds fans at the same service station on the way to see Palace win 2-1 at Coventry

Going 2-0 up at Grimsby, Andy

Gray scoring on his debut, them getting a goal back, but winning 3-1.

On the way home we change at Newark and meet up with London-based Leeds fans. Everything is fine, not a hint of animosity. We disembark at King's Cross all singing together and the police try to segregate us.

A 1-1 draw at Mansfield (£1 to travel) and some bloke got his head stuck in the window. A 1-1 draw at Hereford and they paraded a bull at half-time. 0-0 at Walsall, 0-0 at Wrexham.

Losing 4-1 at Birmingham, not going back the next season and missing a 6-0 win. Losing at Bournemouth and Blackburn, winning 3-1 at Cambridge. Arriving 20 minutes late at Reading just in time to see us go one down and getting soaked to the skin. Travelling to Oldham the night before New Year's Eve. Being stitched up in the Full Members' Cup at Forest and all those trips to Brighton. Bring back Rachid Harkouk. That, my friends, is supporting Palace.

Fan of the Week

by Dennis Brunskill

MY FIRST recollection is being taken by my father to see Palace as a treat on my tenth birthday. It was the final game of the season against the mighty Wolves, and Palace won 4-1. By the time I had entered through the children's entrance at a very muddy Whitehorse Lane End, Palace were already 2-0 up. Danny Light, a short mighty-mouse type of player scored the first against a a giant looking Wolverhampton defence. From that game onwards, I fell in love with C.P.F.C.

By the start of the 1968-69 season, I had attended every home game and a few selected away matches. One match that sticks out was one against Blackpool which was being screened by ITV but was abandoned. I wonder if a tape still exists in the vaults?

Although the conditions were snowy, the action on the pitch was red hot. That winter was very cold indeed and, due to postponements in late January, there was a month without football.

That period to a football crazy youngster was unbearable but when Palace came back they were unstoppable.

They concluded that season with a 3-2 win over Fulham securing promotion to the first division for the first time in their history. The incident that sticks most clearly in my mind was the sight of ex-Palace hero Johnny "Budgie" Byrne (my Dad's all time favourite player), who was in the twilight of his career, seeming to be rather annoyed at the brilliant second half comeback Palace had staged after being 2-0 down.

Anyway, he kicked the ball viciously at the, now, new stand roof stanchion and a brick fell down and landed on a small boy's head. From then on, I knew it was going to be Palace's day.

Probably my greatest memory came at the start of 1969-70 when I first saw Palace in division one. It was not even surpassed by a replay trip to Wembley in 1990 against the same opponents, Man United.

I was right in the middle of the Whitehorse on that blisteringly hot late 60s day as Palace took to the pitch to an amazing welcome. I recall the team was greeted by the Palace Dollies. I wonder what happened to those young ladies? Looking through the old programmes, some of their comments seem funny now.

The game had been billed as an exciting encounter and it lived up to every bit of its hype. It was end to end stuff and probably a fair result in the end. Palace, after that, found the going quite tough and sadly I was present for a few severe thrashings. But there was one gleam of joy when my Grandad, who I had always idolised, sent a letter to the club and was included in the programme as "Fan of the Week". I subsequently featured in the F.A. Cup programme for the cup tie against Chelsea on February 5, 1970 and also in the following week's issue for the division one match with Burnley. Fame at last.

As part of the prize for being "Fan of the Week" I received two tickets to the home match with Sheffield Wednesday, which we lost. I took my Nan and sitting a couple of seats along from us was injured centre-half Roger Hoy. It was to him that we owed so much later on in the season.

Even to such a loyal fan as myself, it seemed all too certain that the Palace dream of first division status was at an end. But Roger Hoy's superb goal against Man City saved Palace from relegation.

Cast into the pit for all eternity

by Tony Robertson.

BUT FOR a freak of chance that had me born to a family that had connections with the Crystal Palace area, I might have grown to manhood with a comfortable, optimistic outlook on life.

As it is, I have developed a strange, bitter, twisted view of fate. This is due in great measure to my very early exposure to Crystal Palace FC.

Had it not been for my family, I might have taken up some less masochistic hobby, like beating myself about the shoulders with a cat o' nine tails.

WE ARE PALACE

Neil Everitt

My descent into football purgatory began one Saturday afternoon in 1967 when my grandfather decided I should be sworn into the Palace brotherhood. The game chosen for this 'coming out' was against Hull City and, at the tender age of seven, and accompanied by my 10-year-old uncle, the three of us made a pilgrimage to Selhurst Park.

I can still remember the thrill of it all. The muddy banking that graced the top of the Holmesdale and Whitehorse ends, the smell of soggy hamburgers and the wonder of going through the turnstiles having paid money to some old figure with yellow teeth.

Of the match itself, thankfully I can remember nothing. We lost 1-0, end of story. What made the game stick in my mind was an incident that had nothing to do with the game.

Mid-way through the first half I remember being so fascinated by the football that anything seemed more exciting than what was happening on the pitch. A quest for excitement led me to test my own keen skills by kicking a large stone into the crowd.

One of the Palace faithful felt the sharp pain of the stone on his calf and turned to let fly a salvo of abuse that made me cry. It was not the last time I was to cry while watching Palace.

From that day on I had to defend Palace through school days when every other kid supported Chelsea and then at work where everybody seemed to 'support' Liverpool. I have stuck to my task with the faith of a missionary, but I cannot help but feel that had my grandad taken me to some other club, life might have been slightly less of a struggle, but perhaps less fun.

Flares and Fedoras

by Nick Rawling

I STARTED going to Palace in 1972-73 when John Jackson saved a penalty from Martin Chivers to help us draw with Spurs.

Jackson was one of my early heroes as were Peter Taylor and Alan Whittle.

Whittle's permanent "morning after" appearance, as well as his skillfully dyed hair, endeared him to all at the Palace. I was indeed honoured to follow his four around Addington Palace in a golf pro-am. That day he sported Farah and Pringle – surely a premonition of his stylish days of 1976.

Peter Taylor appears in my memory as a demented Norman Wisdom, flying down the wing and whacking in great crosses. I remember an evening of celebration for his first England under-21 cap against Czechoslovakia at Selhurst Park. And why not? Palace were getting gates such as the 38,000 against Millwall which was not bad for the third division. Ahhh, Millwall ... whose supporters trashed my blue fedora with the red ribbon to the ground. Maybe they were right, it did look ridiculous on an overweight 13 year-old with natty Wrangler flares. Later we gave them Phil Barber – the Lord moves in mysterious ways.

Like some others, who have written in *Eagle Eye*, I was strangely not at the Palace versus Burnley game of 1979. I was probably at home staring blankly at the wall and listening to Joy Division. I emerged enough to see Vince Hilaire on a number of occasions and marvel at his skills, as well as his ability to fall over, later revived by Eddie McGoldrick. Inevitably it is the teams of Steve Coppell that provide the most memories. The joy of seeing Ian Wright's hat-tricks against Plymouth, Birmingham and Wimbledon. Jim Cannon's camp salute to the Holmesdale, the orgasmic explosion on the Holte when Mark Bright equalised in the F.A. Cup semi final against Liverpool and the way he almost took McMahon's head into the net with it. Losing my voice for three days after and seeing Geoff Thomas Christmas shopping in the Drummond Centre – he was wearing slacks.

There are also bad or surreal memories such as going to Shrewsbury and driving past a lone farmer who gave us a thumbs down salute.

THE TAMING OF THE SHREWS

Shrewsbury Town are called the Shrews. They are one of football's nice clubs. Like the small animal with which they share their name, they've never hurt anybody. Except us.

Shrewsbury endeared themselves to the footballing public in the late 1970s with some stirring F.A. Cup victories

They were evil ... there's no doubt Shrewsbury Town are the work of the devil. Tony Matthews recalls the worst bits

over Man City and Ipswich. I was among those who took to "quite liking" Shrewsbury. If only I'd known what fate had in store for us.

It was only when our 1980s decline set in that Shrewsbury changed from an innocuous mouse-like creature into a dreadful monster.

They had us under a spell. We spent eight years together in division two, during which time Palace only beat them twice. To say they were a jinx is like saying Charles Manson had an attitude problem. Even in our promotion season, they took five points off us. It took one of the best goals of Ian Wright's career to earn us even one point but, if that was disappointing, it was nothing compared to Gay Meadow.

We were on a winning streak while Shrewsbury were going down with barely a victory all season. As we got off the train we predicted the end of the hoodoo. "Palace will win 4-1." What possessed us to be so confident I don't know, but we were soon two down and not even their dozen fans and the two inflatable fish they were holding could believe it.

I couldn't watch, and stood with my back to the game reading the programme. Other Palace fans, in various stages of despair, vented their feelings on our bemused players. Angry gestures were exchanged with Ian Wright. It was April 1.

We were powerless; fighting against superior odds, Shrewsbury had us by the short and curlies, always had and always will.

Promotion brought sighs of relief. No more Shrewsbury; we were free from their clutches at last. Their very name

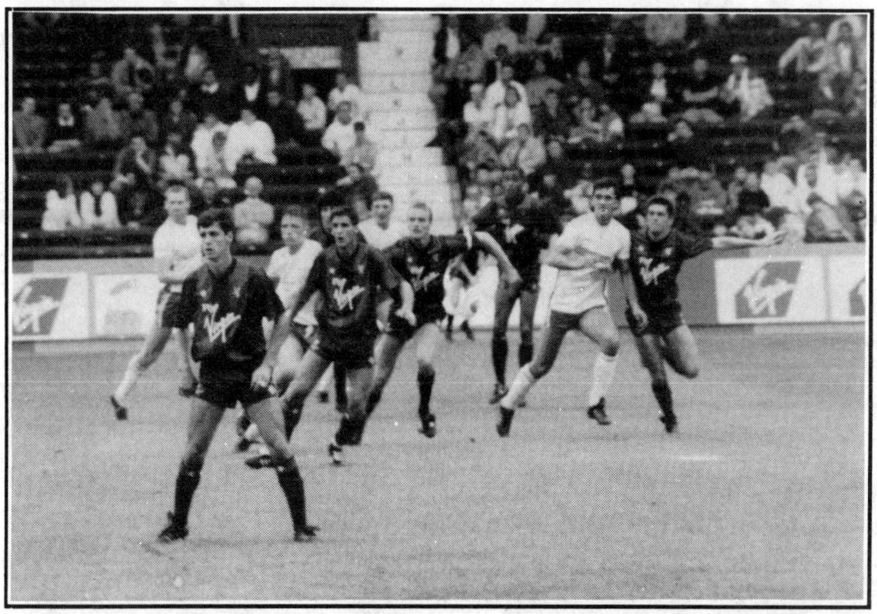

Paul Wright/NUDA

Promotion chasing Palace are held to a draw at Selhurst, 1988

created havoc at Palace. In our first season back down, they did the "double" over us when we thought we were just going through a bad phase. Our illusions would soon be shattered.

In 1982, under Alan Mullery, Palace's good start actually included a home victory over Shrewsbury. But things went down hill fast and even a "creditable" away draw at Gay Meadow thanks to Doris Hinshelwood's penalty couldn't disguise what a bad season it had been. We struggled in 1983-84 and the two draws with Shrewsbury came in handy, but no-one could escape the truth. We were happy to scrape points from a side that had no right to be on the same pitch as us. Doesn't that sound arrogant? Well, we were still living in a time when we thought of Palace as "a sleeping giant".

Steve Coppell had replaced Mullery but we still struggled and results took a turn for the worse when they thumped us at 4-1 Gay Meadow giving Coppell his first taste of managerial defeat.

We'd only chalked up two wins when they came for the return in November and took another point. This was a classic example of the bad luck that dogged us against Shrewsbury. We roared into a two goal lead only for Henry Hughton to be forced to deputise for the injured George Wood. Sensing that Dame Good Fortune was riding to the rescue, the Shrews took advantage.

Visions of a heroic performance were soon shattered. Henry let the ball trickle down his arm while attempting to punch clear. They crept back to Shropshire, sniggering about the hold they had on us, while lumps of hair torn out by the long suffering souls on the Holmesdale fluttered by in the wind.

It was more of a surprise that Tony Mahoney scored than it was that we didn't win the next encounter, but the Coppell magic was beginning to work and at the start of 1985-86 the impossible happened; Shrewsbury 0 Palace 2. The jinx was broken.

Unfortunately the Shropshire bastards turned up on a Sunday in early December to halt our five match unbeaten run. In those days of tiny crowds, an unbelievably huge 8,253 came along to see us move into the promotion frame. Beating Shrewsbury was a formality. The law of averages said we had to turn them over. But Hackett's goal confirmed that the jinx was back. The fair-weather brigade ran away once more.

We missed the play-offs in 1987 after they'd held us goalless at Gay Meadow and, in a farcical match at Selhurst, beat us 3-2 despite Ian Wright scoring with a cross that the keeper threw into his own net. In 1987-88 six more points would have sent us up as champions. We scored 86 goals, but only got one against the Shrews – and that was a consolation goal. After the home defeat we lost only one of the last 11 but missed out on the last day of the season, and it was their fault. How we hated Shrewsbury.

This fixation with Shrewsbury may seem odd, but I warn you now they are never more than a couple of seasons away.

Waterlooville sunset

Hy Money

High flying Hilaire. Vince leaps Ipswich's Paul Cooper.

Vince Hilaire and Billy Gilbert were players of contrasting style. But as members of the young Palace team of the late 70s and early 80s they both delighted Selhurst Park. Interview: David Kemp. llustrations: Jason Axell

A black, wet January night and I'm standing in the car park of Beazer Homes Premier League side Waterlooville. I've been there about 20 minutes having banged on various doors and tapped on assorted windows trying to find a way in. By now I'm wet and cheesed off in equal proportions when, out of the blackness, comes a voice."Who you lookin' for mate?"

"Billy Gilbert."

"'Ang on, I'll get 'im," says the voice, which by this time is standing next to me. The owner of the voice sprints off into the darkness. Ten minutes and a lot more rain later, no Billy Gilbert.

I go around the back of the main stand and try a door I haven't previously seen and there is the subject of my hoped for interview. Standing next to him is the vaguely familiar guy I'd met earlier, now recognisable as Vince Hilaire.

Vince and Billy, once starlet members of Palace's Team of the 80s, are now joint player-managers of Waterlooville FC which sets me up nicely for the first question. Have you always been mates? "Yeah," says Vince. "We both joined Palace at the same time, when we were 13, then of course we spent four years together at Portsmouth."

"Five for me," Billy corrects, "but four years together."

From the juniors both players swiftly moved through a period in which they earned F.A. Youth Cup honours to star in Terry Venables' highly rated young team, but it all went sour quickly. "Obviously there was a huge void when Venners left," says Billy. "He brought us up with John Cartwright and it was hard to replace a character who was larger than life. He had such stature and such knowledge of the game."

Vince certainly missed Venables. "I think one of our big problems was that, from the time we joined under Malcolm Allison, who I always likened to John Wayne, and then Terry and John Cartwright, we found it difficult to motivate ourselves when other coaches came because they had made such a huge impression on us."

By the time Dario Gradi was appointed Vince feels that the players had been

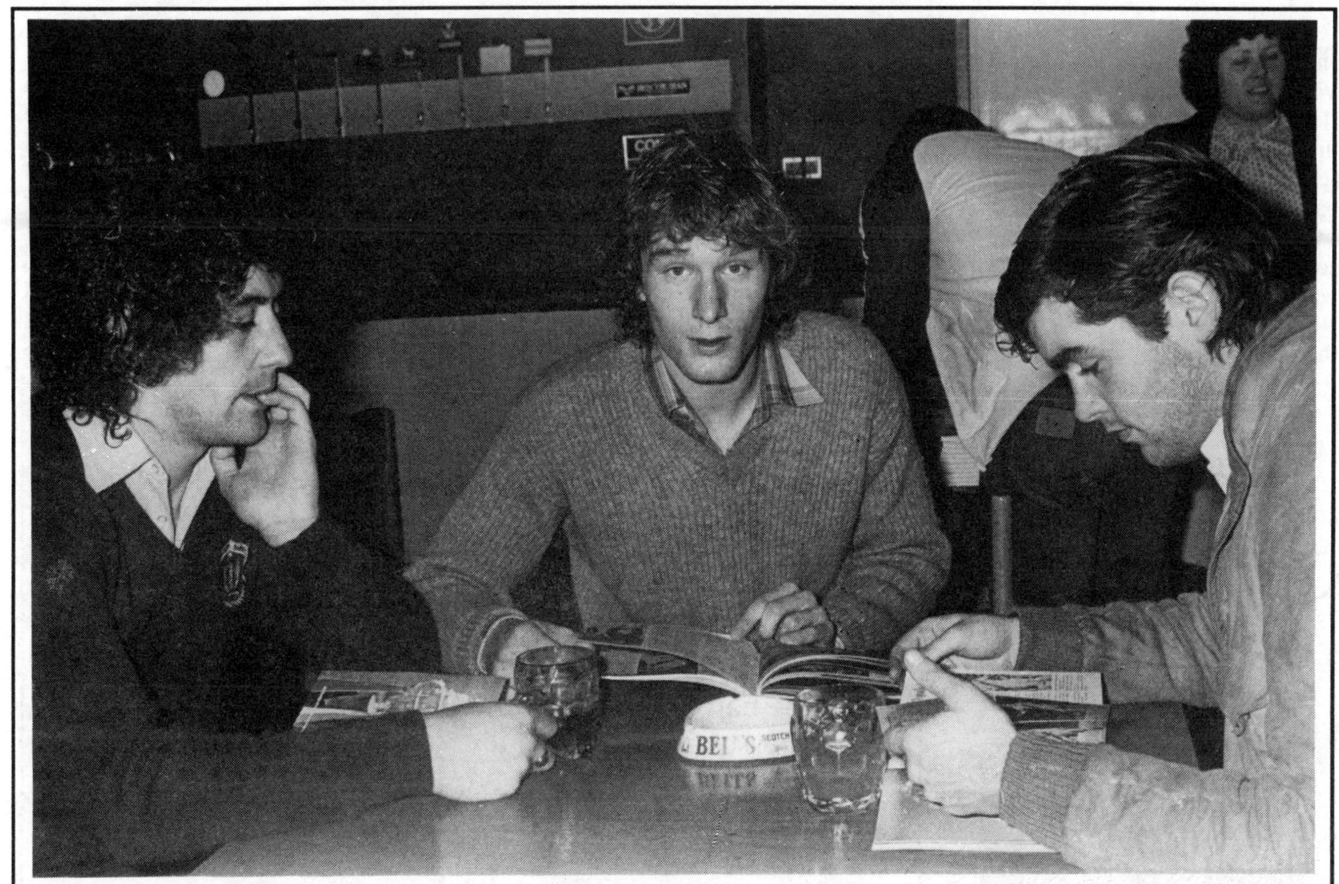

Hy Money

A behind the scenes shot of Billy Gilbert

wrongly tagged. "They would say Billy Gilbert's a troublemaker, Vince Hilaire's inconsistent."

But who are "they"?

"Different people, Dario was just another manager who came along. It wasn't a case of not wanting to do well."

So was it, perhaps, to do with a feeling that Gradi was Noades man? "That made no difference really," says Vince. "We all played our best for the various managers that we had, but we just felt that nobody could fill the void in knowledge that Mal, Terry and John Cartwright gave us."

Palace were busy cutting costs and Billy feels Noades really wanted them to go. "I think the offers we got from Mr Noades, considering that we had stayed through a very bad period, indicated that he really wanted us on our way. He has done a really good job at the club, but at the time we felt we would be better off at other clubs. He never really wanted to make us welcome there. Everything at the club was being cut back, the youth team, everything."

Vince agrees although he blames himself in part: "It was really take it or go. We were still from the old regime. As kids we were treated as well as the first team and, speaking for myself, it meant that I just didn't have any values until it was too late. I didn't realise what it was all about until my early 20s, and I'd been in the first team since I was 17. We left at 24 but that was after six seasons in the first team. Palace really had to cut back. I remember when we went to Calais. That showed how far Palace had gone. We really enjoyed that trip, we were sleeping ten to a room in bunk beds. It was a real eye opener, especially after we were used to going to Sweden."

I moved the subject round to favourite memories, starting with Billy: "Probably in my mind was the Leicester game in the F.A. Cup third round in January 1984. It was funny, the weekend before the club had an offer from Portsmouth and it was all arranged that I was to leave the club after that Cup game, but obviously I mucked myself up a little bit there." Billy mucking himself up meant scoring a brilliant headed goal straight from a corner a few minutes from time and then clearing off the line at our end in injury time.

Vince's favourite game was against West Ham: "Being an Eastender, I always remember my first game for Palace against West Ham in division two in August 1978. Billy scored from about 45 yards." Gilbert adds: "It was my first goal in the first team."

As members of the side that won the championship in that season what stands out? "I would like to have remembered a lot more about the Burnley game," says Vince. "But I got a bang on the head early on, so I was in a bit of a daze. Being young lads we should have appreciated the whole occasion more. but it was over so quickly, you know, finish, game over and we were off to America and then back to the first division. The good thing about it happening so fast was that we didn't give people too much respect and that's probably why we started so well. But we started believing our press and Venners started believing his press. You have to remember that, from being young kids who were always winning games, we lost a few in division one. It was the first time we'd been consistently beaten and we couldn't handle it and, more important, Terry couldn't handle it."

Billy believed Venables was actually "head hunted" by QPR in the close season after the first year in division one. "There was a lot of talk that Mr Bloye had interviewed Howard Kendall for the post and it was a case of Venables and Bloye playing each other off. As Vince said, Venners took losing badly. He was brought up to be a winner all the time, as we all were. The strange feeling was not knowing how to get back on the winning track."

How difficult was it to motivate yourselves after he had gone? "I know it was wrong really," admits Vince. "But I don't think we gave every manager that took over a fair crack really."

Billy is not so sure. "Maybe not effort wise, but on coaching ability we could sum them up within a week to see if they were up to the standard we were used to. I don't want to criticise, we had some good coaches there, but when you got young people coming in saying you should do this and do that and we had been brought up to do it a different way and be successful at it ..."

So what was it they had learned?

"We were always taught to play from the back," says Vince, who still believes in the basic theories of the Venables era. "I think there's a lot of talk about getting the ball forward too quickly in the game. Venners taught us to pass the ball to the back and keep possession, but only if you could do it."

In training he used to use a ploy which got people to play out of position, what was the thinking in that? "It was to get people to realise their strengths and how to exploit them. Kenny Sansom would always rotate with Jerry Murphy, Paul Hinshelwood used to swap with one of the strikers, that sort of thing. Venners could really bring out the best in the players and perhaps that was shown when some of them went to other clubs and didn't perform nearly so well. Dave Swindlehurst was a case in point, he got his moves because everyone thought he was a big bustling centre-forward who could put it about a bit, but in fact he did well when he went to West Ham, another footballing side."

After Venables a string of managers tried at first to steady and later to raise the sinking ship. Billy feels angry at some of the chopping and changing. "Whenever a manager looked like he

"We were always taught to play from the back. I think there's a lot of talk about getting the ball forward too quickly in the game. Venners taught us to pass the ball to the back and keep possession, but only if you could do it."

– Vince Hilaire

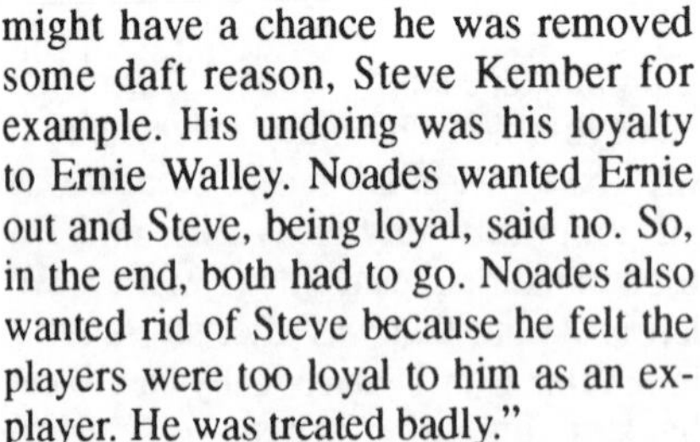

might have a chance he was removed some daft reason, Steve Kember for example. His undoing was his loyalty to Ernie Walley. Noades wanted Ernie out and Steve, being loyal, said no. So, in the end, both had to go. Noades also wanted rid of Steve because he felt the players were too loyal to him as an ex-player. He was treated badly."

For the supporters, the blow was hardened by the arrival of Alan Mullery. But Billy and Vince have better memories of him. Vince liked him because the ex-Brighton boss was prepared to be straight while Billy also saw hidden qualities. "He may not have been the best tactically but his enthusiasm really got you going. But although he was inspiring you couldn't get by on that. All players need to be coached and we weren't." Although Vince and Billy are still together their links with other players have been severed. "Jerry Murphy has disappeared off the face of the earth," says Vince. "We've been trying to get in touch with Peter Nicholas, we want him to play a friendly for us. Billy still speaks to Steve Kember and he is in touch with Paul Hinshelwood."

And what about Palace, do they still have affection for the club? Being one to notice these things I raised a point I'd read about Vince in a Leeds programme that Leeds and Portsmouth are the first results he looked for. A lot of Palace fans would be surprised and hurt by that. "I do still feel affection for Palace. I did get goaded there when I went back once, not racially though. It wasn't the game I got sent off in, that was just stupid. It was the year before in an evening game and Palace won. I was

a bit disappointed by the reception. It might have been me because we lost, perhaps it wasn't as bad as I remember."

Billy also has fond memories although things finished on a low note. "We both look back on our Palace days with affection. We were there a long time. It was just the last year when Mr Noades took over. I hold my hands up to him now, he's done a good job but when we first came people didn't realise how bad it was."

I saw Billy and Vince play for Waterlooville against Moor Green. Vince curled a delicate free kick to local hero Ricky Burnside to flick in, followed by a run of Ricardo Villa proportions to walk in a second. At 2-0, Billy took himself off before his knee gave way forever, only for Moor Green to pull one back.

I was left wishing that they were a bit younger and still with us. After a commiseratory beer (Palace had lost at Hillsborough) I asked where their ambitions lay. Both wanted success and to return to full-time football, Waterlooville are aiming for the conference in 1993-94.

And what about their partnership? Vince, with a knowing smile: "Billy does all the work, I get all the glory."

CRYSTAL PALACE

A COMPLETE FARCE 1971-1989

Right. My name is Carpark, Peter Carpark. I've been invited by all the chaps to tell you my story. I have to warn you that both the contents and delivery of this story might offend some of you. It's the story of a voyage through time and space, a personal quest for a footballing grail that started on November 13, 1971 in Croydon, London Town. It's a story of passion, intrigue and heartache: some of it will make you laugh, some of it will make you cry, but there is one guarantee ... IT IS A TRUE STORY.

ONE ERNIE WALLEY, THERE'S ONLY ONE ERNIE WALLEY....THANK GOD

Neil Everitt

Neil Everitt

Contents:

Early Days at the Cavern
And the strain is already starting to show

Eighteen years gone, my youth wasted, as bald as Chris Jones and what have they ever done for me? Bastards!

Well now it's my turn, Noades, Smillie, Barron, Ernie Walley ... ha! Hold on to your hats!

Carpark: story of a Palace fan
Chapter One: Home draw against Ipswich.

I've come of age, I suppose. Eighteen years of this nonsense and I still turn up, despite the immense travelling problems that living in Ambridge brings. I hear you laugh, or possibly not, but I tell you I've really come of age. Most of you were about three back in '71, unaware of the horrors and joys

Hulton Deutsch

Yogi Bear blasts another humdinger past poor old Sheff U. Wonder if he realised that sad old Palace fans would still be banging on about this game 20 years later, talking about it as if it was yesterday. That's sad, with a capital "S"

to follow, exploring carpets eating rusks. Me? I was a sallow, intense little brat who, up to this point, had supported Liverpool from a distance. I cried when Charlie George scored the winner at Wembley. I still cloud over when I think of Thompson and Callaghan.

I modelled my playing style on the violent tackling and acnoid ferocity of Tommy Smith. It was in this mode that I broke Procter's tooth in the playground. But John, honest, it was an accident.

I was being driven by my father to see Palace. We cruised past the new Whitgift Centre in our outmoded Ford. We spoke of cricket, golf grips, pastry, Bobby Charlton's hair style, informal stuff. We walked up Davidson Road – a walk that was to become a ritual – and approached the new Arthur Wait Stand.

We sat. It was awful, I've always hated it. The rain pissed down, Palace were crap, bottom of division one or thereabouts. The programme cost 6p, away fans were at the Whitehorse End, Palace were yet to beat another London club in division one, they had no real "stars" and the great white hope was Alan Pinkney, top scorer in the Football Combination.

It was a 1-1 draw. The attendance 18,462. I remember three incidents: David Payne slicing the ball into touch

Worst and most embarrassing chants ever (a taster)

- 'One Andy Higginbottom, only one ...' (aaaah!)
- 'Ernie Walley's Red and Blue army'... (not for long!)
- 'What's it like to run at home?'... (by 30 fans cacking themselves in the away seats at Millwall)

The "I should have chosen another career" top ten

- Brian Bason – nowhere man
- Steve Ketteridge – unspeakable
- John Lacy– still useless in amateur stuff
- Mick Hill – dreadful
- Tommy Langley – pathetic shark
- David Price – ooh, I'm pooped
- Bill Roffey – couldn't keep the ball in play
- Tony Mahoney – ?
- Alan Pinkney – eeek
- Billy Hughes

Bubbling under: too many to mention

as he attempted a cross; and the "two" Ipswich goals, one disallowed, both screamers from Miller. Oh, and John McCormick.

Chapter two: I fall in love

So what? But I went again and I fell in love with the club that day.

We were playing Sheffield United, who'd had a brilliant start to the season.

They had Tony Currie, Alan Woodward and Trevor "annoying headband" Hockey. We had John Craven, Wee Willie Wallace and Tony "I can only stand on that one" Taylor. They were fourth in the league, we were bottom. It pissed with rain. We would go down by three or four. But things, as the poet said, fell apart and...

- we ruined them
- we strolled past them

Brighton's Firm

- we ran the midfield
- we scored five
- and we had a hero called Hughes, not Emlyn but genial Yogi.

He went mental and just took on the whole Sheffield defence. If he didn't go round a defender he just ran over him, and then, from any range, he would just blast the ball at the goal. He scored twice and old John Mac roared in a 30 yarder one minute from time. The crowd – an impressive 26,296 – went apeshit. People actually chanted – just a massive steamroller ... *PALACE, PALACE* and the Sheffield players died a death. Changed utterly. That was it. I was a fan. However s*** Palace were to become, whatever crap was being churned out by club propagandists, it stayed with me.

And underneath it all was the realisation that Palace were potentially crap, sometimes unwatchable, but that just once in a while they would turn it on and make it all worthwhile.

And we always had somebody to watch: Yogi, The Don, Vince, Ian

Spammy Lee's letters page

Dear Spammy,
Am I right when I say that Alan Mullery signed the Pathetic Sharks to play for Palace during the '82/83 season?
yours puzzled
Petula Clark
Downtown Cheam

Spammy says ... Yes, Pet, well spotted. Alan completed the trio when he swooped to sign Chris Jones on a "free" from Man City to link up with Tommy "run in a straight line" Langley and Ian "your ball Mabbs I'm knackered" Edwards.

By the way Pet, I'm still a big fan.

Dear Spammy
I was sauntering down the terracing to my favourite spot on the Holmesdale one May morning a couple of years ago to see my favourite team play Portsmouth. Imagine my surprise when I was subjected to a violent beating by a group of fans wearing red and blue – they were Pompey fans.

What a silly mistake – I hadn't read the clear signs outside the ground telling me that Palace fans were not welcome.

When the scars had healed I have to admit I saw the funny side of things though. The laughs my wife and I have had since.
Yours, frighteningly cheerful against the odds,
Nigel Nice-Person,
Noades Road, Purley

Spammy says ... You creep. I hope you took a good beating.

Dear Spammy,
Have you, I wonder, noticed the remarkable similarity between Julie Goodyear, our erstwhile limp wristed goalie and Paul Barron, TV barmaid Bet Lynch in *Coronation Street*.
Are they by any chance related?
yours, worried
Tel Venners

Spammy says ... Dear Tel, nice of you to get in touch. Yes, you have every reason to be worried. You spent nearly £400,000 on Julie Goodyear and then tried to fool the fans, the paying public, into thinking she had first division experience.
Well, it was a pretty feeble effort soon scuppered when we noticed Goodyear eyeing up Billy Gilbert at corners. Also that time at Spurs when she revealed some of her ample cleavage to the Shelf after some heckling. God, it was so embarrassing. I have to admit that Paul Barron did a pretty good job pulling pints down the 'Rovers'.

Dear Spammy,
Am I right in saying that Norman "bites yer legs" Hunter was sent off when playing for Bristol City against Palace in the F.A. Cup third round on January 29, 1979?

Was it for the third atrocious foul on Steve Kember or for the rash late challenge on Jim Cannon?
yours, painfully accurate,
Nigel Lawson
No fixed abode

Spammy says ... Well, you know you're right, you smug git or you wouldn't have sent in the letter, would you?

Actually, Hunter was sent off for being a blunt, no-nonsense, I'll call a spade a spade, hatchet-faced Yorkshireman, whose feeble back pass let in that Polish forward back in 1973. I've certainly never forgiven him for the kicking he and Wor Jackie "giraffe features" Charlton gave worthy old John Craven back in '72.

In fact I hate Leeds, even if Scotney does support them, their fans always beat us up and they always were dirty bastards. Ha, ha ... remember the Cup in '76 and Dave's header ... *Eagles*. Oops, must calm down. Back to the question: he is filth, he should have been shot with the rest of the Revie crew. Also we stuffed Bristol City 3-0 and my dad went. Ice on the terracing.

The "I wish to end my career at Palace" top ten

- Wyn Davies – at O.A.P. stage
- Bobby Tambling – still bloody good
- Gary Locke– remember that run?
- Neil Martin – crap, pure desperation
- Ally Brown – I ask you. He was so slow.
- John McCormick – Steptoe Senior. Great.
- Chris Jones – Co Co The Clown.
- Venables – well he was
- Charlie Cooke – a genius
- Paddy Mulligan – I liked him, went to West Brom.

Wright etc. Other clubs just don't understand, we are magic. Back to earth. Sorry, it got a bit serious.

Chapter three: One Big Mal please (and a milkshake for the old man)

The rest of the Bert Head days were often thrilling but certainly never as "heady" as those in store for us under the ultimate hype-master, Big Mal. His days started officially in March 1973 with a win over Chelsea, some green shirts and a headed goal by Jim Cannon.

But I must go back a bit and give you a bit more Head (no Wayne, you depraved ...): Boxing Day 1972: Palace 3, Southampton 0. It is pretty amazing that I can still remember anything at all but the memory still lingers of The Don making a diagonal run across the Scummers' defence with absolute poise and control and at incredible pace before scoring, I think, his first goal.

The great impression that I always had of him was of a player running on his toes, always set to skip away from a challenge. Apart from Best and Peter Thompson, I always rated Rogers as the greatest dribbler of a ball in post-war English football. But then I'm tired and nostalgic and not a little tipsy ...

Back to Big Mal: we loved him, simple as that. He nearly sank the club but in just over three seasons made it famous. That first game against Notts County back in division two was typically farcical: it all went according to plan for the first 20 minutes or so as we attacked with the Don putting us in front. But hold on, something's not quite right. Why do Palace have no defenders on the goal line at corners? Why is Bobby Bell trying to dribble the ball out of defence a la Beckenbauer when we know he's only good at thumping it into touch or to some unfortunate chaser like John Craven (who of course went on to *Newsround* fame)?

Why have the players got nicknames like "Donkey" or "Earthworm" on their track suit tops? Why is there a callow youth called Hammond in goal after years of Stonewall Jackson? Why are the fans trailing out early as the County winger destroys the ponderous Roffey on our new specially widened pitch? Why? Because that's what Big Mal wants.

I will skip an entire season. Let's start again shall we? This time in division three: the first game against Brighton since division three south days; the day that the famous Brighton Ruck was commenced. I went there with the Old Man and the rest of the Carparks. We didn't know where the ground was; we asked a local old salt and he pointed us in the direction of a plume of smoke on the horizon.

When we arrived at the ground there seemed to be no segregation and a battle was in progress as territorial rights were established. I confess I didn't see much of the game, so busy was I with the adventures of my fellow travellers but it did all seem to be a most excellent adventure, one that has been repeated many times and which demands a separate chapter in this marvellous tale. We lost 1-0, squandering many good chances; my only memory involves a header from Whittle pinging over the bar.

Poor old Alan: a body as flexible as an elastic band. I may add that by the time we next met the Seaweeds we had a good team and we stuffed them 3-0; with the added joy of seeing a few intruders on massive old Aunty Holmesdale persuaded to leave as they posed outside the tea stall (near the gates for what is now the away terrace for all you youngsters out there).

When Palace archivists discuss Big Mal it is to the Cup Run that they turn; I shall arise and do this, but would like to mention a few pieces of terrace activity first. The Old Man and I had been joined on the terraces by the elusive Johnny Ludicrous, whose first game that I recall was the awful Cup defeat by Wrexham in 1974. Nil-two, it pissed down, even through the Old Man's golfing top; Mick Hill hit the post, unfortunately with the ball rather than his head; dreadful. But John was mainlining from then on, ignoring the lure of Chelsea but still practising those guitar licks back at Shelvers Way. Bernie, Colin the Schwab, Andy Morris all turned in the occasional appearance, while the Hung party congregated on another part of the terrace. On to the Den ...

At the start of the Cup run after seeing off the upstarts Walton and Hersham by a 1-0 landslide we travelled, with a little attack of the collywobbles, to the Den. It was my first time as they say; we asked a copper for the Palace end

A portrait of the Arsenal as a young fan

Once upon a game, and a very poor game it was, there was a donkey coming down along the wing and this donkey that was coming down along the wing met a nice old man named Johnny Humphrey.

Wayne told him that story: Wayne looked at him through a glass: he had a hairy nose.

He was Johnny Humphrey. The donkey came down the wing where Geoff Thomas lived: he knew David Platt.

Oh we hate Arsenal and we hate Arsenal

He sang that song: that was his song

We are the Arsenal ... HATERS

When they hit the net first it is a pain and then it gets dull. His father was out on the golf course. That was a good choice.

Written by Jimmy Joyce aged six. It was Jimmy 's first trip to the Palace.

Terrace talk with Wayne Holton

Crystal Palace 1 Arsenal 4, September 14, 1992

After the third Arsenal goal: Well, that's ruined my f****** weekend.
As the ball was passed to Humphrey: "No not to him ... " (Red Ted)
At half-time: "Why have we been chasing Sinnott for three years?" (Anon.)
Before the first Arsenal goal: "What did I say, he's absolutely f****** useless." (Carpark)
After the fourth Arsenal goal: "I think I'm going to be sick." Girl making her way up the Holmesdale to leave the ground.
Before the game: "No, but really, I think Palace will give them a good hiding." (Wayne)
After the game: "What did I tell you, we always lose to Arsenal, I'm never coming here again." (Wayne)
After Palace had scored: (directed at the silent Arsenal fans in the seats) "You're not singing anymore, you're not singing anymore." (The Holmesdale)
After this chant: " .... " (those witty Arsenal fans)
As they read Noades explanation (on his race comments) in the programme: "What a complete load of old b*******." (the entire crowd)

Exclusive: Not The Nodes interview

Peter Carpark met Don Nodes in the murky corners of his local watering hole: The Europark. Wayne Holton taped the interview, bought the drinks, and drank most of them.

Carpark: Give us your view of the Ian Wright affair?

Nodes: He is definitely not for sale. Don't believe any of the rumours that you've read in the press. I love that boy, he's like a son to me – we'll never let him go (starts to weep)

Carpark: But Don, we sold him to Arsenal ...

Nodes: Have we? Are you sure? I though Chelsea were after him ...

Carpark: Erm, no, I think that's Bright, but he's gone as well ...

Nodes: Oh yes, how silly of me, I can't tell them apart. Well, of course, he's a lovely lad as well, they all are, great lads ... anyway how much did we get for Ian?

Carpark: Two and a half million ...

Nodes: Well that should buy a nice mink for 'er indoors, ha ha ha ...

Carpark: What do you think about her taste in T-shirts, Don?

Nodes; Look, if I were you sunshine, I'd change the subject. (To Wayne) Oi you get us another drink ...

Holton: What would you like, another rum and black?

Nodes: Yup and this time make it a double

Carpark: A lot has been said about your special relationship with Steve Coppell. How does this work?

Nodes: It's fairly straightforward. Either he does what I want or there's no money.

Carpark: So Steve doesn't have much say.

Nodes: No, that's the way I like it in busin ... er ... soccer. People work best when they know where they stand. I like to call a spade a spade, me.

Carpark: So I've noticed.

Nodes: You're not some kind of red are you?

Think of a Palace official that every Selhurst supporter admires. Peter Carpark caught up with one of the club's great heroes

Carpark: Why do you think you're such a hit with the fans, Don?

Nodes: They like a bit of honesty and I think I know what they're really after. We've got away from all this terracing because there's not enough money in it. Your average fan wants to spend around £50 a time for an executive box so he can bring the wife along, have a bit of nosh and watch *Grandstand* if the game gets boring.

They can also buy the video if they miss any of it. That's what its about, my dream is to fill the whole stadium with boxes like that.

Carpark: But what about the fans who want to stand and watch?

Nodes: I don't really think they're proper fans. They're not true supporters.

Carpark: What about the rumours of a new stadium to be shared with Wimbledon and even a merger?

Nodes: There's no truth in any of the rumours. Sam Hammam and I are definitely not planning to level Brixton Hill and turn it into a huge shopping complex with a football pitch in the middle. And we are not going to merge and call the club Whiteman palace Hammades PLC.

and he helpfully ushered us into the Millwall home end. Thanks mate, no I mean it ... just wait. Palace had lost only one game at home that season (to the Seaweeds) and were top of the third. Looking back, it is easy to see why. We had a great team: Evans, Jimbo (at left back) Jeffries and Wall at the back; Chatterton, Holder and Martin Hinshelwood in midfield; Swindles, David Kemp and Peter Taylor up front. For this game Stuart Jump was playing at the back with the more assured Hammond in goal.

Palace played some brillo football: the excellent David Kemp, similar to Jeff Bourne in stature, played a delightful one-two with Swindles that left the ape who was marking him kicking air instead of calves as he had intended.

However, the attrition of the Lions, on and off the pitch, was what I most remember about the day. I remember a group of Palace fans near the gate at the Millwall home end, one clutching a bottle of gin, attempting a drunken *Eeee-aaaggglessss* about a quarter of an hour into the game and being told to shut the f*** up by a diminutive Millwall skin aged about 12. They did, it was that kind of atmosphere. Swindles scored; the Palace end was rucked – official line of pitch invasion – and we were thankful to emerge unscathed onto the streets of Lewisham. But those were the days ... *Next Chapter: Come in Steve Perrin your time is up, aka Why didn't they ask Evans?*

Another poem

Crystal Palace

Dear Palace I must confess
Of writing this is not the best
But I just had to let you know
That in the EE book I'll go
Because I have as others do
A passion for a team – oh who
Is this? I hear you ask me why
And I do watch them on Sky
It's hard to cos I do not own
A dish or cable in my home
But then I go to selhurst Park
And watch my team, they're off the
mark
The team is never a disgrace
I've supporters gear all round the
place
I'm sure you won't bear me no malice
When I confirm it's Crystal Palace
A poem is so hard to do
When your team only rhymes with
two
Words from the Oxford Dictionary
But never mind – they're
extraordinary
They bring us joy and pain as well
Have you been with them to the Dell?
The team are great the captain strong
He urges his team on and on
Tho' glory in the cups is few
Remember Liverpool and who
Can forget Everton at Wembley
Were you there too just one of many?
The highs and lows we have to face
For Palace in the Premier race
We know that our team will not topple
Steered by our manager
Steve Coppell
Despite the press who seem to side
With teams that I cannot abide
Particularly one you know
Who poached our Wrighty – our hero
Once a man but now a crass
Left the hallowed turf of Selhurst
grass
And went to join the Arsenal Arse
Done a shameful thing oh what a
farce!
Kissed his shirt and left hell
For us past fans who served him so
well
Now sad to think what's in his mind
The Arse have ruined him for
mankind
But let's not dwell on crap like that
Let's look forward to many England
caps
For the star players we have now
Can do it for us all and how!
We must be strong we must not fade
We'll be the team of the decade

Jenny Modeste

EL TEL

Palace hero or bandito?

Allsport

Robert Deeks appraises the reign of Terry Venables and his subsequent career, as it affected Palace, at a time when the man once tipped to be England manager faces a battle to save his career and reputation ...

There are two views among Palace fans as to the standing of Terry Venables in the history of Palace.

To many, he presided over a wonderfully optimistic period and they feel it was actually Venables who masterminded the 1976 F.A. Cup run.

In his first season as manager he took us out of the third division, where we had languished for far too long, in a frantic and glorious last gasp win at promotion rivals Wrexham.

He then assembled a talented young side from the youth team and led us to the second division championship in front of more than 50,000 fans. For a brief moment in October 1979 we were top of the first division and were the Team of the 80s (there, I said it).

But the team began to struggle and in 1980-81 it all began to go wrong. Many felt that Terry was not given the support that he deserved by the board and was not provided with the cash from the infamous Sainsbury's scheme that was needed to strengthen the young team.

To others, he was a clever manipulator. He inherited a rich crop of youngsters, recruited by Malcolm Allison and nurtured by John Cartwright, and when that team began to struggle, he struggled. He failed to put things right and before his image and reputation could be tarnished he left for QPR.

Then, just to rub our noses in it, he purchased half our team at bargain basement prices and we went down to the second division, bereft of cash and optimism.

QPR were promoted shortly after and went to the Cup Final in 1982. From there, of course, Venables went to

Barcelona and then Spurs where he has become embroiled in a scandal following a court battle for control of the club with his former partner Alan Sugar.

For the first time since he left, perhaps, many Palace fans now have sympathy for the man.

The truth about Venables is, as with many things, not as clear cut as the scenarios I have outlined. The main bugbear for most is the manner of his departure from Selhurst and the decline which followed. But how much responsibility should be laid at his door?

> **It would have been easy for Palace to keep Terry, all they had to say was that compensation couldn't be agreed. Terry found out they had approached two other managers behind his back before asking him if he wanted to stay on. It was poor reward for the loyalty he had shown them four years earlier, when he had the chance to go to Arsenal ...**
>
> FRED VENABLES, TERRY'S FATHER

Terry Venables' standing and success at Palace attracted much attention and he turned down the chance to coach Arsenal to pledge his future to the Eagles. He became manager of the England Under-21 team which by 1980 contained half the Palace side. The club had a string of young internationals; Kenny Sansom, Billy Gilbert, Vince Hilaire, Peter Nicholas, Jerry Murphy, Ian Walsh, Terry Fenwick and even Paul Hinshelwood.

In his recent book, Fenwick said that Glenn Hoddle wanted to leave Spurs for Palace just to play under Venables. With the youth policy working so well, Venables added an astute buying policy with purchases at the right time such as Jeff Bourne, whose goals got us out of division three, and Steve Kember, whose experience helped us back into division one.

Gates averaged 30,000 in 1979-80 and even now it is difficult to see why things went wrong. When Venables left in October 1980 we had just one league victory from ten starts. We were bottom and attendances were falling – 16,000 for his last match against West Brom. Incidentally we won our next two matches under Ernie Walley but the mini-revival was a false dawn. We were relegated long before the season was out with just 19 points – a record low at the time. Venables however was turning QPR around and he even got them to play on a plastic pitch.

What really sticks in the throat for most of us was the way he came back time and again to buy half our team.In addition, he took Alan Harris, his right hand man, and then youth team coach George Graham.

Palace's new chairman Ron Noades complained that the club was in a dire financial position, wage bill too high, gates too low. With Palace apparently so eager to unload players at knock down prices, we should I think be careful about blaming Venables for the depletion of our team.

They were players he knew and anyway he had a point to prove after coming in for criticism about their performances. But it gave us a reason to be angry with him.

In *Eagle Eye* issue 19, Dr R.K. Ashton a friend of Venables suggested that he didn't actually want to leave Palace but, due primarily to friction created by nonpayment of a promotion bonus, he was told by the board that: "Terry, you must go."

Ashton also stated that a member of staff at QPR confided that Venables took a long time to get over leaving Palace. That would appear consistent with what Terry said at the time.

I recall seeing a TV interview with him the day after he left in which he said QPR had come in for him and the Palace board had done nothing to make him feel that he was still wanted. He also said that Raymond Bloye was muttering about his health and he said if you don't feel wanted and somebody else wants you, then you should go.

Ashton added that QPR had made an earlier bid for him in the summer of 1980 and although Bloye had decided to give him "one more chance" he had already sounded out Howard Kendall of Blackburn and John Bond of Norwich as possible successors.

There is no doubt, as has been demonstrated by his confrontation with Sugar, that Venables is not one to bow to board pressure. He was allowed a free reign at QPR by Jim Gregory and was on the verge of buying a big stake in the club when he left for Barcelona.

On his return to England and Spurs he seemed to have an uneasy relationship, first with Irving Scholar and then Sugar. It is probably reasonable to conclude that Bloye similarly thought Venables was getting too big and he wanted to get rid of him.

One must also question why, just three months later, Bloye sold out to Ron Noades. Noades offered a clue in an article for the programme in April 1981, when he wrote: "Somewhere in the last 18 months, the old board for reasons which only they know, found themselves unable to support their manager. They may have had justifiable reasons, I don't know, but once that happens the result is inevitable."

Although Noades laid much of the blame on what preceded him, Palace's decline was also due in no small part to what followed under his leadership. His first manager, Dario Gradi, brought some poor players to the club and through these dark days the resentment grew.

Terry Venables was our main link to the days of so much promise and optimism. We felt betrayed, jilted. He had run off with someone else and we were bitter.

Perhaps only now is that bitterness beginning to heal for many Palace fans. How ironic that following his defeat at the high court the rumours that he would buy into another club mentioned Palace as possible candidates.

Whatever the future holds, I hope we can settle on a more balanced view of the past. If Steve Coppell deserves to remain a Palace hero then I think Terry Venables does too.

I have a DREAM

Whenever Palace are down on their luck, Jonathan Scarlett puts on his pyjamas and goes to bed where he not only saves the club but improves on its past record, slightly

I have a fantastic dream, I dream that I am by far the greatest footballer that has ever lived. In every way, I am far superior to all the players that have gone before me or the ones that will follow, my kind come along once in the lifetime of a solar system. I have a degree in philosophy and am a fully qualified doctor. I smoke 50 cigarettes a day and down eight pints of whisky on a quiet night out and yet I am as fit as a fiddle. Oh, I almost forgot, I have a Nobel Peace Prize as well.

The extent of my footballing skill is such that I make Pele look about as good as Sinbad from *Brookside* playing in a charity match. My silky skills are married to enormous power and strength to create a formidable combination. I can juggle the ball over my head and knock it back with my heel a thousand times while standing on one leg eating a water melon. I can kick a ball further, harder and with more swerve than thought possible by eminent physicists. Every single aspect of my game is perfect, my control and first touch are perfect as are my passing, heading, tackling, distribution, shooting and coin tossing. But perhaps my greatest asset is my pace. My 7ft frame can run 100 metres in 5.65 seconds and that's on a muddy pitch wearing flippers and concrete shinpads. To make the description easier let's just say I am super-human. In fact I will settle for being called a football deity. I play for Crystal Palace.

I don't know how I started playing for the Eagles, but the dream begins when I make my debut as a sub at Old Trafford. Palace are 3-0 down with 20 minutes left. Steve Coppell calls me over from warming up and tells me to go on and get him a goal. I feel enormous pride as the linesman checks my studs. "The substitute for Crystal Palace is number 14, Jonathan Scarlett."

I race onto the pitch to cries of *Who the f****** hell are you?* from the United faithful. I clap the massive band of Palace fans that have made the journey and take up my position in the centre of midfield.

My first touch as a professional comes when Nigel rolls the ball out to me on the edge of the box. I turn, look up and chip a startled Peter Schmeichel from 80 yards with a delightful lob. From the moment I connect with the ball I am running towards the Palace fans with arms raised. They wonder what the hell I am playing at until they see the ball in the back of the net. Pandemonium!

A minute later, I time my run perfectly to beat the offside trap and head for the corner flag. The United fans, in their ignorance, go "aaarrrggghhh", but I know better. I sense that an Andy Thorn punt upfield is going to pass over the corner flag.

I glance across to the goal and as the ball comes over about eight feet off the ground I jump and from the most acute angle volley the ball into the top corner. Not content with that, I land perfectly with my feet together (style is as important to me as scoring). Even the United fans are cheering.

The inevitable equaliser comes with three minutes left. I am in my own box when I spot Bobby Bowry making a great run down the right. I hit a very long ball out to the left hand side and the Palace fans groan as Bruce, Pallister, Irwin and Parker all follow the ball. What they don't realise is that I have put an unbelievable amount of swerve on it and they are left gasping as it spins back in and stops dead at Eddie's feet. He takes it in his stride and scores a great goal.

In the last minute I am fouled and we are awarded a penalty. I am on a debut hat-trick. The referee places the ball on the spot, but I don't think it's fair so I pick the ball up and walk to my own penalty area and put the ball on the Palace penalty spot. Without taking a step I power the ball eighty yards past Schmeichel. Palace have a famous victory. I shrug my shoulders and go over to the Palace fans as if to say "Was that, OK? Have I done alright on my debut?"

I am mobbed by the Palace players and supporters who have run onto the pitch. Needless to say, none of the goals are selected for *Match of the Day's* goal of the month competition.

The next day, the tabloids are going mad and every big club in England is after my signature. The tabloid headline writers have a field day speculating "Scarlett is a Red" and the ridiculous "Scarlett Fantastic!".

Manchester United offer £20 million and a shortsighted Palace accept. The press conference is screened live on all four channels. I am wearing a Manchester United shirt sitting next to a grinning Alex Ferguson and Ron Noades. The camera focuses in on my pen as I sign the contract but instead I write "Bollocks" and rip my shirt off to reveal a Palace one underneath. I kiss the badge and tell a stunned Ferguson I wouldn't sign for him if United were the only club in the world. I start singing *who's that team they call the Palace ...?* at the top of my voice.

But the next day I do sign for someone else ... AC Milan bid £500 million. However, the contract states that I don't have to play for them for 30 years and Palace get the money up front. It's quite a good deal, because the money is index-linked and inflation proof. In actual fact Silvio Berlusconi goes bust within five years because of all the money he's forked out and so I don't have to join Milan anyway.

My next game is at Anfield in the quarter finals of the F.A. Cup and it only takes five minutes before I open the scoring. I am bearing down on goal about 40 yards out when Mark Wright and Torben Piechnik try to sandwich me. I have read their intentions and flick the ball between them. As they converge to block me, I spring over them and do a triple somersault landing on the other side. I run on and curl the ball into the top corner. A minute later we get a second. Palace are awarded a free kick when Nigel Martyn is fouled in our six yard box. They put a wall up (or at least they should have done) but it makes no difference. The ball is touched to me by the Ninja and I hit a thunderbolt that leaves David James floundering. Then I dribble around the entire Liverpool team twice as if the ball is tied to my boot. I reach the goal line and stop, waiting for them to catch up before stooping to knock the ball over the line with my head.

My sixth goal is the real peach. From a Liverpool corner I fire the ball against my own post and it rebounds back with such force that it screeches into the Liverpool net in front of the Kop at the other end.

The icing on the cake is my, and Palace's, ninth. From a cleared corner, I back-heel the ball into the net ... from the halfway line. At the final whistle the all seater Kop is on its feet applauding. I walk over to them and "flick the Vs", but they are so in awe of me that they just run over to join in with the big

Palace conga that is weaving its way round Anfield and eventually leads through the streets of Liverpool where I am given a civic reception.

On the steps of Liverpool Town Hall, the moment is momentarily spoiled when Graeme Souness accuses me of being dirty. I say: "That wasn't dirty, but this is ..." and poke him in the eye. The whole crowd cheers and Souness goes off crying.

Palace reach the Cup Final and I shake the hand of every single Palace fan that has made the trip up Wembley Way. When the teams are introduced to the Queen she grabs a reporter's microphone and announces to the crowd that she has always been a Palace fan, in fact she named all her houses after the team.

She pledges to pump all her spare money into the team (anything that Jack Walker can do for Blackburn, Palace can do 100 times better). We beat Arsenal 20-0 and the referee calls the game off with half an hour to go to prevent the north London wretches suffering further. I only score ten, but in my defence I do set up the other ten. In fact my tenth is so special that the Queen runs down from the Royal Box and gives me my Knighthood there and then on the pitch. The game is held up for about 20 minutes during the ceremony.

Palace become the dominant force in world football and the clubs that used to think they were big can no longer compete. Liverpool, Everton, Arsenal, Spurs and Manchester United become so bad at football that they are forced to take up lesser sports like golf, cricket and ice hockey.

Needless to say, in my dream, Palace

go on to win all three domestic trophies and the European Cup every year for decades. In one particular European Cup Final in Italy one year the Pope was so impressed by the divine performance that he made all the Palace players saints.

WELCOME TO CRYSTAL PALACE FC
BANK OF CRYSTAL PALACE
PALACE ELECTRIC CO.
CPFC TELECOMMS
PALACE RESERVES VERSUS A COMBINED REAL MADRID + BARCELONA TEAM IN THE EUROPEAN CUP. ONLY 127,000 TURN UP....

Never again will Palace sell players to a bigger club because we are the biggest. Yet, despite all the success and the unpopularity it usually brings, Palace become the most popular team in the whole world but especially so in south London (which is all that matters). I am totally committed to Palace because I come from the ranks of their fans. Indeed, all through my career I refuse to play for England because I don't want to lose my form or get injured. The same goes for all the other players at Palace and there is a fantastic team spirit with Steve Coppell at the helm.

I continue to make the headlines during the course of my incredible career. In one game, I am so angered by the abuse directed at Chris Armstrong by Millwall supporters that I kick the ball so hard that I knock the whole goal into the crowd, trapping the guilty bastards in the net. I then go into the crowd and throw the net over the stand to set an example to the other thugs.

In another game Palace score a goal that is a result of a move in which every Palace played touches the ball and Nigel scores with a diving header. The Dutch version of Total Football pales into insignificance as a footballing philosophy in comparison to Palace.

Even David Lacey of the *Guardian* cannot resist singing the club's praises. He sets up a Palace appreciation society and is often seen extolling the virtues of the team to unsuspecting passers by. Every player develops into a superstar because they know if anything happens I will be there to cover for them. Palace take over from the Big Five and are known as "the Big One". Palace fans take over production of *Match of the Day* and all the goals of the month are Palace goals.

As well as doing incredible things on the playing side, I also revolutionise things off the park. I buy out Ron Noades for starters. Millions of people try to take advantage of the free season ticket offer made possible by the Milan money and the dosh from the Queen.

But I stipulate that only those who are bona fide Palace fans can attend. I don't want any glory boys or girls, only those that have suffered with Palace in the past. Everyone is allowed to love us but only the true Palace fans can support us and watch us play. All away games are free for Palace fans and transport to and from games and free meals at service stations are laid on. We take an average away support of 50,000 and often have to help small clubs financially by building them away ends to accommodate our support. I build a new ground for us at Crystal Palace with the reserve and youth teams remaining at our spiritual home, Selhurst Park.

Each side of the new stadium is an exact replica of the original Crystal Palace glass building with 100,000 seats and there is room for 100,000 in the terrace areas. The stadium glistens in the sun and I arrange a sponsorship deal with Death cigarettes and we wear an all black kit with the skull and crossbones on the front. Eric the Ninja looks wicked in his eye patch.

The PA pumps out very, very loud revival reggae and jazz funk, south London becomes an independent state and the envy of impoverished north Londoners who need passports to get in and are escorted out of town at dusk. We have the strongest economy in the world and the highest standard of living for all residents.

I play for Palace for 40 years before I retire at sixty-something still at the peak of my powers. I leave the club in good shape on and off the pitch. With the team at the very top of the world I go back to doing what I love most, being a supporter.

■ Ed's note: the season after John retired, Palace were relegated.

TICKER

Not a player who immediately springs to mind in the great scheme of things, Kevin Taylor was vital to the transitional Palace of the mid-1980s. By Mark Gardiner

The Mullery years ... you can't really appreciate what being a Palace supporter is all about unless you lived through those golden seasons. Less than three years after the Team of the 80s it culled Palace fans as easily as myxomatosis felled bunnies. Teams with vague tactical formations exhibiting a range of football skills from crap to mediocre. Consider the nonentities who wore the sashed shirt: Langley, Brown, Lacy, Strong, Lindsay, Fashanu. Strong men wept when comparing our promotion midfield of Nicholas and Murphy to the shambles of ... well, Nicholas and Murphy. Both quit football to join Chelsea.

Then Steve Coppell arrived with strange ideas such as playing right footed players on the right and left footers on the left. As he gained experience he later outgrew this childishness. During his first season, Coppell made some astute buys including Alan Irvine an effective right winger to replace Vince Hilaire and man-mountain Micky Droy. The midfield was still run by Nicholas and Murphy although in July 1984 Coppell paid Derby £15,000 for 23 year-old Wakefield born Kevin Taylor. He sat in reserve awaiting his chance.

Although we were more solid, we still struggled and reached our nadir with a 5-0 home defeat by Wimbledon. Nicholas left for Luton and Murphy, waiting to see his contract out, left shortly before the end of the season. Taylor made his debut shortly after as a sub against Wolves as part of the reshuffle forced by that week's injury to Kevin Mabbutt. His impact was minimal and it was only Droy's introduction, forming a solid barrier with Jim Cannon and George Wood, that kept Palace out of danger.

At the start of 1985-86 Taylor, for some unfathomable reason tagged "ticker", was injured and the midfield was manned by Tony Finnigan and new signing Steve Ketteridge, offering work rate but little else. We started with a flourish thanks to goals from Barber and Gray but five games without a win prompted Ticker's return against Millwall. He played in front of the back four which became a back three when Droy was banished for upsetting the delicate Mr Fashanu. One down at half time, Ticker inspired the ten men to fight back with a beauty from Barber and a tap in from Gray. After a two game lay off with injury Taylor became a fixture for the rest of the season. He scored his first goal, a late equaliser against Oldham followed by an even later winner by Ian Wright.

Neil Everitt

During two and a bit seasons, he scored some important goals and considering he wasn't exactly in the Bryan Robson mould 15 in 99 appearances was favourable to that of Murphy and, later, Geoff Thomas. Those of you who bought the Ian Wright video (and haven't dumped it yet) can see a 25 yard smasher from Ticker against Ipswich in the game that marked the start of the Wright 'n' Bright partnership. Taylor was also the best penalty taker of recent years, with a deliberate style compared to Andy Gray's hit and hope efforts. He finally missed one at home to Birmingham when the score was delicately poised at 0-0 which so demoralised Palace that we scored six within the hour. Taylor handed the responsibility for future penalties to Gray.

Taylor was also a leading figure in "resolving" on-field disputes, and could often be seen advising referees of the error of their ways; strong rumour had it that in a game at Plymouth he even protested when the opposition were taking a kick-off. He was dismissed early in the game at Grimsby in April 1986 which effectively ended our promotion hopes. During the following season bookings, mostly for dissent, earned a suspension over Christmas and the new year including the rare cup win over Forest. Taylor, Gray and Wright formed an argumentative trio which kept referees busy and would have done Arsenal proud.

In 1986-87 Coppell strengthened the squad with Anton Otulakowski, Gary O'Reilly and Mark Bright. Ticker surprisingly finished equal top scorer with eight league goals the same as Wright and Bright. It appeared that Palace had a settled team which could push for promotion the following year.

Surprisingly two of our more effective players were absent when the new season started. Alan Irvine had been sold to Dundee United, while Ticker was injured and unhappy. Apparently his wife had been "unable to settle in the south" and both wanted to return to Yorkshire. Coppell's response was to strengthen his team with Neil Redfearn and Geoff Thomas. When we started the season with a flood of goals the supporters forgot their old favourites.

Ticker reappeared in a league cup drubbing of Newport but was barely recognisable. He paled in comparison to Thomas. Ticker played two more league games (both lost), and made his final appearance as a sub in the second leg at Somerton Park where he suffered the indignity of being replaced by Alan Pardew. Shortly after, Taylor moved to Scunthorpe where his name regularly appeared on the scoresheet. There seemed few regrets on either side.

It may seem strange to those brought up on dynamic midfield performances from Thomas and Gray that a player whose time at Palace covered just over two years and who disappeared leaving barely a ripple should be the subject of such appreciation. Kevin Taylor was not in the mould of those who succeeded him. He was a solid ball player. But he injected much needed spirit into midfield and with Gray formed a midfield which gave us self-respect. He had a cool head when the ball was at his feet although he tended to lose it when confronting opponents or officials. He contributed significantly to the Crystal Palace revival.

ONE TEAM AT SELHURST

The ground sharing arrangement with Charlton could have fostered a fierce rivalry between the clubs. But, although they hate us, we couldn't give a monkey's about them which says more about Charlton than anything. This selection of articles sum up a unique relationship.

Steve Dixon, then editor of Voice of the Valley, wrote this piece upon the "historic" first meeting between two ground sharing clubs.

Four years, four miserable years. And by the time this sorry chapter in the history of Charlton Athletic Football Club is finally brought to a close, it will have been five years since that desolate September afternoon in 1985 when the men in charge of Charlton made the damaging and ulitmately incorrect decision to sever the link between the club and ground and with it sacrifice the bond between the club and fans.

The announcement, in the form of that wretched piece of A4 paper headed "Message to our Supporters" came with the contrived irony of our third meeting with Crystal Palace that season – no doubt so the arch-villain Ron Noades could be on hand to defend this most improbable deal.

"We don't want you at Selhurst," sang the Palace fans in the Seed Stand that afternoon and we didn't want to go there. But with Noades laughing all the way to the bank and the equally guilty Fryer content to play along, Charlton did indeed take up residence at Selhurst Park in October 1985.

So what are the lessons to be learnt from this, the first ever ground sharing scheme between two league clubs?

That the agreement is wholly in favour of the landlords, to the detriment of the tenants. That the tenants could be expected to be treated as second best wherever possible. And perhaps most importantly that the club and ground cannot be separated without a loss of ifdentity and goodwill so necessary for a football club to survive.

By now, of course, many of the initial difficulties have been ironed out, although just as many still remain. Match days at Selhurst are probably very similar for Charlton and Palace save for a few minor differences.

Away fans at Charlton are allocated the Holmesdale End in its entirety as opposed to that horrible little corner used to accommodate Palace's visitors. Also the two clubs situated their junior enclosures at opposite ends of the mains stand, otherwise arrangements are pretty identical. The major difference must be the attitude of the supporters.

Palace supporters can be comfortable in their own ground, but Charlton fans are rarely enthusiastic about the regular journey around the South Circular to SE25 and conversation among the shopping trolley dodgers often seems to involve the time taken to reach the ground, or the apparently endless administrative delays in the Greenwich Council decision making process so vital to Charlton's return to the Valley.

Everything about a Charlton matchday seems borrowed and unfamiliar. The Club Shop, for example, with Charlton and Palace souvenirs hanging side by side. The supporters club operating out of a red and blue striped portakabin in the car park.

The ticket offices for which a reason for existence has yet to be found.

Those ridiculous signs all around the ground that miraculosuly appear at Chrlton matches welcoming people to Selhurst Park and perhaps the greatest insult of all those hideous portakabins at the edge of the Holmesdale, looking for all the world like those toilets you see at pop festivals, adorned with the emnblem of a once proud club.

This is the legacy of ground sharing, a scheme heralded by its chief instigator as the first of many, but happily for football a forecast that has proved to be incorrect and, indeed, this particular arrangement which so nearly brought Charlton Athletic to its knees is about to end.

If, when Charlton leave, Noades plans to move to the National Sports Centre do not get the necessary council approval do not be surprised to see another club's badge installed in the space that Charlton have occupied for the last four seasons.

Wimbledon are the hot favourites so any thoughts among the Palace faithful that they are about to have their ground 100% to themselves could be dashed

A day at the Palace ... with no Palace

Barrie Greene was dragged along to watch Charlton v Spurs. The match didn't capture his imagination, but the stadium did

IT WAS a choice between fatherhood and conscience that brought me back to Selhurst Park, even though our lads were absent – on their usual away day kamikaze mission.

A wise choice it turned out to be. Following Palace to Derby to watch their abject surrender would have been too painful.

My son supports Tottenham. My house has pictures of Gazza and Terry Vegetables side by side with my little collection of Palace heroes.

How could I refuse to take him to see Charlton abuse our sacred turf against a Spurs team about to sell all and sundry.

I told my son I was on a scouting mission for Steve Coppell and would report to him after the match.

To make me feel even more out of place I stood on the Holmesdale for the first time in about ten years – a Sainsbury's sufferer I am.

My first realisation that this was to be an afternoon of observations was when I saw the box offices outside the ground for the first time.

This invention of Uncle Ron Noades has served to baffle and irritate customers ever since. Built on the hill, the narrow windows were at different heights from the ground with the window for under 16 tickets being the highest – good planning this. Inside the ground we emptied our bladders in what must surely be a listed building. What other reason could there be for the Holmesdale toilets to still be standing.

On the terrace, I was able to view our new scoreboard in all its glory – most commendable, it really does take one's eye and mind from the grocery store behind. I wonder which Palace director owns the company which supplied that, or am I being cynical?

Charlton's "Robin" has the same neck trouble as the Palace "Eagle". Head cocked to one side, it pranced about the pitch with all the enthusiasm of John Salako trying to lose his marker. At least our feathered friend kicks a ball about. The Charlton programme, similar in layout to Palace's, is full of informative information, a boast ours cannot match.

The teams provided little to stimulate us and I began to survey Selhurst Park. I was quite moved.

It's not so bad really. The view above the Whitehorse is of houses rising to meet the trees of Grange Park. It's rather pretty. Yes, we are the "homely" club.

However, the old stand roof has not seen a coat of paint since 1924. If we can afford to buy Mark Dennis we can surely build some toilets and paint a roof.

The game was mediocre but I found it a pleasant change to watch football without the tension. Half-time was only spoilt by Palace's 2-1 deficit. Charlton took the lead in the second half, but Spurs equalised through Thomas (Mitchell not Geoff) and as the sun broke through I felt quite content.

On the field Gascoigne proceeded to win the match with two pieces of pure brilliance which reminded me of Supa Al. Back at the other end next week. With my tranquilisers and clean pair of pants.

---

almost immediately.

Bearing in mind recent history Palace and Wimbledon could be facing a merger particularly if one of the sides were to surrender their first division place come next May.

Charlton meanwhile will be much better off back at a redeveloped if sadly more compact Valley. In the years to come neither Palace nor Charlton fans will look back on this sordid ground sharing arrangement with any affection, although it could be said that our rent money helped get Palace into the first division.

Or is it an unfortunate coincidence that Palace always sign a new player after we've had a couple of good attendances?

For Palace supporters to see Charlton colours all over their ground must be galling in the extreme and they will no doubt be upset to see Charlton supporters in their places in the event of this first match at Selhurst between the two sides with Charlton as the home team.

But for Palace followers the inconvenience has been minimal compared with what their Charlton counterparts have had to endure.

Although we have reluctantly formed new habits it is still an apparently endless journey through unfamiliar streets in alien areas to a bleak and unwelcoming ground with the only prospect of a return to our rightful home on the horizon as an incentive to continue to attend.

For Charlton the real tale of these last four years is a question of what might have been. Had promotion been achieved at the Valley in the 1985-86 season in front of massive crowds instead of the paltry gatherings at Selhurst then the enthusiasm that accompanies promotion to division one and while no one is suggesting that the Valley would have been overflowing every week there is no doubt the attendance would have been much greater than 8,501 that saw the opening game in division one against Sheffield Wednesday – our first in the division one for 29 years.

Fortunately this sorry episode is about to draw to a close and only time will tell whether the damage done to Charlton over the past four years can be repaired, but in the meantime let football supporters nationwide, and not just those of Palace Charlton and Wimbledon, remain vigilant to ensure that nothing like this ever happens again.

"Let us remember that this fixture marks the beginning of the end of ground sharing, an ill conceived idea that very nearly led to the demise of a great club. Let us hope that as a notion it goes the same way as Top Score, mergers, and with luck, the Full Members Simod Data Systems Waste of Bloody Time Cup. Please Mr Noades, no more bright ideas.

STEVE DIXON,
VOICE OF THE VALLEY FANZINE, 1989

I've got the Selhurst blues

Martin Whybrow took an afternoon off to visit Selhurst Park's reluctant co-habitants play West Ham and wishes he hadn't.

Palace had won on Oldham's plastic the night before and all was right with the world. So I decided to take the heretical step of going to see Charlton play in our red and blue Mecca.

We've had our fair share of setbacks (David Price and Brian Bason spring to mind) but they pale into insignificance compared with those of Charlton (lack of ground, support and now form).

And to cap it all the Minister for Sport, Colin Moynihan, has come out of the closet (presumably a very small closet) and declared himself a lifelong Charlton supporter. The shame, the embarrassment. *The Voice of the Valley* ran a "spot the Minister" competition. Mind you, should the horrible little man deem it his duty to show his face at a match he would no doubt turn up at the Valley. Not that he should mind, a football ground bereft of both supporters and players seems to fit in with his ideas for the future of the sport quite nicely.

Moynihan, not surprisingly, did not turn up for Charlton's encounter with West Ham. Wasn't he the lucky one? The omens were not good, bottom against second bottom and things took a turn for the worse before a player had even stepped onto the pitch, West Ham deciding we would have to watch Ray Stewart rather than Alan Devonshire.

Only Liam Brady stood out from the panicky shambles. Not that he wasn't gulity of the long aimless ball upfield, it was just that he hoofed the ball with the outside of his boot. True class will always shine through.

Charlton were not without their admirers. "Played" yelled the guy behind me, then applauded wildly as John Humphrey booted the ball over the Old Stand.

Steve McKenzie, once of Palace, is now decidedly barrel-shaped. He failed to show the form that once fuelled Malcolm Allison's belief in him. Has he ever? Colin Pates looked bemused. If he's joined Charlton for first division football then the end of the season could be tinged with irony.

Every team has its scapegoat and Charlton's is a number 11 called Paul Mortimer. A trifle unfair, he was no worse than anyone else.

He strategically started limping after half an hour but Lennie Lawrence was having none of it. This despite the fact that the crowd were baying for their saviour Paul Williams at an early stage.

He of course was on the bench. He came on, merged into the impermeable mess and nothing improved.

West Ham also have a saviour. *There's only one MacAvennie*, sang the Holmesdale. West Ham are also a club with tradition – a tradition for slagging some poor sod off. It was Geoff Pike, now its John Lyall.

Leroy Rosenior isn't too popular either. Mind you by the time he'd been caught offside for the umpteenth time he'd hardly endeared himself to me.

Ray Stewart revealed that his acting is as subtle as his football. His rendition of a pole-axed victim of a Carl Leaburn elbow showed him to be straight out of the Vince Hilaire school of theatricals.

The linesmen's flags and the trainers competed for man of the match award while I enjoyed the witty repartee from th terraces which reached new heights with "Get yer eyes tested, ref."

One point each was a travesty. Selhurst Park echoed not to the chants of *Eagles* but to a chorus of *what a load of rubbish*.

It was enough to make you cry and you would not have wished it on anyone … except the Minister for Sport.

Neil Everitt

Charlton v Palace 1985. Jim Cannon gets above Steve Thompson

Llantrisant doesn't have too much to recommend it at the best of the times. "The hole with the mint in it," as they say in these here parts.

It was a filthy night, a South Wales special, a goal-keeper's nightmare. Yet tonight there was one redeeming feature. At two minutes past eight, George Wood ambled into the hotel carrying the air of a public school housemaster who climbs mountains and plays number eight for the county rugger team. In truth, at 41, he keeps goal for Inter Cardiff in the Konica League of Wales and only missed playing European football this season by one point.

For the childlike among you, yes, he does wear glasses and no, he didn't drop his pint.

"I come from Lanark, more

down and had a chat and Mullers sold the place to me.

"Even when I was at Blackpool I'd thought of Palace as a high profile club and it was a fair signing on fee, although nothing compared to today. I could have got more by going to Coventry, but I was happy with it. If you're happy you sign."

Initially he played for a struggling side. "Stevie Coppell's first year was just as bad. I thought when I joined that we'd be going up in one or two seasons, unfortunately I didn't realise there had been so much turmoil behind the scenes. It didn't really make for a good team spirit."

Nevertheless, George is surprised that Palace didn't do better. "I liked Alan Mullery, he was a good per-

BY GEORGE

When George Wood arrived at Selhurst Park on a free transfer from Arsenal, Palace were going through a bad time. By the time he left nearly four years later, the revival was well under way. By Matthew Simmonds

a rugby area," he explains. "Basically I was always a goalkeeper. My first club was East Stirling and then I moved to Blackpool." While at Bloomfield Road he played against Palace a couple of times. "We beat them 1-0 at home and then at Selhurst Don Rogers scored a cracker but we came back with two in injury time to win the game. It was the first time I had played at Selhurst Park."

After another six years or so, he returned with Everton in the first division. "Mike Flanagan scored in the first two minutes. It was a great cross from Vince Hilaire and he came in at the near post and hit it far corner. But John Burridge had one of those days where his head got the better of him.

"He came flying out and Andy King just clipped two beneath him. Palace were just pounding us in the second half but we got a third and that was the end of it."

The year before George came to Palace he went with his country to the World Cup Finals. Everything was going well and he was Arsenal's first choice.

"That's the ups and downs of football. I got sent off against Aston Villa and Pat Jennings, who I'd been keeping out, came in did well and I was out. Whatever Pat did was great, whatever I did was average."

Although displaced, he was settled in north London and his daughter had just started secondary school. "I read in the paper that Palace were looking for a keeper and Alan Mullery phoned me up and said: 'Do you fancy coming to Palace in the second division?' I came

sonality and good for his players. But a lot of the lads had lost confidence getting hammered week-in, week-out. We'd only just escaped relegation the year before and it just followed on. Some of the players had outstayed their time at Palace, they'd gone a bit stale and didn't have the same enthusiasm. We could have been good enough to get into the first, we had a lot of good lads there."

Predictably George praises his cental defenders. "Billy Gilbert was outstanding in his last season before moving to Portsmouth and Jim Cannon was very unlucky not to get a Scotland cap, he would get in the Palace back four every time. Later Micky Droy and Jimmy were outstanding."

One thing that did disappoint George was the manner of the league cup

George Wood

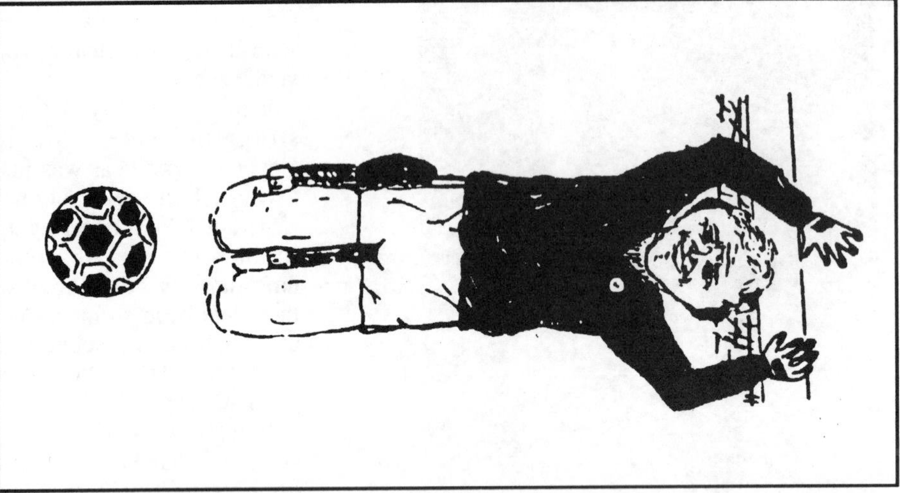

"I couldn't believe he'd never played pro football. As soon as I saw him in a practice match I thought 'Hmm, put him in the side Saturday.' He was a chirpy, cocky lad and the other players couldn't believe he'd never played at any club before."

George Wood's First Impression of Ian Wright

defeat at Peterborough. "We lost 3-0 in the second leg and went out on penalties. That was the one time I was disappointed with Mullers.

"The lads were diabolical on the night, but it was only 2-0 at half time and we were still in front. But he took us in and said: 'Get back out there, you bunch of useless f****** so and sos.' He did the whole bit and instead of trying to say something constructive, say where we were going wrong and tightening us up he sent us straight out in the pissing rain. We stood there in little groups in the rain, no good for team spirit. Mullers was so frustrated by the whole situation that he'd just had enough. He knew he couldn't motivate them and it was time to get new boys in but his hands were tied financially."

Vince Hilaire was one who needed a fresh start. "He never quite made it. I remember playing Middlesbrough and Kevin Mabbutt got sent off and Billy Gilbert followed straight away for arguing, shock horror! Anyway, we were down to nine men and under enormous pressure, all we did was give the ball to Vince and he took it into the corner for two minutes at a time and they couldn't get it off him."

After Mullery departed, Palace brought in Steve Coppell. "I thought 'great'. He set about things brilliantly, weeded out a few hangers on and brought in a lot of new players. The first year we struggled because we were learning together. I was older than Steve, a lot older, but all he had to do was mention scoring against me for England at Wembley and that would shut me up! It was my mistake as well. Butch Wilkins had a shot, it swerved and it was raining and instead of pushing it away, I tried to catch it. Fair dos to Coppell, he was quick. It was only a couple of feet, but before I could fall on top of it, he'd whipped it away and scored. So I could never give him any stick. I've got every respect for him and Ian Evans, they really complimented each other."

When Ian Wright turned up, George was immediately impressed. "I couldn't believe he'd never played pro football. As soon as I saw him in a practice match I thought 'Hmm, put him in the side Saturday. He was a chirpy, cocky lad and the other players couldn't believe he'd never played at any club before. It just shows. How many people are playing park football like him? Incredible!

"Andy Gray on the other hand was a headstrong boy. He didn't treat some people very well. He upset one or two of the senior pros and was a fool to himself. If he'd had Mark Bright's nature who knows what he could have achieved. Perhaps he's quietened down."

As a senior pro George also used to put in extra work with the younger players. "A quick cup of tea and straight out again. Wrighty sometimes used to come back for extra shooting, and Mark Bright.

"The only time I had a specialist trainer was Bob Wilson at Arsenal. I wasn't that great at training, I'd always come in the bottom half on cross country runs. Then again, I was with Budgie Burridge when he was a youngster at Blackpool. He'd always beat me on cross country, but anything up to 200m or 400m and I'd slaughter him. I was quick for a big lad. Training is a psychological thing. If you know you're training well you carry that out onto the pitch. I liked to play out on pitch in 5-a-sides and practice games and scored lots of goals. I once played up front for Blackpool reserves against Burnley when they had Gerry Peyton in goal and I scored with a header and a left foot volley."

Although it was once rumoured that Mullery had considered playing George up front during one particularly severe injury crisis, all his memories of Palace are from between the sticks. "My best save was in a 1-1 draw at Wimbledon. John Fashanu had already given them the lead with a free header into the bottom corner and not long after the same thing happened. This time he hit it from about eight yards, right in the top corner. I just threw myself and managed to get a hand to it and knock it over the bar. When I touched it I didn't know if it'd gone over of not, I was so close to the line. It was good to get something out of that game, we always got hammered by Wimbledon. I played in the 0-5 game.

"One Christmas we beat Brighton 2-0 and I got man of the match. Because it was Brighton it meant so much, I also played in the 6-0 win at Birmingham. When it was 0-0 they had a corner and it came across and someone blasted it right in my face from six yards and knocked me out. We went straight up the other end and scored. And a clean sheet is like a hat-trick for a goalkeeper.

"The worst moments are when someone comes up close and hits it at your feet, and the punters go: 'Oh God it went through his legs!' Those are always the most difficult to save.

"Performance is really down to confidence. You put on a new pair of gloves one week, you feel good, it's pissing down but you catch everything. Next week, bone dry, same gloves, same ball you drop everything!"

Certainly that was the story at Dean Court where George had what he regards as his worst game. "I made one horrendous mistake, the other was Jim Cannon's fault, but he was God and used to get away with everything. We still won 3-2 though!"

Being a footballer doesn't just involve football though. There's often other things going on, publicity stunts for instance.

"They knew I was interested in ornithology and was a qualified bird ringer so Stevie came up and said: 'We've got this idea for a photo session'. We did these shots with an Imperial Eagle from the Russian Steppes, I'd never seen one before. It took off about three times!"

Getting the footballing Eagles soaring though took longer than anticipated. "We always had bogey teams, Shrewsbury, Barnsley and so on. Games like those cost us promotion in both 1987 and 1988. We lost games we should have won.

"It was basically down to bad defending from the front. I believe you attack from the back and defend from the front.

"We lost 3-2 to Reading at Christmas 1987, it was late on when Moran scored their winner, a free header at the back post. Everyone expects the keeper to come for them but you're at the near post and you've got to get across.

"The defenders just let the ball go. At the time it was the easy option to blame the keeper. I can tell you my bad games ... in six matches I made mistakes that I never normally do. Probably the stick I got at the time was justified, but it still hurt.

"People have short memories, I saved a couple of penalties and did quite well. I didn't do so well at Villa, but there was a reason I didn't find out until later. I was making handling errors because I had a crack across the bone at the top of my thumb.

"I went to Cardiff on loan straight after the Leicester game and played four games and then went for an X-ray. It didn't show anything but they decided to send me for a scan and I found I'd cracked the bone. X-Rays didn't show it because another bone was hiding it.

"I'd played 20 games for Palace that season with a cracked thumb. I made mistakes because underneath my glove my thumb was so heavily bandaged that I could hardly get any movement. It's not an excuse, but people didn't know it at the time."

Leicester was where it came to a head. Palace had led 4-2 "I hit a clearance wide down the line. Unfortunately it didn't go out but straight to their geezer who hit it back first time along the ground and rolled it into the net.

"There were three or four of our lads running back, leaving it to each other. Gavin Nebbeling could have cleared it off the line. I thought that's it, I've had enough. If I'd played in the next game I'd have probably ended up in the crowd fighting.

"I went to Stevie and said: 'That's it, I'm going to retire.' I was 35 and I'd had enough of football, I wasn't enjoying it anymore. But we were second when I left that's how bad a season I was having."

George recalls a small section of fans who had a go. "Even when I'd just signed from Arsenal they were at me. I did reasonably well over four years. No one player in the world is everyone's favourite.

"I get a lot of letters from Palace fans and a lot came to see me when I was at Cardiff. It was great to see them.

"Three years on the trot I was involved in the player of the year. You can't go from being popular to being slaughtered, that hurt me most.

"I have three player of the year cups and keep the programmes of every game I played in. I wish I had a video collection. I did have one but lost it in transit when I moved to Wales."

One of George's funniest memories comes from his days at Ninian park and involves another old Palace favourite.

"I was at Cardiff with Ian Walsh. He was very injury prone and only played about three games in two years, although he always looked like he'd score. We were playing this match and he was on the bench. Frank Burrows told him to warm up and he ran down to the corner flag. When he got back to the dugout he said: "I've done my hamstring!"

What does George think of the present team? "Steve Coppell's best signing was Eric Young. He didn't half make a difference to the defence. He's the main core and under-rated. People don't give him enough credit. He's outstanding for Wales. Thorn and Young do a good job. They're not there to play, but if they can play it's a bonus."

George Wood has played nearly 700 games in the Football League and competed in almost every major domestic derby worth mentioning Scotland/England, Liverpool/ Everton, Cardiff/Swansea, Spurs/Arsenal and, most glamourous of all, Palace/Brighton.

He played for Scotland in the 1982 World Cup albeit as a sub in each game.

The night after this interview in the same monsoon conditions he kept a clean sheet as Inter Cardiff secured a 1-0 victory at Welsh champions Cwmbran, perhaps the big boned hands that kept goal for Palace from 1983-88 will see European Champions Cup action next season after all.

Not bad for a goalkeeper whose age is greater than the IQ of the average terrace boo boy.

Palace: the Coppell years

Hy Money

Crystal Palace's new manager Steve Coppell with "Uncle" Ron Noades

We won at Ninian Park to relieve the pressure, but we were still too close to the relegation zone for comfort. We needed Mabbutt. And there he was ... coming over the horizon to whip the second goal past Charlton on Easter Monday. Two more points needed and four games to get them. But you could never be sure with Palace, the sooner they were on the board the better. Chelsea were champions, and Wednesday were nearly there too. They only needed to beat us at Hillsborough to go up. We took the game to the nervy Owls, but a pliant referee wasn't about to disappoint the home fans so, as soon as it was convenient, they were given a dubious penalty and we grumbled our way home.

If we're talking dreadful, Swansea had far greater claim to the title than us. Cannon and Mabbutt, the same pair that had seen off Charlton in the previous home game, dealt with the Swans and we were safe. Mullery had conjured up a vast improvement. Although we finished three places lower in 18th place, we'd achieved it with two games to spare. His relief at keeping us above the relegation dotted line for the second time was short lived though. He was out of a job.

Speculation about our new manager ended when Noades appointed Wimbledon's Dave Bassett. After Dario Gradi joined Palace in 1981, Bassett assumed the manager's chair at Plough Lane and made his reputation by taking Wimbledon into the second division. Just the man to get Palace back on the rails, he moved into his office – and then straight out again. It wasn't right. How could he preach loyalty to his players when he wasn't loyal himself? Or, perhaps, as the cynics suggested, he took one look at the mess and didn't fancy it. Four days later, we were back in the market for a manager. One man who wanted the job was former Palace centre-half Ian Evans, who'd just called it a day at Barnsley. Also tipped was Lou Macari, while his old Man United colleague Steve Coppell was in the running.

Coppell's career was cut short by a knee injury sustained in the match in which England made certain of qualification for the 1982 World Cup finals. Although Coppell played in Spain, the injury deteriorated and late in 1983 he announced his retirement. At 28, he emerged as a stone cold certainty for the Palace job and Evans became assistant manager.

The league's youngest manager had an immediate problem. Billy Gilbert and Vince Hilaire, had had enough. They were disappointed with Mullery's dismissal and, as both were out of contract, they asked to move. Coppell tried to convince them to stay, but they were adamant. Gilbert joined Portsmouth while Hilaire went to first division Luton, who offered £50,000 plus striker Trevor Aylott. Coppell had little option but to accept. With a little money available, he bought experienced replacements in Alan Irvine, the former Everton winger, and Arsenal's reserve centre-half Chris Whyte.

Coppell's managerial career began as Mullery's had ended, with a home match against Blackburn. Under Mullery, we had lost 2-0 in front of a crowd that barely topped 5,000. Coppell's team got a draw in front of a curious 6,764. But it was one of Mullery's favourites, Cummins, who got our goal. Two days later, on Bank Holiday Monday, Coppell enjoyed his first victory. In an unspeakably drab and awful League Cup match, Peter Nicholas gave us a slender victory over Northampton. Only 3,752 watched – a new record low at Selhurst Park. The first Coppell defeat followed – a 4-1 pasting at the hands of those great spoilers Shrewsbury. Another Coppell acquisition, ex-Arsenal left-back Brian Sparrow, scored our consolation but the cause wasn't helped when Aylott was sent off after two minutes.

We then endured a pitiful early season defeat at the Goldstone, before Coppell got his first league win. Former Fulham and Brentford player Tony Mahoney and Murphy scored to beat Sheffield United 2-1. Almost 10,000 saw Palace beat Leeds 3-1 and we set off on a nine game run without a win. The improved crowds drifted back down towards the 4,000 mark, discouraged that the new man was not about to work an instant miracle.

"I've wanted to go since the summer when Billy Gilbert and Vince Hilaire left. Once they went I felt the club didn't want to go places; otherwise they wouldn't have allowed them to go."

– PETER NICHOLAS, WHO LEFT FOR GO GETTERS LUTON IN FEBRUARY 85

On Saturday, October 27, 1984, Jim Cannon broke Terry Long's appearance record. When Long was assistant to Malcolm Allison, he had told Cannon he would be making his debut, so it was appropriate that he should be on hand to commemorate Cannon's feat.

While the interminable struggle continued on the pitch, stories circulated to the effect that Noades wanted a millionaire to buy the club, raising the hopes of a sizeable proportion of the support who disliked him intensely and wanted him "out". But he qualified the announcement by explaining in the programme that he was in fact looking for a millionaire chairman who "could provide funds to achieve the recovery which we would all like to see. The club is not being offered for sale as some papers have suggested and I do not intend to see the steady progress in our recovery stopped in any way."

For most of us, the steady recovery was a figment of Noades' imagination and this impression was heightened by a new low in our first ever league meeting with Wimbledon. Nicholas put us ahead from the spot but mid-way through the second half Bassett introduced a midget striker called Andy Sayer and within five minutes he'd given the lumbering Whyte such a roasting that Palace were 3-1 down. Mahoney, a Coppell signing who could so easily have been a Mullery acolyte, scored a pointless goal right at the end but the disgruntled supporters were not placated. Worse was to follow. With Palace in the mood to give someone a beating, Mahoney and Murphy gave us a commanding lead against the old bogey team Shrewsbury only for Wood to sustain a gash on his knee. Hughton, not the tallest of players, deputised for the big Scotsman and conceded two goals – the second saw the ball trickling down his arm as if he was attempting some mad Harlem Globetrotter trick before settling gently into the net.

It was Whyte's last game for Palace. The club kept things close to their chest but it transpired that there was some trouble involving Whyte and the police and the player was returned to Arsenal. He had not been that great a player but later in his career, after a successful spell with West Brom, he joined Leeds and won a league championship medal.

The Palace-Shrewsbury match was a turning point of sorts – the first of a nine game unbeaten spell which suggested we really were improving. Barber's introduction to the team added some sparkle and, after months of trying, Aylott broke his goal drought. He remains the butt of many Palace jokes even today – many grounds have echoed to the taunt *son of Aylott* after an opponent has missed the target – but in those early weeks he was genuinely unlucky. He still carried the hallmark of a first division striker who had, at one stage, scored in nine successive games for Luton and been part of their swashbuckling first season in division one. But try as he might the ball wouldn't go in and eventually his confidence and determination began to sag. Aylott finally hit a useful run of form with four goals in five games, four of which ended 1-1, while the other was a 3-0 home win over Oldham. But he couldn't maintain that form.

The last match before Christmas was at Grimsby and such was the depths to which Palace had fallen that our 3-1 win was greeted with the Fiat Performance of the Week Award. The week before, in a 1-1 home draw with Cardiff, a young striker called Andy Gray, who Coppell had snapped up from Dulwich Hamlet for a nominal fee, replaced Mahoney. At Blundell Park, the ebullient Gray scored his first goal for the club after Barber had given us the lead. Nicholas wrapped things up. But our star midfielder was not a happy budgie. Although he scored the winner in the Boxing Day match with Charlton, after Steve Gritt had gone in goal for the visitors and Mabbutt had delighted us all by leaping off the bench to score the first, Nicholas's attitude wasn't right.

He was dreadful in the 5-0 drubbing by promotion chasing Oxford when John Aldridge was allowed to run riot and, on New Year's day, he was substituted in the goalless draw at Notts County. To the fans' disappointment he wanted to move and Luton were prepared to pay the £150,000 we had laid out

Neil Everitt

November 1984. Phil Barber gets past an Oldham defender in Palace's 3-0 victory

to bring him back from Arsenal. With Nicholas gone, Palace went off the boil and there was a disaster of immense proportions looming.

It was the blackest day in Selhurst history. The "dark ages" of the early 80s brought many disappointments but this was our lowest ebb. Palace 0 Wimbledon 5 – a living nightmare when a couple of prize donkeys called Paul Fishenden and Steve Ketteridge had a field day. The Dons scored three goals from the same move and Palace just watched them do it. The humiliation was almost unbearable and the plaintive cry "Noades out" was never louder or more heartfelt.

We ambled through the rest of the season without being in much danger of relegation but offering little hope of anything to lift us out of this mediocrity. Attendances still hovered around the 4,000 mark, only doubling for the visit of Brighton when Aylott's goal secured a point.

What many of us had hoped for was a Chelsea-style miracle and instant promotion. But although that was impossible Coppell quietly began to assemble a decent side, even if the results were not yet apparent. He introduced another promising youngster, Tony Finnigan, a friend of Gray's, who had been released by Fulham. Along with Gray, Barber and a young ex-Sutton striker, Steve Galloway, who was touted as a prolific scoring prospect, there was a feeling that Palace were at least on the right track. What was needed was patience. But after years in the doldrums, every game seemed like an eternity.

Mabbutt's goal in our victory against Charlton on Boxing Day turned out to be his farewell present. His long fight for fitness was over, at least at Palace. After three games in the unfamiliar number 7 shirt he made his final appearance in the 3-1 home defeat by Sheffield United on the same day that Micky Droy, a free transfer from Chelsea, made his debut.

Droy, at 6'5" one of the biggest players in the league, made a goalscoring debut but it was his defensive prowess that was more valuable. This bearded, grizzly bear of a man was just what Palace needed to replace Whyte and bring some extra solidity to the back four. Along with Cannon and Wood, he formed an experienced nucleus to a side whose average age got younger by the week. We finished 15th again which, on the face of it, was no better than Mullery had achieved. But after a long hibernation there was just a hint that we were beginning to awake from our slumber. Coppell put the emphasis on youth and his team had a vital ingredient - hunger.

"Playing with Trevor Aylott is great. I have always wanted to play up front with him and got the chance against Manchester City the other week."

– Andy Gray Explains Why He Never Dreamed of Pele, Geoff Hurst or Bobby Charlton When He Was a Boy

Palace started the 1985-86 season on a Sunday with a 2-0 win against Shrewsbury. It was a great performance, particularly by Barber who scored the first goal and set up the second for Gray. Chris Beale from Banstead was among the away support: "We were greeted by police dogs at the station, who behaved like the hounds of hell. We were barged down a little alleyway while the dogs snarled and snipped at us. Everyone came back from the game singing *Going up, Going up*. We'd finished the season before in 15th place and then we'd gone to Shrewsbury and beaten them. It was big stuff. Really big stuff. Where are your tattoos?"

We hit the headlines in the early part of the season not for actions on the pitch but because of a sensational new ground sharing arrangement with Charlton.

Charlton had spent a lot of money in the summer attempting to buy their way out of the second division but Palace had beaten them at the Valley in the league cup in August and returned on September 7 confident of repeating the dose. What happened before the match reduced the game to an insignificant side show. Palace and Charlton were to share Selhurst Park commencing almost immediately. It was a fait accompli. The match went Charlton's way because they were awarded three penalties, two of which were dubious in the extreme, although they did miss one. Palace, presumably expecting an outcry, put a brave face on the revolutionary scheme.

"Palace fans will have heard with interest the news that Palace and Charlton are to lead the Football League field in a ground sharing arrangement here at Selhurst Park.

Merger mania

For a few weeks, it was merger mania. Following Robert Maxwell's initiative to turn Oxford United and Reading into the Thames Valley Royals, Fulham and QPR announced plans to amalgamate into a new club called Fulham Park Rangers.

Speculation was rife that Palace and Wimbledon were heading the same way. Supporters of all clubs began to organise protests and detecting the attitude of the fans, Palace decided to sound out the idea in a questionnaire in which Noades pointed out:

"1. Crystal Palace FC has never approached the Wimbledon club with a view to a merger or encouraged an approach from them.

2. Wimbledon FC have spoken to us and several other south London clubs about their future because they feel they must vacate Plough Lane.

3. In the best interests of Crystal Palace, the directors and I have to consider whether a merger with Wimbledon would be to the benefit of our club.

4. I have always made it clear – to the Wimbledon club and to the media – that in any merger two items are not negotiable

a) our identity i.e. our club name
b) our management i.e. all our staff".

The club received 2,289 completed questionnaires producing a 9-1 majority for "no merger".

The figures were:
Lifeline: for 87 (10%) against 750 (90%)
Club and season ticket holders: for 55 (7%) against 727 (93%)
Palace supporters: for 35 (6 %) against 591 (94%)
Non Palace supporters: for 1, against 22
20 people abstained

Over all, 93 per cent were against and any plans that may have been in the offing were shelved.

"Arrangements such as this are commonplace on the continent and, in our view, it is only surprising that it has taken so long before one has come about in this country. Selhurst Park is a model ground in terms of safety, having met every requirement of the Safety of Sports Grounds Act and it is therefore ideally suited to much greater use than our club alone requires. The agreement between Palace and Charlton is for seven years, with the option of a seven year extension, and it will be worth at least £65,000 a year to Crystal Palace FC. Charlton approached us initially with their proposal which financially was an offer we could not refuse. Already a number of other London clubs are considering it and it will be most interesting to see how many other clubs have followed the lead established by the Palace and Charlton.

There was nothing we could do but accept it and try to ignore the ugly Charlton crest which joined the glorious Eagle on the Old Stand. Our victory over Charlton in the league cup on a 3-2 aggregate set up a glamour tie with Steve Coppell's old club Manchester United. Palace, at home in the first leg, drew 21,506 predominantly lapsed Palace supporters. In an electric atmosphere, Coppell's young braves forced United onto the defensive. Only a string of outstanding saves from England keeper Gary Bailey kept Barber in particular at bay. As was customary with big clubs, Peter Barnes scored on the break to give the reds an undeserved lead to defend at Old Trafford. Large travelling support backed Palace all the way in the second leg, but the game was sealed after just 60 seconds when Norman Whiteside scored. After that Palace did well enough and had chances to reduce the arrears, but United were satisfied.

During the summer Palace had picked up a kid called Ian Wright from a Sunday team called Ten-Em-Bee. Raw and unco-ordinated at times, he was nevertheless enthusiastic and very quick. He had a way of running on his toes which made him appear to be always on the alert.

Coppell put him on the bench, introducing him for short spells to unsettle tiring defences. The crowd took to the new recruit almost immediately and when he scored a last minute winner to complete a remarkable Palace fight back which turned an 89th minute 1-2 deficit against Oldham into an unlikely victory, Coppell promoted him to centre forward. But Wright wasn't ready. He looked lost in the 1-0 defeat at Portsmouth and returned to the bench for a few more months.

Palace were having an erratic season. Not good enough to challenge stylish Norwich, the powerhouse kicking of Wimbledon or the big spending of Charlton, we were let down by an inability at times to put the ball in the net and a general frailty throughout the side. But it was still a vast improvement on recent seasons. Everyone could see the club was beginning to emerge from its decline. Droy and Cannon stood firm in the middle of defence, although the midfield was distinctly lacking where Irvine was a tricky and effective winger but Finnigan was more artistic and less inclined to get stuck in.

We moved for Derby's Kevin Taylor. A stocky, powerful player who settled to his task immediately, running the midfield with clinical efficiency and living up to his nickname of "ticker". The young stars, Barber, Gray and Finnigan all had potential and, by Christmas, Wright was ready for another crack at it.

As usual, Palace managed to ruin everyone's holiday spirits by losing 3-1 at home to Wimbledon in pouring rain. The Holmesdale had never been so sparse. That was followed by a 2-0 defeat in the annual grudge match at the Goldstone and an early exit at home to Luton in the F.A. Cup. This match had been postponed from the Saturday in order to preserve the pitch and give Charlton a chance to face West Ham on the Sunday for the benefit of ITV's cameras. Palace's attendance of 9,886 to see an unusual Friday night match would have been greater had we been able to play on a Saturday and so we were the first to lose out on the ground sharing deal.

The following week, Palace and Charlton met for the first time on Selhurst soil as sharers. The atmosphere was unpleasant although tempered by the fact that Palace were the "home" side. Charlton's eventual promotion ensured we would all have to wait for the day when we would play "away" in our own ground. Goals by Finnigan and Taylor saw off Charlton and kept us in touch with the leaders, but just how far we had to go was illustrated by a breathtaking Norwich performance at the end of January. We were more comfortably beaten than the 2-1 scoreline suggested despite a brilliant goal by Barber, certainly the best of his career and one of the more outstanding Palace efforts of recent times. After that, Palace's form picked up considerably. Wright found the net to win matches against Blackburn at Ewood Park, Middlesbrough and Fulham.

Fulham had long been Palace's *bete noir*, but were now on the slide. They'd lost most of the players who had taken them to within a whisker of promotion and we gave them a real going over at the Cottage in what many of us saw as revenge for all the times we'd outplayed them without reward. Wright popped up for another winner although we contrived to "only" win 3-2.

We exacted revenge over Brighton for our Christmas defeat with a goal by Paul Brush, a left back who had been purchased after a long career at West Ham. Neither Hughton nor youngster David Lindsay had looked comfortable in the full back roles and by the end of the season both were out. We'd tried Nebbeling there while an experiment with Terry Howard, a classy defender on a four game loan, came to an end because we couldn't afford the £30,000 Chelsea were after.

On April 1, Palace went to promotion chasing Wimbledon with one or two pundits beginning to push our claims for a late burst into the top three. Wimbledon had won all three previous meetings but were surprised by our improved power and commitment. In the end, although they took the lead, the Dons were lucky to get away with a draw. The increasingly lethal Wright struck our equaliser.

Two further victories, over Bradford City and Portsmouth kept us in contention, although we had a lot of ground to make up and a complete disaster at Grimsby just about finished it. Chris Beale's favourite Palace experience was the trip to Blundell Park: "I went by myself. Nobody else would go. It was a mistake. I don't know why I went. I don't recall any previous interest in Grimsby except that the season before, we'd lost 2-0 at home to them on the last day of the season. Gary Lund, or someone like that, had scored for them.

"I think the real reason I went was because Palace were still technically in with a chance of promotion (even though in our heart of hearts we knew we weren't). Blundell Park was abysmal, all these people had bought seat tickets which turned out to be lumps of driftwood nailed to the floor. I think the real reason I went up there was to see the Findus Family Stand. It was a sort of giant freezer section, multiplied by about a hundred. It was like an enormous fridge with executive boxes and a great big Findus sign. So I suppose I've seen the biggest frozen food compartment in the world.

"A load of lads turned up at Euston and one of them wasn't even wearing a T-shirt. All he had with him was a copy of *Penthouse* and a bottle of vodka. He went all the way up there with nothing else. They turned up drunk and he was poured into the station and collapsed in front of everybody. I remember the train pulled in through somewhere like South Grimsby and all the Palace lads were looking out of the windows at disused warehouses and giving it a load of prattle about 'they've got no money up here'.

"I can't remember a lot about the match, except it was terrible. You should have seen the way Kevin Taylor got sent off. He sort of flew into the air in a quarter-pirouette and elbowed this Grimsby player right in the face. Everybody could see it. It was so obvious – a bit like Jack Ruby assassinating Lee Harvey Oswald – there was no question about it. Yet when he landed, Taylor did this brilliant 'Mr Innocent' act. The look of shock on his face when he was sent off was a picture. He couldn't believe it, even though he'd laid this bloke out!

"The carriages of the train had been used to take soldiers up to the Somme or something. It really was bad. The whole thing was an almighty blunder."

John Ellis of Whetstone also went to Grimsby: "Kevin Drinkell scored a hat-trick. We tried to get fish and chips before the game because it was 'a fishing town'. But all they had at the fish shop were cornish pasties. The Russians must have sucked all the fish up with those floating hoovers of theirs and left no fish for us. I went up with Ian, a mad policeman, and this girl he was going out with at the time. He had a moustache and was a fascist, he became a sergeant in the end.

"We got as far as Grantham and then we had to get on a little train to complete the journey. But when we stopped at Grimsby there was no platform. We got off in a siding and had to jump off the train. It was unbelievable, even old ladies had to jump down. We were met by all these police with dogs. It was like that Frank Sinatra film *Von Ryan's Express*, where they all escape from the train, absolutely charming. There was all this mist coming in from the sea and it was freezing. The special going up was terrible but the journey back was just as bad. The highlight was the 'zit trolley'. A bloke would come round and if you were lucky you got ham sandwiches and apple pies. But, on the way back, there was

Andy Gray celebrates his winner against Derby with Tony Finnigan

only about half a mars bar and a can of Fanta between the lot of us." And there, dear reader, you have an eye witness account of what being an away fan is all about.

A major disappointment was the poor attendances. The 21,000 odd who had turned up to see Man United were patently not prepared to return just on the basis of the odd good result. In December, we had a chance to go third if we beat Shrewsbury at home. But Gary Hackett struck for Palace's bogey team and what was then considered to be a tremendous crowd of 8,253 went home unimpressed. The penultimate home game against relatively attractive opponents, Leeds United, pulled in just over 6,000, as did the last home match against Sheffield United. In between, Millwall finally put paid to any lingering hopes of promotion at the Den. Former Cambridge forward Andy Higginbottom and Ketteridge replied for Palace.

Our hopes for the new campaign were based on a sparkling destruction of Barnsley at Oakwell on the last day of the 1984-85 season. Wright scored the first double of his career as the Yorkshiremen were crushed 4-2. He'd scored nine goals in 16 full starts with 16 more appearances as substitute. That was the same as Barber and just one behind Gray.

Palace finished fifth, a fine effort considering that resources were so limited and, if Barnsley was anything to go by, the team was about to take the second division by the throat and scare it to death. Ironically it was to Barnsley that we travelled for our first match of 1986-87. It was a far from easy task, but Palace again came through with flying colours. Wright was on the mark again along with Brush and Barber in the 3-2 victory. Barber then scored to see off Stoke in our first home match.

Following the fire at Valley Parade, Bradford City had moved into temporary accommodation at Bradford Northern Rugby League Club's Odsal Stadium. Palace were first to visit the third division champions at their temporary HQ and secured a third successive victory with goals by Irvine and Ketteridge. City had played their first four home games at Elland Road and Leeds Road.

Another small signal of progress was our exemption from the first round of the league cup. Bury were our far from enticing second round opponents and Palace bored the meagre 4,017 to tears by failing to break the visitors down. In the return, we had to withstand an onslaught by the third division team before Wright won it with a touch of pure class – a spellbinding run topped off with a finish from an acute angle. We had suffered a couple of setbacks in the league. A John Gregory penalty robbed us of a point against fellow promotion hopefuls Derby and we were caught by a Sheffield United break away just after we'd equalised at Selhurst Park. That was followed by a 3-1 home drubbing by Reading before we beat Millwall in a match marred by some of the visitors' cretin fans attacking Palace supporters in the Arthur Wait enclosure. By way of consolation, Palace went top and the man who put us there was a cheap import from Millwall, Anton Otulakowski.

Otulakowski had been purchased for £12,500 with money provided by the supporters through a new scheme. Lifeline had been launched by the club with the intention of providing funds for players. For £8.66 per month, supporters were entitled to enter a prize draw while contributing to the well being of the club. Otulakowski unfortunately didn't turn out to be the wisest investment. He made just 12 appearances before succumbing to injury – something that had blighted his career – and he never played again.

If you're top you're there to be shot at goes the old cliche and Palace were forced to take cover as Leeds scored three,

Birmingham four, and Shrewsbury, Plymouth, Grimsby and Ipswich three each in consecutive matches. At this rate our defence would see us relegated by Christmas. Yet we were capable of so much more, as we demonstrated with a tenacious display against first division Nottingham Forest in the league cup. Irvine and Gray gave us the lead and only a late goal by Garry Birtles secured a replay for Brian Clough's aristocrats. We put up a superb defensive display and the City Ground rang to the choruses of *Eagles*. But Forest were a touch too strong.

Droy, who had given remarkably valuable service and become a cult figure, was now on his last legs. In his last appearance, Tommy Tynan had a field day for Plymouth and Coppell was forced to make a change. Gavin Nebbeling, so long the understudy, was given another chance to establish himself alongside the evergreen Cannon. Nevertheless we still looked shaky at the back.

Coppell's reaction to our defensive uncertainty was to buy a striker. Mark Bright's claim to fame was that he had followed in Gary Lineker's footsteps at Leicester. Lineker had been too hot a property for the Foxes to hang onto and when Everton's cash prised the young England forward away, Bright was introduced to the City faithful. His first task was to fire two goals past Lineker's new club, giving Leicester a 3-1 win and putting a smile on the face of football lovers the length and breadth of the country. But the fairy tale went sour, he failed to score regularly and the crowd were happy to be shot of him, helping him on his way with some friendly racist abuse.

The stumbling block was Bright's pelvic injury. In any case, he wasn't too keen on coming to London. Palace had been bitten too often with injuries, and with Otulakowksi a recent reminder of how not to waste money on crocks, there was some doubt whether Bright was the right man. But the tall striker took his place in a reshuffled pack alongside Wright. The first victims of the new rhyming strike force of Bright 'n' Wright were Ipswich, who had been relegated the previous season but were looking for a swift return. Bright marked his debut with a looping fluke of a goal, but our defence was still all over the shop and Town soon established a 3-1 lead. A sixth successive defeat looked certain until Taylor produced a thunderbolt from 30 yards and Wright, with his third goal of the season, brought us pounding back to grab a breathless point.

The rot hadn't quite stopped and Oldham took the points in our next match at Boundary Park. After that we recovered and Bright was on target against Sunderland in our first win for nearly two months. Portsmouth were the new pace setters and they beat us 2-0 at Fratton, after which we went goal crazy. For the first time since August 1980, we scored five in a match. On a muddy day, Brian Horton the Hull player manager, whose Brighton connections were not forgotten, rounded off a joyous afternoon by being sent off. The star of the show was Finnigan who ran the visitors ragged and completed the rout with a spectacular solo effort.

Palace were an odd side. Often lazily disinterested, a goal would spark a frenzy of attacking and excitement, almost like feeding time in the Piranha tank, after which there would be a long period of quiet. The home match with Birmingham was a prime example; after 43 uninspired, goalless minutes in which Taylor had missed a penalty, everyone was just nodding off. Then Wright scored from close in. Palace were aroused and the shocked Blues went in two down and 20 minutes into the second half it was six. Then it died again and the latter stages were spent at half pace.

A major Palace failing was their ability to turn it on against better sides while succumbing to opponents of more humble status. In the Cup, we got another crack at Forest and this time Irvine's strike on a treacherous, snow covered pitch ended the Clough Cup dream for another season. Although bad weather interrupted the league programme we showed our erratic side by losing our next home match to Barnsley.

More agony followed in the last minute at Reading. We were given a penalty only to have our celebrations, tinged as much with relief as joy, cut short when the referee consulted his linesman and changed his mind. Thus we slipped to another silly defeat.

A taste of the glamour we had been missing was offered by the away trip to Spurs in the F.A. Cup fourth round. Had Gray's finishing been steadier, we could have been two up before Spurs were gifted a goal despite a foul on Wood. But the killer was an own goal by another Lifeline signing, Gary O'Reilly. It didn't help that O'Reilly, who had joined from Brighton the week before, was a former Spurs player. Four-nil was harsh, though the supporters had a great time, handing out the first of what would become numerous lessons in the art of singing to Tottenham's fans. It was significant because everybody realised the sort of following we could have if we could gain promotion.

After the rout of Birmingham, the goals, both for and against, dried up. The five wins in the last 12 were all achieved by the odd goal and a new pattern was emerging. Bright and Wright, whose transfer had been made permanent, were developing a lethal looking partnership. They began to grab the lion's share and the more they scored, the more they wanted – and the less everybody else got.

Towards the end of the season, Pompey came to Selhurst for the third successive year in search of points to help them win promotion. And for the third successive season, we denied them any reward. We were a little way short of the last play-off place and had to win to keep our slim hopes alive. For Pompey, a point would be enough. Enormous travelling support arrived and the police upset the home fans by allocating the Holmesdale to Portsmouth, even though a considerable number of Palace supporters were already in position.

The match was a tense and sterile affair until, with a few seconds left, teenage substitute John Salako, who'd made a name for himself with his phenomenal scoring exploits in the reserves, beat Alan Knight. His shot was going in anyway but poacher Wright got a final touch to make sure. Pompey, notorious for having the worst disciplinary record in the league, lost their rag and former Palace star Vince Hilaire thumped Andy Gray into the seats in the Old Stand. Hilaire got his marching orders and the laughing Palace fans made their plans for the last match at Hull.

To reach the play-offs (a new system designed to generate revenue by offering showdown matches at the end of the season while maintaining the interest of also rans such as us) we had to win and hope Ipswich slipped up. Hull were not easy opponents, they were still in relegation trouble and had everything to play for. A couple of thousand Palace travelled north, but we returned home empty handed. Palace turned in a lethargic performance and Hull's Alex Dyer scored two spectacular goals to upstage Bright and Wright.

It was a disappointing but not unexpected end. At least we could comfort ourselves that the team could and would get better. Coppell clearly knew what he was doing and was extremely popular with the supporters, who recognised just how much he had achieved. He had given us back our self respect. Coppell's influence spread throughout the club. In March 1983, for example, Noades had said: "We have made our intentions clear by restructuring our youth system to concentrate on the younger age groups. That foundation will lay the foundations for future security ..." What it actually achieved was the decimation of Palace's youth policy and it was not until Coppell had undertaken a rebuilding programme that players began to come through the ranks once more.

The manager established a centre of excellence, run by Peter Prentice in conjunction with the F.A. Scheme which allows young players to join clubs at 11 years old for a trial period of one month. They attached themselves to a club for a maximum of three years after which, if up to standard they could sign Associate Schoolboy forms with the possibility of an apprenticeship. Each club was allowed a maximum 30 schoolboys which involved as many local schoolboys of District or County standard as possible.

While Coppell was astute enough to have one eye on the future, he had to deal with more immediate problems. Kevin Taylor, our inspiration in midfield, wanted to leave. He was replaced by two new midfielders. The first was Doncaster's highly rated Neil Redfearn, who Palace had been chasing

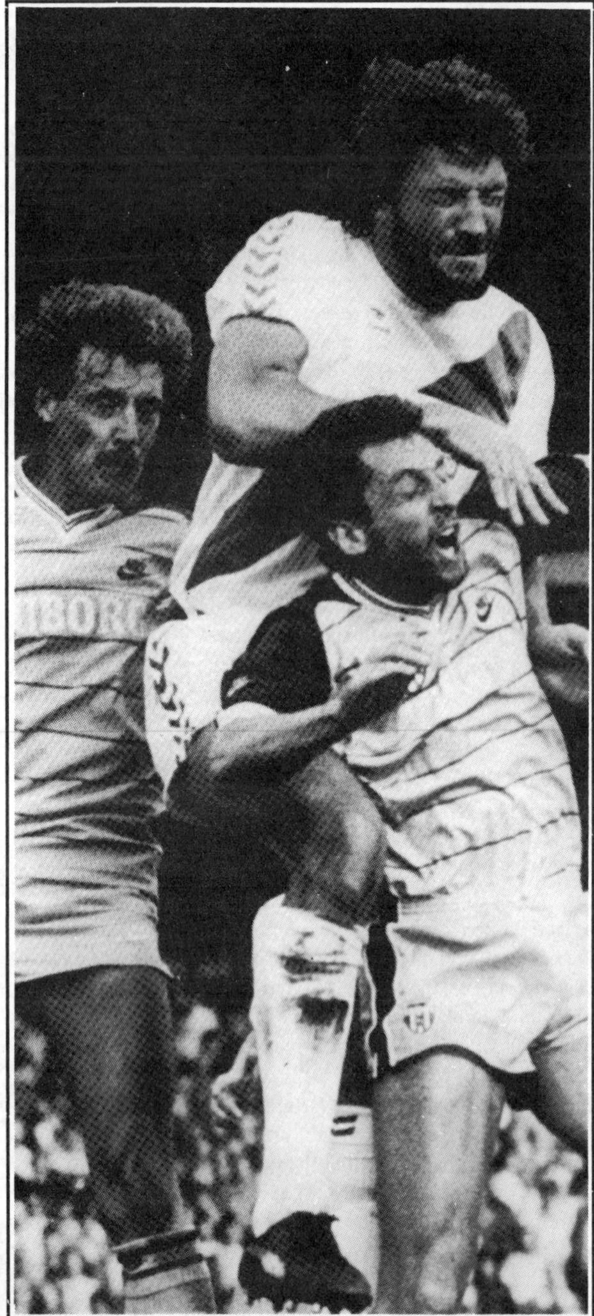

Neil Everitt

Micky Droy in typical pose against Sunderland (on the left is former Palace star Dave Swindlehurst)

throughout the summer. At £80,000, he represented a major investment while the second player was a relative unknown. Geoff Thomas of Crewe was one of a crop of good young players produced by former Palace boss Dario Gradi. We forked out another £50,000 for the lean youngster with the spiky blond hair.

Although Palace lost to Dave Bassett's Watford in a testimonial for Len Chatterton, Redfearn looked an outstanding prospect. Thomas was more ungainly, but proved more effective as the season got under way.

We didn't start too well and threw away a two goal lead at Huddersfield. We then had to come from 2-0 down against Hull with two Gray penalties given by referee Kelvin Morton at a stage when it looked as if a home defeat was on the cards.

Palace, in their usual frenzy after grabbing a couple of quick goals, were only halted by the ferocity of a late summer storm that lashed into the players faces. But after two draws, we lost to a last minute goal at Barnsley to find ourselves close to the bottom of the first league table of the season. It was early days but such was the sense of hope and optimism, that even this came as a bitter blow.

The second successive home drenching on the Holmesdale was tempered by a storming performance against Middlesbrough. Another double for Bright took his tally to five in four games while Thomas scored his first goal. Palace earned plenty of praise for their performance but the destruction of 'Boro was nothing compared to what was to befall poor Birmingham at St Andrew's.

Their programme mentioned, hopefully, that they were looking forward to the chance to set the record straight after we had rubbed their noses in it the previous season. Instead, the Eagles repeated the dose. Bright was on the mark again and, to the accompaniment of clattering seats as the home fans got up to leave, Redfearn, Thomas and Gray with two, including one from the penalty spot, made it a rout. To the delight of the travelling fans, Cannon strode up field to blast home number six and Birmingham's commercial department spent the next week answering requests for the video with a weary: "Whereabouts in London do you want it sent?" The camera work was shaky and there was no commentary except for a City fan heard shouting: "You're a disgrace to the Midlands, Blues."

All eyes were on the Pride of London. WBA, who'd appointed former Man United boss Ron Atkinson to take them back to the glory days of the mid-70s, were the next visitors. In a match billed as a master versus pupil clash between Big Ron and his former United protege Coppell, it was the young buck who came out on top. Two more for Bright another for Redfearn and a goal at last for Ian Wright, who'd suffered a mini drought while his colleagues were helping themselves, shattered Albion's experienced campaigners. Unable to cope with the onslaught they resorted to kicking and had Tony Morley sent off for their trouble.

With 13 goals in three matches and plenty of press attention, Palace's crowd reached a vast 9,000 for the visit of Leicester. Thomas gave us the lead with a powerful first half drive and everyone expected it to be lambs to the slaughter. Instead City equalised and we looked uncertain. Then Wright broke through and Palace sat proudly on top of the division.

A midweek trip to Sheffield United brought an early goal and we looked set to return with maximum points until Tony Philliskirk survived the offside appeals to poke home an equaliser – his first goal for a year.

Reading's ground is miles from the station and the bus takes such an eternity that you begin to wonder if you're really going the right way. It was pouring and the Palace seats in the rickety stand were soon sold out leaving the late comers to pick a spot behind fences more suited to keeping intruders out of weapons research establishments.

At Reading, Richard Shaw made his debut as a substitute for the unfortunate Brush, who'd been running to clear a harmless ball when his hamstring went. Reading raced away and from the cross Gray ran the ball into his own net. It was appalling luck, just the sort of misfortune that in previous years would have brought defeat. Instead, in the space of 17 second half minutes, Palace ripped Reading apart.

Then came three defeats in four games, each offering a new lesson. The first was handed out by Ipswich. Aware of the potency of the home forwards, they packed their defence and, marshalled by the headband sporting Ian Cranson, played a robotic offside trap before catching us with two sucker punches on the break. We realised we had better get used to timid opponents coming for draws.

Lesson two; the Gay Meadow jinx was not going to go away just because we'd become a decent side. Shrewsbury 2 Crystal Palace 0, which prompted a telling match report in Palace's newly born fanzine *Eagle Eye*: "Umm."

Lesson three: big clubs get all the breaks. After Bright had sunk Millwall, Palace suffered the sort of 4-1 defeat at Villa that suggested this wasn't going to be our year. Suspect penalties, bad luck and vicious policing all played a part in a miserable evening which finished with Villa's first home win since relegation the season before. It also gave Villa boss Graham Taylor a chance to assess the qualities of Gray, now settled comfortably alongside Thomas in midfield.

Lou Macari had lifted Swindon from fourth division obscurity to the fringes of the second division promotion race. Swindon didn't look likely to surrender their lead until Bright pulled a goal out of nothing and then won us a penalty and three points.

After whipping six unanswered goals past Newport in our two-legged league cup tie, we travelled to Old Trafford for a third round glamour tie with Man United. Unfortunately, for the first 20 minutes, we were overawed and allowed Gordon Strachan to dictate proceedings. United eased into a two goal lead after which we came to terms with the fact that United, despite an imposing ground, were nothing special. Irish under-21 defender Ken O'Doherty, a close season signing from University College Dublin, pulled a goal back and if an appeal for what looked a blatant penalty had been granted, we may well have earned a replay.

We crossed the Pennines for the top of the table clash with Bradford City, now restored to Valley Parade, and met our match for the first time. City's midfield dynamo Stuart McCall dominated as Palace were soundly beaten.

On November 3, Ian Wright celebrated his birthday with a hat-trick as we hit the goal trail against Plymouth. The season before they had been in the hunt for a play-off place and had successfully stifled us at Selhurst. This time they had no answers. Gray finished off the rout with a powerful run and shot to make it 5-1.

Had our finishing been better we would have had at least five more at Dean Court on the day that Man City beat Huddersfield 10-1. Palace had fought back from being two pathetic goals down after four minutes – George Wood allowing a soft header to slip under his body and a Jim Cannon back pass failing to find the keeper – to lead by half time. Bright with two first half goals had enough chances for a double hat-trick in the second half, but he squandered the lot. Nevertheless it was a great win.

At this stage of the season there was no reason why Palace should not get stronger and go on to take the title. Aside from an in-form Bradford, nobody had got the better of us and although there were plenty of pretenders to the crown, partly because the play-offs kept so many teams in contention, none looked to have the all round ability of a rampant Palace.

There are numerous reasons why we failed. But perhaps the most significant was the sale of Andy Gray. Aston Villa, one of Palace's more potent rivals, approached Coppell about signing Gray and were told he was not available. Gray was apparently informed of Villa's interest but was not concerned. Villa then made their interest known in the press fuelling further speculation which unsettled the young midfielder, who suddenly decided he liked the idea of moving to the more glamourous surrounds of Villa Park after all. Palace resisted, but a player who was rated in the £500,000 class became unmanageable and, to the fury of the Palace supporters, he was sold for a cut price £150,000.

At a management/supporters "forum" a few weeks later, Coppell explained that Gray had become an unsettling influence on the other players and the manager felt he had to sell him before he disrupted our prize possession Wright. "I did the best possible deal I could on behalf of Crystal Palace," said Coppell in the programme opposite the page which carried details of Gray's replacement, Glenn Pennyfather of Southend. Pennyfather had impressed earlier in the season with his performance for the third division club as they knocked first division Derby out of the League Cup. But other than that the diminutive midfielder was little known.

After losing to Blackburn, we cruised to a 3-0 win over Leeds, although the victory was less convincing than the final score suggested. We were nevertheless one of the two form teams in the division. The other was Man City and the meeting of the two clubs was eagerly awaited.

Palace travelled north to face a City side in confident mood. Beforehand, most of us would have settled for a draw but the match proved to be a turning point for both clubs.

City led 1-0 when Bright and the home keeper Eric Nixon got involved in an "altercation". Nixon was sent off and Redfearn equalised from the penalty spot. Bright then added two more to seal a tremendous victory. The win was not achieved without cost. Bright had a broken arm and missed the next six matches.

Without our spearhead, we travelled to Ipswich on Boxing Day and in front of a huge Palace following, went straight behind when David Lowe latched onto a weak Nebbeling back pass to shoot beyond Wood. After that, it was all Palace. Redfearn potted a penalty and Wright grabbed two more as the home support was silenced.

Although we conceded a late consolation it was the away support who left Portman Road singing Slade's festive hit: *"So here it is, Merry Christmas, everybody's having fun ..."*

It was Reading who spoilt our Christmas two days later. We went down to exactly the same score by which we had beaten Ipswich. New Year's day brought more toil and it took substitute Dennis Bailey, a striker picked up from Farnborough, to snatch victory over Barnsley.

The following day, Palace went to Leicester and George Wood, for so long a reliable giant in the Palace goal, had a nightmare. With the supporters increasingly impatient to see the fruits of the club's labours rewarded, Wood, who'd been making silly errors for some time, came in for intolerable stick. Palace raced into a 4-2 half time lead and looked set for another feast of goals. Instead Wood made another dreadful error, hitting a clearance straight to the feet of a home player and we dropped a vital point. That signalled the end for the veteran Scot. Coppell was given £100,000 to invest in Man City's Perry Suckling and Wood departed for Cardiff.

In the winter months, Palace's form dipped noticeably. We

dominated promotion rivals Middlesbrough in dreadful conditions at Ayresome Park but came away with nothing and were robbed on Oldham's plastic pitch. Hopes of another six goal dose against Birmingham were never realistic although Bright scored his first goal since returning to the team in a 3-0 win.

"WHY GRAY HAD TO GO"

"...when Villa made their initial approach to us Andy still expressed his wish to stay at Selhurst Park ... However the following week Andy announced he had reconsidered his position at the club and, three days later, he handed in a written transfer request in which he stated: 'I have been unhappy at Crystal Palace for some time.' The Palace management were now in a most unenviable situation, faced with an unsettled player who was becoming increasingly difficult to motivate and whose influence among the other players was disruptive."

- Crystal Palace FC

At West Brom, we did everything but score. In an unbelievable match, Don Goodman stole the points with Albion's only serious attack while their keeper Peter Hucker had an inspired game. Hucker's goal always led a charmed life against Palace, he had been at QPR in the early 80s when the hooped horrors regularly stole undeserved honours against us. Making it worse was Albion's Kenny Swain claiming in a radio interview that his team had outplayed us and then, walking back to the station, a group of Palace supporters had another unpleasant encounter with the notorious West Midlands Police. Phil Huffer of Forest Hill says: "We were strolling back when a police van drove by very slowly, the back doors were open and inside were a couple of policeman taunting 'come on Palace, if you want to have a go, come on'. Needless to say there were no takers. How can you have any respect for them when they do things like that?"

Palace had another nightmare against Shrewsbury in which Wright showed his irritating side by selfishly wasting a hatful of chances while others were in better positions.

We had now slipped from promotion probables to play-off hopefuls while Millwall were looking the part more than us. We travelled to the Den hoping to restore the balance. After an incredible miss by Bright, Palace fell behind and looked to be heading for another damaging defeat when Cannon popped up at a late corner to bundle a disputed goal over the line. Palace went potty while Millwall furiously claimed handball.

With that snatched point in the bank, we faced another promotion battle, this time at Selhurst. Again we fell behind, which was fatal because Bradford were more than satisfied with a point. Although Barber levelled the scores it was nowhere near enough.

We often dominated opponents without reward and a perfect illustration of this came on a fine Sunday afternoon in Swindon where we came from behind to lead with goals by Wright and Bright. Such were the celebrations that when Pennyfather had a perfectly legitimate looking third goal ruled out, nobody seemed worried. It was almost inevitable that Swindon would equalise and so they did – in the last minute.

Bournemouth looked relegation certainties and even though referee Kelvin Morton sent Wright off for a second over enthusiastic tackle, our ten men were too good for them. Morton made amends by awarding two penalties, one of which was retaken, and we won 3-0.

At Stoke we fell behind, equalised, had a goal disallowed for no apparent reason and, after Alan Pardew, a £7,000 buy from Yeovil, missed an easy chance in the last seconds, were forced to settle for another draw. After draws in each of the opening two matches, we hadn't drawn again until after Christmas. Now we couldn't stop and it was costing us promotion.

The return of Andy Gray, whose outspoken views about Palace and their fans made him the target for non-stop abuse during the Mercantile Credit tournament at Wembley, was eagerly awaited. His profile was not included in the Villa programme pen pictures, nor did his name appear on the back page team sheet, but it was greeted with fifteen and a half thousand boos when it was announced over the tannoy. His every touch was met with howls of derision and on one occasion an apple core bounced off him.

Palace had to win but fell behind early on. In the second half, Wright, shaping up for a strike, was hauled down ... by Gray. In the absence of the substituted Redfearn, Wright took the penalty himself. Gray's error delighted us all but another draw wasn't enough and our chances of overhauling the leading clubs became more remote. Even a play-off place began to look in doubt.

Palace had never fared well at Home Park but this time it was vital. There was no "special" but seats had been reserved on a service train which arrived at one o'clock with Palace fans, wondering where the ground was, filing past non-plussed policemen, who were presumably waiting to escort us to the ground. They said nothing as we passed by.

Strolling through the park which leads to Plymouth's ground the train party was attacked by about half a dozen thugs. It was like something out of a second rate Cowboy and Indian film as the aggressors appeared on the horizon, ran in with fists flying and were chased off. Belatedly the police arrived and the Palace supporters were escorted by a fat police sergeant past little kids playing school football matches while their parents shouted "Argyle" and other hurtful things at us.

It was still so early that the ground wasn't even open so we stood about and snoozed under the trees until a gate man could be found – the bloke who operated the turnstile looked as if he actually lived inside. Anyway, we entered and ordered burgers and tea in an empty stadium while the PA announcer talked rubbish and played the scratchiest records in the world – all middle of the road hits from the mid-60s. On one occasion he was playing the Ken Dodd classic *Happiness* and must have nipped out for some reason. The needle stuck and we were treated to five minutes worth of *Happ ... Happ ... Happ ... Happ...* until he returned and jogged the stylus back to ... *Happiness*.

It was an appropriate song for Palace because we could have won more comfortably than the 3-1 scoreline suggests. It was a vital victory and we waited for a train that didn't set off for London until six o'clock enjoying the efforts of the excellent local paper to put a brave face on Plymouth's abject failure.

After years of being ignored by television, Palace now had a vital game with play-off rivals Blackburn. The Lancastrians had hit the headlines with an early attempt to buy their way out of division two by siging Osvaldo Ardiles and Steve Archibald and attracting much press interest in the process. ITV couldn't resist it and broadcast highlights of the match at the less than convenient time of 9.30am on the following Sunday morning – such was their commitment to football – and they wonder why nobody gave a toss when Sky took the Premier League contract off them. They got more than their money's worth from Palace. After Suckling had saved Archibald's penalty, Bright gave Palace the lead and, in the second half, Thomas headed in a long throw from substitute Salako.

It was all to play for. Palace needed to beat Leeds at Elland Road and then Man City in the last game at Selhurst. But it was too much and we fell at the first hurdle. Although we dominated proceedings the vital break wouldn't come and Leeds won with a dodgy penalty. Still, if Palace could beat Man City and Millwall did us favour by stopping Blackburn from winning, we would take the coveted last play-off place.

Millwall hadn't lost at home all season, but with the championship already in the bag they had nothing to play for. In fact they had less to than that. If they didn't try too hard they could deny us. We made heavy weather of beating City who'd fallen away since we'd beaten them at Maine Road, but eventually Nebbeling and Thomas broke the deadlock at the exact moment that an unidentified radio station

"They've got the right type of players – hungry players – and I would imagine Crystal Palace is waiting to take off. I don't imagine they'll get in the first division this season and I'm sure Steve, deep down, would be pleased about that because at this stage of their development I don't think they're ready. But they play football, they've got a good shape and they've got two finishers – Wright and Bright – and while they've got those they've always got a chance."

LEICESTER CITY MANAGER DAVID PLEAT WITH A PERFECT ASSESSMENT OF 1988 VINTAGE PALACE

A feast of football – the Mercantile Credit Centenary Festival of Football

Do you remember the first time you saw Palace at Wembley? No, forget the F.A. Cup Final (if you were lucky enough to get a ticket). I'm talking about the Mercantile Credit Football League Centenary Festival of Football.

It was 1988 and Palace were only outside chances for the play-offs, even with Wright and Bright. Once we realised we'd qualified for this tournament there was the usual mad rush for tickets, overall Palace sold 7,000, far more than our allocation. But no other team, apart from Tranmere, shared our enthusiasm (it was their first time too).

In all less than 20,000 fans turned up from 16 clubs in a 100,000 capacity stadium. Eventually the big day came and the Palace fans all went up by tube for £1 – it was called a special saver day or something. When we arrived and had bought programmes we realised our game had been drawn last – and it was only half past nine. After a whole day of boring games, bar Tranmere beating the F.A. Cup finalists Wimbledon, Palace's turn finally arrived. Even though most games had been drawn and settled by penalties there was an air of expectancy from the noisy Palace contingent.

From the excitement of Jim Cannon leading the team out until the final whistle we only had a couple of chances and it finished 0-0 against first division Sheffield Wednesday. And so it was a penalty shoot-out to decide who would meet Wigan (honest). Neil Redfearn scored but Phil Barber missed and Perry Suckling couldn't prevent Wednesday progressing 2-1.

After such a long wait it was little reward and even big Jim Cannon looked choked at the end. Yet the day still holds special memories for me when to be honest if you'd told me that in two years we would be in the top flight and taking on Man United for the F.A. Cup I wouldn't have believed you.

Even to this day, I get angry with people who refer to the Cup Final as our first game at Wembley. How could they forget so easily an event that was so important to everyone at the time.

David London

Mercantile Credit Festival of Football

(part of the Football League's centenary celebrations)

Prize money
Winners: £60,000
Runners-up £35,000
3rd & 4th £15,000 each
5th to 8th £5,000 each.

There were 16 clubs, eight from the first division, four from the second and two each from the third and fourth in a two-day eleven-a-side knockout.

The qualifiers were decided by effectively starting a league competition from scratch. The best four clubs in division two over 16 games from the start of November would go to Wembley.

This was the situation when Palace had completed their games:

	P	W	D	L	F	A	Pts
Blackburn	13	10	3	0	22	7	33
Villa	13	9	3	1	25	10	30
Palace	15	9	1	5	34	24	28
Millwall	14	9	1	4	26	16	28
Leeds	13	9	0	4	26	17	27

Leeds eventually pushed above Palace into third place and Millwall would have denied the Eagles a place at Wembley had they not conceded a last minute goal.

It was announced to the yawns of a disinterested public that Elkie Brooks would top the bill in a Gala League Centenary Concert at the Royal Albert Hall.

The show "promises to be a night to remember, particularly for fans of Elkie, and also generally for lovers of showbiz and football" gushed the Palace programme. It is not thought that quite so Palace fans snapped up tickets as for the sporting occasion.

announced that Millwall, who'd been losing at half time, had drawn level. Selhurst went crazy – or at least sections of it did. Others, tuned in elsewhere, weren't so sure. The celebratory pitch invasion was premature and by the time most fans spilling across from the Arthur Wait at the end of the match had reached the Old Stand, Millwall's 4-1 defeat had been announced to groans from Palace and cheers from the jealous City followers.

The best news we could receive after the disappointment of missing the play-offs was to hear that Wright and Bright were prepared to stay in the belief that we would achieve promotion in 1988-89. Certainly, we had the ability to do it but Palace had disappointed so often in the past that there were few prepared to stand up and proclaim that promotion would be a formality.

The season was delayed. Swindon had undertaken ground improvements in the summer which were not ready and so what looked like a difficult trip was postponed. Our opening fixture was at Selhurst against Chelsea, who'd just been relegated but had invested in experienced players to get them back at the first attempt. Jim Cannon had finally retired and numerous central defenders were linked with us during the summer but in the end went elsewhere. Suddenly, a week before the season was due to kick off, we bid for Fulham's Welsh international Jeff Hopkins. A tribunal set the fee at £240,000, well above Palace's valuation, but Coppell had already committed himself to the deal and we were forced to cough up. Hopkins was suspended for the first two matches and so we started with Nebbeling and O'Reilly in central defence. The pace of Gordon Durie made life difficult and he gave Chelsea the lead but, shortly after, Redfearn capitalised on defensive uncertainty to equalise.

Palace had more problems for the home game against another relegated team, Watford, the following Saturday. Coppell drafted Thomas into an emergency centre-back role in place of Nebbeling without success, the Hornets made the most of the reshuffle and we slumped to a 2-0 defeat.

We just could not get out of first gear – drawing the next four against opponents we'd had high hopes of beating. The palace fans had another bad experience at the hands of the West Midlands police at Walsall and one youngster of about 12 years was ejected for blowing a duck quacker.

But finally it all fell into place with a 4-1 mauling of Plymouth in which Alan Pardew astonished everyone with a beautiful shot for the fourth goal. Pardew was not a crowd favourite, many fans thought he made little contribution. Nevertheless he formed the midfield partnership with Thomas and Palace announced their arrival as serious contenders with a sparkling 2-0 win over unbeaten Ipswich in an atmospheric evening game. Palace's crowds were much healthier now. Although only 7,000 showed for the dubious delights of a frustrating draw with Shrewsbury, both the Watford and Ipswich games had topped 10,000.

In fine fettle, we travelled to Ewood Park seeking our first away win. We looked certain to get it when we took a 3-1 lead. Such was the Palace dominance that it was surely a question of how many we were going to get.

Enter referee Mr J.J. Timmons who did everything he could to hand the initiative to Blackburn with numerous unfathomable decisions, including a penalty award for a legitimate tackle that that was barely in our half let alone in the box. Rovers took advantage of the lifeline the referee had thrown them to go 4-3 ahead. Gary O'Reilly levelled the scores but we were denied even a point by a last minute winner. The sneering Blackburn fans trotted happily home knowing they had been gifted the match. What they weren't to know was that revenge would be exacted later in the season.

Bradford City had missed out on promotion at the very last in 1988 and, unlike Palace, they had paid for their failure with the loss of their star player Stuart McCall. But they were still a force to be reckoned with and Palace's victory with a goal by Wright from Redfearn's cross was a fabulous result. The away support really found their voices at Valley Parade and it was apparent that when push came to shove the noise generated particularly away from home would be invaluable.

Back on home soil against Hull, Wright scored again impressing the England Under-21 selectors who were watching from the stand. Redfearn followed up with a penalty winner in a laboured victory over Oxford in midweek.

We were then set back on our heels by a silly defeat at Stoke when, having hauled ourselves back into the game, we fell to a late sucker punch and came away with nothing. Barnsley held us at home and then the much taunted Trevor Aylott scored one of Bournemouth's goals in our 2-0 defeat at Dean Court. There was more trouble in the first minute at home to Leicester the following week when Mike Newell scored a screamer. After that it was all Palace and 4-2 flattered the visitors.

Suckling's leg injury had kept him out of action since the Watford match but former Crewe keeper Brian Parkin, who we had swapped for our reserve keeper Dean Greygoose, was proving an able deputy. However Parkin was beaten five times at West Brom in a match in which Palace's three goals should have been enough to have given us a comfortable victory. Had Wright not missed a last minute penalty, we would have had our second 5-4 defeat of the season. That really summed Palace up. We had the best striking pair in the division but one of the worst defences and while that persisted, any thoughts of the championship or even outright promotion were out of the question. It wasn't just a case of the number of goals conceded, it was the unsettling effect the defence had on the supporters and the rest of the team. Points for our promotion rivals Man City and Leeds in drab goalless draws at Selhurst Park only served to enhance the feeling that we weren't quite good enough. In between Alex Dyer, a £200,000 buy from Hull, scored direct from a corner to give us victory at Birmingham. Dyer had scored a splendid consolation for the Tigers in their 3-1 defeat at Selhurst Park earlier in the season and, after his double at Boothferry Park at the end of the 1986-87 season, it didn't take the wags long to conclude that he had been signed purely to stop him scoring against us.

In the Boxing Day encounter at Brighton, Palace again gave a terrible performance. The only real entertainment was the appearance of a gangling midfielder from Colchester, Rudi Hedman. As the Goldstone echoed to the chants of *Rudi, Rudi, Rudi* we wondered why we had paid £40,000 for him.

We recovered from our Brighton malaise with a superb win on Oldham's plastic carpet on December 29 and followed that with a 4-0 defeat of Walsall, who'd discovered that, after years of chasing promotion from division three, they really weren't good enough for the second. Walsall vied with neighbours Birmingham for the title worst team seen at Selhurst ever (aside from Charlton of course). They were so bad that it was only amazing that Palace, who were 4-0 up within 47 minutes, did not double their score at the very least. John Salako who had come on as a substitute must take the blame for some profligate finishing. One remarkable incident in front of a laughing Holmesdale saw two Walsall players tackling each other.

With Palace back on the rails we faced Chelsea, the runaway

leaders, at Stamford Bridge where a Dorigo free kick settled the outcome.

In pouring rain we got bogged down in the mud against Lou Macari's long ball exponents from Swindon. Mark Bright finally turned the match our way with two goals to cap a brilliant individual performance when others weren't pulling their weight. Bright had had a lean start and there were some who muttered about dropping him. But others believed that, although unsung, he was the senior partner in the Wright 'n' Bright show. Bright matched his flashier and more famous pal virtually goal for goal but also won an endless stream of headers, holding the ball up brilliantly and feeding Wright with a stream of chances. The service was not quite so prolific the other way round although Bright often cashed in on half chances created by Wright, who relied more on individual brilliance. Palace based their entire game around them and it made no difference how cautious the opposition was, they all succumbed in the end.

The Full Members' Cup had evolved into the Simod Cup and Palace made good progress, including a superb win at first division Middlesbrough in the quarter final. With two minutes left it stood at 1-1. Then Colin Cooper picked the ball up for Boro and from fully 40 yards hit a screamer which swerved and dipped over Suckling. The 17,000 Boro fans went mad. They were so confident of victory and a semi final at Nottingham Forest that they were announcing coach bookings when Barber and then Wright popped up within the last 30 seconds to steal the game back. The 100 or so Londoners went mad, dancing for joy on the empty terrace, while furious north eastern nutters sporting T-shirts despite the biting cold stared us out.

There were suspicions of skullduggery in the draw for the semi final which gave the two "big" clubs, Forest and Everton favourable home draws. But perhaps that was just our lack of confidence. Nevertheless, the semi final at Forest attracted 4,000 travelling fans who had grounds for complaint after being roughly treated by the Nottingham constabulary. Our team was equally badly treated by Forest who stormed Suckling's goal in the first half only to be denied by the defiant Palace keeper. Eventually a stunning goal by Neil Webb gave them the lead their football merited. Palace roared on by their balloon waving followers fought back and Wright hooked home an equaliser to send the travelling hordes crackers. After that, we gave as good as we got, but the game turned on an appalling decision by the referee, who sent off our left back David Burke for an innocuous challenge even though he'd not been so much as spoken to. We were a couple of minutes away from extra time but it was too much to ask when Forest snatched a goal against our disorganised defence. The third goal gave the score a look we did not deserve. That was the closest we'd been to Wembley since 1976 and it was a major disappointment. The competition has since been discarded and will no doubt be forgotten before very long so it's worth recording for posterity just how much the matches against 'Boro and Forest meant to us at the time.

Another bizarre sending off came at Ipswich where our 2-1 victory failed to reflect our superiority. This time it was Hopkins who was dismissed following an infringement by Pemberton. Both had dark spiky hair with just a hint of gel and the referee later admitted he'd made a mistake. Hopkins' punishment was down graded to a booking.

Wright had been the main torturer of Ipswich and he started in equally thunderflash fashion against another of our promotion rivals, Blackburn. But after we'd gone in front so early we found it difficult to keep the momentum going and Rovers came back. With seconds remaining, Wright got away and set up Bright to save us an undeserved point.

Bright added two more as Bradford demonstrated just how rapidly they'd declined since the early stages of the season, but in midweek at Oxford the old direct-from-a-corner trick backfired on us when an Oxford effort sailed beyond everyone and into the top of the net. Again Palace were denied by myopic refereeing when Barber was tripped and should have had a penalty. Worse was to follow when Bournemouth cruised into a three goal lead at Selhurst with a couple of brilliant efforts – one from Mark O'Connor and another from Ian Bishop.

Palace fought back and had Barber steadied himself when shooting late on we might have saved a point. But we had slipped down the table and it was the Cherries who looked more likely to be playing first division football in 1989-90. Our biggest problem was in midfield where we'd lost Geoff Thomas to a long term injury. Pardew and Pennyfather just weren't up to the task and Coppell decided to try former Reading midfielder Dave Madden. He'd had injury problems of his own and had been unable to train properly, but he added bite to the midfield. It was a crucial moment. Madden's determination gave us fresh heart. We only got a point at Barnsley when we should have had more but Bright's penalty beat Sunderland and Barber curled in a peach from just inside the penalty box to give us a Good Friday win over Watford, who were one of our main rivals for the play-offs. Watford's crowd seemed to be under the influence, they were the quietest supporters you could possibly imagine.

Neil Redfearn who'd had a problem with being regularly substituted at Palace had joined Watford because, as he put it, "I want to go back up north". He was out of action for the match against his old club and was reduced to doing the Watford prize draw at half-time. He got some abuse but responded with a cheery wave which won him a few Brownie points.

We needed maximum points over Easter and it was Brighton who stood between us and getting them. The match can still be found in the *Guinness Book of Records* thanks to our favourite referee Kelvin Morton. This match could be called the 5-4-3-2-1 game – five penalties, four to Palace, three missed, final score 2-1. Bright put the first penalty away after Wright had opened the scoring with a blistering shot from near the by-line – a goal he said was his best ever for Palace. With Brighton down to ten men following the sending off of Mike Trusson, Bright had a chance to make it 3-0 but saw his kick saved. Then Wright put another penalty against the post and Brighton reduced the arrears with a penalty of their own which Alan Curbishley, whose long association with both Brighton and Charlton marks him down as a very sad specimen, converted. Palace had another attempt from 12 yards and when the taker was revealed as none other than John Pemberton everyone guessed right – it was the wildest attempt since Peter Taylor nearly put one in orbit against Millwall back in 1976. We could console ourselves with the knowledge that we had won, but goal difference between ourselves and the increasingly catchable Man City was tight to say nothing of the missed opportunity to punish Brighton in a manner they would never forget. Equally unforgivable was Shrewsbury. It wasn't until we were two adrift that the team realised that the right to victory had to be earned. Too bloody late!

Palace made amends after that with five straight wins, the best of which was at Elland Road. It was a rainy night and only 442 Palace fans made the trip, the figure was given to us by the police at the ground. We started brightly and Wright put us ahead. Leeds recovered and with 26,500 madmen baying for an equaliser they duly got one. But for once we were composed under pressure and our new penalty taker, the impressive Madden, sent a flimsy spot kick slithering beyond Mervyn Day to give us the points. The ball came to a halt six inches over the line with Day face down in the mud while the Palace fans jumped for joy. The final whistle was greeted with *going up, going up, going up*, sung with increasing conviction. Oldham and Hull were unexceptional matches, as always, but we got what we wanted, maximum points and two clean sheets for Suckling.

The defence continued its mean streak with a 2-0 win over Portsmouth but it's here that the Palace management showed a lack of ambition continuing to talk of scraping play-off places when the more perceptive had identified that rather more was possible. City had been crushed 4-0 at Blackburn.

At Plymouth, Bright upset the home fans with his attitude and his looping fluke of a goal. Pemberton, meanwhile, managed to get sent off while the bench were holding up his number card to be substituted. This upset Coppell who got a talking to from a local Bobby. But the fans dancing with delight because Barnsley had beaten Man City. The Sky Blues were definitely blowing up.

Our match at Maine Road looked likely to decide second spot and City manager Mel Machin confessed "We have had a couple of bad results recently and the fear element has started to show itself. In the first 20 minutes against Barnsley we couldn't get out of our own half. Players were making silly mistakes." Palace still needed to win though and the best we could do was draw. Pardew could have won it for us but missed his chance for glory. Would he ever have another?

What more or less finished it for us was a draw at Leicester, where Madden scored two penalties in more confident fashion than he'd managed at Leeds. As we screamed for the whistle, Suckling was pressurised (or fouled) into dropping the ball for a last gasp equaliser. Had we held on we would have had a great chance because City had lost a three goal lead at home to Bournemouth.

In the rearranged match with Stoke Madden scored another penalty But we could have done with at least one more goal. With one match left, the table looked like this:

	P	W	D	L	F	A	Pts
1. Chelsea	45	28	12	5	93	48	96
2. Manc. City	45	23	12	10	76	52	81
3. Palace	45	22	12	11	67	48	78
4. Blackburn	45	22	11	12	74	77	77
5. Watford	45	21	12	12	70	48	75
6. Swindon	45	20	15	10	66	51	75

City needed a draw at Bradford. If they lost and we won by five then we would reach division one. It seemed unlikely but a combination of factors brought it to the verge of reality, so much so that some City fans were in tears shortly before the end of their match at Bradford.

"Welcome to all the Birmingham City supporters who have travelled down today in fancy dress – we'll have some of our Family Enclosure people come and see you this afternoon – we hope you enjoy your day with us whatever the result," said the Palace programme which was in party mood. So were most of 17,581 who saw the Eagles take on doomed Birmingham. The Blues' fans had come down in fancy dress for a farewell to division two party. But hundreds of thugs, out for a drink and a fight, provoked ugly scenes which made every national paper. Coming so soon after the deaths of 95 fans at Hillsborough everyone was horrified. The police and clubs were caught napping and nobody came out with any credit. The match swung our way and news came through that City were losing. Palace, delayed for half an hour by the hooligans, were four up. But City equalised with three minutes left meaning anything we did was academic. We had an eight day wait before facing Swindon in the play-offs.

That's another defence terrorised! The dynamic duo celebrate. This time their victims are Sunderland

Hy Money

GOING UP

Palace had left their pursuit of Man City a little too late. And so we were forced to get promotion the hard way, via the play-offs. Each of our opponents: Swindon, Blackburn and Watford were dangerous ... it was going to be a nerve wracking affair.

We'd have been happy to have qualified for them the year before, was one Palace fan's frank assessment as others complained bitterly about the play-off system outside Ewood Park.

We'd just lost 3-1 and on the evidence of the evening's entertainment our chances of first division football were zero. It didn't make it fair though. The play-offs are a disgrace. They generate large crowds so they are proclaimed a success but they are inherently unfair and football considerations should always take precedence over money, although in the modern world this is never the case.

We can at least speak without malice. Palace were triumphant in the 1989 play-offs, a rare occasion from our point of view when justice was done and in the home matches with Swindon and Blackburn we saw minor classics – matches that we will take with us into old age. So what are we griping about?

Football is an unfair game at the best of times and never more so than in cup competitions. Conventional wisdom has it that anybody can win a cup, but the best teams are the ones successful in leagues. If you believe that to be true, there can be no justification for completing a 46-game marathon with a four team knock out competition designed to favour teams who were inferior over the course of a season.

The 1993 season threw up probably the most extreme case. Portsmouth, twelve points clear of Leicester, were denied Premier League status by a couple of West Ham goals, and then knocked out by Leicester who met Swindon, at Wembley. That the final should be staged at the hallowed stadium between teams who finished fourth and fifth devalues genuine appearances there.

The play-offs take no account of fatigue, injury or suspensions, which would not normally take effect until the following season.

Whether the play-offs have also affected standards by allowing poor teams to enter higher divisions before they are ready is a moot point. Of course supporters want to see their team go up and that thirst for success will ensure the play-offs remain to blight English league football.

This is how Palace won through in their first and, hopefully, last play-offs.

Neil Everitt

> **"Oh and Gennoe's lost it ... it's a goal from McGoldrick, is it?"**
>
> Martin Tyler, ITV Commentator
> Blackburn v Palace Play Off First Leg

The concept of using Wembley for the play-off final had yet to be dreamt up in 1989. That meant Palace would have to play four gruelling matches in order to reach division one.

To give the team that finished third at least some semblance of an advantage, however flimsy, Palace faced Swindon who had come sixth with the second leg at home. This didn't appear a very good deal. Watford, who had finished fourth, had faded badly and looked the easier meat. But they faced fifth placed Blackburn at Vicarage Road.

We travelled to Swindon on May 21, 1989. On a blisteringly hot afternoon, car after car hurtled west along the M4, red and blue scarves flapping from windows with only an occasional black and white scarf for Fulham, on their way to Bristol Rovers, chugging by.

You could see that Palace were in town just by looking at the Swindon car park. Row upon row of gleaming new cars, everything from Astras to Mercedes and a couple of tractors in the corner which presumably had brought the home fans! The County ground was packed. It was throat-stretchingly uncomfortable.

It was remarkable that nobody passed out as the scorching sun beat down upon unprotected heads – there was no cover at the Palace end and no chance for most to get liquid even at half time. The heat also affected the noise of the crowd. Palace who had been so vociferous all season were subdued, partly because of the tension and partly because to sing would have put even more strain on parched vocal cords.

The teams lazed in the sun too, offering precious little to sing about, which was just as well. There were one or two moments at either end but nothing to seriously trouble the scorers until Jeff Hopkins, flashing at a low cross sent the ball spinning into his own net beyond Suckling.

The Palace fans were left to watch the laughable, but nonetheless irritating, home support head home singing the promotion anthem *going up, going up.* We had an anxious wait until Tuesday night to see if Palace, notoriously unpredictable, could overturn the deficit. The official attendance for the home leg was 23,677, a figure that to most Palace fans will always seem ridiculously small.

The answer probably lies with the decision to allocate Swindon two compounds of the Holmesdale, an area they woefully failed to fill.

Compound one meanwhile was packed to bursting and with the Arthur Wait enclosure in fine voice Selhurst in the dark came alive as it so often does. It was the atmosphere at this match, rather than the Blackburn game, that many fans recall as being truly white hot.

Palace hit poor Swindon with a typical Bright and Wright blitz overturning the visitors' advantage well before half time. That left 45 minutes in which to hold out.

The atmosphere became unbearably tense with the realisation that a Swindon "away goal" would destroy a season's hard work.

It was here that Rudi Hedman enjoyed his finest hour. His commitment and determination as a makeshift central defender settled those around him and Palace eased through with no more than their own paranoia to disturb them. Now it was Swindon's turn to listen to *going up, going up, going up.*

Blackburn had had a tougher time disposing of Watford than informed opinion had expected but they finally lined up to face Palace in the final showdown.

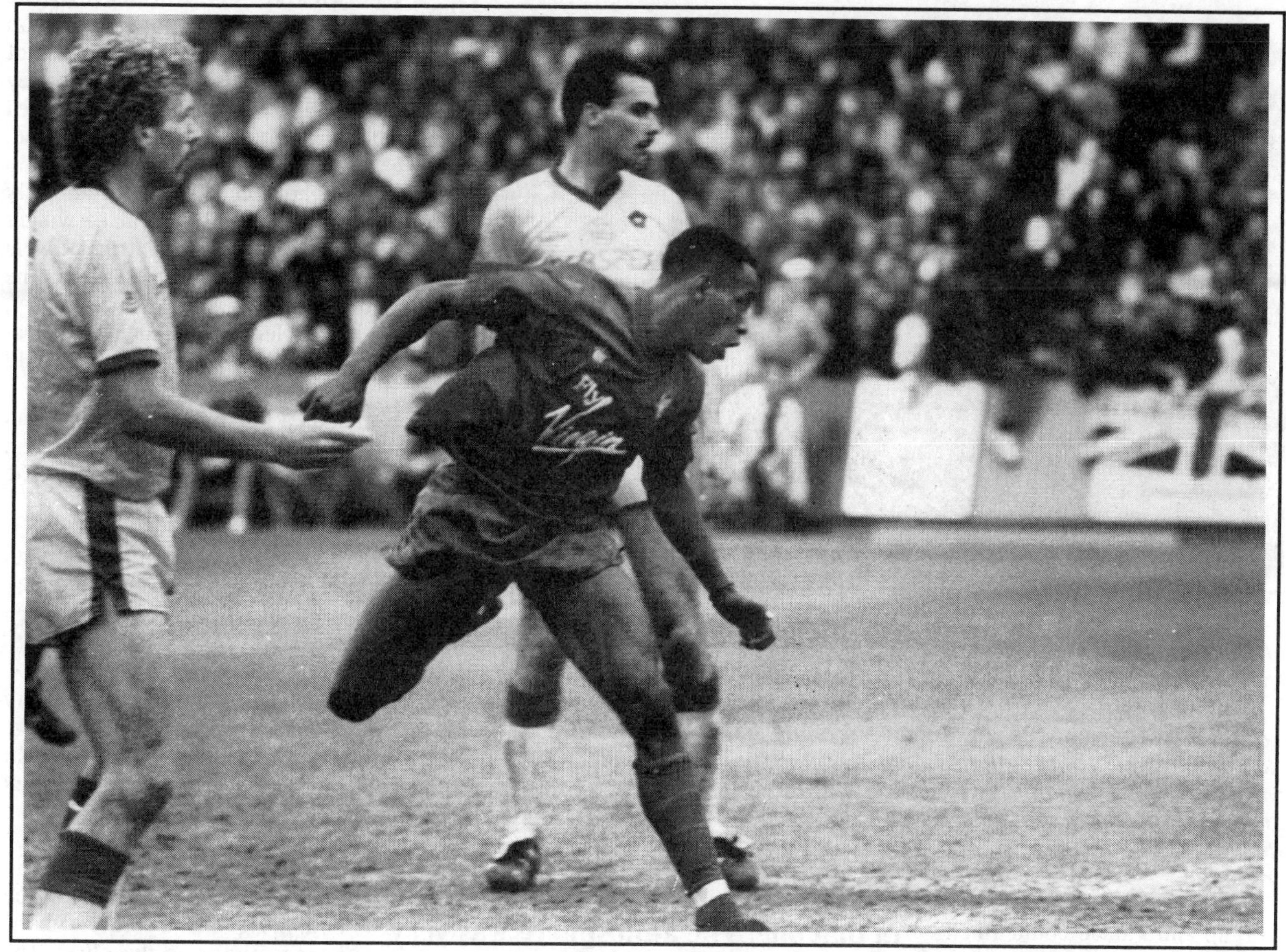

Colorsport

Ian Wright ducks between the Blackburn Rovers moustaches to make absolutely sure for Palace

Ewood Park, the home of the lower placed team, staged the first match. We were greeted by grimy Lancashire rain and were escorted along the scenic route which consisted of boarded up houses, boarded up shops and muck.

The covered end housing the away fans echoed for 15 minutes before the match to an endless chorus of *Stevie Coppell's Red n Blue Army.* So much effort was put into this that many voices had given up the ghost long before the team arrived. The support during the match never reached those heights until the last few minutes.

For anyone who was there it ranks as one of the all-time low points of supporting Palace. The Eagles' display was abject and we fell behind to two swift goals by Howard Gayle. The defence was a shambles with neither Hedman nor Hopkins able to cope with the rampaging home forwards.

Two down and on the ropes, Gayle stepped up to apply the *coup de grace* with a penalty.

But in front of his own fans he put it wide and for the first time there was a glimmer of hope. The glimmer turned into a ray when with two minutes left Eddie McGoldrick got the vital touch to a goalmouth scramble.

The delirious travelling support was still singing the praises of our undeserving team when Simon Garner popped up to restore the two goal advantage and apply "more drama," as ITV's commentator Martin Tyler put it.

The Palace fans reacted badly to this third goal and there was a scuffle with the police before we were taken back to the trains to return in sullen silence through pitch dark England.

Our team had been so soundly beaten that even the most blindly optimistic could not foresee a comeback at Selhurst. Our defence was just too incompetent to keep Rovers out.

The more we thought about it, the worse it got. If we conceded a goal, which they were bound to, we would need to get at least four. But hope springs eternal if you are a Palace fan.

The tickets were sold well in advance of the first leg and it was a 30,000 capacity crowd that welcomed Palace with balloons and a fierce roar. The pubs beforehand had been full of confident talk and there was an air of determination.

Referee George Courtney, on his first ever visit to Selhurst Park, started the game and we made a lively opening hoping to make immediate inroads into Rovers' lead. But it was that fragile defence of ours that had the crowd on its knees in agony as Ian Miller found himself unmarked within six yards. It could have been all over within six minutes, but fortunately he swung wildly and the ball sailed into the Whitehorse leaving Burke and Suckling exchanging bemused glances.

That was Blackburn's big chance and they didn't take it. Now they would pay.

The recovery began in earnest after 16 minutes when, as *The Sunday Times* put it, Palace "began to tease and to induce all manner of chaos in the hesitant Blackburn defence".

Dave Madden picked up a loose ball in midfield and slipped it out to Phil Barber on the left. He controlled it neatly and rolled it into the path of Alan Pardew. Unchallenged, the former Yeovil midfielder raced to the edge of the box and crossed. Ian Wright met the ball and although his first effort bounced off the back of a defender he had enough presence of

mind to flick it past the grounded Terry Gennoe as he fell.

Big Match commenator Brian Moore: *And Ian Wright, socrer of so many goals, has brought a lot of joy to south London as you can see ... Suddenly an afternoon of real possibilities here.*

One-up and Palace could smell blood. McGoldrick was next to break through only to be denied by a despairing combination of Gennoe and Hendry. Corner to Palace.

Going up, going up, going up!

Wright was on the case again, he crossed from the right and from outside the box Madden hit a stinging volley that flashed past Gennoe's left hand post.

One Dave Madden,
there's only one Dave Madden

Eagles, Eagles, Eagles (to *Amazing Grace*)

A free kick to Palace and Bright and Colin Hendry jumped for the ball, which fell to Wright who lashed a volley from the edge of the box to which Gennoe, this time, got a hand.

Moore: Blackburn very much under the cosh at the moment.

Under the cosh was right, the *Guardian* said the first half onslaught was of "Tyson-on-Bruno" proportions. Palace had run Blackburn ragged, but now they resorted to air-raids. The ball, hoisted high, dropped near the Rovers' corner flag, apparently on its way out. Nicky Reid watched it go without spotting Wright's sprint from 25 yards away to stick a foot in and hook it back into the path of Barber, who crossed deep once more. Under pressure from McGoldrick, Rovers conceded yet another corner. Moments later, Barber tried another lob goalwards. Bright this time gave chase and as he moved alongside Hendry, he was bundled over in a three way clash, with Gennoe toppling over the top. The ball ran loose and three desperate defenders lunged at it. David Mail's faintest touch glanced it agonisingly wide of the post. Bright, felt he should have had a penalty, and his protest would not have impressed the lip readers watching on television.

> **"I'm not the nervous type, but I was in that one. The atmosphere was very hostile at Palace. I found it frightening, intimidating ... we had a great chance when it was 0-0. Not long after, they scored and you could sense a feeling spreading through the team that we'd had it."**
>
> - Simon Garner, Blackburn Rovers

Olé, olé, olé, olé, Eagles, Eagles

Blackburn returned to their dressing room battered, but still protecting their lead. For all Palace's whirlwind efforts the seeds of doubt remained. Would Don MacKay be able to pull his troops together?

We kicked off, attacking the Whitehorse, and Johnny Pemberton took an instant time out to enjoy one of his frequent chats with George Courtney after leaving Scott Sellars in a crumpled heap in front of the Arthur Wait stand. The Blackburn free kick went straight to Pardew, who hacked clear. It fell nicely for McGoldrick and the Palace winger set off on a run straight at the Rovers defence. As he approached the box he was dispossessed. At the same moment, a panicking Hendry took a wild swipe at Bright's ankles. Before anyone could see if the referee had noticed, Nicky Reid bundled McGoldrick to the ground and Courtney waddled rather than ran into the box– his arm pointing to the spot.

Selhurst Park momentarily went bananas, but as the tension bit deep into 30,000 nervous systems you could hear a collective heart beat. Madden faced the goalkeeper in silence.

Moore: And now it's all down to Terry Gennoe in the Blackburn goal and Dave Madden of Crystal Palace. I doubt whether he'll ever take a more important kick than this one ...

Madden ... stepped up and planted the ball firmly into the bottom right hand corner with the keeper diving to the other. The *Observer:* "Blackburn's big, strong men sank into their boots."

Was there ever a louder roar at Selhurst Park than this one? Thirty thousand voices all waiting for the same moment, all shouting that same word in unison ...

YES!

Moore: There's the look of relief on that man's face and there's the look of joy on theirs.

Going up, going up, going up!

Palace, in front on away goals, pressed relentlessly, going for the Blackburn jugular. Barber crossed and McGoldrick headed agonisingly wide with Bright, who had followed in, unable to get the diverting touch.

Now Blackburn, for the first time since the sixth minute, mounted an attack. Gayle cut in from the right and shot low and hard from 20 yards into Suckling's midriff. Any other game and it was a straightforward save, in this game it was greeted like the second coming. Thank the Lord.

Perry, Perry, Perry!

Shortly after, Courtney sounded full time. The cheers are muted by the knowledge that, although the battle is over, the war is not. Could Palace keep them out? Or would tension change the nature of the match?

Eagles, Eagles, Eagles

The first period was comparatively quiet. Nerves taut. People too tired and frightened to sing, except for the occasional plaintive cries of *Come on Palace, Come on*

Of the limited action, the most dramatic moment followed a Pardew floater from deep in his own half. Wright outpaced the gasping Mail, brought the ball down with a deft touch, and shot. But Gennoe timed his move perfectly to deflect the ball away with his body. The crowd heaved, almost sick with the strain.

Blackburn breathed again, but not for long. They were squeezed back to their own lines. Wright beat his man on the left and crossed to the edge of the six yard box where O'Reilly got up to join the front men. He acrobatically hooked the ball across the face of the goal, no more than six inches past both the post and Bright's desperate attempt to touch it home.

The teams turned round and Blackburn came again, looking to steal it. A free kick by the corner flag was headed out and Garner, who'd been a virtual spectator, met it with a volley from the edge of the box. This was the shot which would put Blackburn into division one. Except Suckling, with a flying leap, tipped it over the bar to gasps of relief.

"Play offs are cruelty to animals. But there was justice in the result. We were the third best team in the league and we've proved it."

- Steve Coppell

Garner sank to his knees knowing he would come no closer.

Every Palace fan wanted to have Perry Suckling's babies. We'd plenty of experience of maternity, we'd just had kittens.

As the seconds ticked away, thousands of young fans edged the pitch waiting for the moment when, after eight years of anguish, Courtney would signify that Palace were back in the first division. Still every soul was tortured by the knowledge that one slip would wrench it away. The fans half dared to encroach but were held back not by fences or police but by the fear that if they touched the hallowed turf they would undo the magic of a sensational afternoon.

They waited for the whistle, and waited, and waited. Within touching distance of the fans, McGoldrick received the ball wide on the right, beat his man and floated a tantalising cross between the two central defenders. Wright arrived and with a little nod, sealed a momentous afternoon.

Brian Moore: *That's made it certain now ... that's ... made it absolutely clear for Crystal Palace.*

The fans could no longer contain their joy. Arms aloft, they raced on.

Off, off, off, off

Still horrified that anything might spoil a perfect day the invaders were cleared by the mass disapproval of the rest. As the pitch cleared, Selhurst Park echoed

Brian Moore – your comment?

That's the part I like ...

And Palace are in business now ...

What a good crosser of the ball he is ...

That's made it certain now, that's made it absolutely clear for Crystal Palace ...

Liverpool, Arsenal, Tottenham and the rest, we're on our way to meet you now ...

Andy Ward

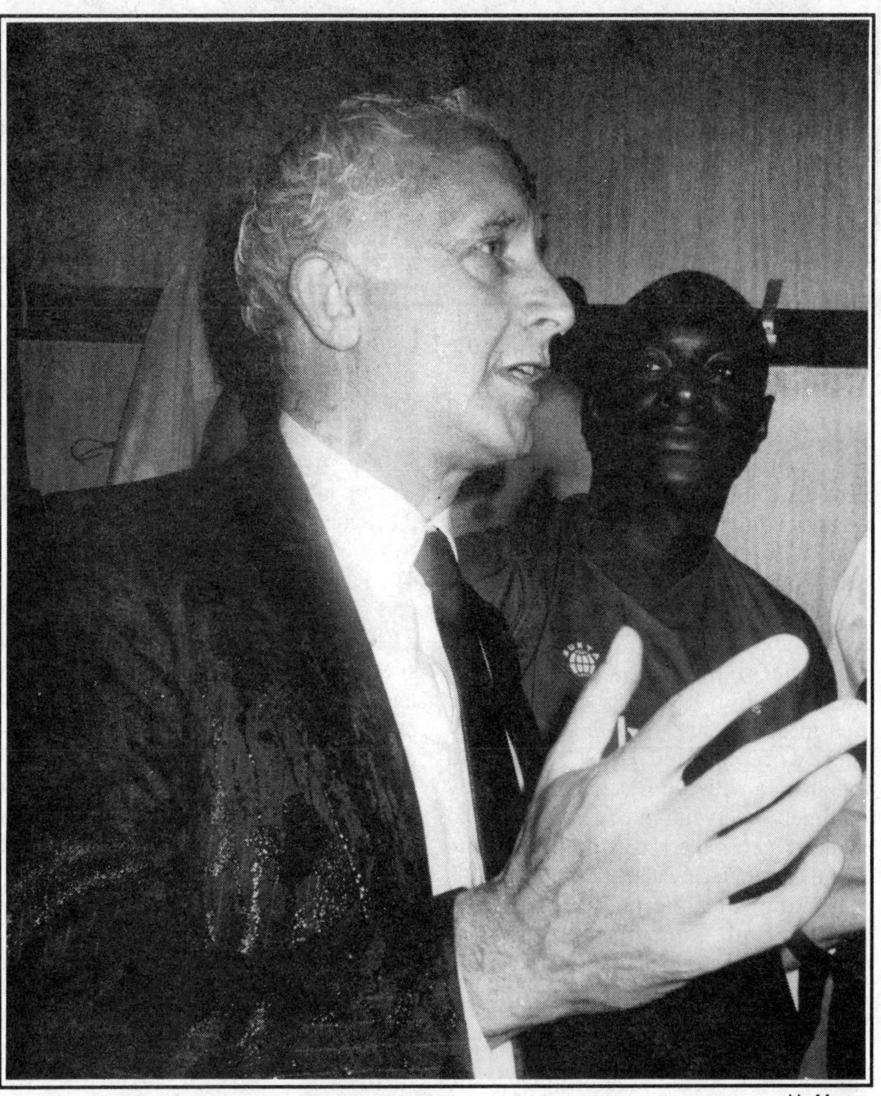

Hy Money

Ron Noades expensive suit get a champagne dry clean

Hy Money

Champagne Charlie: Another explosion from Ian Wright

with noise, unable to contain the sound.

Going up, going up, going up!

Blackburn had known all along that they were dead. They tried, but their legs, weary from backing off, would not respond and they could do nothing to change the script. Palace had never been so determined, so sure footed, so devastatingly effective.

A hopeful punt was collected by Suckling while Hendry, in desperation, tried to bundle him over the line. Angry fans were denied the chance to remonstrate with the Blackburn player by the timely intervention of a steward, who bounced across the six yard box pleading with them not to invade.

Suckling took the goal kick, Bright jumped and Courtney presumably sounded three shrill blasts not that you would have heard it if he'd used Motorhead's sound rig.

Bright and Wright raced into each other's arms seconds before they were engulfed in a tidal wave of supporters.

Wright, lifted high by his adoring fans, was relieved of his shirt. Practically insane with joy, he wore a smile you could light a city with.

Moore: Arsenal, Liverpool, Manchester United and the rest, we're on our way to meet you now!

The Palace fans stayed behind for the best part of an hour to hail their heroes and *The Sunday Times* reported: "Amid scenes of rampant and intimidating hysteria at Selhurst Park … thus ended an exercise in greed that these furious play-offs represent; thus was avoided the injustice that would have happened had Blackburn, who finished fifth in the table leap-frogged Palace who were third." It would be a most fitting epithet but for a more unlikely source for a classic conclusion.

The *Sunday Sport,* hardly noted for its sports coverage, put it bluntly into perspective: "The Team of the Eighties will end the decade where they started it – in the first division." And this was written under the headline: "Up yours El Tel."

Faced with a succession of winding-up orders, Palace kept both their nerve and their best players and on Saturday their courage and indestructible ambition was rewarded when the play-offs, which were the brainchild of their chairman Ron Noades, restored them to the first division after an absence of eight years. The system is about money rather than merit, and Saturday's frantic affair before a full house of 30,000 was entirely typical. Never mind the quality feel the wad. At least we had the right result.

- Joe Lovejoy,
The Independent

PROMOTION

Steve Amos compares the Palace teams of 1969, 1979 and 1989 which earned us promotion to division one.

The Crystal Palace team of 1969 was an experienced and hard working bunch of aged artisans, cobbled together and highly motivated by old Bert Head.

Despite all the talk of declining standards it's hard to imagine such a limited team making it into the first division these days. But what they lacked in finesse was more than made up for in sheer enthusiasm and commitment.

The team lacked any real stars, but probably the two outstanding players were goalkeeper John Jackson and midfielder Steve Kember.

I genuinely believe that Jackson was one of the finest players never to play for England. If he'd been in goal instead of Peter Bonetti I'm sure England would never have lost to West Germany in the 1970 World Cup quarter-final.

Jackson did as much as anyone to ensure that Palace got into the first division, and more than anyone else to keep them there.

Steve Kember was only 20 when that team won promotion and was probably at the peak of his form.

In those days he was a midfielder with class and vision and appeared certain to have an international future.

Only when he joined Chelsea did he deteriorate into a mundane midfield ball winner. Chelsea had already allocated the more creative role to Alan Hudson so after leaving Selhurst Park, Kember was never the same player.

The rest of the team may have lacked first division quality but it did possess some real characters.

There was John McCormick, a £1,000 signing from Aberdeen, who stood like a craggy Scottish peak in central defence. Alongside McCormick, Roger Hoy was a big favourite with the crowd until injury prematurely brought his brief career with Palace to an end.

The team also boasted Mark Lazarus, who played for nearly every club in London including three spells with QPR.

The team had no outstanding striker – Cliff Jackson was leading scorer with 14 – but still managed to score a total of 70 goals with almost every player finding the net.

1969

	P	W	D	L	F	A	Pts
Derby Co	42	26	11	5	65	32	63
Crystal Palace	42	22	12	8	70	47	56
Charlton	42	18	14	10	61	52	50
Middlesbrough	42	19	11	12	58	49	49

1979

	P	W	D	L	F	A	Pts
Crystal Palace	42	19	19	4	51	24	57
Brighton	42	23	10	9	72	39	56
Stoke C.	42	20	16	6	58	31	56
Sunderland	42	22	11	9	70	44	55

1989

	P	W	D	L	F	A	Pts
Chelsea	46	29	12	5	96	50	99
Manch City	46	23	13	10	77	53	82
Crystal Palace	46	23	12	11	71	49	81
Watford	46	22	12	12	74	48	78
Blackburn	46	22	11	13	74	59	77
Swindon	46	20	16	10	68	53	76

Like the Glaziers of 1969, Terry Venables' young Eagles had no outstanding goalscorers. But they made up for it by playing sophisticated football based on rock solid defence.

The team conceded a mere 24 goals, a crucial statistic when one considers they only managed to score 51.

Like John Jackson before him, John Burridge performed heroics in goal. But unlike Jackson he played behind a back four of the highest class.

Paul Hinshelwood was a solid and consistent right-back, while at left-back Kenny Sansom was already establishing himself as England's finest since Terry Cooper.

In the centre of defence, the great Jim Cannon was partnered by Billy Gilbert, who had yet to develop his mastery of the suicidal back-pass and the pointlessly conceded free-kick.

The defence was so strong that a future England international, Terry Fenwick, was rarely even considered for the side.

In midfield Peter Nicholas was tough and competitive, yet with the vision to hit a defence splitting pass usually to Vince Hilaire who could generally beat the entire defence three or four times before falling over and claiming a penalty.

If Vince did get a cross in it would generally land on the head of Dave Swindlehurst who occasionally scored. Alternatively it would fall to Ian Walsh and end up in the higher reaches of the terraces.

The one department in which the team of '89 surpasses the team of '79 is up front.

Ian Wright and Mark Bright were in a different league from any of their predecessors at Palace, with the sole exception of Don Rogers at his brief but brilliant peak. Wright, was capable of scoring a whole range of goals from tap-ins to thunderbolts while Bright was more of a traditional centre-forward. Their mutual understanding was invaluable.

The rest of the class of '89 was closer to the team of '69 than that of '79 winning through more on determination than class.

The defence was shaky, although surprisingly they conceded less than both Chelsea and Man City who finished above them, and the midfield virtually non-existent, although it lacked the presence of Gray and the injured Thomas, which was remedied immediately on entering division one.

Phil Barber, Alan Pardew and Dave Madden all played above themselves to take Palace up while Eddie McGoldrick, who made it immediately clear upon his arrival that he didn't want to be called Eddie the Eagle arrived halfway through the season to run, wiggle and fall over with almost as much dexterity as Hilaire.

If it was possible to select 11 players from the three promotion winning teams what would you get? A predominance of the players from the class of '79 with Wright and Bright providing some much needed firepower.

My combined team would be: Jackson, Hinshelwood, Cannon, Gilbert, Sansom, Kember, Nicholas, McGoldrick, Wright, Bright, Hilaire. subs: Thomas, Swindlehurst. Team manager: Steve Coppell, general manager Bert Head (well, we don't want El Tel back do we?)

TAFF

Ian Evans had two spells at Selhurst Park, the first as centre-half and captain and the second as assistant manager. He spoke to Laurie Dahl

Mention George Best to most people and they will waffle on about silky skills, European Cup Finals and how modern footballers are not as good as in the good old days. Mention George Best to a Palace fan and you'll spend the next hour listening to a foaming at the mouth rant about how he Ian Evans' leg and what we'd do to him if we met him …

Ian Evans is one of those people who can do no wrong in the eyes of the Selhurst faithful, even coaching Millwall is an acceptable pastime for one of Palace's favourite sons. It's 16 years since the audible crack of bone signalled the end of the road for Evans at Palace yet the memory still makes people wince. "The goalkeeper had the ball and threw it out to Bestie who was wide left, to our right," says Evans. "The ball came away from him and I went into a block tackle. I felt a pain in my left leg and a pain in my knee. Apparently he jumped at me two footed."

So was it a bad tackle? 'I didn't have time to assess the situation, it just happened. I was carted off to the Mayday hospital, a bit of a rough ride in the St John's Ambulance and then one of the nurses came in and I was in my football kit but I swear she asked 'Road accident?' And then the porter was taking a sneaky look at my X-Rays and I could see him out of the corner of my eye going 'Urgh'. And I asked him: 'Well what's the matter then?' And he said: 'You really want to know?' And I said 'yeah,' and he said: 'It's broken.' It was a stupid question, my leg was bent round. I knew it was broken myself.

Did Best come to see him? "No, I had no contact with him, not even a card. I think, reluctantly, Fulham decided to send me a bowl of fruit via Kenny Sansom. But not even a representative came. Although Les Strong called in."

It was terrible blow for Evans who had been an instant hit at Selhurst having stepped down from first division QPR and had won 13 caps for Wales since joining in a deal which took Don Rogers to Rangers and brought Terry Venables to Selhurst.

"Terry was senior pro at Palace and before that at QPR, all the other players looked up to him and would listen with interest when he was talking. He was a very organised sort of chap and had his books and his writing and his views on the game – he wrote a book called *They Used to Play On Grass* where he predicted plastic pitches and other innovations. Because of the sort of character he was, it was no surprise when he made the progression through to coach and then manager.

"Gordon Jago was manager at Rangers and I'd been in and out of the side as a youngster, just bits of games at the back end of the season, so I told him you either stick with me or let me move on because he'd bought Terry Mancini and Frank McLintock and a couple of other centre halves. To cut a long story short, I got a call on my day off to go to see chairman Jim Gregory at his office in Roehampton pending a transfer. That's all that was said, so on the way from my home in Wokingham I wondered. Where is it? Would I say no? Would I say yes? Anyway, I got to the door and I saw Malcolm Allison and I thought, who's he manager of? Crystal Palace? That's alright because I won't have to move house. He took me in a room and told me the wages and this and that, blah, blah, and I said: 'Smashing, thank you very much.' And he said: 'Do you want to speak to Terry?' And I thought what's Terry got to do with this? Terry came in and said 'What do you think?' And I said: 'What do you mean what do I think? I'm going, I'm signing for Crystal Palace.' And he said: 'You don't know what's going on do you? It's me and you and Don Rogers going the other way.' Anyway, the deal went through and it wasn't until years later that I realised Terry was 50/50 about whether he wanted to go or not. He told me I'd tipped the balance because of the way I went about it. 'I felt I couldn't let you down,' he told me, 'so I went through with it'. I've got a lot to thank Venners for in that respect.

"I didn't think of going from QPR to Palace as stepping down because I was playing reserve football anyway. If anything, I was stepping up, although I'd tasted first team football at QPR It made me feel wanted for starters. It's amazing what a transfer does for you.

"I enjoyed working with Malcolm, he was a big character, full of life and different ideas. I think that to carry out his ideas and methods he would probably need the best 11 players in the land, he was so far ahead of his time he probably expected certain players to do things they weren't capable of. But they would have been good ideas for a national manager – he would have had them playing all sorts of systems and doing all sorts of things."

Malcolm and Steve Coppell are like chalk and cheese when it comes to management styles. How did Ian become Steve's assistant in 1984? Was it true that Ron Noades wanted him to become assistant, but Steve wanted Lou Macari? "No, I don't think that was the case. I had that conversation with Steve and said to him that obviously a lad who'd played for Man United and had so many England caps must've come across somebody he wanted as an assistant. But Steve said Lou wanted to be his own man and, although he'd always been friendly with Dave Watson, he wasn't sure that was the right thing. So he was prepared to meet me on Noades' say so and have a day with me. We agreed to give it a go to see how we got on and I said if at the end of the day he didn't want me then so be it. But we got on well enough.

"Steve sat back early on and wanted to pick it up as he went along. He let me do all his coaching and was quite happy to assess what was around him both player-wise and on his own staff. But he became more and more involved and more and more thoughtful about how he wanted the team to play. I got on really well with him, he's a smashing fella and I'm sorry he had to resign because he's been the most successful manager they've ever had. But you're only as good as your last result and your last season and that's all people remember unfortunately."

How bad a mess were Palace in? "There were things you couldn't do, places you couldn't go because bills hadn't been paid, you couldn't buy this, couldn't do that, everything was done on a shoestring. But over a period of years, a certain amount of success allowed us to do other things."

Would you have liked to be manager at Selhurst? "No, I was happy to stay with Steve. I said to him all along, believe it or not I don't want your job. If you get the sack, I'll go too because I'll take it as a comment on me as well. I believe the same with Mick McCarthy here at Millwall. I don't want his job, I've been a manager and you can shove it as far as I'm concerned. I got enough rein and enough say at Palace and I do here too. I used to talk to Steve before training, telling him what I was going to do and asking him if he wanted me to do something over and above what I had planned, or if he didn't want something. He used to sit down in the morning or the night before and say 'we'll have a bit of that and a bit of that'.

What was Steve's routine? "On Mondays Steve would be in his office discussing the ins and outs of the game, who did well, who didn't. After discussing the match we'd go out and train. Monday in football is the same as everywhere else so we'd just do some light general stuff, ball work. Fitness was Tuesday, with hard work all day, but perhaps we'd get the ball out for 15 minutes. If they'd played well on Saturday and got a good result we'd generally let them have Thursday off. Then we're looking towards Saturday with what we call pattern play, setting things up in front of goal, attack against defence, crossing, shooting, trying to create what should happen on Saturday, building up play down the flank, telling the players how, when and where to make runs. Friday would be working on set plays, corners and free kicks. Steve was very strong on this aspect and it turned out to be quite fruitful for Palace. On the morning of the match we might come in at 11, go and train on the pitch, do corners and free kicks, go and have a bite to eat relax and get ready to play at three o'clock.

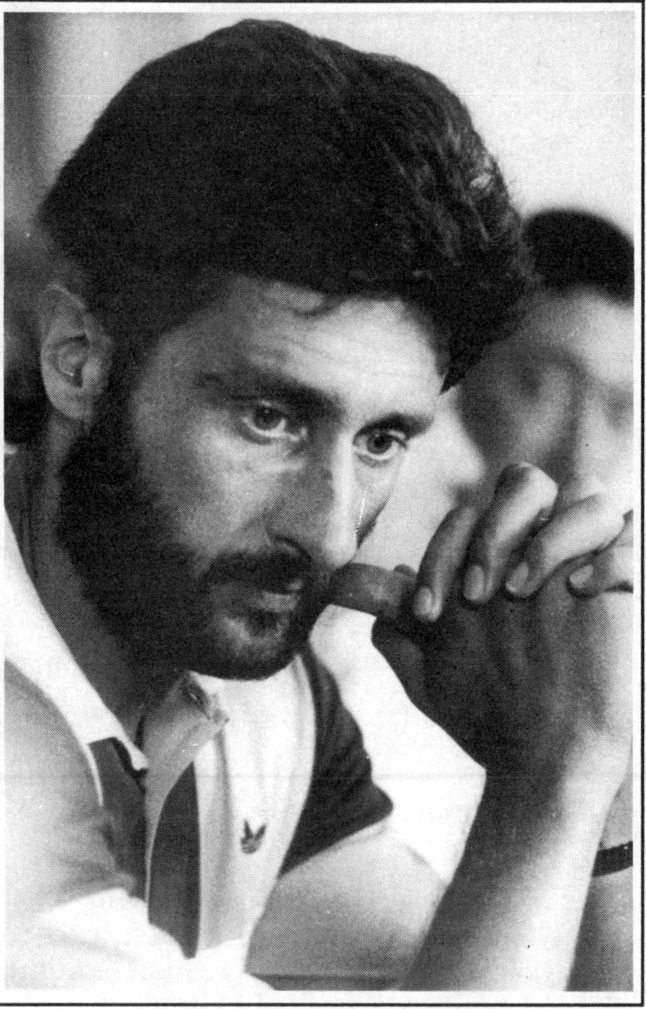
Hy Money

"Steve didn't really mix with the players socially, maybe the odd pint, but he didn't make it a regular thing. I did though, I was in Dorking and so those who lived in the south, Jim Cannon, Kevin Taylor and Alan Irvine lived around Croydon, and we had a pint before we went home. If we were on tour there'd be camaraderie, there wasn't any season when there wasn't, there were no cliques. Even the black lads mixed well, irrespective of what was said on Channel 4 two years ago. Tony Finnigan, Andy Gray, Wright and Bright, they were a good bunch of lads. I've never known Palace as anything other than a closely knit club whether as player or assistant manager.

Nevertheless when the chance came to manage Swansea, Evans packed his bags for the land of his father. "Why I went to Swansea God only knows. As soon as I left, Palace got promoted. I went in March and they got up, so I'd like to take a little bit of credit for that, a little bit for those two months plus the previous five years hard graft. I know Stan Ternant came in and Ian Branfoot and good luck to them."

The highlight at Swansea was the "brilliant" performance of John Salako on loan. "The fans loved him, he played against Panathinaikos for me and scored. I also think it did him the power of good. I tried desperately to buy him and I came very close for less than a pittance but football's all about ifs and buts and if I could have done the deals I wanted to do I'd probably still be there now. While he was playing well for me he kept pushing his price up. He was a big fish in a small pond and it lifted him because he was always brow beaten at Palace. Salako may have enjoyed it at the Vetch, but Evans' memories are less fond.

"Swansea was the worst 12 months of my life. There were a lot of things I did wrong, basic things. My biggest mistake was going there alone and not appointing somebody I knew, who I would be comfortable with."

The fans were loyal to Terry Yorath weren't they? "He'd left under a cloud and the chairman kept going on, Terry this and Terry that and then 'Oh sorry, Ian, I shouldn't be saying that about Terry.' I was very unpopular with the fans because of the way I spoke, I'm Anglo-Welsh. I had letters from kids saying piss off back to London, my dad hates you, you London so and so, untold letters like that. They gave me a real rough time and there was nothing I could do, but I'd like to think I influenced a lot of the players there. I didn't make enemies with the players, I coached and managed them the best I could and I think they accepted that. I keep in touch with a lot of them and they ring me and ask for advice. It was a torrid time. My wife suffered terribly because she had to sit in the stand on occasions when I was getting diabolical abuse and not from some sections, but from a full house. I hope you don't have to experience anything like it, it's the only profession in the world, unless you're a stand up comedian, that you get abused as much as you do when you're a football manager. It was a bad move all round."

After Evans left Swansea he was offered a position with Millwall where he worked with Chris Armstrong. "Chrissie was a reserve player with me. We used to work early in the mornings, shooting and crossing and showing him where to go and what to do.

"Then Mick took over and asked me to join him and we started to use Chrissie in the first team. We went to Ireland and it looked as if he and Jon Goodman would be our front two, He was frightening defenders, he was quick and strong and knocked them about. We had a league game and then Orient in the league cup and the next minute, Palace, £1 million offer. We didn't quite think he was worth that and it was a good deal for us and it gave him a nice move into the Premier League. He's done well."

The Nineties ... same old Palace

From Wembley pride to relegation despair

1989 and Palace are back: Richard Shaw gets in a tackle against Aston Villa

Neil Everitt

On a glorious August afternoon, 5,000 Palace fans welcomed their team's return to first division action at Loftus Road with a massive balloon reception.

To everybody's surprise, Andy Gray turned out not for Rangers, the club he had joined from Villa a couple of months earlier, but for Palace. The player who had become a hate figure at Selhurst Park following his acrimonious departure rejoined the fold for £500,000. Palace also paid £50,000 for Mark Dennis, a highly talented left back with a wayward reputation both on and off the pitch. But it was goodbye to Gavin Nebbeling, who made the short journey to Craven Cottage.

Despite the passion of the supporters Palace were beaten by two goals from QPR's new signing from Aberdeen Paul Wright, who hasn't been heard of since.

The first visitors to Selhurst were Manchester United, prompting recollections of our first ever division one fixture back in August 1969. Our first goal of the season came in the last minute when Wright got away from the United defence to cancel out Bryan Robson's strike.

"I was very impressed with Southampton and Crystal Palace, not two clubs you hear and read about, but both played excellent football against us. As for technique, the two Palace strikers were very impressive."

Liverpool's Glenn Hysen
On his First Impressions of English Football
Including a 9-0 Victory Over Palace

On the following Saturday, the heavens opened and Coventry completed the misery for the drenched supporters with a thoroughly negative display capped by a Brian Kilcline free kick that snivelled past the unsighted Suckling. Coventry lived up to their reputation for being horribly dull and the disgruntled faithful made their way home saying: "If that's division one, let's go back to Barnsley."

With just one point from three games, a victory was vital and we were fortunate enough to have another home game, this time against Wimbledon. Thomas opened the scoring with a streaky first half goal and then Wright hared past the Dons' gangling centre-half Eric Young to settle everybody's nerves. With our first victory in the top flight under our belts, we set off for Anfield not expecting a great deal but getting a good deal more than we bargained for. The 9-0 defeat will live forever in the memories of those who witnessed it and prompted Steve Coppell to remark: "This will haunt us for the rest of our lives." Palace winger Phil Barber missed the game but he was certainly affected saying: "I remember coming in and turning on Ceefax and there was a whole page for the Liverpool scorers."

Yet although news of the rout hit the front pages it was not the humiliation that outsiders believed.

The attitude of our players and supporters ensured that Crystal Palace left Merseyside with their heads held high. Our reputation was, if anything, enhanced. At least Palace was in the public eye. The match also served to make the players more determined. The Southampton fans tried out the taunts of *9-0* but they were outsung on the terraces and outfought on the pitch. Jeff Hopkins was credited with what was really a Russell Osman own goal to earn us a deserved point. Two matches later, Palace were comfortably in the top half of the table following wins over Nottingham Forest, with Wright again applying the killer touch, and Everton, where Alan Pardew stunned his fan club with a run and calculating finish.

There was no doubt that the first division was fun. The supporters sang themselves hoarse as the team supplied tremendous entertainment at both ends of the pitch. It was enthralling stuff.

We advanced to the third round of the league cup on away goals, fighting back from a home defeat against second division Leicester. Even then, in a crazy game at Filbert Street, we survived City's Wayne Clark hitting the crossbar in the last minute of extra time with Suckling grounded.

It might have been better if he'd stolen victory because having failed to make the most of our dominance over Forest in round three we made our exit in a replay that at one stage threatened to become a repeat of Anfield. We were three down in 20 minutes, including yet another own goal for Hopkins, and did well to keep it to five. The papers followed the management line of blaming the hapless Suckling for the debacle although his back four was non-existent. Certainly his confidence had gone as was illustrated in one of the most remarkable Palace matches ever.

Millwall were comfortably placed in the table and had been top at one stage. But they met their match when Palace served up an eccentric performance even by their own weird standards. Television commentator Martin Tyler was left gasping at the sheer volume of scoring opportunities. It began badly when Hopkins surpassed himself with a 35 yard own goal, before Pemberton left Terry Hurlock puffing and blowing as he charged down the the line to cross for Wright to stab home the equaliser. From a corner Wright got a touch to Thomas's header and then McGoldrick made the most of hesitant Millwall defending to hook the ball back for Bright to slot home. In the second half Palace had enough chances to be four or five goals clear before static defending allowed Tony Cascarino to head Millwall back into contention. With Tyler about to make a telling comment about the pathetic Palace defending, Steve Anthrobus appeared unmarked to send the visiting support wild with joy and Palace looked likely to lose a game they should have won at a canter. But

"Direct, dangerous and deadly!"

MARTIN TYLER ON IAN WRIGHT'S EQUALISER V MILLWALL

STEVE COPPELL sat on the table in the middle of a hushed Crystal Palace dressing room and told his players they had made it into the record books.

Not only that, they'd put Palace on the map.

Liverpool boss Kenny Dalglish popped his head round the door and told the Palace lads they'd done well to keep going.

The score hadn't done Palace justice, according to Kenny. They deserved to score four.

But even four wouldn't have been enough — it was the night Palace let in **NINE** in front of the Kop.

The Sun

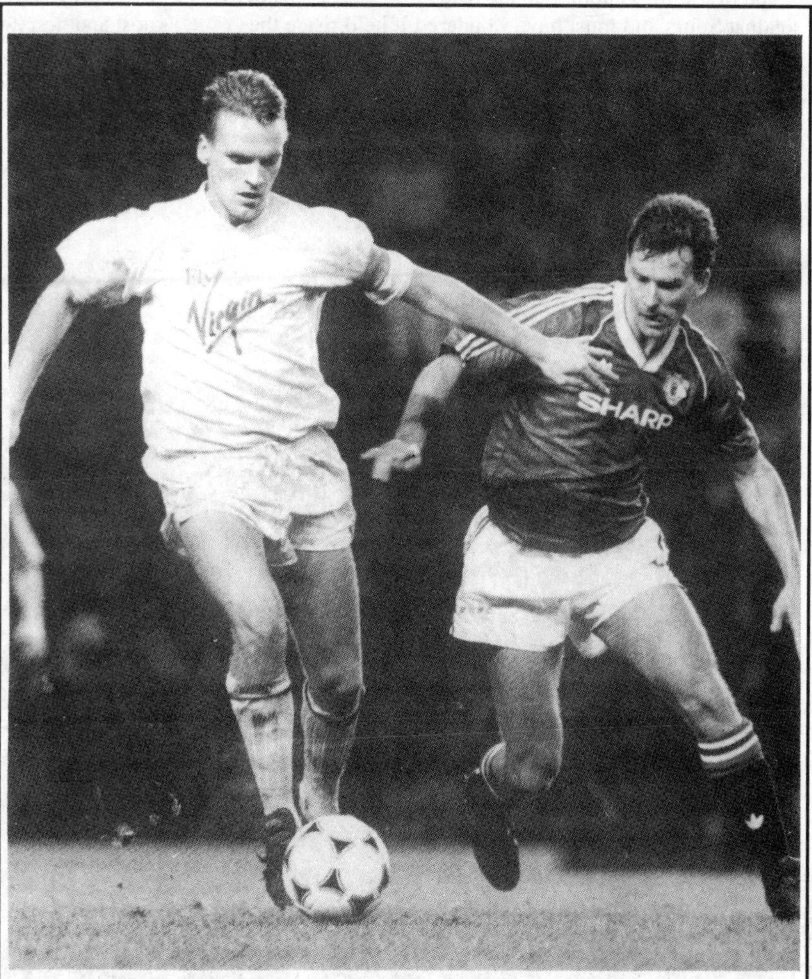

Neil Everitt

December 1989: Man United 1, Palace 2. Geoff Thomas gets the better of "Captain Marvel" Bryan Robson.

with a minute to go, Wright fed his partner and Bright launched an unstoppable shot past Brian Horne. Even then Millwall had three golden opportunities to make it all square but Palace clung on and their exhausted supporters went for a lie down in a dark room. For Millwall it was the beginning of the end. Their season collapsed and they were relegated, Palace had now settled comfortably around 15th position where we would stay virtually unmoved for the rest of the campaign.

As the season progressed, the team evolved. Coppell had promised to give the players who'd earned promotion a chance, but he made one or two telling changes. The first was in goal where a long standing interest in Bristol Rovers' England B goalkeeper Nigel Martyn was followed up with a £1 million bid. Brian Parkin who'd had one outing after Suckling was dropped for the Luton game went west in part exchange. Luton's equaliser in that match followed a farcical incident in which Alex Dyer, attempting to clear, hit his own crossbar.

The first million pound goalie made his debut in the derby against Spurs and must have wondered if he'd made the right decision. He was beaten three times in a thunderous match in which Paul Gascoigne had an unpleasant little set to with Gray. And we got a snapshot of vintage Mark Dennis into the bargain. He ran 35 yards to throw a haymaker of a punch which luckily for those nearby didn't land on anyone. Palace had just pulled the game back to 2-2 when a cruel deflection from a free kick sealed another home defeat.

"All Charlton Athletic supporters want their team to beat Crystal Palace more than anything else and all Palace supporters want their side to beat Charlton more than anything else."

CHARLTON MANAGER LENNIE LAWRENCE, BEFORE THE HISTORIC PALACE "AWAY IN THEIR OWN GROUND" MATCH, SHOWING HIS TOTAL MISUNDERSTANDING OF THE SITUATION. PALACE FANS COULDN'T CARE LESS ABOUT CHARLTON. WE HATE BRIGHTON AND AS FAR AS WE ARE CONCERNED CHARLTON DON'T EXIST

The defence had been ridiculously porous since the departure of Jim Cannon. It needed a strong commanding figure and Coppell decided that this man was former Wimbledon defender Andy Thorn who returned to south London for £650,000 from Newcastle and, despite being referred to as a "trainee Tony Adams", by a Magpie fanzine, he did indeed bring greater stability. It didn't stop Palace getting the occasional thrashing though, there were too many inconsistent players for that.

Thorn made his debut at Old Trafford where United had threatened to run riot only to be held up by international class goalkeeping by Martyn. Then a piece of sheer genius by Wright spun United's defence round and Bright powered home the equaliser. Struggling United had no answer when Bright flicked a cross between Jim Leighton and his near post and despite the obligatory Old Trafford injury time which prompted one wag to remind the referee "come on, I'm missing *Blind Date*," we were more troubled by our own anxieties than by United's attack. And just a reminder for

A classic Palace moment. Andy Gray is about to take a free kick v Millwall. With no interference the ball went out for a throw by the corner flag

United fans and football writers everywhere; after Palace had taken the lead, the visiting supporters taunted the pressurised home manager with *Ferguson out*, and the thousands in the seats around us joined in! Where are they now?

While we were kept behind, we peered through the executive boxes at the TV screens showing the draw for the 1990 World Cup finals until the bastards inside drew the curtains. A less pleasant bunch of away fans might have put the windows in.

This was the first and only time in history that south London had all four of its league clubs in the top flight at the same time and Palace's long awaited fixture with Charlton – where we played away in our own ground – was staged in November. Thorn marked his home debut with a first minute goal. Justice was done because the Charlton keeper should have been sent off for bringing Bright down when he had a clear run on goal. Charlton, being the whingers they are, had moaned solidly since their promotion that they were never awarded penalties, but Pemberton and Hopkins changed all that with a cretinous piece of defending. Mark Reid missed with the kick and Palace held on for three more points.

Hopkins was still struggling to come to terms with the higher quality of football and this was emphasised by another howler at Highbury on New Year's day in which he took three goes at passing to Arsenal's striker Alan Smith. Palace were 4-1 down at half-time, but Arsenal, being Arsenal, took their centre forward off and shut up shop.

In the F.A. Cup we made a meal of overcoming second division Portsmouth at Selhurst, falling behind before squeezing into the fourth round with a last minute Andy Gray penalty which he had earned with an outrageous dive.

In round four we faced third division Huddersfield without Wright. Seeking a measure of revenge for the Anfield humiliation Palace battered Liverpool at Selhurst only to be denied by Bruce Grobbelaar, some frantic defending and the woodwork. Rush had given the visitors the lead and Beardsley extended it with a shot that Martyn should have saved. But in pouring rain Palace paid for their unstinting efforts with a long term injury to McGoldrick, who had tormented the Scousers all afternoon, and Wright, who in attempting to finish off a move in which he had rounded Grobbelaar, fell badly in a challenge with Barry Venison.

Coppell, meanwhile, substituted Pardew only to find he had two other players needing to come off and so Palace finished with ten men. That didn't stop Salako hitting the post with a scorching long range effort which only emphasised what an unfortunate afternoon it had been.

It transpired that Wright had fractured his leg and so we moved Salako into attack to partner Bright. Initially it paid dividends. We crushed Southampton despite failing to capitalise on a 3-0 lead and Salako also scored at Forest. That was merely a consolation, Brian Clough's team destroyed our ponderous defence, quite literally walking the third goal into the net.

And so to Huddersfield. Even without Wright, we had too much firepower for the third division promotion seekers, but in round five, fourth division Rochdale offered stiffer resistance. Eventually Barber broke the deadlock although Martyn was forced to make a point blank save in the last minute to spare us a replay.

The quarter final paired us with Cambridge and miraculously Wright was back. It was a welcome boost, especially with Bright serving a suspension for a sending off

Continued on page 311

Leads, leads and leads and leads ... we all f****** hate leads

Top flight football brought Palace tougher opponents and points were more difficult to come by, but this still doesn't explain why Palace found it so difficult to win comfortably either at home or away.

Throughout the first four and a half years of first division and Premier League football virtually any Palace victory was accompanied by near heart attacks in the seats and on the terraces with desperate calls for pacemakers.

The tradition actually began in the second division against Brighton in that infamous match when at 2-0 up we were awarded two penalties in the space of two minutes and missed both of them. In the end, although our penalty tally had risen to four, we scraped a 2-1 win in a match we should have coasted.

It was that day that grey hairs began to appear on my teenage head. However it was in the first division that this unique phenomena really gathered pace.

Of eight home league wins only two were by more than one goal. With the infamous Palace defence making walking down a motorway blindfolded appear a safer option, most of us spent the last minutes of even the most mundane match on our knees deep in prayer. How we survived the late onslaughts of Everton (2-1), Millwall (4-3), Norwich (1-0) and Rochdale in the F.A. Cup (1-0), I'll never know.

All five of our away wins were by the odd goal and, on many occasions, we threw our hard earned leads away. Against Derby (home and away), Aston Villa, Luton and Chelsea – who scored a last gasp equaliser having been completely outplayed – we blew it. Man City and Sheffield Wednesday were both gifted points after we'd built up 2-0 leads. And most famously, our inability to hold onto our advantage manifested itself in the F.A. Cup Final.Opposition goals in the last ten minutes cost Palace 11 points and a place in the top ten. It also cost us the F.A. Cup.

The following season, the arrival of Eric Young sealed some of the gaps. This stopped the haemmorhage of late goals but we continued to let leads slip to give ourselves an unnecessarily hard time in the closing stages. Most notably against ten-man Coventry, Palace were left thanking Nigel Martyn for a fortunate escape with all three points, after we had been 2-0 up. Southampton and Derby were also allowed back into matches they had been played out of.

Finger nails are fashionably short at Selhurst Park, bitten to the quick every other Saturday. Even in the season of boredom only relegated West Ham, right at the end of the season and Everton were beaten by two clear goals. It all adds up to fears for my health, my life expectancy reduces week in, week out and I haven't left school yet.

Cris Lehmann.

A *nightmare* on Anfield Road

Stuart Watt recalls the 9-0 defeat at Anfield

To see the team you love humiliated is not my idea of a good time. I imagine the radios carrying Capital Gold's commentary were being switched off all over London as stunned Eagles winced at their team's collapse.

The optimistic had hoped for an away win, some thought we might sneak a draw, most realised we'd probably lose – but no-one thought it would be so bad. Listening to your team being thrashed on the radio is, I'm sure, more painful than being at the game itself. As it turned into a rout most of us were having too good a time to be depressed, we left that for the lightweights who'd stayed at home. We were trying to enjoy ourselves somehow, if only to avoid a suicidal desire to throw ourselves in the nearest river. At times, the Mersey seemed the only option. With a quarter of an hour gone, Palace won a free kick just outside the Liverpool penalty area. Thomas struck it beautifully; the ball beat the wall, sailed past Bruce Grobbelaar, hit the post, bounced across the goal and was thumped clear. Seconds later, Liverpool swept upfield and McMahon scored a brilliant goal. Two-down and you could tell it wasn't going to be our night. Thomas was also involved in the other low. We were six down and thinking things couldn't get much worse when, of course, they did.

Having been awarded a penalty the captain was given the task of converting it. We were ecstatic ... something to cheer at last. Fools! We should have known better than to hope for a goal that night. Thomas put his head back and wellied the ball into row 40. The Liverpool fans reacted as if they'd won the double in the last minute of the last game of the season; we felt like the team they'd beaten. Perhaps Grobbelaar had frightened him. We were close enough to see the look on our man's face as he placed the ball and his short, hurried run up. He knew he wasn't going to score before he kicked it. We desperately wanted to cheer a goal: Thomas couldn't score from a penalty, Gray couldn't score when clean through, clearly Palace weren't going to oblige so there was only one other team to cheer.

As the floodgates opened, we temporarily changed allegiance and joined in with the celebrations. I think the police, who'd earlier told us we could only stand up and cheer "when" Palace scored, felt sorry for us so they just let us get on with it. Having spent all that time and effort to see a midweek game in Liverpool, we were determined to enjoy it. We cheered and sang, encouraging Palace to achieve something ... anything. But vocal support wasn't enough. Just before half time, with everyone nearly hoarse from singing *Stevie Coppell's Red n Blue Army*, if there was any justice there would have been a spectacular Eagles' goal to bring us back into the match. But there is no natural justice and, to prove it, Rush materialised in the six yard box to net Liverpool's third.

Only Gray lived up to our expectations, showing he had skill and determination and was capable of kicking people if necessary. Palace tried hard and kept running but for the most part failed to get the ball. Once Liverpool had it they wanted to play with it until they scored, only allowing us a few touches from the kick off. Even Wright and Thomas were made to look like little kids playing the first XI at school.

We could sing *You're Not Getting Ian Wright* because Liverpool obviously didn't need him and everyone in the ground knew it. We sang all the same and enjoyed every second of it. In fact I enjoyed virtually the whole night. Hearing the roar that greeted Aldridge's goal, hearing the Kop sing *You'll Never Walk Alone*, having a post-match pint bought for me by a sympathetic Scouser – all these were worth being there for. My team may have been thrashed but just for that night I didn't care.

The Moana Geezer

David Kemp meets that rarest of creatures, a Man United fan who reckons he's a proper football supporter

This is sort of a confession I suppose. It wouldn't interest Esther Rantzen, but it does help provide an insight into one of the most common phenomena in football today. Who put the "Moan" in Moan United? Read on dear reader ...

I know someone – work with him, actually – who is a Moan United fan. Originally from Manchester, he still has close links with the place and regularly attends home and away matches. He is something of an anomaly as he rubs shoulders with the Little Moreton-in-the-Marsh Reds, and all the others, who are of course fanatics who go twice a season and then moan because they can't get a ticket for the final. Anyway, this guy I work with, we went to the first leg of the Youth Cup Final together and it was on leaving the match that I was given a rare insight into how these boys regard themselves and their place in the cosmos.

I engaged in a little good natured joshing about the genuineness of the United mob.

Our red friend was suitably miffed and informed me that he was a long standing supporter, which I conceded, and that, and here comes the good bit, he had supported them through thick and THIN!

This magnificent piece of overstatement did not sink in immediately. But, rather like Paul Ince, it became increasingly more irritating over the course of the next hour or so. It was only when we were back on the M25 that I realised the full implications of this smug statement. Summoning all my oratory skills, I yelled: "What bloody thin?"

Cup win after Cup win, Cup Winners Cup, numerous second places in the league (ho, ho, ho), league cup, hardly anorexic is it? More Bernard Manning waistline actually. Since he'd been a Red, I forcefully enquired, had they spent aeons in division two? Or a painful period in division three? Lost a billion times to Shrewsbury? How about losing to Aldershot? Rotherham? Grimsby? Hartlepool? Hull? ... nope.

My pipe cleaner body fought to control the car all the way round to drop Cyril Smith off at his car and slowly drove home down the M4 to ponder the inequalities of life.

So remember, when Robson's lace snaps and he spends the rest of the match abusing the ref, or Ince spends a game rearranging cheek bones with his elbows, these boys have played for Moan United through thick and thin.

Neil Everitt

F.A. Cup 1990

Palace had never reached a Wembley final and when they were drawn against invincible Liverpool in the F.A. Cup semi-final it was too much, even for the most optimistic, to hope for a change of fortune.

Daily Star: They fell about laughing on Merseyside when Liverpool were drawn against Palace in the semi-final – and why wouldn't they?

The Sun: It dawned as Palm Sunday but by the time the shadows were lengthening last evening, it was Barmy Sunday … the day football went absolutely and delightfully stark, raving mad.

■ Let's start in the BBC TV studio with the thoughts of QPR midfielder Ray Wilkins: [on Steve Coppell]: He's got an unenviable task, they are facing Liverpool and it's going to be a hard afternoon for them. [On our best chance]: The hardest part for Palace is when the game becomes a football game

Commentator John Motson (opening cliche): Semi-final day has a flavour all of its own

■ Liverpool had more fans than Crystal Palace who took up only 16,000 of their 18,000 allocation "because they sold to members only".

■ Six members of our squad are injured including Ian Wright

You say that you love me
All of the time
You say that you need me
You'll always be mine
And I'm feeling Glad All Over
Yes I'm Glad All Over

Motson: It's going to be an uphill battle for Crystal Palace. But the thing they've got on their side is nobody expects them to win.

Eagles, Eagles, Eagles

Motson: A feast of football coming up for you … Crystal Palace in the red and blue stripes will kick off. Playing in the first half from left to right and they are, to say the least, underdogs. Four-to-one against Crystal Palace to win this match were the odds.

Terry Venables (analysing): They're going to play it as tight as they possibly can.

Motson: As far as central strikers are concerned, Mark Bright having to plough something of a lone furrow I would think.

Motson: Liverpool team, of course, packed with big match experience, nobody more so than Hansen.

Motson: It's a promising moment for Palace because there is a feeling if they can get at Liverpool it may be from set plays.

Eagles, Eagles, Eagles

Motson: Here they are again chasing the double of league and cup.

Venables: I think they're competing very well in the early stages of the game, Crystal Palace, they know they've got to … I'm just concerned that they're going to pull them all over the place.

Motson: Richard Shaw staying close to Peter Beardsley I've noticed.
Motson: Hansen looks to be in his usual commanding form here.
Motson: Well there was a question mark about whether the big occasion would get to the less experienced side.
Motson: This precise Liverpool build up which has become so familiar.
Motson: But there's no inferiority complex about this Palace side although they lost 9-0 at Liverpool earlier in the season. Everybody's made so much of that, its almost had a counter reaction in the Palace camp …
Motson: He loves to run with the ball Andy Gray, but he had too many grey shirts around him then.
Venables: Andy Gray's very dynamic. He's a little bit hit and miss at times, a little bit inconsistent, he's inclined to go by three or perhaps fall over the ball but he certainly is a danger.
■ McMahon gives the ball to Pardew, who gives it back. McMahon advances, Rush times his run, collects the pass, draws Martyn and flicks the ball into the right hand corner of the net.
Motson: And Ian Rush, the ace goalscorer, once again, makes it look so easy.
We're on the march with Kenny's Army,
We're all going to Wembley
Venables: The runs that Rush is making behind Thorn all the time is a constant worry to O'Reilly, he doesn't know whether to go with him or play him offside.
■ Within ten seconds O'Reilly brings Rush crashing down
Motson: No disrespect to Gary O'Reilly, Steve Coppell was disappointed that Jeff Hopkins wasn't going to be fit for this semi-final.
Motson: They really were down to their last 13 senior players and now they're a goal down too.
Venables: [Palace] are trying to put a little aerial work in now and this is where Hysen will come into his own. He certainly is magnificent in the air.
■ Rush is injured.
Venables: [Palace] are trying to play offside and it's a really dangerous gamble … for what they've gotta lose, they've already come unstuck once.

Aston Villa
Villa Park, Birmingham B6 6HE
Telephone: 021-327 6604
№ 0944
F.A. CHALLENGE CUP
SEMI FINAL TIE
Sunday, 8th April, 1990
CRYSTAL PALACE
v
LIVERPOOL
Kick-off 12.00 noon
S. M. STRIDE
Secretary
£7.00
Including V.A.T.
K
TERRACE
STANDING
You are advised to take up your position not later than thirty minutes before kick-off.
This portion to be retained.
HOLTE END TRINITY ROAD ENTRANCE

Motson [on Rush]: He's a bit like Marco Van Basten when you said the only way to stop him is to tie his legs together.
Hark now hear the Palace sing
And Brighton run away
And we will fight forever more
Because of Boxing Day
Venables: They've set about the job quite well, Crystal Palace.
■ Burrows hacks down Gray.
Motson: And that's the second offence by David Burrows, George Courtney already had a word with him once.
Venables: [Andy Gray's] inclined to want to lay on the ground a little while.
You dirty northern bastards
■ Bright crosses, Hysen struggles and Palace push O'Reilly and Thorn up for the corner.
Eagles, Eagles, Eagles
Motson: I feel sometimes, Liverpool are a little bit vulnerable at set pieces defending.
Venables: They're sticking at it.
Motson: Geoff Thomas is having a good match in midfield, number eight, leading the side well.
■ Rush limps off.
Venables: Perhaps we won't be seeing more danger from Ian Rush after all. [Palace] can't be sorry he's gone off I shouldn't think.
Ole, Ole, Ole, Ole, Eagles Eagles
■ Burrows hacks down Gray.
And it's Crystal Palace, Crystal Palace F.C.
We're by far the greatest team, the world has ever seen
■ O'Reilly, Pemberton, Barber and Salako string together a neat movement, Gillespie clears. Barber's shot is blocked.
Venables: I think they've done very well. They're certainly not out of the game yet. If they can pressurise them the way they are and make them give the ball away they've got a chance to get some encouragement from that and I certainly … corner kicks, I just feel that they might get a bit of good fortune on that as well.
Stevie Coppell's Red and Blue Army
■ Palace attack but Liverpool clear and counter.
Motson: This is where Liverpool can be so dangerous.
Venables: It's been a good game. Crystal Palace have done very well, they've caught Liverpool continuously in possession which is not always a very easy thing to do. They've worked very hard, I think the two midfield players have competed against McMahon and Whelan very well and Thorn has organised well at the back.
Motson: But Liverpool lead 1-0 … and it's difficult, in some circumstances, to see Liverpool letting a game go when they have the chance to take a grip on it, we shall see …
We're going to Wembley,
We're going to Wembley,
You're not, you're not
Maybe it's because I'm a Londoner
That I love London town
Maybe it's because I'm a Londoner
That I think of her …

HALF TIME, HERE COMES THE SECOND HALF (THIS IS THE GOOD BIT)

■ Liverpool come out and the camera lingers on Barry Venison, substitute for Gillespie.
Bring on the Palace, Bring on the Palace
Motson: There's Ian Rush back changed, disappointing end to the day for him but his goal may still prove priceless, we shall see.
■ Palace come out to *The Liquidator* by Harry J

"I think they're playing with a lot of determination and they look, physically, fractionally stronger than Liverpool. Technically, I think that Liverpool are better than them. But the biggest problem they've got, I think, is Hansen and I think that if Mark Bright pushes across and closes Hansen down quicker ... they've got to gamble a little bit more and I think that being one down at half-time they will gamble this half."

MALCOLM ALLISON ON PALACE, HALF TIME INTERVIEW FOR BBC TV

All Stars
Eagles, Eagles, Eagles
Motson: Well let's see what Palace can do about it now in the second half as they attack the Holte End here at Villa Park. John Pemberton, a lovely run early on. And a chance for Barber ... and Venison ... and it's a shot ... and it's a shot and ... it's there! By Bright! It's Mark Bright straight from the kick-off. After John Salako's shot didn't quite get there, Bright's certainly did and Palace are level. What a dramatic start to the second half and Liverpool are stunned.
Motson: Well, it was John Pemberton here who takes so much credit ... it was an inspired run ... the cross met first of all by Venison, then Salako ... off target ... but Mark Bright hammers that left footed into the unguarded goal.
Motson: Well what a start to the second half for Crystal Palace. They are level and Steve Coppell is back in business.
Ole, ole, ole, ole, Eagles, Eagles
Motson: That was without question the sort of run that can turn a match and its put this one right back on the boil.
Daily Mail: As a sporting moment it rivalled Devon Malcolm knocking Viv Richards' leg stump out of the ground at Sabina Park.
We're on the march with Stevie's Army
We're all going to Wember-leee
And we'll really shake 'em up
When we win the FA Cup
Cos Palace are the
greatest football team
The Sun: To Palace's credit, when they sensed blood they hardly looked back.
Motson: And that's a foul by Venison on Barber – quite a stiff challenge in actual fact – and it gives Terry Venables a chance to reflect on how this semi-final has turned.
Venables: Pemberton. I didn't know where he came from. The pace he showed was just fantastic, John.
Motson: He's a great lad off the pitch John Pemberton, he's had, er – as so many of Steve Coppell's players have – experience in the lower divisions at the places like Rochdale and Crewe. Being part of this occasion means so much to him and he seemed to suddenly make up his mind he wanted to leave his impression on the semi-final.

Motson: Andy Gray has got a low flash point at times. He got involved there with a couple of Liverpool players and George Courtney having to administer his first serious lecture of the semi-final. He's a volatile character Andy Gray, but he's very talented. And Geoff Thomas the captain may have to go forward and just, er, also receive a warning word on behalf of his team.
And it's Crystal Palace
Crystal Palace F.C. (loud)
And it's Liverpool
Liverpool F.C. (louder)
And it's Crystal Palace FC
We're by far the greatest team
The world has ever seen (loudest)
Motson: It's Liverpool 1, Crystal Palace 1 and if you were making a cup of tea and, er, taking rather a long time over it I suppose you could conceivably have missed the goal before you got back in front of the television.
Venables: Well Liverpool were just caught completely cold weren't they? I think they were still having a cup of tea in front of the television.
Motson: Its put this game back in the balance and from a neutral point of view, who's complaining?
Motson: And there's a late challenge there, a late challenge. Steve McMahon got involved with Phil Barber and that was after the ball had gone.

Neil Everitt

Supa Al's finest moment

You dirty northern bastards
Motson: Mind you the game's played so fast these days, er, quite often those look worse than they really are.
Venables: Unless you're on the receiving end of it, John.
Motson: Anyway Barber's alright I'm pleased to say and Palace are alright at the moment, it's their supporters who are celebrating with chants of Eagles, Eagles, which of course is the club nickname.
Daily Express: At the heart of it was McMahon's battle with Palace captain Geoff Thomas, a heavyweight contest this, with the ground-side advertising hoarding coming off worse at one stage as they clattered into each other. Complaints and oaths hit the air, particularly from McMahon, and Palace knew at last they had arrived in this game.
■ Houghton gets away from the defence but slices his shot high and wide
We love you Palace, we do, we love you Palace, we do
We love you Palace, we do, oh, Palace we love you
Que sera, sera, whatever will be, will be
We're going to Wembley, Que sera, sera
Venables: They did gamble and the gamble did pay off.
Eagles, Eagles, Eagles
Motson: Palace are playing with a renewed optimism now. They're pushing people up alongside Bright and around him and getting far more bodies in the Liverpool penalty area than they managed in the first half.
Ole, ole, ole, ole,
Eagles, Eagles
Motson: And he looked offside, but he's not, here's Bright. Ball's out now.
Motson: Majestic was the word Ray Wilkins used to describe the Liverpool captain. But, er, I don't think he was expecting that the second half to start quite like that.
Sing when you're winning
You only sing when you're winning
Hark now hear the Palace sing
And Brighton run away
And we will fight forever more
Because of Boxing Day
Motson: Palace whose main priority this season is survival in the first division, they feel they're only a few points away from that now.
Motson: That's a loose ball by John Barnes' standards, Terry.
Motson: Palace are playing a lot more football now aren't they?
Motson: Such a big day, er, er, particularly for the Palace players and their families because they haven't been used to this kind of thing and Steve Coppell, of course, has as a player.
Que sera, sera
Whatever will be, will be
We're going to Wember-leee
Que sera, sera
Venables: It looks like Crystal Palace are relishing the day so far more than Liverpool.
Motson: And Liverpool's passing seems to have broken down
Eagles, Eagles, Eagles
Al, Supa Al, Al, Supa Al
Al, Supa Al, Supa Alan Pardew
Motson: Liverpool with a lot of defending to do at present and they're not doing it with a great deal of composure I have to say … Barry Venison there getting into a real mix-up
Motson: Barnes and Barnes again, Houghton's in the middle and Beardsley's there as well for Liverpool, it hits Richard Shaw – a few hopeful appeals for handball, nothing serious … and here come Palace with Thomas and, on the far side, Mark Bright's there again. Andy Gray's in the middle this time, so's Thomas and there's Thomas, oh, and Grobbelaar grabbed it on the line. An extraordinary 60 seconds.
Venables: There's a fantastic change of ends there, from being 2-1 up, they could easily have been 2-1 down, John.
Motson: It's developing into a really good game this semi-final – sometimes they're nervous, tense affairs without much incident but in this second half especially, the game in general has really come to life and the crowd joining in to lift the occasion …
Oh my lads
You should've seen us coming
Everywhere was red and blue
Everyone was running
All the lads and lasses
All with smiling faces
Walking down the Holmesdale Road
To see the Palace aces
Motson: Well the sheer uncertainty of the F.A. Cup is what gives it its glamour isn't it? Its magic and, er, you can never predict what's going to happen in these one-off occasions, can you?
Motson: Grobbelaar so athletic on his line to make a save that could just have tipped the scale in this cup tie we'll have to wait and see how significant it proves.

"Now it's Hysen getting forward for Liverpool … and falling over in the process."

JOHN MOTSON

Ole, ole, ole, ole,
Eagles, Eagles
Motson: I'm sure Nigel Martyn would have admired it from the other end.
Motson: Bright, still giving Hansen some difficulties.
We love you Palace, we do, Oh Palace we love you
Motson: And Barnes picks it up from Beardsley and look at McMahon in space … it's McMahon for Liverpool … forward run … Nigel Martyn doing precisely the right thing getting out the full 18 yards to block Steve McMahon. And here Palace were really opened up …
Venables: Last five or ten minutes, John, looks like Liverpool are picking it up a bit more and they're getting back into the game. From now on there should be more spaces appearing and that's the sort of opportunity Liverpool like to take advantage of.
South London la, la, la, South London la, la, la
Motson: Well certainly the painful memory of that 9-0 defeat now wiped from Steve Coppell's mind as Crystal Palace hold Liverpool in this semi-final indeed have taken the game to them for much of this second half. But, as Terry Venables says, Liverpool showing in the last five minutes that there's a resilient edge to them that we know all about.
Motson: Beardsley to Barnes … and the flair players beginning to get into the game a bit now. Barnes, and Beardsley forces Andy Thorn across.
Venables: They're getting so close that every time a ball is passed a foot's just appearing.
Motson: That's a foul … Alan Hansen … on Mark Bright … and a free kick to Palace which could spell a bit of danger. They've got, er, Gary O'Reilly I notice going forward to help Bright in there. And now they've waved Andy Thorn up as well.
The Sun: Gray sent his free kick deep into the Liverpool defence and there was O'Reilly to crash the ball home.
Motson: … and Palace … are they in front? Yes they are!
Motson: Liverpool stood there and couldn't really believe it. And Gary O'Reilly from the back, found room in the penalty area and from the set play which people felt would be a Palace strength, or maybe a Liverpool weakness, O'Reilly drives the ball past Grobbelaar and just for a moment the whole crowd

seemed to freeze. But it was a good goal and it's 2-1 Palace.
Motson: Let's just gather our thoughts because Gary O'Reilly has enabled Crystal Palace to come from 1-0 down to lead 2-1 against the holders and the hot favourites. What a story we could have in the making here, but this is Barnes for Liverpool.
Motson: Well, opportunity beckons for Crystal Palace the underdogs. Kenny Dalglish now is the worried man
Que sera, sera, whatever will be, will be
We're going to Wember-leee
Que sera, sera
Motson: Well, Gary O'Reilly who played in the 9-0, that's his first goal of the season. He wouldn't have been playing if Jeff Hopkins had been fit. What a story that could be.
You're not singing, You're not singing
You're not singing anymore, You're not sin-ging any-more
Motson: And listen to their supporters at the moment
Motson: Is there going to be an upset? Or will Liverpool, with all their experience of the big occasion, come late in the game as they've done so often before?
Eagles, Eagles, Eagles
Motson: Nigel Martyn's save from Steve McMahon suddenly becomes very important
And it's Crystal Palace, Crystal Palace FC
We're by far the greatest team
The world has ever seen
Motson: Corner. Barnes is in there, Whelan's in there and Barnes again ... oh, and away almost on the line ... Geoff Thomas I think ... the captain ... corner again. Barnes again. And this time it will be claimed. It was a vital clearance and I'm pretty certain it was Geoff Thomas behind Nigel Martyn who got the ball away from danger.
Liverpool, Liverpool, Liver-pool
Motson: Just over a quarter of an hour of the 90 minutes remaining. I put it that way because if Liverpool were to equalise now we could well be into extra time.
Motson: Barnes is hovering there. Oh its Burrows, what a save by Martyn. But was he offside anyway? I've got a feeling there may have been a flag but Martyn didn't know that did he? He had to make the save and how well he did it.
Venables: It was really a fantastic save there, it looked in no doubt he'd score.
Motson: There are 14 minutes left in the F.A. Cup semi-final, if the score stays this way.
Que sera, sera, whatever will be, will be
We're going to Wember-lee, Que sera, sera
Motson: McMahon ... looking for Barnes. O'Reilly's stretched here. And he needed a bit of help. A corner's been given. He felt he was pushed, Gary O'Reilly, but I think he struggled a bit to match Barnes' pace to be honest.
Eagles, Eagles, Eagles
When Geoff goes up
To lift the FA Cup
We'll be there, we'll be there
Motson: Barnes ... that's trickled off O'Reilly. Liverpool are forcing a succession of corners.
Eagles, Eagles, Eagles
Motson: Venison ... looking for Beardsley ... well Liverpool have really got to fight for their lives now. It's a free kick, Salako on Houghton. Ten minutes to go and trouble here for Palace, possibly. Mark Bright has gone back to help them defend. Barnes, Whelan and Hysen waiting to come in, in a line of three, as Staunton and Venison address the ball ... Staunton to Venison ... right across the goal ... McMahon ... aaahhh, it's there, it's 2-2, Steve McMahon. So the free-kick now works for Liverpool and a more unexpected one it was too, how they worked that.
Venables: They just got caught napping there, Crystal Palace, on a free kick that had a lot of invention in it.
Motson: As true as an arrow from Steve McMahon.
Liverpool, Liverpool, Liverpool
Motson: And, as they used to say in Bill Shankly's time, and since, you never rule Liverpool out. And with ten minutes to go it's all square again, but what a semi-final
Motson: Where do we go from here? Extra-time perhaps?
Venables: I don't know where we're going, but I'm certainly enjoying it, John.
Motson: Well you, I think, Terry, 40,000 inside the ground and millions at home what a football match ... Beardsley. Oh look at this ... Staunton. Penalty! Pemberton on Staunton. George Courtney has pointed to the spot and Pemberton is distraught. Well, I'm not sure about that from here. Staunton is in the box there's no doubt about that, but was he pushed? Well the referee couldn't have been closer could he? You couldn't fault George Courtney's positioning and poor John Pemberton has now been booked as well.
We love you Liverpool, we do, Oh Liverpool we love you
Motson: And in a couple of minutes the whole scene here has changed. Steve Staunton was the player who went down. Liverpool have been given a penalty from which they've had mixed luck this season. They've missed a few, they've scored a few. But now the million pound goalkeeper Nigel Martyn has to face John Barnes. The Palace players are talking to Barnes I'm not sure what's being said. George Courtney has booked Pemberton, he's given the penalty kick and the cup holders could strengthen their grip on the trophy here.
Motson: Barnes scores. The goalkeeper went the right way but the kick was true in the corner and Liverpool lead by three goals to two. And from being 2-1 up, Palace are suddenly dumped on their backsides and can't really believe what's happened to them, most of all Pemberton.
Alan Pardew: After their first goal Liverpool just turned away as if they would get another nine. But when they went 3-2 up they were running around cheering. They were over the moon. They were that relieved. That spurred me on. It showed how rattled they were.
Venables: To be fair, it looked like Liverpool weren't gonna do it.
We're on the march with Kenny's Army
We're all going to Wember-lee
Eagles, Eagles, Eagles
Motson: It's a corner to Palace ... because you couldn't rule out a third goal for them now, could you, the way this match has gone.
We shall not, we shall not be moved
We shall not, we shall not be moved
Just like a team that's gonna win the F.A. Cup
We shall not be moved
Motson: Was it a penalty, Terry?
Venables: I ... the decision is like the game, it could have gone either way.
We're on the march with Kenny's army
Motson: And that's Shaw, high and wide.
When the reds go marching in, when the reds go marching in
I wanna be in that number, when the reds go marching in
Motson: John Pemberton's had such a mixed afternoon, remember he made that Palace equaliser and then, as Staunton got forward, well he did make contact with his back but my view was it took Staunton a little while to go down.
Venables: Well, they'll argue about that one in the, er ... up and down the country, everybody's watching in the, er ... millions of homes and we'll let you be as good a judge as us.
Motson: It's opening up again for Beardsley on the left. It came via Pemberton, but he's got enough pace to shake Beardsley off.
You'll never walk ... Alone ... You'll never ...
Motson: Just under three minutes, Liverpool 3, Crystal Palace 2
Alone ...

... in one of the most exciting semi-finals, well, certainly the second half, that I can remember ...
With hope in your heart ...
And you'll never walk ...
... and the emotions on the bench, well they must feel they've been on a rollercoaster ride over there ...
Walk on, walk on ...
Steve Coppell is standing. His team were less than ten minutes from Wembley, let it be said, they're now less than three minutes away from going out ...
And you'll never walk alone
... Thomas, and Bright's in there, and Thomas. Staunton. Gray! Gray! Three-three! Gray for Palace! They're back in it and Liverpool's defence are all over the place.
Motson: It's a free-kick again – a set play – well Grobbelaar did punch it but not far enough, only to Geoff Thomas ... it spun up off Staunton's chest. The man who actually got the penalty for Liverpool has now virtually delivered the pass for Steve Coppell's side to equalise.
Motson: Two minutes to go. Liverpool 3, Crystal Palace 3 and this one is going down in semi-final folklore.
Venables: John, I think this might bring the fans back.
Motson: Well, I think if we had more football like this, more excitement like this, er, it would generate even more of an increase at the gates than we're having at the moment. It's great stuff isn't it? The televison audience must be on the edge of their seats too.
The Sun: The most dramatic and compulsive live viewing since Neil Armstrong took that first, small step for man on the moon!
Motson: Here's Bright, foul by Hansen is it? Yes. Now, twice from free-kicks Palace have scored ... what sort of finish could we be in for here?
Motson: Three-all, extra time beckons now ... but hold on, free-kick again. So, once more, O'Reilly and Thorn take up their positions and once again Gray prepares to launch the ball in ... oh, against the bar, by Thorn I think. Against the crossbar in the dying seconds.
Ole, ole, ole, ole,
Eagles Eagles
We're proud of you,
We're proud of you
We're proud of you,
We're PROUD

EXTRA TIME

Motson: ... three waiting in the centre for the cross for Palace, Salako provides it, Thomas is there! Grobbelaar missed it ... is it? No, the whistle's already gone, Glenn Hysen I think must have been pushed. Alan Hansen, I think, put the ball in his own net in the end, I don't know whether I've got that right, but it seemed as though he did, maybe he'd heard the whistle.
Venables: Liverpool look to be lifting it up a bit now, five minutes, as I've said there's spaces opening and they're playing the ball the better at the moment ... and they're making the chances.
Motson: There's been so much incident and excitement that it's probably drained the players emotionally as well as physically I would have thought.
Venables: It's certainly slowing down now, John.
Ole, ole, ole, ole, Eagles, Eagles

SECOND HALF

Venables: Well, I think there's been such a turn around so often in this game, I think now at this stage they'd both settle for a replay now, I think.
Wilkins: They [Palace] look very, very tired now and I think

> □ACCORDING to a much-loved cliche, soccer is an international language . . . well not quite.
> This is how the American media were alerted to that Palace triumph by the agency AP:
> "Andy Gray ties the game with three minutes left in regulation and Alan Pardew wins it in overtime as Crystal Palace upsets Liverpool 4-3 Sunday in the semi-finals of the English Football Association Cup."

"Palace's journeymen deserved to go to Wembley for their first final for their indomitable spirit alone. And so do their 16,000 magnificent fans whose colour, humour and noise contributed so much to a glorious day at Villa Park a year after the tragedy of Hillsborough"

BRIAN SCOVELL, DAILY MAIL

We're the famous Crystal Palace and we're going to Wember-lee

I expect there are thousands of stories from that day in April 1990. I have so many memories of the most astonishing day in Palace history: having my glasses sent flying by my girlfriend as the balloons flew up at the start, sitting in a pub in Handsworth afterwards surrounded by curious Rastafarians while we stared into our pints in disbelief, wondering why John Pemberton crossed himself as he came out for the second half and the almost orgasmic realisation that, after all these years, Palace had finally made it. But perhaps my most bizarre moment of that time came on the Monday after the match. I was still in a deeply comatose state, a little like Arthur Fowler in *EastEnders* after he had nicked the Christmas Club money.

As a worker in a medical charity I was due at an important meeting at University College Hospital and I had to meet the head of the surgical department.

A combination of celebration pernod and paraquat and pornographic thoughts of a creature with the top half of Darryl Hannah and the legs of Phil Barber, meant that I was a good 15 minutes late.

As I entered the hospital I could see the consultant bounding up to me and I imagined my brilliant medical career fading out like an Alan Pardew pass. He reached me out of breath: "Well, well," he blurted, "well, what do you think, will Ian Wright make the final?"

KEITH MILES

Wayne was in tears, the Old Man, after more than 20 years of torture was euphoric, the boys down the 'Poachers' could not be silenced and even I sipped gently on some fizzy water late into the night. Oh God ... now calm down.

PETER CARPARK

The madness of the terrace was only improved upon by the mayhem of the boys on the pitch. With the multi-regional followers of Liverpool only singing when they're winning Villa Park belonged to Palace. On the terraces and on the pitch. Leaping, leaping, leaping around the Holte end. This is incredible.

LAURIE DAHL

John Motson: 15 seconds after O'Reilly's goal and with 18,000 Palace fans going barmy he says: "Palace, are they in front? Yes, they are!" Disbelieving sod, he must be from the Planet Scouse. And as for Ray Wilkins saying Palace *HAD* to do it in normal time because Liverpool would be fitter ... words escape me.

MARTIN EVANS.

that is the nervous energy creeping into the match now.
Motson: Well, it's certainly pulling at the nerve ends this one isn't it?
Venables: Once he's inside the 18 yard box now, John Barnes is looking to hold onto that ball and really frighten the opposition.
Motson: [Liverpool] they're forcing the issue at the start of the final 15 minutes
Come on Palace, Come on Palace, Come on Palace, Come on
Motson: Looks as though he's really enjoyed the game, the Palace keeper, and I suppose it's one the players will look back on and say, well it's something to be a part of, but not if you lose.
P...A...L...A...C...E... Palace, Palace
Motson: And McMahon curls one, drifting away from the far post.
Motson: Forward by Thorn, looking for Bright, Hysen is with him, tried to turn inside him, corner to Palace ...
Motson: Well, they made such good use of their set plays, Crystal Palace, that you wouldn't rule them out now. Andy Gray has gone across to take it.
Motson: Thorn flicked it on ... and it's gone in! Pardew! 4-3, Palace! The flick on by Thorn made all the difference, Liverpool are caught out again by the set play and it looks like Alan Pardew who bundled it in ... and it's back with Steve Coppell and the underdogs again.
Ole, ole, ole, ole,
Eagles, Eagles
Al, Supa Al,
Supa Alan Pardew
The Sun: I saw Bruce Grobbelaar flapping like a Zimbabwe house sparrow at lobs and crosses that produced Palace's remarkable victory.
Motson: Well there's a Sunday team down in Surrey called the Nomads who'll be watching this game today, because they cancelled their fixture today I'm told because their coach and manager is Alan Pardew and it may be that he's written the last chapter in this game, or dare I say that?
The Sun: This was blink and you miss it football – amazing stuff ... a year ago, English football was engulfed by the black shadow of an appalling tragedy. The sun shone in Manchester and Birmingham yesterday. And English football produced a worthy if inadequate tribute to 95 people who could not be there.
Motson: There are eight minutes left and I have to keep saying it, don't rule Liverpool out.
Sing your hearts out, sing your hearts out,
Sing your hearts out for the lads
The Guardian: Take a brilliantly sunny if chilly day, four sets of enthusiastic and well behaved supporters, attaking football on all sides and one shock with maybe another to come, and all seems right with the world of football. The picture is by no means all gloom and despondency.
Motson: The tension inside the ground is quite fantastic. I hope it's coming across at home.
Venables: Dare you say it, it looks as if Crystal Palace, for the first time, are gonna go to Wembley in the F.A. Cup. They're still playing good football, Liverpool, but it's just a case of set pieces.
Motson: Steve Coppell has done his homework.
Motson: Six minutes away from Wembley, Crystal Palace, they were eight minutes away in normal time can they hold it on this occasion ... seven goals in a semi-final ... Palace fans singing ...
Que sera, sera, whatever will be, will be
We're going to Wember-lee
We shall not, we shall not be moved
We shall not, we shall not be moved
Just like a team that's gonna win the F.A. Cup
We shall not be moved
Motson: It's really academic now, but I suppose in the light of cold appraisal somebody will wonder what would have happened if Rush hadn't been injured.
Motson: This is Houghton, there's danger, Barnes! Ohhh, and Nigel Martyn, that save might have been worth a million pounds, you never know.
We are Palace, we are Palace
Super Palace from Selhurst
Eagles, Eagles, Eagles
We're proud of you, we're proud of you,
We're proud of you, we're proud
Motson: Well now, do you see a last minute dramatic recovery by Liverpool and that man [Dalglish] or not?
Venables: Well, you can't rule it out, but I don't think so, I think that, erm ... Crystal Palace are on the way.
Motson: Well, it's your old club, you were with them the last time they got to the semi final, 1976, and this man now [Coppell] must be thinking my goodness how close we are. Against all the odds in many ways.

"The old chap tried to focus through watery eyes on the scene of joy and colour. Around him young supporters danced and cheered. 'I can't believe it, I just can't believe it,' he choked to himself. A veteran fan of more than 50 years, the old chap found it hard to grasp the reality of his team reaching the F.A. Cup Final."

DAVE McCLELLAND
CROYDON ADVERTISER

We love you Palace we do
Oh, Palace we love you
Motson: There's a minute to go at Villa Park, Crystal Palace are that close to Wembley, to putting out the holders and the favourites Liverpool, to destroying the dream of the double, can they hold on?
Ole, ole, ole, ole,
Eagles, Eagles
Motson: The ground booming with noise from Palace supporters, look where Glenn Hysen's playing now, centre forward.
Motson: 4-3 to Crystal Palace coming up to the end of extra-time, Geoff Thomas getting tangled up with Ronnie Whelan, shouts at George Courtney, gets nothing, on by Hysen, Barnes, there's danger here, turns it in ... but there's not now.
Motson: We are up to the end of the 30 minutes of extra time it's only a question of what George Courtney the World Cup referee decides to add on for stoppages. Bright, on his own up front for Palace, We are on the verge of a real turn up here. Andy Thorn battling away, and Geoff Thomas ... Andy Gray ... and Bright's made a curving run to stay on side that was brilliant actually, at this stage of the game. He'll want to try and hold it up if he can ... well, I don't condone time wasting but in Palace's situation you can forgive it today can't you? After all we've been through here.
Motson: The ref has given a goal kick, he's looked across at his linesmen, he's checked his watch again, when will he blow? Crystal Palace 4 Liverpool 3 and Crystal Palace are at Wembley! They've beaten Liverpool, whose dream of the double is destroyed in one of the most amazing matches, surely in the recent history of the F.A. Cup. Steve Coppell runs off and the Palace supporters celebrate.
Daily Mirror: The joy of this incredible victory belongs to Palace and the chief architects of the win, Mark Bright and Andy Gray, celebrated by running over to their jubilant fans, where they lost their shirts in the kissing and the hugging.
The Daily Express: Palace are known as the Eagles. Isn't there a kids' comic called something very similar? Perhaps that's the answer because this was pure fantasy, undiluted by anything approaching realism.

CUP FINAL DAY

Palace captain Geoff Thomas with Manchester United's Bryan Robson

Glory, glory Crystal Palace. The most wonderful day in Palace's history was not Cup Final day but April 7, 1990 at Villa Park. Winning the semi-final was the achievement, Cup Final Day was the reward. There isn't very much to say about the Cup Final except it was everything we had dreamed it would be.

The build up was the thing. As you get older so the child's delight in waiting for Christmas and birthdays to come and being overcome with the unbearable suspense evaporates, but reaching the Cup Final returned us all to a childlike state.

Being able to parade through London in red and blue and knowing that everybody knew who you were and where you were going. Being part of something the whole world was watching and becoming part of history.

The trains to Victoria packed with happy faces, excited voices, reading Peter Gillman's article in the *Independent* magazine telling Britain what it means to be a Crystal Palace supporter. We really are a breed apart, something different. Seeing the Duke of York pub slowly fill to bursting. The side street where the banner for the musical about the life of Buddy Holly pronounced "This is a show you will never forget!"

The good humour of the whole day. The tourists on their open top buses snapping away at this great English spectacle and with no malice we gave them everything we had, determined to savour every second of a day we never imagined would come for us.

Boarding the tubes and watching the unsuspecting passengers' faces drop as they were submerged in a sea of fans and then the relief when they detected our good nature and listened to the singing and the banter.

Wembley Park station; and knowing that you were nearly there and just catching a glimpse of the twin towers. Into Wembley Way and for many of us the first sight of United fans. The friendly mixing, the jeers and catcalls but no aggression. Walking up Wembley Way as slowly as possible not wanting the day to go too quickly. The colour of the Palace fans and United looking positively drab in comparison.

Silly things like wanting the "Palace" parachutists to land in the centre circle and hoping the United ones missed. Watching Wembley fill, listening to the Palace getting their singing going. *You say that you love me, all of the time ...*

They put *Abide With Me* over the tannoy to make it sound loud, but we were going to sing it anyway. We'd waited so long to be part of this we weren't going to miss our chance.

Then the teams, the noise, all those balloons, seeing Stevie Coppell bringing Palace out of the tunnel. How we paid for this. Not with money, we paid on the terraces of Barnsley, Hull and Reading. This is what you get for loyalty

Gary Chapman

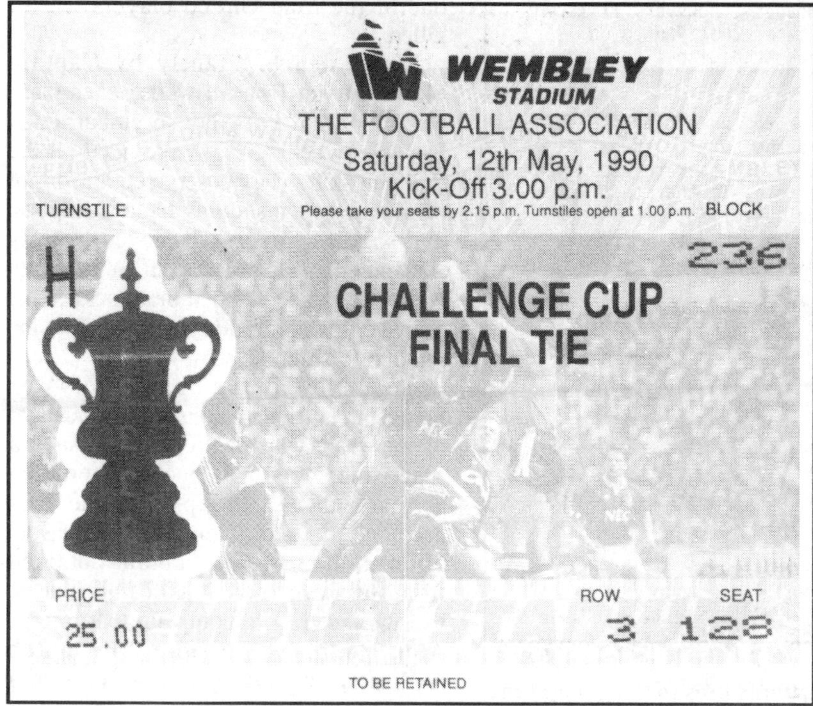

WEMBLEY
STADIUM
THE FOOTBALL ASSOCIATION
Saturday, 12th May, 1990
Kick-Off 3.00 p.m.
Please take your seats by 2.15 p.m. Turnstiles open at 1.00 p.m.
TURNSTILE
H
BLOCK
236
CHALLENGE CUP
FINAL TIE
PRICE
25.00
ROW
3
SEAT
128
TO BE RETAINED

Top: The Palace fans begin to gather outside the Stage Door at Victoria
Right: Wembley bound, Peggy Witheroe in a dress she knitted for the occasion

---

Defeat: "Off you rant about Robson's deflected header and Hughes' strike through O'Reilly's despairing legs with only six minutes left. Now you are in your stride you give it both barrels. The replay, oh God. The anger, the hurt, the dreadful kit, the penalty that should have been, the game that should have been, their keeper who should never have been. The despair and frustration wells up from where bitter pain is stored inside you. It's always there, somewhere, hidden from view mostly, but there all the same, maturing, fermenting, hardening and distorting. A dream torn asunder, a golden future smashed into a thousand excuses which all begin "if only". The fact is that 1989-90 was a major success for the club, but you can't bring yourself to feel that it was."

MATTHEW SIMMONDS

THE VALLEY PARTY

Please reply to:

54 Sherard Road
Eltham
London
SE9 6EP

21st April 1990

Eagle Eye Magazine
30 Manor Court
Whetstone
London N20

Dear John/Tony/other jammy bastards,

Don't ask me why, but for reasons best known to themselves, and totally beyond my comprehension, I am requested by my Valley Party colleagues to offer our heartfelt (or should that be heartbroken ?) congratulations on your victory in the semi finals of some nondescript cup competition, the title of which escapes me.

I find it quite extraordinary that you should succeed in one of the competitions that was not invented by Noadesy, however, it is the desire of both our candidates and associates that you go on to Wembley and represent South London in true traditional fashion by being stuffed out of sight.

Following my prediction that Supa Al would score the winner in the semi (see VOTV 19), I have just been down to the betting shop and put my life savings on Mark Robins to take the cup back to Old Trafford. At least one Robins will be able to claim that this has been agood season, because it's been a disaster for us.

May it rain solidly on Cup Final day so that all your brand new souvenirs get soaked, and I hope that all your video recorders refuse to function. Let's hope the Queen isn't too upset at the thought of sitting next to Noadesy for half the game.

Yours most begrudgingly,

Steve

Steve Dixon
Valley Party

P.S : Enjoy the day !

A wonderful piece of sportsmanship from Charlton's fans to their long time tormentors at *Eagle Eye*

We're not biased but ...

It is the bitterest pill for any fan to swallow. We lost and no amount of hypothesising will change the fact. Should we have wasted our time trying to stop United instead of playing ourselves? Was it a penalty? Should so and so have played? Does it matter?

It was still a privilege to be there on both occasions and I will never forget the best support Wembley has ever seen. But what detracted from the whole occasion for me was the lack of credit for Palace in the press. It only serves to compound our misery and I feel it is not only unwarranted but yet another example of the love affair between the newspapers and the establishment clubs. This is from the *Daily Typical*:

By Denis George-Busby

THANKFULLY good football won the day last night when a wonderful Manchester United triumphed over cynical reprobates Crystal Palace in the F.A. Cup Final replay at Wembley.

Lee Martin's second half stunner gave the Red Devils the result they deserved and ensured Palace got what they deserved – nothing.

Right from the start the south London scum (who were lucky even to be at Wembley having denied fabulous Liverpool the rematch with United that the whole country wanted to see) played with the intention of kicking United out of the game. So cyncial was their play that one would not have been surprised to see Arnold Schwarzenegger out there in one of the horrible black and yellow tops that Palace wore. It was a surprise that one of the Man United players wasn't killed.

United, led brilliantly by Captain Marvel Bryan Robson whose exemplary behaviour and fair play so embarrassed Palace's wrecking crew, provided all the flair and skill. They deserve credit for not retaliating to the spoiling tactics. Hughes, that striker supreme, displayed honesty and integrity and was the uncomplaining victim as Palace wielded their tackles like a scythe in a cornfield. They had done the same to Rush in the semi-final.

One could only feel happy for Alex Ferguson, surely a candidate for manager of the year, who has assembled such a great side. As for Palace? Is there any normal right thinking person who does not hope they get relegated next season. Thomas their bestial captain obtained from the lower divisions, of all places, had the temerity to complain that referee Alan Gunn, who handled the match brilliantly, should have awarded him a penalty for an innocuous incident that in any case clearly took place six yards outside the box.

■ Two Liverpool supporting friends in Bradford told me after the replay that we deserved to lose. I've had a difficult time trying to defend Palace's tactics. I tried to explain that we didn't set out to break legs but the game turned out that way. United were hardly vicitms of circumstance. Although I don't believe we are a neutral's best friend, what can we do?

One of the Liverpool fans says the tone of the game was set by Andy Thorn. It's hard living with such people because they are so bloody snobbish when it comes to football and are now gloating in their own little way.

Michael Grace

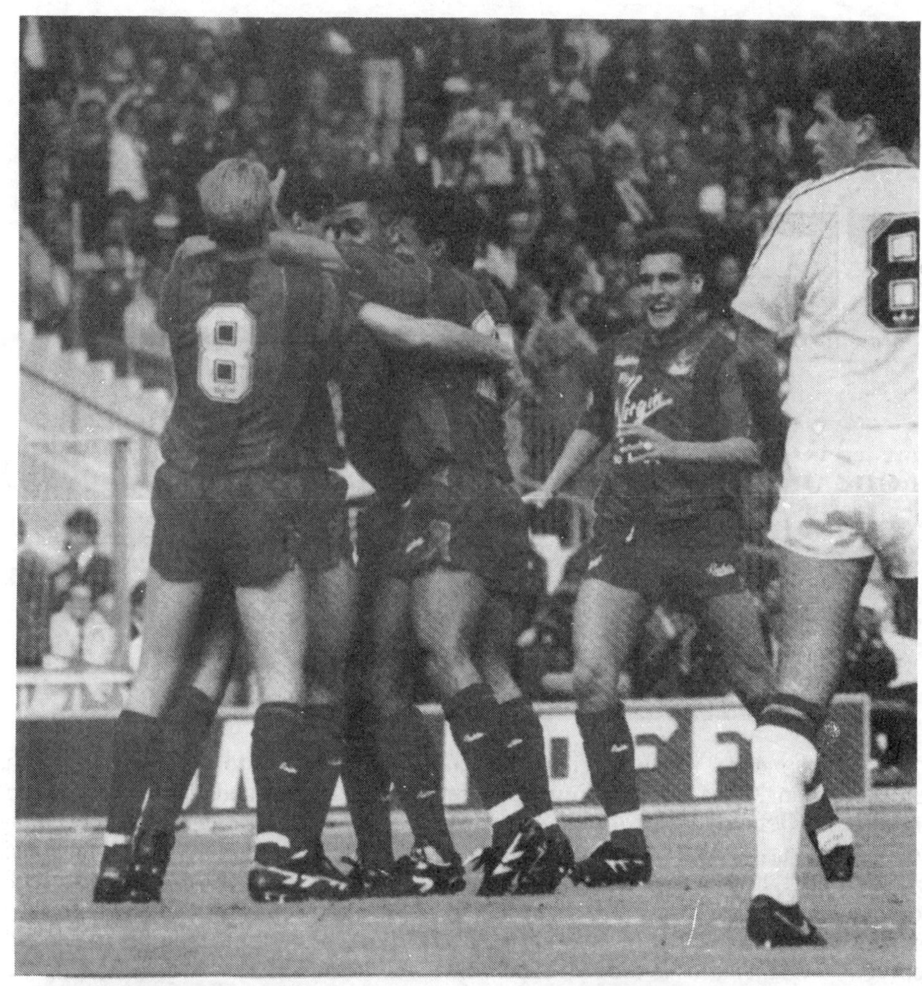

Left: Neil Everitt's photo captures the celebrations of Palace's first goal. Gary O'Reilly is mobbed by Geoff Thomas, Mark Bright and John Salako while John Pemberton is about to land on top of them.
Below: The Eagles gather outside Wembley. Gary Chapman wearing shorts, cut short a trip to Australia to get back for the Final

Within three minutes Wright had scored the first distinguished goal of the game, and shown up how much we had all been missing. Collecting the ball on the left, this player, who had cost Palace peanuts comparatively, raced around Pallister, who had cost Manchester United £2.3m, as though he were a telephone pole, and struck his splendid cross-shot past Leighton.

BRIAN GLANVILLE, SUNDAY TIMES

THE LIFE OF O'REILLY

Gary O'Reilly was one of the first players to be bought by Palace with Lifeline money. He might have seemed like another cheapo signing but the ex-Spurs and Brighton player gave the club more than value for money. Here Gary looks back on his Palace career with Neil Witheroe and Laurie Dahl

Gary O'Reilly joined Crystal Palace at a time when the club was emerging from one of its blackest periods. Steve Coppell had built the nucleus of a side good enough to challenge for promotion but Palace were still financially weak and, in an attempt to speed up the recovery process, the club introduced Lifeline, a prize draw scheme to help buy players.

Lifeline was an instant success. Asked to put their money where their mouths (and hearts) were, the fans stumped up and cash became available for some modest investments. The first players signed with the help of Lifeline were Anton Otulakowski from Millwall, Mark Bright from Leicester and, for a fee of around £40,000, Brighton's big central defender Gary O'Reilly.

"If I didn't want to go I wouldn't have left Brighton," says Gary. "But I was happy to come and be part of the set up. The fact that it was the supporters' money was great because it was an interaction from a lot of people. Everybody feels they have a part of you and part of the club which is a good thing.

"Originally I imagine Lifeline was there to buy five and nearly six figure players, but promotion means the players become seven figure purchases and the money goes to supplement those purchases rather than buy them outright. You raise the money and you have to put your trust in those in charge to spend it wisely."

Brighton, of course, were Palace's greatest rivals. Was Gary aware of the animosity? "Without a doubt. It's a big thing. It's not an Old Firm in the sense of Rangers-Celtic, or maybe a Tottenham-Arsenal, but Palace against Brighton down here is a big thing. Down here they look forward to it. Having played for both sides I know what it means to each set of people.

"Even my friends called me 'foreigner' after I'd left. They were joking, but they couldn't understand why I'd gone to Palace."

> **"It's a big thing. It's not an Old Firm in the sense of Rangers-Celtic ... but having played for both sides I know what it means to each set of people"**
>
> GARY O'REILLY
> ON CRYSTAL PALACE V BRIGHTON

The reason Gary had to go was simple, Brighton had financial difficulties far worse than those at Selhurst. When he explained the position to his friends they understood. He made his Palace debut against first division Forest in the F.A. Cup. It had been snowing and there was some doubt whether the game would go ahead. "I got there about 25 minutes before the kick-off. Although I'd left in loads of time but the traffic was solid as soon as I crossed the M25. I didn't know any short cuts and I was getting a bit worried. Late for my debut. What a start."

But the day ended happily with Gary on the winning side after Alan Irvine's goal had seen off Brian Clough's men.

"I liked the idea of beating Forest. For Palace to win then was great, it meant a lot and picked everyone up."

The fourth round was an even bigger challenge and Palace took thousands of fans to White Hart Lane to see O'Reilly and company take on Spurs, the club where he had begun his career and for whom he had won a UEFA Cup medal.

Then, calamity, slap bang in front of the Palace fans. "I put one in our net for them. It happens. I don't think we were second best, we could have won but we didn't play well and we didn't win."

Gary followed up by conceding a penalty at Stoke in the league. "Again it happens, I don't really remember. I reserve the right to forget the bad bits. There's not a defender in the league who's not going to give away a penalty from time to time. Occasionally it's deliberate, or you can mistime a tackle or perhaps the referee will interpret a challenge in a different way to you and with the new laws you can end up being sent off for the most innocuous things which is a shame."

These early incidents, coupled with his Brighton background, might easily have affected the crowd's attitude. Was he aware of this? "No. Alright I'd rather it hadn't happened, but you have to get on with it and if I started to worry about those sorts of things when I went out then I wouldn't be doing what's best for me, the team or the supporters. You can't worry about what people are saying."

There were other disappointments too, but as Palace progressed the team became more focussed. The defence that had leaked five goals at Blackburn and West Brom tightened up. Yet O'Reilly doesn't recall a specific turning point where a mid-table outfit suddenly became promotion winners.

Instead he recalls that Steve Coppell spelt out what could be achieved. "Steve liked to call it the comfort zone. He told us we could be in the comfort zone, and it wouldn't be a problem. We could finish eighth if we liked, but it meant we'd just see out the rest of the season. Or we could do it. We could push ourselves and get promotion. Players were pushed and everybody was made aware of the necessity of promotion, we were pushed to get up and this whole body came about. Even losing both away play-off games, we still had belief and desire and it came through."

While the play-offs put everyone through the mill, Gary had other problems. "I'd had an injury that kept me out for a month. I went swimming first thing every morning, came into training, sat on a bike, cycled, went nowhere – it had one wheel. The day before the Blackburn game I trained for half an hour for the first time in a month. I went home thinking I'd love to play but I couldn't really see myself making it after only half an hour of five-a-side. But I prepared as I normally would. I'll be available, I thought, I probably won't be asked but I'll be ready. Then I got a phone call at ten o'clock on Saturday morning. It was Steve Coppell: 'Are you fit enough?' I said let me think about it, because it was not just me. If I said I was fit I had a responsibility to the other players.

"I played with a bandage on my knee and to be honest I never felt tired. I was carried along. It was probably the greatest atmosphere of my life, fantastic. I hadn't played in any of the other play-off games. I'd watched them, I'd been to Blackburn in the week before and I watched us lose and it was so frustrating.

"Sometimes at Selhurst Park people can be a bit quiet and you can hear mumblings, but this was so positive. Everybody was just willing us to win. I was so keyed up I don't remember the incidents in the game, all I can remember is winning. We played extra time and it didn't bother me one bit. There was this point in extra time when I knew we'd won it. Just inside. I didn't say anything. Sometimes in a game you get that feeling – we know we've got this, this is ours."

O'Reilly was one of the few who had played in the first division before. "I'd been there with a rather good Spurs

Colorsport

team. We had Clemence, Roberts, Perryman, Ardiles, Hazard, Galvin, Archibald and Crooks. I got a UEFA Cup medal for being in the squad and a couple of shirts I'd swapped. They were a very good side but that doesn't mean Palace were second rate. I was lucky enough to be involved in a very strong team but, man-for-man, not many of the Palace players would have got in that Tottenham team.

As the importance of the matches both in the second division and then in the top flight increased, so did the animation with which the supporters, desperate to keep what had been won, expressed their opinions over what was still a notoriously leaky defence. What was Gary's view? "Selection was nothing to do with me. It's nice to think that the supporters would want me to play, but its the manager's decision and that's what he's paid for. I was a player and played as well as I possibly could, hopefully to my potential, and then Steve decided. He would shake up and move his formations. If he felt a player didn't quite suit the formation he would leave him out or bring another in. It was entirely up to him.

"I see players as a unit, a complete team. It's up to the management to work it out, it's not player against player, it should be the management who decide the whole approach.

"I went into the first division with a unit that wasn't as strong as many of those we were competing against, let's be honest. However, it was up to us to prove ourselves. And by the end, we'd begun to pick up results, win games rather than nick them, collect points away from home and, in the end, we had the right to be there. We were written off as soon as we were promoted so I was quite pleased to say 'we're here and we're staying'. And we had character – that's why we got promotion, that's why we got to the F.A. Cup Final and stayed in the first division. We had a sense of direction."

Mark Bright and Ian Wright were the stars up front and Gary recognises that the rest were there to provide them with service. "They were both world class moaners. Moan, moan, moan, moan. They used to rip John Salako to shreds because he would turn in, turn out, stand on it, fall over, get up, go for an ice cream and come back and they'd still be waiting for the cross. So you can imagine the conversation. But I didn't mind because I understood them. They made runs and they wanted the ball. The team were all on the same wavelength and we got on well. But, when Mark and Ian had left, Eddie McGoldrick scored more goals. They always made him cross, but all of a sudden there was no demand and he got double figures for the season having got six in four years. You traded Eddie's goals for the Wright and Bright show.

"Our game was functional. Ian and Mark had an almost telepathic understanding and they were very focussed. Why play a lot of football that doesn't bring out the best in them. You play football that does that, and Steve decided early on that he would tailor the style to Mark and Ian. And it was productive.

"When you consider the resources Steve had, both financially and in terms of players, he did an extremely good job. It wasn't pleasing to the purists but in the end you are judged on how little or how much success you achieve. Steve was thoughtful and shrewd enough to come up with a system to suit the players he's got. But although the team was built around Ian and Mark they were still part of it. They understood that they were part of the team."

Palace had a lot of growing up to do, not least after their destruction at Anfield. As one of the central defenders that night what does Gary remember? "I can laugh about it now and obviously we laid it to rest in the semi-final, but what stuck out was our supporters. They were superb and never stopped trying to get behind us.

"If we'd been told we'd have to lose 9-0 before we could go on, we wouldn't have fancied it. I don't see it as a turning point so much as a wake-up call. What it did was make us stronger. It made everybody say 'right that's not going to happen again', and we went away to Southampton straight after and got a draw and we were unlucky not to come away with three points. It sparked us, although it didn't kick in straight away. It hurt the whole club. And the press wouldn't let it lie, they kept poking away at the wound. Later when we got to the semi-final we had a really strong focus of 'we owe you'.

"The semi was a chance to do something about it especially after we'd lost at home. And everybody looked at it as 11-0 down. I watched the video afterwards and Bob Wilson and Ray Wilkins had us written off. I couldn't wait for the end of the game to hear what they had to say. They were nailing the coffin lid down and I was pleased as punch to have that happen.

What was the feeling before the semi? Most fans expected defeat but were heading for Villa Park to prove a point anyway, was that how the players saw it?

"We were training at Mitcham, working out the pattern of play, and during this practice match it just started to click. I got that feeling; I think we'll win this. I didn't say anything to anybody, but I just thought to myself this feels good. The preparation and everything was right and we had such an incentive to do well and when we came out onto the pitch at Villa Park everywhere was red and blue and we thought, we own this place, this is ours.

"People from outside the stadium who got there late said there were red and blue balloons everywhere, they wondered what was going on. The Liverpool supporters were brilliant, too, they gave us a big round of applause. I walked over to the Holte End afterwards and they were clapping. They didn't have to do anything. It was the same when we got beaten 9-0. They gave us applause because our supporters never stopped singing."

Palace may have had a score to settle but the match looked to be running to script when, the "ace goalscorer" slipped Gary's clutches to make it look so easy. "Ian Rush, all credit to him, he has been a superb player and it's just as well he didn't get any more. It happens for you sometimes. He left through injury, they changed the structure and it worked for us."

What about the goal to put us ahead for the first time? "Shoot, shoot. It was one of those. Ball, shoot, net, goal, thank you. You don't even think. I don't see myself as a calculating striker, I've put my fair share in Row Z. It was such a concerted effort and there were nine really good reasons on everyone's behalf."

And so to Wembley. What is it like to play in an F.A. Cup Final? "It was great stuff, the record and everything. I'm a

"I was so keyed up I don't remember the incidents in the game, all I can remember is winning ... Sometimes in a game you get that feeling, we know we've got this, this is ours."

– Gary O'Reilly on the Blackburn play-off

big Beatles fan anyway and we went to Abbey Road studios and the four scorers stood on the Zebra crossing, just like on the *Abbey Road* album, for the cover of *Glad All Over*. It was just a big thing. I can't hold a tune but I enjoyed it. Once you actually get through there's a load of things, so much is happening.

"We had things people wanted us to wear. Before the game we had to wear certain sunglasses and when the cameras were around you had to make sure you were reading a certain daily paper. It's an absolute circus. But you get involved in a big, big thing. Over a hundred million people watched it live. The F.A. Cup is the single domestic final that attracts that sort of attention. Everybody in the world wants to know about you. But I had the advantage of having seen it before and could take it with a pinch of salt. I didn't get involved with too much and on the day I did my own thing.

"I remember when Brighton were there they were on the pitch with their cameras and I didn't want any of that. It was a big day for Palace and myself, but I was there to play football and to win, not to be a tourist and be seen wandering up and down in a club suit.

"I did my warm up routine as usual – a stretching routine I'd had for years – why change it for the Final? Some players were relaxed, some were really tense, some have an exclusion zone around them, others don't stop talking. Some can't get out of the toilet. I was just getting myself ready, thinking about my opponent."

Gary's opposite was Mark Hughes and it proved to be a real ding dong battle. "You know what you're getting yourself into. You don't expect him to kiss you. You expect a certain amount of aggression and he gives it to you. It's whether you can contain him. He is a quality player and he's difficult and quality players will force you into errors and create something from nothing.

"We were six minutes from winning, we had another bite at it and it never happened. That's the way it goes. We were there, we earned the right and it was great. It hurt afterwards when I looked at my medal and it said 'runners up' on the back. It meant that much to me and I wanted one with 'winners' on it. I'd been at Spurs in the early 80s, when they'd won cups but I was on the periphery and I wanted some of that. As Ian Wright said, it's what every schoolboy dreams of doing. You go out kicking about with your mates and you dream of scoring a goal in a cup final. That happened to me, so you can imagine what a thrill it was. It means so much to me to have actually done it. I wouldn't let anyone take it from me but it's painful to look at.

"But the fans went through all the anxieties because it's worse to watch than to play I can tell you and at least I got a medal."

And that kit? "Yellow and black stripes, we looked like bees! It came out the day before the replay and we appreciated our sunglasses. Funnily enough that was the last game I played that most fans would have seen although I went on the tour to Italy and scored again."

The impact Palace had made earned an invitation to a prestigious tournament in the Italian Alps. "I got a big kick out of Italy. After we'd been to Wembley I sat and watched a lot of the members of Fiorentina and Sampdoria playing for half a dozen countries in the World Cup and I thought, yeah, let's see what you can do, let's see what you can do against Gary O'Reilly.

"You need that test to try yourself against the best and Italian football is by far the most skillful football that I've watched. English football is brilliant, but I love Italian football for different reasons. I got a big kick out of scoring against Fiorentina and beating Sampdoria. The Palace fans were doing a conga on the terrace and we met them on the streets. I'm sure they got as big a kick out of it as I did. It was real fun.

"I would have liked my career to take off after that but it didn't happen. I'm not angry, I'm disappointed that it didn't go as I hoped but you have to get on with it and it's no use worrying about it."

Shortly before Palace were relegated, Gary, who had returned to Brighton, announced his retirement through injury. A sad ending just three years after so much glory.

"I did the commentary for the radio on Brighton's last game of the season and about a thousand people stayed behind to cheer the Palace result. You can't say horrible people because Palace fans probably did the same when Brighton went down the year before. But I was probably the only one in the Goldstone who was not happy because we put a whole lot in to get there.

"We finished third and by rights we should have been promoted anyway but we had to go out and prove it again. We worked hard for that, everybody did. So it was disappointing to hear about relegation."

So has it all been for nothing? "Go back and compare the club from when I joined in 1987 and look at it now. It's a revelation.

"You have corporate entertainment areas downstairs, you have boxes over Sainsbury's, its fantastic and its being developed again. When you think what the club has achieved in six years, not bad.

"Alright you can say we should have won that cup, we should have beaten Man United and been in Europe, but you can't. That's it. You deal with what you've actually got.

"If someone said six years ago you'd reach an F.A. Cup Final, play in the Premier League for four seasons and get all these developments you'd have said no chance.

'Everything has progressed. There are certain things you will never be happy about, but to be honest you can win 10-0 and someone on the terraces will be standing there going 'bloody rubbish, why didn't we score 12?'

"Its the old cliche you can't please all the people all the time."

THE PARTNERSHIP

Jeeves and Wooster, Regan and Carter, Reeves and Mortimer. All great double acts, but not a patch on Bright and Wright. Mark Gardiner looks back fondly at a new concept for Palace ... two goalscorers

Hy Money

Being a Palace supporter during the early 1980s meant being guaranteed plenty of goalmouth excitement. Unfortunately most of it was at our end because the Palace strikers of the day were conspicuous by their absence. During those barren years only the hugely underrated Kevin Mabbutt (10 in 1982-83) and Andy Gray (10 in 1985-86) reached double figures in six seasons. The likes of Langley, Edwards, Brown, McCulloch, Wilkins, Evans (top scorer with seven in 1983-84 – all away from home) and Aylott delighted the fans with their skills – other teams' fans.

In the 1985 close season Steve Coppell signed a 22 year-old from Ten-Em-Bee (or Greenwich Borough depending on which argument you last heard) who had been rejected by Brighton and Millwall.

My first sight of Ian Wright was at a pre-season friendly against West Ham. Typical friendly fare – unlimited subs, bugger all team info, Frank McAvennie in midfield for the Hammers. Then late in the second half a stocky looking white midfielder trotted unannounced onto the pitch – "Hmm, Ian Wright looks useless," followed by a lithe young black striker "Andy Higginbottom eh? Make a note of him." As we all know Higginbottom went on to glory with Palace and England while ...

Coppell had a solid formation for the season and for the first time for many a year, the fans actually saw something that Crystal Palace could actually call a football team. Gray and Barber looked the business up front and scored a hatful of goals (well, they did by Palace standards). Wright made his full debut against Charlton in the league cup without showing any real promise. His big moment came as a late substitute against Oldham, popping up with an even later winner, a near post header from an impossible angle, and injuring himself with the ferocity of his celebration. He repeated his super sub act against Blackburn in the next home game and we became aware of the impact a fresh Ian Wright could have on tiring defences. A new hero was born and although he finished with what now seems the miserably low total of nine goals from 32 appearances (16 as substitute) he was a fixture in the Palace team. His willingness to chase any hopeful punt and reach it with his pace meant he fitted perfectly into a side with our midfield's capabilities.

The following season (1986-87) saw Ian initially partnered by Barber and then Gray, but neither seemed to offer long term hope of an effective striking force. So, in November, Steve finally found his man in Leicester's reserves. Mark Bright had come from Port Vale to replace some bloke called Lineker (who I believe made it big in Japan). Steve sold Palace to Mark on two counts. First he wouldn't cop racial abuse from Palace fans (unlike some of the less liberal minded Leicester supporters) and secondly because we had a young striker who was going to be big news. On his own admission, Bright took a look and liked what he saw, which came as no surprise to Coppell who believed Bright was intelligent enough not to be fooled. At £75,000 this was Steve's best transfer deal, although Bright's pelvic complaint made insurance a problem and meant that the striker was a bigger gamble than many appreciated.

Richard Saker/Allsport

In their first game together Bright and Wright scored. They were the business, although neither set the world alight initially (17 goals between them), the partnership grew and they became firm friends. Mark sought perfection from his partner and from the start his encouragement or admonition of Ian on the pitch was vital. Wright recalled in his video (tucked on every Palace shelf unwatched waiting for his departure from Arsenal) that at bad moments he would hear Mark saying: "Come on, keep going, you'll get something."

It is probably fair to say that without Mark Ian would have become one of the good strikers who never quite made it at the top grade.

The next two seasons culminating in promotion saw Bright 'n' Wright run roughshod over second division defences. No matter how badly Palace played – and both our midfield and defence were capable of plumbing the depths – we always had a chance because of the those two up front. Remember the look of terror on the defenders' faces as they came after them again. Walsall, Birmingham, Plymouth they'd virtually capitulate before the kick off. In those days Mark was more valuable to the team given the style of play and it was probably his injury sustained in a small contretemps with Eric Nixon at Maine Road (allied to Gray's sojourn at Villa Park) that cost us the championship in 1988.

It seemed to everyone outside the club (and to many Palace fans) that Wright was the star of the show. They underrated Bright's contribution while all the attention was focussed on this new young firebrand. While it is fair to say that Ian scored more spectacular goals, Mark occasionally weighed in with a beauty. If you were to examine the goals they scored you almost certainly find Mark laid on as many for Ian, if not more. Both were excellent players in their own right and proved it when the partnership was broken.

The first division brought new challenges and Ian took to it like a duck to water while it looked as if Mark might be out of his depth. But a couple of goals at Leicester in the league cup and at home to Millwall broke the drought and they were off again. While the rest of the team had to adapt pretty quickly and needed strengthening with the incoming Martyn and Thorn, our strikers gave us cause to believe no game was out of reach. Mark with a little help from Pembo gave me my greatest moment as a Palace supporter with the equaliser in the F.A. Cup semi at Villa Park while Ian's explosion from the bench in the final after returning from a fractured leg has gone into Wembley folklore.

The following year (1990-91) was our best year although something had changed. Ian no longer chased everything that moved, be it ball, opponent or referee. He seemed reserved and maybe fame and an England cap had gone to his head, I think it might have been then that he decided to leave, although the race row may have been the last straw. When he left for Arsenal, I could not but wonder what might have happened had we reached Europe, either by hanging on for another seven minutes in the Cup Final or by UEFA maintaining their ban on Liverpool.

It was ironic that he should score his last goal, as he did the first against Oldham, although not nearly as ironic as the goal which relegated us. After his Coca Cola Cup antics, I don't care anymore.

Mark soldiered on with a succession of partners and a barren run of 18 games without a goal after he'd scored 13 in 15 matches. His departure did not make sense because like many people, I'm sure Chris Armstrong would have benefited hugely from his presence while the 15 guaranteed goals Bright would have given us would definitely have kept us up.

Both have gone on to be just as successful with other clubs although they play for teams packed with talent, which Palace sides often did not possess. Although they've proved themselves individually, I believe neither would have been as successful without the other. I count myself lucky to have seen them play for Palace. To have one outstanding striker is great, to have two was heaven.

Russell Cheyne/Allsport

Colorsport

Colorsport

Three heroes of the early 90s: (left) Phil Barber, (centre) Geoff Thomas, (right) John Salako

he'd earned by lashing out at Sheffield Wednesday's Lawrie Madden. Cambridge were bidding to become the first fourth division club ever to reach the F.A. Cup semi finals and there was no reason to believe they were not capable of further progress, especially against a notoriously inconsistent Palace. In a tense and uneven encounter we endured a couple of hairy moments but eventually a bobbly old goal by Thomas secured victory.

Almost by accident, Palace were through to the semis. What better way to win a cup? Avoid the big clubs and headline making performances and let everybody wonder how on earth you'd got there unnoticed.

Of course, the Palace haters could point to an unbelievable amount of Cup luck – the toughest team we'd played was Pompey languishing in the nether reaches of division two. Such good fortune couldn't last and sure enough it didn't. Liverpool despatched QPR in their quarter final replay at Anfield and we prepared for a big day out at Villa Park.

We were without Wright once more because an innocuous, but clumsy, tackle by Paul Blades of Derby had fractured his leg again. He was stretchered off with most of us assuming that our Wembley dreams had gone to casualty with him.

The other, lesser, avenue to the twin towers was closed by Chelsea in the Southern Area Final of the Full Members' Cup, now sponsored by Zenith Data Systems. In the league we bobbed along, still suffering the occasional trauma such as a 4-0 defeat at Everton after which we were branded by former Liverpool defender Tommy Smith as "the worst team ever to play in the first division". It was certainly a dreadful performance, but what Smith did not take into account was that Palace were equally capable of moments of sheer brilliance. In the week prior to the semi final we travelled to the Den to nail the coffin lid shut on Millwall's relegation season. We played brilliantly and a flying header by Andy Gray sealed a 2-1 win against the dispirited Lions. In midweek, we faced Norwich where O'Reilly who'd had a goal against Millwall disallowed, stuck one in his own net.

As a reminder of where the neutral sympathies lay for Sunday, April 8, the Norwich fans joined in with the Palace chants of *No Scouse at Wembley.* But finding people who genuinely believed it would happen was rather more difficult. The *Guardian's* David Lacey described Palace not as minnows but as "mincemeat". Like many other sports writers, he forgot the errors made in writing off Wimbledon before the 1988 F.A. Cup Final against Liverpool.

But were Palace really capable of an upset? In our heart of hearts, most of us doubted it, the defence would not be able to soak up the inevitable punishment to which Liverpool would subject it and anyway the Reds were infallible.

What happened on that bright but chilly Sunday afternoon finally helped to put Palace in football's history books. A club that, with occasional exception, had been ignored for most of its existence suddenly became the most famous in the land for a couple of glorious days.

Everyone wanted to know us, the streets of London were paved with red and blue and we floated on air. Liverpool 3 Palace 4 is one of the most famous F.A. Cup results ever, a moment we had waited for all our lives. It is still impossible to adequately describe the emotion of the occasion, although that won't stop the 15,000 nut cases who were there from trying if you so much as mention it in passing.

While waiting for a golden conclusion to a fabulously enjoyable and exciting season, Palace picked up the points they needed to ensure survival. We drew with Arsenal at home the week after Villa Park with a blistering equaliser by Gray while Garry Thompson, who had been signed as striking cover for Wright, got one of the goals that beat relegated Charlton in our home game. But Palace hadn't become a perfect side over night as the 3-0 thrashing by Chelsea, in which O'Reilly was sent off for two chopping tackles on Gordon Durie, illustrated. Nevertheless we survived comfortably and turned our minds to applications for Final tickets – a task complicated by a tiny allocation of just 14,000 and the numerous permutations of club members, lifeline members and season ticket holders who wanted them.

The last match of the season was at home to Man City who, for obvious reasons, wanted a Palace victory at Wembley almost as much as we did. The match was played in a party atmosphere in which City supporters descended on south London dressed as the Blues Brothers in black suits and ties, white shirts and shades. Unlike the Birmingham fans of a year before they were good natured and the Palace fans joined them after the match in a massive singalong incorporating such classics as *Glad All Over, Blue Moon, You're the pride of Manchester, We beat United 5-1* and *You're Gonna Win the Cup*.

On a brown pitch – the grass had been treated for the summer but had died off because of exceptionally hot weather – Andy Gray hit a free kick from fully 40 yards to give us the lead and Pardew made it 2-0 within five minutes. But the referee, sensing the amazing atmosphere, decided a draw might be nice and so gave City a dubious penalty and allowed a handball by Niall Quinn to go unnoticed for an equaliser. It prevented us reaching our highest ever league placing but, what the hell.

Cup Final day passed in a dream. The scenes at the Duke of York at Victoria, where police closed a side road full of singing, dancing and drinking fans were beautiful to eyes accustomed to fences and grey second division terraces.

Walking up Wembley way, United supporters chanting *what's it like to see a crowd?* were greeted with choruses of *you lost to City 5-1*. Yet the atmosphere was friendly. Although our support was heavily outnumbered it was already apparent that Wembley was ours. Most supporters will tell you that the moment the teams came out of the tunnel, although it still had a dreamlike quality, was the first time that everybody truly began to believe what was happening to us. It had to be a sunny day at Wembley and it had to be Ian Wright's day, literally bouncing off the bench to put us within seven minutes of ecstasy.

Few of us had bargained for spending Saturday night anywhere else other than in the pubs of south London. Camped in the car park at Selhurst queueing for replay tickets was not an option that had been considered. At least our consolation for United's late, late equaliser and a night under the stars was another trip to Wembley.

During the week, Palace seemed to become more bullish in their predictions of victory but the replay was a dreadful let down. United changed their goalkeeper, omitting the out of sorts Jim Leighton for the on-loan Les Sealey. It was not an act of great sportsmanship either for their unlucky keeper or towards Palace, but they got away it. But that is just one excuse because in the end we should have beaten United. Had we repeated our performance of the previous Saturday we would almost certainly have done so. Instead the game featured a number of unsavoury incidents and a single breakthrough by Lee Martin which took the Cup to Manchester. We should have had a penalty when Thomas was tripped in the area by Brian McClair, we had one or two half chances, but in the end we lost. As United's car horns sounded in celebration, we tried to come to terms with the fact that it was over and there would not be another chance. We'd played United four times that season and lost once, in the one that mattered. We were actually better than them, we finished higher in the league and, in Wright, Bright, Gray, Thomas, Thorn and Martyn, had better players than they, for all their millions, could offer. But we lost and it still hurts.

The press made great play of the sporadic violence and bickering that marred the replay, tarnishing England's showpiece occasion. An early challenge by Bright on Sealey was singled out although there were others. The statistics showed that the foul count was exactly even and United were equally culpable. It takes two to tango, but one to make a scapegoat.

In the close season, the arguments raged. Some letters to the *Croydon Advertiser* expressed shame and sadness at the Palace performance while others expressed their pride and outrage at the criticism.

Palace prepared for the new season with a pre-season trip to Italy where they met Fiorentina and Sampdoria in a four team tournament. The team was strengthened by the acquisition of Glyn Hodges from Watford for £400,000 and Wimbledon's gigantic central defender Eric Young who, at 29, seemed a little over-priced at £850,000. The season began with Palace fans having to beg steal or borrow identity cards to breach Luton Town's away fans ban. The hundreds inside illustrated just how much of farce the scheme, politically motivated by the Hatters' chairman David Evans, really was. Young marked his debut with a goal but we had to settle for a point.

Despite Wembley, there were few pundits prepared to predict any more than a slight improvement on our first league season. But Coppell had assembled a powerful defensive unit in which he replaced John Pemberton, sold to Sheffield United, with Charlton's £450,000 John Humphrey. This didn't go down at all well with most supporters, who were loyal to Pemberton despite his often wildly erratic football. He was an endearing character and with the memory of his surge down the Villa Park flank still fresh in our minds, Humphrey, a quieter character but defensively more solid, had a hard act to follow. He was also considered to be a Charlton man. Lennie Lawrence's reluctance to sell him and stories of Humphrey's lack of desire to come to Palace didn't help. His form at the start was not impressive and the fans, aware that he didn't like us took a long time to take to him. Nevertheless with Young and Thorn resuming the solid partnership they'd formed at Wimbledon and Richard Shaw comfortably settled at left back, Palace had a unit comparable to any in the league. Martyn was being tipped for international honours as were Gray and Thomas in midfield while Wright and Bright were increasingly potent up front. As a bonus, Palace finally had John Salako, energised by Villa Park and Wembley, performing to his true potential.

The first home game was a battle royal with Chelsea in which Gray and the Blues' new £1.7 million signing Dennis Wise had a tiff and were banished to the dressing rooms. By that time we were winning with a typically blasted Gray penalty. His technique was to try to put a hole in the back of the net and if necessary the goalkeeper too.

In the second half Wright turned Erland Johnsen inside out to make it 2-0 before Tony Dorigo reduced the arrears. It was our best ever start to a first division season, unbeaten for 10 games. It wasn't perfect, there were laboured victories over Sheffield United and Southampton and a lucky home draw with Forest, but balancing that were such sparkling performances as the 3-0 victory at Carrow Road on a hot afternoon when Norwich were taken to the cleaners.

For stats freaks we also recorded the landmark of 1,000 league victories when we beat Derby 2-0 at the Baseball Ground on September 29. We hovered around fourth place and as the season progressed we even began to think quietly in terms of the championship. But often it was sheer determination that carried us through and it became noticeable that we never pasted anyone. Scorelines of 1-0 and 2-1 became the order of the day (the exception was a 4-3 extravaganza against Wimbledon) and although there was pleasure to be gained through riding high in the table some of the fun had gone. Indeed one newspaper complained that the Palace of old would not have beaten Manchester City at Maine Road in such clinical fashion as this one. We'd lost some of our endearing zaniness. But we feared no-one, not even the leaders Arsenal, who were fortunate to escape with a point, from a 0-0 draw, particularly when Salako had a goal ruled out on a marginal offside decision, or their closest challengers Liverpool.

By December we were in third place and just after Christmas we beat the Scousers in a televised clash at Selhurst Park, confirming that the Villa Park victory was no fluke. Unfortunately our next game at Aston Villa on a day of torrential rain ended in defeat. We would have lost even had the most ludicrously offside goal in history by David Platt been disallowed. It set us back just when talk of a championship challenge was growing in authority. The winter months brought something of a decline and we made a disappointingly early F.A. Cup exit after failing to beat Forest in another live TV match at home. The tie turned into a saga not least because of the bad weather which forced three postponements. We had taken the tie to a third game with a Salako lob from the half way line over the stranded Mark Crossley but collapsed in the third match, 3-0.

Our cup interest was restricted to the Zenith Cup where we overcame Bristol Rovers, Brighton and Luton to set up a Southern Area Final with Norwich.

After a lean spell we regained form and confidence, although we lacked the fluency of the early part of the season, and there was a brilliant victory at Leeds with a last minute Salako goal which put some daylight between us and the Elland Road club who were hot on our heels for a UEFA Cup place.

Ian Wright finally got the international recognition his club performances deserved with a first cap in the friendly against Cameroon at Wembley. One could argue with some justification that he merited a place sooner but, once again, being at Palace probably didn't help his cause. It was a bitterly cold night but a large and vociferous following of Palace fans made the effort to get to Wembley to support him. As the season progressed Palace introduced a couple of younger players into the side, but the unhappy Hodges departed to struggling Sheffield United where, after a loan spell the home fans arranged a fund to help pay for him.

Gareth Southgate and Simon Osborn were the first members of an outstanding youth team to come knocking on the first team door. Southgate played in the first leg of the Zenith Southern Area Final at Norwich, where we earned a 1-1 draw, and acquitted himself well. We finished the job in the return with goals by Wright and Bright while Alan Pardew, relived his semi final glory of a year before with arguably his best performance for Palace.

After the ticket restrictions for the F.A. Cup Final, seats at Wembley for the Zenith were available in abundance. Many took the opportunity to take their family and friends and Palace boasted support in excess of 35,000 compared to around 15,000 for opponents Everton. Despite the best efforts of Sky TV to inject some glamour and importance

"Both teams face a difficult season so a point each to start with was probably a satisfactory result."

ITN COMMENTATOR AFTER THE FIRST GAME OF THE SEASON, AUGUST 1990 – WE FINISHED THIRD.

Geoff shows the sheep shaggers

Geoff Thomas' England B debut – Wales v England at Vetch Field Swansea Tuesday, February 5, 1991

A bollock freezing night and that unsmiling Scottish face drove his Merc into the Swansea City car park almost over my toes. Thoughts of Villa Park coursed through my body, instant anti-freeze. What is it about Mr Dalglish? What is it about his team that makes me want to tap on his window and sing: "Who put the ball in the Scousers' net ...? Half of Crystal Palace!"

The game. Steve Bull really does bring his own personal fan club. Hundreds of them shouting "sheep, sheep, sheep shaggers" on the North Bank. Good for them.

A tight game, unremarkable save for Gary Mabbutt's girth, a Mark Walters' turn, Paul Davis' 25-yard free kick winner and the appearance of one Geoff Thomas.

I can hardly contain myself as the tall figure settles into the midfield as a second half substitute. "Come on Geoffrey Thomas," I roar, the quiet of the North Bank amplifying my call.

"When Geoff goes up to get his losers' medal," croons Dr Alan Watkins beside me. Honestly, these university lecturers might have letters before and after their names but they don't know anything about football if they like Man United.

Geoff runs up and down a bit before he first touches the ball. Nothing special, nothing fancy. "Well in, Geoffrey Thomas," I encourage at 150 decibels.

"Must be his dad," says some clever cloggs to appreciative sniggers. Perhaps they had been studying my CPFC/Brazil ski-hat.

A corner. Geoff is on the edge of the box. The header out is poor and Geoff cocks his lethal left foot ready to hammer it in. He swings and connects with air ...

"Aaaarrrgghhh ..." from Watkins and the strange faces around me, as they stare pitifully at my hat. I'm rooted to the spot, mortified while they patronise and intimidate me,

"Just giving the Taffs a chance," I bleat unconvincingly and, changing the subject, "coming for a pint in the Builders after?"

Matthew Simmonds

EVERTON are set to turn League form upside down and claim the Zenith Data Systems Cup at Wembley on Sunday... but it's going to be close!

Based on performances in the competition so far this season the two squads are evenly matched with the Merseyside outfit just having the edge.

But it's the superior goal power of the 'Toffees' that will see them win the day against Steve Coppell's high-flying 'Eagles'.

into the game and the desire of Palace fans to actually see their team land a trophy, there was no disguising the fact that this was a second rate competition. The match itself was at times unwatchable, at times brutal and just occasionally brilliant. The best bits came in the second half when, after Thomas gave us the lead with a death defying header and Everton's Polish winger Warszycha made the most of a fortuitous bounce to reply, Martyn saved us with a couple of great saves. In the first half of extra time, Wright outstripped the Everton defence from a big kick by the keeper to drive past Southall and in the second period, Salako headed the third and Wright made absolutely certain with a delicious first time finish which left a dejected Southall standing. Soon after, the keeper was sitting. Much was made of his one man protest, but whether this was aimed at Palace or at the incompetence of his team-mates only he knows. And so Geoff Thomas, named Man of the Match, collected Palace's "first major trophy," although many would argue that the second and third division championships were of far greater significance. Nevertheless it was a good day out. It gave us another trip to Wembley, something we would have sold our souls for five years earlier, and a little consolation for the F.A. Cup Final defeat.

In the league, we chased Liverpool and Arsenal to the tape. Our championship hopes, slim as they were, had been blown away in January and February but we were in the hunt for a European place until the very end of the season when reports were filed that there was a possibility that UEFA might decide on an early end to Liverpool's three year ban from the continent following the carnage at Hysel.

Had UEFA decided not to lift the ban, Palace would have qualified in third place. Now we had to get second spot with a side that had picked up one or two injuries and was tiring. The end came ironically at Anfield where a patched up team missing Gray, Young, Thorn and Bright played superbly but were robbed by an Ian Rush goal which followed a blatant foul, an offside header by John Barnes and a criminally unjust own goal by McGoldrick, who'd been quite brilliant in an unfamiliar sweeping role.

And so we missed out on Europe. It wasn't Liverpool's reinstatement which was annoying so much as the incompetence of the Football Association. They made no attempt to represent Palace's interests in the matter, leaving us high and dry at the end of a campaign in which the club had believed there would be the prospect of European football. The F.A. could and should have asked for special dispensation for Palace. Germany was a reunited country yet two East German clubs were still allowed to enter the UEFA Cup. It should not have been beyond the wit of this country's football administrators to call for a preliminary match between Palace and the fourth East German side Chemie Halle, who were not even considered good enough to merit a place in the following season's Bundesliga. The F.A. has always been more concerned about the interests of the big clubs than the likes of Crystal Palace. They let us down very badly. Coppell called then "chocolate soldiers", the supporters had harsher terms at their disposal. The sad thing was that the F.A. seemed genuinely unaware of a problem so busy were they patting themselves on the back for getting Liverpool reinstated.

An Ian Wright hat-trick devastated Wimbledon in our final away match and his second goal was scored from just outside the centre circle. It was Wimbledon's last match at Plough Lane, their owner, Lebanese businessman Sam Hammam, announced that the Dons would become Palace's new tenants at Selhurst Park to mild protests from the sparse home support and weary disinterest from the visitors.

We finished the season with a 3-0 drubbing of Man United at Selhurst, a result tempered by the appearance of £15 million worth of second rate reserves as United rested their players for the Cup Winners' Cup Final against Barcelona later that the week.

During the summer of 1991, many Palace supporters felt that, having just finished third, we were in a position to attract a couple of top players to the club. However two third division players, Bradford's Lee Sinnott and Chris Coleman from Swansea, were the only imports. Aside from coach Ian Branfoot, who left to take up the manager's post at Southampton, two popular players also moved on. Phil Barber, the last survivor of the pre-Coppell days, and Garry Thompson, who moved to Millwall and QPR respectively.

John Salako made his England debut on the summer tour of Australia and caught the eye. He was hailed as the best player of what most people regarded as an unnecessary and unsuccessful tour. Geoff Thomas and Ian Wright also added to their collection of caps, although both embarrassed themselves with bad misses.

The season had something of a false start. Palace's first two games against Leeds and Spurs were postponed, due to unfinished building work at Selhurst and Tottenham's Cup Winners Cup preliminary round excursion to Stockerau. We eventually began the season with a defeat at Man City, where two appalling penalty decisions denied us a winning start. Our first home game, against new tenants Wimbledon, was the most dramatic match of what was to become in purely footballing terms a dull season. Soon after John Fashanu had put the Dons ahead, Richard Shaw was carried off following a bad tackle by the big forward. Then Martyn received a red card for upending Robbie Earle having rushed way out of his goal towards the left wing. Salako took over in goal to outstanding effect and Palace's ten men battled their way into a 3-1 lead helped by Wimbledon having Terry Phelan and Vaughan Ryan dismissed. Wimbledon then hit the post, their first shot anywhere near the target since Martyn's dismissal, before reducing the deficit to 2-3. Only world class, one-handed save by Salako, of which Martyn himself would have been proud, ensured victory. After a scrappy victory at home to Sheffield United, we won 1-0 at Villa Park with an early Wright goal. It was a performance that had Palace fans dreaming of the championship, and not without justification. It was our first game in a new Brazilian style strip (apparently Bright and Wright's idea) and, so good was our football that it could have easily have been produced by the mighty South Americans themselves. Further confirmation of Palace's potential came with a 2-2 draw at Everton, despite the sending off of the influential Thorn. But from there, it all went wrong.

A Channel 4 television programme, *Critical Eye - Great Britain United*, broadcast on September 12, reflected attitudes towards black footballers. Ron Noades was one of a number of Palace people interviewed. His observations on black players included: "I don't think too many can read the game ... when it's [the ball] behind them it's chaos ... when you're getting into mid-winter in England, you need a few hard white men to carry the artistic black players through ..."

Noades' remarks caused an unholy row, with threats of reports to the race relations board and calls for the black players in the Palace team to refuse to play. Two days later, we lost 4-1 at home to Arsenal. The Palace players, with the exception of Andy Gray, were barely interested and it was later rumoured that some had to be coaxed by Coppell before they would take the field at all.

The poisonous atmosphere pervaded the terraces, Palace fans created little noise, a silence which showed that they were as appalled as the players at the chairman's remarks. It was a terrible moment for the unfortunate Perry Suckling to return to the Palace goal, in place of the suspended Martyn. Arsenal scored four unopposed goals and Palace's championship dream died on the spot.

"Palace are the sort of team whose ties light up in the dark, 'aura' is not a word one would associate with their football."

David Lacey of the Guardian on Coventry Manager Terry Butcher's Belief That There is Something Special About Palace

The following Tuesday, we suffered another home reverse, 3-2 to struggling West Ham with a performance that was just as half hearted, but then we won by the same scoreline at Oldham the following Saturday as things appeared to be returning to an even keel. Wright ran half the length of the pitch to score a memorable goal. Although the supporters didn't know it, we'd seen his last appearance for Palace.

Wright's £2.5 million transfer hit the papers the next day and on Monday, September 23, he joined Arsenal. Although he stated that his reason for signing for the Gunners was because they could offer him European football, many people thought it was rather more than co-incidence that he decided to leave Palace within two weeks of Noades' comments. This opinion was further strengthened when it transpired that he was ineligible to play in Europe (Arsenal were in fact eliminated by Benfica before he could get a game).

The bad press that had stalked the club since the Cup Final reared up again again as the papers speculated about who was going to be next out the door at Selhurst. These really were bad times for Palace fans. However with £2.5 million to spend on a replacement, we were just as concerned about who we should buy. Southampton's Alan Shearer and Brian Deane of Sheffield United were apparently top of the Palace wanted list, but it transpired that neither could be prised from their clubs. The discovery that both were priced in excess of £3 million when they were, at the time, inferior to Wright, increased our dismay. There was little doubt then as there is little doubt now that we should have realised far more from the sale of the greatest asset in English football. Whatever the reason for his departure it was bad business by Palace.

With neither Shearer nor Deane available, we moved for a surprise third choice, Sunderland's highly-rated Marco Gabbiadini, who was happy to make the long trip south for £1.8 million, Palace's most expensive signing ever.

Gabbiadini's debut, in the re-arranged game against Leeds on October 1, was overshadowed by a disastrous injury to John Salako.

On his home debut for England against Germany, two weeks earlier, Salako had been substituted after crashing his knee onto the goal post. In the Leeds game, he fell awkwardly after an innocuous aerial challenge with Mel Sterland. His cruciate ligaments suffered horrific damage and doubts were aired as to whether he would ever play again. It was devastating. We had lost two England strikers within two weeks, but it was an even bigger blow for the player, who had emerged as a leading candidate for a place in the squad going to the European Championships in Sweden. In the final minutes of the game, Gabbiadini earned the free kick from which Bright headed home to wreck Leeds' unbeaten record.

Gabbiadini's first league goal came in the 2-1 win at Coventry, a game that also marked the debut of former Charlton midfielder Paul Mortimer, a £500,000 replacement from Aston Villa for the sidelined Salako. After a non-descript goalless draw with Chelsea, Gabbiadini played his best game in an Eagles shirt in a thoroughly deserved 2-1 victory at Anfield. Not only was this our first ever win at Liverpool, but it served to finally lay the ghost of September 12, 1989. The 3,000 travelling fans celebrated as only Palace fans know how - non-stop singing and hundreds of balloons in the new Brazil colours of gold, green and blue.

A Thomas goal then gave us the points at home to Southampton and in spite of all our difficulties we had risen to fifth place. This in no way meant that everything in the garden was rosy. Palace were slaughtered 5-1 at Forest and a depressed Coppell offered Noades his resignation after the game, which was refused out of hand. But it was all downhill from there. We scored more than one goal in only five of the remaining 27 games, two of which were against Norwich (3-3 and 3-4, on Leap Year Day)

After an early exit from the F.A. Cup at the hands of Leicester, where Young was sent off for using an elbow, we had two awful 1-1 draws with Man City and Leeds. Another bombshell was on the way … Gabbiadini was sold to Derby for £600,000 less than we'd paid for him. In his 15 League games he'd scored just five goals and been called "incredibly average" by assistant manager, Alan Smith. Coppell, meanwhile, admitted that he had not seen him play before his big money move to Selhurst. The fans generally gave Gabbiadini their backing, willing him to be brilliant. Although he had not performed well, many felt for him and realised that he didn't fit into the Palace system. It was not as if replacing Wright would have been an easy task in any case.

David Whyte who, like Wright, was signed from Greenwich Borough, was drafted in for the home game against Coventry but it was Andy Gray, who grabbed the headlines after missing a penalty and then being substituted to a chorus of boos from large sections of the Palace crowd (and cheers from others), who thought he might have missed it deliberately. Gray had been in superb form earlier in the season and deservedly won his first England cap against Poland. But he had been unfairly substituted at half time by Graham Taylor and his form seemed to desert him. At the same time he allegedly refused to train after a bust up in which he said he would not have signed a new contract if he'd known that Palace were going to sell Wright. Gray was placed on the transfer list and left to rot in the reserves, until Spurs came in for him, ending his third spell at Palace.

Whyte made headlines for the right reasons at Chelsea a week later. He produced one of the finest individual performances by a Palace player in recent seasons, tormenting many people's choice for England Paul Elliott so much that he was hailed as the new "Messiah". Geoff Thomas' season however was undoubtedly affected by an embarrassing miss for England against France at Wembley. He was unfairly ridiculed by certain sections of the media and seemed affected.

While everything the first team did seemed to turn to dust, the youth team reached the F.A. Youth Cup final for the first time since 1978. But they eventually went down 6-3 on aggregate to a strong Manchester United side which included Ryan Giggs. However some of our other young players such as Whyte, Southgate, Osborn, Simon Rodger, Dean Gordon and Jamie Moralee, all of whom made their league debuts during the season, gave Palace fans reason to believe that the future was bright. And there was another international to add to the growing list when, towards the end of the season, Martyn made his full debut against the CIS.

Mark Bright, the subject of speculation linking him with Chelsea and QPR among others, finished top goalscorer with 17 league goals despite playing alongside seven different partners.

The final position of tenth was disappointing after the successes of the previous two years and it was clear from letters to the *Croydon Advertiser* that Palace fans felt that a new partner for Bright and a change from the long ball system was needed to turn things around. The most disturbing thing was that Palace had become boring. For the first time there was open dissent aimed at Steve Coppell from sections of the support. His blinkered tactics and unnecessarily negative approach made watching Palace a chore. Many supporters claimed they only attended because of some misguided notion of loyalty. With Noades charging top whack for the pleasure, the most common complaint was that Crystal Palace did not provide value for money in what has been tagged "the season of boredom". Palace in 1991-92 finished in an unaccustomed mid-table position and played drab football yet we'd sold our most famous player, seen several players gain international honours, become embroiled in a high profile national debate about racism in football, reached the F.A. Youth Cup Final and made a record signing and sold him for two thirds of the price after just 15 games. That's Palace when they're boring!

As part of their pre-season preparations, Palace became the first team to tour South Africa since the lifting of the sporting ban imposed in protest against apartheid. The visit was taken very much with goodwill in mind and the players held coaching sessions with local youngsters. Palace played two matches beating Kaiser Chiefs 3-2 in the first and then going down 2-1 to Orlando Pirates. Coppell later said in an article for the *Guardian* that the tour had been financially enticing but had wreaked havoc with his pre-season plans because of injuries which had been picked up.

Another disruptive influence was the on-off Geoff Thomas saga with Arsenal appearing as favourites to win the £3 million race for the midfielder's signature, then being replaced by Blackburn. With Jack Walker's millions backing any move he saw fit, Kenny Dalglish looked all set to pay the figure Palace wanted. Ironically, it was against Blackburn that Palace started the season. Thomas still hadn't signed and appeared in red and blue stripes rather than blue and white halves. He was non-existent throughout. The same could not be said of Alan Shearer who scored twice after Palace had forged ahead through Bright and then Southgate. Right at the death Osborn saved a point with a header. The other bonus for Palace was the return of Salako after his long term injury although many fans were not impressed that he was being hailed as "like having a new player". The general feeling was that Palace should have bought new talent during the summer but, aside from the £250,000 acquisition of Darren Patterson from Wigan as cover for the already ample number of central defenders at Selhurst, Coppell showed no interest in strengthening the squad.

Most commentators predicted another mid-table finish for Palace although there was growing pessimism among the fans. We travelled to Oldham with Thomas' move finally settled. He wasn't going. Most were secretly pleased although couldn't resist the cruel suggestion that Blackburn's interest cooled after they'd seen him play. We

Cut-price Marco on his way

MICHAEL HART reports on a £600,000 los

MARCO GABBIADINI is poised to join Derby County for a fee of about £1.2 million — £600,000 less than Crystal Palace paid for him only four months ago.

manager Steve Cop- record £1.8

Gabbiadini agreeing terms with the Second Division club, who are still hopeful of clinching a promotion place this season.

Ideally Cox would like

Coppell had no one to fill void left by Wri England's John Salal would have been a central att

Sixteen things never heard at Palace matches

1) Sinnott kills the ball instantly
2) McGoldrick keeps his feet despite Stuart Pearce's scything tackle
3) And the referee gives Eric Young the benefit of the doubt
4) The crowd are baying for Mortimer to come on
5) Williams milks the applause as he celebrates his hat-trick
6) Old pals Gray and Thomas help each other to their feet after another titanic but fair collision
7) Osborn delayed just long enough before releasing Armstrong with a pass of slide-rule precision
8) The Palace goal followed a mazy run from the back by Shaw followed by an inch perfect cross
9) Liverpool are bemused by Palace's repertoire of free-kicks
10) Steve Coppell fields an unchanged side for the fifth successive match
11) Cool as a cucumber Thomas strokes home the penalty
12) Thorn resists the temptation to bring the forward down
13) Bould/Adams/Keown is penalised for climbing on Armstrong
14) With the defence expecting a lob onto Young's head, Thorn fools them by releasing Humphrey into the vacant space on the right wing
15) Palace's possession football frustrates Forest who seem unable to keep the ball for more than a few seconds
16) Coppell has realised that despite their height and experience Arsenal's/Everton's/Shrewsbury's central defenders are vulnerable to the high ball

Tony Humphreys

Marco Gabbiadini

Neil Everitt

shared the points with Oldham, Spurs and Sheffield Wednesday and then lost at home to Norwich pinning us down the table in 18th place. *The Sunday Times* said: "If it was value for money you were after, the Sainsbury's adjacent to Selhurst Park held infinitely more appeal."

Palace now had a new £1 million striker. After only a handful of games for Millwall Chris Armstrong had made sufficient impact to prise open the Palace wallet. His first game was in a heartbreaking last minute defeat at Old Trafford. We'd been genuinely unlucky and we took our good performance into the first 20 minutes at Villa Park before collapsing in the most astonishing manner. Palace were suddenly on the rocks.

Without a win in seven games there was more bad news when another hero departed for pastures new. Mark Bright moved to Hillsborough with Paul Williams coming south in part exchange. The Bright/Armstrong partnership had lasted just two matches. Williams had an excellent reputation as a quality footballer but was hardly a prolific scorer. Was this how Palace intended to survive, sell the one player guaranteed to get a notoriously shot-shy team goals.

At least at home to Oldham we had a great chance to collect our first three points of the season. Armstrong and Williams hit it off immediately, but Coppell's negative approach handed the Latics the initiative and the lead in the first half. Having fought back Palace were too fragile to hold on. Our need of a win was desperate and it came at Everton where the home side were torn a part by a first half performance that had the visiting support pinching

Pitch battle, but not for the fans

I'd never been to Loftus Road before, but I can only assume that it is a last game tradition that the fans are allowed onto the pitch to salute the players in the directors' box at

It's the end of the season and the police are going to be bored on Saturday afternoons

the end of the game.

If this is the case wasn't it obvious that the away fans would want to do the same? So why weren't they prevented from doing so?

At the last game at Selhurst Park, the stewards taped off the ground to prevent invasion and promised the players would do a lap of honour (for what it was worth) and I don't remember seeing one fan on the pitch.

Obviously coloured tape would not prevent them if they wanted to get on but as a deterrent it worked well.

This is what the stewards at Loftus Road should have done to ensure away fans remained where they were and allowed the home fans to have their fun.

But having spent a whole season with the police keeping fans apart as if they were lepers, the last match was suddenly a chance to mingle whether they were in a celebratory mood or not. Inevitably a small incident occurred, and I mean small.

It involved no more than half a dozen guys at most and could have been handled by trained stewards. But no. Three days after the Los Angeles riots the local police saw the letters LAPD in front of their eyes and went charging in truncheons blazing. Within seconds one fan was on the ground with a policeman kicking him, Rodney King eat your heart out. But that wasn't all. Thirty seconds later the cavalry arrived with a speed that would have made General Custer green with envy.

I've never seen anything so over the top or frightening. Suddenly there was a riot on the pitch which only involved police.

I kept my eye on the policeman kicking the fan. I don't know whether he was a QPR or a Palace fan and I don't much care. If I could have got close enough I would have taken his number and reported him. It was unnecessary brutality.

I doubt the game I love will ever lose the bad reputation it has while the police behave the way they do.

The irony of this situation was that we were allowed to leave at the same time, no keeping us behind like naughty schoolchildren which is my pet hate at away games.

That was only because there was no police outside to supervise, they were all on the pitch. Among the fans that mingled outside the topic of conversation was what a cock-up the police had made of the situation inside.

I believe the solution to incidents such as this must be that stewards are properly appointed and trained (and paid). We don't need an expensive police force at every game when they could be out catching murderers or terrorists or unsuspecting motorists.

Sue Darnell

themselves in disbelief. Armstrong, Williams and Salako ran every which way dragging the Everton defence out of shape as we built a 2-0 lead which could easily have been doubled.

It wasn't just the result but the manner in which it was achieved that was so pleasing and the performance at home to Southampton the following Saturday promised more entertainment and more goals. Unfortunately Palace met the Saints at their most cynical. An outstanding performance by their keeper Tim Flowers allied to wayward finishing by Salako left us highly frustrated and in the last minute Ian Dowie bundled in an undeserved winner for Southampton.

Palace went to Coventry in atrocious conditions and earned a 2-2 draw in a surprisingly entertaining game. The attempts to play football and abandon the long hopeful hoof prompted compliments but we weren't getting the results. Man City, Ipswich, where Southgate missed a last minute penalty, Arsenal, where Wright scored his first winner against his old club, and Chelsea extended the barren spell. We were in deep trouble and only Forest, who were having a shocking season kept us off the bottom. *Match of the Day* took a look at the "other end of the table" in our clash at Selhurst Park where Palace repeated their past failings against Cloughie's team by failing to take their chances and then conceding a late equaliser. And there was more bad news when John Salako learned that his injury while training with the England squad was a recurrence of his earlier cruciate ligament problems. Palace would have to do without their star winger for the rest of the season.

"I wouldn't have signed a three-year contract had I known the club was willing to let Ian go."

ANDY GRAY, DAILY MIRROR, JANUARY 28, 1992

"He [Gray] probably doesn't like Marco Gabbiadini and Mark Bright.'

RON NOADES IN THE SAME STORY

Our record against Liverpool since the 9-0 humiliation of 1989 had been good but they paid us back in spades at the end of November to the tune of 5-0 and Palace were in such disarray that the chances of avoiding relegation seemed remote. We returned for a fourth round league cup match with a patched up side including debutants Bobby Bowry and George Ndah, who'd made a fleeting appearance as substitute in the league game and the patched up team gave a performance as brilliant as the previous Saturday's had been dreadful. Coleman gave the Eagles the lead and had Mike Marsh been properly punished for his professional foul on Ndah he would not have been on the field to take Liverpool's dubious penalty equaliser. Nevertheless pride was restored and the revival continued with our first home league win of the season with a slice of good fortune. Brian Deane's early header for Sheffield United appeared to have crossed the line but the referee waved play on and Palace eventually secured

Steve Morton/Allsport

One of a brilliant crop of young players around which Palace will build their future. Simon Rodger takes on Wimbledon's Lawrie Sanchez during our 2-0 victory at Christmas 1992

the points with a strike by Armstrong and a firecracker by Southgate. That was the first of five wins on the run which took us to 15th place just after Christmas. But injuries, bad luck, bad play and mystifying tactics brought us four straight league defeats and a cup exit at second division Hartlepool, who "giant killed" us with a dubious late penalty and then added insult to injury by setting a new record for failing to score in 11 league games immediately after.

Our last hope of glory was in the league cup. Immediately after we had been labelled "Hartle-fools" the kids who had done us proud by knocking out Liverpool in round four faced Chelsea. In sodden conditions, Palace took advantage of a silly mistake to slide into the lead and adapted to the puddles better even after Andy Townsend had equalised. George Ndah's first senior goal gave us the lead and another of "Coppell's Babes" Grant Watts, who watches Palace from the Holmesdale with his father, nipped in for number three.

In the semis we drew the short straw against Arsenal, a tall order for such an inexperienced team, and Steve Coppell brought further criticism raining down on him with his negative selection for the first leg at Selhurst. It backfired and the tie was all over as contest before half time. The second leg was a formality except for the antagonism between Wright and his former supporters after he kissed his Arsenal shirt in front of us. That finished him as far as Palace fans are concerned. Wright is no longer a Palace hero.

The thought that supporters would openly criticise Steve Coppell and even call for his resignation would have been unthinkable at any time before but as the team spluttered and coughed, an increasing body of opinion believed it was time to make a change. The fiasco at home to Tottenham when the very left footed Richard Shaw, playing at right back to incorporate Lee Sinnott on the other side, was ripped apart was a classic example of bad planning and organisation. Palace were rubbish and after pulling ourselves clear we had slipped back to 19th place.

Amazingly we then went to Blackburn and produced two brilliant goals, one by Armstrong and one by Rodger, his first goal for Palace, to secure three unexpected but nonetheless vital points. Aston Villa and Man United were battling for the championship but Villa didn't look too special when Bowry's shot from the edge of the box beat them at Selhurst the following Tuesday. After we'd been robbed of a deserved point at Hillsborough by a Danny Wilson goal from Martyn's poor clearance we picked up vital points with five draws and an excellent victory at fellow strugglers Sheffield United. The Palace support left Bramall Lane singing *staying up, staying up*. And surely we were. Although we were 18th, there was daylight between us and the four clubs below. We had a good defence, a number of decent young players and the irrepressible Armstrong knocking in the goals. It would surely be enough. But the seeds of our destruction were sown at Sheffield when Armstrong was sent off for dissent joining Young, suspended for an accumulation of points, on the sidelines. It meant we went into the Easter period without two of our most influential players.

The home match against QPR was unspeakable rubbish but we stole a point with an own goal by England full back David Bardsley, but on Good Friday, live on Sky TV, the heavens opened and so did our defence allowing Wimbledon a free afternoon in which to help themselves. Armstrong and Young returned for the Middlesbrough game where after 61 blank minutes Rodger's deflected free kick set us on our way to our biggest victory since promotion in 1989. We drew at Leeds while Oldham, Forest and Middlesbrough faltered. We were now at the stage where we were virtually uncatchable. Although we lost to Man United it seemed that one more win would do it. Faltering Ipswich had just secured their own safety with a victory over local rivals Norwich but they were torn apart by a stylish and powerful Palace performance. The players did a lap of honour at the conclusion of our home season. We had two away games to come and were eight points clear of Oldham who had three games left but a superior goal difference. One more win would see Palace safe but if Oldham couldn't get three

Allsport

Chrissie Armstrong, a player many feel will eventually become better than Ian Wright

ATALANTA
Home ground: Comunale stadium, Bergamo (capacity: 42,000).
Position last season: eleventh.
A team with no big names, Atalanta have established themselves as a solid mid-table side, staying safely in Serie A since 1988, after 20 years spent yo-yoing between the top two divisions.
British equivalent: dull but deadly Crystal Palace.

Even *Radio Times* had a go at boring Palace. This is from the magazine's guide to Channel 4's Italian Football coverage.

Neil Everitt

A sickening end at Highbury. The Palace bench watch helpless as our Premier League life ebbs away. From left: Simon Osborn, physio Dave West, coach Steve Harrison, assistant manager Alan Smith, John Salako, kit manager Spike Hill, Andy Woodman, coach Wally Downes and Steve Coppell.

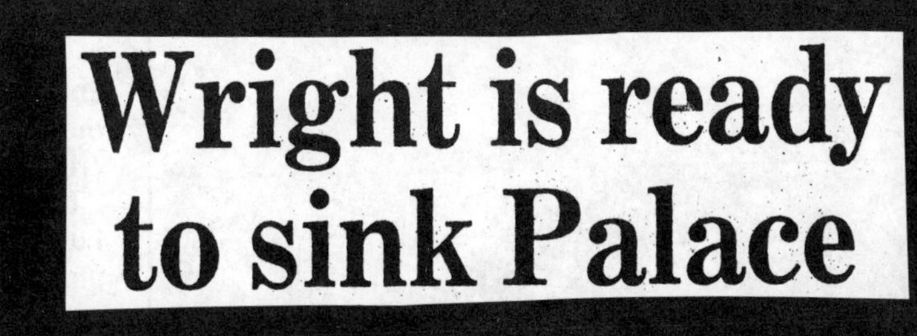
Wright is ready to sink Palace

victories, something they had not achieved since their own promotion two years earlier, then we wouldn't need even that.

On the Sunday after Palace had beaten Ipswich, Aston Villa's title challenge came to a limp end with a home defeat to the desperate Latics. The telling moment aside from Nick Henry's first half goal was when Villa hit the bar.

The mathematicians were hard at it. Palace didn't look so safe after all not least because after a long midweek journey to Manchester City they faced a difficult last game against their bogey team Arsenal and their hated former striker Ian Wright. Oldham had two home games first against Liverpool and then Southampton both desperately ordinary teams with little to play for.

Palace took the game to City and Thomas, finding the old fight and spark that had been missing for nigh on two seasons, had a header cleared off the line while Tony Coton produced a couple of inspired saves. Those who travelled up went through agonies at the news that Liverpool's £1 million keeper David "Calamity" James had made crucial errors to give Joe Royle's team an advantage. There was no need for calculators now. Oldham had to win their last match and hope Palace lost.

It took next to no time for Wright, who'd declared himself fit after injury to breach the Palace defence and put us behind. Oldham meanwhile had taken the lead then lost it against Southampton. As they forged ahead once more, Palace tried everything to get back into the game. Soon after we had gone behind, McGoldrick had missed a good chance. There numerous scrambles and Seaman nearly fumbled a shot from Southgate into his own net but as it became clear that Oldham were going to win, the radios were switched off despite rumours of a Southampton fight back. We pressed forward but were caught against the run of play. There wasn't even time to pray for a Southampton equaliser. Palace, after four seasons, returned from when they came. To be relegated in such circumstances was heartbreaking.

If the truth be known, many neutrals were pleased to see us go down. Palace had not won any friends with their football. That didn't make it any better for those of us who love the club. What hurt most was that we felt that the young players would have brought brighter and more enjoyable football to Selhurst Park. The *Independent on Sunday* noted as much after we had beaten Ipswich: "Only arithmetic and the improbability of an Oldham revival now stand between Crystal Palace and Premier League football next season. A display of much character and even some style … and then a well deserved lap of honour. The cheers may have been of relief but they were no less resounding for all that."

Steve Coppell's resignation brought to an end the greatest era in our history. He took us up, he took us to Wembley, he won us a trophy and gave us a team full of internationals. But our decline had become ingrained and in the end he couldn't take the necessary action to save the club. Something should have been done to arrest it, but it wasn't. It's easy to say but, after nine years of unprecedented success, who would have wanted the task of sacking Steve Coppell?

Our young players are still with us and under Alan Smith they must prove themselves in the first division. We know they have the ability, but it's more difficult to earn promotion that it is to stay in the Premier League. Had Palace taken a little more care, we would not be in this situation. Such is life when you're a Palace fan.

As for Palace fans, they like to get their disappointment in early. Amid the celebrations, at least one long-sufferer among the 30,000 throng had already mapped out the team's future. Back to the second division around 1993 in time for promotion in 1999.

THE GUARDIAN AFTER PALACE HAD BEATEN BLACKBURN IN THE PLAY-OFF FINAL IN 1989

STEVIE

Steve Coppell took Palace from the lower reaches of division two to the top of division one and to Wembley. But his reign ended in disappointing failure. Mark Gardiner assesses the Coppell era and wonders what went wrong.

Ben Radford/Allsport

The departure of Steve Coppell means the end of an era for Crystal Palace. During his time at Selhurst, Palace fans experienced many highs but over the last two years Steve endured many criticisms as the dream turned sour. But were those criticisms justified?

The major complaint was over the buying and selling of players. A number of turkeys arrived at great cost and swiftly departed. Yet the expulsion of Paul Bodin because he "didn't fit in with our style of play" was made to look ridiculous when we switched to a sweeper system. Deals involving Gabbiadini, Mortimer, Sinnott and Bodin cost the club a great deal of money with little return and led to the charge that Coppell was a poor judge of expensive players.

Everyone accepts that he could pluck players from non-league or lower division ranks but examine how some of his big money buys justified their price. McGoldrick, Thorn, Martyn and Young were were well worthy of the investment. Every manager, even the greats, has bought poorly at some time. Brian Clough's record on million pound players was not exactly flawless. Coppell's record was no worse.

On the other hand Palace's record on selling top players is not good. The departures of Ian Wright, Andy Gray and Mark Bright were all for less than most Palace fans believe was due to us. Ian had a clause in his contract which he exploited, I believe perhaps after being "tapped" on an England tour, at an unfavourable time of the season. Andy's career has virtually sunk without trace since leaving us for the second time.

The latest charge is that Palace have made a £2 million loss on

Coppell – a view from afar

When Palace were promoted to division one, there was only one certainty: one day we would be relegated. It even happens to the big clubs so inevitably our turn would come. That doesn't make it any better when it does. It was with

Ray Kalinauskas observed demotion from the colonial outpost of Perth, Western Australia.

much trepidation that I finally plucked up the courage to switch on the radio for the weekly broadcast of the match of the day on the BBC World Service. Everyone in the world seemed to know that Palace needed a favourable result against the Gunners to stay up. We're no strangers to this kind of drama. I remember having to beat Burnley to stay in division two nearly a decade before. Hearing that Ian Wright had done the unthinkable was devastating, particularly when combined with the news that Oldham were doing the business against Southampton. I switched off in a daze with the same feeling I had just before Hartlepool scored the goal that knocked us out of the Cup. I realised our time was up.

I listened to the post-match interviews only to confirm that it had really happened. The sense of loss was quite overwhelming, particularly the knowledge that an era had finished. Despite relegation, there are lots of good players in the side and unless we go up straight away the chances are that a different Palace XI will take us back to the top flight.

So why did we go down? The loss of Wright and Bright; everyone knew that Ian was worth three times what Marco Gabbiadini was worth, but that's how we replaced him. Mark Bright had to follow eventually and Chris Armstrong on his own was never going to be able to completely fill the void.

Buying some players either not good enough or not suited to our style. Apart from some dodgy buys in his early days (does anybody remember Pennyfather, Suckling or Otulakowski with much happiness?) Steve's major blunder for me was Lee Sinnott. Gabbiadini had a goalscorer's pedigree but he was obviously a guy who liked the ball to his feet and Palace's style demanded a mobile player prepared to chase. Letting good players go. Every manager does this. It's a hazard of the profession, but from a fan's point of view a couple of players must be mentioned. Stan Collymore – was he really not the answer up front? Paul Bodin – don't we like players with flair? And Glyn Hodges – my biggest heartbreak – if only we'd held onto him, things would have been okay.

In Alan Smith we retain a link with the Coppell era. Whether or not this proves to be a good move will only be obvious in a year or two. Unfortunately Palace do not seem to be a club able to attract managers of the highest credentials. Had we survived a year or two longer in the Premier Division we would have begun to develop a tradition. Now we are back to uncertainty and a very tough division. The loss of Eddie McGoldrick and Geoff Thomas (how did a player lose £2 million off his value in a year?) will not assist our promotion hopes. If everyone else can be retained and if John Salako gets fit then perhaps we can make it back straight away. Realistically if we finish mid-table and avoid further catastrophe I think 1993-94 won't be too bad a season. There are good young players at the club. Now they must grow up quickly if Palace are to be successful. The acquisition of one or two experienced midfielders and somebody to complement Chris Armstrong would seem obvious moves. But will Alan Smith be allowed to spend the money generated from the sale of Geoff and Eddie? I hope so.

I am optimistic for the future of Palace, but in my heart suspect we could be in the first division for a number of seasons. It's up to the fans to support them and do as much as possible to get the club moving again.

by Ray Kalinauskas, illustration: Jason Axell

Stan Collymore after he left us for £150,000 and moved to Forest for £2 million. Rubbish. Not many fans saw anything special in Stan the Man and if he was so obviously talented why did he end up at Southend instead of being picked up on the cheap by a Premier League club? If Steve is guilty of overlooking a natural talent then there are 21 other Premier managers equally responsible. Perhaps Stan, like Jamie Moralee, found his natural level. Meanwhile will we double or treble our investment if (God forbid) we sell Chris Armstrong.

The style of play was another bugbear. The long ball game played by Palace differed from that of Sheffield United and Wimbledon in that Steve always found room for wide men in his teams (from Irvine to Rodger). No-one complained when Wright and Bright were banging in the goals and we were winning.

Only when we started losing did this really become an issue. On tactics I can remember when the only thing our back four could do was launch mass charges up field as an offside trap. We were so successful that Wright and Bright had to knock in 50 plus goals a season to compensate for the leaky defence.

In later years Steve became more adventurous in employing sweepers and man-to-man markers – remember Villa Park and Wembley? When you are tactically brave you will screw up occasionally. My criticism was that in 1992-93 we became too cautious in team formations.

Steve stated that he resigned because he wasn't ruthless enough to tear the club apart but I think he's a bit self-effacing here as Palace heroes like Perry Suckling, Gary O'Reilly and John Pemberton would testify. Bear in mind that, of the 11 who won the play-off against Blackburn, six did not play for the club again after the Cup Final 12 months later. My feeling is that after nine years of pressure Steve needed a break. Okay I'm a Coppell supporter. All the above are only my opinions, but these are facts: Steve Coppell led Palace to our highest ever league placing, our best records in both the F.A. Cup and the League Cup and a Wembley triumph in the Zenith Cup. We were on the brink of European soccer and gained the national spotlight one fine lunch time at Villa Park. Steve Coppell was Crystal Palace's most successful manager.

SOME PEOPLE ARE ON THE ...

How many fans have felt in need of a stiff drink after watching Palace? For one group of fans, Palace wouldn't be Palace if they were sober

Every club has supporters groups attached to it, from the benign East Grinstead reds to the more sinister ICF or Bushwhackers. Palace is no exception. Down the years we've had the Melbourne, the Palace Action Campaign and today you will hear of the Witton Arms, the Addiscome Eagles, the Pigeon Lot and the engagingly named Orpington Pissheads, a collective dedicated to the noble pursuits of drinking and following Palace.

They are based in the British Queen at Locksbottom where on any night you're sure to find at least some of them slaking a thirst. They also boast many "associate members" outside the area. At home games you will always find them at the Cherry Trees in Norwood Junction while London away matches involve a visit to the Duke of York at Victoria. Paul James takes up the story: "There has always been a strong Palace following in this area. The 'pissheads' came together a couple of years ago when we realised there was enough of us to arrange mini-buses and coaches to away games. Our main aims are to go to all the away games, have a few beers and a chat with the opposing fans and a good laugh – no aggro. When we're further afield we like to find a pub near the away end where there's a good mix of supporters, like the Aviary in Nottingham. One of our best days was at Notts County in 1992, we had about 28 members there.

The away leg of the Youth Cup Final against Man United in 1992 is also fondly remembered. "We met in the Queen at about 11.30am," says Paul, "we had a mini bus arranged and left at about 1pm with a couple of cases of lager, a case of cider and half bottles of vodka on board ... and there was only eight of us drinking! We arrived in Manchester around 7.30 and nearly didn't get in after having to ask a copper where the away end was (there wasn't one!) The team did us proud and afterwards we went to Oldham to see the mates we'd made there on an earlier trip. We got out of their social club at about 2am and made it back to London about 10.30am the following day."

The friendship with Oldham fans has been one of the best things to come out of their travels. "It was in the Autumn of 1991, Wrighty's last game before he became an Arsenal bastard. Eight of us went up on the train and were due to meet up with some others at a pub we normally drank in, but it was shut so we had to go elsewhere. We met these Oldham fans and they said to come back after the game. We had time to kill and although we were a little uncertain because we'd won 3-2, they were really pleased to see us, the result was immaterial to them. We drifted into the town centre and at about 7.30pm we realised we were in danger of missing the eight o'clock train from Manchester to London. But the Oldham lads just phoned their wives to pick us up and, thanks to them, we managed to get the train. We promised to keep in touch and now we visit each other regularly."

The friendship was strong enough to survive the relegation battle of last season. "Obviously we were devastated when we went down, but no-one blames Oldham. They just kept apologising. It's good that one of us stayed up, at least they are a club supported by real fans. It's things like this that don't get reported in the papers."

Anyway, division one has its advantages. "We're quite looking forward to visiting Barnsley, Grimsby, Derby and all the old haunts. There's a lot more interest in these away games and people are looking forward to having some fun, although hopefully we'll bounce back up because the division is basically crap. We have the players to do it," he says.

Another pisshead, Pete Mahoney, says there is an art to getting the balance between drinking and football right. He recalls a couple of times when he didn't manage it: "Sheffield Wednesday in February 1993. We went by mini bus, I was the only one who felt like a drink. By kick-off time I was out of it." A similar thing happened at Leeds where the police were a little less tolerant and threw him out after taking photographs of him for their rogues gallery. Adam Young and James had a similar experience at Southampton where after downing 12 pints, Paul apparently had to be propped up against a wall, neither could remember a thing about the match and had to check the papers the following day to find out who'd won.

"My favourite away trip of all time was Grimsby in 1984," says Paul. "We went up on the train travelling early to beat the Inter-City alcohol ban. We had a sports bag full of beer and wine. By 11 o'clock several Palace fans had been arrested for drunkenness. In fact the police saved the life of one who nearly fell off the train, they just managed to catch him in time. Somehow the same bloke was smuggled into the game, but when our third goal went in whoever was holding him up must have let go and he was last seen rolling down the terrace! On the way back the train stopped at Newmarket and a load of London based Leeds fans got on. We thought there might be trouble but instead we had a few beers together and played cards all the way home. It was a great trip not least because we were bottom of the league and that was our first away win of the season."

Andy Ingram achieved one of the most bizarre ejections from a football ground at QPR. For singing a song from the Wizard of Oz. "They had lots of yellow lines all over the place and this copper was hassling me about standing slightly on one of these lines. So I gave him a rendition of *Follow the Yellow Brick Road* accompanied by a little dance down the terrace, as you do after six pints of Tennent's Extra. Two of them then marched me out of the ground. They put down on the charge sheet that I was 'obstructing a fire exit'."

The Pissheads have had a brief flirtation with media stardom and proved painfully accurate in their assessment of the club's fortunes. Andy Brown recounts the time that he, Paul and John James were interviewed by Capital Gold. "It was Andy Gray's last game for us at home to Coventry. We lost 1-0 and he appeared to deliberately miss a penalty, but we were especially crap. The interview took place before the game and I remember Paul's final comment 'the club's going down the pan' did not go down well with the expert panel, Terry Neil in particular. I think a letter should be sent to Capital Gold to tell them where they heard it first."

Mention Wembley and thoughts inevitably drift to the Mercantile Credit. Ingram: "I spent loads on really good tickets next to the Royal Box. We played Wednesday and drew 0-0. It went to a penalty shoot-out and Barber missed. I remember Steve Coppell saying afterwards: 'We had a penalty competition in training and Phil won it.' I expect everyone else had to kick with their other foot!"

The 9-0 defeat at Liverpool: "On the train we really thought we were going to win. As the goals went in Palace just sang louder and louder. It will never be matched. You had to feel for Perry Suckling, he'll get a great reception when he comes back this season. The F.A. Cup run is a sore point with some. Paul explains the lengths to which he and his brother went to get a ticket. "We got there really early to beat the road blocks but we still couldn't get one. Just before the game, Gary O'Reilly's dad pulled up asking for directions to the ground. He asked us if we all had tickets and we said we hadn't. If there'd only been two of us I reckon he'd have sorted us out. But we were locked out with 700 other Palace fans. We tried everything to get near the ground. Standing tickets were changing hands for £40. Others were so desperate they were cutting across allotments and drainage ditches to get in, only to find the police ready to turn them back dripping wet.

Chris Armstrong brings the conversation into the present. James believes he is following in the recent tradition of great Palace strikers. "We're going to make him an honourary member or our president, because he lives in Orpington." Paul is still bitter abut the sale of Mark Bright, though. "He would have kept us up, simple as that."

Relegation came as a bitter blow. "I wanted to jump on the track at Highbury tube station. We had potentially such a good team. If we keep the side together and don't lose too many players, we'll be okay. We've got some good young players coming through; Rodger, Ndah, Southgate and Tim Clark. The club's got a good future. Maybe a year in the lower division will do us good and we'll come back a stronger team."

Somewhere in the background a derisory voice pipes up: "That's a typical Palace fan speaking: 'Maybe going down will do us good.'." The speaker turns out to be an Arsenal fan and just what the hell do they know about relegation anyway?

■ Orpington Pissheads: Paul James, Martin Young, Adam Young, Andy Brown, Pete Mahoney and Andy Ingram

Thorny and the Ninja

If you want to score against Palace you have to get past these two first. In the early 90s, Palace's defending was often naive but a taciturn giant and a greyhound loving Londoner changed all that. By Tony Matthews

I doubt whether Eric Young or Andy Thorn care what opposition fans think of them. But it worries me from time to time that they are wholly misunderstood.

Palace's long ball style and the press campaign to discredit our challenge to the Big Five purists (it's easy to be a purist when you can afford to buy any player that shows promise) often prompts other supporters to suggest that Messrs Thorn and Young are a couple of thugs with no talent.

Nothing could be further from the truth. No-one is disputing their fearsome looks or powerful style (when were central defenders ever noted for their beauty?) but the point that is often missed is that they are defenders of genuine quality.

It is a proud boast for Palace fans that they are willing to give any player a chance to prove himself at Selhurst Park. But most of us have opinions about opposition players and make our own judgements about who we would like to see at Selhurst in Palace colours. And so, in the same way opposition supporters now judge him, we shuddered when Eric Young was signed. A gangling Wimbledon player of ferocious looks, we assumed he would be a typical Plough Lane donkey, more a disciplinary liability than a defensive asset. We'd blown £800,000 of the club's hard earned Cup Final revenue on a player who we thought, at 29, might be past his best.

Well we were wrong. Eric, of the brown headband and spidery legs, resumed his partnership with his former Wimbledon colleague Thorn as if they'd never been apart and Palace had a defensive solidity not seen since the days of Cannon and Gilbert. As the fans warmed to the big man, the headband brought him the nickname of Ninja (the Mutant Turtles were popular at the time) and "you'll never beat the Ninja," has echoed across football grounds the length and breadth of the country ever since.

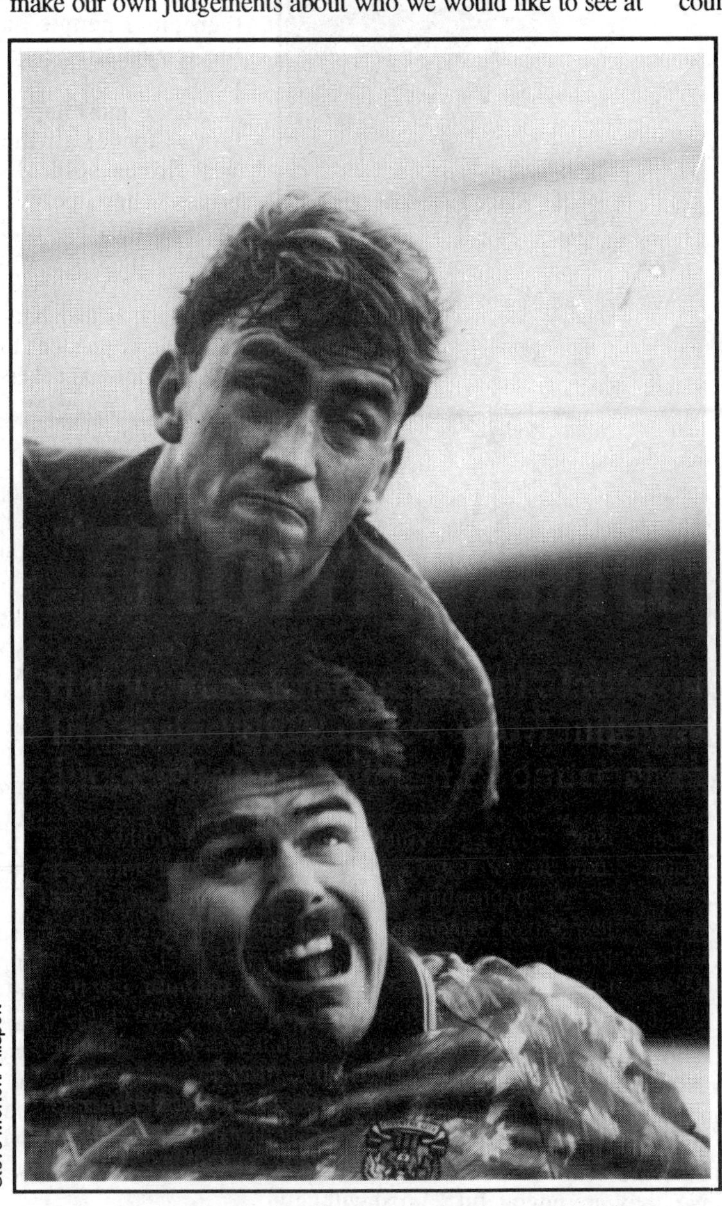

Steve Morton/ Allsport

Andy Thorn gets above Coventry's Micky Quinn

Thorn, who arrived from Newcastle, mid-way through our first season back in division one, endeared himself to the Palace support by opening the scoring against Charlton on his home debut. His presence for the rest of the campaign was a major factor in Palace's survival and march to Wembley. He was instrumental in the defeat of Liverpool in the semi-final with his terror inducing presence at set-piece attacks and he nearly spared us an extra 30 minutes agony, crashing a header against Bruce Grobbelaar's crossbar.

Four years on and the presence of Eric and Andy still gives us belief. Pessimism comes easy for Palace fans but we know that while we have them we can beat anybody, even if we dare not say so. Eric still has great pace and the sight of those long legs stretching to remove the ball from an onrushing forward is a tonic to every faint heart. He recently broke our international appearance record. Fifteen caps at Palace with a realistic chance of more to come and perhaps even a trip to America for the World Cup finals. Don't tell us he's not a quality player.

Thorn's strength is his ability to read the game. Any break, any danger and you know he'll be there. Don't let the hoofs into the stand fool you, he's doing the job we need. He has often attracted the interest of other clubs and if he played for a club with a bigger name, he would surely have won international recognition by now. That might send the snobs on the quality papers up the wall, but it would be every bit as deserved as the recognition the papers so willingly give to Adams, Ruddock and others. Thorn is more than their equal.

Thorny has also turned the back header to Nigel Martyn into an art form. Giant goal kicks glanced off the back of his head, or by beating a forward to nod back to head into the arms of the keeper, we don't expect him to make mistakes and he rarely does.

Thorn and Young formed the backbone of the defence upon which Palace's best ever league placing was built. Other fans may hate Eric and Andy, but wouldn't they just love to have both the immovable object and the irresistible force at the heart of their defence?

Mr £

Who is Ron Noades? The Norwegian Crystal Palace supporters' club chairman Tor Øystein Vaaland met the Palace chairman in the autumn of 1992. Here, he reflects on the man some fans love and some fans hate.

Ron Noades lies buried in a soft office chair with his feet placed on the desk. He gazes over his left shoulder through the window and out onto the Selhurst Park pitch. He sighs and declares his longing for a bigger and better stadium, with a 42,000 capacity. But then you have all these so-called supporters who criticise. They simply don't understand what it's like to run a top club as a modern business.

"We came tenth last year, but people didn't call the season successful," says Noades. "Perhaps it wasn't for them, but in other places like the north of England other clubs' supporters would have been more than satisfied. Steve Coppell comes from the north and can't understand this attitude in London. We've got Palace up amongst the best, but people don't understand how good that is with our limited resources. We are lacking in traditional support. Before this season began we had sold just 3,500 season tickets. Blackburn Rovers had sold 10,000. It's embarrassing."

Hy Money

Ron Noades is chairman of Crystal Palace. He is a businessman. He doesn't love Palace, but he does want the club to do well. Then he will earn more money.

"I treat my players like stocks. Ian Wright was 28 years old when we sold him, and we ... well, how long could we have expected him to play at the same level? Not long. It is possible that we sold him a year too early. Well, yes, maybe one year too early ..."

That was Mr Noades' only admission throughout our one and a quarter hour conversation. Even his worries about reduced attendances did not provoke self criticism. No, they are ungrateful, those people out there, those who don't come to see Palace play. They should support the team better than today. Higher attendances would give the club more money, better players and, in turn, a better team – and then more people on the terraces, he suggests.

"What is most important is to get all the VIP boxes sold, 48 boxes where people are served food and drink during the matches. If all these are sold it is economically the equivalent to 5,000 additional tickets being sold each game," says Noades.

Quite big and a little heavy in his body, not a typical Palace player, not an athlete, Ron Noades nevertheless moves quietly over his office floor to a huge, high cupboard.

He picks out plans for a superb new Selhurst Park. "Look here, drawings for a stadium with seats for 42,000 people. You should know that we were ahead of the Taylor report with regard to an all-seated stadium. If it had been up to me, and without considering any feelings, I would have sold all the players and built a new stadium in record time and then started with the team and football from afresh. It's with a big stadium that we can rival the likes of Arsenal and Spurs. Don't you agree?" he asks. I nod willingly.

"But why is it so expensive to watch Palace at Selhurst Park?"

"It isn't. It's cheap. The *Mirror* and other papers are lying. In fact most of our seats are cheaper than last season."

"But it costs quite a lot, say £14 or £15 ... "

"It varies. On one stand there is access to a cafe. One can't say £9 here and £14 there. Last year the most expensive seat without food was £20, this year it's £18. Besides, it's cheaper for pensioners and children in the stands as well, not only on the terraces. Crystal Palace is the only club with such a deal. The only increase since last year is from £6 to £8 for members in the terraces. People moan about prices and the next minute they moan that we don't buy enough players ... what sort of mentality is that?"

Well, what sort of mentality is it?

"It's the English nature. Here you have to fight against all the papers, not like in America where the press supports you, or in Italy where the top teams are the people's heroes. The British press won't help football, they want to sell papers and that means criticism. 'Greedy chairmen' I read in the paper – you've surely seen it – when we asked for £40 million from the TV stations this spring. After having been cheated for years we are all of a sudden greedy. No, in America everything is different ..."

Is that because football is first and foremost a business?

"Yeah."

But wouldn't you call it stupid or bad business to lose £600,000 on Marco Gabbiadini?

"We didn't lose anything on Marco Gabbiadini. We sold him and made a profit before he lost his value. If my manager hadn't sold him I would have been very critical. Not now. My relationship with my manager is very good."

What do you think of the independent and critical voices around Crystal Palace such as the fanzine *Eagle Eye*? "They are trying to be satirical but they are mainly stupid. For example they called Alan Pardew a donkey on the front page and that's terrible.

"They put out a magazine you would not want your children to read, if you know what I mean. Well, they have improved a little, they have cut out the swear words, so it's not as bad as it used to be."

Do you think it's okay that somebody is criticising, that someone cares while others like you have to give the answers.

"Yes sure, but they don't want to listen to the answers. When I had the bars built here at Selhurst Park they said I first had to buy players. The ordinary supporters do not understand that we cannot buy players. They don't understand that you must also spend money on other aspects of the club's activities."

Ron Noades buys and sells players and buys and sells clubs. Proudly he says that he owned Wimbledon and Crystal Palace at the same time for a three week period.

"I bought Wimbledon while they were a non-league club. It took a year to get the club into the league and the first year we won the fourth division. In 1980, I bought the majority of shares in Crystal Palace to be able to move Wimbledon here to Selhurst Park. Everybody got angry and there was a big fuss with people saying I couldn't move a second club in here. Because of these reactions I had to sell the shares in Wimbledon, but for three weeks I was, in fact, the owner of both Wimbledon and Crystal Palace."

In 1991, Noades was branded a racist after a comment to a Channel 4 television programme about black players.

"The black players needed the strong white players to help them through a hard English winter," he said, but nevertheless he boasted about their elegance and technique. I asked him why he said things such as this.

"The remark was taken totally out of proportion. At Palace half the players are black, as well as some coaches. The interview was taped and Channel 4 cut it in a certain way to twist my words consciously."

But why did you say it in the first place?

"When I managed Southall it was me who wanted black players. Because of me we got Cyrille Regis, to mention one you might know.

"You probably don't know Southall. It's an ethnic minority area where 99 per cent of the population are Asian. And then they accuse me of being a racist ..."

But why did you say what you did?

"The interview was cut to pieces and Channel 4 fed the papers with my replies beforehand so the scandal erupted. I got an 11 page script. Everyone who wanted a copy got one and I gave some out to a selected few."

But are you saying there is a difference between black and white players?

"Well there was, but the difference is now less. The blacks are technical. we saw that when we were in South Africa during the summer of 1992. But on the other hand they are not as well organised or tactically skilled. The difference is less so in England than Europe or elsewhere."

Do you have a better relationship with Channel 4 today?

"I don't talk to them. I don't trust journalists, they misuse me."

Then Ian Wright was sold shortly after the remark scandal?

"It had nothing to do with that. The reply did not create problems in the club, neither at that time nor afterwards."

■ This article first appeared in the Norwegian Palace fanzine *Orne Blikket (Eagle Eye)*. Reproduced with permission of Tor Øystein Vaaland.

Jason Axell

A PASSION FOR PALACE

Father and son Ken and Keith Sinclair served on the Palace board. Here they tell Phil Huffer and Tony Matthews about their days as directors of Crystal Palace Football Club.

What's the difference between a supporter and a director? Not a lot according to Ken Sinclair. And he should know, he's been a Crystal Palace fan for more than 40 years and was on the Palace board from 1974 until 1977.

Ken was born in Thornton Heath and has supported Palace since the 40s, but more regularly since the 70s. He and his wife Yvonne introduced their son Keith to Palace and his addiction – he went to every game for five years – was such that he followed his father onto the board for an eight year spell from 1984 until 1992 – a period that spanned some of Palace's greatest and worst moments.

It wasn't until Palace were in serious trouble that Keith decided to join the board, so what made him take the plunge? "The chairman Ron Noades was still very much an outsider – a Wimbledon man. I think he wanted respectability and at the time he didn't really have anybody on the board who was a Palace supporter and so he asked my father to rejoin the board."

But Ken – although he supported Noades and his plans – didn't want a directorship because he "realised how difficult it was to combine outside business interests with running a football club". The senior partner of a firm of stockbrokers at the time – Ken is now semi-retired – he strongly believes that "football directors can't really do much for a club".

"Many of them are a bit of a waste of space – glory seekers who don't really add very much," he says, which he feels, is especially the case at a club like Palace, who have a chief executive to run things. Keith, however, in "the *naïveté* of youth" thought he might be able to contribute something.

In July 1984 – a month after Steve Coppell had been appointed manager – Keith joined the board. The financial sum involved was around £12,500, although nowadays an interest free loan of around £100,000 is required from any one aspiring to the Selhurst boardroom. Even if directors don't add much to the well-being of the club, the money they bring is a great help. "It gave Palace a little more credibility at the bank, which was demanding more financial stability," says Keith. "We were all fanatics and we felt Ron had battled away and we wanted to help."

Keith was keen to be involved. "At the time Ron and I chatted about it and, unlike many clubs, the directors didn't really have a set role. I lived in Guildford and the idea was for me to get involved in the youth side, which I did for a while. But after I was married, my wife got a bit upset with me disappearing to football twice a week and doing other things as well, so it became very much a match day orientated thing. "In those days I still went to all the games and there were so few directors that often there was either just Ron and myself or I went alone. I got a real buzz out of it."

For many directors the social side, before and after matches, is the be-all and end-all and Keith has mixed feelings about this. His fanaticism was not welcomed among people who fancied themselves as more genteel. "I don't particularly like football club directors. To be honest I didn't get on all that well with most of the other Palace directors. We didn't have a lot in common and most of them weren't that interested in football. They got the same buzz as I got, but I was looked upon in a poor light for my vocal support for the club, which annoyed me. It culminated in a disagreement between myself and Ron at the Cup Final because I wore a hat and scarf in the Royal Box and supported the club visibly."

Despite this, Keith loved going into the famous board rooms at Old Trafford and Anfield. "Man City was great. The best and plushest was Everton while the worst was Newport County." Both men also enjoyed the chance to mix with football's personalities. Ken remembers the spirit of Big Mal's days: "The Cup run was terrific, Malcolm Allison was a grand guy. I rated him as a coach and it was always entertaining. Palace was a wonderful place to be." Years later Keith had the pleasure of Mal's company for the F.A. Cup semi-final at Villa Park. "He knew his stuff. Even when Liverpool were ahead he turned to me and said that Palace were going to win the game."

Mal's was spot on and afterwards Keith was able to enjoy the discomfort of Liverpool's directors. "I've never seen a set of men so disappointed. They were very bad losers and barely spoke to us. They were gutted. They had the game won and were on their way to Wembley. They'd got their coaches and hotels booked. I would have loved to have gone up to them and screamed in their faces."

And it wasn't just the Palace men who were smiling, support for the underdog was widespread. "The Aston Villa people were wonderful to us because they wanted us to win." While occasions like Villa Park were wonderful experiences Keith wanted to be more than just a glorified fan. He had joined the club to do something. In the early days, Palace held regular board meetings. "Mostly we discussed money matters. If Steve wanted cash we'd have to decide if we could afford it. I recall one hastily assembled Friday night meeting, we cobbled together the money to buy Perry Suckling. At the time, the club didn't have the cash and it was a big step." And a significant one; Suckling's heroics eventually helped Palace reach the first division.

Even so, Keith agrees that most directors "don't know their arse from their elbow" when it comes to football. "I know as much as anybody else who stands on the terraces but that's it. I certainly wouldn't allow my opinion of a player to influence whether or not we gave Steve the money for him."

Ken believes that directors should be honest about their lack of understanding: "I actually believe in footballers running football, with people like Noades taking the lead and making the tough decisions."

> **"Malcolm was a grand guy. I rated him as a coach and it was always entertaining. Palace was a wonderful place to be."**
>
> KEN SINCLAIR

But his son found, as time wore on, that board meetings became more of a rarity. Noades ran the club as a dictatorship and Keith decided to quit. "I came to the conclusion that my input was zero and my view was less than that.

"My enthusiasm began to run out. The way the whole thing ended knocked a lot out of me. It was a bit acrimonious but you still don't lose the love for the club you support."

Ken once had a chance to take over at a southern football club but didn't believe he could change his team. "Without an allegiance there is no passion. It's got to be our club right or wrong."

Both of the most recent Palace chairmen did change sides, however. Ray Bloye was a Chelsea supporter, although Keith says: "He didn't really know what a football was. He just wanted the glory." Noades, of course, was Wimbledon's chairman and, before that, had been in charge at Southall.

Ken uses the state of the club under Bloye to emphasise what a good job he believes Noades has done.

"You need somebody who will devote themselves to the club. He's a professional chairman. I think he gave the supporters what they wanted – first division football. He rebuilt the club and I supported him."

Palace, post-Bloye, were in a mess. If it hadn't been for Dick Varey, "a Geordie who loved the club and football", Palace would have collapsed a lot sooner than they did. The Sinclairs say Noades turned the club around. "To give Ron his due, he lived from hand to mouth," says Keith. "They hadn't seen the books when they took over and it was shock. Noades saved the club, although I believe he did so because he wanted the glory and to be in the papers. That's his ultimate ambition." Ken agrees: "Without Noades there wouldn't be a Crystal Palace today.

"I think he got a bit of a rough deal but people now appreciate what he's done. The supporters never read balance sheets and don't realise the state the club was in," says Ken.

So will Noades be around for a long time? "Whichever way you look at it, he controls 91 per cent of the club through its holding company Altonwood. He built it and will be very reluctant to give it up. His wife, Novello, is now on the board of that company and, the way I perceive it, he wants his son to get involved."

But Keith found it equally difficult to find out what the finances were, even when he was on the board. Today he has even less idea but intuitively feels things are not good. So what of the future for Palace?

"Panic buys are wrong and Coppell was prone to that. The signatures of Bodin and Mortimer were enormous mistakes." The poor attendances are also bad news. If Noades has built the club to survive on, say, 20,000 gates and they only reach 15,000 then its a problem. But Keith doesn't believe the low crowds are particularly Noades' fault. "Its symptomatic of football as a whole."

Most fans see Noades as an abrasive character who has often criticised them unjustly. Is this in part why he does not receive as much credit as, perhaps he should? "I have to say, Ron was always willing to talk to the supporters and to give his view. He never hid from them which is more than most would do," says Keith.

So would Keith ever rejoin the board? "I don't think so, not with Noades there. I'd love to run it and I think it would give me immense satisfaction. But I'd have to be in charge."

LOCAL INTEREST

Unlike many local papers, the *Croydon Advertiser's* coverage of the club doesn't stop at reports. Sports Editor Dave McClelland reveals a little of his work.

Many people would consider that Dave McClelland has the best job in the world, indeed he probably thinks so himself. He is the man who gets paid to watch Palace play.

A local lad who lived in Thornton Heath and supported Palace as a boy he is the *Croydon Advertiser's* sports editor.

He joined the paper straight from school and learnt his journalism with the Advertiser Group completing the usual NCTJ courses. He has been with them ever since.

"I worked as a news reporter first and moved to sport covering Sutton United then Croydon and eventually Palace."

McClelland has been sports editor for seven years and is only the third since the war, following on from Gerald Williams, who later became a BBC tennis commentator, and John Matthews.

"People might think I do nothing else but Palace, but the club accounts for only 15 per cent of my job. We do four pages of sport of which the first page of the second section is devoted to Palace. But Croydon is a large area and there is a lot going on, athletics, boxing and other local football down to Sunday League level. A lot of my work is involved elsewhere. We work to deadlines and Monday and Tuesday are devoted to local football.

"Concentration on Palace doesn't really start until Wednesday. I cover the home matches but not always the away games. I spend all Wednesday on Palace although the report is done on Monday. You don't want to be a copy of the Sundays and Mondays so I look for something a bit new so I don't hurry the report. Midweek matches affect us, though.

"I don't do so many away games – only the important ones – we can usually get a feel without being there. There are a few links with other local papers where they might be able to provide us with information, but it's not usual. If I ask the Hartlepool chap he's not going to be able to approach it from the angle we want because he doesn't know anything about Palace. Basically I just watch the match and occasionally if it's not an important game I might do a bit of PA work there's no opportunity to write for the national press because in the Premier League they all send their own correspondents. I'm still a supporter but obviously my professional interest has changed things and I can't stand up and cheer in the press box, it's not done.

"After the match I attend the press conference and although Steve Coppell was notorious for not attending, the opposition manager might be there and I usually get a reaction from a player."

Regular news and views are sought from the club. Over the years the degree of resistance has varied. McClelland remembers Bert Head was always positive. "He held a meeting every Monday morning for the press and was always keen to push the club. Steve Coppell was not a pushy fellow and less forthcoming.

"We have to smell certain things out for ourselves, we've got to keep in touch and know what's going on. One of my biggest problems is that things often happen on a Thursday when we're ready to go to press. The signatures of Marco Gabbiadini [and more recently the resignation of Coppell] are examples. With the Geoff Thomas transfer, I actually had three different stories written to cover all the eventualities.

Bert Head was something of a father figure at Palace whereas Malcolm Allison was not terribly good to work with. He was a national figure and was more concerned with the cameras than the local press. He did a column for us. We went to see him once a week and he would throw out a few ideas from which we would write a piece. But Malcolm projected the club.

Terry Venables was difficult in a different way. "He had so many other things going on. Being manager of Palace was just one of his involvements. Alan Harris used to be the one to speak to."

Dario Gradi was already a familiar figure to McClelland because he had been at Sutton United. "He was a nice bloke but not really big enough for the club. I don't think Steve Kember took to the job. I don't think he liked the pressure and was happier out of it. Jim Cannon had always wanted to be a manger and I thought there might be a role for him. Steve Coppell was a different character, he got the respect of the players because of his career as a player. In the early days he did brilliantly. He made good purchases like Thomas and Redfearn but I thought they ought to play a different way. He made a genuine attempt to do this but things went badly, the home defeat by Southampton for example, and so they regressed to their old ways."

When a controversial story breaks, supporters speculate on how much the *Advertiser* can delve into the background. McClelland assures that the relationship between the club and the paper is a professional one. "People think I'm quite close to the players but that's not a good thing because you've got to write about them. If I was Nigel Martyn's best friend it would be difficult to write objectively about him. You've got to maintain a distance."

That doesn't stop the club occasionally attempting to use the paper. "In his early days at the club, when John Matthews was sports editor, Ron Noades used to storm down to our offices to make his protests and demands known." From the paper's point of view it wants stories that will sell copy and if Noades is prepared to make ill-thought out comments it will have no qualms in using them. "I didn't prompt Noades to describe the 14,000 league cup crowd against Forest as a disgrace. He's very outspoken." The fans have their chance to reply though. "Letters come in spasms, but I always try to leave space because it provides the fans with an outlet."

Occasionally Noades comments to the *Advertiser*, such as his criticism of Coppell's management both during and after the relegation season, were picked up by the national press. What is the relationship between local and national papers? "They are quite different. A rule of thumb is to look for direct quotes. When I write a story I always check it and hope there's some truth, but with national papers it's often 90 per cent speculation. The nationals do their own thing although they might occasionally ring me up. On match days they tend to form a little clique – partly because they don't like to let anyone out of their sight in case he's got an exclusive. They also work together.

Has McClelland ever wanted to move onto the national press? "I've not had any serious ambition to do so. I'm not the type. It's a different job, there's more travel involved and I don't do that style of writing. The years have gone by and I'm still happy here."

The highlight was the Cup final. "I never imagined Palace would grace Wembley. In the end it just happened. I had been to Wembley before to cover Palace players' international appearances and I did the Amateur Cup Final in 1963 when Sutton met Wimbledon. The press box is massive it was a great day. The Promotion nights were fantastic too especially in 1979. As for players? "Johnny Byrne shades Ian Wright out of the picture. Byrne's ball playing was wonderful.

A successful Palace helps the *Advertiser's* sales especially in North Croydon where support is strongest. The club's happy, the paper's happy and the fans are happy, it's only the letters column that suffers.

Club photographer

There are loads of photographers. All lined up by the goal waiting for that moment when the forward rises and the ball flashes past the despairing fingers of the keeper. It's our goalkeeper of course.

Up the other end there is a lone figure, just one guy waiting for a Palace strike. Everyone who follows Palace knows who it is. Neil Everitt's photos of Palace in Action have taken up a couple of pages in the programme since the late 1970s, he also takes them for the *Croydon Advertiser* and the *South London Press*.

Neil became club photographer in a haphazard way: "Keith Payne was the Palace photographer and I succeeded him. I took a while to decide because I was a fan on the terraces and I was going to lose a great deal. It is a different perspective but there are other benefits. I'd taken pictures on one of the pre-season tours to Holland and Germany. I had no money and I was thinking of selling the cameras but the commercial manager Tony Shaw asked me to do some pictures. I think the first one I did was Grimsby away in 1976. The club sorted out accreditation – at one stage I didn't miss a game for seven years."

Neil had been a steward on one of the coaches a job that was not without incident: "It was 1978, the year Forest won the league. They'd been away and we were at Notts County. We arrived at one of the service stations and these kids in the back had gone quiet. We went to get a tea and I lost sight of them. They had gone to the side of the motorway where the Forest coaches had just arrived.

"The Palace kids were making the usual hand signals. I told them to stop being silly, but they reckoned they could have Forest. The next thing I knew the kids were storming past me back onto the coach and the Forest fans were coming across the access bridge. And they weren't kids, they were blokes in their 30s. We couldn't leave because the driver wasn't around and I thought we'd had it. But just then the lads from the Melbourne pulled in and set about the advancing Forest. That gave us time to make our escape. We left them to it, to the sight of flying bricks and smashing glass.

His devotion as a fan has had to take a back seat to photography. "Often I don't know what's happened during the match. I'm more removed from it now although it can still get to you. The Cup Final was a nightmare, I was on sea sick tablets because of nerves. The semi final was better, I was crying when we were 2-1 up. It's probably the greatest game I ever did, apart from the first goal. But nobody got a photo of it because Bright was too close even though most of the photographers were ready. I did get pictures of the celebrations."

One wonders why he doesn't set his sights beyond Palace and the local papers. The answer is that he doesn't need the hassle of Fleet Street deadlines and besides he already has a job, as editor of a trade magazine.

"I just turn up. The *Advertiser* and *SLP* have a standing order. I only put up what I think's reasonable. It really depends on the day. I look for pictures of a Palace attack, if there's not much happening I might move so I can actually get something ..."

The job has its hazards although they are few and far between: "I'd been going through a bad time, not getting any good pictures. Alan Irvine and a Fulham defender came at me. I should have moved, but I knew if Irvine got there I'd get a great shot. The next thing I knew, the Fulham player had hit me and I cut my head with the camera. But considering the number of games it's rare for anybody to come near me."

PICTURE PALACE

Hy Money's photographs have captured the life of Crystal Palace F.C. From the joy of promotion to the misery of semi-final defeat

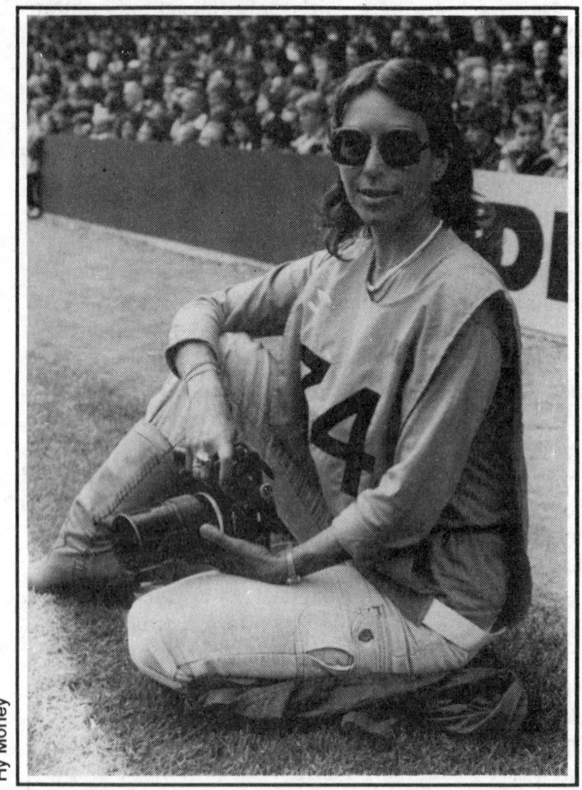

Hy Money

Hy Money opens a filing cabinet stuffed with photos that would make any Palace fan cloud over. Inside is the story of Palace in the 70s, not only on the pitch but behind the scenes. Pick up any picture and it tells a story; Yogi Hughes receiving treatment to ghastly looking injuries, players celebrating the births of their children, Ian Walsh being pursued by Peter Nicholas and Steve Kember after scoring against Burnley in 1979 and the unbelievable sight of more than 50,000 smothering the pitch on a May night in 1979.

Hy's work goes beyond football, she is one of Fleet Street's top photographers and along the walls you will find every kind of celebrity from Nookie Bear to Elizabeth Taylor, but her career began by accident at Crystal Palace.

"I was always snapping, taking photographs of my children often for the benefit of my family who lived abroad. It was my son who dragged me along to Palace. He wanted to go to the Palace as a birthday treat and I thought he meant Buckingham Palace. I was horrified when he told me he meant Crystal Palace. They were thrust upon me."

"My husband was supposed to take them but had to play cricket. I couldn't believe it. I didn't want to go. I didn't even know how to get to Selhurst Park. I was so nervous, I couldn't believe it. But I can still visualise the colour and the atmosphere. There was such a buzz, such energy. I was surprised at how family orientated it was. Then I saw the people sitting by the side and I just wanted to be there. I was captivated by the movement and the effort. It was visually exciting. It was Kevin Keegan's first away match for Liverpool and I got a photograph of him signing autographs. I just had to get closer."

Hy says she was so inspired that she pestered Palace for a press pass. "I went back so many times and they just ignored me. Eventually I insisted on seeing the head man. I was so determined that they relented and I got to see Bert Head. I told him how wonderful it all was and he pressed a buzzer to his secretary and said: 'For God's sake give this woman a pass and get rid of her!'."

Hy had won her first battle, but there were others to fight. Football photography was, and still is, a male preserve. The professionals gave her a hard time. "They said: 'Oh look what we've got here, have you got your knitting in your bag darling? Have you got your crochet with you?' I was literally quivering." That was nothing compared to the abuse from the terraces. "I have a distinctive jacket in Palace colours which made me an easy target for opposing fans. I've put up with the cries of 'Get em off' and worse. I've had staples fired at me, been stampeded on, and used to get comments when Malcolm Allison was there because of his reputation as a womaniser. They assumed I was there because of him."

Yet nothing would put her off. She made a small breakthrough when some of her photos of her children were used by family magazines. "I thought this is a jammy way to earn money so I kept snapping. I realised that it was the photograph that counts not the name."

Hy went to every Palace match as well as the reserves. Eventually her commitment paid off. "One of the reserves got called up for the first team and I was the only one who had a picture. I began working on a regular basis and although nobody came up and asked it evolved until I was the official club photographer. Then Malcolm Allison came and that was the big time, because he was always in the news."

As the only female sports photographer. It's no easier for a woman to get on now than it was 20 years ago. "The Photographers Association tried to stop me from joining the NUJ although they couldn't because I had work in so many publications, they were also annoyed because there had been a programme about me on television after such a short time. The old hard core still don't talk to me, they talk around, about and over me. The new ones look at me and say 'what's this funny old bird doing here?'"

One of the most embarrassing incidents was a clash with Brian Clough. "We were beating Forest. I was minding my own business taking photographs when I got a call ... 'Oi you, get off the pitch.' I tried to ignore it but he persisted. He said: 'No place for women, get off the pitch.' A steward came and asked me to leave 'just to keep the peace' but I refused. The next thing I knew Terry Venables was there and Clough said: 'I want her off the pitch,' but Terry said: 'Stay where you are.' And Clough was going: 'I see, I see, it's like that is it?' It was so uncalled for." As a postscript, a year later Clough came up and hugged her in view of other photographers. "I was not impressed I felt he was just using me.'

One of the more depressing moments came at Ninian Park while Cardiff were celebrating their escape from relegation on the night Palace went down to the third in 1974. I was in the Cardiff dressing room and they spotted me and were shouting: 'Wor we've got a bird here!' They threw me fully clothed into the bath with my cameras and films. I got up screaming I was furious and came home on the milk train in a Cardiff City tracksuit. But Hy wouldn't change a minute of her career.

"It all started that day when that cricket team was a man short. I've travelled all over the world with my cameras. It changed my life."